No Star Too Beautiful

Other works edited and translated by Joachim Neugroschel

Great Tales of Jewish Fantasy and the Occult

*The Shtetl: A Creative Anthology of Jewish Life
in Eastern Europe*

*The Dybbuk and the Yiddish Imagination:
A Haunted Reader*

The Golem

The Complete Short Stories of Marcel Proust

No Star Too Beautiful

Yiddish Stories from 1382 to the Present

EDITED AND TRANSLATED BY

Joachim Neugroschel

W. W. NORTON & COMPANY

NEW YORK / LONDON

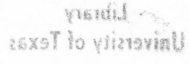

Permissions have been granted by the following:
Asch, Sholem. "The Story of Beautiful Marie." Translated and printed by permission of David Mazower.
Elberg, Yehuda. Selection from *The Empire of Kalman the Cripple* is reprinted with permission of Syracuse University Press.
Karpinovitsh, Avrom. "Zubak." Translated and printed by the author's permission.
Korn, Rokhl. "The End of the Road." Translation printed with permission of Dr. Irena Kupferschmidt.
Leivick, H. "He." Translation printed with permission of Ida Leivick.
Rosenberg, Yudl. "The Golem." *Great Tales of Jewish Fantasy and the Occult.* Copyright © 1976, 1987 by Joachim Neugroschel. Reprinted with permission of the Overlook Press.
Rosenfarb, Chava. Selection from *Bociany* is reprinted with permission of Syracuse University Press.
Singer, Isaac Bashevis. "The Mirror." from *Gimpel the Fool.* Copyright © 1957, renewed 1985 by Isaac Bashevis Singer. Reprinted by permission of Farrar, Straus and Giroux, LLC.

Some of the Yiddish works that Neugroschel translated for this anthology may still be in copyright, but because those Yiddish publishing houses no longer exist, it was impossible for him to track down any possible estates. Every effort has been made to contact the copyright holders of all of the selections. Rights holders of any selections not credited should contact W. W. Norton & Company, Inc., 500 Fifth Avenue, New York, NY 10110 for a correction to be made in the next reprinting of our work.

The editor is grateful for two generous grants he received from the Jacob T. Zukerman Culture Foundation of the Workmen's Circle.

The text of this book is composed in Electra with the display set in Locarno Light and Locarno Italic.
Composition by Adrian Kitzinger
Manufacturing by the Haddon Craftsmen, Inc.
Book design by JAM design
Production manager: Julia Druskin

Library of Congress Cataloging-in-Publication Data

No star too beautiful : Yiddish stories from 1382 to the present / edited and translated by Joachim Neugroschel.
p. cm.
ISBN 0-393-05190-0
1. Yiddish literature—Translations into English. 2. Jews—Literary collections.
I. Neugroschel, Joachim.

PJ5191.E1 N62 2002
839'.108—dc21   2002069222

W. W. Norton & Company, Inc., 500 Fifth Avenue, New York, N.Y. 10110
www.wwnorton.com

W. W. Norton & Company Ltd., Castle House, 75/76 Wells Street, London W1T 3QT

1 2 3 4 5 6 7 8 9 0

I've seen so many storm the sky. No star
Was far too beautiful or far too far.

—Bertolt Brecht, *Mother Courage*

CONTENTS

Yiddish—The Longest Journey

*I*N THE BOOK OF NEHEMIAH, Jews who have returned from the Babylonian Captivity (586–516 B.C.E.) attend a prayer meeting that is not unlike a gathering in a modern Reform synagogue: there is no segregation of the sexes, and apparently none of these Jews knows Hebrew. So when the readers "instructed the people in the Law . . . they did read from the Book of the Law of God in translation to make it intelligible and so helped them [the worshipers] to understand what was read." (8:8)

The biblical passage needed to be translated since these Jews, who were born and raised in Babylon, had abandoned Hebrew as their everyday language, using it only for liturgical purposes and for setting down the biblical scriptures. Instead of Hebrew, the exiles had developed a new Jewish vernacular known today as Aramaic—actually Judeo-Aramaic: Babylonian with borrowings from Hebrew. The original name of this language, *Targum*, means "translation"—in accordance with its function of rendering the Bible into everyday parlance. When these Babylonian Jews brought their new language to their ancient homeland, they maintained it for over half a millennium.

This was not the first Jewish vernacular, and it was far from the last: since then, some two dozen Jewish languages have evolved worldwide, and a dozen are still spoken in the twenty-first century.

. . .   .

NOW LET'S LEAVE the ancient homeland and fast-forward to the German town of Worms in A.D. 1272. In a makhzor (prayer book for the Jewish holy days), some virtuous soul had written a rhyming couplet in a new Jewish language, though in Hebrew letters:

Gut tak im betage/swer dis makhazor in bes hakenes trage—"A good day is given the man who bears/Into synagogue this Book of Prayers."

This new tongue was a blend of elements drawn from southern and central German dialects and from Hebrew and Aramaic, as well as two Jewish Romance vernaculars (Judeo-Italian and Judeo-French) that Jews spoke before migrating to German areas a couple of centuries earlier. Having also passed through Bohemia, they picked up a few Slavisms—the earliest in the new tongue (curiously enough, one of their names for God was "Bog"—from Old Czech).

During the Middle Ages, masses of speakers of the new Jewish vernacular then moved from Germany to Slavic territories, especially Poland, where they added a huge number of Slavic words and forms to their own tongue. Throughout its history, this language has had a variety of names, including Yiddish-Taytsh (Judeo-German) and Jargon (not necessarily a pejorative term). However, the name that won out in modern times is Yiddish (literally, "Jewish").

The journey of the people and the language did not stop there. Some Yiddish speakers returned to Germany, Holland, or northern Italy because of pogroms, expulsions, or other anti-Jewish measures. Indeed, the golden age of Old Yiddish literature took place in northern Italy from 1474 to 1600. Then, in the nineteenth and early twentieth centuries, millions of Jews fled from tsarist Russia (which included such areas as eastern Poland, Ukraine, Byelorussia, Lithuania, and Latvia); Jews also left western Poland (which belonged to Austria-Hungary until 1918). And these migrants and refugees spread Yiddish all over the earth: to Western Europe, South Africa, Palestine (and then Israel), South America, and particularly North America.

Eventually, however, Yiddish lost its various strongholds. It was destroyed in Europe chiefly by the Nazi genocide and by the Soviet tyranny, and, in the rest of the globe, by the mass linguistic and cultural assimilation of Jews or by the exclusive demands of Zionism's creation of modern Hebrew.

The year 1382 shows the earliest extant literary manuscripts in Yiddish — the start of Yiddish written literature (we may assume the existence of previous oral traditions such as folktales, fairy tales, sermons, and other works). If we shoot forward to 1929–30, we find that three Yiddish publishing houses in Eastern Europe issued three different Yiddish translations (one by Isaac Bashevis Singer) of *All Quiet on the Western Front* by the German novelist Erich Maria Remarque. These editions were catering to a huge Yiddish readership with various degrees of literacy: after all, by 1939 there were probably some eleven million Yiddish speakers worldwide. Along with countless translations of past and current authors, lots of Yiddish households naturally owned earlier and contemporary Yiddish books. By now, many outstanding Yiddish writers had already been gathered in complete multivolume editions: Mendele Moykher-Sforim, Sholom Aleichem, Yitsik Leybesh Peretz, Avrom Reyzen, Dovid Pinsky, to name just a handful.

In the six centuries since 1382, Jewish life and Jewish literature have gone on an excruciatingly bumpy ride. Countless Jewish manuscripts and books have been destroyed by Christians. On the other hand, many were saved because Jews refuse to destroy texts containing the name of God; instead, they lay them to rest in a storeroom known by the Hebrew term *genizah*. Such caches, especially the one in Cairo, have yielded troves of Yiddish and Hebrew documents — some almost whole, some tattered.

The dissemination of written Yiddish finally took off when the printing press made it more widely available. In 1534, a publisher in Cracow, Poland, printed the first Yiddish book: a bilingual concordance to the Bible. In 1686, a publisher in Amsterdam brought out the first Yiddish periodical, a biweekly, thus initiating over three chaotic centuries of Yiddish journalism in many different countries.

THROUGHOUT ITS HISTORY, Yiddish has contended with Hebrew and Aramaic as the languages of the Jewish religion and, later, with neo-Hebrew as Zionism's spoken and literary language. Few Yiddish writers started out with Yiddish; most wrote their early works in Hebrew or, during the modern era, even Polish, Russian, or German. Quite a number of authors wrote belles lettres and/or nonfiction in both Yiddish and Hebrew, perhaps translating their works from one tongue into the other. Such overlapping has led many critics to see Hebrew and Yiddish writing as forming one literature in two languages. But this oversimplification ignores the multiple and partly separate audiences. Until modern times, nearly all women were excluded from the study of Hebrew and could rely solely on Yiddish texts (or, starting in the nineteenth century, on texts in non-Jewish tongues). Furthermore, while most men had some knowledge of Hebrew, there were enough men who were likewise dependent on Yiddish texts—to the extent that they could get away with reading secular material. In the nineteenth century, when the Haskala, the Jewish Enlightenment, addressed the Jewish masses, whose knowledge of Hebrew was inadequate, these writers, who hated Yiddish, nevertheless had to use it in their satirical works. Such authors demonstrated that Yiddish and Hebrew were separate and unequal—and yet they enriched one another in a constantly fluctuating osmosis. But by the 1920s, numerous factors, especially the successes of Zionism and socialism, had led to the almost total divorce of Hebrew and Yiddish.

The story of the Yiddish story is as rich and tempestuous as any aspect of Jewish life. From the outset, narrative themes could be religious or secular, their sources Jewish or non-Jewish. These facets were sometimes fused, sometimes sharply distinguished.

The squabbles between Hasidism, the rabbinate, the Haskala, communism, socialism, Zionism, assimilationism, Yiddishism, Reform, Conservative, and Orthodox Judaism have provided one raison d'être, lots of subject matter, and loads of inspiration for Yiddish fiction. Pitched battles among these various causes and movements are far less frequent in the twenty-first century; still, without them, Jewish stories, past and present, would be unbearably dull.

In the modern era, Yiddish has had numerous additional functions, one of which was to help create a secular Jewish life as well as a transition to non-Yiddish assimilation. The explosion of Yiddish belles lettres in the nineteenth and twentieth centuries; the development of Yiddish theater, journalism, publishing, cinema, radio; translations of foreign literature (both past and present); the decay of the shtetl; the network of Yiddish schools in Eastern Europe; the profound religious traditions— all these elements contributed to forming a fragile mosaic that the modern era has totally shattered.

. . .   .

ONE OF MY goals in compiling this anthology is to show the overwhelming variety of Yiddish fiction (form, diction, structure, etc.) from its pre-Yiddish roots and medieval debut to its modern traditions and experimentations. Often unique, sometimes parochial, sometimes of universal interest, mirroring realities or conjuring up fantasies, admonishing or diverting, appearing in prose or verse, describing a Hasidic wonder or squirting venom at such hagiography, crystalizing as a sketch or an animal fable or a short story or a novella or a thousand-page novel, cultivating terseness or garrulousness, forging a tight or loose plot or absence of plot, covering a single page or spinning an endless saga, focusing on dialogue and/or narrative, drawing on or attacking the supernatural, Yiddish stories run the full gamut of human creativity—as proved by the tales that I've presented here.

ACKNOWLEDGMENTS

I WOULD LIKE TO thank the many people who have helped me enormously with directions, explanations, suggestions, recommendations. In alphabetical order: Dina Abramovicz, Zachary Baker, Dan Ben-Amos, Marc Caplan, Amy Cherry, Itzik Gottesman, Kim Guise, Eli Katz, Aaron Lansky and his National Yiddish Book Center, Sid Leiman, Max Mermelstein, Edna Nahshon, Simon Neuberg, Dovid Roskies, Mordkhe Schaechter, Jeff Sharlet, Michael Steinlauf, Dov Taylor, Erika Timm, Iosif Vaisman, Bina Weinreich, Seth Wolitz, Neil Zagorin, Sara Zfatman, Harry Zohn—and countless employees of countless libraries.

PART ONE

The Old Yiddish Period:

1382 to the

Mid-Eighteenth Century

NEGLECTED AS YIDDISH culture may be, the Old Yiddish period is even more overlooked. Whereas educated people in other European cultures have at least passing acquaintance with their early history and literature, many cultivated Yiddish speakers, lacking an education in Yiddish, assume that Yiddish literature was launched in the nineteenth century. Yet a rich Yiddish literary tradition actually began way back in 1382 (perhaps before that in oral form) and spread forth in manuscripts, then books. Unfortunately, these texts disappeared over the centuries, and most Old Yiddish works were not published or republished until the second half of the twentieth century.

Scholars disagree about whether these earliest texts were in Yiddish or simply Judeo-German — German with a sprinkling of Judeo-Romance and Hebrew/Aramaic words and phrases. Whatever the language, it was written in the Jewish alphabet, therefore making it accessible almost purely to Jewish readers.

Yiddishists divide the history of the Yiddish language into proto-Yiddish (ninth to mid-twelfth century); Old Yiddish (1250–1500); Middle Yiddish (1500–ca. 1700); and New Yiddish (1700 to the modern era). However, literary genres and stages follow their own development, which doesn't necessarily parallel the evolution of a

language. I would therefore extend the term "Old Yiddish" to cover
the period running from 1382 (the year of the earliest extant Yiddish
literary manuscript) to the mid-eighteenth century. The discovery of
printing certainly helped circulate Yiddish texts; but Yiddish literature formed a kaleidoscope that didn't always reflect the dating of
linguistic phases—especially since the Yiddish language blossomed
in a vast geographic network, with a variety of users, dialects, and
audiences (including wealthy patronesses) for Yiddish literature.

Labels like "Middle Ages" or "Renaissance" don't necessarily
apply to Jewish history: unlike Western Europeans, Ashkenazi Jews
didn't pass through a medieval period that led to a creative rebirth
of classical culture. Nor was the Jewish Enlightenment, the *Haskala*,
truly identical with the German *Aufklärung* or the French age of
Lumières.

The versatility and sophistication of early Yiddish literature was
thrilling and provocative. The writers were of course profoundly
influenced by the sacred texts: the Jewish Bible, the Babylonian
Talmud, the Mishnaic interpretations—and their commentaries.
One example of this impact is Moshe Esrim Vearba's *Shmuel-Bukh*,
the *Book of Samuel* (1544). This verse romance, based on the biblical
story of King David and colored by the world of Christian chivalry,
is hailed by some scholars as the national epic of Ashkenazi Jews.

Old Yiddish authors penned homilies for women, guidance books
for men, medical manuals for physicians and patients. They translated prayers and other liturgical and theological texts, including biblical concordances. They invented plots and characters and they
drew on the international treasury of folktales and fairy tales. They
frequently adapted Gentile stories, dechristianizing and even judai-
cizing them: see Yitskhok bar Yehudah Reutlingen's Yiddish version
(1580) of the German sixteenth-century folk book *Emperor Octavian*.

The difference between a Jewish and a Gentile story is captured
in Old Yiddish terminology: the Old Yiddish noun *histórye* (Gentile
history, story, tale) as opposed to the Old Yiddish *mayse* (a Jewish
story). According to Erika Timm,* the *histórye* was a marginal genre.

---

*In *Beiträge zur Geschichte der Deutschen Sprache und Literatur*, vol. 117, no. 2
(Tübingen, 1995), pp. 243–80.

Appearing first in the late sixteenth century, it consisted of stories "whose non-Jewish derivation, made clear by non-Jewish names, indications of social status, and so forth, must have been obvious to the average Jewish reader." Despite rabbinical disapproval, says Timm, the *history* endured until the late eighteenth century, and though peripheral, it exerted a certain pressure on Jewish writers, challenging them to come up with "*mayses*," Jewish stories, often judaicized plots, to edify and entertain, especially on the Sabbath. In modern Yiddish, the word *history* has all but disappeared, while *mayse* is now a generic term for all sorts of Jewish and non-Jewish tales. Sometimes, however, in the face of modern borrowings like *novelle* (novella), *dertseylung* (tale), or *legende* (legend), *mayse* can also mean "fairy tale," "Hasidic fable," and so on.

Now let's begin our journey through Yiddish fiction with one of the very first Yiddish literary works—an Old Yiddish verse narrative about Joseph and Potiphar's wife.

ANONYMOUS

Yiddish literature begins with a version of the biblical tale about Joseph, Potiphar's wife, and her lust for the slave boy. Some observers claim that prior to the modern era there is little about sex and/or romance in Yiddish literature; this brief and vaguely obscene narrative should help dispel that illusion.

The earliest source for this piece is a midrash (Tanh.uma, Vayeshev 5), which actually talks about "citrons" (etrogim) as the fruit that is served. The Yiddish poet changed it to "apples" (perhaps because of an unfounded tradition that apples were the forbidden fruit in Eden). A later source is Sefer ha-Yashar, Vayeshev 87a–87b, which became the basis for Israel J. Zevin's modern Yiddish adaptation, "Zlikhes Libe" in Der Oytser fun ale Medroshim. Zevin uses "oranges" (apelsínen). A tongue-in-cheek German*

*(New York: Tashrak Publishing Company, 1926), vol. 1, pp. 166–68.

version of the "luncheon" appears in Thomas Mann's Joseph and his Brothers: *the ladies who lunch are likewise served oranges.*

Although rooted in religious tradition, the Old Yiddish version of this midrash, as Eli Katz points out,* is narrated with the most courtly and courteous trappings—a mythical realm for the Jewish audience.

Virtuous Joseph (1382)

I will sing wonders, if you have the time,
Of how virtuous Joseph quelled his heart so fine
Whenever his master's wife asked him
To lie with her and commit a sin.
To the lovely lady he politely said, "Never!
I would have to repent such a wrong forever.
All your orders I would fully obey
If they did not harm my soul in any way."
     And so purposefully the master's consort
Gathered the worthy ladies of her court.
The lovely and noble hostess spoke so courteously:
     "My slave is the most lovable that a lady can see.
His eyes are like stars, like gold is his hair—
My heart loves him more than I can bear.
His face and his speech are so regal that he
Ought to rule an entire country.
Virtue and worthiness are his constant guides,
Virtue at his right hand, worthiness at his left side.
I told him I wished him to lie with me,
In my orchard, I would serve him as need be.
But there is no way I could ever see
His beautiful features properly.
Pure and clear are his eyes and bright
As the morning star and the sun's own light.
My heart is tormented by desire,

* "Six Germano-Judaic Poems from the Cairo Genizah," doctoral dissertation, 1963.

This hero has conquered me and my fire.
Now follow me, ladies, all of you.
I want to show you the beautiful Jew."
    The ladies exclaimed, "Don't make such a fuss!
How could a little Jew appeal to us?
We need some proof!" the ladies did say.
    They stood up and followed her right away.
She ordered her servants to bring chairs that unfold,
With silk cushions and inlaid with gold.
The ladies all sat in a courtly way.
Then the rich, sublime, and virtuous hostess did say:
    "Joseph, my slave, please come here and stand
Before these lovely ladies, as I command."
    Joseph obeyed her speedily,
He stepped forward so courteously.
Next, apples were brought, so alluring and red,
For the worthy ladies. And the hostess said:
    "Bring us knives, the finest to suit,
So that these worthy ladies can peel their fruit."
    The servant quickly brought the knives, and
Each lady took a knife in her hand.
    "Peel your apples," said the hostess fair.
    They did so while at Joseph they did stare.
And soon their hands were cut and gashed.
    The smart and worthy hostess was very brash:
"Look, worthy ladies, why have you lost control?
You've cut up your fingers—a heavy toll!"
    They were very ashamed, they peered around.
They didn't know what they had found.
    "Joseph, my slave," the lady said, and
"Pour the beverages with your snow white hands."
    He served them mead and clear wine apace.
He was deeply ashamed, with a crimson face.
Joseph poured with his snow white hands,
His eyes on the guests, his heart with God, and
After he poured, their goblets were at their lips,
But they stared at him without taking sips.

Their complexions were no longer bright,
And they held the golden goblets very tight.
Their love was so deep, they couldn't stand the sight,
And they had to admit that their hostess was right.
    The ladies arose and kissed his head.
"You deserve to rule your own kingdom," they said.
    Now witness the wonder of the hero's victory
Purely because he quelled his heart, you see.
    A short time later, he gained dominion
Over Egypt, and his virtues were legion.
    For the sake of God, friends, learn from this tale:
Your love should be chaste without fail.
And if your love is always chaste and wise,
You will enter holy Paradise.

ZALMAN SOFER (dates unknown)

*W*ritten in verse (with a demanding rhyme scheme—ababccc), this narrative dialogue draws on the following biblical references:

"Noah planted a vineyard and he drank of the wine, and he was uncovered in his tent" (Genesis 9:20–27). Noah's son Ham tells his two brothers, who then cover their father. Upon awakening and learning what has happened, Noah curses Ham's descendants.

Moses and the children of Israel, who are plagued with thirst, "tempt the Lord" by asking, "Is the Lord among us or not?" (Exodus 17:1–7). God tells Moses to smite a rock: water flows out, and the people drink. But Moses loses the possibility of reaching the Promised Land.

After Lot and his daughters survive the destruction of Sodom and Gomorrah, the two girls, believing they are the last human beings alive, get their father drunk, have sex with him, and bear a son each (Genesis 19:31–38).

The Yiddish text, transliterated into modern Hebrew script, can be found in M. Basin, 500 Years of Yiddish Poetry (New York: Literarisher Ferlag, 1917). I am also grateful to Erika Timm for showing me her transliteration (Trier System).

Debate Between Wine and Water (1517)

"I'M CALLED THE offspring of the grape," said the wine. "People drink me fervently, and I'm very fine. I can make people joke and jibe, I can drive away their terrible pains, I can delight their hearts."

"Stop talking," the water snapped. "Remember the way you sinned with Noah in the ark. You can't hold a candle to me, I please both rich and poor."

"I'm praised all the time," said the wine with envy, "when girls get married and when babies get circumcised. I am a hero above you, and you can't get ahead of me—people say blessings over me."

"How can you boast like that?" the water shouted bitterly. "You come from me—I'm your father, you were cut by my rain. You really shouldn't say those things, you should honor me in front of honorable people."

The wine instantly replied: "You're not being fair. You made a great man commit sins—Moses, the servant of God. He nourished us with Heaven's bread. For your sake he had to taste death. And that's something we lament all the time."

"Why do you keep talking and talking?" said the water. "Hold your tongue. The Red Sea was split down to its very bottom and it rose on both sides, so that the holy people of Israel walked across without getting their feet wet."

"You should praise me," the wine cried haughtily. "I am poured on the sacrificial altar, two quarts of me each day. People pay high prices for me and they store me in a fine tent while they spill you on the ground."

"Don't brag at my expense," the water yelled. "I'll tell about how you made Lot's daughters commit a horrible sin. Lot poured wine down his throat, and that's nothing to flaunt, for he made both his daughters pregnant!"

ZALMAN KHASAK *(dates unknown)*

The Holy Days taking part in the free-for-all are: Hanukkah (the Feast of Lights); Passover (commemorating the Exodus of the Jews from Egypt); Shevuoth (commemorating God's gift of the Torah to the Jews); Rosh Hashonah (New Year's); Yom Kippur (Day of Atonement); Sukkoth (harvest festival); Ninth of Av (the destruction of the Temple); and Purim (the salvation of the Persian Jews from destruction at the hands of Haman, the shah's wicked adviser).

This humorous narrative has an intricate rhyme scheme, which I haven't even tried to capture: aabccbdedefgf, whereby the g-line remains unrhymed. This device—the "orphan line"—was used in medieval German poetry to lend a touch of disharmony, of dissonance. In this Yiddish debate, the dissonance may reflect the sometimes harsh if comical argument. As the penultimate line of each stanza, this orphan is part of the conciliatory finale spoken by Purim:

> God grant that next year we will be
> In Jerusalem with all our tribe.

The War of the Holy Days *(1517)*

OLDENDORF, GERMANY

NOW, MY DEAR friends, do you see what you're doing? The Holy Days indulged in arrogant boasting, in envy and hatred and warfare. Hanukkah tried to fight them all and carry the day by force: "I want to present this to people so they'll understand this whole business. The Greeks failed to remove one small measure of oil, enough to burn for one day—but the light lasted for eight days. Heaven worked this great miracle: the good Lord made a great sign to every single person."

"I don't wish to put it off any longer," said Passover, stepping forward.

"I want the prize. On my day they started to tell the story, God chose my night and He also parted the Red Sea."

Hanukkah said: "I'm so delighted—I've got my revenge. No one can stomach your food, people cook a lot better on my day. Young and old are cheered by the sight of me. So keep quiet, you talk too much!"

"You shouldn't break off with me," said Shevuoth. "Why, you're one of us. On my day God gave us the Torah and gave each man a crown as well. God Himself spoke to us."

Hanukkah replied very sagely: "I've seen a lot of cake and milk with you—you've simply lapsed into a fever because all the meat was fed to the dogs. I won't say a word about your great offense. Just take your cheese and butter and leave the land."

"Well, let me complain too," said Rosh Hashonah, the holy start of the New Year. "I'm stronger than you, for the world was born on my day, and people have to blow a horn to scare off Satan."

Hanukkah sneered: "You've lost to me; you are godly half the day, but I don't need to pray very much. Instead, people have to read from the Psalter. That's prohibited on your day, but I can enjoy it."

"Hanukkah, I've taken my aim at you—for you're nothing compared with me," said Yom Kippur, the Day of Atonement, the unique day. "On my day God forgives Israel for all its sins, and the children of Israel are just in all their bonds, like the pure and holy angels."

Hanukkah said: "I'm longer than you and hotter. You belong with the Ninth of Av in the summer. I'm good at gobbling and guzzling, but people suffer grief and hunger with you, and they also have to go barefoot. Someone who hates you can't repent his sin."

"You're throwing out the baby with the bathwater. You always have the least provisions, so I'll give you another day. My name is Sukkoth, and people will know Israel because of me when the sun is hottest."

Hanukkah said: "I'm superior to you!" And they began to curse one another. "With you, people sit in snow and rain, but when I come, they heat their homes. I've shut your mouth—you want to battle with me, and that makes me very angry."

"It's no miracle that you've promised the Holy Days, and they've shattered their share. But I, Purim, I'll catch you. On my day they cook the best and not the worst. Israel was saved, and Haman was hanged."

Hanukkah replied wisely: "You are my inferior, for I last a whole eight days, and even that, I feel, is too brief."

Purim said: "You are the master and I am the servant. God grant that next year we will be in Jerusalem with all our tribe."

ANONYMOUS

The manuscript of this story, which belongs to the overall international fairy-tale stock, can be found in Trinity College, Cambridge, England: Codex F 12.45. A transcription has been prepared by Erika Timm (Trier System). Another version of the text is included in the later Yiddish Mayse-Book *(1602).*

A Tale of Mainz—
The Two Half Brothers (ca. ?1520)

I'VE BEEN TOLD that years ago a rich man lived in Mainz as a leader of the Jewish community. He had a beautiful wife, who, however, died, leaving him their son. A short time later, he took another wife and he had a son with her. The two half brothers were raised together as full brothers. They loved each other very much and they studied the holy Jewish writings together day and night until they became great scholars.

Their father, however, loved his first son more, while his second wife loved her own son and hated the older one.

Now in the same town there lived another rich community leader, and he had a daughter whose beauty was unrivaled. He would have liked to give her hand in marriage to one of the half brothers, but he didn't know which one. If she married the older boy, then the second wife wouldn't like it, and if she married the younger boy, then the father wouldn't like it since his older son was the firstborn.

They finally decided that the two half brothers should go on an ocean voyage for three years, whereby each son would be given a hundred ducats for his pouch. Upon their return after three years, the one who had studied harder and had more money would marry the beautiful girl.

The two half brothers liked the idea, for they both loved her, and each boy planned to study so much that he would get the girl.

So they ordered some bread—that is, biscuits. Each brother then took a hundred ducats for his pouch, and they boarded a galley. The father and the mother, who accompanied them to the harbor, each told his or her son to study hard so that he would marry the beautiful girl. The girl's father, who likewise saw them off, told them: "One of you will marry my daughter—the one who studies harder and acquires more money, so I can see who is the more skillful."

The two boys set sail, and the moment they reached the high seas, the younger son devised a cunning plan to cheat his brother and get the beautiful girl for himself. One night, when the older son was asleep, his younger brother filched all his bread, leaving him without food. Then he went to the crewmen and gave them fifty ducats to testify that he hadn't robbed him, nor were they to sell him any bread, so that he would starve to death.

Upon waking up, the older brother, unable to find his bread, began shouting: "Who's taken it?" No one responded, and he didn't want to get beaten into the bargain. He had to keep quiet. After hungering for a day, he took his hundred ducats and tried to buy bread from the sailors, but nobody wanted to sell him any. The starveling went to his half brother and said: "Dear brother, for God's sake—sell me some bread! Otherwise I'll starve to death."

The brother replied: "I love you, but I love myself more than you. A tempest may come, forcing us to remain at sea for a long time. If that happens, I myself won't have enough food, and both of us will die. It's better if only you die. But if you give me your hundred ducats, I'll sell you ten loaves of bread."

The older brother thought to himself: "I'll give him the hundred ducats so that I won't starve to death. If God helps me, I'll find a way to survive with my knowledge of the holy books." And so he forked over the hundred ducats and took ten loaves of bread.

As they sailed on, a gale arose and it tossed the galley to one side, so that they spent nearly a year at sea. Many of the crewmen starved to death. The older son, who had no bread left, once again approached the younger one: "For God's sake, give me some bread."

His brother replied: "I'll give you some only if you let me poke your eyes out. That way I'll be certain you won't marry the beautiful girl."

The older son thought to himself: "Dear God, what should I do? I'm bound to die." And he said to his brother: "Dear brother, poke my eyes out, but give me your word of honor that you will let me live and that you will guide me to people who can take care of me by the will of God."

The younger son gave him his word of honor and then he poked both his brother's eyes out. He fed him until they reached a port, where the younger son and his blind brother disembarked. The younger one thought to himself: "I'd better not guide my brother to other people. My parents might eventually find out about him. But killing him wouldn't be right either. I'll let him live, and I'll just leave him here. That way, he'll die on his own, and my parents will never be the wiser."

So he abandoned his poor brother and went away.

We will now let the blind brother sit where he is, and we will write about the younger brother, who could still see.

The younger brother found a ship that would take him home. He boarded the ship and sailed home after being away for only a year. When he returned, he was lovingly welcomed by his mother. His father then asked him: "Where did you leave your half brother?"

The son replied: "Dear father, my brother was not very skillful and he wasn't used to the ocean. Unfortunately, he died on shipboard after being ill for six months. I spent more than two hundred ducats of my own money on him, and I have another two hundred left. I simply earned my money on the ship, and if I'd spent another two years in the cities, I would have acquired a lot more money."

The father was horrified, but his wife was delighted that her son would get the community leader's beautiful daughter. She then hurried over to tell the girl that the younger son would marry her. The mother also said that they ought to have the wedding very soon.

But the girl's father replied: "I'd rather stick to my promise and wait out the full three years. Perhaps the half brothers had a fight, and your son then quickly sailed home first and wants to marry my daughter before your stepson shows up. The older son may be at a great yeshiva and may still manage to come home in time. In that case, I'll have broken my word. That's why I don't want to have a wedding until the three years are up. If the older brother doesn't return at the end of three years, then I'll let the younger one marry my daughter." The girl's father knew that she preferred the older brother. So they agreed to wait the full three years.

And now let us leave the younger brother, who tried to amuse his fiancée for the next two years, and let us again write about the blind brother, whose younger brother had left him on the seashore, so that his father and his stepmother could only assume he was dead.

The poor man had been sitting there for a very long time, nearly starving to death. At times he stood up and wanted to go somewhere, but he only fell into the filth. He then thought to himself: "How can I walk if I'm blind? I'll sit down again and recite all the prayers I know by heart—until I die." And he tearfully recited his prayers until he fell asleep.

He now dreamed that an angel came and told him: "God has heard your prayers. Reach beside you and you'll find some herbs. Rub them into your eyes and you'll be able to see again."

The older brother awoke from his dream and he thought to himself: "Dear God, I dreamed such a beautiful dream. If only it were real!" And he pulled out all the herbs he found beside him and he rubbed them into his eyes. And . . . he could suddenly see as well as he had seen before, and his face was more beautiful than ever.

Now since he could see again, he traveled to a land called Armenia, taking along the herbs that had restored his sight. Eventually he reached a town called Kulbakh, where he stayed at an inn. The innkeeper, a wealthy man, gave his patrons six months' credit for food. That was why the older brother wanted to stay there.

Within a week he saw that the innkeeper had only one child, a beautiful daughter, who was blind. The brother thought to himself: "My prospects look good."

That evening, when they were about to dine, the brother went to the innkeeper and said: "Dear innkeeper, I have no money to pay you for food, but I'll try to recompense you in a different fashion. You have an only child, and she's blind. I hope to God that I can make her see again."

The innkeeper replied: "Dear friend, you're trying to do the impossible. My daughter was blind when she emerged from her mother's womb. If you could really make her see again, I would give you ten thousand ducats. I'd also send you to the king, who has a blind son. If you could cure him, the king would give you half his kingdom."

The brother then said: "I'd like to give it a try." He took the girl into a private room and rubbed the herbs into her eyes and—she could see again, and she had a beautiful face. The innkeeper immediately gave the brother the ten thousand ducats. Holding him by one hand and his daughter by the other, the innkeeper took them to the king and said: "Your Majesty, I am bringing you my dear daughter, who, as you know, was blind when she emerged from her mother's womb. But this man cured her. I hope he can also cure your son."

The king said: "Dear innkeeper, if he makes my son see again, then you'll become my viceroy, and I'll give him anything he desires."

The brother then made the king's son see again. The king was overjoyed and he said: "Ask for three wishes, and I'll make them all come true."

The brother's first wish was that the king's son should marry the innkeeper's daughter. His second wish was that the king should give him two hundred thousand ducats. And the third wish was that the king should purchase the town where his father lived and make the son its ruler.

The king's son promptly married the innkeeper's daughter, and the king then gave the brother the two hundred thousand ducats. Next the king wrote a letter to the king of Mainz and offered to buy the town for three times its value; he would then install a ruler. They came to terms, the king sent the payment, and the inhabitants prepared to ride out and meet their new ruler. The town of Mainz was handed over to the Jew, the son of the community leader.

And what did the son do? He took thirty prominent young men and ten ordinary ones and he bought them fine horses and dressed them in red. The son said to them: "Come ride with me to a town called Mainz, and I will reward you. This town will become mine. My father lives there and my stepmother and my fiancée. Once we're there, don't reveal who you are until I say so."

He then set out with his companions, and they reached Mainz, where they were welcomed very respectfully by the inhabitants, as is the custom when a new ruler arrives. The Jews in Mainz asked only that the new ruler be good to Jews.

It was now three years since the two half brothers had originally set sail, and the younger brother ran after the girl's father because he wanted the wedding to take place. When the father then began celebrating the wedding, the ruler found out and he thought to himself: "I have to make sure that my brother doesn't get my fiancée."

The ruler set out and he too attended the wedding, where the Jews welcomed him very respectfully. When the ruler saw the bridegroom sitting next to the bride, he sat down at her other side and hugged and kissed her in front of the bridegroom. The Jews were terrified, but they didn't dare say anything. And so the day passed, and the ruler returned to his palace.

The next morning the ruler told his ten ordinary men: "Go to the wedding, where each of you will take a stick and smash all the pots used for cooking and take their meat. And when you see the bridegroom, throw filth at him, and act malicious toward the Jews."

And that was what the young men did. As a result the Jews were terrified of the new ruler.

On the third day of celebration, when the bride and groom were to be wed under the canopy, the ruler took all his thirty prominent young men, dressed them appropriately, and gave each one a prayer thong, while he himself drew a beautiful prayer shawl over his head. He sent ahead all kinds of Klezmers [musicians] and then attended the wedding.

And all the Jews began to laugh, saying that the ruler was so charitable, while the Christians thought that he was crazy. The ruler then stepped under the canopy with the bridegroom, and when the bride was escorted to the groom's side under the canopy, the ruler stood on her other side. They launched into the benedictions, and when the groom was about to slip the ring over the bride's finger, the ruler produced a ring and slipped it over her finger before the groom could manage to do it. Next, the ruler's men drew their swords and took the bride to the palace.

The Jews followed the ruler and said: "Give us back our bride. If you don't give her back to us, we'll go and complain to the Pope."

The ruler answered: "Let the bride remain in the palace tonight, and I'll do nothing to dishonor her. And if she doesn't agree to become my wife in the morning, then I'll let her go."

So the bridegroom had to go home in shame, and the girl's father and mother went home, bitterly weeping.

Once they had left, the ruler went to the bride and revealed who he was, and he told her so many things that she believed him. She hugged him and kissed him, and spent the night in great joy.

He said to her: "Dear bride, when your father and mother come here tomorrow with the entire congregation, don't tell them who I really am. Just say, 'Dear father, I want to marry the ruler and I never want to hear or see my fiancé again.'"

In the morning they came, and the ruler brought the bride from the chamber and said: "Dear girl, if you wish to go home to your father and mother, I won't stop you or force you to stay."

The bride said: "Dear father and mother and congregation, I want to marry the ruler and I don't want to marry my fiancé or ever hear him or see him again."

And so everyone went home, saying: "The hell with a bride who wants to be a Christian."

Once all the congregants were back home, the ruler had a lot of cows slaughtered and he threw a marvelous banquet. He again summoned all the congregants, and when they arrived, he locked them up in a large room, saying: "I won't allow you to go home until you dine with me, because I have married one of your Jewish girls."

The Jews were terrified and they said: "Dear lord, we are not permitted to eat your food."

The ruler replied: "If you don't want to dine with me, then you will all have to die."

When the Jews heard that, they were terrified and they thought to themselves: "It's better for us to eat nonkosher food than for all of us to die and let them take our children."

The Jews began to eat and they acted very merry and cheery with the ruler, but their hearts weren't in it.

After the meal, the ruler began to speak: "Dear friends, don't think that the food you ate was not kosher, it was definitely kosher. I am as Jewish as you." And he revealed himself to his father and to the congregation. The congregants were overjoyed, and so were his father and his parents-in-law. But his stepmother and the first bridegroom, who was his half brother, were terrified. The ruler told them about how his brother had poked his eyes out and how God Blessed Be He had come to his, the older brother's, aid.

He then had the younger brother's eyes poked out, but he kept him at his table and he did not do to his brother as his brother had done to him, stranding him on the seashore.

Thus no one should rely on his great cunning or shrewdness, for whatever God wills must be done, as you can see from this story. And so the older brother, together with his wife, remained very wealthy until the end of his life.

The End of the Tale of Mainz.

ELI BOKHUR *(?1469–1549)*

A woman marries her husband's murderer and then, fearing her son's revenge, tries to do away with the boy. He escapes and makes it through diverse adventures until, depending on the variation, he kills his stepfather, possibly his mother, and possibly marries his true love.

Bovo actually began life in the tenth century among the Danish invaders in England (his story was paralleled in Historia Danica by Saxo Grammaticus). The oldest extant version of Bovo's narrative was probably the Anglo-Norman Boeve de Haumtone (first half of the thirteenth century), while the oldest manuscript of the metrical English romance, Sir Beues of Hamtoun, was composed in the early fourteenth century. Sir Bevis of (South) Hampton then kept resurfacing in numerous prose or verse adaptations written in different languages, including French, Welsh, Russian, and Italian.

The Italian version, Bovo d'Antona, in ottava rima (stanzas with an abababcc rhyme scheme), caught the eye of Eli Bokhur (aka Elias Levita), a Yiddish writer and Hebrew teacher who had settled in Italy around 1496. His dazzling Yiddish masterpiece, Bovo fun Altona, retaining the metric structure of the Italian text, was composed in 1507 but not published until 1541.

Later that century, back in England where it all began, William Shakespeare turned the oft-treated story of the original Danish Amlethus into a play: he called it Hamlet.

Bovo of Altona *(1507; publ. 1541)*

Chapters 1–3

WE SHOULD PRAISE God eternally and proclaim His wonders, for He is revered and venerated by pious souls. He is powerful both on earth and in Heaven. His praise is unfathomable, no one can laud Him enough, for His praise has no end or cease. May His Holy Name strengthen me, so that I may succeed in completing this task of rendering an Italian book into Yiddish. May He help me to take great care and not miss out on anything, so that people won't laugh at me. Now lend me your ears and let's get going.

THEY SAY THAT long ago a duke with many fine qualities ruled Lombardy. This dear man, whose name was Guidon, had no equal far and wide. A great hero in all battles, he wore his crown honorably in a town called Altona. This was where he had spent his life, and he was now sixty. The Italian book tells us that the highborn duke had never married and had never been corrupted by women. But when he reached old age, he felt very cold, though he was warmly covered. No matter how much he was warmed, it wasn't enough, he was freezing to death. So his wise warriors said to him: "Your Grace, take our advice. Send out men to search everywhere and find a young, warm girl. She should warm you and take care of you." The duke would have been doomed had he remained a bachelor any longer.

The daughter of the duke of Burgundy was chosen. The duke of Lombardy liked this girl, who'd be good for him. She was known as the beautiful Brandonia. Indeed, her beauty, which was beyond compare, was renowned as far away as Babylonia.

In many respects Brandonia had a wonderful life with the duke, who gave her anything her heart desired. Her days were fine—but her nights were awful. She warmed the duke in good ways—I can say no more. But at last the fun came to an end: beautiful Brandonia became pregnant and then bore a son by the grace of God. No one had ever seen a lovelier and more graceful boy than this one, whom they named Bovo—and you can imagine how delighted his father was. The duke asked his friend, Count Sinibald, to be Bovo's godfather, and the count obeyed. Deep in a forest several leagues from Altona, on top of a steep hill, Sinibald lived in Sansimon, the most fortified castle that anyone had ever seen.

The duke said to Sinibald: "Take my son, have your wife nurse him, and provide him with everything. And if he cries, have somebody sing to him."

Sinibald took the young lord and brought him to his wife in Sansimon. She was very glad to nurse the baby, but she didn't know what else to do with him. They watched him develop and grow strong and bold, and by the age of ten he had already overpowered two or three athletes. Sinibald taught him how to fence, to joust, to tilt, to parry. The boy wanted to kill and wipe out everyone — his mind was so swift!

Sometimes, together with four or five servants, he would ride over and visit his mother. But she didn't love him, she hated him because of his father. She couldn't stand the duke, she didn't feel the slightest bit of joy with him. Once, she began talking to herself: "Oh me, my parents have made me so miserable. May God give them both diarrhea. How could they have been so mean and given me that old fart! I'm going to think of some way out, even if it kills me. I don't want to waste away here and turn moldy and rusty. I'm going to get a fine young man who'll feast with me just as I wish."

Brandonia had a servant named Ritsard, who was very good at being evil. One day, Brandonia summoned him to the chambers built for her by the duke and she said to Ritsard: "If you promise not to betray me, I'll confide something very important and also pay you a thousand ducats. But if you don't obey me, you'll regret it. I'll shout for help and tell them you tried to violate me — which will cost you your life."

Ritsard replied: "Gracious lady, no matter what you ask of me, there's nothing under the sun that I won't do for you." However, he had practically dumped in his pants and he was shaking as if he had a fever. "Once I get out of this ditch," he thought to himself, "you won't throw me in a second time."

Brandonia then said: "You are to go to France and visit a proud young hero, Duke Dodon of Maience. My husband once stuck a knife into his dear father's belly. Tell Dodon that I want to help him avenge his father's death. Show him this letter: I'm asking him to come to Lombardy so he can kill my husband. My husband has a menagerie in that forest, and I'll send him out to hunt. Tell Dodon to wait there with his men. He won't have a long fight or skirmish. Just tell him to do it right. Next, he should come here straight across country and capture the town. I'll scream and cry loudly — if I'm not laughing too hard. Then I'll marry him, we'll have the wedding very soon. And I'll be with him day and night — making up for lost time!"

Ritsard took his leave and rode away, carrying the letter. But then he thought of his decent master and loudly bemoaned what Brandonia was planning. He repeatedly felt like turning back, but the devil wouldn't let go of him. Ritsard's luck ran out as he rode on and finally arrived in Maience. He headed toward the palace, where he dismounted and tied up his young horse. Entering the hall, he gave Dodon Brandonia's message and her letter.

Dodon read the letter two or three times, then showed it to his wise counselors. Furious, he told his men: "Grab some clubs and beat the messenger! Throw him in the dungeon—the traitor must hang! I don't trust that conniving whore Brandonia! She thinks she can entice me there. They betrayed my father and now they're planning to betray me."

Ritsard was terrified and he said: "Gracious lord, don't give yourself away. Please send out and investigate, and I'll come over to your side. If you find I've lied in any way, you can skin me alive."

Dodon thought: "I'll run the risk. If he's lying, I'll find out. There's one thing that's believable: no young woman wants to have an old man." He then said to Ritsard: "Hurry back and tell her to get ready, tell her I promise to help her."

Ritzard went home and brought Brandonia the news. Now listen to what she could devise when she felt it was the right time. One Sunday night the Creator must have tortured and tormented her. She fell ill and she groaned and shrieked—no one could get her to stop. She was spewing out her very innards. Brandonia then said: "I'm doomed! I'm going to die! My mother wants to shatter my heart!"

The duke now came to her: "You dear girl, what's wrong?" He handed her the glass for tears and said: "My darling, catch your tears in here and tell me what you desire. I'll do anything for you. Tell what you want, and if it exists in the world, I'll get it for you."

Brandonia replied: "If I dared bother you, I'd ask you for a very small favor. Go hunting tomorrow morning for some wild prey, which I'll eat in a soup or a stew. If you can do that for me, dear lord, I think I'll recover fully."

The duke then lay down with her, and they conversed until dawn, when he quickly got out of bed and sent for his armor. He also ordered his servants to blow the trumpets since he wanted to go hunting with all his men.

Upon seeing this, Brandonia said: "Dear lord, please, don't wear your armor—I won't hear of it. You'll be too hot. You're not going to joust with anyone. And I also think you should take only two men along. That's enough company. Leave the others at home."

The dear fool let her convince him. That very same morning the pious and honorable duke heedlessly rode out with only two men and with his hawk on his arm. Meanwhile Duke Dodon, the destroyer of the land, was concealed nearby in the forest, waiting with four hundred armored men, while Duke Guidon hunted with his hounds. When Dodon felt the moment had come, he and his men came charging out and they shot arrows that lodged in Guidon's flesh, inflicting deep wounds. The poor duke died on the spot. Next the invaders galloped into the town. "Dodon! Dodon!" they shouted as they burned and massacred.

When she recognized him in the distance, Brandonia hurried over and took him home—and he had to lie with her. (Gentlemen, that should tell you what misfortunes come from evil women. A wife cuts her husband into bits and pieces so that she can dishonor him. All misfortune comes from women. Just look at what King Solomon wrote in his books: all his days he looked for a pure woman but never found her.)

Loud weeping and wailing could be heard throughout the town, and many people shed bitter tears—burghers and aristocrats, rich and poor, merchants and shopkeepers. Why, even a rock would have felt pity. The townsfolk shouted: "Alas, alas! Our dear ruler!"

Many people wanted to get even and avenge his death. They grabbed their swords and spears, intent on killing the murderer. But Brandonia sent for them and spoke sweetly: "What do you want to start with us two? It's happened—make the best of it! The old duke, Guidon, may have shown you great trust, but take a look at my dear Dodon, the young, strong, proud giant. He's going to give you presents—fields and meadows and vineyards, and you won't have to pay any tolls or taxes or interest for an entire year. So follow my advice, pledge your friendship and your loyalty to Dodon."

The townsfolk mused: "Why should we put up a fight? We'll keep our anger to ourselves." Against their will and with deep regret, they swore their allegiance to Dodon.

Meanwhile, Bovo, terrified of the uproar, had concealed himself. Sinibald, his pious godfather, who had no idea where the boy had gone, was very worried. He combed the house all morning—every nook and cranny, and behind every vat and every sack. Next he searched every corner of the stable.

Bovo had lain down under a large manger, and when he heard his decent godfather, he quickly emerged and threw his arms around him. "Dear godfather," said Bovo, "what's happened?"

Sinibald told him everything, including the bad news about his father. Next Sinibald hurried off to find the old noblemen who had kept their allegiance to Guidon. He told them to get ready and flee with him and Bovo to Sansimon Castle.

That night they stole away in three groups, weeping and wailing in the nasty rain. There were easily sixty men, one of whom was the traitor Ritsard, who had brought Dodon the letter. But none of these lords knew about his betrayal. In fact, they trusted him blindly, they didn't realize that he had changed and that he wanted to continue his treachery.

"We shouldn't wait any longer," Ritsard mused. "I'm going to sneak off and find Dodon. I'll inform on them all, I'll make sure he has them arrested."

Ritsard swiftly galloped back to town and told Dodon everything, naming every single man who had brought Bovo to Sansimon. Dodon was furious: "Just wait till I get my hands on them—I'll beat them to a pulp!" He then quickly spoke to his strong warriors: "Go and catch up with them! Goad your horses, dig in your spurs!"

They replied: "Gladly, Your Grace!" And they sped away like lunatics!

After his betrayal, Ritsard rejoined the conspirators: "Dear comrades, let me advise you. Ride slowly with the boy. What's the rush? You don't have to be afraid, we're safe, there's no one to be scared of."

So they slackened their pace. But soon they glimpsed a large enemy battalion half a league behind them, it was galloping cross-country on both sides. Sinibald said: "We're in trouble! If we don't flee, we'll be done for!"

Ritsard said: "I'll go and find out who they are and where they're heading." No sooner said than done. He whizzed off like an arrow from a bowstring, and upon reaching the pursuers, he said: "Step on it! They've spotted you! If you don't hurry, they'll escape!" Then he swiftly rode back—a cunning traitor.

Sinibald had a highly honored son, who was known as the strong Tirits, for he could fight ten men at once. Now, riding at the head of his comrades, he saw Ritsard hurrying to and fro, and it dawned on him that Ritsard was a turncoat. The son said to his father: "Didn't you notice? Ritsard has betrayed us. I can see his treachery—I want to kill him, by God!" Tirits dashed over and thrust his lance into Ritsard's belly. The traitor plunged down and bit the dust. His neck was broken, not a peep came out of him. His treachery was avenged—may it happen to all traitors!

After killing him, Tirits returned and said: "If you want to go to bed with a whole skin, then stay a league ahead of our enemies."

The pursuers maintained their speed, and Sinibald's men fled on and on toward Sansimon. Bovo, however, couldn't keep up. His horse was very high — too high for him! When he dug in his spurs, the horse reared and then kicked out. Bovo had to jump down and he fell on his back. The pursuers came racing over and they grabbed him. Meanwhile his comrades reached Sansimon and dashed across the drawbridge. When they realized they had left Bovo behind, they lamented loudly.

Bovo tried to remount his horse, but failed. Dodon's men captured the poor boy and carried him back to Altona. After closing the gates, they were delighted to take him to Dodon and Brandonia. The two of them looked him over but hardly spoke. So we'll leave them for now and go back to Sansimon.

Sinibald and his men didn't want to wait. They galloped out of the castle, burning and catching and robbing and grabbing anything they could lay their hands on. This was the wise course to take. Otherwise they would have been doomed. They filled Sansimon with enough food and supplies for an eternity — cattle, lumber, iron, as well as wine and oil and grain. Four hundred men were holed up inside — and the devil himself couldn't have stormed the castle.

Duke Dodon was furious: "I won't stand for that. I'll wage war even if it costs me all the territory that I've conquered!" Now Dodon had a highborn brother in France, a man known as the strong Alborigo. When Dodon summoned him, Alborigo came riding with a thousand lances. Next Dodon sent his brother and all his warriors to Sansimon, which they surrounded completely. But each man inside merely gave them the finger and stuck out his bare behind. Nevertheless they had to keep quiet, and so the war dragged on and on, as you will hear.

After some three long years, Dodon himself rode out from Altona together with his lords and barons and he pitched his tent in the field. One night, when everyone was fast asleep in the battle zone, Dodon began shouting bloody murder. They all awoke, terrified, and Alborigo asked his brother what horror had taken hold of him. Dodon replied: "I have to laugh at it myself. I dreamed that Bovo came galloping over me and cut my throat."

Alborigo said: "Listen to my advice. Your dream wasn't just a figment. I swear to you, brother, on my honor, you're going to have problems with that boy. You've got to get rid of him. Don't ask any questions; go tell his mother that she should secretly kill her son."

Dodon said: "Hurry and tell my wife about my dream. I'm sure that when she hears about it, she'll have her son exiled or even executed. She loves me too much to let the dream come true!"

Alborigo said: "I'll go gladly!" He rode into town and told Brandonia the whole business.

She was aghast, but she didn't want to argue with Dodon. "Tell him," she said, "not to worry. I'll see to it, I'll take care of Bovo. Dodon won't have to go to confession."

While Alborigo brought back her answer, Brandonia (may she be stricken with an awful disease!) tried to figure out a way of executing her son in secret. She finally hit on a plan and sent for Bovo on the spot. Upon entering, he said: "Mother dear, what is your wish?"

She said: "I felt like seeing you. Let's go for a walk." Taking his hand, she led him through several rooms and then locked him up in the last chamber. Since the poor boy was yelling and screaming, Brandonia wanted to make certain no one heard him. So she locked all the rooms leading to that last one and she hung two curtains over each door.

Bovo was extremely upset. He wondered: "When is this going to stop? How could my mother have forgotten me here? I'd really like to eat, damn it!" He started shouting and he shouted loudly for three days and nights. Brandonia, that evil woman, was afraid somebody might hear his yelling, and she thought to herself: "I'll sneak a certain herb into his food, it will paralyze him. Why make him suffer for a long time?" She prepared some roast chicken and rubbed the herb into the meat. Then, summoning her old chambermaid, she said: "I've left my darling son all alone in a room. He's been there the whole day. Bring him this chicken and tell him to enjoy it. I've forgotten all about him, but ask him not to hold it against me."

The chambermaid took the food and quickly brought it to Bovo. Upon unlocking the door, she found him sitting there, barely conscious, hardly able to talk, almost on his last legs. Crawling over to her, he grabbed the chicken with both hands and was about to shove a piece into his mouth. But the chambermaid, who loved him for his father's sake, stopped him and said: "Dear boy, listen to me and don't eat even a morsel if you value your life. Your mother has an evil goal, she wants to murder you. She's poisoned the chicken. If you eat it, you'll be sorry."

The Italian manuscript tells us that a puppy dog had come running in the moment the chambermaid had opened the door. Tearfully, the chambermaid said to the boy: "If you don't believe me, I'll prove it to you." She tore off a piece of chicken and fed it to the puppy, and before it even swallowed the food, its throat swelled up and it choked to death.

When Bovo saw that, he began to flail his arms about. "Oh, God! How awful! I'll make myself vulnerable! If I come out, I may be seen." He broke into a run and dashed across the town, through muck and filth. Ignoring everything else and racing past the people, he headed for the town gates. His hair was tangled and his cheeks had lost their beautiful color; he looked so awful that no one recognized him.

Bovo walked through the gates and cut across the fields. No path was shown to him, no horse could have kept up with him unless it had been ridden by a giant. But then Bovo's strength began to ebb, and he sat down in a meadow. After resting briefly, he hurried on. Soon he reached the coast and he rested again. Every limb of his ached, and he was so hungry that he munched grass. Eventually he fell asleep on the shore. He slept all night, and no one woke him.

In this place, which wasn't so far from Scaivonia, Bovo slept for three hours into the day. All at once a large galley came sailing—this is absolutely true! She was coming from the Barbary Coast. A man on deck, who spotted Bovo lying on the beach, said to the merchants: "I can see somebody not far from here. If my eyes don't deceive me, he's been killed."

Another man said: "Let's get him aboard. We can easily find out who he is."

Four men sprang into the small rowboat and brought the poor boy back to the galley. He looked as if he were ready to be buried. Not a hair was stirring on his head; he was dead to the world. They tried to revive him with sugar and with herbs, and they rubbed his entire body with vinegar and medicinal water. At last he began to awaken.

Upon coming to, he was amazed to see the people who had resuscitated him. Peering around, he wondered: "Was I paralyzed? Or was I blind? How did I get into this galley? Did the devil carry me?" They told him where he had been and how they had brought him here. Bovo was now fully recovered.

These people made a great fuss about his indescribable beauty; they were very fond of the boy and took very good care of him, so that he quickly did whatever they asked. No sooner did they make a request than he fulfilled it, and he served all the merchants, singing cheerfully, joyfully, exuberantly. Now, since each man wanted to keep Bovo for himself, a battle royal broke out. One man said: "I saw him first." Another said: "I revived him." A third one said: "I carried him on my back." A fourth one said: "I'd rather die than let any of you get him!"

They were ready to bash one another's heads in and they brandished their weapons amid shouting and mayhem. Bovo quickly grabbed an oar and, whacking so hard that it bent, he got them to lay down their weapons. The boy then said: "I swear to you, don't fight over me. Come to your senses, you decent men, and back off. Follow my advice and stay in one place. I tell you, you won't lose out. Just listen to me. I promise I'll serve you all until we reach a port, where you'll sell me as a slave and share the money equally."

The men agreed to this settlement, Bovo got them to shake hands all around, and there were no more hostilities. They continued sailing, sometimes through a wind, sometimes in fair weather, and they all chatted with Bovo. He told them a lot of things, and they asked who his parents were and if he had any kith or kin.

Bovo replied: "The good Lord has punished them: they're poor and they live on charity in Nuremberg. My father is Hungarian and my mother is French. She left me to starve to death—she's a nasty piece of work. I was a nasty boy, I would have shit in my pants before I'd suffer anymore. So I ran away."

The merchants laughed a good while, giggling into their sleeves. But then all at once, after another two or three leagues, a wild storm arose, and they hurried to reach land. Trembling with fear, they hoped to reach the port of Ancona. But then they were blasted by a horrible tempest, by wind and rain, thunder and lightning. Trying to save their lives, they dumped their cargo into the sea, and each man recited a blessing. Within a short time, they were pushed very far, with the water flooding in on all sides. The sail was shredded, the rudder was shattered, the water gushed all around, up to their backs—they were practically swimming. But then God brought them luck: in the middle of the sea, they saw an island, and so they moored the ship there, keeping it immobile. Nor did they spare a single straw.

Now the wind began to weaken, and when they saw that they were near a lovely city in Flanders, they steered in that direction. The city, Armonia, was ruled by a wealthy king named Arminio. The citizens sighted the galley and they fired signals. The king and his lords climbed to the palace roof and watched the galley as it drew near and then dropped anchor in the harbor.

Seeking a diversion, the king and his lords went down to have a look at the galley. The king chatted with the merchants, and they said: "Your Majesty, would you like to buy a boy? We'll sell him to you at a fair price." Bovo was the boy they offered, and they displayed him to the king. Bovo had lovely hair and a peaches-and-cream complexion, and not a single defect could be found in him. The king inspected him front and back and had him trot to and fro, putting him through his paces like a horse that's up for sale.

And so, dear gentlemen, reflect on how a duke's son came down to such a low level. That's why no man should ever rely on land or money, for he never can tell what may become of him or what misfortune may afflict him. You see, the world is like a ladder: one man climbs up, the other comes sliding down.

ANONYMOUS

Mayse no. 1, Codex hebr. 495, Bayerische Staatsbibliothek, Munich.

The sources of this mayse *are ecumenical. According to Erika Timm,[*] this legend debuted in the Apocrypha (first Christian century), and then was adapted in turn by Philo Judaeus, St. Augustine, the Talmud (Pesakhim 118a), and the Koran. At first oral in Yiddish, the story was set down in Hebrew during the thirteenth century and then rendered into the vernacular, whereby the oldest extant Yiddish version, a rhymed text, was written down in 1382–83.*

*Timm, op. cit., vol. 117, no. 2 (1995).

Abraham's Childhood

ROVERE OR REVERE, ITALY, 1584–86

THIS TALE CAN be found in Bachya's commentary on the weekly biblical portion entitled Lekh-lekha [Genesis 12:1–17:27] and on its midrashic
interpretation.

We learn in this midrash that God Praised Be He said to Abraham our
Father: "I am God, who brought you out of the fiery furnace."

And this is what happened to Abraham:

AT THE HOUR of his birth, a star arose in the east and devoured four stars
on the four sides of the heavens. King Nimrod [who founded Babylon
(Genesis 10:8–12) and who, according to tradition, became Abraham's
adversary] asked his wise men what the occurrence of this eastern star
meant.

They replied: "It means that at this hour a son was born to Terah, and
his son will ultimately bring forth a nation that will inherit both this world
and the next. If you wish, we will fill his home with silver and gold and
we will kill his son."

King Nimrod then sent for Terah and said to him: "Yesterday a son was
born to you. Go and bring him to me, and I will kill him and fill your
house with silver and gold."

Terah answered: "You speak to me like someone who tells a horse,
'Come here, let me chop off your head, and I will reward you with a
whole house filled with barley.' The horse replies, 'You fools, if you chop
off my head, who will eat the barley?' The same is true if you kill my son:
Who will inherit the silver and the gold?"

The king said, "I have heard that a son has truly been born to you."

Terah said, "Yes, but then he died."

The king said, "I am talking about a living son."

Terah thereupon hid his boy in a cave, where he spent three years.
God Blessed Be He put two windows in the cave: oil went through one
window and fine white flour through the other. And when the boy turned

three, he left the cave and saw heaven and earth and he wondered in his heart: "Who created all this?" And he then prayed to the sun all day.

When it was evening, the sun went down in the west and the moon came up in the east. Upon seeing the moon and the stars around it, the boy thought to himself: "The moon must certainly have created all this and me, too. And the stars are the servants of the moon." So he stood all night and prayed to the moon.

When day came, the moon went down in the west and the sun came up again in the east. The boy thought to himself: "I can see that the sun and the moon have no power. There must be a Lord above them, and I will pray to Him."

He then went to his father and said: "Dear Father, tell me: Who created heaven and earth and me?"

His father replied: "My god, whom I have—he created all this."

The boy said: "Dear Father, show me your god if he is powerful enough to create all this."

The father showed the boy his idols.

Abraham then went to his mother and said: "Dear Mother, prepare a good dish for me so I can honor my father's god with it."

She made him a good dish, and the boy took it and placed it in front of the largest of the idols. But the idol said nothing and ate nothing. So the boy went back to his mother and said: "Dear Mother, prepare a better dish than the earlier one."

She prepared a better dish, and the boy placed it in front of the largest idol. But the idol said nothing and refused to eat anything. The boy was then imbued with the prophecy, and he recited the biblical verse: "They have mouths but they speak not; eyes have they but they see not" [Psalms 115:5, 135:16]. He now took a flame and burned up all the small idols, and he took some fire and placed it in the hand of the large idol. In the end the large idol also burned up.

When Terah came home and saw that his gods had burned up, he asked: "Who did this?"

Abraham said: "I didn't do it. The largest god grew angry at the others and he burned all of them up."

Terah said: "My dear son, I see that you are not intelligent, for they have neither the power nor the life to do that. I myself carved them out of wood."

Abraham said: "Dear Father, your ears should hear what your mouth speaks! If they have no power, why do you believe in them?"

The father heard what his son said. He then went to the king and told him that Abraham had burned up the gods in a fire. The king sent for the boy, and when he came, the king asked him: "Your father has told me that you burned up the gods. Why did you do that?"

The boy said: "I didn't do it. It was the largest god who did that."

The king said: "How could they have done what you say? Is there any living breath in them?"

Abraham replied: "Your ears should hear what your mouth speaks! If they have no power, why do you believe in them and why do you neglect Him who created heaven and earth and why do you believe in a piece of wood?"

The king said: "I created heaven and earth with my power."

Abraham said: "Let me tell you something: I left the cave where I was hidden for three years and I saw the sun coming up in the east and going down in the west. If you can make the sun come up in the west and go down in the east, I will admire you as a god and worship you. But if you cannot, then the same God who gave me the strength to burn your idols will give my hands the strength to kill you."

The king asked his wise men: "What should we do to this boy?"

They replied: "This must be the boy who, we said, will bring forth a nation that will conquer this world and the next. We therefore advise you to do to him what he did to our gods."

The king instantly had the boy thrown into a fiery furnace. But the Holy One Blessed Be He said: "I will protect him, for I am One, and he is the one man who has recognized me, and you, [the archangel] Gabriel, should protect Daniel's companions Hananiah, Mishael, and Azariah [Daniel 1:6f; 3:1–30]. Abraham recognized me at the age of three."

Now the Holy One Blessed Be He came down and protected Abraham, so that nothing happened to him. And the people standing around the fiery furnace saw that the boy was protected, and many of them now believed in God Blessed Be He since Abraham believed in Him and trusted in Him, as the biblical verse says: "Blessed is the man who trusteth in God Blessed Be He" [Jeremiah 17:7].

ANONYMOUS

A transliteration (Trier System) of this tale has been prepared by Erika Timm, and a facsimile of a virtually identical later version is included in Eli Katz's Book of Fables.*

Printed in Verona in 1595, and lacking a rabbinic endorsement, The Book of Cows, a Yiddish collection of thirty-five fables, may have been a reprise of an earlier anthology. According to Katz, these stories ultimately derive from Aesopian and Arabic traditions that circulated in Hebrew versions. One Hebrew source, Mishlei Shu'alim (Fox Fables), says Katz, contains 119 Aesopian tales written by a French Jew, Berechiah ben Natronai ha-Nakdan, in the late twelfth or early thirteenth century. Another source was Meshal ha-Kadmoni, which, drawing on Indian and Near Eastern literature, was written in Hebrew by Isaac ibn Sahula (thirteenth century). And finally, there is Der Edelstein, a Middle High German text penned by Ulrich Boner in the fourteenth century.

The fables (and each moral) gathered in The Book of Cows are all cast in rhyming couplets, each line containing between three and six beats. After an abortive effort to render "The Peasant and the Scribe" as a poem, I finally succumbed and opted for prose. But

> *For better or worse,*
> *Here's the first page in verse:*

> *Beyond the Stura River, they say,*
> *A peasant lived in his crude way*
> *In a large village, and a few*
> *Other peasants lived there too.*
> *He went to plow his field each day.*
> *And he wasn't brainy in any way,*
> *He was quite stupid like men of his ilk.*

*(Detroit: Wayne State University Press, 1994).

His garden also had a lot of silk—
Worms like to spin that kind.
Now one day he made up his mind:
He would take his silk to the fair.
"Nobody will bamboozle me there.
They'll have to pay some pretty pennies
Inside the walls of Venice."
     The peasant could think of nothing more—
He planned to rake in money galore.
The trip would last three days and nights,
And he looked forward to the delights.
For this long journey he did prepare.
The summer was so torrid here, etc.

The Peasant and the Scribe

FROM *THE BOOK OF COWS*
VERONA, 1595

THEY SAY THAT a very crude peasant lived in a big village across the Stura River, where a number of his companions resided too. The peasant, who was neither wise nor shrewd, neither smart nor sensible, went out to plow his field each day. He also had a garden with lots of silk, the kind spun by worms.

One day he decided to take his silk to market. He thought to himself: "It won't be easy for anyone to bamboozle me. They'll have to pay through the nose inside the walls of Venice." He was totally engrossed in his idea and planned to make a bundle—it would cheer him up no end.

The overland route takes three days, so he prepared for a long trip. Since the summer was extremely hot, he took along a flask plus a pouch containing three ducats. That way he'd have everything he'd need.

Early in the morning the peasant strapped the pack harness tight so that the donkey could lug a heavy burden. Tying on a pair of saddlebags, the peasant crammed the huge amount of silk into one bag while leaving the other empty. Since the off-kilter load made the donkey stand lopsided, the peasant filled the left-hand saddlebag with many small or large stones he got his hands on. The packs had to be well balanced, for the peasant was heading to faraway places.

However, even though he thrashed and flogged his donkey and drove it brutally, the weight was too heavy, the animal could barely drag itself along. All at once the peasant encountered a man, who, though lacking money and property, was in a fine mood. His life was dedicated to intellect and wisdom, but his clothes were torn and tattered and covered with patches. The peasant, who was scared by the very sight of this shabby and seedy man, thought to himself: "He must be a highwayman!"

The stranger said to the peasant: "You don't have to be scared of me — I'm not the devil out of hell."

So the peasant walked toward him, greeted him courteously, and asked: "Where are you from, my friend?"

The stranger, who was a scribe, asked him: "Where are you coming from and what town are you going to? Please tell me, my dear friend — I'd gladly keep you company."

The peasant said: "I'll explain how I got here. I'm a rich merchant and I'm taking a load of silk to Egypt. For it is written [Leviticus 19:9]: 'Thou shalt not wear mingled cloth.' People need silk for the ritual fringes."

The wise scribe answered: "Fine! Then let's travel together. I know I'll enjoy your company."

The peasant said: "I'd certainly like to join forces with you. But please tell me what line of work you're in."

The stranger said: "Actually, I was born in a large town filled with intelligence and wisdom and with many admirable sages and scholars. In fact, I'm coming from there now. All my life I've been accustomed to studying and writing, but I'm so poor that I had to leave home. I plan to make my fortune, for I've got lots of different skills. I hope I can make use of them in Italy if I meet the right persons. I'd like to find people who want to hire a *melámed* [elementary religious teacher] to tutor their children — I know I can do it. I've already taught the Siddur [Daily Prayer Book] and the commentaries of Rashi [eleventh-century exegete].

"If I found a respectable man, I'd go to work for him. I can guarantee that my charges will make great strides within a semester. I'll teach them everything that God has taught me. I'll also raise them properly: I'll get the boys up early in the morning and take them to synagogue, I'll have them pray fervently as if every day were Yom Kippur and Rosh Hashanah. I won't let them skip a single word and I'll make sure they stay in their seats instead of running around and fighting and roughhousing with the bad boys. I won't let them associate with the troublemakers or talk and shout in the synagogue. They won't harass one another, they'll recite the prayers correctly and omit nothing. They won't play any pranks or pinch each other the way bad boys do. They'll pronounce every word distinctly and complete each blessing with an amen.

"The teacher must be a good guide so that the children will behave in the synagogue. Otherwise he has to slap their hands and put some fear in their hearts. That way he'll win them over to the Torah and the prayers. These pupils will be lauded throughout the community and honored more than any other pupils.

"Well, I'm both wise and clever, thank God. I'm renowned among sages and unique among teachers."

When the scribe was done, the peasant said: "You've been talking a blue streak and you seem to have a stock of good words. But I haven't really been listening because of my donkey. His load is heavier than usual, he's about ready to keel over. Once I get him moving again, you'll have to repeat everything you've said. My poor donkey is wobbling as if he were sick—I can't get him to budge, he just digs in his heels."

The peasant tried to force the donkey, but the load was too heavy, the animal couldn't walk, its legs buckled, it fell flat on its face. The peasant was both terrified and furious, he growled like a bear, he yelled and screamed.

The scribe said: "You're doing it all wrong. Your stupidity is obvious in a lot of ways. Oh my! Why holler so angrily? It just goes to show what a fool you are! Grab hold of the tail, we'll pick the donkey up again and remove everything he's carrying. You won't suffer any damage—I'm giving you some excellent advice. C'mon, let's get started!"

The peasant began unloading, and the scribe, following his own advice, wanted to help. Upon grabbing the sack of stones, he said: "Now I see why the donkey can't haul this load you've forced on it. No wonder it collapsed."

The peasant said: "I'll tell you the truth! I filled one saddlebag with silk, which I want to sell in Egypt. Then I had to fill the other side with these stones."

The scribe said: "You've been waylaid by your own stupidity. You weren't smart enough to put half the silk on one side and half on the other. The donkey would have a much easier time walking and it wouldn't have fallen so miserably into the mud. That's why you ought to take my advice."

The peasant did what the scribe told him to do. The scribe then went on from where he'd left off, blowing his own horn. He said: "My wisdom can't be fathomed." And he kept talking in that vein.

The peasant said: "Tell me quickly! What's it all about? If you're so smart, how come your clothes are so ragged and threadbare? Who can believe you're so wise if you wear such awful stuff and you can't help yourself and you have such bad luck in everything you try? Who's going to listen to you?"

The scribe said: "Let me explain it to you. The sages made a pact, which they confirmed by fasting to make sure it was heeded. Their agreement was that no melámed should ever get rich, otherwise he would no longer enjoy his work. That's why I'm so poor. Nevertheless, I'm still a teacher."

The peasant said: "I don't like what you've told me and I don't want to travel with you. You've had such misfortune and hardship, nothing you do works out, and you hardly ever succeed at anything. So I'd rather get rid of you. Just go your own way, or else we'll get into a big fistfight. And I certainly don't need your advice either. I'd be better off traveling alone. Your bad luck made my donkey collapse—he practically broke all his limbs. It was all your fault. I don't want to boast about your company and I certainly don't welcome your advice. I don't care how heavy the load is—I want my donkey to carry the stones, and I'd rather travel by myself. I'm sure I'll manage, I don't need to hear your babbling—everything you say is a lie."

THE PEASANT COLLECTED as many stones as before and put them on the donkey's back, forcing it to stoop. Then he drove the donkey very hard.

Quite early on the third day he reached his destination, the town where he planned to hawk his silk. The merchants came hurrying over. One merchant paid a tidy sum for the silk and said: "Is this all the silk you've brought?" The merchant thought to himself: "He must have more silk for sale in the other saddlebag." Out loud he said: "Tell me, my dear quick-quack, what do you have in the other bag?"

The peasant said: "There's nothing there—just stones to balance the weight."

The merchant thought to himself: "It's so wonderful that the peasant brought these stones from a foreign country!" When the merchant touched the bag, he saw how many whetstones were inside, and he thought to himself: "The peasant must have brought them on purpose. He must have learned that the king and his council have raised a hue and cry throughout our country. They've decreed that all swords and knives have to be sharpened because the king is planning to attack his enemies, and he wants to start immediately." The merchant said out loud: "These whetstones are just what I need."

He promptly took the peasant to a place where he said a lot of friendly things to him. "Just tell me what you want for the stones."

The peasant, who didn't know about the royal edict, couldn't believe his ears. He said: "Don't make fun of me! I'll swap them for a bunch of old shoes."

The merchant said: "That's fine! Just see how much you can charge. You don't have to be ashamed of this merchandise."

The peasant said: "Well then, seriously, I'll take a thousand pounds."

The merchant immediately emptied the bag on the table and gave the peasant ready cash.

The peasant went home. Who could be happier! Just look at what luck can bring. He said: "Since my donkey carried a heavy load, I'll give him more fodder today, some extra oats."

The peasant led a merry life and never even dreamed of crying. After all, he'd gotten a thousand pounds for some ordinary stones.

EVERY WORD OF this fable is true—just ask Joel the Whipper. And there are two lessons you can learn here.

First of all: a melámed is expected to teach with goodwill—as this fable points out—and with good cheer. Happy the man who does so and who guides his pupils for their own good and not for appearance's sake. Nor should he let his work get him down, like the peasant, to whom the scribe divulged his business. If a man wants to be an excellent mentor, he ought to take this advice to heart. That way he'll ply his craft with pleasure and honor.

As for the second lesson of this fable: If you're poor, then people will disdain your opinions and heartfelt thoughts, even today. A man who can't help himself or bank on himself (and there are many such paupers!) can't give anyone good advice. He has to walk barefoot with everyone else and he won't find favor with anybody. No matter how wise he may be, he'll remain a laughingstock. He can speak with the best of intentions, but he'll be shrugged off like a barking dog, and his counsel won't bring him luck.

By disregarding the scribe's advice and following his own instinct, our peasant got a great deal of use from his stones. Had he listened to the scribe, he would have lost his thousand pounds and ended up in the filth. No one should lend an ear to an unfortunate person, for his recommendations seldom pan out. But if you ask a fortunate person, God will bless you through him. Luck always wins out, even if something appears to go against nature, just as luck was with our peasant because he ignored a luckless man. That's certainly why fortune smiled on him.

If you need advice, then always ask a man who's got a star shining on him and who's going through a favorable period. Stick with him—you'll have lots of luck and God will give you a happy and prosperous life.

JACOB BEN ABRAHAM OF MEZRITCH

(dates unknown)

Six Tales from *The Mayse Book* (1602)

The Mayse Book (Story Book), published in Basel in 1602 (and reprinted nineteen times during the next two centuries), contains some 258 tales that run the gamut of Yiddish narrative modes—chiefly ethical/religious, but also entertaining. As Sarah Zfatman points out,* the stories were probably told in spoken Yiddish, set down in Hebrew, and then adapted into written Yiddish, which was read both silently and aloud to an audience. According to Jacob Meitlis,† the texts fall into three groups: some 150 Talmudic/ Midrashic stories; the Rhine-Danube cycle; and the international novella.

A still undetermined number of the Talmudic and Midrashic stories may have been transmitted through The Well of Jacob (En Yaakov). *This*

**Yiddish Narrative Prose from Its Beginnings to "Shivkhe ha-Besht" 1504–1814* (Jerusalem: 1985), in Hebrew.
† *Das Ma'assebuch* (Berlin, 1933).

Hebrew compilation of Aggadic legends (mostly from the Babylonian Talmud but also from the Palestinian Talmud) was begun and commented on by a Spanish exile, Rabbi Jacob ibn Habib, who lived in Salonika and died in 1515–16). His labor was continued by his son. A two-volume edition of En Yaakov *was printed in 1522, and expanded versions were published in the aftermath. Those Ashkenazi Jews who could read Hebrew were familiar with this work, although it was not translated into Yiddish until the nineteenth century.*

1. The Jewish Pope

THIS IS THE story of what happened to Rabbi Simeon the Great, who lived in Mayence on the Rhine. Now Rabbi Simeon, he had three big mirrors hanging in his home. And in these mirrors he could see everything that had happened or was to happen. Also, at the head of his bed he had a spring that flowed from his grave at the cemetery. Rabbi Simeon was a great rabbi. And he had a son named Elhanan, and he was still a little boy. Now one day, the shabbes-goyeh, the Christian woman who did the chores on the Sabbath, wanted to heat the room as she usually did. So she picked up the child and went away with him. The maid, who was in the house, didn't ask any questions, for she thought the goyeh would bring back the child. And everyone else was in synagogue.

So the goyeh took the child and went off and had the child baptized. She thought that she had thus made a sacrifice to God, for in olden times people set great store by baptism.

Now when Rabbi Simeon the Great came home from synagogue, the maid wasn't home, for she had run after the goyeh, but she couldn't find her. So Rabbi Simeon didn't find his maid or his child. All at once, the maid arrived and screamed frightfully. Rabbi Simeon asked the maid why she was screaming. The maid said to him: "Dear Rabbi, may God protect us. The shabbes-goyeh took the child away. And I don't know where she's gone with him."

They looked for the child everywhere. But they couldn't find him. The child was gone. The parents wailed and moaned about their beloved child, as we can well imagine. Rabbi Simeon fasted day and night. But the good Lord, Blessed Be He, did not reveal what had become of the child.

Now the child had gone a long way, falling into the hands of Christian priests, and they raised the boy, who became a great scholar. For his mind came from Simeon the Great. And the boy went from one university to another, until he arrived in Rome. Here he zealously learned many languages, so that he became a cardinal in Rome and his fame was so great that people couldn't praise him enough. And he was greatly respected and also very handsome.

At last it happened that the Pope died, and the youth, being very intelligent and knowing many languages, became Pope. Now he knew quite well that he had been a Jew and came from Mayence and was the son of Rabbi Simeon the Great. But he felt so well off that he remained among Christians, as one can imagine, for he was so highly respected.

One day he thought to himself: "I want to try and bring my father from Mayence to Rome." So he wrote a letter to the bishop of Mayence, for he was the Pope after all, and all bishops served under him. And he told the bishop of Mayence to prohibit the Jews from keeping the Sabbath, circumcising their sons, and letting their women go to the ritual bath. The Pope knew his father would be sent to him to try and rescind the decree. And that was what happened. When the letter from the Pope came to the bishop, the bishop immediately informed the Jews about the misfortune. The Jews lamented to the bishop. But the bishop showed them the letter that had come from the Pope. Therefore he couldn't help them. If they wanted to plead their cause, they ought to go straight to the Pope in Rome.

Now who could be more miserable than the poor Jews? They did penance, prayed, gave alms. Finally, they made up their minds to send Rabbi Simeon the Great with two other rabbis to Rome to see the Pope. Perhaps the Holy One Blessed Be He would work a miracle for them. However, they still circumcised their sons on the sly, for they had gotten permission from the bishop to do so, but in great secrecy.

The three Jews got underway and went to see the Pope in Rome. When they arrived, they went to the Jews there and told them what had happened. When the Roman Jews heard this, they were greatly surprised, for they said that since time immemorial they had never had a better Pope for Jews, for he couldn't live without Jews and always had Jews around him secretly, and they had to play chess with him. Nor had they heard anything about the dreadful decree.

"We cannot believe that the decree came from the Pope. The bishop must have issued it himself."

So Rabbi Simeon the Great showed them the Pope's letter and seal, and the Jews had to believe him, and they said: "You must have committed some terrible sin in Germany."

And the Jews of Rome also did penance, and prayed, and gave alms. And the community elders went to the cardinal, whom they knew personally, and asked him to intercede.

The cardinal said: "The letter was written by him personally to the bishop of Mayence, so there's nothing much we can do."

He promised he would do his best and told them to draw up a petition, and he would make sure that the Pope would get it. And he would do his best to help them.

So the Jews drew up a petition and gave it to the Pope. As soon as the Pope read the petition, he saw how matters stood. And he had the Jews come to him personally. Thus Rabbi Simeon came before the highest cardinal, and he presented them to the Pope, saying these were the Jews from Mayence and they wished to speak to him personally. The Pope ordered that the eldest should come before him. Now Rabbi Simeon the Great was the eldest among them, and he looked like an angel of the Lord. And the moment he came in, he fell to his knees. There sat the Pope with a cardinal and they were playing chess. When the Pope saw Rabbi Simeon, he was deeply shocked and asked him to stand up and have a seat until he was finished playing. For he recognized his father right away, even though the father didn't recognize him.

When they had finished playing, the Pope asked him what he wished. The great rabbi told him, weeping and wailing, and wanted to prostrate himself before the Pope. But the Pope wouldn't let him, and he said: "I have heard your wishes, but strange reports came from Mayence, and that was why I had to issue my decree."

The Pope began a Talmudic discussion with Rabbi Simeon, and he very nearly beat him, God forbid, so that the rabbi was amazed that there could be such a mind among Christians.

They remained together half a day, until the Pope said: "My dear scholar, I see that you are very learned. The Jews did not send you in vain. I have Jews here every day, they play chess with me. Why don't you play chess with me? Your matter will not turn out badly."

Now Rabbi Simeon was a master at chess, peerless throughout the world. Yet the Pope checkmated him. The great rabbi was astounded. And thus they once again began speaking about faith, and Rabbi Simeon heard highly intelligent things from the Pope, which greatly astounded him. Finally, when he had lamented for a long time and told him his wishes, the Pope asked all the cardinals to leave. Then the Pope threw his arms around the rabbi and wept. And he said: "Dear old father, don't you recognize me?"

The father replied: "How do you know me, your royal highness?"

The Pope said: "Dear old father, didn't you once lose a son?"

When the great rabbi heard this, he took fright and said: "Yes."

The Pope said: "I am your son Elhanan, who was taken away from you by the shabbes-goyeh. What the sin was that caused it, or what the grounds were, I do not know. I believe that He Whose Name Is Blessed wanted it to happen. And that was why I issued the decree, hoping that you would come to me yourself, which is what happened. Now I want to become a Jew again. I will therefore annul the edict."

And he gave him letters for the bishop of Mayence, revoking the somber edict.

Now the son asked: "Dear father, can you give me advice as to how I can atone for what I have done?"

Rabbi Simeon said: "My dear son, do not worry, you are one of us, for you were only a child when you left me."

The son said: "My dear father, while I lived so long among Christians, I knew that I had once been a Jew, and the fine life I led, as you can see, prevented me from returning to the Jews. Can I have atonement?"

The son said to the father: "Go home in the name of the God of Israel and bring the letters to your bishop, but don't say anything else about me, I will soon be with you in Mayence. But I want to leave something behind me here, which will be good for the Jews."

Rabbi Simeon went back to the Roman Jews and showed them the letter, stating that the edict, with God's help, had been annulled. They were very happy.

Rabbi Simeon and his comrades returned home and brought the letter to the bishop, stating that the edict was annulled, praised be God, and they were all very merry. And Rabbi Simeon told his wife the whole story. When she heard that their son was the Pope, she wept and wailed. But Rabbi Simeon said to her: "Don't grieve, we will soon have our son with us again."

Meanwhile, the Pope wrote a book against the Faith and locked it up in a vault and ordained that any man who was to become Pope had to read that book. And a short time later, he started out with a great deal of money and moved to Mayence, where he once again became a respectable Jew, and in Rome no one knew what had become of him.

The next day, Rabbi Simeon the Great commemorated the story with a poem to be recited on the second day of the New Year. Therefore, do not believe that this tale is made up. It most certainly happened, just as is written here.

Some people say that Rabbi Simeon the Great recognized his son by the way he played chess, because he used a certain gambit that the father had taught him when he was a little boy. And now he had made that same move when playing with his father. The rabbi realized that this must be his son. May the good Lord, Blessed Be He, forgive us our sins through Rabbi Simeon's merits. Amen. Selah.

2. The Pious Jew

A PIOUS JEW died, leaving many wonderful books, which the heirs sold to strangers. And when the other pious Jews saw this, they were pained that the children should be selling off their father's books. Now in the same town there was a great sage, and he said to the pious people: "Don't feel so bad that the books are coming into strange hands. Let me tell you why this is happening and how he sinned. That man never wanted to lend a book to anyone. For he said he was an old man and his books might confuse him and he couldn't see very well. 'Others might ruin my books. So I won't lend my books to anyone.' But a man should not act like that. And since he never lent his books to anyone, they are now coming into strange hands."

3. Hillel and the Convert

A NON-JEW CAME to Shamai and said: "Convert me to Judaism by teaching me the entire Torah while I stand on one foot." But Shamai drove him away with a measuring rod that carpenters use.

So the man left Shamai and went to Hillel and asked him whether he could teach him the entire Torah while the man stood on one foot. And Hillel converted him by saying: "I will teach you the entire Torah while you stand on one foot." And he went on: "Just follow this biblical verse, 'Do unto others as you would have them do unto you.' That is the basis of the entire Torah. Everything else is an interpretation of the Torah. Go and study it further."

And that was how Hillel taught him the entire Torah while the man stood on one foot.

4. The Man Whose Wife Had No Fingers

ONCE THERE WAS a Jew whose wife had no fingers on her hands, and the man didn't realize this during her lifetime.

Rabbi Joseph said: "How chaste the wife must have been, for the man never realized during her lifetime that she had no fingers."

But Rabbi Hiyye said to Rabbi Joseph: "No. There is nothing particularly chaste about her for covering her body, for it is the custom of every woman to cover her nakedness, all the more so this woman, she had to cover herself so that her husband wouldn't see her. Her husband, however, must have been very saintly, for he never knew that she had no fingers."

5. Joseph the Sabbath Observer

THERE WAS ONCE a man named Joseph the Sabbath Observer. He had gotten his name because he would buy whatever he could to honor the Sabbath. Nothing was too costly for the Sabbath. If any good things came to the market, he would buy them. No fish was too expensive for him.

Now Joseph had a neighbor, who was very rich, and he would always make fun of Joseph, saying: "What good is it for you to honor the Sabbath like that? It doesn't make you any richer. I never honor the Sabbath so much, and yet I'm richer than you."

But Joseph was a good man and he didn't care, he trusted in the good Lord, who would make up for everything.

In the same town, there were astrologers, and they said to the rich man: "My dear friend, what good is it for you to be so rich? You can't eat a good fish for your money. We have seen in the stars that that your money will come into the hands of Joseph the Sabbath Observer. He eats a good morsel for his money."

The rich man believed the words of the stargazers, and he went and sold all his property and bought gems and pearls for the money and strung them all together on the headband of his hat. He planned to move to another country, thereby making sure that Joseph would not get his money. And so the rich man sailed across the ocean. But a wind arose when he was on the water, and the wind was about to drive the ship under. It blasted away the rich man's hat, which plunged into the water. Along came a huge, powerful fish and swallowed the hat. The rich man was now impoverished.

Once, on a Friday, the eve of Sabbath, a fisherman caught a large fish and he brought it to market. Everyone bargained for the fish, but the fisherman wanted a high price, so that all the customers left, unwilling to buy the fish. Everyone said: "No one but Joseph the Sabbath Observer would buy that fish. He buys all the large fish; they're never too expensive for him."

And then Joseph, that good man, came to the marketplace and wanted to buy fish for the Sabbath. Thereupon he saw the large fish for sale. He was overjoyed that he could get such a large fish for the Sabbath, and he thought to himself: "Even if the fish costs me a hundred ducats, it won't be too expensive." He started bargaining for the fish. The fisherman wanted a very high price. And he was glad that the man bought it and took it home in high spirits.

When Joseph cut open the fish, he found the string of gems and pearls that the rich man had lost. And thus the prophecy of the stargazers came true: The rich man's wealth came into the hands of Joseph the Sabbath Observer. Joseph was very happy at becoming very rich, for the string of precious stones was worth a kingdom.

Then an old man came to Joseph and said: "If a man borrows a great deal for the Sabbath, the Sabbath will pay him back a great deal." This means: The man who honors the Sabbath with good things will be paid back doubly by Him Whose Name Be Praised. Amen.

6. *Philiman and Satan*

THERE WAS ONCE a pious Jew named Philiman, and every day he would say: "Let an arrow fly into Satan's eye!" And he would curse Satan every day. Once, on the eve of Yom Kippur, Satan disguised himself as a beggar and came up to Philiman's door and said: "Dear friend, give me a piece of bread, for God's sake." And he went on: "On such a holy day, when every Jew sits at a table in his home, I have to eat outside in the street."

So Philiman asked him into his home and gave him a piece of bread.

And Satan spoke again: "On such a holy day, when every Jew sits at a table, I have to sit in front, without a table and eat all by myself."

So Philiman asked him to sit at the table as well.

Now that Satan was sitting at the table, he took on the appearance of a sick, ugly man full of scabs and pus, and the saliva drooled out of his mouth.

Philiman said: "Act properly. Why do you behave in such an ugly way?

Satan, who had disguised himself as a beggar, said: "Give me something to drink as well."

So Philiman gave him a goblet of wine. When Satan was about to drink, he spat into the goblet. He did this to spite Philiman and hurt his feelings, because Philiman cursed him every day, as you have heard. When Philiman saw him drooling into the goblet and then dropping it, he yelled at him: "Hey! Either drink properly or go away."

Whereupon Satan fell back and pretended to be dead. Then a voice came from the street: "Philiman has killed a man in his house." Philiman fled and hid in the synagogue. And when Satan saw that Philiman was so unhappy, he set out and he told Philiman: "I am Satan and I disguised myself as a beggar, I wanted to hurt your feelings because you curse me every day. So, do not curse me anymore."

To which Philiman replied: "What should I say, you Satan, you Evil Spirit?"

Satan said: "Pray to the Holy Blessed Be He to take the Evil Spirit away from you, and to prevent you from stumbling and committing sins, just as King David, may he rest in peace, also prayed to the Holy One."

YAKOV BEN YITSKHOK ASHKENAZI

(1550–1624/28)

Tsene-Rene, the so-called women's Bible or family Bible, rendered into colloquial Yiddish, was aimed at readers who knew little or no Hebrew — some men and just about all women. First published in the early seventeenth century and then constantly revised, this standard household item, still available today, has gone through some 220 printings.

In excerpting, and commenting on, the lean and linear biblical narra-
tives (Pentateuch, Haftorat, and Five Scrolls), the author weaves in quo-
tations from diverse exegetes as well as other parts of the Bible. He thereby
entwines two different modes of time: the irreversible time of biblical his-
tory and the to-and-fro of the time-tripping clarification. By drawing on var-
ious sources, the "discussion" reflects the oral debates and analyses, plus
the question-and-answer processes traditional in the study houses (to which
women have no access).

Noah and the Flood

FROM TSENE-RENE (?1608–22)

THESE ARE THE GENERATIONS OF NOAH [Genesis 6:9].

King Solomon (may he rest in peace) said: THE RIGHTEOUS MAN WALKETH IN HIS INTEGRITY [Proverbs 20:7]. Now this means that a man should follow God's commandments for the sake of God and not for boastfulness. There are people who give alms and then go and tell others about it. In so doing, they commit two wrongs. First of all, they brag and show off. And secondly, they humiliate the pauper by disclos-ing that he has received their charity. That was why King Solomon said: THE RIGHTEOUS MAN WALKETH IN HIS INTEGRITY: BLESSED ARE HIS CHILDREN AFTER HIM. The man who walks in simplicity and modesty and does not boast is righteous and he deserves to have children as pious as he himself. And that was why King Solomon said: MANY MEN WILL PROCLAIM THEIR OWN GOODNESS: BUT A FAITHFUL MAN WHO CAN FIND [Proverbs 20:6]? Lots of people shout about their charity and good deeds, but a pious and true man — who can find him?

It is well known that the righteous have three virtues. Firstly, if a man is pious, he is considered righteous. And if he is even more pious, then he is considered flawless. The third virtue is called *hishalkhus* ["walking with God"], which means that he always walks whole with God. And Noah had all three virtues. That is why the Torah says: THESE ARE THE GENERATIONS OF NOAH: NOAH WAS A RIGHTEOUS MAN AND PERFECT IN HIS GENERATIONS, AND NOAH

WALKED WITH GOD [Genesis 6:9]. Noah was righteous and whole-heartedly good. He never questioned God's actions and he always walked whole with God.

Noah's name occurs three times [in that verse, 6:9] for the following reason. First, he saw the world when there were houses and people; then he saw the world devastated by the Flood; and thirdly, he saw the world again with houses and people.

Now the verse says: IN HIS GENERATIONS. This means that he was a righteous man in his time, when all other people were evil. And had he lived among pious people, he would have been all the more pious. However, a few Sages offer the opposite interpretation: in *his* generations he was regarded as a righteous man, but in Abraham's generation he would not have been regarded as righteous, for Abraham was more pious than Noah.

And the Torah tells us that Noah was righteous, and it was because of his righteousness that God saved him from the Flood. AND THE EARTH [ORETS] WAS FILLED WITH VIOLENCE [6:11]—the world was filled with thievery and robbery. FOR ALL FLESH HAD COR-RUPTED ITS WAY UPON THE EARTH [6:12]. All creatures had cor-rupted their way—that is, they fornicated indiscriminately. Even the cattle and beasts and birds mated outside their species, and people wor-shiped idols. AND THE LAND [ORETS] WAS FULL OF VIOLENCE, the land was filled with thievery. And it was because of all this thievery [*gzeyla*] that God sealed His decree [*gzeyra*]. For while fornication and idolatry are worse than theft, your common sense should tell you that you must not steal even if it were not prohibited by the Torah. On the other hand, copulation and idolatry are evil only against God because God pro-hibited them. But theft is evil against both men and God. And the Flood came because people refused to believe that God can renew the world and they refused to believe that God pays attention to man, rewarding the righteous with good rewards and punishing the wicked with their just desserts. For they said: "God is in Heaven and pays no attention to human beings. It's all the same to Him whether a person is pious or evil."

That was why God brought the Flood. And Noah, the righteous man, and his children survived. This shows us that God rewards the righteous with good rewards and punishes the wicked with their just desserts.

MAKE THEE AN ARK OF GOPHER WOOD [5:14]: God told Noah to construct a huge ark, like an enormous ship upon the water, and to

coat it with tar both inside and out. Now God could have saved the righteous man, Noah, and his children without the ark. But God told Noah
to keep building it for one hundred twenty years so that people would ask
him, "What are you going?" He would then tell them that God would be
sending a Flood, and perhaps they would repent.

Our Teacher Bachya [Jewish ethical writer, eleventh (thirteenth?) cen-
tury] writes: "Why did Noah not pray to save the world from destruction
as Abraham prayed? For when God told Abraham that He wanted to
destroy Sodom and Gomorrah, Abraham prayed over and over for those
evildoers. And the Prophets did the same in their time. However, Noah
saw that his generation did not have ten righteous men, so he could not
pray for its survival. After all, Abraham had stopped praying for Sodom
and Gomorrah since ten righteous men could not be found."

A different interpretation is as follows: "Noah did not pray for them
because for a hundred twenty years God kept warning them to be pious,
but they paid Him no heed."

AND THIS IS THE FASHION WHICH THOU SHALT MAKE IT
OF [6:15]: God told Noah to make the ark three hundred cubits long and
fifty cubits wide and thirty cubits high, with a window to let in light. The
ark consisted of three floors: the top story was for the people, the second
story for the cattle, beasts, and birds, and the bottom story for waste and
refuse.

I WILL ESTABLISH MY COVENANT WITH THEE [6:18]: God
said to Noah: "I will keep my oath to thee: the fruits and the grains will
not spoil in the ark, and the wicked will not kill thee because of the ark,
and thou shalt come into the ark with thy sons and their wives." The
Torah prohibited Noah from mating with his wife in the ark. That is why
the biblical verse says: "The husbands separate and the wives separate."

AND OF EVERY LIVING THING OF ALL FLESH, TWO OF
EVERY SORT [6.19]: God commanded Noah to take one male and one
female of every creature into the ark. And God commanded him to take
such cattle and beasts and birds as did not mate outside their own kind,
and the ark did not take in those that *had* mated with a different kind.
And the cattle and the beasts and the birds came by themselves. And those
that were taken into the ark were certainly good. And Noah had to bring
sufficient food so that all creatures would have enough to eat and drink.

FOR THEE HAVE I SEEN RIGHTEOUS BEFORE ME IN THIS
GENERATION [7:1]: God said to Noah: "Thou art the only righteous

man in this generation." And that is why the verse does not say "righteous and flawless" (*tamim*) as before. This teaches us that we should not fully praise someone to his face.

And God commanded Noah to take seven pairs of all kosher animals and birds in order to sacrifice them at the end of the voyage. . . .

I WILL CAUSE IT TO RAIN UPON THE EARTH FORTY DAYS AND FORTY NIGHTS; AND EVERY LIVING SUBSTANCE THAT I HAVE MADE WILL I DESTROY FROM THE FACE OF THE EARTH [7:4]. . . .

. . . AND NOAH WENT IN . . . BECAUSE OF THE WATERS OF THE FLOOD [7:7]: This means that Noah boarded the ark because of the great water. For Noah still believed that God would not send the Deluge, and so he did not enter the ark until he was forced by the waters.

THEY CAME TO NOAH [7:9]: All creatures came to him. And every creature that was accepted remained in the ark. At first the rain was gentle, so that people might still repent. But when God saw that they refused to repent, He sent a deluge of hot water, and the people were scalded.

. . . AND THE WATERS PREVAILED UPON THE EARTH AN HUNDRED FIFTY DAYS [7:24], the waters rose and fell during one hundred fifty days. AND EVERY LIVING SUBSTANCE WAS DESTROYED [7:23]. . . .

AND GOD REMEMBERED [8:1]: God remembered Noah and the cattle and the beasts, and He calmed the waters. Now Our Teacher Bachya asks: "Why were the birds not remembered? The answer is: The cattle and the birds were created with man on the sixth day. So God remembered them with man."

AND THE ARK RESTED IN THE SEVENTH MONTH ON THE SEVENTEENTH DAY OF THE MONTH, UPON THE MOUNTAINS OF ARARAT [8:4]. Now Rabbi Moshe ben Nakhman [thirteenth-century philosopher] writes:

"At first it rained for forty days, and during those forty days the waters rose and rose until they were fifteen cubits upward and covered all the mountains. And all the wellsprings and windows of Heaven were opened, and the waters were in their strength for one hundred fifty days. And then God sent a strong wind. And so the wellsprings and the windows of Heaven were plugged up, and the places where the waters went out were shut, and the ark floated on water four cubits deep until the first day of the month of Tammuz [June-July]. After that, they could see the mountain peaks on the tenth day of the next month, Av [July-August]. Noah then opened the window of the ark. And three weeks later, he sent out the dove to see if the earth was dry. And thirty days after that, he opened the covering of the ark."

AND HE SENT FORTH A RAVEN [8:7]: Noah then dispatched a raven to see if the water had receded. But the raven did not want to leave. He said: "I and my wife are the only ravens in the ark. If I am destroyed, there will be no more ravens on the earth."

But Noah refused to let the raven back into the ark. He said: "You cannot be used for food [because you are not kosher] or for sacrifice [because you are not pure]."

God said to Noah: "Take him back, for he will perform a mission in the days of the prophet Elijah." What happened was that [centuries later] the prophet Elijah was in a cave, hiding out from Ahab, King of Israel, and he had nothing to eat. But the ravens brought him meat and bread from the palace of Jehoshaphat, king of Judea.

ALSO HE SENT FORTH A DOVE FROM HIM [8:8]: God dispatched a second dove. Now Our Teacher Bechya asks, "Why is the phrase 'from him' used in regard to the dove but not in regard to the raven? This shows us that the clean birds were with Noah in his room while the unclean birds were kept separate. That is why the phrase 'from him' is not used in regard to the raven."

AND LO, IN HER MOUTH WAS AN OLIVE LEAF PLUCKT OFF [8:11]—the dove came flying back with a leaf from an olive tree in her beak. Now the question is: Where did the dove get the leaf since all the trees on earth had been uprooted? The answer is: It did not rain in the land of Israel, the waters from other lands came flowing here, and so the trees in the land of Israel were not uprooted.

Now a few Sages tell us that the dove brought back a leaf from the Garden of Eden. So the question is: How did Noah know that the waters had flowed away since the leaf came from the Garden of Eden, where there was no Deluge? Well, Rabbi Moshe ben Nakhman writes: "The gates of the Garden of Eden were locked to keep out the waters of the Flood. Then, when the waters receded, the gates were reopened: the dove flew in and plucked a leaf. She could have brought a better leaf, but she brought an olive leaf, which is bitter, to show Noah that it is better to eat a bitter leaf from God's hand than sweet food from a human being's hand."

THE EARTH DRIED [8:14]—and when the earth was completely dry, Noah and his household still did not leave the ark, for Noah said: "God commanded me to go into the ark, so I will not leave without His permission."

WHILE THE EARTH REMAINETH, SEEDTIME AND HARVEST, AND COLD AND HEAT, AND SUMMER AND WINTER, AND DAY AND NIGHT SHALL NOT CEASE [8:22]: "There is a time when man must sow on the earth and reap, a time of cold and a time of heat, a time of summer and a time of winter, and they should never cease. And I will never again kill all men at once as I did with the Flood." Nevertheless, some will be born and some will die. That is why the verse says that there will be reaping and sowing—that is, people will be born and will die. And how will they die? Because of cold and heat. That is why the verse says, COLD AND HEAT, for when the summer or the winter leaves, many illnesses arise.

However, according to the author of *The Generations of Isaac*, God meant that "I will not bring down another Flood, but I will curse mankind with cold and heat. The heat will burn the grain, and the cold will stunt its growth. . . ."

. . . AND GOD SPAKE UNTO NOAH, SAYING, GO FORTH OF THE ARK, THOU, AND THY WIFE [8:15–16].

AND NOAH WENT FORTH, AND HIS SONS, AND HIS WIFE, AND HIS SONS' WIVES [8:18]: Now one may have a question. God told Noah that he could go out together with his wife—that is, live with her in order to have children. And why did Noah not wish to live with her? Yet the verse speaks of Noah with his sons, but mentions the women separately. Now there were three reasons why Noah did not wish to live with his wife.

The first reason was that he was afraid that another Flood would come upon his children. That was why Noah said, "Why should I have more children?" So God swore to him that He would never bring another Flood.

The second reason was that Noah feared that wild beasts would kill his children, because men had been sinning since Adam. So a wild beast had the right to kill people, for the beast said, "I am no worse than man when he fails to observe the Torah." But God told Noah, "Thou need not fear the wild beasts, for I will make the beasts fear men. AND THE FEAR OF YOU AND THE DREAD OF YOU SHALL BE UPON EVERY BEAST OF THE EARTH, AND UPON EVERY FOWL OF THE AIR, UPON ALL THAT MOVETH UPON THE EARTH, AND UPON ALL THE FISHES OF THE SEA; IN YOUR HAND ARE THEY DELIVERED [9:2]. But the verse right before that one says: AND GOD BLESSED NOAH AND HIS SONS, AND SAID UNTO THEM, BE FRUITFUL AND MULTIPLY, AND REPLENISH THE EARTH. This also meant that you men should not fear the wild beasts, and you should live with your wives in order to have children."

And the third reason was that Noah imagined that his children would become evil and murder one another. So God said, AND SURELY YOUR BLOOD OF YOUR LIVES WILL I REQUIRE; AT THE HAND OF EVERY BEAST WILL I REQUIRE IT, AND AT THE HAND OF MAN; AT THE HAND OF EVERY MAN'S BROTHER WILL I REQUIRE THE LIFE OF MAN [9:5]. "If a man murders another man, then I will kill the murderer. And if a beast kills a man, than I will kill the beast." . . .

I DO SET MY RAINBOW IN THE CLOUD, AND IT SHALL BE FOR A TOKEN OF A COVENANT BETWEEN ME AND THE EARTH [9:13]: God said to Noah, "I will give thee a sign that I will keep My promise, that I will never send another Flood. And if human beings are evil, I will let it rain, and I will place a rainbow in the sky to show them that I ought to wage war against them and bring a Deluge to drown them. But I will keep my promise."

And that is why both ends of the rainbow point down to mankind. It shows that God has made peace with us and that He does not want to harm us.

Two Spells from Medical Manuals

With slightly modernized spelling, these two Yiddish texts can be found in Max Erik, Di Geshikhte fun der Yidisher Literatur (Fun di eltste Tsaytn biz der Haskole-Tkufe) *(Warsaw, 1928), pp. 45–46.*

In presenting various kinds of cures, Jewish medical manuals included brief anecdotes, spells to ward off the evil eye, malignant spirits, demons, and so on. Like the spells presented here, they constitute an intriguing narrative folk genre.

The first tale has not yet been dated, though, as Erika Timm pointed out to me in a private letter (December 19, 1999), "Such spells were set in verse until the fifteenth century."

The second tale, attributed to Yuda ben Yakov Darshan, was included in The Book of Life-Saving Remedies (Sefer Matsel Nefoshes, *Amsterdam,* 1651).

Anonymous Medical Manual (?16th–17th century)

THE PROPHET ELIJAH was walking along when he suddenly ran into a demon. Elijah asked him: "Where are you going?"

"I want to go to X son of X." And he approached the sick man and his father. "I want to eat his flesh and drink his blood."

Elijah thereupon said: "I forbid you to do so by God of Abraham, by God of Isaac, by God of Jacob: you are not to eat his flesh or drink his blood or harm him in any way. Let this be true in the Name of God and in the Name of Holy Israel."

ATTRIBUTED TO
YUDA BEN YAKOV DARSHAN

A Spell Against the Evil Eye (Symptom 35)

IN THE NAME of the Lord God of Holy Israel.

The prophet Elijah was walking along when all at once he encountered a demon angel. Elijah asked him: "Where are you going?"

The angel said: "I want to go to the home of X son of X and sit at his head and in his brain and in his eyes and in his body and in all of his two hundred forty-eight parts and in all of his three hundred sixty-five veins, and I want to eat his flesh and I want to drink his blood."

Elijah thereupon said: "Just as you don't have the power to drink up all the waters of the sea, you likewise mustn't have the power to inflict any harm in any matter or any form anywhere on earth.

"If X was kicked by a donkey, he need not worry, and if he was kicked by a horse, he need not worry. If a man has given X the evil eye, then let the man's arms and legs drop off. And if a woman has given X the evil eye, then let her breasts and her legs fall off.

"In the Name of the Lord God of Holy Israel. Amen. Just say that three times."

ANONYMOUS

*F*or detailed information about this folk narrative, see Sara Zfatman in Studies in Jewish Culture, in Honour of Chone Shmeruk, *in Yiddish (Jerusalem: 1993).*

The West Indian Tale

PRAGUE, CA. 1665

We have a lovely tale at hand,
It's come to us from a distant land,
That land is West India, and
Many people in the world
Call that area the New World.
Our tale's about a wife who let her spouse
Leave her and their house
To go abroad, for he couldn't read
The holy books. Here are his deeds.
In the end, upon returning,
He had money and pious learning.
So now do hurry
To buy this story.

THIS IS THE tale of a man who was a terrible ignoramus: he knew nothing about the Jewish faith, though he did know that he was a Jew. Moreover, he lived near a Jewish community.

He had a wife, but she died. So he married a maidservant from that congregation, which he seldom visited, though he was wealthy. His new wife saw that her husband was completely unschooled in the holy writings. He never put on a prayer shawl and prayer thongs, and when he got up in the morning he went straight to the stable to see how his livestock was faring, or else he went out to his field. Upon coming back to eat, he touched the bread without washing his hands or saying grace. Nor did he have any children.

When his new wife, poor thing, saw what he was like, she said: "Why are you so ignorant? You never pray and you never put on a prayer shawl and prayer thongs the way other Jews do."

Her husband replied: "I don't know how to pray and I don't know what a prayer shawl and prayer thongs are."

The wife wanted to teach him how to pray, but she couldn't teach him. "I can't sit back and watch you going on like this. Why don't you go to the congregation? Take enough money along. You can give it to the town rabbi and explain your situation. Tell him you're completely ignorant about the Jewish faith and that you want to learn all about it. He'll instruct you and teach you what you have to do. You may have a lot of money, but if you die ignorant, you will never have any rest in the next world."

The husband answered: "Dear wife, I'm going to do as you say."

Taking along enough money, he traveled to the Jewish community. When he arrived, he asked where he could find the Jewish "parson," for he didn't know the correct Jewish terms. They directed him to the town rabbi and they all wondered what he was after. The rabbi received him and asked him what he wanted. He didn't realize the visitor was Jewish, for he was dressed like a wealthy farmer.

The man explained that he was a Jew and that he wanted to learn how to read the holy writings, for he knew nothing about the Jewish faith. "I've got two hundred guldens here, which my wife gave me for my studies. Please teach me so that I'll know what a Jew should know.

The rabbi replied: "Dear son, if you wish to learn, then I will try to teach you." Taking the money, he went on: "This will be good for me."

He ordered fine Jewish clothing for the man and took him to synagogue and instructed him what to say. The worshipers recited *Kedusha*, the sanctification of God's Name, and when they exclaimed, "Holy, holy, holy," they got up on tiptoe with each "holy," as is customary. This tiptoeing greatly upset the visitor, who then dashed out of the synagogue and hurried home.

Upon his return, his wife asked him why he was back so soon, to which he replied: "Dear wife, the rabbi took me to a Jewish church, and the people there were hopping and shouting so much that I was happy to get out!"

His wife started crying and she said: "You don't have to act like that. I know that's what they do. Just do this: take some more money and go back to the rabbi and study."

And the man did so. And the rabbi said: "Dear son, you don't have to act like that." The rabbi took him to the synagogue again. Here the yeshiva boys began arguing, splitting hairs, as is the custom. But the man thought they were arguing about him. And so he once more hurried home to his wife.

Upon seeing him, his startled wife cried out: "Almighty God, why are you back so soon?"

He explained that the students had formed an alliance, and they were shouting so loudly that he felt his life was at stake. If he hadn't run away, he would have been killed.

His wife retorted: "I know perfectly well that they behave like that. But just do this. Take some more money and go back to the congregation, and don't come home again until you know how to study the holy writings. If you act so strange again I'll run away from you and never come back and I'll deny that you're my husband."

He agreed not to act strange any more. He took some more money, went to the rabbi, and handed it to him, saying: "Dear rabbi, make a great effort, and when you teach me, I'll obey you."

The rabbi answered: "If you keep acting as you've done before, I'll be cheating you out of your money, for if a man wishes to study, he mustn't act like that."

The man promised not to do it again.

The rabbi then began teaching him the Jewish alphabet, prayers, and the Pentateuch, and the man learned earnestly. He complied with his rabbi's teachings and learned proper behavior. He learned at length what a decent householder should know; and he became a kosher slaughterer and examiner. The man spent a total of two or three years with the rabbi. Since he understood everything, he gained everyone's love.

One day he felt he should go home to his wife, and he told the rabbi he would do so if the rabbi agreed. The rabbi said: "Yes." He also asked the rabbi what good deeds he should perform so that he might enter Paradise like other Jews, since he had previously spent his days badly.

The rabbi answered: "When you have guests, rich or poor, be generous with food and drink and everything else. When you have poor guests, give them great charity. Study the holy writings for an hour each day and fast one day a week. You will then certainly enter Paradise."

Next, the rabbi bought the man as many prayer books and holy writings as he needed, and he blessed him and sent him home to his wife.

And the man went back. When he arrived, his wife was overjoyed. She welcomed him and said: "Dear husband, what have you learned?"

And the man replied: "I have learned what a Jew should know—writing and reading and other things too."

Who could be happier than his dear wife?

The man ran his household very honestly. When guests came he treated them well, he gave great charity to the poor, and he obeyed his rabbi in every way.

The news of his charity spread, so that many paupers came to him, and eventually he ran out of food. One day, when he was visited by a rabbi with many students, he said: "Dear rabbi, I would gladly receive you with all due honor and respect and give you money, but I have none left." He went on: "Dear rabbi, what should I do to nourish myself?"

The rabbi replied: "Let me give you some advice. Leave home and hire yourself out to a householder, and I'll take in your wife. Perhaps the good Lord will help."

And so the man put his wife in the rabbi's care and then set out in tattered clothes and with a bundle on his stick. And he wandered for a long time.

Eventually the man came to a dark forest, where he trudged around for three days without eating or drinking until he was on the verge of dying. But in the end, the good Lord helped him get out of the forest. Now the man saw a beautiful castle in front of him. He thought to himself: "There must be people inside, and they'll feed me for the sake of God."

When the man drew closer, he saw that the gates were all open. He entered but neither heard nor saw anyone. He came to a dining hall, where the tables were set and decked out with all sorts of good things. The man sat down and ate and drank, and he was fully refreshed. He then wondered where he was, and he didn't know where to go. "I'll stay here. People will come and show me the way."

And as he sat there, he saw a huge battalion with a queen approaching the bridge. And when they reached the hall, they pounced on him and shouted: "This is the right man! We've found the man we've been seeking for such a long time!"

They had him sit down at the table, next to the queen, and they said in unison: "This is our lord and king!" And they danced and sprang about, and treated him joyously all day. He let them play with him, though he didn't know what it was all about.

When night fell, they escorted the queen to a beautiful bedchamber and had the man lie with her. He went along with it all and felt as if he were in Paradise, just as his rabbi had said that he would earn Paradise if he gave a lot of charity. These people treated him like a king, and the queen fell in love with him. And he stayed in the castle for almost seven years.

One day, when the man had lain with his queen, she became pregnant and she eventually gave birth to a son, who was named Solomon. The man then dreamed about his first wife. Upon awakening, he lay there and sighed bitterly. His queen said: "Why are you sighing so bitterly?"

He replied: "I had a dream about my first wife, but I don't know where she is."

His queen said: "I know where she is. But let me tell you who I am. I am a she-demon, and all my people are demons too. You've been here for almost seven years now and you've had every heart's delight, you've gotten everything you've desired, and you've been well served by all your subjects. Now if you stay here for a full seven years, you'll have to stay forever. I will always remain as young and beautiful as I am now, and we will all live forever—and so will you, if you remain here. I'll let you choose, because you're so pious and you feel compassion for your wife. If you remain here, you'll have enough for all time and you will be treated like a king. Otherwise you can return to your wife. You have three days to think it over."

The man hugged and kissed her, but he was distressed, for he loved her and their son Solomon and he wasn't sure how to deal with his conflict. He wanted to go back to his first wife for he had promised her he would return and not abandon her. When the queen saw that he had made up his mind, she sent for the tattered clothes he had worn, and she had him take off his elegant garments and put on his original ones, and they gave him back his bundle and his stick.

The queen than took him to a room and filled his bundle with gold and money, and she said: "Do as you like with it, you will never be able to spend it all in your lifetime. Your son Solomon will succeed you as king, for we have to have a king who comes from human seed. So that should make you feel less miserable about leaving our kingdom behind."

Then Solomon spoke: "Well, father, since you want to go back, let me give you three things, which you should keep eternally for my sake. The first thing is a candle that will never go out as long as you hold it in your hand. The second thing is a stick: whenever you come to a body of water, strike it, and no matter how deep it is, you will be able to go across. The third thing I'm giving you is a ring. If ever you get arrested, God forbid, take the ring in your hand and you'll escape. Don't give it to any person no matter how deeply you care for him. However, if you lose everything and you get into trouble, call out 'Solomon!' three times, and I'll be with you and I'll help you."

The man then blessed his son and hugged him and hugged his wife and said farewell to them and started out.

AFTER WALKING FOR a day, he got lost and didn't know where he was. He found himself in a dark, dense forest, where he couldn't see anything. Taking hold of his candle, he walked right across the forest. On the other side, he encountered a stranger, who asked him: "How did you manage to get through the forest?"

The man explained that he had a candle, whereupon the stranger asked if he could borrow it. The man gave in and lent him the candle, even though it was prohibited.

Continuing on his way, the man came to another dark forest, darker and denser than the first had been. He thought to himself: "If I only had my candle, I would manage to get through." So he felt and groped his way out.

Next, the man came to a large body of water. Taking his stick, he struck the water and then got across it safe and sound. Upon reaching the other side, he encountered a stranger, who asked him for the stick. The man gave in and handed him the stick. He then continued on his way. Next, he came to another body of water, which was deeper than the first, so that he had a hard time getting across.

He then went on until he came to a town. It was evening and the gates were closed so that he couldn't enter the town. Upon finding an old cottage outside the gates, he thought to himself: "I'll spend the night in this cottage."

Inside he found a lot of chained prisoners lying there. He went up to one person and felt very sorry for him. He asked: "If you have faith in me, I'll free all of you with a ring that I have." And they all said: "Fine!"

The man gave them the ring, and they all freed themselves. They went away with the ring, and he was alone now, without the three things. All he had left was his bundle of money.

Since it was day now, the man went on. However, it was the eve of the Sabbath, and when he was taken in by a Jew he asked him to safeguard his bundle. The householder, noticing that the bundle was heavy, looked inside, saw the money, and took it, replacing it with three beakers.

On Sunday the man asked for his bundle, suspected nothing, and set out on his way. But then the householder and the judge came dashing after him. The householder accused the man of stealing his beakers and he had him arrested. While sitting in prison, the man thought to himself: "If I had listened to my son Solomon, I could easily escape now. However, my son did say that if I found myself in a difficult situation, I should call him." He then called: "Solomon, Solomon, Solomon!"

His son appeared instantly and said: "Dear father, what do you wish from me?"

The father lamented: "Dear son, help me, advise me how to get free."

The son said: "Dear father, I told you: let no one be so dear to you that you give him the three things I gave you. Well, it's happened, and tomorrow you'll be put on trial. Keep up your spirits, I'll be with you. No one will be able to see me. According to the rule, a defendant is allowed to have a defender. So ask for one. When you're questioned, look around and I'll be standing next to you in a green robe. Tell them you want me and no one else as your defender, and I'll take care of freeing you. Keep up your spirits, you have nothing to worry about."

The day came, and the man was taken to court. The Jewish householder accused him of theft. The judge then said: "Answer the charge!"

The man asked them to give him a defender. The court agreed. The man looked around and said: "I want the man in the green robe and no one else—he should be my defender."

The defender stood up and said: "How can the householder claim that my client robbed him? After all, my client left his bundle with him for safekeeping. The householder then took all the money and put the three beakers in its place. The pious man trusted him and didn't bother checking the bundle when he got it back. He simply started out again. And now this evil man wants to kill him! You'll see I'm telling the truth: if you dig under his threshold, you'll find everything. After that, let justice take its course."

They arrested the householder and sent men over to his house. Upon digging, they found exactly what the man in the green robe had said they would find. They gave the defendant back all his money and, after hanging the householder, then let the man continue on his way.

His son Solomon then appeared to him again and said: "Dear father, if you had listened to me, you wouldn't have been in such a terrible situation. I was the person who borrowed all those things—I wanted to test you. You've got your bundle back, and here are your candle, your stick, and your ring back. Let no one be so dear to you that you again give him these three things. For I will never come to you again. You have enough money, more than you can ever use up in your lifetime. You can spend as much of it as you like, but you'll never manage to spend it all. Go home to your wife. You'll find her in a field tending sheep; she'll be wearing a red dress, for the yeshiva students treated her so terribly that she couldn't remain with the rabbi. She is still pious and honorable—you don't have to doubt that for an instant. And you won't recognize her."

Father and son said goodbye to one another and went their separate ways.

The father went to where the son said his wife would be. And there she was. The poor thing sat in the field, tending the sheep. She wore a tattered red dress like a wretched pauper. The man greeted her and she returned his greeting. He invited her to come with him since she was sitting there all alone. But she said she already had a husband, though he wasn't with her. He then told her to come with him, he would give her a hundred guldens. But she refused. Then the man hugged her; he burst into tears and said: "I am your husband. And this is what happened to me while I was away."

He then indicated all the features by which she could recognize him. And he redeemed her from the shepherd. The couple then joined a wonderful community, where he bought a beautiful house. He became a wealthy man and a community leader, he gave a lot of charity, and was highly respected in the community.

Thus every man should pray to God to give him such a wonderful wife. Let him study the holy writings and earn the privilege of entering Paradise, and he should have a good life. May we all be a lot better off very soon. Amen. Selah.

YIFTAKH YOSPE BEN NAFTALI HA-LEVI *(1604–1678)*

A transcription of this story into the modern Hebrew alphabet is included in Sara Zfatman's excellent book The Marriage of a Mortal Man and a She-Demon *(Jerusalem: Akademon Press, 1987). A romanization of the story was done by Simon Neuberg (Trier System).*

The author, known as Yospe Shammes, was born in Fulda, Germany, in 1604 and moved to Worms, Germany, in 1623. After penning a few nonfiction books in Hebrew, he wrote several tales that belong to different genres but are all set in Worms: Sefer Maase Nissim *(The Book of Miracles). Despite the title, only some of the tales deal with the supernatural. It is not clear whether the original manuscript was in Hebrew or in Yiddish, although Simon Neuberg opts for the latter.* *Neuberg, who supplies rich data and analyses, tells us that the collection was first published in Amsterdam in 1696 by Yospe's son, Leyzer Liberman, who made some revisions and also added a story of his own plus a poem by his son.*

Yiddish literature is filled with (usually erotic) tales about Jewish men seduced or shanghaied into sex and even marriage by female demons. This complex theme may hint at an underlying fear of conversion to Christianity.

The Queen of Sheba in the House of the Sun

FROM *THE BOOK OF MIRACLES*, NO. 2
AMSTERDAM, 1696

THE HOUSE KNOWN today as the House of the Sun is a large stone structure next to the synagogue. But long, long ago it was called the Devil's Head, and it was the home of a well-respected man. However,

---

*Afn Shvel, 314 (April–June 1999), pp. 10–14.

he was poor and didn't want anyone to find out. This caused him great distress.

One day he went to his storeroom and wept bitterly because of his great poverty. All at once the Queen of Sheba appeared. He had never seen a more beautiful woman — her hair was like spun gold. She said to him: "If you sleep with me every day when the bell strikes twelve noon, I'll make you so rich that few people will match you in wealth."

The man gave in and he slept with her. Every day at twelve o'clock she then visited him, accompanied by two attendants, who carried her gold basin, in which she kept her golden hair. When she lay with the man, the basin was placed on the floor, next to the bed. Her attendants remained outside the storeroom until she got up again. Whereupon they reported to her and followed her out.

The Queen of Sheba ordered the man not to breathe a word to anyone and she said she would kill him if somebody found out. The man obeyed her fully. Every day, when he had lunch, he went down to his storeroom and lay in the bed with her. And she kept her promise, she brought him lots of gold and silver. The man became very rich and purchased luxurious clothing for himself and his wife, as is customary among the rich. On the Sabbath and on holidays his wife wore beautiful garments, and her fingers were covered with rings. It was all more than enough.

The man's wife said to him: "I wonder how you've gotten all this wealth. I haven't seen you doing any business."

The man was very annoyed: "What do you care? If I've got it, I've got it!"

His wife had to hold her tongue. But then one day she said to him: "My dear husband, please tell me what you do in the storeroom at noon every day and why you always stay down there for such a long time."

The husband replied: "I've gotten into the habit of taking a nap at noon every day."

She asked no further questions, but she thought to herself: "He must have a good reason for going down to the storeroom every day at the same time — and I'm not allowed to go. Something's fishy."

So one day, she took the man's storeroom key and had a locksmith make a duplicate for her. The husband was in the storeroom, and after a while she slowly unlocked the door and went in. And there she found her husband lying with the Queen of Sheba. The wife saw how beautiful the queen was and she saw the basin next to the bed and the queen's beautiful hair in the basin.

The wife sneaked out of the storeroom and slowly shut the door, making sure not to awaken anyone, so no one would realize she had been in the storeroom.

When the Queen of Sheba woke up, she said to the man: "You have to die now, for you've revealed our secret. Somebody was inside this room and saw us sleeping together."

The man swore that he knew nothing, that he had never said anything to anyone. Because of his pleading, she didn't harm him, she let him live. But she said: "You will never see me again, I will never visit you again, and your wealth will vanish. I'm taking it all back, and you'll be poorer than ever before. I've got two children from you. I'm going to twist their necks and kill them. Three days from now, go across the bridge [*gisa*] that spans the Rhine. Take several people along, and you will see a coffin floating down the river. It will contain the bodies of the children I bore you. I want them to be buried here, by the Rhine." The man did her bidding: three days later he crossed the bridge and saw the coffin floating down the Rhine.

And within a short time he was again terribly poor.

Therefore never be led astray by money. God grants everyone what he deserves. Amen.

MOSHE VALLIKH (*dates unknown*)

*I*n Yiddish, animal fables are more of a written than a spoken genre. *Framed in rhyming couplets with lines of varying lengths, these two renowned fables go back to Aesop.*

Despite some differences, this collection, The Book of Fables *(Sefer ha-Mesholim) (Frankfurt-am-Main, 1697) is pretty much a knock-off of* The Book of Cows *(1595). According to Eli Katz,** *Vallikh replaced most Italian derivatives, made the overall diction more contemporary, mellowed or abandoned sexual and vulgar material, and discarded Christian and Jewish references that he considered nonessential.*

---

*Katz, *Book of Fables.*

Two Fables from *The Book of Fables* (1697)

The Cat, the Mice, and the Bell

A cat and also many a mouse
Inhabited the very same house.
The cat was always their foe
(And even today that still seems so).
The mice had to complain and cry
As lots of days and years wore by.
Their situation was bad because
The cat caught them everywhere in her claws.
    The mice took urgent counsel to see
How they could cope with their enemy
And keep the cat from pouncing on them
Suddenly and trouncing them.
Since she couldn't get under the eaves, they began
To gather there and work out a plan.
They were in a dither, they didn't know
How to escape their ferocious foe.
The mice huddled with one another
And put all their heads together.
They desperately wanted to drive her away,
And this was what they agreed that day.
A long debate about a solution
Finally led to a conclusion:
They would hang a bell from her neck, and the bell
Would ring loud and clear, and its ringing would tell
Where she would go and where she would stay.
Then they could keep out of her way,
And she'd never sneak up on the mice.
    They bought a bell that was so nice,
And so cheerful was its clang.
They wanted to use a thick cord to hang
The bell around her neck—and that would
End her wicked ways for good.

But this was something no mouse dared to do
(Every word of this story is true).
They failed to agree on who would tie
The bell and so they suffered—oh my!
They couldn't put their plan into action,
They couldn't work as a single faction.
Let them weep and wail about their decision
Because they couldn't carry out their mission.
    It was all for nothing, and that's why, they say,
Cats hunt mice to the present day.

The Fox and the Stork

A fox and a stork were very close, they say—
Which you can still find today.
They cared for each other, those two.
They were loyal friends and true.
    The fox once invited the stork to a meal.
Oh, how honored the stork did feel.
    "Don't mention it," the fox said.
"Today! you're going to be well fed.
I'll serve you every kind of dish,
I'm sure you like chicken and fish."
    The stork was so very hungry that
He hurried over. Right off the bat
The fox took him by his wings and
Said, "Please sit at my left hand.
Let's get started. It's time we ate."
And the fox served him oatmeal on a flat plate.
"Just eat as much as you desire to
And don't take anything home with you.
C'mon, tuck in. There's nothing that
I've forgotten. I've used enough fat
And the seasoning is the best."
The host was deriding his guest.
    With his paws the fox picked up the food.
"It's so well cooked, it's so very good."
He was teasing his friend, who couldn't eat

Anything with his long beak.
    The fox then said to the stork:
"Would you need a shovel or a fork
Or even a silver spade
To eat what I've made?
Oh, well. It doesn't matter anyway.
You can eat in the Italian way.
Now don't be shy. If you
Don't help yourself, what can I do?"
    Whenever the stork opened up
His beak, the food would drop.
The stork was hardly overjoyed—
In fact, he was very annoyed.
But his annoyance he didn't reveal.
    "Is this all you've cooked for our meal?
Back home I've got a lot more food—
Kreplekh that are very good
And delectable almond rice,
Which I know you'll find very nice.
And every kind of Purim treat.
Why not come to my home and eat?
I'm sure you'd find it delicious.
And I'll prepare the finest dishes.
"I've fattened lots of geese and chickens there,
And I'm well prepared with all my fare.
I'd like to reciprocate.
I'll use the most elegant silver plates."
    The fox said to the stork, "That's fine.
But be sure to serve me good wine.
I don't like wine with a bad taste.
So tomorrow I'll come to your place."
    The stork hurried home all the way
And then labored so hard the next day.
He prepared a generous spread
As if a great lord were to be fed.
He sent his servant for the cow's milk
While he did other chores of that ilk,
When all was done, a carafe he did buy

With a long, narrow neck, and he filled it high.
So when the fox showed up at his door,
He was promptly offered food galore.
    The stork said, "I'm sure it's fine.
I know that we will have a good time.
I've cooked up a lot of food,
And the beverages are very good."
Then at last the victuals were brought.
"I've given it a lot of thought,"
He said, "particularly
Because of the banquet you offered me."
    The stork began to mock the fox:
"Please, my friend, I don't want to coax.
Dig in and eat your fill. Just munch.
Otherwise you'll miss out on your lunch.
I'll eat everything I find—
Why take so long to make up your mind?
You don't want to eat, it seems?
Or perhaps you don't like my cuisine?
Perhaps you ate before you came,
Or perhaps you feel sick? What a shame!
Or is sniffing the food enough for you?
Look inside the carafe—please do!"
    The fox could see the food very well—
Why couldn't he do more than smell?
The stork had given him tit for tat
For provoking him, and that was that.
The fox went home so very hungry,
And he was also very angry.
But if he hadn't hoodwinked his friend,
He wouldn't have suffered in the end.
The stork outfoxed the fox, you see.
He got back at him for his trickery.

This fable is aimed at a world where a man
Bamboozles another if he can,
And fawns on him and flatters him
Only to make a monkey out of him.

Furthermore he taunts and mocks
And jeers at him, just like the fox.
So he ought to be justly repaid,
And retaliation he'll seldom evade.
A man who wants to be treacherous
Is neither pious nor virtuous.
He'll get exactly what he's earned—
Which is something the fox has learned.

GLIKL BAS YUDA LEIB *(1645–1724)*

(a.k.a. Glikl of Hamelin)

The untitled memoirs (1691–1719) of one of the earliest female Yiddish writers contain a number of comforting, edifying, and/or entertaining stories that derive from both Jewish and Gentile sources. For just about every tale, Glikl indicates an origin, though perhaps leaving out more precise data. Thus we are intrigued to learn that she found this story "in a book written by a worthy Jew"; and though left ignorant of his identity, we can marvel at Glikl's wide learning and at the wealth of Jewish and non-Jewish literature available to her in oral or written form. Citing linguistic reasons, Chava Turniansky concludes that for this story Glikl copied a Yiddish translation of a Hebrew text.*

The Tale of the Pious Jew

FROM MEMOIRS (1691–1719)

I'VE ALREADY MENTIONED that my father married off my sister Hendele. Why dwell on it? I've talked briefly about how my mother had

---

*In *Studies in Jewish Culture in Honour of Chone Shmeruk* (Jerusalem: n.p., 1993), pp. 153–177, in Yiddish.

been a miserable orphan, but she had had faith in God, and He helped her honestly and richly. This is demonstrated by the following story. While some children are not as well off as others, most people are, thank the Lord, well off and they have their piece of bread. If you trust in the good Lord with all your heart, then He will not abandon you. "Trust in God, and God shall protect thee. Praised be He forever and ever."

Here is a lovely tale and a comfort for all stricken hearts. It teaches us that we should never give up our hope for God's help and never doubt in God's help. This was the case with the pious Jew in this story: even though he was afflicted with poverty, misery, and every kind of anguish, he endured them all patiently and never strayed from God, and God so graciously helped and assisted him, as you will now read.

ONCE UPON A time there was a pious man who had two small sons and a pious wife. He also had a little money to get by on. This man was unfit for any business; all he could do was study the holy books. However, he very greatly desired to earn more so that he might support his wife and children without gifts or help from other people. But fortune did not smile upon him, and he had a lot of debts, alas, which he could not repay. Since nobody cared to vouch for him, his debtors took him to court, and the judge ruled that whereas the man could not pay his debts and had no guarantor, he would have to go to prison. And that was what happened.

His pious spouse cried and cried. She didn't know how she could provide for herself and her two children. And she also had to provide for her husband in prison, alas. As she sat there, moaning and weeping, an old man who was passing by asked her why she was crying. When she saw that he was a decent and venerable old man, she told him about all her troubles.

The old man then said: "Stop crying, God will help you again. And since your husband studies the Torah, God will not forget you. God does not abandon a Jew who is learned in the holy texts. If He does not help him in his youth, then He will help him in his old age. I know that you will have a great deal of trouble and that you and your husband and your children will go through a lot of suffering. But in the end God will be good to you if you endure all your adversities patiently."

He comforted her some more and advised her to become a laundress and earn money by washing other people's shirts. "That way you'll provide for yourself and your husband and your children, so long as you're not ashamed to ask people to let you do their laundry."

The wife felt comforted by the old man's words. She thanked him amiably and said that she would follow his suggestion. The old man then left, and she never saw him again. She went into her home, made supper for her husband, and comforted him: he shouldn't lose patience and he should keep on studying the holy texts. She told him she'd work day and night to provide for him and their little children. Now the pious man finally broke down, and he and his pious wife cried bitterly, begging the good Lord to take pity on them.

The wise and pious wife pulled herself together first and she said: "My dear husband, yelling and crying won't fill our bellies. I'm going to go and see what work God grants me so that I can earn some money and keep you and our children alive."

The pious man replied: "Go ahead, my dear wife. That will help us."

And she went home to spend the night with her children.

The next morning she got up very early while the children were still asleep and she went from house to house, inquiring whether there was any laundry to be done. The townspeople felt sorry for her and let her do their wash. And so the poor woman became a laundress. The town lay by the sea, and every day she would go there with her two children to wash clothes and spread them out to dry on the grass.

One day, when she was doing the wash, a boat came sailing along, and the seafarer, upon seeing how beautiful she was, steered the boat over toward the shore. He was amazed at her beauty.

The woman said: "Why do you look at me so amazed?"

The seafarer replied: "My dear lady, I feel very sorry for you. Tell me: how much do you charge to wash a shirt?"

The woman said: "Sir, I get two groschens for washing a man's shirt because I have to clean it thoroughly."

The seafarer said: "My dear lady, I'd be glad to give you four groschens if you wash my shirt clean and fine."

To which she said: "Sir, I'd be glad to wash it."

She took the shirt, washed it very clean, and spread it out to dry on the grass. While waiting for his shirt, the seafarer kept scrutinizing her as she washed it. Then she dried the shirt and folded it very neatly. The seafarer couldn't bring his boat to dry land, so he stopped one cubit away. He wrapped the four groschens in some paper and tossed the money over to her. She took it, and he said: "Hand me the shirt here into the boat."

So she handed it to him in the boat—whereupon he grabbed her arm, dragged her aboard, and quickly sailed away. She screamed from the boat, and so did her two children from the beach. But it was no use, she was already far out to sea and no one could hear her.

The two children no longer saw or heard their mother, so they ran to their father in prison. Weeping bitterly, they told him everything that had happened to their mother.

When the father heard their story, he wept and screamed, and then said: "God, my God, why do You leave me in such misery? I have no one left now to feed me in prison."

And weeping and lamenting, the man fell asleep. He dreamed that he was in a vast wilderness teeming with wild beasts that stood over him, ready to rip him up and eat his flesh. The man trembled in fear and terror. But as he looked all around in his misery, he saw a large herd of sheep and cattle moving his way. When the wild beasts saw them, they abandoned the man and dashed after the cattle. Making his escape, the man came upon a castle standing by a river filled with boats. When he entered the castle, the people there had him sit on a royal throne, and he was joyous about being with his seafarers.

But now he woke up. Thinking about the dream, he said to himself: "The dream signifies that my misery will soon be over. God will help me again and He will bring me joy with seafarers because a seafarer caused me grief."

During that period, the king died in the town, and the people of the country made his son king. In order to have a good name for himself, the new king exempted the town from paying taxes for three years and he also released all the prisoners in the town. The Talmudic scholar was one of those released from prison and he was now reunited with his two sons. He walked and walked through the marketplace but could think of no way to earn even a penny in order to buy bread for his children. Looking up, he saw a ship about to sail for the East Indies.

So he said to his children: "Come with me! Since your mother was abducted by seafarers, let's go aboard this ship. Maybe we'll find your mother, and God will help us come together again."

The man went to the seafarer and asked him to take him and his two children along, for he was so poor that he couldn't even buy a morsel of bread. He told the seafarer about everything that had happened to him. The seafarer felt sorry for him and so he took the man and his two children aboard and let them eat and drink as much as they liked.

When they reached the middle of the ocean, God sent out a powerful tempest. The boat shattered, and everyone was drowned except for the Talmudic scholar, his two children, and the seafarer who had fed them. He and the scholar were each holding on to a plank, and the two children were clinging to a single plank together. Then the sea tossed them ashore in different countries.

The scholar found himself in a vast wilderness, an area inhabited by savages. He was seen by the daughter of the king of the savages when she was grazing the sheep and cattle in the wilderness. The girl was almost stark naked though she was covered with hair and she wore a loincloth of fig leaves over her private parts.

The king's daughter came up to the castaway and expressed her love for him so he would marry her. He was so frightened that he likewise expressed his love and said he would marry her. The other savages saw this and began whistling. Next, the savages, young and old, came bounding out of the mountain caves they lived in, and they all ran over to him to drink his blood and eat his flesh, and their king was among them. The scholar was so terrified that he could scarcely breathe. When the king's daughter saw this, she told him not to be afraid. She went over to the king, her father, and begged him to spare the stranger's life because she wanted to marry him. The king gave in and he spared the man's life.

The scholar had to lie with her at night: he was her husband and she was his wife. Although he often thought about his beautiful and pious wife, who had been abducted from him so miserably, there was nothing he could do. He patiently put up with everything and he kept up his hope that the good Lord would help him again and take him back to his pious wife and their dear children.

After they had lived together for a while, the princess became pregnant and she bore him a son, a savage. The man tended the cattle in the wilderness every day. By now, he had been living among the savages for two years and had to eat the meat of wild mules and other beasts, and he and his savage wife had to live in a cave in the mountains. He too was covered with hair and he looked like a savage.

One day he was standing on a hill in the desert, not far from the sea, and he was thinking about his ordeal, about losing his wise and pious wife and their children. Worst of all, he would be wasting his remaining years living with mindless savages, and in the end, once they got tired of him, they would eat his flesh and break his bones, and he would not be buried next to other good Jews as is proper for a good Jew. "For all those reasons," he thought to himself, "the best thing would be for me to run down this hill, run over to the sea, and drown myself just as my two dear children were drowned." He didn't realize that the sea had cast his boys ashore in a different country. He felt that by drowning himself, he would find them and be happy with them in the afterlife.

He made his confession to God with hot and bitter tears. And when he was done, he ran toward the sea, intending to drown himself. But then he heard a voice calling out his name: "You desperate man! Why are you despairing, why do you want to doom your soul? Go back up the hill where you were standing and dig a hole. You'll find a chest full of money and precious stones—a huge fortune. Drag the chest down to the beach and stand there for a while. A ship carrying people like you to Antioch will come sailing by. Shout at them, ask them to take you aboard and save you and your chest. Eventually you'll become a king, you'll be well off, and you will experience the end of your woes and the start of your joys."

When the scholar heard this, he climbed back up the hill and began to dig as the voice had ordered him to do. In this way he found the chest of gold and precious stones. He dragged the chest down to the beach, and when he looked up, he saw a ship carrying passengers and approaching the shore. He yelled at them, asking them to come over and take him aboard, for he was a human being just like them. They heard his voice, they heard him speak the way people speak, so they headed toward the beach. He then told them about everything he had gone through, and they took him and his chest along. When he was already aboard, his savage wife recognized his voice. She then picked up their savage child and dashed after the scholar. Spotting him on the ship, she called out to the scholar to take her along.

But he made fun of her, saying: "I have nothing to do with savage beasts! I've got a much better wife than you!"

When she heard that he didn't want to come back to her, she was so angry that she grabbed her child's legs and tore him in half. She hurled one half to the ship, and she was so furious that she ate the other half. Then she ran away.

The scholar sailed off with the other people. Soon they reached land, an island, and they disembarked. The scholar now opened the chest: it was filled with gold and priceless jewels. Delighted, he paid for his passage and brought the chest to a hostelry.

That night, lying in bed, he thought to himself: "If I could buy this island from the king, I would build a castle and a town. That way, I'd have a livelihood and I wouldn't have to be afraid that someone might steal my fortune."

The next morning he went to the king and purchased the island, which was several leagues long. He then built a castle and a town, and eventually an entire country was built on the island. The inhabitants regarded him as a ruler and he was revered like a king. He thought about his wife and their children and about losing them so miserably. And it occurred to him:

"Since my wife was abducted by a seafarer and since all seafarers have to sail past my castle, I will issue a decree that no ship can pass by without registering with me. Otherwise the ship will be doomed along with everything and everyone aboard."

He issued the decree, and all the seafarers registered with him and they ate with him. A long time wore by, but he learned nothing about his wife and children. Once, around Passover, the scholar was having lunch and he felt very joyful. His servant entered and told him that a rich shipowner, who had just arrived, had requested that he not be kept waiting long.

The scholar replied: "Today's a holiday, so I can't ask him what he's carrying. He'll have to wait until after the holiday, but have him come up and join me in my meal."

When the shipowner came, the scholar welcomed him and offered him a seat. The shipowner asked if his case could be taken care of right away. But it was no use, the man had to remain and eat with the scholar.

The scholar asked him where he was from and whether he had a wife and children. The guest told him where he was from and said that he had two wives. Once of them was at home, and she had borne him three children. "I consider her a good housewife. But the other one is delicate and not fit to do housework. She's very intelligent, however, and that's why I always bring her along. She can watch over the ship, she collects my money from the people, records all transactions, and overseas everything. But I've never slept with her. I've never mated with her."

The scholar asked: "Tell me, my dear shipowner, why haven't you mated with her?"

The shipowner replied: "She already had a husband, who was very intelligent, and he taught her a riddle. And she says: 'The man who solves the riddle must be as intelligent as my husband, and I will let him sleep with me. Otherwise I'd rather be killed than let anyone sleep with me — or else I'd take my own life. It's unsuitable for a crude peasant to ride the king's mount.'"

The scholar then said: "Dear shipowner, please tell me the riddle."

The shipowner replied: "This is my wife's riddle:

"'A bird without wings flies from heaven to earth and alights very nicely on a sapling. The bird makes the sapling sway to and fro. Then the bird can no longer be seen. He strengthens the sapling until it bursts into the most beautiful blossoms. The sapling draws all the strength it can receive. But suddenly, the sapling withers and it is utterly contaminated. The bird flies away into the air and he starts to sing, to roar, and he shouts: "Oh, you gloomy sapling, who drained your strength? When you wanted it so badly, you couldn't get it. And now that you've received strength from me, you've dried up. What good is it to you?"'

"That, your majesty, is her riddle, and I haven't managed to find the solution."

When the scholar heard the riddle, he shuddered because it was *his* riddle, and he realized that this had to be his wife.

Seeing how frightened the scholar was, the guest said: "Your majesty, why are you so frightened?"

The scholar answered: "Dear sir, I'm very surprised by that wonderful and intelligent riddle. I would love to hear it from the woman herself. You may have forgotten something or added something. So if *she* tells me the riddle, I'll think about it and perhaps I'll solve it."

The scholar sent one of his servants to summon the woman, and the messenger ran very fast and said to her: "Get ready to accompany me to the ruler. You're invited to eat and drink with him — you and your husband."

When the good woman heard that, her heart began pounding, for she didn't know why she was being taken there. She was worried that she might go from one misfortune to an even greater one. But what could she do? She had to go where she was told. She put on lovely attire and adorned herself with jewelry as befits a woman who has to appear before a king.

Upon entering the castle, she was announced to the king, and he ordered his servants to bring her in. They brought her in, and she was asked to be seated next to the shipowner. The scholar welcomed her but was still uncertain whether she was his wife. He didn't quite recognize her face. Nor did she recognize him. After all, many years had passed since they had separated. Their appearance had thoroughly changed, and so had their clothes. The scholar kept silent and they sat there, eating, drinking, and making merry. But the scholar was unable to make merry. He seemed lost in thought.

The shipowner then said to him: "Your majesty, why aren't you merry? Why are you absorbed in dark thoughts? Are you bothered because we've been eating and drinking for such a long time? We'll stop and thank you and then go our way."

The scholar replied: "No, no. You are both my cherished guests. But I've been thinking only about the riddle. I'd like to hear it from the woman herself."

So the shipowner told his wife to tell the king the riddle. She did so, and he asked her: "Where did you get that riddle?"

The woman said: "Your majesty, I had a pious husband, a great rabbi, and he would always tell me such ancient tales, stories, and riddles. And no one can solve these riddles."

The scholar asked: "If someone does solve the riddle, will you be truthful and admit he's right?"

She replied: "Your majesty, there is no one on earth who knows the solution except for my former husband."

The scholar replied: "Well, I'm the man who can reveal its meaning. The bird that flies from heaven to earth is the human soul. It alights on a sapling—that's the human body. The human body is like a tree that grows very beautifully. Green and with branches—that's youth, which is like a beautiful pleasure garden. And when the bird makes the tree sway to and fro—that's the soul, which rules and turns all the body's limbs and makes them flexible. But no one sees the bird because the soul is buried in the body. And the tree draws all strength and then withers—that's a human being who is dissatisfied with what he has and who wants everything he sees and therefore he sometimes loses what he has, and injustice devours justice. And suddenly, a man dies and leaves everything behind. So the bird flies into the air—and that's the soul. The soul laments over the body and says: 'So long as you lived, everything was not enough for you, and you did not rest and you did not sleep until I brought you wealth. And now you're withered and you're leaving everything behind and you're dying. What use is it for you or me? If you had done good with your wealth, we would have arrived safely.'

"That is the solution to the riddle," the scholar concluded, "and the solution is true. If you admit truthfully that I have guessed right, I will take you back."

She looked up, peered hard at the scholar, and recognized her husband. She sprang to her feet, hugged him, and the two of them burst into tears.

They were so overjoyed that they had a huge banquet.

The terrified seafarer fell to his knees and begged for his life. The scholar said: "Since you never mated with my wife, I will spare your life. But because you took something that wasn't yours, I will take what is yours."

The scholar took the seafarer's entire wealth and then let him go. The scholar and his wife remained deeply pious and fully joyous and very wealthy. They told one another about everything that had happened to them. And they were terribly unhappy about their children because they thought they had drowned.

Now a big heatwave set in, and no one could sleep at night. There were a lot of ships, and the sailors came on deck, into the open air, to while away the night by talking with one another. The scholar's two sons were among those sailors but they didn't realize that their parents were nearby. The two boys said: "We'll tell one another riddles to while away the night."

The sailors were all satisfied with the idea and they agreed that if someone solved a riddle, he would be paid ten guldens by the riddler, but if he failed to solve it, he would have to pay the riddler ten guldens. They then said: "Let the two boys give us a riddle, because they're more intelligent than we are."

The two boys said: "We saw a very beautiful maiden, who couldn't see with her own eyes. She has a lovely and tender body, but the body isn't there. The maiden gets up every morning, never shows herself all day long, and never returns until night, adorned with lots of jewelry. Such jewelry has never been created and doesn't exist in the world. You can see her when you close your eyes, but when you open them she vanishes. That is the riddle, and now give us the solution."

Everyone was surprised at the riddle and said it was too difficult to solve. An old merchant who was among them offered a solution, but the two boys refused to accept it, saying it was the wrong answer. And so they argued until dawn and they didn't know who should pay whom the ten guldens. The skipper then said: "Listen to me! We'll go to the king in his castle and he'll decide which of you is right."

All of them agreed and they went and appeared before the king, who asked: "What do you want so early in the day?"

They told him everything, including the business about the ingenious riddle and the old merchant's answer. When the king heard the riddle, he was terrified. He looked at the two boys and recognized them because they weren't yet fully adult. The king said to them: "How do you know that the old merchant's answer is wrong?"

They replied: "Your majesty, our father was a learned man. He thought up this riddle and he also provided the solution. That's why no one can solve it but us and our father."

The king said: "If I gave you the right solution, would that mean that I am your father?"

They replied: "If someone gives us the right solution, then he has to be our father, for he never in his life told the riddle to anyone but us, his children, and we've never told the riddle to anyone else."

The king said: "Listen to my solution. Perhaps it's the right one:

"To my mind the beautiful maiden is the youth of young boys. All they think about all day long is beautiful maidens and all they see in their dreams is a beautiful maiden. But she herself sees nothing with her eyes when she appears in a dream in the dark night. So eyes don't help. If your eyes are open, you see nothing. That's why the beautiful maiden can see nothing with her eyes. She leaves in the morning. When a man opens his eyes in the morning, the dream leaves, and she remains absent all day long until the night. Then she reappears with her beautiful jewelry, which has never been created and doesn't exist in the world. That's easy to understand, because the man has seen the jewelry only in his dreams — it has never been created and it doesn't exist in the world.

"Now that's the solution. If you tell me I'm right, I'll accept you as my sons."

The boys were astounded at the solution, they exchanged glances and realized that this man was their father. They were so overjoyed that they burst into tears and they were too frightened to speak. The parents leaped up from their chairs and they hugged and kissed their children. And they all wept so loudly that they could be heard far away, and people learned that the boys were their children. The boys finally pulled themselves together and began to speak, and they and their parents told each other everything that had happened to them. And they were all ecstatic.

The king gave a huge banquet for all his people, and everyone was overjoyed. He was a king now, and his boys were princes. And he told them that they should be pious and serve God very zealously, and He would always help them. For if God wants to treat a man badly, all his friends will keep silent. They won't help him and they won't give him any advice. They will avoid him and say that he has turned out badly. And so that man will remain alone. Not one in a thousand people will tell him, "You are my friend." But if God does good to a man, then his enemies will keep silent, no matter how great their number.

The sailors saw all these things, heard all these words, and many of them became Jews, and a lovely community developed.

From that we can see that a man must endure everything patiently and put up with it, and also help the poor. If he can't give them anything, God will nevertheless remind him to do good and He will protect him against all evil, He will redeem us from our long and harsh Exile and take us to our Holy Land, and all sad hearts will be joyous.

> From that we can see
> That a man must suffer patiently
> And he must endure
> And also help the poor.
> If he can't give them what he should,
> God will still remind him to do good.
> And we can also expect
> That He will protect
> Us against all that's bad.
> God will redeem us from our sad
> And long Exile and
> Take us to our Holy Land,
> And all hearts that are mournful
> Will be joyful.
> In writing down this tale,
> I hope that the good Lord will
> Pity us and answer our prayers too.
> If we were pious, God would do
> As we wished. But because

Our sins are too great and our remorse
Is too weak, we must keep waiting for our
Good Lord to set the hour.

IN WRITING DOWN this tale, I hope that the good Lord will take pity
and answer our prayers. If we were pious, God would do as we wished.
But because our sins are too great and our remorse is too weak, we must
keep waiting for the time that is fixed by the good Lord.

I FOUND THIS story in a book written by a worthy Jew.

ANONYMOUS

*The sole extant copy of this fairy tale is in the Offenbach Collection at
the Bodleian Library, Oxford. Sara Zfatman dates it around 1714–22.*

*Drawn from the international array of folktale and fairy-tale motifs, this
anonymous narrative may be a source for Rabbi Nakhman of Braslev's
(1772–1810) tale, "The Lost Princess."* The Braslev text was then "completed" and also parodied in both Yiddish and Hebrew by Yoysef Perl
(1773–1839) as "The Story of a Lost Prince."*

The Princess and the Seven Geese (1714–22)

HERE IS A wondrous and very useful tale, which has never before
appeared in print. Anyone can follow it as a good example. First of all:
you should beware of uttering any curse whatsoever, for you never can
tell whether it might take effect. Secondly: no matter how miserable you
may be, you should always maintain your faith in God, as my benevolent
readers will see.

---

*See Joachim Neugroschel, *The Dybbuk and the Yiddish Imagination* (Syracuse, NY:
Syracuse University Press, 2000).

. . .   .

THIS STORY IS about a king of Jerusalem. His name was Hyrcanos and he had seven sons, who were peerless in every way. Still, the king and the queen prayed for a daughter, and God answered their prayers. The queen became pregnant and gave birth to a girl, whom they named Esther. There was no such other child under the sun. On her forehead she had a small golden star, which everyone marveled at.

When the girl turned one year old, she fell ill, and all the doctors despaired of curing her. Eventually she became so weak that they feared for her life. All the doctors and her parents and her seven brothers stood around her bed in great sorrow. Suddenly, an excellent doctor cried out: "Oh, you dear people! If I could get fresh well water quickly, I might be able to do something to help the child, God willing!"

Now who was more joyous than the parents? The seven brothers instantly took a silver pitcher and ran to the well themselves. Every brother wanted to draw the water and each one said: "I want the child to recover because of me!" And as they crowded around, the pitcher dropped into the well.

Their mother, in great distress, waited for the water. Then the boys came back and told her what had happened. The queen assumed they had dropped the pitcher deliberately so the girl might die. The mother thought her sons were envious because everyone paid more attention to the girl than to all the brothers together. In her anger the mother exclaimed: "A curse on you! I hope I never see any of you again!"

And, because it was a bad time, no sooner had she spoken those words than seven geese stood there and flew away. Other lords then dashed to the well and drew water, and the girl began to recover. However, the queen was weary and felt faint, she wanted to kill herself, and she refused any solace, especially when she learned that the seven brothers had dropped the pitcher accidentally. Now they were gone, and the girl was left alone.

The parents wouldn't allow the girl to be exposed to daylight, and they guarded her like the apple of their eye. The girl grew up, and she was peerless, and she studied all kinds of subjects and languages.

Now on the second night of Sukkoth, the Feast of Tabernacles, it was the custom in Jerusalem for all girls to go to the Temple and watch the festival of water-drawing. The king's daughter also appeared before her parents and, bowing down to the ground, she dolefully said: "Dear, loyal, honored parents. Since I stand in such high favor with you and since I'm your beloved only daughter, I haven't spent any time among other people. Now today is the seventh day of Sukkoth, and so I humbly beg you not to turn down my request. Allow me to see the holy place and the Temple. I would like to forget all about my life by praying for the holy repose of the Shekhina, the Divine Radiance."

The king and the queen gave their permission. And the instant people learned that the princess was coming, a huge crowd gathered. Everyone wanted to see what she looked like. Arriving with the entire court, she walked along regally, and as she did so, she heard two lords conversing. One said to the other:

"Dear brother, have you ever seen such a beautiful girl in your life? There's probably no artist who could capture that fire."

The other lord said: "Yes, but what a girl! You should have known her seven brothers, who were cursed because of her. You'd be amazed!"

Having never heard about her brothers, the girl instantly felt faint. She said: "I'm losing my strength." She tearfully went to the queen and said: "Noble and most worthy empress and dear, loyal mother, I've overheard something. Have I ever had a sister or a brother?"

When the mother heard that question, she cried out: "Oh, you dear child, you've reminded me of my great torment, for which I can never find any solace!" And she told her the whole story.

After hearing it, the daughter promptly went to her chamber and tore her clothes. Lamenting in her misery, she fell to the floor and said: "My God and my Lord and my Creator, why did you answer my parents' prayers and bring me into the world, which caused my dear seven brothers to be cursed? I therefore ask you for advice: how can I save them?"

Finally the girl went back to her mother and said: "Dear mother, did you see where my brothers left and where they flew to?"

Her mother replied: "Who can tell? They flew toward the forest of Lebanon, and that forest is endless."

Fearing the queen's disapproval, the daughter didn't reveal her plan to her mother. She quickly made up her mind. Several days later, taking along food and drink, the girl stole out the back and through the pleasure gardens. Upon reaching the Kidron River, she ferried across in a small boat and then entered a forest, where there were no paths or trails. She trudged along for an hour or even two or three and, peering around, she called out her brothers' names, but received no answer. Eventually the girl reflected and then said: "Oh, what have I done—going into the wilderness like this? I'd rather go home and pray to the Almighty day and night in order to redeem my brothers."

Turning around, the girl thought she was heading home, but instead she wandered further and further into the forest. Night came, and because she was terrified of wild beasts, she climbed up a lofty fir tree, where she stayed until dawn. Within three days and three nights, she had consumed all her food. However, she was familiar with herbs and roots. She also wept and shouted at the heavens each day, asking for strength and help, so that the good Lord granted her grace and shielded her against harm.

But now we will leave the princess and tell about the king and the queen.

When it was time for the servants to report to the king, they said they had no idea what had become of their beloved daughter. Her parents were so horrified that they nearly lost their minds. The king sent out men to look for her and to announce that if anyone brought him any information that person would receive immense grace and fine presents. Well, you can imagine the grieving and lamenting.

But here we will leave them in their deep sorrow and go back to the princess.

After wandering through the wilderness for six months without finding her way out, the girl fell to her knees and gazed up at the sky. With dreadful cries and a heavy heart, she began to weep bitterly and then said: "You dear Almighty God, Who created the entire universe and rules it, all secret thoughts are exposed to You. You test the very core of our consciences and You reward each person according to his deeds. You know very well that I am a very beloved only daughter, and You placed my father as king over Your beloved nation Israel. In the brief time that You have let me spend in this world, I have always helped people who are poor and wretched, and I have always hated pride. It was not out of whimsy that I wandered into this forest. I am not after something that is useful to me and that I deserve. No. I am looking for my dear, loyal brothers, who were banned from human society because of me. Therefore I beg You, Lord of All the Universe: if it is Your holy will to remove me from this world, lead me to my dear parents, so that they may know what has become of me. Do not let me die in this wilderness, do not let me become the prey of wild beasts."

Her heart was so heavy and her tears were so profuse that she finally blacked out and fell into a deep sleep. When she awoke and started wandering again, she saw a marvelously huge and beautiful castle in the distance. No other castle like it had ever been built. And she was very happy to see it. She said: "I love You and thank You for bringing me back to human beings." And she hurried over.

Entering the castle, she passed from room to room and saw wonders of silver and gold and all kinds of jewelry. But surprisingly enough, she didn't find a single person. She continued searching in room after room until she reached a large kitchen, which was adorned with all kinds of silver and gold utensils. A fire was burning, surrounded by seven pots containing food and with a ladle leaning against each pot. And since no one was there to cook properly, the food in one pot was still uncooked, while the food in another pot was slightly burned. So the girl stoked the fire, cooked the food properly, and ate a bit from each pot. Then she removed the pots from the fire and went into the dining room, where she sat down behind the stove. She said: "Dear God, I want to see who's going to come here and consume the food."

Sitting there and musing, she suddenly heard a loud commotion. Seven geese came flying in, and they spoke to one another like human beings. The table was set and they sat down to dine. The girl thought: "Oh, God, Who has the power to grant all wishes—let these people be my brothers!"

Now she heard them talking to each other: "The food tastes good this time, as if it were cooked by human hands."

Another said: "How could a human being come to this wilderness?"

The third one said: "Perhaps our parents went to such great lengths to look for us or else our sister has grown up and has sent out people to look for us."

The fourth one said: "If it were our sister, I would kill her myself. It's because of that beast that we were all cursed!"

The fifth one said: "That's nonsense! What did she do—the poor, sick, miserable infant? It was our mother who cursed us—but she didn't mean for the curse to come true!"

The sixth one said: "The child had to survive so that she would be a comfort to our parents."

The seventh one said: "My dear brothers, there is no one on earth who can help us aside from our sister, and if she died, then we must remain cursed forever and ever!"

Finally they all began shouting in loud, lamenting voices: "Dear Almighty God, please tell us whether the girl is still alive." And they burst into tears.

Upon hearing all this, the princess could no longer contain herself. She sprang out from behind the stove, shouting and weeping, and she said: "Oh, you dear, loyal brothers! I'm your dear sister! I've come here to help you!" And all the brothers threw their arms around her.

They were so happy that they didn't know what to do next. They said: "Dear, loyal sister, we don't have much time. We'll describe our situation. You see, this castle is not a real castle, our food and drink are not prepared by human hands. We become human for only one hour every day, and when the hour is up, we turn back into sorrowing geese and fly away. We ourselves don't know where we fly. In God's name we will help you to return to our parents, so you can complete their family for them. But we cannot help ourselves, and as you have heard, you can't help us either—you'd lose your life. So we'd rather remain cursed forever!"

Upon hearing that, the girl tearfully said: "If you won't tell me how I can help you, then I swear by heaven that I will kill myself right in front of you all."

When the brothers heard that, the eldest brother said: "Dear, loyal sister, if you want to help us, you have to remain mute for seven years plus seven months plus seven days plus seven hours plus seven minutes and never let on who you are, and for three and a half years you must not set eyes on any person. But given your noble upbringing, how could you endure this?"

When she heard that, she replied: "My dear brothers, I'm a noble and delicate princess, yet I've managed to survive in the wilderness for almost a year eating nothing but leaves and grass and never changing my royal clothes and appearance. How is that possible? God has brought me here to help you." And even though the brothers tried to dissuade her, she went on: "I can't stand this sorrow anymore, I'm ready to help you body and soul." And she tearfully hugged and kissed each brother and said goodbye.

And then seven geese were standing there and they flew away.

The girl also left with a heavy heart and wandered through the forest for many years without knowing how long she was there. One evening she came to a wood, where she retired to a lofty tree to spend the night. That same night a young king named Aristobulos came riding with a large retinue. They had been in the desert, where they had caught lots of wild beasts. The king had reached the forest that same night. The hounds, smelling a human being in the tree, refused to go on. The hunters then saw the girl and called to her, asking whether she was human. But she didn't respond. So they got her down and brought her to the king. The instant he set eyes on her, he was dazzled by her great beauty and radiance.

Taking the girl aside, the king addressed her in many languages. She displayed honor, modesty, and courtesy toward him but never uttered a word.

When they reached the king's town, his mother asked him what he was going to do with this girl, whom he had found in the wilderness and who hadn't yet learned how to speak. He replied: "I may have found her in the wilderness, but she's a human being all the same and she must come from a noble family. And if she can't speak, who can tell why?" And so, over his mother's objections, he made the girl his queen. Eventually she became pregnant.

Some time later, the king said to his mother: "I have to go to Rome about an important matter. Please take care of my dear, loyal queen and help her with any problems—not as a mother-in-law but as a mother." The king's mother promised him a great deal, but her heart was very evil.

A short while after the young king said goodbye and started out for Rome, the young queen began to feel very sharp pains: it was time for her to give birth. However, her old and cursed mother-in-law permitted only one midwife to attend to her. But God helped, and the young queen easily gave birth to two boys, each with a gold star on his forehead. When the old woman saw that, she ordered the midwife to tell no one what had happened, otherwise she would have her killed in a horrible way.

Putting the twins in a basket, the old queen gave them to a servant and commanded him on pain of death to carry them to the desert and chop them to bits. Next she took two puppies and forced them to lie down with the young queen. The old queen thereupon spread the news that the young queen had brought two puppies into the world. That way, the king would kill her.

When the servant carrying the basket arrived in the desert, he clutched his sword in one hand and took one baby out of the basket. The baby laughed at him so charmingly and played with his little hands. The servant thought to himself: "How can I harm this child?" But then he mused:

"If I bring them back, I'll lose my life." He took out the other baby and was about to kill it. But the baby's little hands played with the servant's face, and he began to laugh at the servant in a lovely and friendly way. The servant thought to himself: "How could I have such a cruel and cursed heart? I can't possibly harm these dear, joyful babies. I'd rather be killed a thousand times myself!"

The servant took the babies, placed them on the ground, and said: "Almighty and merciful God, I can't help these children, so I'm placing them under your protection." He then went home and received great gifts from the old queen.

Meanwhile, after the servant left the babies, a lioness came along and pounced on them. But when the lioness noticed that the babies came from a sublime and noble royal dynasty, she brought them to her precious den and nursed them along with her own cubs.

Now let's get back to the young king. When he arrived home and found two puppies with his dearest queen, he was very upset: "I know that I had a good, pious queen."

But the old queen said something shameful to him: "I told you not to take the wild animal. Now you can see what's happened."

The young queen was finally sentenced to be burned at the stake, and a huge crowd of spectators gathered, covering hill and dale. Her period of silence had long since ended, and she could speak now. But she didn't realize that and she preferred to be burned.

Meanwhile her brothers had turned human again and they came among people. Planning to go to their parents, they bought good horses. As they rode across the desert, they came to a lion's den, where they saw two children playing together. They also spotted the gold stars on their foreheads. The horsemen shouted to each other: "Dear brothers, those are offspring of our sister." Since the old lioness was away, the brothers jumped into the den, swiftly took the children under their coats, and galloped off.

Upon reaching the town and hearing the shouting, one brother said to the others: "We'll watch too. It must be strange to see a queen being burned at the stake."

When they went up close to see her, a huge fire was blazing. The queen was brought in with a puppy hanging on either side of her and her ladies-in-waiting escorting her and weeping bitterly. The queen rested her head on one lady's shoulder and gazed at the ground. The king walked behind her, lamenting loudly: "If only I could burn up with her!" But the old queen, who walked at his side, was overjoyed. And when the young queen saw the fire, she fainted.

As the brothers drew closer, they instantly recognized their sister. Brandishing their swords, five of the brothers rushed to her defense, and the eldest said: "What has this noble heart done to deserve getting burned at the stake?"

The other two brothers opened their coats and said: "These must be her dear children!"

Then the midwife came and fell to her knees in front of the king and said: "I got the babies myself from your queen, but I was terrified that your mother would have me killed!"

Next the servant came. He too fell on his knees and he said: "The old queen gave me these children and ordered me to kill them in the desert. Have mercy, your majesty—that was what she ordered me to do!"

The brothers shouted: "Loyal sister, start speaking! Look at us, we're your brothers! Don't you recognize us!"

The king immediately ordered his doctors to awaken his queen. They did so, and when she came to, she looked around and recognized her brothers. She was so happy that she burst into tears: "Praised be Almighty God! Blessed is the time and the hour that I saw you! I was about to be burned alive for your sake."

When the king heard that, he was so joyous that he flung his arms around her: "Are you Esther, the daughter of mighty King Hyrcanos of Jerusalem? Praised be the Almighty, who has blessed me with you!" The king then issued an order: "Take the old, cursed beast immediately and throw her into the fire!"

His order was carried out, and the king and all the people were filled with joy. Then the king said: "Let's not waste any time! We'll all go to your parents in Jerusalem and we'll have a proper wedding there and bring them joy."

So the king and the queen as well as her seven brothers, together with all the lords and a huge retinue, traveled to Jerusalem in great splendor.

Now everyone can imagine how their arrival lifted all the heavy hearts. And may God also bring us joy very soon and deliver us from our bitter exile and very soon send us the Messiah from the House of David. Amen.

ANONYMOUS

Till Eulenspiegel was a legendary Low German traveler and prankster. The first cluster of tales about him appeared in 1510, in a High German edition published in Strasbourg. Various collections then came out over the next few centuries. The first extant Yiddish translation, identifying our hero as Aylen-Shpigel, was completed by Benyamin Merks in 1600 and was followed by various editions. In 1735, a Yiddish book printed in Prague included five stories that were not traditional—and these are the texts that are translated here. All this background information can be found in Hermann-Josef Müller's excellent paper, "Eulenspiegel im Land der starken Weiber."

As I mentioned in the introduction of this section: from the mid-sixteenth century to the mid-eighteenth, Yiddish distinguished between mayse *(a Jewish tale) and* história *(a non-Jewish tale). The anonymous 1735 author of the Aylen-Shpigel stories was following a Yiddish tradition of secularizing the Christian references. Although Till doesn't quite become a Jew, the Yiddish versions provide a vague Jewish flavor, mainly through borrowings from Hebrew and Aramaic (Müller lists sixty-six in the entire collection). Given his pitfalls and pratfalls, this Till can easily be accepted as the token Gentile in the roster of legendary Yiddish funnymen (like Motke Khabad and Hershel of Ostropolye).*

Five Stories about Till Eulenspiegel

FROM ADVENTURES OF AYLEN-SHPIGEL
PRAGUE, 1735

AYLEN-SHPIGEL WAS BORN in the county of Brunswick, two leagues from the town of Wolfen-Bitel in the village of Knetlingen. His father was a peasant. Aylen-Shpigel had a face like a monkey, because his mother

*Jiddische Philologie, Festschrift für Erika Timm (Tübingen, 1999), pp. 197–226.

had looked at a monkey during her pregnancy. By the age of four, he was already a rascal, and all the neighbors complained about his pranks. Then his father died, leaving the poor widow in complete indigence. . . .

1. How Aylen-Shpigel Came to the Land of Strong Women

AYLEN-SHPIGEL CAME TO a strange land, where the women governed while their poor husbands had to do the housework. Furthermore the wives would beat them for almost no reason. If a woman gave birth to a boy, they would promptly chop off his right thumb, so that as a grownup he wouldn't hold a sword in his right hand and rebel against the women.

These women also had poisonous fingernails, and if a wife scratched her husband, drawing even one drop of blood, he would die within twenty-four hours, and no doctor could save him.

Now when Aylen-Shpigel came to this country and saw that the women were in charge, he asked several men: "Why are you such fools? Why do you let the women dominate you?"

The men replied: "We have no thumbs on our right hands, and even if we managed to overcome the women, they would still get the better of us—all they have to do is scratch us slightly, and we'll die."

Aylen-Shpigel was so afraid of these women that he left the country.

2. How Aylen-Shpigel Was Fooled by the Monkeys

AYLEN-SHPIGEL MET A merchant who had only narrow-brimmed hats in stock whereas wide-brimmed hats were the latest fashion. The merchant was very distraught because of his narrow-brimmed hats, which he couldn't sell. He therefore lent Aylen-Shpigel a thousand such hats, which were to be paid for within six months. Aylen-Shpigel took the hats and boarded a ship that was sailing to a country where people wore narrow-brimmed hats.

But the ship encountered a nasty wind and she took water, so that all the hats got wet. Then the wind drove the ship to a strange land. However, the crew and the passengers were happy to be ashore. Aylen-Shpigel laid out his hats on the ground to dry them in the sunshine.

Not too far off there was a forest teeming with monkeys. Meanwhile Aylen-Shpigel left his hats out overnight and, together with the other people, he went back to sleep on the ship.

In the morning, before the people awoke, the monkeys came. Each monkey donned a hat and then jumped around in the trees. Aylen-Shpigel got up and wanted to check his hats. But they were all gone, and he had no idea who had taken them. After looking around, he peered up at the treetops, where the monkeys were leaping about in the hats. One monkey doffed his hat and bowed to another monkey. Aiming to get back his hats, Aylen-Shpigel climbed a tree, but the monkeys quickly sprang from one tree to another. He tried to jump after them, but he fell to the ground, nearly breaking his neck.

Aylen-Shpigel then thought to himself: "I've heard that when monkeys look at a person, they ape everything he does." So Aylen-Shpigel got all the people off the ship to come with him under the trees where the monkeys were. Each man removed his own hat and tossed it on the ground, and they all returned to the ship. Now, climbing down from the trees, the monkeys threw off their hats and went away. Aylen-Shpigel hurried over and got back all his hats.

3. How Aylen-Shpigel Caught the Monkeys

AYLEN-SHPIGEL WANTED TO get even with the monkeys for causing him so much trouble with his hats, so much effort and labor. Noticing that they imitated everything they saw a person doing, Aylen-Shpigel picked up two basins, one filled with water and one with pitch. He then went under the high trees, where the monkeys were. Taking the basin of water, he washed his eyes for a long time so the monkeys could have a good look.

Next Aylen-Shpigel went away, leaving the basin of soft pitch under the trees. The monkeys climbed down from the trees and washed their eyes with the soft pitch, smearing their eyes until they were blind. After which, Aylen-Shpigel came hurrying over with the rest of the men. They caught several hundred monkeys until the ship was full and then they continued their voyage.

4. How Aylen-Shpigel Was Captured by the Dogheads

ABOARD SHIP AGAIN, Aylen-Shpigel was very upset, for the sailors didn't know where to go or where on earth they were. They kept sailing and sailing until they reached a strange land. This was the land of the

Dogheads. But Aylen-Shpigel and the others didn't know this. He and forty men went ashore to buy food. Now the Dogheads came and captured them all and put them in large cages, where they were fattened on nothing but raisins and almonds. They were fed by elderly women, and the one who fed Aylen-Shpigel was a friendly widow, who had amiable conversations with him about all sorts of things.

Aylen-Shpigel asked her: "Why are we locked up? Why are you fattening us and what do you plan to do with us?"

"When you're fat, we're going to roast you and eat you. It'll be good for you to be buried in our bodies. That way, you'll never have to worry about dying from a long and ugly illness."

Aylen-Shpigel asked her: "Do you people ever eat one another?"

The woman replied: "No. We only eat our enemies."

Aylen-Shpigel asked: "What makes you think we're your enemies?"

The woman said: "How can you not be our enemies if you caught the poor monkeys and bound them up and tied them down in the ship? We released the poor monkeys from your brutal hands and sent them back to their forest."

Aylen-Shpigel asked: "What's your connection with the monkeys?"

The woman said: "When we die, our souls are reborn in monkeys, and from there our souls pass into mice, which is why we never kill a mouse. When we find a mouse nest, we feed milk to the young until they grow up and run away. One part of our soul is reborn in animals, and that's why we never eat them. If any of us kills an animal, he is put to death. After three incarnations, our souls reach the afterlife, where they are bathed in a large brook. As soon as they are bathed, they forget everything they experienced in the world and they are reborn. Then they come back into the world and pass into new people."

Several days later, the Dogheads took eight fattened men out of the cages, but Aylen-Shpigel wasn't one of them. The women tied the hands of the eight men and brought them to a large fire. They danced around them three times, then killed them by beating their heads with a wedge, and roasted them in the fire. One of the men was blind in one eye, so they threw away his head, saying: "His head isn't healthy, we mustn't eat it."

The Dogheads gobbled and guzzled all night long, getting so drunk that they slept part of the next day. That same night Aylen-Shpigel found a hole in his cage and crawled out. He also helped his companions to crawl out, each from his own cage. They quickly boarded their ship, sailed away, and came back to a German land.

5. *How Aylen-Shpigel Became a Peasant*

WHEN AYLEN-SHPIGEL grew old and could no longer support himself, he married a widow, a peasant woman with a small nest egg. Aylen-Shpigel drank away the money day and night. Now once, when he was drunk, he collapsed in the street and fell asleep. At this point the king happened to be driving by and he saw Aylen-Shpigel sleeping in the filth. The king ordered his servants to take Aylen-Shpigel to the royal palace, undress him, put him in a beautiful bed, and let him sleep. The king also told his servants what to do when Aylen-Shpigel woke up.

At last he woke up, looked around, and saw that he was lying in a beautiful bed. He didn't know what had happened to him. Finally the servants came and said, "Your Majesty, don't you wish to get up?"

Aylen-Shpigel didn't wait to be asked twice, he did as they suggested. He thought to himself: "If I'm a king, then I'm a king." They dressed him like a king, in very costly garments, and then set the table, where he was served, surrounded by many counts and princes. For three whole days Aylen-Shpigel gobbled and guzzled like a peasant, as was his habit. He drank to his heart's content every evening.

During the third night, while Aylen-Shpigel was asleep, the king ordered his servants to remove Aylen-Shpigel's beautiful garments, dress him in his old clothes, and take him back to the filthy street where they had found him. There he slept until daylight.

His wife had spent three entire days looking for him and on the fourth day she finally found him lying in the filth. Waking him up, she said: "You bastard! You got so drunk that you're lying in the filth! Where've you been so long? This is the fourth day that you've been gone."

Aylen-Shpigel figured that his three days as king had only been a dream. And all the food and drink during those three days had also been a dream. He told his wife he'd been sleeping and dreaming for three days. To which she said: "You bastard! Come home and forget that whole business. You can see that a person's life is just like a dream, it's got no substance. Only the man who's got something good in this world has a good dream, so to speak, and that's that."

PART TWO

Hasidism and Anti-Hasidism,

Mysticism and Moralism:

Eighteenth and Early

Nineteenth Century

*T*he seventeenth and eighteenth centuries launched one of the most dreadful eras in Ashkenazi history, especially in Poland and Ukraine. Caught between warring nations—Cossacks, Tartars, Ukrainians, and other groups on one side versus Polish aristocrats, partisans, and other groups on the opposing side—Jews were unwarrantedly perceived as enemies by all sides. Amid these upheavals, Jews suffered not only constant instability but also horrible tortures and massacres that devastated and wiped out huge segments of their communities. And this age of pogroms actually continued even beyond World War II, constituting one of the main themes of Yiddish and Hebrew literature.

As if those ordeals were not enough, Jews endured profound internal conflicts, particularly with the rise of Hasidism and its ensuing adversaries. These struggles were dominated by two crucial and opposing figures: the Baal-Shem-Tov and the Vilna Gaon (Genius).

In the 1730s, a man named Israel ben Eleazer (?1700–1760), who called himself the Baal-Shem-Tov (the Master of the Holy Name), gained renown as a miracle healer and charismatic leader. He supposedly worked cures and expelled demons as well as achieving states of mystical exaltation. Moreover, he viewed prayer as the basic way of communicating with God who, according to the Baal-Shem-Tov and his followers (Hasids), was omnipresent—even in human agony.

This new movement, stressing joy, humility, and gratitude in worship by ordinary Jews, rejected the elitism of the earlier mystical tradition, which was based on the scholarly perusal of holy texts. As a result, Yiddish could replace Hebrew in worship and prayer—a concept that was anathema to the anti-Hasidic factions, who furthermore despised an intrinsic feature of Hasidism: the sect leader known as the *rebbe* or *tsadik* (saint) or *guter-yíd* (literally, good Jew). Hasidic literature, in Yiddish and/or Hebrew, abundantly describes the doctrines, the miracles, the lifestyles, and even the melodies of these tsadiks. Eventually, Hasidism was fragmented by the rivalries between various Hasidic sects, which fought constant verbal and even physical battles with one another—as well as with the anti-Hasidic *Mitnagdim* (literally, opponents). For all the internal and external warfare, the rationalism, the secularization of Jewish life, and the modern genocide, a few Hasidic sects are still thriving today—mainly in Israel and the United States.

The other core figure of Ashkanazi life during the eighteenth century was Elijah ben Solomon Zalman (1720–1797). Nicknamed "the Vilna Gaon" (Genius), he penned commentaries on the Bible, as well as other sacred texts, including a Cabalistic magnum opus, the *Zohar*; this demonstrates that he was never a foe of mysticism per se. In his approach to the sacred texts, however, he promoted exact readings, with interpretations based on common sense. Yet he also delved into secular areas such as mathematics. His chief complaints about Hasidism were as follows: It encouraged personal religious experience over the studying of the Torah and the Talmud; it replaced the standard Lurianic prayerbook with the Askenazi prayerbook; and it went way overboard in prayers.

The Hasidic sects continued to fight with one another and with the Mitnagdim; and both sides, in turn, eventually had their skirmishes with the Haskala (the Jewish Enlightenment).

DOV BER BEN SHMUEL OF LINETS

(*dates unknown*)

In Praise of the Baal-Shem-Tov, *a hagiographic "biography," was compiled by Dov Ber ben Shmuel (the master's erstwhile scribe). His collection was published in several Hebrew, then Yiddish editions. In narrating the Baal-Shem-Tov's life, the book describes his—and also his followers'—various mystical deeds, wonder cures, and other miracles. These tales circulated orally, in books, and in pamphlets. Printed in Hebrew or Yiddish or both, they form a powerful corpus within the two literatures and are still being reprinted today in various Hasidic communities.*

From *In Praise of the Baal-Shem-Tov* (1815)

The Baal-Shem-Tov and the Hungarian Highwaymen

THE BAAL-SHEM-TOV WAS in a place flanked by high mountains. A very deep valley lay between the mountains, which were as steep as a wall. Once, the Baal-Shem-Tov was walking on a mountain, lost in thought. He was walking on one side of the mountains, while there were highwaymen on the other side. And when they saw that he was lost in thought, they said: "He's going to fall into the valley." But when the Baal-Shem-Tov approached the brink, the mountains drew together, forming a flat surface. And when the Baal-Shem-Tov walked away from the brink, the mountains drew apart to their earlier state. And this kept happening as he walked to and fro.

The highwaymen saw that the Baal-Shem-Tov was a godly man for God was with him. So they went over to him and made peace with him. They said to him: "We see that you are a godly man. So we ask you to pray for our success in the place we are going to."

The Baal-Shem-Tov said to them: "If you promise not to rob any Jew, I'll do what you ask."

The highwaymen swore an oath. And from then on, whenever they had a conflict, they would ask the Baal-Shem-Tov to judge the matter.

Once, two highwaymen came to the Baal-Shem-Tov and asked him to settle their argument. He did so, but one highwayman was unhappy about the verdict. He therefore waited for the Baal-Shem-Tov to fall asleep, and he then went to his home to kill him. When the highwayman lifted his hatchet over the Baal-Shem-Tov's head, someone—he didn't know who—grabbed hold of his hand. He was beaten, thrashed, and injured until he could no longer speak.

When the Baal-Shem-Tov awoke, he saw the bruised and bloody man and he asked him: "Who did this to you?"

The highwayman didn't have the strength to answer, and the Baal-Shem-Tov left. The next day the highwayman came to him and told him everything.

One day the highwaymen came to the Baal-Shem-Tov and said: "We know a shortcut to the Holy Land—through caverns. If you come with us, we'll show you the way."

So the Baal-Shem-Tov went with them. And as they walked, they came to a pit filled with clay and water, and a plank lay across the pit. And they leaned on the beam that stood in the water. The highwaymen went first. But when the Baal-Shem-Tov was about to go, he saw the "flaming sword which turned every which way to keep the way of the tree of life" [Genesis 3:24]. And the Baal-Shem-Tov stepped back, for it was dangerous for him to go any further.

How Odem Behaved Toward the Baal-Shem-Tov

THERE WAS A Hasidic master named Rabbi Odem [Adam], who found some mystical writings in a cave. Rabbi Odem was very poor, he lived in a small cottage, and he and his wife wore ragged clothes. One day his wife said to him: "I'm ashamed of going to synagogue in my ragged clothes."

Rabbi Odem replied: "Before you leave for synagogue, go to the chest in the bedroom and take out any garment you wish for. But when you return from synagogue, you have to put the garment back in the chest."

For many years Rabbi Odem's wife had clothes in this way. Whenever she wanted to go to synagogue or to market, she would go to the chest in the bedroom and take out any garment she wished for. Then, when she returned from synagogue or from market, she put the garment back in the chest. The congregation was astonished because she wore a different dress in synagogue each day: where did her husband, who was a pauper, obtain such expensive clothing? They asked his wife, and she revealed the secret to them.

Eventually the story reached the emperor, and when he had it investigated, he learned that it was true. Rabbi Odem now enjoyed the emperor's favor, but he remained poor for he didn't want to indulge in the pleasures of the world. And even though the emperor wanted to make him a rich man, Rabbi Odem declined.

Now the emperor had a minister who hated Jews, and this minister was very angry that a Jew should enjoy the emperor's favor. One day Rabbi Odem invited the emperor to a banquet, and the emperor accepted the invitation. This infuriated the Jew-hating minister, but the emperor said that he would attend the banquet. At the time stipulated by Rabbi Odem, the emperor set out together with all the cabinet ministers, including the Jew-hating minister; the emperor knew that Rabbi Odem would do wondrous things.

However, the Jew-hater kept trying to persuade the emperor to turn back. He said: "You'll see that we'll all be insulted. How can such a pauper serve a banquet for an emperor and his ministers?"

But the emperor paid him no heed. When they approached the town, he dispatched messengers to find out whether there would be rooms suitable for himself and his retinue and whether preparations were being made. When the messengers returned, they said: "We heard nothing, we saw nothing regarding a banquet. All we found was a tiny, hunched cottage."

But the emperor pressed on anyway. He thought to himself: "It will truly be a great miracle."

This is the story of the banquet:

In a different country a king threw a banquet for another king. The king built palaces for two years, he prepared food, tableware, and gold and silver sideboards, and very many servants. And when the time came that Rabbi Odem had stipulated for the emperor to attend the banquet, those palaces, together with all the food, the tableware, the sideboards, and the servants, were transferred to the town where Rabbi Odem lived.

Upon arriving in the town, the emperor found a large palace with several floors and ceilings. It was made of the most beautiful glass, which is known as crystal. The glass ceilings were filled with water, and there were fish swimming to and fro.

The emperor rode into the palace with all his ministers and with all his servants and horses. People instantly appeared and welcomed the emperor and all his ministers with great reverence. Rabbi Odem, the Hasidic Master, then said: "Eat and drink to your hearts' content, but nobody is to remove anything from here." He then went on: "Let everyone stick his hand in his pocket, and he will take out whatever he desires."

The emperor began. He named something that he wanted and he found it in his pocket. All the ministers followed suit. When it was the Jew-hater's turn, he said something to Rabbi Odem. The rabbi replied: "Stick your hand in your pocket." The minister did so, and when he pulled out his hand, it was smeared with excrement, and the stench was awful. The emperor had the minister tossed out into the street. The Jew-hater washed his hand with water, but it was no use, his hand continued to smell. He asked Rabbi Odem for help, and Rabbi Odem told him: "If you agree to stop hating Jews, you will be helped. If not, your hands will remain dirty forever, and you will never get them clean again."

The Jew-hater agreed that he would start loving Jews.

Before they left, the emperor secretly removed two beakers from the sideboard. As the emperor rode away, the palaces disappeared. The only things now missing were the food and drink they had consumed and the two beakers. When the news reached the emperor that the palaces had gone with all their preparations and had come back whole, the emperor wrote a letter to the king: "You should know that a Jew here brought me your palaces, we ate the banquet you had prepared, and I am sending you the two beakers as evidence."

ANONYMOUS

A typical Yiddish genre is the tsadik tale, the usually hagiographic description of miracles worked not only by the charismatic leaders of various Hasidic sects but also by biblical figures such as the prophet Elijah

*and historical celebrities such as Moses Maimonides. Transmitted both
orally and in pamphlets from the eighteenth century to the present, these
stories were the particular targets of anti-Hasidic challengers, who saw the
genre as part of the corruption of Jewish life. Because of the destruction or
unintelligibility of many of these pamphlets, I've relied on modern reprints
and retellings. But the stories are best read in conjunction with the tales of
the Baal-Shem-Tov—and the anti-Hasidic potshots.*

Stories about the Tsadiks

How Elijah Entered Heaven Alive (based on II Kings 1–2)

FROM ALE MAYSES FUN ELYE HA-NOVI (1911)

WHEN THE DAY came on which the prophet Elijah was to die, he knew
he wouldn't pass away like other people: he would enter Heaven while
still alive. And he didn't want to die in the company of others, so he
decided to keep to himself on his last day. In fact, he would even conceal
his demise from Elisha, his disciple. Elijah said to him: "Stay here. I have
to leave, for God has sent me to Beth-El."

But Elisha swore that he wouldn't let him go alone, he would go with
him. For God, Blessed Be He, had revealed to him and to all the other
young prophets the day of Elijah's death. So Elisha followed Elijah to
Beth-El. Next they went to Jericho. They were trailed at a distance by fifty
of the young prophets, who yearned to witness Elijah's end.

When Elijah and Elisha reached the Jordan, Elijah took his mantle,
rolled it up, and struck the water with it. The Jordan divided, the water
parted and remained like that on either side. Elijah and Elisha walked
across the entire Jordan on dry land, while the fifty young prophets
remained on one bank of the river.

Elijah then asked Elisha: "What should I bequeath to you before I'm
separated from you?"

Elisha said: "I want my spirit of prophecy to be twice your spirit of
prophecy."

Elijah said: "You're demanding too much. Still, if you're privileged to
see me when I'm taken from you, then I promise you that you'll get your

wish. But if you don't see me, then you won't get what you're asking for." Now the Sages said that "a friend should not be separated from a friend when they are discussing the Torah." So as they strolled along, they began talking about the Torah.

All at once a fiery chariot arrived with fiery horses, driving the two men apart, and Elijah went up to Heaven in a whirlwind. The angel sent to bring him did not gain control of him so easily for Elijah and Elisha were absorbed in the Torah. That was why the angel had the fiery chariot appear between the two men. Elijah automatically stopped studying; the angel therefore instantly had power over him and was able to take him up to Heaven while Elijah was still alive.

The holy Zohar says that when God sent a second angel to take Elijah up to Heaven, the Angel of Death expressed his opposition. But God told him that when the world was created, it was immediately decided that the prophet Elijah would enter Heaven alive. The Angel of Death said that if this happened, other people would make demands and ask to be taken to Heaven while still alive. God replied that Elijah was not like other people and that he would be able to keep the Angel of Death away from the world altogether.

God added: "If you want to have power over Elijah, then go down to him."

The Angel of Death promptly did so. The moment Elijah saw him, he threw him to the ground and trampled him—he wanted to destroy him altogether. But God wouldn't allow it.

The holy Zohar also says that when Elijah entered Heaven, his spirit separated from his body and became a holy angel like any holy angel. He carries out missions for God in this world, and all of God's miracles in this world are performed through Elijah. When Elijah comes down to this world and appears to people, he has a body like any human being.

Rabbi Shimeon asked how it was possible for Elijah to enter Heaven alive. As we know, not all the Heavens together can hold even a particle of the things of this world. The secret lies in Adam's book, which says that a spirit will come down to the world. He will have a physical body and he will call himself Elijah, and with his body he will enter Heaven in a whirlwind and in a cloud, and in that cloud his spirit will leave his physical body and will enter a pure body of a radiance, with which he will be able to fly to Heaven and join the angels. The physical body will remain lying in the cloud, and when Elijah has to go down to this world, he will first go into the cloud. There he will take off his Heavenly body and put on his physical body, in which he will appear in this world. And those two bodies will enable Elijah to be in either world.

When Elisha saw Elijah flying up to Heaven, he shouted: "My father! My father! You protect Jews better than all their armies with all their weapons!"

When Elijah was then fully concealed from Elisha's eyes, Elisha ripped his clothes as if Elijah had died. Elisha now saw Elijah's mantle lying in front of him: it had dropped off Elijah when he had flown to Heaven. Elisha picked it up, took it to the Jordan, and struck the water with it, say-ing: "Where is the God of Elijah—the Lord who will give me the power to work the same wonder as Elijah?" The Jordan then divided and the water parted, and Elisha crossed the Jordan on dry land.

The young prophets, who were in Jericho, saw all those things from a distance and they told one another that Elijah's spirit of prophecy was resting on Elisha. They all went to him and bowed to him with their faces on the ground in order to show that as of today they would be subservient to him as they had been to Elijah. However, the young prophets failed to understand that Elijah had flown to Heaven with his body while still alive. They thought that Elijah's spirit had left his body high up among the clouds and that the whirlwind had dropped his body somewhere in the mountains. The fifty young prophets therefore decided to look for Elijah's body so that they could eulogize him and bury him in great honor.

For three days they looked and looked, but they couldn't find the body. Now they understood that Elijah had flown to Heaven alive.

From then on Elijah would never show himself openly until the Messiah came. Once the Messiah comes, Elijah will again show himself to the entire world. For now, only the tsadiks are privileged to see Elijah's revelations, but in secret, so that no one else can see him.

IN THE DAYS when Jehoram reigned as king of Judah, he consolidated his power through murder and cruelty, putting all his brothers to the sword. He also went in evil ways by marrying one of Ahab's daughters.

One day he received a letter from Elijah with a harsh prophecy from God. The prophecy said that Jehoram would soon have a dreadful end: a great epidemic would afflict his entire household, bringing terrible ill-nesses, and Jehoram would die a horrible death.

Everything written in the letter came true. According to calculations, the letter reached King Jehoram seven years after the demise of the prophet Elijah. How was the letter written by Elijah and how did it reach King Jehoram? Many different explanations were offered by the interpreters. But the truth will not come out until the writer of the letter reveals himself to all Jews. He will then illuminate our eyes. May it happen in our days. Amen.

The Salvation of a Soul

FROM *SIPUREI HARI* (NO PLACE OR DATE)

BEFORE ACCEPTING A student, Rabbi Isaac Luria, the great Cabalist, would test him to see whether he was capable of studying the secrets of the Cabala. If he saw that a candidate was uncertain, he would tell him to go to some yeshiva and study the Talmud.

One day a young scholar came to Rabbi Luria to study the Cabalistic secrets. The rabbi asked him whether he had a wife. The scholar replied that he was still a bachelor. So Rabbi Luria said: "If that's the case, marry a pious woman. Then I'll take you on as one of my students."

The bachelor asked him: "Rabbi, where can I find my soul mate?"

Rabbi Luria replied: "At present in Egypt. Go there, and when you arrive, go and study in Rabbi Betzalel Ashkenazi's study house, and within a short time you'll be offered a wife. Accept the offer, for she is your soul mate for now."

The young scholar said goodbye to Rabbi Luria and went to Egypt. He began studying in Rabbi Betzalel Ashkenazi's house of study and he soon grew famous for his great wisdom.

Within a short time he was offered the hand of an orphan, who had a dowry of two hundred ducats. The young man accepted the offer, and the wedding soon took place with a great deal of fanfare. All the sages of the city attended the celebration.

The orphan, who came from a fine family, was a loyal wife. She made sure he studied day and night, while she opened a shop to support them. They lived very happily.

But their joy was short-lived. Eight months after the wedding the wife caught cold and, after keeping to her bed for a short time, she died.

Broken and despondent because of his grief and misery, the scholar wanted to leave Egypt. He returned to the Holy Land, hoping to find solace by studying under the holy Rabbi Luria. With a mournful face he entered the rabbi's house of study and asked to be accepted as one of his students.

Rabbi Luria said to him: "I see you're very surprised that I told you to go to Egypt and get married. And what was the result? I'm going to reveal a secret to you, so you'll understand and you won't complain about God's ways.

"You should know that the orphan's soul had already been in this world one generation earlier. And your soul likewise lived a generation earlier. The two of you were business partners, and the orphan's soul embezzled two hundred ducats from you. Heaven therefore ordained that your partner's soul should return to this world and do penance for the great sin of theft. And she became your soul mate for a brief time. You got back your two hundred ducats as her dowry, while her soul achieved full salvation, so that she had nothing more to do in this world."

The scholar found comfort in those words. He studied diligently for a long while, then he married again, this time in the Holy Land, and he became one of the famous geniuses in the country.

A Tale about Moses Maimonides

FROM MAASE FUN RAMBAM
VILNA, 1913

WHEN MOSES MAIMONIDES lived in the city of Algiers, the capital of the kingdom of Barbary in the land of Africa, he was considered a great man and he was esteemed and acclaimed everywhere. Everyone praised and honored him. He was also very influential among the lords and judges in what was called the "divan" (the court of law) in the capital. However, one of the lords, whose name was Peri and who was wise but also wicked, had hated Moses Maimonides for a long time because he was envious of his wisdom.

One day the Jews of the capital came to Moses Maimonides with a problem. They were concerned about a keg of wine that had been touched by an Egyptian who lived in Algiers. Maimonides ruled that the wine was therefore not kosher so that Jews were not allowed to drink it.

Another problem was then presented to Maimonides: a lizard had crept into a barrel of olive oil. Maimonides ruled that the lizard should be thrown away and that the oil was kosher and could be consumed.

The Jewish elders thereupon went to Judge Peri and complained about the two judgments. Peri was furious, and his anger burned inside him: "So for him I and my nation are worth less than a lizard. Now's the time to get my revenge." Peri decided to kill Maimonides, who, however, found out about the plan either from his holy spirit in Heaven or from his friends.

Maimonides took his treasures of gold, diamonds, and money, and he went to a boatman and said: "I feel very sad. Please take me to another shore so that I can unburden my heart, and I'll pay you.

The boatman replied: "I'll do what you ask of me."

The two of them boarded the small skiff, and the boatman fell sound asleep. Maimonides, who could miraculously shorten the trip, placed the boatman in the stern of the skiff. Then Maimonides brought his wife and children, and they sailed hundreds and hundreds of leagues from Algiers within a quarter hour. The skiff halted, and at that very instant the boatman awoke. He saw that he was in a foreign country and he heard a language that he didn't understand. He trembled and he shouted very bitterly. He figured that Maimonides had worked magic.

When Maimonides heard the man shouting, he calmed him down with gentle words: "Don't worry, within a quarter hour I'll get you back to Algiers. But be careful. When you return to Algiers and wake up, you should cleanse yourself. I'm going to place a document in the stern of the skiff. You must toss this document into the sea. And if you say anything to anyone, you will die immediately."

The boatman said: "I'll do what you tell me." And he swore an oath. Maimonides then paid him his fee and sent him away. Within a quarter hour the boatman was back in Algiers, and he did what Maimonides had ordered him to do.

Several days later Maimonides reached the city of Cairo, which is the capital of Egypt and the residence of the king of Egypt. It wasn't long before the subjects and all the great men of the country praised Maimonides to the king, for Maimonides had worked great feats and wonders with his medical treatments. Within a year the king of Egypt exalted him for his great wisdom and science. The king raised Maimonides' chair above those of all his other subjects and he loved him dearly.

Maimonides' fame spread through all the lands and it reached the ears of the boatmen who sail the ocean. They in turn carried his fame to Judge Peri, who thus found out that his enemy had escaped to Egypt. Peri was very annoyed and upset because the king of Egypt had exalted Maimonides.

Meanwhile the three-year alliance with the king of Egypt had come to an end, and it was time for another three-year alliance. So the judges of Algiers sent Judge Peri to the king of Egypt in Cairo. The morning after Peri's arrival, Maimonides summoned the angel of fire and told him not to let any fire burn anywhere in Egypt. Loud shouting was then heard throughout the land and also in Cairo, because they were unable to light a fire anywhere. And the shouting lasted for six days throughout Egypt.

When the king heard this, he asked all the wise men who knew about these things: What could be done against this prodigious thing, which was afflicting his entire country? But none of the wise men could explain it to him. The king then asked the great physician, Dr. Maimonides.

Maimonides replied: "Long live the king. I recall that when I was in the city of Algiers one of the judges was a great magician, the likes of whom couldn't be found in the entire land of Barbary. His name is Peri, and I've heard that he arrived in Egypt six days ago to renew the alliance. But his real plan is to use his magic to destroy your country and murder you and your children and your wife and your subjects. After that, he'll become the king of Egypt and Arabia."

Upon hearing this, the king said: "Yesterday Judge Peri told one of my subjects that you fled Algiers in the afternoon of such and such a day in such and such a year because they wanted to execute you for cursing God, the divan, and the entire country."

Maimonides replied: "May the king live forever and shield his country and all its inhabitants against evil. Not only is Judge Peri a great magician, but he also plans to use his magic to conquer many nations and become their king. And he also wants to shed blood uselessly with his magic."

With the king's permission, Maimonides went home and then returned to the king with the document that he had had at the beach the afternoon of the day that Judge Peri had said that Maimonides had fled Algiers. Maimonides also had the letter he had received within several days—the letter to the lord of the gates in Cairo. The king believed Maimonides and he declared Judge Peri guilty.

Next the king conferred with his advisers about what to do with the magician Peri. Eight days after his arrival, Judge Peri mounted a chariot drawn by eight mules in order to go to the king and renew the alliance as well as to denounce Maimonides.

Judge Peri had a huge and very beautiful dog, which he loved dearly. And the dog joined him in the chariot. The instant the dog stepped into the chariot, he sprang out again and released large flames from his mouth. The fire grew bigger and it was bigger than all the houses in Cairo, it burned the houses and the people until it became a huge conflagration. Judge Peri stood there amazed, for he had never known that his friend the dog could release fire from his mouth, a fire that kept growing and growing endlessly.

When the common people standing near Peri's chariot saw the evil deed, they shouted, "Magician! Magician!" The magician greater than all other magicians had not been in Egypt for many years. So they decided to kill him and his dog. Otherwise the whole of Egypt could be destroyed. And they suddenly cut him and his dog into smithereens and the [sir-hamishtelekh] and they smashed his chariot into a thousand pieces. Each person then picked up a piece of the judge's bones or skin or the bones or skin of his dog and took it home and put it in a clay vessel for a long time as a warning to criminals not to imitate a magician like Judge Peri.

And the king and Maimonides were no longer angry.

The Angel

FROM *IN DER VELT FUN KHSIDES*
WARSAW, 1938

ALTHOUGH HE WAS the only child of the Preacher of Mezritsh as well as his spiritual heir, Avrómele had a completely different manner of worship: he was entirely removed from the whole earthly world. Day and night he was absorbed in study and service, in fasting and penance — beyond all understanding. In this way, Avrómele deviated from his father, who, like the holy Baal-Shem-Tov, taught his followers that you serve G-d not with fasting and penance but — quite the opposite — with food and drink, and with joy instead of sadness.

Avrómele's conduct made him seem more like a divine angel than a human being of flesh and blood. That was why the Hasidic world nick-named him the Angel.

The Angel modeled his behavior after that of the holy cabalist Rabbi Isaac Luria, and his closest friend was the most respected of the preacher's students, the man who became Rabbi Shnéur Zalman of Ladi (of blessed memory). Together they studied exoterics and esoterics — revealed things and concealed things — day and night.

Old Hasids tell us that the Angel was fearful to look at. In general he was rarely seen for he almost never associated with other people.

At fifteen he married his first wife, and though he lived with her for ten years, he was so removed from the world that he scarcely knew her.

Widowed at twenty-five, he resolved never to marry again. Needless to say, his decision was a harsh blow for the preacher. Since the Angel was his only child, his lineage would be terminated!

Hasidic legend tells us that the Angel was a man of peace; he had a holy and polished body with no earthly needs whatsoever and a soul without the slightest flaw.

However, his father, the preacher, fully recalled the testament of his great rebbe, the Baal-Shem-Tov, who had assured him that since the Messiah wouldn't be coming all that soon, his soul would descend again to this lowly world and reside in one of his children. That was why the Preacher of Mezritsh, in his deep distress, argued with his holy son:

"The Torah wasn't given to angels, the whole universe is full of the Good Lord's majesty. He is everywhere, in every gesture and in every human step."

"You *can* find Him everywhere," the Angel replied. "But you *have* to find him in spiritual deeds . . ."

"I order you to have children!" the preacher snapped.

The Angel did not respond. Later on, however, he explained himself to his friend, the Rabbi of Ladi. "I cannot disobey my spiritual father, the Lord of the Universe, by obeying my earthly father. . . ."

But in the end the Angel gave in and decided to marry a second time. There are different theories about why he changed his mind. Some people say that he was ordered by Heaven to carry out his father's wishes.

Upon learning that his son had finally agreed to remarry, the preacher sent two messengers to Kremenits, to the great preacher Feyvish, the author of *The Teachings of the Sages*. They were supposed to ask Féyvish for the hand of Gíttele, his twelve-year-old daughter, for the holy Angel.

The messengers set out in a luxurious coach, taking along a number of things, including many gifts, many jewels for the bride—because the Preacher of Mezritsh had ordered them to bring her here immediately.

The messengers pulled up outside Feyvish's house in Kremenits, but they couldn't find him, he was at the synagogue. Only his wife was at home. Upon hearing the proposal, she burst out laughing: "What are you talking about? Marrying a twelve-year-old girl to a widower who's more than twice her age?"

Ignoring her words, the messengers asked where her husband was, for they were fully convinced that the twelve-year-old bride was the Angel's soul mate. Finally the mother gave in and sent for her husband to come quickly.

When he heard the proposal he accepted it with all his heart, he actually danced with delight. It was no mean thing being related to the Preacher of Mezritsh and having the holy Angel as a son-in-law! "We agree, we agree!" the father joyfully exclaimed. "May the wedding be blessed!"

The messengers now took out the expensive garments and presents for the bride, they had a banquet fit for a king, and the next day they set the time at which they would take the bride to Mezritsh for the wedding.

The marriage was celebrated with utter merriment, the Preacher of Mezritsh took part with all his friends—there had never been such a wedding!

THE DUBNO PREACHER
(Dubner Maggid) *(1740–1804)*

Sermons have wielded great influence over religious and secular works in Christian and Jewish culture. Martin Luther King Jr.'s speeches are basically sermons; but the most familiar American literary example may be the title and epigraph of Ernest Hemingway's For Whom the Bell Tolls, *both derived from a sermon by John Donne. Still, popular as this novel may be, few of its readers believe that Donne's sermon—or any sermon—is intrinsic to their lives. For Yiddish speakers, however, sermons, especially the parables used by preachers, are an integral and familiar part of their everyday experience. Indeed, sermons are a crucial, if at times soporific, component of Jewish culture throughout the world.*

The best-known Ashkenazi preacher was probably Yakov Krants, the Preacher of Dubno (1740–1804), whose oral sermons were written down by his followers and eventually published in Hebrew, then Yiddish. Tradition focuses not on his full sermons but on the more entertaining parables contained within. These stories are liberated from their homiletic constraints and usually provided with a moral. Krants, an anti-Hasid who was close to the Vilna Gaon, the poster boy of anti-Hasidism, drew his parables from so many sources that he might almost be called one of the first Yiddish folklorists. Ironically, his material was so eclectic that a few of his parables, such as "The Prince Who Forgot Who He Was" (p. 119), sound like Hasidic tales. Furthermore, since the Krants stories that have come down to us are told about Krants (in the third person), they sound very much like Hasidic hagiography. Ultimately, when the Haskala made headway, the Dubno Preacher, like the Hasids, attacked it with all his furious might.

True to literary custom, I've stuck to parables rather than whole sermons. For a detailed introduction to the world of Jewish sermons, see Marc Saperstein, Jewish Preaching 1200–1800 *(New Haven: Yale University Press, 1989).*

Parables

A Parable about a Parable

THE DUBNO PREACHER was once asked: "How come a parable can have such a powerful effect on a person?"

To which the Preacher replied: "I'll explain it by telling you a parable." And this is the parable he told:

Truth once walked through the streets, as naked as on the day he was born. People refused to let him enter their homes. Anyone he encountered would dash off in terror. As Truth wandered in great misery, he ran into Parable, who was all decked out in beautiful clothes with splendid colors.

Parable asked: "Tell me, my friend, why are you roaming around in such a dejected mood?"

Truth replied: "It's awful, brother. I'm old, very old, so nobody wants to have anything to do with me."

"People don't dislike you because of your age. I'm very old myself. Yet the older I get, the more they love me. Let me tell you a secret about people. They want everything to be all gussied up and a bit disguised. I'll lend you clothes like mine, and you'll see that people will love you too."

Truth followed the advice and put on some of Parable's clothes. Ever since then, Truth and Parable have walked hand in hand, and people love them both.

A Question with a Parable and an Answer with a Parable

ONCE, WHEN THE Dubno Preacher was visiting the Vilna Gaon, the latter asked his guest how long it took him to create a parable.

The Preacher replied: "Give me a line from a holy book, and I'll ask you a question with a parable and answer the question with a parable."

They agreed to open the Sidur [Daily Prayer Book] lying on the table. The Gaon would indicate a line, and the Preacher would use it to ask with a parable and answer with a parable.

They opened the Sidur, and the Gaon pointed to the line that went: "Jews pray to God, expecting Him to answer their prayers as he answered Abraham's prayer on Mount Moriah."

"Let me ask a question right here," the Dubno Preacher began.

"Once there was a shopkeeper in a shtetl, and he had two steady customers: one was the town plutocrat, the other was a pauper. One day the rich man's daughter was getting married, and, as is customary, everyone was sending presents. The shopkeeper spent fifty rubles on a costly gift and sent it over to the rich man's home. A short time later the poor man likewise married off a daughter. Now what should the shopkeeper give him? Not an expensive present—something for two or three rubles. That would be enough for a pauper.

"The pauper was so upset that he went to the shopkeeper and said: 'What's this all about? The rich man has everything, so you send him a gift worth fifty rubles, but you send me such a cheap trifle!'

"The shopkeeper was beside himself at the man's chutzpah: 'You pauper, you beggar! What are you complaining about? The rich man buys so much from me, he provides me with almost half my income. But how much do you buy? Half a herring, a quart of kerosene, a kopek's worth of matches—plus I often have to give you credit, and it's agonizing to get you to pay your debt. So how can you compare yourself to the rich man?'

"Now that's a question for us Jews. How can we have the chutzpah to expect the good Lord to answer our prayers as he answered Abraham's prayer? After all, God profited greatly from Abraham—lots of good deeds and dutiful actions. We Jews, however, are poor in good deeds, we pay God with a psalm, a Benediction, a 'Hear, O Israel'! And we're often in his debt and even go bankrupt!

"That's the question, and now I'll answer the question with a parable.

"Once there was a Jewish farmer, a very simple, ignorant man, who knew little about the Jewish religion. But he had a lot of money and he wanted to buy himself some ancestral prestige. His son had a good mind, so the father sent him to the yeshiva in town. The boy studied hard and became known as the best scholar there. A few years later the director of the yeshiva died, and people wondered whom to replace him with. They considered the excellent student, the son of a rich peasant. But opponents argued that it would be unsuitable to appoint the son of such an ignorant man. Someone then suggested that if the father donated twenty-five thousand rubles to the school, the son would be given the great honor of becoming its director. The peasant seized the opportunity. It was no small matter having such a son! And he handed over the cash.

"Years later the peasant's son died. And since the grandson was an eminent genius, the congregation wanted him to follow in his father's footsteps. Someone reminded them that when the father had become director, his father had donated twenty-five thousand rubles to the yeshiva: so the grandson should also contribute the same amount.

"'No!' said one of the congregants. 'The grandfather had to pay because he was ignorant and illiterate. But this man's father was an outstanding scholar, so we have to appoint him with the greatest respect and with no contribution.'

"And that's the answer to the question. Abraham had a father, Terach, who worshiped idols; so the son had to contribute a great deal. But we Jews have a wonderful father, Abraham; and so God has to answer our prayers, even though we don't give a lot."

The Two Watches

A MAN OWNED two expensive watches. He was very proud of them and he would show them to all his friends. When he was old and about to leave this world, he gave each of his two sons a watch, telling them never to sell the watches. The old man's death was followed by a bad period for his sons. They grew poorer and poorer, and because their plight was crushing them, they thought about selling the expensive watches. But since they were ashamed to flout their father's will in front of one another, each man sold his watch in secret. One day, when the two happened to meet, one asked the other what time it was. His brother replied: "I've forgotten my watch at home. Where's yours?"

The other answered: "I've forgotten my watch too . . ." Both of them realized that each had sold his watch.

"Did you at least get a good price?" the older brother asked.

The younger brother replied: "I got very little, because the man I sold the watch to is no expert. So I had to take what he offered."

"Listen," said the older brother. "I handled it differently. First I had my watch evaluated by experts, then I found a rich merchant, who paid the correct price."

"Well," said the younger brother. "I was smarter. You sold the watch to a man who knows its value. And if ever you want to buy the watch back, the merchant will charge more than he paid. But I sold my watch to a man who doesn't know its value, and he'll be happy if I pay him the same price that he paid me."

MORAL ▩ The wise man looks beyond the present time. A man can get a good price and still cheat himself.

Man and Beast

ONCE A FEW small shopkeepers got together, saying: "Why should each of us have his own shop and compete with the rest of us and lower our prices and make a pitiful living? Let's merge all our little shops into one big, fine store. We'll hire a capable man to run the business, and we'll share the profits equally."

The small shopkeepers went along with the proposal, and the new business started out quite well. The manager ran the store very adequately, distributing the profits carefully, and the partners lived decently, in peace and quiet. A bit later, however, the manager started embezzling and siphoning off some of the money. When the partners realized he was dishonest, they started behaving indecently themselves, robbing, cheating, and swindling one another.

MORAL ▨ Each bird, beast, and head of cattle gave some of its qualities to man, and all the animals were partners in creating him. So long as man behaved decently, all living creatures likewise behaved decently. But in the years before the Flood, when men abandoned the road of righteousness, the birds, beasts, and cattle also left the strait and narrow path. And that was why the Flood came upon all of them.

The Prince Who Forgot Who He Was

A KING ONCE got angry at his son and drove him from the palace and the city. The young prince wandered about, starving and without knowing where his feet were taking him. Late one evening he arrived in a village and, knocking at a peasant's door, he asked whether he could spend the night. The peasant looked at the boy with the beautiful face and the radiant eyes and he liked him very much. Feeling sorry for him, the peasant took him on as a farmhand: the boy would help him milk the cows, tend the poultry, and do light chores around the house. In exchange the boy got food and drink and a bed. Naturally the peasant didn't know that the stranger was a prince.

The prince grew accustomed to his work and his new kind of life until he completely forgot that he was a prince. As long as the peasant was alive, the boy had an easy time and enough to eat and drink. But then the peasant died. His son, his sole inheritor, was an evil man. He forced the boy to labor very hard, beyond his strength, and he gave him very little food. Life for the boy was, alas, so harsh and bitter that he wished he were dead.

Meanwhile the king remembered his son and he missed him deeply. His anger had waned long since and his paternal feelings had revived. The king grew sadder day by day, not knowing where his son was or how he was living.

The king then conferred with his advisers, and they decided that he should journey across the country to look for his son. So the king and his suite traveled through his kingdom, and wherever he stopped, he would issue a proclamation stating that anyone with a grievance against another person and any servant with a complaint against his master should appear before the king, and the king would hear him out.

Many people arrived with accusations. They came from the city and from the surrounding shtetls and villages, which were poor and small. One of these plaintiffs was the unhappy prince, who wanted to complain about his bad master. The prince failed to recognize his father. He had totally forgotten who he was and what he had been, and he didn't realize he was standing in front of his own father. He tearfully explained that his master was forcing him to do hard labor, beyond his strength, and giving him very little food, starving him to death.

The king heard him out, and he too began shedding tears, for he recognized his own son. Unable to contain himself any longer, the king exclaimed: "My son! My dear child! Look what's become of you! How could you forget your great background and your pride? How could you forget that a royal crown is waiting for you and that generals and ministers bowed to you in your home? Have you fallen so low that your sole desire is to make the peasant give you a little less work and a little more bread?"

MORAL ▦ It's the same with us Jews. We've so deeply forgotten our wonderful past and our great background that we've grown accustomed to our life in exile, and all we desire is fewer evil decrees and a bit more income. Yet it never crosses our minds to ask God to take us back to our own land and to our ancient grandeur.

Before a Contract and After a Contract

A YOUNG STRANGER came to a rich man in a large city and asked him for a job. The rich man replied: "How can I give you a job? I don't know you from Adam and I can't tell if you're good at anything."

The stranger retorted: "Employ me in your business for a one-month trial period. I'll be content with anything you care to pay me for that month, and you can see whether you should keep me on after that."

The rich man agreed and hired the stranger. Throughout the trial period, both the employer and the employee were satisfied with each other. The young man did everything he had to do and he was paid what his boss wanted to pay him.

When the month was up, the rich man said to the young man: "So far we've acted in a fraternal way. But now we have to get down to business. You've worked as much as you've liked, and I've paid you as much as I've wanted. Sometimes you've done too much work, sometimes less. Sometimes I've overpaid you, sometimes I've underpaid you. But now we'll draw up a contract so that we can accurately gauge your work and your hours. We'll also set down an exact salary for you."

MORAL Initially Abraham came to serve God for a trial period. Abraham himself, with his own mind, realized that there is a Creator in the Heavens, and Abraham, of his own accord, decided to serve Him and live decently. And the Lord did good things for Abraham: He gave him children and wealth and shielded him from misfortune. When Abraham turned ninety-nine, the Lord appeared to him and said: "I am God Almighty. Now I am your Master. We will draw up a contract. From this day forward, you will be my worker forever and you will do specific work."

RABBI NAKHMAN OF BRASLEV

(1772–1810)

A new direction in Hasidic literature was developed by the Baal-Shem-Tov's great-grandson, Rabbi Nakhman of Braslev. Instead of paeans to Hasidic miracles and gurulike rebbes, to the deus ex machina wonders performed by the prophet Elijah, and to the concealed actions of the Thirty-six Hidden Saints (Lamed-Vovniks), Nakhman rejected the traditional elements of Hasidic storytelling. He turned to symbolism and allegory, creating and orally narrating to his followers mysterious tales that drew on talmudic and cabalistic themes as well as folk motifs. The results were elusive and magical myths with their own pungent diction and intricate plots.

After Nakhman's death, his assistant, Nathan, published the stories in a bilingual edition—the Hebrew at the top half of each page and Yiddish at the lower half (unlike side-by-side bilingual texts in other cultures). Thus even the book design was symbolic, Hebrew obviously representing Heaven and Yiddish Earth.

Telling about lost princesses, inscrutable beggars, bewitched princes, enchanted kings, make-believe countries, children whose bodies are filled with jewels, these stories employ an authentic oral vernacular rather than the stilted archaisms of earlier texts. The characters move through unearthly, enigmatic terrains that most readers might not necessarily discern as Jewish—places of survival, of quests for redemption, radical self-confrontation, and struggles with the fragmentary nature of life.

And while Marxist critics have always decried the occult, M. Viner, a leading Marxist historian of Yiddish literature, fell prey to these tales, though warding off their metaphysical seductiveness. Instead, he acclaimed them for using Yiddish as the language of the Jewish proletariat and for describing everyday workers and their lives—a public relations exaggeration, since so many of the characters are rabbis or royals.

Martin Buber adapted Nakhman's tales (and other Hasidic works) into German, destroying their charisma by rewriting them as Grimm fairy tales; and the English translation of the Buber skewings then moved one league further from the baffling charm of the original—completely nullifying its poetic spell.

A Tale of a King's Son Who Was Switched at Birth with a Maidservant's Son

FROM TALES (1815)

ONCE THERE WAS a king who had a maidservant living in his home and serving the queen. A cook is probably never received by the king, but the maidservant had some other kind of chores, smaller chores, to do for the queen.

Now the time came when the queen was about to give birth. And the maidservant was also about to give birth. But the midwife came and switched the babies in order to see what would happen. She took the king's child and placed it near the maidservant, and she placed the maidservant's child next to the queen.

The children began to grow up. The king's son (that is, the boy who grew up with the king, for they mistook him for his son) was raised (that is, elevated) higher and higher until he became very big and became a big creature.

And the maidservant's son (that is, the real prince, who was brought up by the maidservant) grew up in her home.

Both children went to school together. And the king's real son, who was known as the maidservant's son, was by his very nature drawn to royal conduct, but he grew up in the maidservant's home.

And the other way round: the maidservant's son, who was known as the king's son, was drawn by his very nature to conduct that was anything but royal. But he grew up in the king's home, and so he had to behave in royal fashion. And since women have little self-control and cannot hold back, the midwife went and told someone the secret—namely, that she had switched the two babies.

Now since every person has a friend, and the friend has another friend, each one passed it on until the secret was exposed, as is the way of the world. The commoners began whispering about it—namely, that the king's son had been switched at birth. The higher-ups certainly could not talk about it lest the king find out. After all, what could he do in that case? Nothing would help. For one could not believe it entirely—what if it were a lie? And how could they switch the children back? That was why they understood that they must not reveal the secret to the king. However, the commoners whispered it to one another.

ONE DAY SOMEONE went and revealed the secret to the king's son: namely, that he had been switched at birth. "But you cannot investigate this, it would not be proper. And how does one investigate such a matter? I've simply told you about it so that you'd know. If ever there is an uprising against the throne, the uprising would be stronger because of this secret. For the rebels will say that they will take the king's son as their king—that is, the one who they say is the king's real son. That's why you have to make sure you find a way to get rid of that boy."

Those were the words of the man who revealed the secret to the maidservant's son, whom people mistook for the king's son.

The king's son (that is, the boy who was called the king's son) went and began playing tricks on the father of the maidservant's son, who was actually the boy's own father, and the son made a point of causing him trouble all the time, to force the father to flee with his son.

While the king was still alive, his son (that is, the maidservant's son) had little power even though he caused the king a lot of trouble. But then the king grew old and died.

The maidservant's switched son, who was called the king's son, mounted the throne. And he now did further bad things to the father of the maidservant's son (the son was actually the king's son, while the father was actually the father of the maidservant's real son, the son who succeeded to the throne, for the two sons had been switched at birth).

The new king treated his real father very badly. And he did everything secretly; he didn't want anyone to know since it wouldn't make a good impression.

AND THE FATHER knew that the king (who was actually his son) was playing tricks on him because everyone was saying that the children had been switched at birth. So the father went and revealed the entire matter to his son, the king's real son, who, because of the switch, appeared to be the maidservant's son.

And the father told him that he greatly pitied him either way: "If you are someone else, my child, then I certainly pity you; and if you are not someone else, my child, if you are really the king's son, then you are even more to be pitied. For the man who has become king wants to get rid of you altogether—God forbid! That's why you have to flee, you have to escape."

It bothered him greatly.

But the new king (that is, the maidservant's son) kept playing more and more tricks, one after another. So the prince (that is, the real prince) felt he had to flee. His father (that is, the maidservant's husband) gave him a lot of money, and the prince fled.

The king's son (that is, the real son) was extremely annoyed at being driven from his country for no good reason. He thought to himself: "For what and for whom was I driven out? If I'm the king's son, then I shouldn't be driven out; and if I'm not the king's son, then I shouldn't have to flee at all. What have I done wrong, how have I sinned?"

And he was so distressed that he took to drinking and to visiting houses of ill repute. He wanted to devote the rest of his life to getting drunk and following his heart's desire because he had been driven from his country for no good reason.

And the king (that is, the false king) was a severe ruler. And whenever he heard that certain people were murmuring and saying that he had been switched at birth, he would punish and torture them and get his terrible revenge,

And thus he ruled with an iron fist.

One day the false king was out hunting with his lords. Soon they came to a lovely place, with a lovely stream running alongside it. So the hunters stopped, dismounted, and strolled about, while the king lay down for a bit.

Then he thought about what he had done by driving out the real prince for no good reason. If the prince was someone else, then it was enough that he'd been switched at birth—why should he also be driven out for no good reason? And if he wasn't the prince then he shouldn't be driven out—for how had he sinned?

And the king kept thinking about it and he regretted his great sin and his great wrong and he was at a loss about what to do. But you can't talk about this to anyone, you can't consult with anyone, you're too ashamed. This left the false king very worried, and because of his great distress he told the lords that they would all have to go home. He was so greatly distressed that he had no desire to stroll about. And so they went home.

And when the king came home, he had lots of matters and problems to deal with, and he was so engrossed that he forgot all about his misdeed—that is, his distress and his remorse about the man he had driven out for no good reason.

And the real prince, who had been driven out, had done what he had done and had spent all his money. Now one day he went for a stroll by himself and he also lay down for a bit and mused about all the things that had happened to him, and he started thinking: "What has God done with me? If I'm really the king's son, then all of this certainly shouldn't have happened to me. And If I'm not the king's son, then I shouldn't have had to flee and be driven out." He then mulled: "Well, if the good Lord can actually allow a king's son to be switched at birth and endure those other things, then is everything I've done right? Did I have to do what I've done?"

And he began feeling distress and great remorse in regard to the wicked things he had done. He then went home (that is, to where he was staying) and he again took to drinking. But because he felt some remorse, he was haunted and confused by thoughts of regret and repentance.

One day he lay down for a bit and he dreamed: There was a fair on a certain day and so he went. And he was to accept the very first job he was offered even if the work wasn't respectable . . .

Now he awoke. But the dream had pierced his mind deeply. Some dreams leave the mind quickly, but this dream had pierced his mind deeply. He felt very unhappy about doing what he had to do. Yet he went back to drinking.

Then he had the same dream once again. And he dreamed it many times. This confused him greatly. In one dream he was told: "If you want to take pity on yourself, you should do it" — that is, go to the fair.

He therefore had to make his dream come true.

He went and spent his last money at the inn where he was staying, and he also left his good clothing there. He put on a simple garment, the kind worn by merchants, and he went to the fair.

There he met a merchant, who asked him: "Would you like to be paid for some work?"

He answered: "Yes."

The merchant told him: "I have to herd some cattle. Can I hire you?"

The king's son had no time to think it over because of his dream, which had told him to accept the very first job he was offered. So he promptly answered: "Yes."

The merchant promptly hired him and began using him and ordering him about like a lord with his servants. The king's son began wondering what he was doing. This kind of work was certainly unsuitable for him since he was of royal blood, but now he would have to drive cattle and go with them on foot. But one can't go back. The merchant was ordering him about the way a lord orders about his servants.

So he asked the merchant: "How can I go alone with the cattle?"

The merchant replied: "I've got herders who drive my cattle. You'll go with them." And the merchant handed over some cattle for him to drive.

The king's son drove the cattle from the town and joined the other herders who were driving the merchant's cattle. The merchant savagely rode a horse alongside the herders and he brutalized the king's son.

The king's son was terrified of the merchant. He was afraid that if the merchant hit him with his stick, he would instantly die because he was of royal blood. He was therefore quite scared as he drove the cattle with the merchant riding alongside.

They reached a place and there they took out the bag containing bread for the herders, and the merchant gave them all some bread.

Next they traveled along a very dense forest. Thereupon two heads of the prince's cattle wandered off into the forest. The merchant yelled at him, and so he went after those stray cows. But they fled deeper into the forest. He kept chasing them, but because the forest was so dense and thick, he and his companions soon lost sight of one another.

And the prince, who had lost two cows, was chasing after them, and they kept going and going. And he kept after them until he reached the densest part of the forest.

Here he thought to himself: "I'm going to die anyway, because if I return without the two cows, the merchant will kill me. But if I stay here, I'll be killed by the beasts of the forest."

And the prince went on and he kept chasing the two cows. And they kept fleeing and fleeing.

Meanwhile night was coming on. The prince had never had to spend the night alone in such a dense forest. He heard the roaring of the beasts, who were roaring as is their nature. He thought about it and then he climbed a tree, where he spent the night. And all night long he heard the beasts roaring as is their nature.

IN THE MORNING, when the prince awoke from his sleep, he saw the two cows standing nearby. So he climbed down the tree and went to capture them. But they fled again. Whereupon he chased them. But when the cows found some grass, they stopped to graze. The prince chased them, so they fled again.

He kept chasing them, and they kept fleeing, until he reached a very dense part of the forest, where there were beasts, and the beasts were not afraid of people for they were very far from any settlement.

And it was night again. And he heard the beasts roaring, and he was very frightened. Then he saw a huge tree standing there, and he climbed up the tree. And upon climbing up, he saw a man lying there. The prince was terrified. Nevertheless he was glad to find another human being. And they asked one another:

"Who are you?"

"A man."

"Who are you?"

"A man."

"How did you get here?"

The prince didn't want to tell him about everything he had endured, so he answered: "I brought the cattle to graze, but two cows wandered off, and that's how I got here." He then asked the man he had found in the tree: "How did you get here?"

The man answered: "I came here because of a horse. I was riding a horse and I stopped to rest. Then the horse wandered off into the forest. I chased after him, but the horse kept fleeing, until I finally reached this tree."

The two men agreed to stay together, and if they came to a settlement, they would continue together.

They spent the night in the tree and they heard the beasts roaring and bellowing.

TOWARD DAWN THE prince heard a loud laughter—ha ha ha!—throughout the forest, for the laughter resounded through the entire forest. The laughter was so loud that the tree began shaking. The prince was terrified.

The other man who was in the tree said: "I'm no longer scared of that for I've spent several nights here. Toward every dawn that loud laughter makes the trees shake and shudder."

The prince, who was terrified, said to his companion: "This must be a place of those 'people'" (he meant the demons). "You never hear laughter like that in a settlement. Who's heard such laughter anywhere in the world?"

Then it was day.

They looked and saw the two cows standing there and the horse standing there. So they climbed down and went chasing after them: the prince after the two cows, and the other man after the horse. The cows kept fleeing, and the prince kept chasing after them. The other man likewise chased after the horse, and the horse kept fleeing.

In this way they grew far apart and neither knew where the other was.

Meanwhile the prince, who was chasing after the cows, found a sack of bread, which is a very welcome thing in the wilderness. The prince shouldered the sack and went on chasing the cows.

All at once he encountered another man. At first the prince was frightened. Nevertheless he was a bit glad to find another human being.

"How come you're here?" the man asked him.

"And how come you're here?" the prince asked back.

The other man answered him: "I and my parents and my grandparents grew up here. But you—how did you get here? Nobody ever comes here from a settlement."

The prince was terrified, for he realized this was no human being, since he had said that his parents had grown up here and that nobody ever came here from a settlement. Nevertheless the man did nothing to him, he even befriended him.

And the forest man asked the real prince: "What are you doing here?"

The prince replied that he was chasing after the cows.

The forest man said: "Stop chasing after those sins. Those aren't cows. It's your misdeeds leading you around. That's enough. You've been punished, you've gotten your just deserts. And now stop chasing after them. Come with me. You'll come to what's right for you."

And so the prince went with him. But he was afraid to talk to him or even ask him anything. After all, if that person were to open his mouth, he might gobble up the prince. So the prince followed him silently.

All at once they encountered his companion, who had chased after the horse. And no sooner had his companion spotted him than he signaled that this was no human being, that he was to have no contact with him. He then went over to the prince and whispered that this was no human being.

The man who was chasing after the horse then looked and he saw that the prince was carrying a sack of bread on his back. The man said: "Brother, I haven't eaten for many days. Please give me some bread."

"Here in the wilderness," the prince replied, "nothing can help. My life is more valuable. I need the bread myself."

His companion pleaded with him, he begged him fervently: "I'll give you anything I can give you."

But in the wilderness no gift can be given for bread.

The prince responded: "What can you give me for bread in the wilderness?"

The horse man, who asked for bread, answered the cow man, who was the real prince: "I'll give you myself completely for the bread, I'll sell myself to you as a slave."

And the cow man calculated that it was worth buying a man for bread. So he bought him as an eternal slave. The man swore an oath that he would be his eternal slave, even when they reached a settlement. And the prince said that he would give him bread from the sack until there was no bread left.

THE TWO MEN walked together and followed the forest man. The slave, that is, the horse man, who had sold himself into slavery, followed the cow man, and they both followed the forest man. It was easier for the prince now, for he had a slave. Whenever he had to pick something up or do something else, he ordered the slave to do it for him or pick it up for him.

And together they followed the forest man, until they reached a place teeming with reptiles—serpents and lizards. The prince was terrified and he asked the forest man: "How can we get across?"

And the forest man answered: "How come you don't ask how you'll get into my home?" And he pointed to his home, which hovered in the air.

And they went with the forest man, and he got them safely across and brought them into his home, where he gave them food and drink. Then he left.

THE REAL PRINCE (the cow man) kept ordering his slave around whenever he needed something.

The slave was greatly annoyed that he had sold himself just because he had needed bread to eat at a certain hour. Now he had something to eat, but he would still have to be an eternal slave because of that one hour. He heaved a deep sigh: "What have I done to deserve to be a slave?"

The real prince (his master) asked him: "What high rank did you have that you should now sigh about what you've become?"

He answered that he had been a king, but people had said that he had been switched at birth. For actually, the horse man was the king's false son, who was actually the maidservant's son, who had driven out his friend, who was actually the king's son. When it had occurred to him that he had been unjust, he had felt remorse and he suffered because of his wicked deed and the great wrong he had done his friend. One night he had dreamed he could repent by giving up the throne and wandering far, far away. But he didn't want to do that.

Yet he was always confused by those dreams about what he should do, until he finally decided to do it. He gave up the throne and simply wandered about until he came here. And now he had to be a slave.

The real prince, who had herded cattle, listened to everything the horse man told him, but the prince held his tongue and thought to himself: "I know how to deal with you."

At night the forest man came and brought them food and drink. And they spent the night there.

Toward dawn they heard the loud laughter, which made all the trees shake. The sound of the laughter shattered all the trees. So the slave urged the real prince, his master, to ask the forest man what that laughter was, and the prince asked the forest man: "What is that loud laughter toward dawn?"

The forest man answered: "The day is laughing at the night, for the night asks the day: 'Why don't I have a name when you come?' The day then starts laughing loudly, and then the day comes. And that is the laughter that you hear toward dawn."

That was a great wonder for the real prince, for it was a wild thing for the day to scornfully laugh at the night. But he couldn't ask any more questions for the forest man answered him in that way.

In the morning the forest man left again, and the cow man and his slave ate and drank. Then at night they again heard the wild roaring and shrieking of the beasts, for all the animals and birds were making a hubbub: the lion roared in his way, and the leopard howled in a different voice. And the birds chirped and twitted, and all the other animals shrieked as well, each with a different voice.

At first the cow man and the horse man were so terrified that they didn't really listen to the noises. Then they listened and they heard a melody, the creatures were singing a lovely melody, which was a tremendous surprise. So the two men listened more closely. And so they heard a wondrous melody, a delight to hear, and all the delights in the world were nothing compared with the tremendous delight of hearing this wondrous melody.

The two men now talked about remaining here, for they had food and drink and they also enjoyed a miraculous delight, against which all other delights were worthless. And the slave urged the master (the real prince) to ask the forest man what that was. And the master did so.

The forest man answered: "Because the sun made a garment for the moon, all the beasts of the forest said: Because the moon did very good things for them. For their power, the power of the beasts, exists mainly at night. For sometimes they have to go to a settlement, but they can't go there during the day, they can go only at night, for their power exists mainly at night. So the moon does a good thing for them by shining on them. The beasts therefore agreed to make a new melody in honor of the moon, and that is the melody you hear. All the beasts and birds sing the new melody in honor of the moon, which received a garment from the sun."

And when the master and the slave heard that it was truly a melody, they listened even more closely and they heard that this was truly a very sweet and lovely melody.

The forest man then said: "Why are you so surprised? I have an instrument that was handed down to me from my parents, who inherited it from their parents' parents. My instrument is made of special things, special leaves, special colors, so that if you put it on any beast or any bird, it will instantly start playing the melody that the animals have sung."

Now the laughter resounded again, and the daylight came. And the forest man left once more.

The real prince then set about looking for that instrument. He searched the entire room, but he couldn't find the instrument. And he was too scared to go any farther.

So the master and the slave were afraid to ask the forest man to take them to a settlement.

Then the forest man came and said he would take them to a settlement. And he took them. And he took the instrument and gave it to the real prince and he said to him: "I am giving you the instrument, and you will know how to deal with this man."

They asked him: "Where should we go?"

And he told them that they should inquire about the land that is called "The Foolish Country and the Wise Monarch."

They asked him: "Where and on what side should we inquire about that land?"

He motioned, "There"—like someone pointing a finger.

The forest man then told the real prince: "Go to that land, and there you'll achieve your glory."

And the master and the slave set out.

. . .   .

AS THEY WALKED along, they wanted to find a beast or a cow to try out the instrument and see whether the animal could play the melody. But they didn't spot a single animal. Upon approaching a settlement, they found a cow. They then put the instrument on the cow, and the instrument began to play the melody.

The two men walked and walked until they reached the land they were seeking. The land was surrounded by a wall. You could get inside only through the gates, and you had to walk several leagues until you reached the entrance gates. So they kept walking and they finally reached the gates.

However, the guards refused to let them through. The king of this land had died, leaving his son in charge. According to the king's will, the land, which had previously been called "The Foolish Country and the Wise Monarch," should henceforth be called "The Wise Country and the Foolish Monarch." But if someone now undertook to change the name back to the earlier name, then he should become king. That was why they refused to allow anyone to enter the land unless he undertook to restore its earlier name: "Would you undertake to change the name of the land back to its earlier name?"

If he couldn't do it, then they couldn't let him enter.

The slave urged him to turn around and go home. But his master didn't want to turn around, for the forest man had told him to go to this land and achieve his glory.

Meanwhile another man came along, riding on a horse. He wanted to enter the town. But he too was not allowed to enter.

The real prince saw the man's horse standing there and so he went and put the instrument on the horse. And the instrument began playing the wondrous melody. The man with the horse begged the real prince to sell him the instrument. But the real prince refused and he asked: "What can you give me for such a wondrous instrument?"

The man with the horse said: "What can you do with this instrument? You can put on shows, for which you'll get a gulden. But I know something that's a lot better than your instrument, I have something that I inherited from my parents' parents: the ability to grasp the hidden meaning of words. If someone says something—anything at all—then I can use my inherited ability to understand something different from what's been said. I haven't revealed this to anyone on earth. But I'll teach you how to do it if you give me the instrument."

The real prince, who had the instrument, thought to himself that it would truly be marvelous to grasp the hidden meanings of words. And so he gave the instrument to the man with the horse in order to gain that ability.

And the real prince, who now had the ability to grasp hidden meanings, went over to the gates of the land. Here he realized that he could restore the earlier name of the land, for he could now grasp hidden meanings. He understood that it was possible, though he didn't know how. He thought to himself that he could do it. What could he lose? He then went to the people who refused to let anyone enter unless he restored the name of the land, and the real prince told them to let him enter and he would restore the name of the land.

So they let him enter and they told the lords that there was a man who wanted to undertake to restore the earlier name of the land. They then brought him to the lords of the land, and the lords said to him:

"You should know that we are no fools, thank goodness! However, our deceased king was a genius, compared with whom we are all fools. That was why the land was called 'The Foolish Country and the Wise Monarch.' Then the king died, leaving a son. And the son is also wise, but compared with us he is anything but wise. That is why the land is now called 'The Wise Country and the Foolish Monarch.' Now according to the king's will, if we can find a wise man who can change the name of the land back to its earlier name, that man can be king. The king told his son that if we can find such a man, the son should give up the throne, and that man should be king—that is, if we can find a genius compared with whom we will all be fools. Let him be king, for that man will restore the earlier name of the land, so that we can call it 'The Foolish Country and the Wise Monarch.' For we will all be fools compared with him. So you should know what you are undertaking."

The lords told him all those things and then they said: "You'll be tested to see if you're such a genius. You see, there is a garden that was left by the king, who was a genius, and this garden is very marvelous, for metal instruments grow in it: silver instruments and golden instruments. It's truly marvelous. Now what's the problem? The problem is that no one can go inside. For if a person goes inside, someone there instantly starts chasing him. Someone chases him, and he screams, and he sees nothing and knows nothing. And someone chases him until he flees from the garden. So if you are a genius, you will get into the garden."

That was what all the lords said to the prince. The prince then asked whether someone beat the men who get inside. The lords said: "Someone chases him, and he has to flee in great terror." That was what they had heard from the people who had entered the garden.

He, the real prince, stood up and went to the garden. And he saw that the garden was surrounded by a wall, that the gates were open, and that no guards were posted there. For no guards were needed for the garden. After all, no one could get inside.

When the real prince reached the garden, he saw a man standing there, but it was actually a painting of a man. He took a closer look and above the man he saw a board with writing on it, and the writing said that this man had been a king for hundreds of years. Before his reign there had been wars, but during his reign there had been peace.

Because he could now grasp hidden meanings, the real prince understood that everything hinged on that man: if you entered the garden and were chased by someone, you shouldn't flee, you should stand next to the man. That would save you. Furthermore: if you took the man and placed him inside the garden, every person could enter the garden unscathed. The real prince understood all this because he was able to grasp the hidden meanings of things.

He stood up and went inside the garden, and the instant someone began chasing him, the prince went over and stood next to the man, who was standing outside the garden. That was why the prince emerged unscathed and unharmed. For the others, who had gone inside the garden and had been chased—they had fled in great terror and had therefore been beaten and injured. But the real prince was unscathed and unharmed because he had stood next to the man.

The lords saw this and they were very surprised to see him emerge safely.

Next he, the real prince, told them to take the man and put him inside the garden. They did so. All the lords went into the garden. They entered and emerged safely and completely unharmed. The lords then said to the real prince:

"Although we've seen you accomplish this, we don't want to hand you the monarchy on the basis of one test. We're going to give you a second test. There is a throne that belonged to the old king; and the throne is very high; and near the throne there are all kinds of beasts and birds carved out of wood; and in front of the throne there is a bed; and next to the bed there is a table; and on the table there is a candlestick; and leading from the throne there are paved roads; and they run from all sides of the throne; and nobody knows what sort of throne that is and what sort of roads those are. And where the roads run on a bit there is a golden lion; and if a person walks toward him, the lion opens his maw and devours him. And the road runs on past the lion. And the same is true of the other roads that run out from other sides of the throne: where a road runs on a bit, there is another kind of beast, such as, for instance, an iron leopard. And you mustn't walk up to the leopard, otherwise he will devour you. And the road runs on past the leopard, and the same is true of the other roads. And these roads run on and they run through the entire land. And nobody knows the meaning of the throne and the roads. You will therefore be tested to see whether you know the significance of the throne and everything else."

Then they showed the real prince the throne, and he saw that it was very high. He walked over to the throne and looked very closely. And he realized it was made of the wood of the instrument the forest man had given him: if you put it on a cow or a beast, the instrument would start to play.

The real prince looked again and he saw there was a rosebud on top of the throne, and if the throne had the rosebud, it would have the power of the instrument, which, if put on a beast or a cow, would start to play.

And he again looked closely and he saw that the rosebud moving up the throne was below in the throne [sic]. You would have to remove the rosebud from below and place it above, and then the throne would have the power of the instrument. For the old king had done each thing wisely, concealing everything, so that no one should understand what the king meant, until a very wise man came and grasped and guessed how to arrange all those things in their proper order.

The same held true for the bed: he understood that it had to be moved a little from where it was. And the same with the table: it too had to be moved a little. And the same with the candlestick: it too had to be moved a little from its place. And the same with the birds and the beasts: they too had to be shifted: each bird had to be taken from one place and put in another; and the same with all of them—they all had to be shifted.

For the king had done everything so wisely and in such a way that no one should understand, until a wise man came and understood how to rearrange everything.

And the lion who stood there, where the road ran out—he too had to be shifted. And the same for everything—it all had to be shifted.

And the real prince told them to arrange everything in the proper order: the rosebud was to be taken from below and placed above. And all the things had to be rearranged.

And when each and every thing was shifted, they all began playing the wondrous melody, the fabulous delight, and they all did what they had to do.

And so they gave the kingdom to the real prince, who had demonstrated all kinds of wisdom. And he, the prince, said to the maidservant's son: "Today I understand that I am truly the real prince, and you are truly the maidservant's son."

PART THREE

*The Haskala
(Jewish Enlightenment):
Nineteenth Century*

*I*nspired by the French and then German Enlightenment (and ignoring the antisemitism of Enlighteners like Voltaire and Rousseau), the Haskala began in Germany during the eighteenth century. Its leaders and its followers (maskils), trying to overhaul the standard Jewish education, stressed the importance of secular subjects. At the same time, the maskils wanted to deal with Judaism on an almost purely rational basis by reducing the role of the Talmud and removing what they viewed as superstition, empty ritual, and Orthodox rigidity. The magnum opus of the German Haskala was probably Moses Mendelssohn's translation of the Pentateuch into German (though in the Jewish alphabet). He not only hoped to make it easier for Jews to read the holy text, he also wanted to encourage his brethren to give up Yiddish and become German speakers so that they might claim full civil rights on an equal footing with Gentiles. This cultural assimilation worked, partly because the German Jews, constituting less than 1 percent of the overall German population, yielded to secularization and assimilation.

Early in the nineteenth century, the Haskala then reached Eastern Europe; and while the goals were in many ways similar to the German ones, the maskils had to face a much larger and very different audience, which lived mostly in shtetls and faced far grimmer antisemitism than in Germany. The maskils, who also had to deal with the warfare between the rabbinate and Hasidism (both of which were entangled in desperate conflict with the Haskala), wanted Jews to salvage what they saw as the positive aspects of Judaism, including Hebrew as the language of religion, while taking on the language and culture of their host countries.

Like the French and German Enlightenments, the Haskala worshiped rationality; and like them it could be tyrannically rational and fiercely irrational—not unlike the religions that the maskils attacked. One such irrational component was the hatred of Yiddish. They castigated it as a mishmash jargon—though any educated person knew that a major tongue like English (on which the sun never set) was far more of a fusion language than Yiddish could ever strive to be. Like most Yiddish authors, the maskils, a small cultural elite, at first wrote in Hebrew. But realizing the rather blatant and—for them—insufferable fact that most Jews didn't know Hebrew well enough to read Hebrew works, the maskils reluctantly turned to Yiddish—and thereby helped to create a modern Yiddish literature. Their legacy still pops up now and then both in Yiddish literature and in Jewish literature in non-Jewish languages, for instance, Philip Roth's short story "Eli the Fanatic."

YOYSEF PERL (*1773–1839*)

In 1816, Yoysef Perl, a former Hasid and now a leading figure in the Galician Haskala and a ferocious anti-Hasid, submitted a pamphlet to the Austrian censor. Written in German and entitled On the Nature of the Hasidic Sect as Drawn from Its Own Writings, *the anti-Hasidic text was banned by the imperial censor; nevertheless, the manuscript circulated (it was eventually published in Israel in 1977).*

In 1819, Perl, who was the first maskil to attack Hasidism openly, published a vicious Hebrew satire, The Revealer of Secrets, *attacking the corruption of the Hasids and their rebbes' exploitation of their followers. Hoping to reach a much larger audience, Perl then did a Yiddish version, which was not published until 1937.*

The plot of this epistolary novel (perhaps the first Hebrew, first Yiddish, and thus first Ashkenazi novel, and most likely the first Jewish novel) centers on the efforts of some fervent but shady Hasids to get hold of a mysterious anti-Hasidic book that exposes what Perl saw as the degeneracy of their movement: their forgery, bribery, robbery, smuggling, fornication, and other delights perpetrated by these ancestors of Bugsy Siegel and Meyer Lansky. The book is, of course, Perl's pamphlet.

Dehumanizing the characters through caricature, Perl, who translated Henry Fielding's Tom Jones *into Yiddish, manages to pour out fire and brimstone that far outdoes Fielding or Swift, yet remains cartoonish. Perl may have chosen the epistolary form because it constitutes a basic mass medium of literature — especially if penned in Yiddish.*

For an excellent translation of the Hebrew version, see Dov Taylor's Revealer of Secrets, *(Boulder, CO: Westview Press, 1997). And for an incisive analysis, see Marc Caplan,* Prooftexts *(January 1999), pp. 92–100.*

Selections from *The Revealer of Secrets*

HEBREW VERSION FIRST PUBL. VIENNA, 1819; YIDDISH VERSION VILNA, 1937

1. From Zelik Letitshiver of Zolin to Zaynvil Verkhyevker in Kripen

LAST NIGHT, AFTER evening prayers, I lingered at the home of the Rebbe (long may he live!) and listened to his honeyed words. I was thoroughly delighted, for after praying, the Rebbe (long may he live!) was in pure communion with G-d, and his speech was utterly ecstatic, as it usually is. Believe me: with the good Lord's help I learned more from his sweet words and his concerns than a person could learn from the teachings of another Rebbe. Deep inside me I know that I certainly wouldn't have gotten tired of listening to him for days and days without eating or drinking. But the Rebbe (long may be live!) wanted to smoke his pipe and go to the outhouse. So I brought him his pipe, but then someone else pushed ahead, brought the burning coal, and lit the pipe for him. Seeing as how the Rebbe (may he live many, many years!) didn't want me to accompany him to the outhouse, I headed home thrilled that I'm privileged to be one of the Rebbe's followers and that today the good Lord helped me to hear such holy words from the Rebbe.

When I arrived home, my wife handed me a letter that had been brought by a visitor from your town, and once I saw your handwriting I was all the happier. But when I read your letter, I got all shook up because you wrote that your landowner has a heretical book that was published in Galicia and that attacks our Hasids. According to what you wrote me, the book is really nasty and it makes fun of all true Rebbes. If you hadn't written me, I would never have believed it in a million years. Because to my mind, it's impossible in our time, now that the Messiah is about to come at any moment and the whole world so plainly and openly sees the wonders and miracles our Tsadiks perform almost every half-second—nothing's impossible for them! Why should I bother praising them? Who doesn't know all this?

We're long past the times when Jews fight against us. Now everybody (bless the Lord!)—young and old, kith and kin—knows how much power our Rebbes have. We witnessed—thank goodness!—the horrible public downfall of all our enemies. Who doesn't know that our Hasids are the only ones left in the world and that our Tsadiks can do whatever their hearts desire? They get the good Lord to do anything they like—why, a single word from them can move mountains!

So how can we possibly believe that somebody's dared to write and even publish a book attacking the Tsadiks? Doesn't that foul-mouthed author know that if our Rebbe (long may he live!) wants to, he'll tear him out by the roots? Why, our Rebbe rules the world like a king. Would such an ugly freak dare to write a book attacking a king? The whole business practically gave me a heart attack—I would have easily been melancholy if I hadn't already been so delighted by our Rebbe (long may he live!) and if I hadn't had a shot of liquor after reading your letter. My melancholy was driven away, not even a speck of it remained.

All the same, I tell you, we have to do anything we can against that book. For the time being I'm afraid to tell the Rebbe about the book—it might (G-d forbid!) distress him for a moment. I'm sure he's already heard the story directly from Heaven, but if he hears it down here, he might possibly get upset. On the other hand, I'm afraid that if I tell him, he'll choose to get even with the author personally. Who knows?—he might have the Angel of the Torah burn the man to a crisp, and so on!

Actually, I'd love it if we could see the fiend and settle his hash! Why, we'd rip him to shreds! And if we couldn't, then we'd set the guy on fire—and put an end to him and his book! So let me know what you think: should I continue saying nothing to the Rebbe, and we'll do what we have to, or should I tell him the truth and ask him to deliver the guy into our hands, so we can carry out his sentence?

First of all, you have to do whatever it takes to get hold of the book, so we can find out what disgusting things it contains. Furthermore, we should track down the title and then tell our Hasids to buy up all copies and burn them to hell so that the title will be forgotten in this world. Besides all that, we should find out who that dog of an author is so we can teach him a lesson! If he left out his name because he's scared shitless of our Rebbe (long may he live!), then maybe his unkosher mug is in front of the book because that's the custom among the sinners! If that's the case, then he'll have to suffer even if he's from a foreign country. All the Rebbe (long may he live!) has to do is look at that unkosher mug, and that's it! No one'll know what's become of the bastard! Now don't be lazy, for goodness sake. Get your hands on that book and send it to me. A word to the wise, etc. . . . .

P.S. Last shabbes we had a guest from Galicia, a follower of the Rebbe of Lublin, who sent his best greetings and a couple of little Hasidic tunes. Our Rebbe (long may he live!) added a few stanzas, turning them into whole Hasidic melodies. When you visit us, G-d willing, you'll find them delightful, for they'll show you that our Rebbe (may he live for many, many years!) is really the king of all Tsaddiks.

2. From Zaynvil Verkhyevker to Zelik Letitshiver

I GOT YOUR letter, and it gave me a celestial pleasure to hear about the Rebbe's health and your health. Please keep writing me about his health and yours and about his good deeds and yours.

Regarding the book, you've asked me to write you as to whether I feel that you should inform the Rebbe, the Tsadik. In my opinion, you should continue keeping the matter a secret until you have no choice and you have to tell him. After all, it's possible that Heaven has told the Rebbe nothing as yet. I'm worried that if he suddenly learns about the matter down here, he'll tear the author out by the roots, so that we won't be able to do anything to that bastard! That's why it's better to keep mum for now.

As for getting the book, I've tried in any number of ways, but so far nothing's worked. Once, we deliberately talked to Shloyme about it—his nickname is Hungry Shloyme because he's a big pleasure seeker and not the least bit G-d fearing. But still, he's intimate with the Rebbe, the Tsaddik, and gives him money and he's also a good buddy. I gave Shloyme the Rebbe's best regards and asked him about the book. Now he's got a relative, Freyde Isaacs—she's marvelously capable and also greatly admired by the landowner—and Shloyme said he'd ask her to get the book the next time she visits the landowner. And Shloyme kept his word. What more could you ask for: two days later I visited Freyde, and she gave me the book, which she had filched from the landowner's home the previous night.

I took the book and showed it to my son-in-law, who's from Galicia, where he attended the Austrian schools. And even though, with G-d's help, he's totally forgotten what little he ever learned there, he still knows his German ABCs and he can tell the difference between them and other alphabets. And no sooner had he glanced at the title page than he told me that this book wasn't a German book because he saw a word that began with a *ch*, and they don't have words beginning with *ch*—a German always replaces a *ch* with an *h*. For example, they pronounce *l'khaim* as *l'haim* and *Chanukkah* as *Hanukkah,* and so forth. And he could tell clearly that the whole word he saw beginning with *ch* wasn't German but maybe Latin.

But since I knew very well that the heretical book was in German, I was certain that Freyde had snatched the wrong book. I returned it to her so she could sneak it back before the landowner realized it was missing. Once he realized it, he'd lock up all his other books, and she'd be unable to steal the right book. But if she sneaked it back now, she'd be able to steal the right book some other time.

When I saw that Freyde hadn't been at the landowner's for several days, I spoke to the lessee of the village of Slobidzhik. I know that his landowner, who's related to ours, is always hard up for money. So I told the lessee to promise his landowner he'll dig up some cash for him and also to mention the book that our landowner has and to say he's been hearing great things about it. The lessee is supposed to whet his landowner's appetite for the book, and the moment the landowner borrows it, we can be sure the lessee will get it and bring it to us. I hope everything turns out all right. Goodbye.

3. *From Zelik Letitshiver to Zaynvil Verkhyevker*

WHAT'S BEEN HAPPENING with you? Haven't you gotten the book yet? I wrote you long ago that this is no trivial matter, and you still haven't done anything. Maybe you're being lazy (G-d forbid!), so I have to tell you again: don't shrug this off as insignificant. I hear that book has excited all the lords who've read it, and unfortunately they even want to translate it into Polish. The ones who've read it are laughing their heads off at our Hasids and Tsadiks.

Just today I ran into Councilman Glokhov's agent, and he told me that yesterday several lords had gathered at Glokhov's home for tea. A whole bunch of them had read the book, and that's all they talked about. Some poked fun at the agent and called him a Hasid. One of those bastards suddenly even asked him if he knew why Jews rock back and forth when they pray.

The agent said: "I don't know."

The bastard retorted: "Listen, I'll tell you why. It's because praying is like mating. That's what it says in the Hasidic book *Likutei Yekorim* [*Precious Selections*]."

Another lord asked the agent whether it was true that the Gentile law courts are actually "husks" and the Gentile courts contain "sparks" of holy Jewish justice. A simple Jew can't go to a Gentile court, but the Rebbe can, though purely because he wants to extract the "holy sparks" from the "husks."

Still another lord asked the agent whether he was chatting with them only to pull out the holy sparks and leave the lords as empty menorahs. And they kept asking the agent so many similar questions that he lost track. But all the questions stank to high Heaven—they were so heretical that the agent couldn't stand it. He swore to me that he hadn't gotten a wink of sleep all night—it had practically thrown him from his bed. And when I saw him, he looked horrible (it should only happen to your worst enemy!). So you can see what's going on. Now, for Heaven's sake, don't be lax about pursuing this matter. We're all terrified it might come out, and the Rebbe (may he live many, many days and years!) could get wind of it (G-d forbid!). So I'm urging you not once but a thousand times: don't be lax (for G-d's sake!), be prompt and alert, as befits our Hasids. A word to the wise, etc. . . .

4. *From Zaynvil Verkhyevker to Zelik Letitshiver*

I CAN SEE from your letter that you're very melancholy about the book (G-d help us!). I don't get it. Just remember: I'm not lucky enough to sit with the Rebbe, the Tsadik, to feast my eyes on him all day long and reflect myself in his radiant countenance, which shines like a mirror. And just because I praise him and exalt him publicly, no melancholy can get the better of me. While you see him and hear him singing too, you sometimes get melancholy. I'm sure it's only because you love him so profoundly, you're more lovesick for him than for women, and you're terrified he might get upset by the book (G-d forbid!).

But to my foolish mind, you people have been talking about the book for such a long time that the Rebbe, the Tsadik, has heard the news from above and knows everything about it. However, he probably has his reasons for taking no action at present. And we don't dare ask why he doesn't want to. After all, we don't dare question the good Lord, and likewise, we mustn't question a Tsadik. So I say to myself: you don't have to worry, it's sure to work out. But that's neither here nor there. We still have to do our bit. I'm getting no sleep, though. I'm doing everything I can, but it doesn't help. Maybe the Rebbe, the Tsadik, doesn't want us to get hold of the book. Why doubt him? If he wants us to, we'll get the book in the twinkling of an eye.

The Slobidzhik lessee I wrote you about did what I said. His lord gave him a letter to my lord, asking him to lend him the book through the lessee. My lord then gave the lessee a letter for his lord but not the book. And when the agent asked my lord whether he'd give him a book for his lord, my lord replied: "I've written him about the book in my letter."

Now you wrote me that some landowners at Councilman Glokhov's home had said they'd read the book, and I wonder if those lords still have it, which is why my lord can't loan it out. I'm sure that as soon as they bring it back, my lord will send it to the Slobidzhik lord. However, I was worried he might notice that one of his books is missing, the one stolen by our Freyde — he could hit the ceiling and refuse to lend anyone a book, even the Slobidzhik lord. He'll think it's missing because he lent it out.

So I ran over to Freyde and asked her to go to her landowner's home immediately and sneak back the book without his noticing. Freyde was angry at him because he hadn't summoned her for several days, but I said to her: "Ahasuerus didn't summon Queen Esther for a while, but because the Jews were in trouble, she went to him anyway [even though she was risking her life]!" And so Freyde had to go now too. She headed out immediately, and the instant she came back, I went to her. She told me the lord had taken a book from its shelf and brought it over to a candle to check something in it. Meanwhile she'd put back the stolen book without his noticing. He'd then returned to the shelf, put back his book, and locked the bookcase.

Next they'd chatted about a thousand different things until she'd brought up the right book. The lord told her he hadn't seen it for several days. The Slobidzhik lord had written him, asking to borrow the book, and he had replied that he didn't know what had become of it. But he wouldn't have lent it to him anyway because his relative was scatterbrained, and he refused to let this book out of his home because it wasn't available in our country. A couple of days ago several lords from the region had visited him and they had asked to borrow the book and take it home, but he wouldn't lend it out. So they read a few pages in his home, and the lords who didn't know German asked the others to translate those passages into Polish or Russian. They all praised the book to the skies.

When the lord told Freyde about all that, she asked him: "Is the book so thick that all they managed to read was a couple of pages?"

The lord answered: "Wait, let me look for it. Once I find it, I'll show it to you." He went over to the bookcase, found the book, and showed it to her. Freyde realized it was the very same book she had stolen. The lord opened the book, leafed through it, and then asked: "Freyde, did you know that G-d has a wife and a concubine?"

Freyde laughed.

"Why are you laughing?" the lord cried. "That's what it says in Rabbi Volf of Zhitomir's book." Then he continued: "This is a very valuable book, and since I couldn't find it for a number of days, I have to lock it up in the small bookcase inside the big one."

When Freyde told me all this, I began trembling and I was also furious at my son-in-law, because if it hadn't been for him, I wouldn't have returned the book. But then I thought it over: why was I furious at my son-in-law for not knowing German? How could I really be angry about that? Quite the contrary: he has my everlasting respect. After all, even though an imperial decree had forced him to attend an Austrian school, he still doesn't know the wicked language in which the heretical book was printed. I dashed home and showered my son-in-law with love and kisses for not knowing German. I hope he'll turn out to be a fine fellow (G-d willing!), and we'll manage to deal with the book without his help. Why do I need him to know German? I'd much, much rather get deliverance from somewhere else.

5. *From Zelik Letitshiver to Zaynvil Verkhyevker*

GRANTED, ACCORDING TO your letter, you're not lazy about the book and you're doing what you can to get it, and perhaps the Rebbe (long may he live!) doesn't want us to get it. But the goyish blaspheming of the Tsadiks and all our Hasids is no trivial matter, it gets worse every day.

Today our Aaron Lozer, the innkeeper, told me that some county officials were drinking in his tavern last night and they kept laughing and jeering at our Rebbe (long may he live!) and all Tsadiks and all our Hasids. One of the drunks asked Aaron if wine and not mead could also put a Hasid into a state of rapture. Another said: "Look, Aaron, I'm just sitting here, drinking my wine like the king's son and I'm 'cleaving' to the Father, the King."

Then, when Aaron's daughter handed one of the guzzlers a flask of wine, the bastard asked her if she knew that when a man is studying the Torah he has to strip the Torah naked, for the Torah is like a bride—and those drunks kept talking dirty, which our Aaron couldn't stand. And even I, in retelling it—I felt like collapsing.

I was so upset, my heart was so distressed, that I went to see Yosl. I'm sure you know him, he's one of the Rebbe's followers. He's wonderfully skillful, his handwriting is a miracle of miracles! I told him the whole story, and he practically burst into tears. He then gave me a letter written in Polish and bearing the lieutenant governor's seal: it was addressed to your landowner and it asked if the lieutenant governor could borrow the book for a couple of days. Yosl assured me that anyone who knew the man's handwriting would swear that he had written the letter himself.

I'm enclosing the letter, so (for Heaven's sake!) take it and have it delivered by someone your lord doesn't know. The messenger should tell the lord that he's a special courier. This will get us the book, your lord won't disobey the lieutenant governor. Remember last time, during the final shabbes meal, the Rebbe (long may he live!) said: "Yosi is wonderfully skillful." Now I think the Rebbe (long may he live!) was hinting that we'll get the book only through Yosi. You do know that all our holy tomes, particularly *The Delights of Elimelekh*, tell us that everything a Tsadik says, does, and makes is not ordinary but miraculous. Goodbye.

6. From Zaynvil Verkhyevker to Zelik Letitshiver

I'M SENDING YOU a special courier since the matter is very urgent. As soon as I got your letter, I went over to the market and looked around for a man who my lord wouldn't know and who we could rely on. All at once I spotted the melámed [teacher at the Jewish elementary school] of the village of Verbitsh. He's a follower of our Rebbe, and even though he's been teaching for years, he speaks Polish fluently. He's also a bit of a clown, but he's no fool. I secretly handed him the letter, and he blissfully strode away and brought it to the landowner.

The landowner said that the mail coach from our town to yours would be leaving in two days, and he'd be mailing a response to the letter. The melámed played innocent and asked the landowner whether he shouldn't be sending something to the lieutenant governor. The landowner said: "I've got nothing to send him."

The melámed acted naive and said: "Since I'm not getting what the letter says, please give it back to me."

The landowner told him: "You're a moron! I'm keeping the letter, and I'll mail my answer!"

That's why I'm sending you a special courier. Do whatever you can to get the response off the stagecoach. If the letter reaches the lieutenant governor, he'll start an investigation. He may know Yosl, and the whole business could wind up badly (G-d forbid!).

7. From Moyshe Fishels in Nigrod to Gedalye Balter in Aklu

I MUST TELL you I'm having a fine time (thank goodness!) in my father-in-law's home. My prestige keeps growing daily with him and his entire family. My father-in-law (long may he live!) supports me in every way (with G-d's help) so that I can sit and study the Torah. I've abandoned all business and I stay put in the study house. And I can keep it up if the good Lord helps me for as long as I live. After all, I can't do what others like me do: traipse around idly and chitchat all the livelong day. There's nothing in the world I enjoy as much as studying the holy texts, and all I want to do is keep studying day and night so I can have the privilege of attaining what a man is obligated to attain in this world. And (praise the Lord!) it's been ten years (and may it be a hundred!) that I've been living with my father-in-law and I haven't frittered away a single day.

So it makes my heart bleed whenever I recall that the Jewish court has ruled that I must leave my father-in-law (G-d help me!) because I don't have any children. I can't say whether it's my fault or my wife's. She's already tried a whole bunch of remedies and antidotes that were recommended by old women, midwives, and wonder workers, and she's also paid fees to Tsadiks. But nothing's helped. I know that none of that stuff is worth a plugged kopek, but I had to give in to my wife's endless nagging. Even though she sees that nothing she does can help, she still keeps asking for more remedies—just like a woman.

Meanwhile she's learned there's some kind of Rebbe in your town, and she's driving me up the wall, pestering me to take her to him. I could barely get her to give me some peace till I said I'd write you and find out whether or not there's any substance in the Rebbe. I do hope that you haven't forgotten our old friendship and that you'll guide me to the truth. I beg you, dear friend, tell me the whole truth, for if there's nothing to it, it would be a sin for me to neglect my holy tomes for several days and waste my money traveling. We look forward to your response. Goodbye.

8. *From Zelik Letitshiver to Zaynvil Verkhyevker*

PRAISED BE G-D! We owe it purely to the Rebbe (long may he live!)—thanks to his merits a great miracle has occurred: we got the letter from the post office. We sent the postmaster a present through his agent so he'd give us your landowner's letter to the lieutenant governor. And that's what happened. So what can I tell you? The instant I got hold of the letter, I dashed over to see Yosl.

He threw his arms around me and showered me with kisses. "You simply don't realize," he said, "what a huge favor you've done me with this letter! I'm involved in a big lawsuit, and the lieutenant governor's the only person who can help me! If he'd found out about the letter, he'd have wiped me out (G-d forbid!)!"

Now that you've told us about the letter, Yosl sends you his best regards. He also said that if you need rent receipts for your brother, he'll make them out for free.

Let me also tell you the latest news. A couple of weeks ago, Volf

Dubner the tavern keeper married off his daughter to a Galician widower named Mordkhe Gold. Mordkhe is totally against the Rebbe (long may he live!) and against all Tsadiks. So there's no doubt the man's a big fornicator. He's a worse schlimazl than his father-in-law, who's never had the chutzpah to oppose the Rebbe openly. Mordkhe is an out-and-out heretic, he's practically a goy. He reads the heathen books and talks about Shechem and Joseph and about G-d and about the Rebbe (long may he live!). If that weren't enough, he also keeps inciting his father-in-law to oppose the Rebbe openly. And even though Volf Dubner doesn't have the chutzpah to do anything in public, he secretly attacks the Rebbe (long may he live!) as often as he can and he slanders him behind his back every chance he gets.

Now since Mordkhe sometimes goes shopping in the various shtetls, he may quite possibly visit yours, and sculpture you should know how to deal with him. I'll describe him in detail so you can recognize him on the spot: he's a handsome fellow with lots of curly hair. (Nevertheless when the Rebbe—long may he live—once passed his hand over my face, I saw that he was actually a burned-up cinder and had long hair down the back of his head!) His clothes are splendid, and he always sports a cravat. He talks in a very measured way, he's a big mathematician, and while he occasionally reads a Jewish book, he's never in his life peered into a tome by our Tsadiks.

I also think he's a bit crazy. First of all, he can't endure having a stain on his clothes, he gives alms to goyish beggars, he never drinks liquor, he never smokes a pipe, and he wears a hat [over his skullcap] summer and winter. There's nobody like him in our entire district (thank goodness!)—in fact, I suspect there's nobody like him in our entire country. So you're sure to recognize him by his peculiar features and you'll know what to do with him, because he's no ordinary sinner, he's an anti-Hasidic fiend.

SHLOYME ETINGER (?1803–1856)

Etinger, a follower of the Haskala, was known for his achievements in several genres. His fables, deriving from a number of Jewish and Gentile sources, are not always Jewish in substance, though the author is usually wagging his finger at Jews—sometimes for exhibiting negative human traits, sometimes for specifically Jewish issues. Plugging into a tradition of verse fables, Etinger harks back to the works of the French fabulist Jean de La Fontaine (1621–1695), as mediated through Russia versions, many by the Russian poet Ivan Andreyevitsh Krilóv (1768–1844). Living in tsarist Russia, the first secular Yiddish fabulists preferred to translate Krilóv's fables into Yiddish rather than devise their own. Etinger, however, composed delightful Yiddish verse fables that are fresh and graceful, if moralistic. But no one says you have to heed anything but their entertainment value and their social and political barbs. Etinger had to pay a heavy price for his jabs: none of his works was published during his lifetime—they could circulate only in manuscripts and perhaps orally.

Fables

The Monkey

"Show me a single animal
That I can't mime and mimic well!"
A monkey boasted to her visitor,
A fox who'd come to chat with her.
    The fox retorted right away:
"You wretched jester you, please say:
Who in the world—just tell me, who
Would ever want to mimic you?"
    The moral of this parable?
You can supply it at your own will.

The Three Sons

A householder, a decent man,
Rich in goods and a long life span,
Divided his hard-earned property
Among his sons—in all there were three.

"There's also a ring," he said, "that I own
And I'll give this ring to my son
Who does the greatest good,
The finest deed, as he should."
    After the father's declaration
Each son went off in a different direction.
Three months passed by and then
The sons stood before their father again.
    The eldest spoke first: "You know,
It was some four weeks ago.
My friend gave me the full stash
Of all his jewels and his cash.
He had no document—I repeat:
No IOU and no receipt.
But, on my life, I honestly
Returned everything he'd stored with me."
    "My dear son," said the father, "you
Did what every person should do."
    Now the middle son began:
"I was traveling and then
I saw a child fall into a stream,
And I dashed right over to him—
I flew like a bird instantly
And pulled him out immediately.
Then I took him to the village nearby,
As all the villagers can testify."
    The father went on: "There's no need
To praise you greatly for your deed.
Any man who wouldn't do the same
Ought to feel a lot of shame!
Your action was very fine—very.
But it was not extraordinary."
    The youngest son said: "My enemy fell asleep
While he was tending his sheep.
He lay next to the river in the dale,
He could've easily died—without fail.
At the least stirring he'd plunge down

Into the raging water and drown.
So I woke him up and saved his skin."

The old man held out both hands to him:
"On you, my dear son, the ring I bestow.
Good for the man who does good for his foe!"

The Assembly

A lion drew his final breath,
And the animals were bereft by his death.
There was no one to rule the realm,
So everyone wanted to take the helm.
When the animals realized their quandary,
They discussed it thoroughly
And agreed with one another
That they ought to get together.

At the assembly the animals wondered
Who should reign—and they pondered.

The first candidate was the tiger,
He wanted to be king—if you please.
"No," said the animals, "he's a fighter,
And we want to live in peace."

Then they heard the eldest bear:
He wished to be monarch there.
"This dancer!" the animals did rage.
"All at once in his old age
He decides he wants to be the head!
Let him dance and prance instead!"

Now the stag came hurrying
With sharpened antlers—fit for a king.
Turning on his charm he did say:
"Who's more beautiful anyway?
My desire you should heed:
I want to command indeed."

"What good are all your airs?"
Said the animals assembled there.
"Beauty alone is not enough.

Your mind has to be sharp and tough."
  The fox held his tongue zealously,
But speculated silently:
"No matter who may mount the throne,
I'll outfox him on my own!
Whoever is chosen, whoever reigns —
I'll simply work behind the scenes."
  The donkey, that dimwit, that fool,
Also had a hankering to rule.
"Well," he volunteered, "let's think.
Why shouldn't I become the king?
There's no need to ask any question,
How can anyone raise an objection?
I have an ancient pedigree:
The grandest people have ridden on me.
When Father Abraham was sent,
According to God's commandment,
To sacrifice Isaac, he did ride
My great-great-grandfather to the site.
And Balaam's donkey, who saw the angel appear,
Was my uncle's relative — I swear!
And my father says we're the blood relations
Of many asses in the Jewish nation."
  The horses, who were the donkey's kin,
Agreed one hundred percent with him,
And they all told him that they had
Heard about his great-granddads.
  But the fox's dander was up, and he
Snapped at the donkey angrily:
"Go to hell with your pedigree
And your disgusting genealogy.
Saints and rabbis have ridden on donkeys,
But you brazen fools are no better than monkeys.
  "My idea will appeal to everyone.
Don't forget the old saying: Like father, like son.
Why cogitate and ruminate?
Why contemplate and deliberate?

It's very simple: Our ruler should be
The old ruler's son—don't you see?"
   "Yes! Yes!" the animals yelled that day.
And the donkey didn't even bray.

Just ask the head of any Jewish congregation.
Meetings are alike throughout the Jewish nation.

AIZIK-MÉYER DIK (1814–1893)

Aizik-Méyer Dik was probably the first professional Yiddish writer. One of the most widely read Yiddish authors of the nineteenth century, he wrote this didactic tale both in Hebrew (as "The Panic") and in Yiddish (as "The Town of Hérres").

In 1830, Tsar Nicholas I ordered the minimum age of marriage to be raised from sixteen to eighteen for men and from fourteen to sixteen for women. While the ukaze was aimed chiefly at the peasantry, it was a hard blow for Jews, who frequently married off their very young children.

Although the author was writing mainly for women, whom he addresses throughout, he followed the tradition of starting a paragraph in Hebrew, then repeating the Hebrew phrase in Yiddish. I've tried to mirror this technique by rendering the Hebrew into high-flown English and the Yiddish text into a more colloquial style.

In a typical Jewish literary tradition, the protagonist is the whole shtetl rather than an individual Jew; indeed, the townsfolk are seldom mentioned by name.

Dik's oeuvre, according to David G. Roskies, embodied "the transition from old to new in nineteenth-century Yiddish literature."*

**The Field of Yiddish, Fourth Collection*, Marvin I. Herzog et al., eds. (Philadelphia: Institute for the Study of Human Issues, 1980).

The Panic, or The Town of Hérres

VILNA, 1868

THIS IS THE story of what happened in the town of Hérres during the year 5595 (1835).

A Brief Description of the Town of Hérres

IT IS WRITTEN: It is impossible to accurately depict a nation without first accurately describing the country it lives in, and it is just as impossible to record a story about a Jewish community without first accurately presenting the town it lives in.

Hence—so I feel duty-bound to describe this community's town before telling the story itself.

The town—let its name be Hérres—lies on the northwestern border, near Polesye. Most of the townsfolk are Hasids split into different sects, which all hate one another's guts. Whatever one sect may prize the others despise, and whatever one sect regards as sacred, the others regard as sacrilegious. The only thing they have in common is that they all detest and deride the mitnágdim (anti-Hasids) and the Haskala. The Hasids spend their days puffing away on their pipes and swapping tales about the wonders and miracles performed by their rebbes.

Needles to say, these people are completely down and out, barely earning enough to keep body and soul together. They are divided into two branches. One branch blossoms and bears fruit in the summer, while the other branch thrives in the winter. The latter group sells big cheeses that are flattened every day by hundreds of young men, for then the collectors go about in large cloaks, holding cheeses just for show, walking the streets all day long. At night, the lotteries commence.

In late spring these miserable cheeses are gradually replaced by fruit and cucumbers. For back then the best grain fields in those regions of black earth were transformed into cucumber gardens by a couple of rodents known as gophers. A certain Polish prince, who resided in Russia and had been visiting Poland, had brought back the gophers as a curiosity. Within a short time, these creatures had multiplied so greatly that they spread for miles around Hérres, chewing off the ears of grain just as they started forming seed. The peasants then stopped sowing their grain and remained empty-handed until Russians came from Moscow: the Russians leased the land for gardens and by planting chiefly cucumbers they made huge fortunes.

(When I visited this town, I saw that the Russian farmers drove out the gophers by pouring water into their burrows. In one single day I witnessed the killing of over eighty thousand gophers. The corpses were skinned, for their hides are used in garment linings, and so the farmers managed to get by. Today they once more plant grain, while our anti-Hasidic Jews keep up their cucumber patches in a small area.)

In the winter, at the very first snowfall after Sukkoth (the Feast of Tabernacles), the townsfolk purchase as many as thirty or forty geese, put them in their attics, and feed them oats for several weeks. Next they kill them and skin them and then cook the fat and sell it to the clothing factories. They peddle the goosemeat door to door and the cracklings at county fairs, and they also sell the feathers. But in pursuing this commerce, they lose their hereditary land, while the geese peck away at the attic ceilings, causing the roof shingles to rot. They poke their heads through the holes and all winter long they chatter away from roof to roof, honking at the top of their lungs. It's deafening—especially for a passing stranger who's not used to these rooftop discussions.

The town also has some thirty or forty shops, which raise their prices year after year. These shops are the focal points of local happiness, and the greatest gift you can wish a child is: "May you have your own shop next year!" So you can understand how great the poverty is. You can rightfully say that the people get free lunches at one another's homes, for the doors get no rest—beggars never stop knocking.

No other town has so many attendants and officials at the study house, from no other town have so many Jews moved to the Holy Land. At Purim and at Hanukkah there are more takers than givers, for even the young men of the richer class disguise themselves as Turks and trudge from house to house with small drums and fifes, and they sing liturgic songs that they have learned from Holy Land Jews.

During the four weeks leading to Purim, not even the anti-Hasidic youngsters and sons-in-law pick up a holy book. Instead they are absorbed in the laws of disguise, preparing their costumes and learning the melodies. Needless to say, such cerebral activity cannot proceed without schnapps and snacks. Throughout that period no one has any control over them—no father or mother, no father-in-law or mother-in-law or wife, for that would mean doing something for the collective.

Now it came to pass—one of the star pupils was indulging in this genteel sort of Purim playing when his mother up and died on him. The local clerics excused him from observing the traditional seven days of mourning—not because of the religious laws but because Purim required his exemption.

Upon visiting the town's charity hospital I found a poor, sick woman in one of the back rooms. She lay there unsupervised, in the bitter cold, while the attendant chopped off pieces of wood from the front rooms in order to heat the back rooms. "Your hospital is also sick," I told one of the officials. "It feeds on itself like a diseased person feeding on his own flesh!"

Twice a week all the townsfolk, rich and poor alike, are permitted to go out in public without a belt, without a hat, and without decent shoes. On those days the bath house is heated. You can imagine that a person is going to the bath house, for when you do, you always wear old rags, which no one will steal. But on those days people do all sorts of business in their tatters—on the street, at the market, in the post office. The first time I entered the synagogue, I saw that the worshipers at the eastern wall were wearing odds and ends, their cuffs and collars basted with pieces of drill and patches of twill and yellow-speckled swaddling cloths.

I could barely choke back my laughter. And when I asked someone about the clothing, he replied: "Those are our rich men. They've gotten expensive linings, but they don't have fox skins or rabbit skins for the overlays."

A year before my stopover, the anti-Hasidic parish raffled off a young genius. Hundreds of mothers and hundreds of daughters each scraped together a couple of rubles for a ticket, and the lucky winner got him for a husband.

This poor town is very often visited by another Hasidic rebbe, and it consumes whatever he leaves.

The surrounding countryside is beautiful, but the Jews never get to enjoy it. The walls of houses are very lovely but they are never repaired, for the people have no sense of beauty and purity. Each day is like any other, with no changes, and things liven up only when a Hasidic rebbe passes through. Otherwise the town is as dead as if it were located in darkest Asia.

The Sad Letter in the Synagogue

IN THE YEAR 5594 (1834) it was the Ninth of Av, the holy day commemorating the Destruction of the Temple. In the morning, when the
worshipers were lamenting at the synagogue, one of the foremost
anti-Hasids came in. Now in the Jewish towns, the common people usually pray in the great *shul* [synagogue], while the scholars pray only in the
bes-médresh [study house] and never set foot in the synagogue—it
wouldn't be proper. The householder who entered the synagogue was one
of those who prayed only here.

The newcomer, holding a letter, made a beeline for the town trustee,
who was the leader of the congregation—a respectable man, versed in
both secular and religious law. (This trustee had prospects of earning the
official title of Great Scholar this year; you see, the rabbi, out of weakness, had formed a minyan—ten-man quorum—in his home.) The worshipers were just ending the lamentation known as "Turn Thine ear to
me."

The newcomer, who seemed about to weep, said breathlessly: "Hurry
up, my dear Benyómin! Hurry up and read this letter! It's no simple letter, it concerns the very essence of the Jewish nation."

Those words hit the Jews like a two-ton boulder plunging into the middle of a still lake. The news spread from one worshiper to the next, growing and fanning out through the town with a tenfold impact.

And it came to pass—and when the trustee finished reading the letter,
he burst into hot tears, wringing his hands, tearing his clothes, pulling
out his hair, and twisting his face like the victim of the worst disaster.

"We're doomed! Doomed! We're all doomed!" he exclaimed over and
over. And the worshipers were terrified—too upset to recite the
Lamentations. The trustee, who just minutes ago had looked forward to
seeing the householder, forgot all about the title of Great Scholar. The
congregants, not knowing the contents of the letter, went crazy. Their eyes
were riveted on the two men: the trustee and the esteemed gentleman
who had brought the letter. The Jews were trying to read their faces, hoping to fathom the scope of the disaster, but without much luck. Skipping
the Lamentations the way you skip the second half of the Hagada on the
second night of Passover, they barely managed to pour into the street.
Clusters formed outside every house, people whispered to one
another—and yet nobody knew what to tell them.

The Great Assembly in the Rabbi's Home

AND IT CAME *to pass* — the Jews were standing around in small bunches, trying to figure out what the bad news could be. The ragged and unshod beadles and attendants (of whom, as we have pointed out, there were many) were dashing along the houses, calling to a meeting. They summoned the judges, the scholars, the most solid citizens, and especially the tavernkeepers, who are the wisest Jews because they often confound everyone with their liquor. They also rallied a few of the very simple people in the street, partly because they pitied them for being terribly poor — and the poor made up most of the population.

The whole town was then summoned, and the few stay-at-homes were people in mourning. Once everybody was present, they closed the door, and the trustee addressed them on behalf of the rabbi, who was under the weather:

"You ought to know, brothers, that at any moment now we can expect a ukaze that will cut to our very quick, a ukaze that doesn't concern just a single moral precept, but that touches the sheer survival of the Jewish nation, so that there will be no one left who can call himself a Jew: 'Woe unto us for we have sinned!' The evil decree stipulates that no Jewish girl can marry before the age of sixteen and no Jewish boy before the age of eighteen. This edict is far worse than Pharaoh's edict to kill all the male babies of the Jews, for that ukaze was aimed only at boys, but this one includes girls." He then quoted a Hebrew saying: "'Without kids there shall be no wethers.'" Which he translated: "'If there are no baby goats in town, then pretty soon there won't be any rams either.' If you don't make sure you have kids when you're young, then no one'll take care of you when you're old. And Jews will gradually die out."

He then read them the letter from his relative in the big city — the letter revealing the great secret: the ukaze was about to be issued, so he should marry off his daughter immediately. The congregants were so deeply agitated by both the trustee and the letter that they wept and wailed — there wasn't a dry eye among them. They thought it was the start of the trials and tribulations heralding the coming of the Messiah. The trustee told them it was top secret, they mustn't breathe a word to the townsfolk.

They then sat down around the table and mulled for a couple of hours until the Supreme Jewish Court handed down its ruling: Every Jew who cared about God and about His nation, the people of Israel, should marry off his son, his daughter, or some poor orphans this very day, the Ninth of Av. For the ukaze might easily arrive tomorrow, and then the congregant would "cry out in distress" (as is written in the sacred writings) — that is, he would lament, but it would be too late. And the matter had to remain strictly confidential, a guarded secret, so the townsfolk wouldn't find out (God forbid!), especially the crooks and connivers, and then who could tell what damage it might cause.

The Great Turmoil in Town

AS WE KNOW, the whole town had attended the meeting, so you can imagine that the whole town was not oblivious to the great secret. Indeed, before the crowd even broke up, the hubbub and brouhaha had spread to every last home plus the mill, the bath house, and the poorhouse — and with dozens of lies to boot. That was because a couple of tailors among the beadles had sneaked out for a while during the meeting, and during that while those rumormongers had blabbed everything to a certain wadding maker who happened to be around, and he, in turn, had padded the news a little and carried it to a couple of shops. The town was utterly devastated. Within an hour, everyone had heard the story, together with a lot of added drivel. Within another half hour, scholars pointed out allusions to this decree in ancient tomes, and the Hasids said that their rebbe had known about this drivel long since and had married off his little Shmuel in the nick of time.

However, I'd like to briefly describe what concerns us. No sooner had the flock left the meeting than it split into two parties. One party consisted of matchmakers, the second of in-laws. Ignoring the fact that it was raining, they plodded along the muddy road in their stocking feet, whispering and muttering, depicting how sensible and fortunate this marriage or that marriage would be. By evening, half the town was engaged.

The very first victims were the poor, mostly Hasids, for even the non-Hasidic town rabbi observed a few Hasidic customs. He sometimes took a fee, gave an amulet, showed off his wisdom — no ignoramus he and certainly no fool. He dealt in prayer shawls and knew how to hawk his wares. So however great a fuss the rabbi made among the men, his wife made an even greater fuss among the women, who were far more terror-stricken by the edict than the men were. You see, each woman recalled that she had been divorced by the age of sixteen or at least that her marriage had been on the rocks. And now her daughter wouldn't even be married by that age.

And no sooner did the day turn away—the instant the day ended and the evening star began to twinkle, and before people even ate supper, they had weddings in their homes—silent festivities, no clowns, no klezmers, no rituals: no seating of the bride on the bridal seat, no veiling of the bride prior to the ceremony—the only veil was the veil of secrecy. For that was what the rabbi had ordered, and for two reasons. First of all, it was the Ninth of Av, and secondly, the townsfolk were not to get wind of the weddings. But they didn't dare have a marriage without a license and without a rabbi, a cantor, and a beadle.

Because so many weddings took place that night, they couldn't drum up a *minyan* (quorum of ten men) for reciting the nuptial benedictions. I had the misfortune of living near the synagogue courtyard, where the stampede had begun, and so that night I was forced to attend a dozen or so weddings in order to complete the *minyan*. At each wedding they served only a single schnapps plus a roll with herring. The weddings were like funerals in the throes of an epidemic—God forbid!—when short shrift is given to the burial rites.

How the Panic Grew

AND THERE WAS *light*—by dawn the town was blessed with a huge number of new husbands, and the synagogues, large and small, were blessed with a huge number of new prayer shawls. And the congregations stopped reciting *Takhnun* (the supplicatory part of morning and afternoon weekday prayers) until the eve of the New Year, for each day brought more weddings, as we shall see.

The plague of the Panic lasted much longer than the Ten Plagues of Egypt. In the morning the citizens shuffled about, only half awake, for practically no one had slept or allowed anyone else to sleep: they had all needed minyans. Groups of people had clustered outside every home, shouting, "Mazeltov!" to and fro and replying, "Live a long and happy life!"

After prayers, when the little prayer rooms were filled with a heavy cloud of pipe smoke, the congregations had heated debates about the issue. Some felt that the Great Assembly had hit on a wonderful idea by permitting the weddings of the previous night, and these people viewed it as a fabulous miracle that the nuptials had been celebrated in time, for they heard that the decree had already gone into effect in Byelorussia and that the Jews there were already fasting.

Other people, however, made fun of the whole thing. First of all they didn't believe from the get-go that such a ukaze could be issued; and secondly, even if it *were* issued, it was no big deal. Needless to say, few such opinions were expressed, and they were shouted down anyway and called heretical. It almost degenerated into a free-for-all. Then, around ten o'clock, a certain regional marriage broker arrived—from Minsk or from Pinsk, I can't remember which—and he noisily announced that he had letters from the capital indicating that girls would no longer be allowed to marry until the age of twenty-five or have children until thirty. He was so busy that he prayed in the tavern all on his own. He didn't even want to visit some wealthy men, who, taking pity, had invited him to their homes several times. "I haven't got a free moment," he told the messengers. "You don't see that the world's on fire. For me every minute is now worth its weight in gold. People know about this edict far and wide—praise the Lord."

These words—spoken by the marriage broker, became the talk of the town within seconds, and everyone, young and old, gathered around the tavern where he was staying. They wanted to see him in his good fortune: for just as a cholera epidemic spells good fortune for an undertaker, a Panic spells good fortune for a matchmaker. Furthermore, they all figured he'd be bringing a whole crew of matchmakers, and several rich ladies got their tongues in gear, hoping to have at least a word with him. But he was as unreachable as a great rabbi. There was a rich man named Elyokum, and the marriage broker agreed to stop off at his home, but he refused to set foot inside. The owner had to come out and stand there to discuss a matter—probably concerning his twelve-year-old daughter.

"Do as I tell you!" the broker shouted at the rich man. "Do as I tell you! This is no time to quibble! No time to get finicky! Gone are the happy days when you could be fussy about matches! The world's on fire!" And with that he drove off in his coach. He had sufficiently demonstrated to the citizens of Hérres that the world was out of joint now, a marriage broker couldn't enter the rich man's home, and he had to travel by coach.

That afternoon, the Panic kept spreading hour by hour, so that by nightfall the whole town was affected. The people who had made fun of the news in the morning were now leading their children to the wedding canopy, thereby substantiating the old adage: "Leave in haste, leave in waste."

The night following the Ninth of Av, the well-to-do people over-whelmed by the Panic celebrated nuptials in the synagogue courtyard. They hired a clown and some klezmers, together with a fiddler or a cym-balist or, in a pinch, a drummer—whereby the clown could attend only during the actual wedding service. And so the second night after the holy day brought a lot more marriages than the first night. The town was a shambles.

The Jewish Farmers

THE BITTER TIDINGS — the bad news spread through the surrounding countryside by the third day—with thousands of added horrors. Girls, it was said, had to marry within eighteen days and boys within thirty; wid-ows and divorcées were out of luck, while divorced or widowed men could not marry a fifth time.

The Jewish farmers were totally confused. Tossing away their sickles even though it was harvest time, hundreds of them hitched up their empty wagons and drove to town. They wound up in the marketplace because no other area could hold so many vehicles at once. And before they even managed to climb down and ask if the rumors were correct, they heard the strains of klezmer music and saw whole bevies of brides and grooms being led to the synagogue courtyard from every street and alley. Without bothering to inquire, the farmers realized the scuttlebutt was true and they implored the Jews to help them out with brides and grooms. The townsfolk opened the prayer rooms and schoolrooms and rounded up the orphan beggars, and the farmers then each grabbed a barefoot boy and barefoot girl and drove back home.

The Plutocrats

AND THUS — AND so the Panic mounted day by day. Weddings upon weddings, not to mention engagement parties, took place nonstop. Yet there were some twenty or thirty families in Hérres who remained quite indifferent to the Panic. They were the upper crust, the big merchants, who were neither Hasids nor anti-Hasids. They would pray here or there,

at the nearest synagogue, and they had little to do with the ordinary townsfolk, for they were seldom at home. They had actually been born in large
cities and had moved here after marrying, but were now divorced or widowed. For several weeks they laughed and jeered at the Panic. "No," they
said. "We don't believe the letter that Beryl got from his father-in-law in
the capital. Maybe his father-in-law can't afford the gift he promised his
son, and so he wrote the letter, hoping they'd speed up the wedding without money. And we don't believe the marriage broker either. He's raking
in a fortune and lying his head off!"

But their firm opinion crumbled in less than two weeks, because their
wives didn't rest for an instant, they kept henpecking their husbands,
telling them they shouldn't think they were any smarter than the rest of
the world—especially since they had more daughters than other fathers
did. Furthermore the rabbi had said that by separating themselves from
the community they would have trouble with later marriage proposals.
And who could tell? Maybe the matchmaker was right in saying that a
girl wouldn't be allowed to marry until twenty-five, and then they couldn't
justify themselves before God or the world. Besides, their daughters were
really starting to get scared like Lot's daughters: like them they were afraid
there'd be no husbands left for them since all the boys were being grabbed
up. In short, these rich men were attacked on all fronts, until they finally
caved and were swept away by the Panic.

Still, they wanted to distinguish their weddings from the Panic nuptials, which were like children's games. So they paid the assessor dozens
of rubles to let them celebrate the marriages in public, as is appropriate,
for they thought he might have already received an order to the contrary.
The assessor, who knew from nothing, allowed them to do as they wished.
To make the ceremony more orderly, they hired four poor boys to hold
the canopy poles more than twenty-four hours a day. Meanwhile the two
kinds of klezmers in town formed two parties: one group played under
the canopy while the other group accompanied the bride and groom to
the wedding and then escorted the newlyweds home. And yet there was
a huge throng at each wedding, like the crowd listening to the cantor during the Days of Awe, and all sorts of in-laws kept waiting impatiently for
the in-laws under the canopy to leave. A lot of fistfights broke out, so that
servants had to stand there, maintaining order in the masses of squabbling
and quarreling. You could have readily applied the adage: "A family fight
is a family rite."

The Cantor

NOW IT CAME *to pass*—this was also a golden age for the cantor, who was making a pretty kopek. He just stayed with his choirboys in the anteroom of the synagogue, eating there, sleeping there, writing the marriage contracts, for the pen belongs to the cantor. Every so often he would stick out his head and croon the wedding song: "How grand . . ." His wife peddled wedding rings, prayer shawls, and glasses for the groom to step on, while in the few moments between weddings the cantor would moonlight, slaughtering sheep, goats, chickens, for he was also the town slaughterer.

For a wedding he would charge double what he charged for slaughtering a baby goat. After all, at a wedding two people get massacred. That's why there are four poles holding up the wedding canopy but only two poles for burying a corpse. At a wedding during the Panic, they buried two persons, but at a funeral only one.

During that period no one studied in any study house because everyone had to celebrate some relative's nuptials every single day. Even the childless people got to attend weddings daily because they managed to dig up all sorts of freaks—a cripple, a hunchback—whom they married off. A German passing through town summed it up accurately: "When a Christian has a flock of children, he has one wedding; when a Jew has one child, he has several weddings; if he has no children at all, then he has a hundred weddings!"

The Panic to the Umpteenth Degree

THE GREAT PANIC *did wax larger day upon day*—the Panic spread so much farther each day that pretty soon the whole town looked like one big wedding warehouse, and even transients got married. If a boy or a girl passed through Hérres, then by the time they reached the other end of town they were no longer single, for the town walls had closed in on them, refusing to release the youngsters until they were hitched.

In short, everyone kowtowed to the Panic no matter what his social class: rich and poor, lad and lass. Many children, unbeknownst to their parents, ended up under the canopy. Many serving girls, who'd been sent out to shop for meat, barley, and flour, came back as married women—or didn't even bother coming back. Many little girls who had no boys to

marry ended up with old widowers, whose minds were more in the afterlife than in this life. Many men had to carry their brides to the canopy.
Many had been assaulted off-guard by the Panic and — it should only happen to your worst enemy — they became unexpected husbands.

Just half an hour ago, I spoke with a man who had gone to the market
to sell buckwheat cakes. This dwarf, asthmatic, ruptured, and in his forties, had no intention of getting hitched, especially since he'd been
divorced twice and broken off an engagement with a third woman. Well,
he was trudging along with his buckwheat cakes, the town was peaceful
and quiet. And some thirty minutes later he was standing under a
canopy — by God! — and the cantor was crooning a wedding song. In
short, not even a babe-in-arms was safe from the Panic. During some four
weeks, not a girl or boy was to be seen in the streets, just as you won't find
a white rooster anywhere the day after Yom Kippur (when roosters are
sacrificed).

There weren't enough prayer shawls to go around, so they sliced the
available ones in two. The dead were buried without prayer shawls, for
the rabbi said: "It is written that a bride hath the right of way over a
corpse" — which means: a bridegroom is a lot more valuable than a
cadaver.

Meanwhile the town paid no heed to its livelihoods. The shops were
closed, people went about in their Sabbath best, and everyone who ran
into someone else would wish him "Mazeltov!" without knowing whom
he had married off — for who didn't celebrate a wedding in those difficult
times? Some girls fall asleep during a Passover banquet and thus fail to
eat the wings that signify that they will marry this year — well, even they
got married during the Panic.

Incidentally, the notion that a girl who eats wings will marry this year
derives from a tale narrated in the midrash to Lamentations: A smart
young man traveled from Jerusalem to Athens to collect the inheritance
left him by his father, who had died in that city. The will stipulated that
the inheritance should be paid out only after the boy proved that he was
intelligent. One of the tests took place at the home of the friend whom
the father had entrusted with his fortune. The son was presented with a
whole chicken at the table and was told to divide it into pieces for himself, for the host, for his wife, for his two sons, and for his two daughters.
The son gave the head to his host because he was head of the household.
He gave the innards to the hostess so that she would have a blessed womb.

He gave the feet to the two sons because they were the pillars of the household. And he gave the wings to the daughters, implying that they would soon fly away—that is, marry.

The Two Brothers

AND IT CAME *to pass in the days of the Panic*—during the Panic, when marriages were only temporary, some brides and grooms varied widely in age and pedigree, whereas in more peaceful times nobody ignored even the slightest bit of pedigree. Normally they set up an engagement the way you put up a booth for the Feast of Tabernacles. But during the Panic they would couple off a ten-year-old boy with an eighteen-year-old girl and vice versa: a ten-year-old girl with a young widower.

(This was like the period when Jews in Poland had to get government licenses to open taverns. It was very difficult obtaining such a permit, and the holder could bequeath it only to his wife but not to his children. Many tavernkeepers, who were often as old as eighty and with one foot in the grave, would marry a twelve-year-old girl so she could inherit the license.)

A certain father in Hérres had two sons, one age nine and one seven. The older boy was married off to a girl of eighteen since all the younger girls had already been grabbed up. During the Panic, needless to say, people would miss a match by a day, by an hour, whereas nowadays they have years at their disposal. At any rate, the bond between the nine-year-old boy and the eighteen-year-old girl was as weak as that between silk and rope. Eventually the marriage became so burdensome for the boy that he would hide at the first signs of twilight, creeping into a mousehole so that he wouldn't have to be with that person, who had made his life more bitter than sweet!

Now it came to pass—the father beat his son a few times, so that he tearfully yelled: "Why are you forcing me to be with her? Let Yoshke do it."

That's how far people can go in their insane piety!

The Hat

AND NOW, DEAR lady, my reader, in order to give you a direct and correct notion of the intensity of the Panic in this impoverished town, let me tell you about my hat.

A year ago my wife's parents bought me a fox-fur hat worth four rubles; it came from *Tsomber,* and the top was made of repp. I would wear my hat on snowy days and I also used it to sneak potatoes from the cellar, roast them at the study house, and then carry out the ashes and live embers. Furthermore my hat also served as a pillow when I fell asleep at the study house after supper and I didn't wake up till morning, for I was one of the night guards. Sometimes I'd fill my hat with snow and make small snowballs, which I threw at certain men who were separated from their wives and in constant litigation with them and who were determined to go to the Holy Land. These men, who constituted all the holiness of Hérres, played a major part in the Panic. I couldn't stand them and so I kept pelting them with snowballs and making them shiver, and they would run away from my hat and its stockpile of snow. My hat was virtually condemned to death and, often tattered at the hands of those separated husbands, it eventually wound up on a scarecrow in our garden.

Now during the Panic I would lend my hat out to bridegrooms, and it came back to me and went out again a dozen times a day. The same was true of the other clothing worn by those grooms, most of whom were young boys apprenticed to blacksmiths, chimneysweeps, or the like. They would be whisked off to the canopy so quickly that they had no time to clean up and they got married with sooty faces.

The Sabbaths

EVERY SABBATH A transport of congregants, big and small and in shreds of prayer shawls, would be taken to the synagogue, where, a dozen at a time, they would go up and read from the Torah—just like on Simkhas Torah (the festival celebrating the end of the yearly reading cycle of the Torah). The little congregants would bring along slices of challah and a chicken drumstick and eat while standing on the benches and while the Torah was being read during prayers. Their hair was covered with barley, which their wives had poured out on them during the wedding ceremonies that week. . . . Combs were never used in that town, especially during the Panic, when stuff was falling from all hands.

The new housewives going to the women's section of the synagogue brought along their dolls and jacks, and during the day they poured sand into their veils. On Saturday morning, after prayers, the new couples made the rounds, wishing their friends and neighbors a good Sabbath. So on each Sabbath, the whole town was on the move: fathers-in-law who had been called up in synagogue to read from the Torah were now outdoors, where they bumped into fathers-in-law returning from the entertainment that took place the morning after a wedding. Furthermore, relatives were streaming in from many other towns, as were scores of marriage brokers. In the evening there were meals ushering out the Sabbath, and at night hymns were sung. But in the end, no one slept during the Panic, no one ate, no one did business, no one studied the holy books. All they did was drink and have weddings—there was no time for anything else.

The End

THE PANIC IN Hérres raged on for all of six weeks, and it might have dragged on further if four boys had been left to hold the four poles of the wedding canopy. The whole town was so thoroughly duped that no maid remained with her employer; they had all gotten married and were now housewives without maids. There were no tailors or shoemakers, no crafts or commerce. And then several weeks later the real ukaze arrived: it stipulated that no girl was to marry before the age of sixteen and no boy before eighteen. The decree triggered a rash of divorces, for the townsfolk realized how silly and stupid they had been and they were all ashamed. Along with the countless divorces, there were multitudes of trials in the rabbi's home. Within a few months there were twice as many serving girls as before, and within nine months huge numbers of wet nurses. It was like Egypt, when Pharaoh ordered his soldiers to drown the Jewish male babies.

(According to the Torah, when Moses, as a baby, was set adrift on the Nile, he was found by Pharaoh's daughter. When she looked for a wet nurse, the baby's sister asked her if she should bring a Jewish wet nurse since many Jewish wet nurses could be found along the river, mourning their babies, who had been snatched from them.)

All the couples who had married during the Panic were thoroughly despondent for getting hitched without rhyme or reason, and the most wretched were the incompatible spouses, who simply couldn't live together. The entire assets of a Panic couple consisted of a prayer shawl and a Panic kerchief—a kerchief that the factories had manufactured specifically for the Panic, which had raged throughout the land. Furthermore legions of husbands now deserted their wives, took off for goodness knows where and were never heard from again.

Thousands upon thousands of Jews remembered the Panic, and our young people wept for many years. The ukaze, which had been feared as a misfortune, was then joyfully accepted. Our daughters started marrying much later than at sixteen and our sons much later than at eighteen. And that, dear lady, my reader—that was how far a nation can go astray and make itself miserable if its leaders are ignorant and unworldly and make themselves unhappy with our sacred laws, which were meant to make us happy. As King Solomon said (Ecclesiastes 8:5): "Whoso keepeth the commandment shall feel no evil thing; and a wise man's heart discerneth both time and judgment." This means that if you obey God's commandment, you will be protected against misfortune, but you have to act like a sage in order to determine the correct time and do the correct thing. For example: there is no question that marriage fulfills God's commandment, but it must come about at the appropriate time and after much reflection.

I've told a tale that is not as awful as the real events for I'm sure I've forgotten certain things. I've set down this story in order to show you, dear lady, my reader, how feeble-minded and superstitious people were some thirty years ago. The world would rather be hoodwinked by a defrauded fraud than accept the wisdom of thousands of sages. In Hérres a nincompoop and his letter brought horrible distress to over a thousand families. This idiocy even infected the surrounding towns, for stupidity is as contagious as a plague.

It came to pass—in our time the Marriage Panic stopped, thank goodness. But it has been replaced by a new Panic: the epidemic of Torah scrolls commissioned by craft brotherhoods. Torah scrolls are penned everywhere—in taverns, in tearooms—and they are carried through the streets by whole gangs of men who do the exact opposite of what the Torah commands. Every month brings new gangs, who build new altars: brotherhoods of water carriers, of assistant teachers, of brokers, of road pavers, of bread kneaders. These organizations are based on nothing but sheer arrogance. If a man genuinely wants to worship his God, he can find a place in our empty Great Synagogue or in the prayer rooms. It's a thousand times better to be the smallest among the biggest than the biggest among the smallest.

Come thou forth and harken—come and hear, my dear bread kneader. Where will you find more learning, respect, ethics without studying the holy texts: among your bread kneaders or among the worshipers in the

Great Synagogue or in a prayer room? It's enough for you to be with your fellow bread kneaders all week. On the Sabbath you should come among bigger people and learn from them how to stand, how to speak. As for the money you give your brotherhood, it's better to spend it on your bread kneaders when they are sick or old. Open a bank account, and make sure that everyone shows up to pray. You all want to be beadles, members of the brotherhood board. You want to commission a Torah scroll just for the sake of throwing a banquet to celebrate the start of the project and then another banquet to celebrate its completion.

No, my dear brethren, that's just another Panic—one involving brotherhoods and Torah scrolls. In our time, with the existence of the printing press, an individual doesn't have to commission a Torah scroll. That is the judgment issued in *The Soul of Man* by the great Rabbi Abraham Danzig of blessed memory.

And so, dear lady and reader, our time also has its Panics. I've written about them in various places, but that's only a drop in the bucket. We hope, God willing, to write more about them in the future.

YITSIK-YOYL LINYETSKY *(1839–1915)*

Born into a Hasidic family in Vinitse, Podolye (in tsarist Russia), Yitsik-Yoyl Linyetsky was something of a child prodigy in studying the holy texts. Then, as a teenager, he began rebelling against his father (a rabbi and a Cabalist) and against Hasidic life in general, which he regarded as superstitious, fanatical, and hidebound. To maintain control over him, his father married the fourteen-year-old off to a girl of twelve. But because the boy husband was poisoning her mind with ideas of the Haskala, his father forced his son to divorce her and marry instead a deaf and semiretarded girl. The boy fled several times and was caught, but then managed to escape to Zhitomir, where he divorced his second wife, married a bride of his own choosing, and settled in Kiev in 1863.

After writing poems in both Hebrew and Yiddish, he began composing his virulently anti-Hasidic, semi-autobiographical novel The Hasidic Boy. *In 1867, it was serialized in* Kol Mevaser *(Voice of the Messenger, founded in 1859), the Yiddish supplement to a Hebrew journal,* Hamelits *(The*

Advocate, 1857). *The serial was so popular that readers would line up in droves waiting for each new installment. Skewering all aspects of Hasidic life, especially the blind faith in the rebbe or tsadik (the mystical gurulike leader of a Hasidic sect), Linyetsky eventually softened his stance in the sequel,* The Worm in Horseradish *(1888), and in a revised version of* The Hasidic Boy *(1895).*

His depiction of the heder, *the traditional elementary school for Jewish boys, became part of a legacy that poured fire and brimstone upon this institution — until the twentieth century, when the anger partially turned into a nostalgia for shtetl life, a warm and fuzzy attitude toward Hasidism and the Hasidic masters, and a scholarly approach to Jewish mysticism, especially to the Cabala and its powerful effect on Jewish thought.*

Combining personal horrors with the impact of the Haskala, and inserting didactic passages that recall sermons and homilies, Linyetsky produced one of the foulest and funniest satires on Hasidic life.

Linyetsky also did a number of translations, including a free adaptation of Gotthold Ephraim Lessing's play Nathan the Wise *(Nathan der Weise, 1778–79), which besides being the first blank-verse drama in German was a plea for religious freedom and for the emancipation of the Jews.*

The Hasidic Boy (1867)

Chapters 1–4

Not telling is bitter — your heart bears a stone.
Telling is brutal, a shame of your own.
But shame aside, who cares about honor, if we
Can do some good for the community?

How painful, how agonizing by far,
When you don't even know if you are what you are!

IF MY FATHER had felt even the tiniest particle of the sufferings I've endured, he wouldn't have been so overjoyed in that beginning — God help us! — when my mother took the keys from his hands. But what's done is done! And I'll weep forever because of that horrible minute when I was torn from eternal room and board in Paradise: out of a clear, vast Heaven I had to tumble down into a dark, cramped belly and then put up with a life of endless and dreadful agony—God only knows how come and how long!

Granted, the Torah, which the angel studied with me in my mother's belly, made my dismal situation a bit less harsh. But alas, my angel was a big sleepyhead, especially following the Sabbath repast, when my parents had long since gotten up after gorging themselves on pea-and-pear soup. I now had to hear them discussing me, but I couldn't tell what sort of creatures they were . . . or what might await me from them in life. . . .

Once, on the eve of the Ninth of Av, when Jews mourn the destruction of the Temple, my angel was snoozing away with nary a care in the world because you're not supposed to study the holy texts on that holy day. My parents, who were sitting in front of the house, waiting for the sky to split open, had this conversation about me.

"What do you think, Yosi?" my mother asked my father. "Is it gonna be a boy, huh?"

"What are you blabbering about, you dummy?" my father snapped. "The rebbe clearly said a girl, so how can you ask?"

"C'mon, c'mon, you silly hothead," said my mother in a soft, cheerful voice. "I'm joking—don't take it so seriously. It's just that yesterday the sawbones was grumbling that I'm carrying a boy. He just doesn't know what he's talking about!"

"You crazy thing!" said my father with a mellow expression. "Don't worry! If it's really a boy, the tsadik can change it into a girl, especially since he clearly told us with his holy lips that it would be a girl even before you got pregnant! . . . So what's there to talk about?"

"You're so right, honestly," said my mother, slightly embarrassed. "We've seen the tsadik perform a bunch of similar miracles (long may he live!)."

"You say, 'similar miracles'!" my father replied with an earnest and mocking expression. "Miracles indeed! And what miracles! Oh, wow! . . . Just imagine, you dummy: he turned the duke of Partselivke into a werewolf and with just a wave of his stick he drove away the dark clouds in a pitch-black night so he could bless the new moon. Those feats are a lot more miraculous—so why bring up a trivial wonder, huh?"

"The devil only knows—oh, women!" said my mother, a bit hesitant and embarrassed. "They simply swear by that old geezer of a sawbones.

Whatever he says, they say, is God's own naked truth, and it has to come true just as he said it. Why are you so annoyed? A woman is long on hair and short on brains." After a minute of deep silence she went on with a bold face. "You know what, Yosi dear? When the heavens split open, let's both of us shout out together: 'God Almighty! A boy!' It's sure to come true!"

My father blew up at her chutzpah in going against the tsadik: "You're a numbskull and you're gonna remain a numbskull. I'm not wasting any more breath on you!"

Hearing that conversation, I froze all over. "Oh my God! What am I gonna do if I'm a girl?—God forbid!" I remembered the horrible scenes I'd often witnessed through my window in Paradise. I'd watched the demons dragging the Hasidic sluts into Hell—dirty, grimy, filthy, dejected sluts with shaven heads and empty mouths from which all the teeth had been farted out. And when asked about the desires they'd had on earth, they would gape like a mouse after an earthquake or gawk like a clay golem.

I shuddered all over, I was terrified of only one thing: ending up as a girl in a Hasidic household—God forbid! Still, I was comforted by the hope that I might get lucky and become a genteel lady in an aristocratic Jewish home, like the tiny number of respectable crones who were brought to Paradise. They were so clean, pure, lovely, modest, decent, and smart that I felt thrills and chills from head to toe. But now that I knew what I'd stumbled into, alas, you can imagine my panic. Lucky me! I'd really and truly end up as a girl—God help me!

Granted, there was nothing pleasurable about the Hasidic men in Hell. They too were dirty and filthy, stubborn and poisonous, like the demons of Gehenna—but not like the Hasidic sluts: good-for-nothings, disgusting creatures, scrawny, scraggly, all skin and bones. A man, however—do you know what the word "man" signifies among Hasids? A stinking bedbug, a mute stutterer, a clay golem is lord and master of the smartest, finest, and most beautiful woman! However, I may have been scared out of my gourd, but I was in the tsadik's hands, and it was all as useful as a hole in the head!

I was also astonished that I'd never heard the terms "Rebbe," "Preacher," "Tsadik," etc. in Paradise. But who can tell? Maybe they were busy in Hell, saving the corrupt and foolish souls of the Hasidic sluts. . . . In short, I barely made it through the nine months by the skin of my teeth, I kept shivering minute by minute as I thought to myself: "I'm about to become a girl!"

You mustn't take it amiss, dear reader, that I was so needlessly afraid of some idle poppycock. Please understand that when I was in my mother's belly, I didn't have the brains to realize that once nature does something, it can never, ever be altered. Even if all the Hasidic Rebbes in Poland joined forces with all the yeshiva directors in Lithuania and with all the Thirty-six Lamed-Vovniks [Hidden Saints], they'd still be unable to redo even the tiniest vein under the ear of a moth! Even if you made an ensign out of the Preacher of Zazulnitse's stick and the Tsadik of Nazarenitse's *talles-kotn* [four-cornered, tasseled undergarment worn by Orthodox Jews] and you tied them up with the Rebbe of Rakhmestrivke's Yom Kippur belt, and the chief of the Lamed-Vovniks fanned and fanned with the ensign until the Messiah came, he still couldn't move the teeniest wisp of a dark cloud from its place—much less a human being, the first and last artwork of nature. So how can anyone possibly believe that a tsadik can change a boy into a girl?

While I still didn't have much gray matter at that time, I nevertheless decided that if the good Lord helped me become a boy, I'd prove to the world that all the tsadiks have far less clout with the Almighty than a little sawbones in Strizhevke. But unfortunately, when I first saw the light of day, the angel flicked my upper lip with his finger, and I completely forgot the whole kit and kaboodle. My father then went to the rebbe to consult him about my name, and it was only after the circumcision ceremony, when I heard my name, Itsik, that I first realized I was a boy.

And the rebbe simply turned his lie into a now miracle: "Ah, ah, ah!" Rolling his eyes heavenwards, he moaned to his audience: "Ah, ah, ah! The child has a very lofty soul and to avoid [ruining] my honor, the Shekhina deceived God and made me dream about the word 'female' instead of 'male.'"

So even if I had a lowly soul, at least I wasn't a slut!

But let me return to my birth.

> *And now I'll tell you all the rest*
> *From birth to leaving my mother's breast.*

DURING MY FIRST minute of coming into the world, I saw a large kitchen knife lying at my side with a small and ancient religious book—all this in my mother's bed. Then, during the next few hours, I noticed amulets attached to the curtains and to all the doors and windows of the room. Upon spotting the knife, I nearly died of fright, for I still had some dim reminiscence of what the angel had taught me about how Abraham nearly sacrificed his son Isaac [Itsik in Yiddish]. And so I figured I was in for it too. But since childhood fancies waft away in the blink of an eye, especially in a baby like me, I quickly forgot all about the knife and instead I focused on the small religious book. As I lay there, wondering, "What could it be?", it opened by itself, and I recognized it straight away:

"Damn it!" I cried, dispelling any evil dreams. "Why, this is the exact same Pentateuch that the angel studied with me in my mother's belly and that was worshiped as so holy in Paradise! How dare they put it in such an unclean bed with all kinds of ugly colors!"

All at once, I fell asleep, and when I woke up I observed the childhood amulets surrounding me. I saw a small, painted box holding the names of the Patriarchs and Matriarchs and on top of it an amulet containing the "Song of Degrees" by King David (may he rest in peace). [This song is made up of the first words and names of Psalms 120–34.] The woman was certainly a very welcome sight. I knew the whole bunch of them personally from Paradise, where I'd attended lots of concerts at which King David and a chorus of ministering angels had performed the "Song of Degrees." So I certainly felt very much at home.

But how could I enjoy anything? My little bit of pleasure was sure to turn bad. Just look: right above the box was the fine fellow's name in big letters: *Satan!* Under the box, the dear woman's name: *Witch.* I was cut to the quick! For Heaven's sake: such fiends and witches were being set up to protect such lofty, sacred, celestial people, the first and greatest in the world! And what was the meaning of the lowest line? For the love of me—I couldn't understand a single word! It was silly: in the other world I had been a polyglot, fluent in all the seventy languages. Now even if it had been Tartar or Turkish, would I have caught the slightest hint? I tried different combinations of letters, intricate codes—but to no avail! One more minute of that and my tiny brain would have exploded—if the midwife hadn't dumped me into a trough of hot water.

As if being born wasn't enough, I had to cope with an old witch—a midwife and nanny! Three or four times a day she treated me like a military kidnap victim, an illegal border crosser, tying me up hand and foot, suffocating me in a pillow like a Sukkoth citron wrapped in oakum, puffing on me almost every minute, whispering and yawning. And whenever I yawned, she'd inundate me with spit to ward off the evil eye.

Once I got rid of her and survived the third day after my circumcision, I had to deal with even more troubles, more terrors. Whenever I felt a gnawing in my tummy or got sweaty and feverish or got bitten by a flea or a bedbug, I'd start wailing in pain. My mother or the maid would then shake me in the pillow, twisting all my joints and turning my brain upside down. At best, they'd shove a breast down my throat, almost choking me. Luckily it was a breast! Whenever my mother—that woman of valor!—went to her store, they'd stuff a filthy, sweetish rag into my craw, gagging me for hours on end.

At the age of two months I was plopped into a cradle, but only after it had been used for rocking a cat. Well? It wouldn't have been so bad in the cradle. Believe me: you swing, you sway. It's certainly better than lying on a pillow like a clay golem—but how could I enjoy my stinking life? Rare were the days on which I didn't tumble out of the cradle. On one day one of the four cords snapped; the next day, the nail in the ceiling broke; the day after that, one of the knots got unknotted. And what with all the constant retying, renailing, reknotting, my cradle rose higher and higher, until within a few months I practically hit the roof. There was a good reason why the tsadik had said I had a lofty soul. . . . On the other hand, the loftier my soul, the harder I fell.

Amid my troubles I sometimes felt like playing with Satan on the ceiling, or peering into the candle, or living it up a bit at night. But my mother or the maid, hoping for a bit of peace and quiet, wanted me to sleep straight through. So they'd spook me by telling me about a ghost, a demon, an old witch, a poltergeist, a beggar with a bag, and other such bugaboos, until I was scared of my own shadow. And to this very day, whenever I see things like my own shadow flitting against the moon at night or a distant goat tugging straw from a roof or a moonbeam striking a window in a dark house, I imagine that it must be a fiend, a devil, a phantom, a sorceress—and at those moments, my life isn't worth a plugged kopek!

In short, easier said than done. I was barely one year old and I was already crawling in and out of every nook and cranny, smearing myself with dirt, eating ashes from the stove, getting umpteen injuries a day. And each time I fell, my mother would rip open the seam in back of my diaper, pour in a little water, and wave a kitchen knife to ward off evil. It was as if she'd spread out her arms. My you-know-what stuck out, and then I'd fall again, hurting another part of my body. If (God forbid!) the walls of the room had been hung with mirrors, so that I could have seen my own reflection, I would have died of fright ten times a day.

My head was bloated and scurvy, my face sooty and muddy, my mouth drooling, my nose sniveling. The notch left by the angel's finger above my upper lip was now a putrid, pale red groove for the endless muck oozing from my nose. My hands and feet were wet, filthy, sticky, and my you-know-what looked as if it were sporting a skullcap made of old, sallow, greasy brocade. And really: who was there to take care of me? The maid, who earned six rubles a year plus some primordial calfskin shoes belonging to my father? The poor girl had to clean, nurse, smear, heat the stove, tend the cow, drive the herd, take out the slop buckets, pluck the poultry, wipe her nose, and scratch her head with both hands.

As for my poor mother, I can't really hold anything against her. Aside from keeping her shop and running the household and patching and darning and reading the women's Yiddish prayers and pampering my father with a little celestial pleasure, she would vomit—unable to stand the sight of meat. You do know that a whole crew of Hasids are born in the twinkling of an eye so that every tsadik can have a flock of idlers. And the more the tsadiks strain to produce junior rebbes, the more their followers struggle to breed junior Hasids. So how could my poor father lag behind everyone else? Especially since he was the right-hand man to the Rebbe, who considered him the cream of the crop! . . .

I could have bawled my eyes out, I could have been hurt and even killed when I fell, I could have starved to death and frozen to death, I may have been covered with filth, mud, and mucus—but it was nobody's business. And that was the life I led for three slow, screaming years until my father finally took over my supervision.

> *My father wants me to follow him too*
> *And start becoming a full-blown Jew.*

WHEN I TURNED four, my father began teaching me about duties and good deeds. Now you may think he taught me the same idle customs that the German Jews teach their little children—for instance, God's commandments: they kiss their parents' hands upon getting up and upon going to bed, they thank them for every bit of food and drink, and so forth. You may think that this was what my father taught me, but not on your life—you couldn't be more wrong! In Eastern Europe, decent Jews regard such duties as sinful and they laugh their heads off at them. In fact, my father always taught me the very opposite, to give my mother the finger; while my mother always taught me to yank at my father's coattails. And no sooner did someone enter our home than my parents began harassing and tormenting me:

"C'mon, Itsik, tell him! Well? Get a move on!" They wanted me to say: "Good evening, a tsadik's got his ass on backwards!" And other such sly remarks. Now that's one of the commandments that an adult is obliged to fulfill not according to the Torah, to Jewish Law, but according to basic ethics and manners. For instance, my father taught me not to tie my shirt collar like a hound [?], he taught me to hold my skullcap with both hands all night long to keep it from falling off—God forbid! . . . At Purim I had to turn over on the table eighteen times, for the book of Esther [9:1] describes how the Jews turned the tables on their enemies. At Passover I had to sit with him at the seder till cockcrow. At Yom Kippur I had to abstain from tasting even a crumb of food until twelve o'clock and I had to run around in stocking feet all day long. At Sukkoth, the Feast of Tabernacles, I had to sleep in the tabernacle no matter how cold it got. My father also taught me not to comb my sidelocks except on Fridays, to accompany him to the bath house on the eve of the Sabbath and shave my head down to the scalp, and so on and so forth.

I won't even go into all the commandments I had to obey. However, the bathhouse on Fridays was hell on earth, and I'll never forget it no matter how long I live. The sheer mention of that Gehenna makes me shudder from head to foot. Picture that dark, burning hole. Every Friday my father would drag me to the top level of the steam room and flog me with the birch broom for fifteen minutes before the bath and some ten minutes after. And the steamroom was just child's play compared with the actual comedy of the pure bath—long may it live! It was agonizing and terrifying. And you know that it's easier for a child to endure ten physical pains than one terror!

Imagine a three-year-old who's done nothing but run around all day long in the playful, joyful, beautiful outdoors. All at once my father seizes my hand and takes me down some thirty or forty narrow, crooked, broken, slippery steps—down, down into a dank, dark, deep pit chockful of naked, slimy people shoving back and forth—adults! Do you get it? Adults! Not boys my own age. Every time one of those adults touches me, I feel a sickening disgust, too horrible for words. And it's all the more horrible for being in a gloomy abyss. . . . Every second, you hear something like a dull, distant, hidden splash and a muffled voice like a dreadful echo in a dark, dense, wild forest surrounded by an empty, cloudy, brutal wilderness that you can never go into or get out of in all eternity. . . . And in the midst of those ghastly and fearful ordeals, my father grabs both my hands like a demon, a klutz, and hurls me into the water with all his might and main! I had no idea what was happening to me, I kept wriggling like a poisoned mouse, kicking and flailing, as if looking for my soul in the darkness.

Can you, dear readers, picture my terror? You can? Well, you're lying—as sure as I'm a Jew! No matter what you imagine I went through at that moment, it was a thousand times worse, by God! I can still recall the nauseating stench of the air and the sharp and bitter taste of the bathwater—or rather cesspool. But in fact I emerged so scoured and scrubbed from the steamroom and the bath that even today I still can't clean myself as thoroughly with the finest soaps and the clearest, freshest water. . . .

I can tell you about hundreds of commandments, but you'll merely find them entertaining, whereas for my father they were the very bedrock of Judaism!

And so I spent another agonizing year at home, until they talked about sending me to a heder (Jewish elementary school). On the face of it, the plan was music to my ears, for I was so sick and tired of being at home, by God. I was as neglected as a stray dog, and nobody so much as glanced in my direction more than once a week. My father was engrossed day and night in gathering the donations for the Rebbe, so that aside from making me observe the commandments, my father forgot all about me. My poor mother, for her part, was overwhelmed with the store, the household, and, above all, the infants. One clung to her apron, the second lay in her arms, and the third was in her belly. So the heder sounded like a lot more fun. I figured I'd receive guidance on how to become a decent person—I don't mean like the rich children but more like the offspring of ordinary householders in town.

But then I overheard my father saying to my mother: "You can see, Vitye, that I'm constantly absorbed in earning a living. So why don't you take him to the heder? A Talmud teacher is a different story, but am I supposed to deal with a heder teacher, ha? You can quite understand that it's not my cup of tea!"

"You're so right, by God!" said my mother. "I won't spare any effort. But tell me, Yosi, what heder should I pick? We've got only two heder teachers hereabouts: Nakhmen Crash and Nekhémye Cap. Who's the better one in your opinion?"

"How should I know!" my father retorted. "Nakhmen Crash sounds all right."

"But he butchers the kids, and besides, just the other day, Vekhne told me she's heard from a lot of respectable people that Nekhemye is a much better teacher than Nakhmen."

"Never mind. It's all the same to me," said my father. "But Nekhemye isn't a follower of my Rebbe."

"So what?" said my mother, smiling softly. "He goes to the Rebbe of Zodkivetse, but he's still a Hasid."

"C'mon, you idiot!" my father exclaimed, slightly irritated. "You don't know what you're talking about! Is the Rebbe of Zodkivetse a real tsadik? I personally heard from my rebbe's holy lips that the Rebbe of Zodkivetse is God's clown because his soul was taken from the world of pranksters. A sign of that was that his wedding took place in the darkest night because he was circumcised on Yom Kippur. Do you understand what my heavenly rebbe means—ha?"

"How should I know!" said my mother, as if she'd committed some offense. "I see scads of people going to consult him, and I may be a stupid woman, but that's fine with me!"

"Oh my God!" said my father. "So they go and consult him! So what? People also go to the yeshivas in Lithuania! What does that prove? Just another hoax! This past Sabbath, didn't our rebbe moan and groan about the Lithuanian yeshivas? He explicitly said that they were no better than the government-licensed rabbinical seminaries. Those schools churn out a lot of heretics, and the Lithuanian anti-Hasids eventually become terrible heretics too. And the yeshiva students are what it says in Exodus [12:38], 'A mixed multitude . . . and flocks, and herds, even very much cattle.' And the rebbe provided an interpretation that simply made the heavens reverberate! So what do you know? Why, you're nothing but a kosher cow! . . ."

"Well," said my mother with a pitiful expression. "What do you expect of a woman? You certainly have more knowledge in your little finger than I have in my whole head. So decide what you think best."

From that lovely conversation I already had an inkling of what awaited me in the heder, and I sensed that school might be even worse than home.

And indeed it was!

No painter, no orator, and no writer
Can truly depict a Hasidic heder.

THE FIRST TIME my mother took me to Nakhmen Crash's heder, I nearly passed out. The filth was practically waist-high. Next to the door stood a pail of water and a mildewed and overflowing slop bucket with things floating on the surface—the things that were thrown at Haman's head. The four small double windowpanes were thickly frosted over because of the cold weather, and the frosty growth was wrinkled with zigzagging figures and stars of David. There were pokers and shovels as well as various crooked rings and stripes that were full of flourishes: some were notched deeper and narrower, some were broader and more shallow, some were still fresh and bright, and some were older and icier. Rare were the fresh circles drawn with the help of a kopek and reaching all the way to the glass. And every window was leaking, the water dripping down to the floor.

Three little boys with unbuttoned shirts were rummaging in the mire, crawling about on all fours, always sticking out their you-know-whats. A long, narrow table, equipped with seesawing legs, wrapped in strings, and sporting a stained, charred, scratched-up top, was surrounded by benches—narrow, knotty planks resting on two sliced logs. Sitting on the planks were boys of various sizes; they were entangled in one another, and their backs were all stuck to the wet, freezing wall. In front of every group of ten boys lay a siddur [prayer book], three times thicker and more swollen than at its original publication. . . .

At the end of the table there was an old, large basket filled with cups, and next to it a huge, spotted tomcat was licking away while his tail kept smacking a pupil's head. Through a tiny, narrow doorway in the corner I could see the lower half of the teacher's wife: she was bending over, brandishing a poker, apparently thrusting it into the stove. Whenever the front door opened, she would ram her greasy headgear and sticky, sweaty face out the window like a soldier in a tent (rooty-toot-toot!).

The teacher sat at the head of the table, next to the stove. He had no caftan, and his yellowed *talles-kotn* was doubled over and rubbing against the stove. A torn, smeared, crumpled, ancient skullcap, so shrunken that it looked more like a lid than a yarmulke, was perched on his bald, shaved head like a big, round something-or-other herbal bandage on a gargantuan boil. In one hand the teacher clutched a thick leather whip, while his other hand, creeping into his filthy, unbuttoned shirt, kept scratching the forest of curly chest hair.

Upon entering, we were greeted by a noisy spectacle; the teacher and his belfer (assistant) were cracking their whips. The boys were honking like a gaggle of geese, bawling and howling. All of a sudden, the teacher's wife swept through the house like a whirlwind, carrying a live ember in a dishrag. She dumped the ember into the slop bucket—splash!—and a hissing steam filled the entire room as if water had been poured into a cauldron at a steambath!

My mother left after exchanging a few words with the "professor," and I was on my own in the new institute. No sooner was she gone than the teacher came over to me and said: "Do you see this whip here? That's what you flog a boy with if he doesn't want to learn."

And he cracked it across one boy's head to make sure I understood the meaning of "whip." Next he dragged me over to the table, opened the bloated siddur, and asked me: "Can you read the holy texts?"

"Nnnnooooooo!" I blubbered, trembling with fear.

"Hush!" he half-shouted. "What are you so upset about?" And he pinched my cheek. The pain shot to my heart, and I wailed even louder. So he put me on his lap and aimed his pointer at the first two letters of the Jewish alphabet: "This is *aleph*, this is *beys*."

But seeing the *beys*, I forgot all about the *aleph*, and seeing the *aleph*, I forgot all about the *beys*. The teacher glared at me, things looked bad. So he started telling me that if I wished to study, the angel would drop a kopek into the room. Upon hearing this delightful news, I forgot all about the siddur and gaped at the ceiling. The teacher then reeled off a litany of threats: if I didn't want to study, I'd be flogged with iron rods in the afterlife, fiends would carry me off beyond the Mountains of Darkness, demons would sell me to the Gypsies, I'd have nightmares about ghosts and other horrible bugaboos!

The blood froze in my veins. I hallucinated: the *aleph* was a demon, the *beys* was an iron rod, and the prayers in the siddur were the Mountains of Darkness. Suddenly I launched into a woeful shrieking and I had to be taken home. All night long I was haunted by devils and corpses holding iron rods and bellowing at the top of their lungs: "Say *aleph!* Say *beys.*"

For the whole next month I lay in bed, feverish, more dead than alive. Now I realize that when Hasidic Jews, male or female, read these lines, they'll smile to themselves and claim that I'm simply trying to entertain them and that I don't have them in mind. But actually, just as I was terrified of ghosts, devils, and iron rods, I know that all Hasidic Jews, down to this day, are in mortal dread of fiends, phantoms, and demons, and of being carried off by the devil. They fail to see that they've inherited their fears from the dear, sweet heder.

These adults are merciless toward their small children, whereas they ought to bring them up in a better way so they won't lead panicky lives. But how can parents wean a child away from such terrors if they themselves believe in them as strongly as they believe in God? Is there any shortage of Jewish tales about demons in cellars, ghosts in synagogues, about werewolves, dybbuks, devils? These parents protect their newborns by hanging amulets on doors and windows, amulets containing those mordant names; and they also nail up amulets and talismans in their basements and storerooms. Alas: the more they protect their children, the more terrified the children become. Yet such parents lead their offspring along the same road that their fanatical fathers led them. Indeed, they are *mis*leading them!

After all, no baby has ever been replaced by a changeling. No devil has ever been spotted in a cellar. No ghost has ever been heard praying in a synagogue. And if a gravedigger steals winding sheets from corpses, does he keep a charm, an amulet, a talisman in his pocket? And what about the rebbe's assistant who has to do his business in the latrine at night? There are certainly no amulets or talismans on the outhouse walls. And what does the Rebbe think when he's summoned by the district police chief or the investigator? You don't find any charms in their offices, do you? So is the rebbe scared of finding a demon or a devil there? Not on your life—trust me! The rebbe seems more afraid of—what do you call it?—an even greater surprise.

When a Hasidic Jew reads a Jewish book or a gazette about such idiotic fanaticism and superstition, he says with a smirk: "What? You think the author's wrong? Don't our Jews suffer from all the nonsense and stupidity that he depicts?" Yet this reader fails to realize that he himself is one of "our Jews." And he doesn't change by even a hair's breadth.

As sure as I'm alive, I know that after reading my little book every Hasidic Jew will keep repeating: "The Hasidic boy who says such and such and who writes this or that—might he not be right?" But in the end the reader will forget that all these things lie inside him, perhaps more than in anyone else, and he'll simply deny that he fits the description.

I can assure you I'm not depicting Hasidic life for the sake of telling a story! I simply hope I can save some Hasidic boy by getting him to become a decent person and to reject all those foolish ways that darken his life. By "some boy," I mean all boys. . . . It may be too late for the fathers, but they should not destroy their children's lives!

However, I've digressed too far. Let's get back to my heder. . . .

MENDELE MOYKHER-SFORIM

(?1836–1917)

*A*round 1836 in Kapulye (tsarist Russia), the man who was eventually dubbed the "grandfather" of modern Yiddish literature came into the world as Sholem-Yankev Broido, but later changed his last name to Abramovitsh. After putting out a number of works in Hebrew, he switched to Yiddish, hoping to find a broader audience. His first Yiddish publication was The Little Man, *serialized in 1864–66 in* Kol Mevaser (Voice of the Messenger). *For this Yiddish publication, the author wanted to employ a pseudonym, Senderl Moykher-Sforim—Senderl the Book Peddler. But the editor, Alexander Tsederboym, changed it to Mendele Moykher-Sforim without consulting the writer, who then, accepted it as his lifelong nom de plume and literary persona. Today, he is still affectionately known as Mendele.*

Starting out as a bitter satirist of the internal corruption of Jewish life in tsarist Russia—a stance typical of the Haskala—Mendele eventually mocked the enlightenment for its indifference to the external pressures on Jewish life and for its rejection of what he saw as certain positive Jewish traditions.

Constantly revising and expanding The Little Man (*the first version is included here), Mendele eventually turned it into a full-fledged novel. He wrote a number of plays, short stories, and novels, translating his Yiddish works into Hebrew, and vice versa. He also did a number of translations from other languages, including a free adaptation of Jules Verne's* Five Weeks in a Balloon *(Cinq semaines en ballon, 1862).*

His enormous contributions are best summed up by the Yiddish critic Zalmen Reyzen in his lexicon of Yiddish writers:

> *Not only is Abramovitsh the great and original Jewish writer, who tapped the deepest wellsprings—of popular life, popular culture, and nature—he is also the first great Yiddish author. . . . He raised Yiddish literature from its primitive condition to a high artistic level. . . . He grasped the causes of Jewish poverty much earlier than his Haskala con- temporaries, who blamed all problems of Jewish life on the lack of enlight- enment and lack of education among the Jewish masses. In* The Little Man *. . . he already derided the social injustices that plagued Jewish life . . . but his laughter is bitter. . . .*
>
> *Born into the Lithuanian dialect of Yiddish, he spent a long time in Ukraine and southern Russia. Abramovitsh, who was blessed with a remarkable ear, thus created the first [modern] Yiddish prose style on the basis of our main dialects.* *

The Little Man, or
The Life Story of Yitsik-Avrom,
the Power Broker (1864–66)

I WAS ACTUALLY born in Hypocritia, and I'm called Mendele the Book Peddler. I've been on the road for virtually years on end, going every which way. I'm known far and wide, as I crisscross the Jewish Pale of Settlement, hauling all kinds of books published by the Hasidic press in Zhitomir. I also have prayer shawls, ritual undergarments with the pre- scribed number of tassels, ram's horns, leather prayer thongs, holy

---

* Zalmen Reyzen, *Lexicon of Yiddish Writers* (Vilno: n.p., 1926).

amulets, mezuzas, and wolves' teeth. Now and then I also have brass or copper utensils. And ever since the Yiddish weekly *Kol Mevasser* started publishing in 1862, I've been carrying several issues on and off. But never mind—that's neither here nor there. I'd like to talk about something else.

You see, this year, 5624 (Christian year 1864), I was heading toward Foolsville for Hanukkah. I figured I'd sell wax candles for the holiday and for ushering out the Sabbath. But never mind—that's neither here nor there. Anyway, I arrived on Tuesday, after prayers and, as is my habit, I drove straight to the synagogue. But that's neither here nor there. Upon reaching it, I saw clusters of people, some arguing, some chatting, some laughing, some unheeding. These clusters didn't stay put, three groups would merge into one, and one would break up into three.

How does the saying go, huh: "What am I?—chopped liver?" Which means I'm as good as the next guy, I *am* a Jew, you know! I probably wanted to find out what was going on. Out in the world you have to learn everything, hear everything—it might come in handy. But that's neither here nor there. Anyway, before I even managed to unharness my horse, the clusters approached me. One man said, "How do you do!", another peered into my wagon, a third one groped, a fourth grabbed, as is customary among Jews. The schoolboys—those scamps—actually started pulling hairs from my horse's tail. But that's neither here nor there.

Meanwhile I overheard a conversation:

"Oh, my! Oh, my! Blessed is the True Judge. May the man rest in peace. He was so young too, just in his forties. Oh, my! Oh, my! How can it be? Such a fine person!"

"C'mon! Why are you so upset, Avrom? What's the big deal? How wonderful was his ancestry? Truthfully now, truthfully: how important was the man?"

"With you, Yosl, nothing's important. Maybe Avrom is right. How can it be, how can it be? It's an awful pity! As sure as I'm a Jew—it's an awful pity!"

"Another mourner—Leyb! He agrees with Avrom—what did you say, Leyb?"

"Who, me? What did I say, Yosl? By all means—what did I say?"

"Yes, you, Leyb. You with your pure lips! You just said something: 'Big deal! Itsik-Avrom—the big cheese! He can forgive me or not forgive me: he was as gross as they come. Hard-hearted and a bit of a fool!'"

"What, Yosl? I said that? So long, damn it, I just don't have the time!"

"Okay, so long! Huh, Avrom? Why don't you come along to the study house? We can have a little schnapps. The beadle's got very good schnapps today. Look, Yosl, a little schnapps never hurt anybody. You did the right thing, Yosl, when you tripped up that liar. Honestly, what's the big deal? The man—may he rest in peace—was an ignoramus, a busy-body, a fleecer, and he left enough money."

"That's what I love about you, Avrom. You always like to tell the truth."

I listened to the entire conversation, but that's neither here nor there. It was time for me to unpack my wares. I put the horse back in the shafts, but with its face toward the wagon, I fed it a little chaff and then I got down to work. No sooner had I taken out a Havdala candle, a *talles-kotn*, a pack of tassels, when the beadle of the Jewish court came panting over to me: "*Oy gevalt*, Mr. Mendele, *oy gevalt!* Hello, hello, Mr. Mendele! The rabbi would love you to visit him right now!"

I replied that I would go to him soon. But then I started wondering why he was summoning me on the spot. He blessed Hanukkah candles only when they were in the menora—which I had sold him just a year ago. And why did the beadle come running so breathlessly? Well, be that as it may, I had to go. After briefly reflecting, I took along some candles, a few amulets, a brand-new, hot-off-the-press Yiddish prayer book for women—maybe the rabbi's wife could use it. But that's neither here nor there.

Well, when I entered the rabbi's home, he came toward me, exclaiming: "Oy, Mr. Mendele, oy! How have you been? The good Lord Himself must have sent you—dear, precious Mendele. Mr. Mendele, you're a godsend—it's obviously a miracle, Mr. Mendele!"

But that's neither here nor there. Any other book peddler would certainly have assumed that they'd been eagerly awaiting his wagon and his stock. But I'm no dunce, I wasn't born yesterday. You should know the rule: Cheating makes the world go round! A man intent on buying something he's desperate for pretends he has no use for it, that way he can get it for a song. If, for example, he needs a festival prayer book, he simply haggles over one for the High Holidays or for Lamentations or over a pack of prayer shawls. Meanwhile he picks up the festival prayer book just casually, glances inside, and then puts it back with a vague, wry smile, hinting that "if it's dirt-cheap, maybe I'll buy this too."

Believe me, the whole world is a market. Everybody wants to profit while the other guy loses. Everybody craves a free lunch. But that's neither here nor there. One glance at the rabbi's face and I sensed that he wasn't in a buying mood. Otherwise he wouldn't have let on that he was eager to see me. Granted, the rabbi is a holy man — so help me! But here on earth you have to pull the wool over people's eyes. Even the angels visiting Abraham had to defraud him. You see, while Genesis [18:8] says, "And they did eat," Rashi's commentary says they only pretended to eat. But never you mind, that's neither here nor there.

The rabbi led me into his study, where the judges and all the rich men were sitting, lost in thought. The rich are usually a bit lost in thought, absorbed in worries. Now if you've got money, why in the world do you have to think or worry? After all, you don't need deep thoughts to count your rubles. But that's neither here nor there.

The rabbi then turned to the judges and plutocrats: "Gentlemen, I invited you here with regard to an important matter, but when our Mr. Mendele miraculously showed up in our community, I decided to keep you waiting for a moment until I could get hold of him. I beg you to forgive me. And now, gentlemen, now that we're all here, I'm going to tell you an extraordinary story."

I didn't have the foggiest notion of what it was all about, and I was very surprised. But then I figured: "Don't let me be such an eager beaver. When I get a little older, I'll know everything anyway."

The rabbi (long may he live!) produced a thick envelope from his pocket: "Gentlemen, I received this letter this morning from the new widow of Yitsik-Avrom. Before passing on, he told her to get it to me. You can see my name here, gentlemen. Well, to make a long story short, I'd rather read you the letter. Please have a seat, Mr. Mendele, and please put your candles over there, on the shelf."

I sat down, the rabbi (long may he live!) opened the envelope, shrugged, and began reading.

Yitsik-Avrom's Letter

THIS LETTER, RABBI, contains my complete life story as well as my last will and testament. Please honor my request, Rabbi, and please carry out all my wishes. And I beg you to forgive me for burdening you with such a long document. In the end you'll see how useful my letter is.

. . .   .

I WAS BORN to a poor couple in the small shtetl of Bezlyudi [Nopeople]. I don't remember my father, who died while I was still a baby. My memory only goes back to when I was five. I recall that in my childhood I wasn't considered particularly intelligent. Whenever I'd say or do anything, people would laugh their heads off. I was never fondled, never cuddled, never kissed, never hugged, like other children. If I cried, I was never soothed with candy or toys—all I got was slaps and swats. I never heard the word "pity": I never heard anyone say, "A pity he goes barefoot" or "A pity he's cold" or "A pity his face is swollen" or "A pity he didn't get enough rest" or "A pity he's shivering." All I ever heard was: "Just take a gander at that fine, bloated face, those beet-red legs: he's already starting to play his little tricks"—which meant that I was trembling, that my teeth were chattering.

A pauper's child in this world is one child too many, a thorn in everyone's side. Not even his own parents feel any pity for him unless he's sick. You see, poverty and distress turn the heart to stone. I was in the habit of peering into a person's mouth when he was talking, and I'd also peer into his eyes. One day I stared hard into my mother's eyes. Normally she'd beat me for that, but this time, when I saw that she didn't, I couldn't help asking her: "Please, Mama, who's that little man in your eyes?"

She smiled and answered: "That little man is the soul. He's never in any eyes—never in animal eyes, he's only in Jewish eyes."

When I heard her response, my brain started teeming. From then on, I was preoccupied with the little man. He appeared to me at night: I dreamed that I was playing with him, that I was holding him, that I was a little man myself. In short, the little man simply haunted me. I so badly wanted to be a little man. It was no small matter—after all, a little man is a soul! I wondered how I could catch a little man. One day I thought of a really sharp trick. While my mother was bending over, removing a pot of porridge from the oven, I dashed over and punched her in the head so as to make the little man tumble out of her eyes. You can imagine how much I got pinched and smacked, and I didn't eat the rest of the day, because my mother's forehead had broken the pot.

Another time I suffered an even worse sentence. I was curious to know whether an animal also had a little man. So I went over to a cow in the street, and while I was peering into her eyes, she gored me, mauling me badly and leaving me with a scar on my left cheek. All those thrashings did nothing to beat the little man out of me. Quite the opposite: they beat the thought of him deeper and deeper into my mind.

I attended the Talmud-Torah [the free elementary school for the poorest Jewish children] and I don't think I was an ignoramus about religious matters. For seven or eight years I studied the Pentateuch with interpretations and all of Rashi's explanations. Apparently, you can be a scholar and still be a total fool. The two aren't mutually exclusive. My mother called me a shlimazl, and she was very right. I was certainly the biggest shlimazl in school. So I got the biggest share of beatings.

Ultimately the rebbe whipped and whacked me so thoroughly that I had to stop going to school. You see, he was expounding on the biblical verse, "And Lamech said unto his wives Adah and Zillah, 'Hear my voice'" [Genesis 4:23]. "Lamech," said the rabbi, "was blind, so he was led around by Tubal-cain, the son he had had with Zillah. And when his son beheld Cain, Lamech's grandfather, in the distance, he mistook him for a fox and he told his blind father, Lamech, that he should aim at the fox. But Lamech actually killed Cain. When Lamech found he had killed his own grandfather, he clapped his hands and then beat his son Tubal-cain to death. So Lamech's two wives left him. He begged them for forgiveness: 'Adah and Zillah, Adah and Zillah, Hear my voice.'"

One day the Talmud-Torah was visited by a clean-shaven Jew from St. Petersburg. He and all the beadles were here to test the children. As my bad, bad luck would have it, I was asked to translate that very passage: "And Lamech said unto his wives Adah and Zillah, 'Hear my voice.'" When had I ever spoken with a Jew who was clean-shaven like a Christian priest? I shook like a fish in water, my ears buzzed, my hair stood on end, my eyes kept darkening and brightening as if I were peering at the sun. I felt incapable of reciting the long story about Lamech or the legend about him. But I had to talk and in my confusion I stammered: "Said a fox, Lamech blind, to his wives, Tubal-cain led him around, Adah and Zillah, and he killed him."

The clean-shaven Jew practically exploded! He called over the rebbe and fumed in German: "Is this possible? What are you teaching your pupils? Is this possible!"

The rebbe scratched himself, picked his nose, then jabbered in broken German: "*Mein Herr*, the boy, he frighten, he always good boy—I guarantee!"

The non-Orthodox Jew said to me: "Don't be frightened, my lad, nothing will happen to you. Translate the word *omer* ["said"]. Tell me what it means."

Gawking like a clay golem, I replied: "It means 'fox.'" I had to tell the whole long story. The poor rebbe was in agony, his voice was dark and savage.

After that incident he would constantly harass me, vent his spleen on me, beat me like there was no tomorrow—until I finally dropped out of school.

My mother handed me over to a tailor, hoping I'd learn his trade. But my bad luck wouldn't let up. Life with him was no bed of roses. For an entire year I wasn't granted the honor of holding a needle. My job was to lug wood, sweep up, empty the slop bucket, go to the market for kosher threads, and accompany the tailor when he delivered a garment. I ate garbage.

The tailor's wife was a mean and nasty shrew. She wore the pants in the family and led everyone in the household by the nose. She needed her daily portion of booze and she likewise needed someone to pinch, twist, yank, as well as scold, torment, and chew out. She would run her hands over my face and pat me all over. I thought that an apprentice had to put up with all that, or else he'd never become a tailor—God forbid!—just as you can't become a scholar without beatings. And so, alas, I endured getting smacked around and I never emitted so much as a sob.

One day, just before Passover, my employer said to me: "Yitsik-Avreml, go to the store, get me a kopek's worth of kosher threads, and whip-stitch the front of this dress, then the back. Step on it, you bastard!"

I recall how eagerly I looked forward to the honor of sitting at the table and wielding a needle—it was as if I'd been invited to hold one of the poles of a wedding canopy. So I got going!

After running the errand, I sat down at the table, cheerful and joyful. The tailor crooned a bit of *Kol Nidre* [the prayer recited on the eve of Yom Kippur], a bit of a High Holiday prayer, a march, a tune he'd devised himself, a wedding melody, the comical jingles of a wedding clown. "Get moving, Yitsik-Avreml," he chanted. "Trim the candle! Step on it, you bastard! Step on it, you jerk!" And I stitched and stitched, stitched and stitched the dress or my fingers—whichever I happened to get. But you don't feel a stitch when your heart is blissful.

All at once, a pall was cast on my pleasure. The room began to smell—something was burning. We looked here, we looked there, and at last we found that the back of the dress I was working on was smoldering. You see, when I'd trimmed the candle, a bit of burning wick had fallen off. An uproar, a clamor, and I was inundated with slaps, blows, and punches. I got more than enough.

The tailor tried to convert the back of the dress into the front with sleeves. But for all his straining and struggling he got nowhere! He took out the scrap of leftover material. But, alas, for all his pain there was no gain, he got nowhere. The back had to remain a back.

"Now you listen to me, Yitsik-Avreml!" the tailor shouted. "Get the hell outa here, you li'l bastard! I ain' got no strength to keep hittin' you! When my wife comes back from market, she'll whip you some more! But that ain' nothing compared with what I'll do to you later on!" Studying the back of the dress, he muttered to himself: "I'll cover the hole with a pocket. Why not, damn it!" Then he yelled at me: "Get the hell outa here, you li'l bastard!"

I crawled out from under the table like a kitten. That was Wednesday. On Friday my boss told me to follow him, we were delivering the dress to the innkeeper's wife. No sooner had she looked at it than she blew up! Boom! A pocket in back?

"What the hell is this?" she hollered. "For God's sake! What the hell is this? I refuse to accept a dress like this—it's ungodly!"

"Goodness!" the tailor answered with an angelic smile. "For Heaven's sake, please don't holler, Brayndl. I've made your dress in the very latest fashion. Why, gracious me! All the aristocratic ladies are wearing gowns with pockets in back. Goodness! Only a lunatic would put a pocket in the front of a dress! So wear it in good health! And give my assistant a tip! He wore his eyes out sewing the pocket!"

My boss was the best tailor in the shtetl. People said that he went by the fashion journals. The innkeeper was the richest man in Nopeople. When the fashion-conscious women saw his wife going around with a pocket in back, all of them got pockets in back. But it didn't help me. The tailor beat me within an inch of my life, and I had to run away.

I was then farmed out to other masters, a different one each week. I had no luck anywhere. I was a shlimazl. Each master promptly honored me with a slop bucket, saying: "Carry it, carry it, Yitsik-Avrom! When you get married, I'll bring you wine in a sieve! Carry it, boy, carry it! When I was your age, I carried millions of slop buckets."

Another boss, a shoemaker, kept sending me to outhouses to yank out the hairs from the backs of hogs.

Once a cantor passed through our shtetl, where he celebrated the

Sabbath with choristers. He had a choirboy around my age, and I was so envious when I saw him tweet-tweet-tweeting at the pulpit. I would have given my eyeteeth just to be a choirboy like him. During prayers, when all of us boys were in the synagogue's anteroom, I eyed him respectfully. I felt there was nothing better in the world than being a choirboy, except for a little man. When the choirboy opened his lips, I peered into his mouth and I would have been deliriously happy to jump inside.

Upon coming home, I tried to imitate the choirboy. During the Sabbath hymns I unleashed my voice and tweet-tweet-tweeted to my mother's sheer delight. But I wasn't interested in the hymns, I was simply imitating the choirboy. And when my mother saw that I refused to stop and I wouldn't give her any rest after the heavy pudding, she gave me a sound thrashing and kicked me out.

Where could a boy go on the Sabbath? Why not the synagogue? There I ran into a whole gang of kids. I had assumed I was the only one to imitate the choirboy. But no! They had all done the same thing. Each boy had been thoroughly engrossed. One had squealed, a second had bellowed, a third had roared like a bass, a fourth had bawled like the cantor, yet another had meowed, and still another had chirped and twittered. The innkeeper's son was also in the crew and he'd had a difficult enough time imitating the choirboy. It turned out that all these kids had been kicked out of their homes. The bunch of us went up to the women's balcony in the synagogue, where we shrieked and shouted so much that the beadle doused us with water and drove us out of the building.

Actually I had a nice, reedy voice, so I asked my mother to apprentice me to the cantor, and I kept nagging and badgering her until we went to see him. The poor, bereft widow longed to be rid of a piece of work like me. After having me screech something, the cantor agreed to take me into his choir. I couldn't have been happier—my ecstasy was indescribable.

For over six months I toured the world with the cantor. But my bad luck endured, I had an awful time with him too, more awful than the other boys. I got into serious trouble. While the cantor was praying, we boys had to stare at the worshipers and see if they liked him. At home, he would call out a boy's name and ask him to comment on the cantor's praying. Usually he picked me, almost out of spite, but perhaps he did so because the other choir boys would run off after the service and disappear. When he addressed me, "Avromke!", I would reply, "Cantor, the audience laughed. Honestly, they laughed their heads off!" He would then grab my ear, twisting and twisting, yanking and yanking. I tell you, compared with that torture the beatings I'd received from the tailor's wife were good clean fun!

One day the cantor gave me such a horrible thrashing that I was bedridden and speechless for a whole month. You see, in February we came to a shtetl where he was to perform on the last Sabbath before the Jewish month of Adir: the weekly biblical portion was *Shekalim* [chapter 30 of Exodus]. The cantor prepared thoroughly, for he was eager to be hired on a permanent basis. Saturday evening, a whole lot of people visited him in his room, and he sent for wine and rum to usher out "Queen Sabbath." He was intent on winning over the worshipers. At one point, wanting to send me on an errand, he called out, "Avromke!"

Ha ha ha! I opened my mouth and blurted out: "Cantor, they laughed at you!"

The poor cantor made a horrible face and turned as red as a turkey. The guests were dumbstruck! Thinking that the cantor didn't believe me, I swore, "As sure as I'm a Jew, Cantor! They laughed their heads off—all these people here. Not to mention the man sitting at your side, drinking and whispering to you. Honestly, during the Eighteen Benedictions he practically had kittens!"

The cantor emitted some forced laughter and told the others that I was a simpleton, a blockhead, but that he had to hold on to me because of my marvelous voice. You can imagine what happened to me. I was sick for the next four weeks.

I continued traveling with the cantor all spring and nearly all summer. On the Sabbath following the Ninth of Av, we reached Hypocritia, where the cantor was again hoping for a steady position. He worked with might and main, and they asked him to perform during the Days of Awe, that would settle the matter. Meanwhile I got to know the kids in Hypocritia a little and I gained their respect: when they stole the beadle's ram's horn, I got to blow the first blast. I felt somewhat rooted here, but what good is it if you have no luck?

Now let me tell you how my apprenticeship came to a screeching end. You can imagine how my cantor was slaving away at Rosh Hashanah [New Year's] till he was blue in the face—he was practically climbing the walls. The bass got hoarse because he had to croon along with almost every piece, the poor tenor's falsetto grew raspy because he had to outshriek the bass, but all that came out was a squeal. In short, they did nothing but yell. I was supposed to shriek nearly every minute. . . .

One of the worshipers was a rich and somewhat modern young man, thickset and good-natured, and he liked joking about with children. This man hated the cantor. When the cantor reached some kind of acme in the Eighteen Benedictions and spewed out his spiraling expertise, the clownish young man stole over to me and asked: "Can you make a sour cherry?" He instantly pursed his lips, and his "cherry" was so big that I burst out laughing. At that very moment, however, the cantor swiveled up to a level at which I was supposed to chime in. When the audience saw that the cantor had stopped, they began pounding on their stands. The cantor angrily turned and glared at me; his face was as red as a carrot stew. The bass grumbled that I ought to go on. But no sooner had I started squealing than the rich young man made another cherry. I shrieked with laughter. The cantor broke into a wild gallop, got confused, tore out of his shafts, and skipped a passage in the Eighteen Benedictions while making other mistakes as well. The congregation began to stamp and knock. The women panicked and shouted: "Fire!" Now the men panicked, and everyone stampeded out of the synagogue. In short, the service was shattered.

The day after Rosh Hashanah the cantor sent me packing and fled in disgrace, leaving me, a big shlimazl, stranded in Hypocritia.

At Rosh Hashanah I had eaten in the home of a Jew who was neither rich nor poor, neither Hasidic nor modern, neither gloomy nor cheerful — just your regular Jew. Since I was now alone in the world, like a stray lamb, I thought about it, then went to him and described my misfortune. He listened, saying nothing and stroking his mustache. With a pensive gesture he invited me to stay and had me fed.

Around eleven p.m., when the whole town was asleep and the night was as dark as the inside of a black cat, he took me to some back alley at the other end of Hypocritia. The alley was as still as a graveyard. All you could hear was the rustling of trees, the branches crackling in the wind, and an autumn drizzle trickling on dry fallen leaves. Whenever the wind died down, I could make out the grinding of a distant mill, and when the wind started up again, it brought a mingling of sounds: the crowing of a rooster, the baying and barking of dogs. There were plainly no Jews living here; otherwise there would have been no trees and no leaves scattered on the ground.

The man kept walking and walking, never saying a word. Eventually we entered a small, low-built cottage. A candle was flickering in a tiny vestibule. The man took off his coat and, after telling me to wait, he stepped into the other room. Standing at the closed door, I overheard a conversation in German:

"Good evening, Herr Goodman."

"Welcome, Herr Jacobsohn! How nice to see you. It's been three weeks since you were last here. How come?"

"My dear Herr Goodman, how could I? You know these are the High Holidays, so the local Jews are now more fanatical than ever. You're aware of my situation, you know how dependent I am on them. If ever they saw me visiting you . . ."

"You're perfectly right, Herr Jacobsohn, perfectly right. Yes, you're dependent on them, you're the head of a family."

"Have you completed your book, Herr Goodman?"

"Oh, yes! I'm happy with it. Too bad there are so few people in town who can read Hebrew."

"It's much more upsetting that you're not compensated for your efforts and that you often have to live in such penury—and you even have to suffer aspersions that you don't deserve."

"Believe me, Herr Jacobsohn, the only payment a writer really needs is to be understood. Contempt and poverty merely inspire me to work harder. Suffering for the truth is no suffering. It's much worse cajoling and flattering people, denying who you are, selling your conscience, your intellect, your heart. Do you think it's easy being a hypocrite? It's as difficult as being a thief. The hypocrite, the flatterer must always be on the watch just like a thief. Do you believe that all my persecutors, the Hasids, are happy and religious? Not at all! Some of them persecute me out of envy, jealousy."

"Really, Herr Goodman. With such qualities and such fine thoughts and opinions, you are truly enviable. But do you know why I've come? You've told me several times that you need an errand boy. I've found one for you and I've brought him here. He seems honest, though a bit simple."

"Thank you so much, Herr Jacobsohn. Where is he?"

I grasped little of their conversation—that is, I didn't catch the gist even though I understood most of the words. Some Yiddish was mixed in, and I deciphered the German words because when I'd traveled with the cantor, I'd heard all sorts of people talking. The cantor himself had enjoyed tossing in a German word or two whenever appropriate. He'd often say that he could read music and sing with a German accent.

Suddenly the door opened, and I was summoned into the next room. The man who'd brought me was bareheaded. The "German" shook my hand and said very amiably: "So, my dear young man, you'd like to work for me? It's not a hard job, you'd occasionally have to run errands."

My eyes bulged so stupidly that the "German" smiled. But I liked him a lot. His face was so kind, and he spoke to me so warmly—not like the tailor and the cantor, not even like my mother—that I was instantly drawn to him. At this point, I reached for my lambskin cap, which I wore all year round, in winter and also in summer, when I went barefoot. I raised my cap slightly, then shifted it to one side of my head, then the other, then bent it a little toward my face, then pushed it back, then to and fro, then a wee bit higher. With my other hand I scratched my earlocks and the back of my neck. I didn't have the foggiest idea of what to do with my head and my cap. Finally I screwed up my courage and yanked the cap off. Something like a cool breeze came wafting over my naked head as if all my hair had been shorn. I had to keep touching my head.

"You're a good boy," the host continued in German. "What is your name?"

I was perplexed, just as I had been at school when the clean-shaven Jew had visited. I gaped and gawked, at a loss for words.

"What is your name?" the German repeated.

"I don't know!"

"What do you mean, you don't know?"

"My mother," I replied, "called me Yitsik-Avromtshe, the teacher called me Itshe-Avremele, the tailor called me You-L'il-Bastard-Yitsik-Avreml, and another boss, when he forced me to carry the slop bucket, he'd tease me and call me Itshinoo-Avrominoo. And the cantor called me Avromke. So how am I supposed to know what my name is?"

"Your name is Yitsik-Avrom." The German smiled. "A very nice name . . . handed down to us from the Patriarchs, Abraham and Isaac. That's what I'll call you: Isaac-Abraham, or simply Abraham—the German pronunciation. Well, would you like to stay here, Abraham?"

"You shouldn't beat me or thrash me! Every bone in my body's been smashed!"

The host's eyes filled with tears. Gripping my shoulder, he said to Herr Jacobsohn: "The poor boy has suffered a lot. So young and he doesn't have a whole bone in his body! He's really crude, even simple, but he's good and honest." Herr Jacobsohn kept silently stroking his mustache.

"No!" the German said to me. "I give you my word, I won't beat you. You're a human being just like me and you're also poor. Well, would you like to stay here?"

"Yes, but you shouldn't make me squeal and trill. It hurts my throat."

To make a long story short, I moved into Herr Goodman's home. He had a wife and two little children and he was very poor, but his cottage was spotless, and everything was in its place. The rooms sparkled in every last nook and cranny. His daughter had only one dress, but it was always clean and lovely as if it had only just been sewn. The mother inspected every chink and crevice of their home and she was always cheerful. Her husband sat in his study, writing day and night. He was inundated with books—on the table and under the table. I never had to polish his boots for he seldom went out. On the other hand, his robe and his slippers were tattered.

My work consisted mainly of errands. My boss would sometimes have me deliver a book. It sounds easy enough—but it wasn't! It was harder, by God, than working for the tailor or the cantor. I would bring someone a bill, and the man would scowl and snap at me to come back tomorrow. Tomorrow he'd again say, "Tomorrow." The next day he wasn't in, and when I came back another day, he'd shout, "What does the kid want from me? I can't get rid of him!"

Another man would order his domestic not to let me in. A third man would read the bill, hesitate, and go away without a word. A fourth would say, "Tell your boss I wasn't at home! Understand?" In short, I was kicked around, and if someone saw me coming, he would lock his door or sic a dog or a servant on me. If anyone felt sorry for me and took a book, he would soon hurl it under a bed or a chair and fork over a torn ruble without a serial number.

And that was how I spent a year with the "German."

Herr Jacobsohn would often show up late at night, and if I wasn't too tired, I'd eavesdrop on them behind the door. Once Herr Jacobsohn talked about a certain Dr. Stoneheart, expressing surprise at what he had done. Herr Goodman replied: "All other physicians are very honest and virtuous" (I didn't know what those two words meant). "Why are you so surprised at Dr. Stoneheart! He's a little man, that's why he's such a rich and popular soul."

I was beside myself! How come Goodman himself had said that a little man was the soul and was rich? In my imagination I again strove to be a little man. Seriously! A little man was rich after all.

On another night I heard Herr Jacobsohn talking about Issar Choker and how wealthy and happy he was—a bigwig in town. Goodman replied: "Why are you so surprised? Issar Choker is a little man, and he and the rich man are soul mates."

Welcome! Again the little man! And again my old thoughts! I kept tossing and turning all night and musing: "Issar Choker is a little man, a soul, and he's rich and happy. So it's obvious that if you're a little man, then you're rich and happy, and it's obvious that a person can become a little man if he wants to. And if he becomes a little man, he'll be rich and happy. So I've been doing the right thing wanting to become a little man. Yes, it's right and it's good! But how do I become a little man? How do I pull it off? I can do all the contortions I like, I can stand on my head and whistle, but I still won't become a little man. It would be quite a feat. Otherwise anyone could be a little man, a soul, a rich and happy person."

Those were my thoughts in bed. And when I dozed off, I dreamed that I bumped into a little man in the street: he was all gussied up like a lord—in gold and silver, a living doll! I was so envious that I pulled in my body, tucking my feet under me and holding my breath until I stopped feeling, thinking, seeing, hearing. And all at once I became a little man! As teensy as a flea! I had a grand time!

When I became a little man, everything turned out well. I soon became a soul. I rode in a carriage and led the whole town by the nose. Everyone paid homage to me and people who saw me from a distance pointed me out: "There goes the soul! What? You have a dowry to put in safekeeping? Give it to the soul! You need some arbitration? Go to the soul, by golly!"

Suddenly I began stretching and straightening. Light was pouring into my eyes, and—Good morning, bastard, Yitsik-Avreml! . . . I lay sprawling on my bed, as snug as a bug in a rug. Then I patted myself: yes, it was really me!

"Well," I mused, "never mind. I'll figure out how to become a little man. I have to become a little man."

I reasoned: "When I dreamed about becoming a little man, a rich and happy person, I first stopped feeling and thinking, seeing and hearing. So it's logical that you have to wipe out those things—right? You can't become a little man until you stop feeling and thinking. But how can you do it? How can you stop feeling and thinking? That's the whole secret!"

It struck me that I ought to ask Herr Goodman, but then I changed my mind. Why, if he'd known the secret, he'd have become a little man himself! He'd have been rich and happy and he could've spared himself the embarrassment of sending books and bills.

After viewing the matter from all angles, I decided to leave Herr Goodman and work for Dr. Stoneheart. That way, I'd discover the secret of how to become a little man. I went to a broker and promised him a large fee if he found me a job with the doctor. And the very next day I dumped my good employer and followed the broker to my new place.

The doctor wasn't at home. Madam Stoneheart gave me some chores to do, and I spent the day with my nose to the grindstone. In my heart I secretly longed to see the little doctor. That evening the front door suddenly opened, and in trekked a tall, cloddish man with a huge gut (like my cantor), a behemoth the size of Gog in the Bible. I gaped and gawked at him.

The clod hollered in Russian: "What are you looking at, you numbskull!"

I shuddered and trembled: "Oy, oy, oy—my name is Yitsik-Avreml. . . . My name is Avram. . . . I'm an orphan. . . . I work here. . . ."

"Well, it's obvious you're a big idiot," the clod went on in Russian. "From now on, watch out! The instant I come home, you're to help me out of my fur coat and my galoshes—get it!"

I was so terrified that I fell prostrate on the floor, threw my arms around the clod's legs, and took off his galoshes. Next the clod went into the parlor. I brought the samovar and then waited on him and Madam Stoneheart all evening.

In bed that night, I wondered who the clod was. He was sitting alone with Madam Stoneheart all night—where was the doctor?

I waited on the clod two days in a row. The instant he came in or was about to go out, I kowtowed and took off or put on his galoshes, while he held his arms akimbo and gazed at the ceiling, unconcerned that his big hooves were crushing my fingers. And I still didn't know who that clod, that Esau was!

When the clod was preparing to retire to the bedroom for the night, I went down to the kitchen and with a pitiful face I asked the cook: "Please

tell me, who's that guy who comes every evening and sleeps in the bedroom?"

The cook gaped at me, flabbergasted: "What's that? What? What are
you saying! Somebody's sleeping in the bedroom? What are you talking
about?"

"Honestly!" I cried. "I swear it! As sure as I'm a Jew! As sure as I'm
gonna hear the Messiah's trumpet. May I be hit by lightning if I'm lying!
May God strike me dead! I heard him go into the bedroom!"

"Well, and what about the boss?" the cook asked with a cheery face.
And her eyes glowed like an oven when you're baking challah.

"The boss?" I replied. "I guess he doesn't spend his nights at home. He
must've gone somewhere."

"Hey," said the cook. "I'd like to see it for myself. I'll find some excuse."

Several minutes later the furious cook came storming back, and her
mouth spewed out a torrent of curses: "What? So young and already
spreading vicious rumors? Making up a lot of trash? What's that? You
numbskull, you little creep! Hanging's too good for you! Of all the chutzpah! You snotty brat, you worthless jerk, you bum! You brazen moron! I
hope you die and never get resurrected! Oh, God, oh, God! I hope you
go to hell! I hope you burn for all eternity! For God's sake! What the hell
are you talking about? The boss himself is sitting with Madam in the bedroom and chatting with her!"

"What are you saying?" I began. "My God! What are you saying? That
tall clod—?"

"You can go straight to hell, you little schmuck!" the cook yelled, grabbing the poker. "What's that, you dirty creep? Calling the boss a clod?
Get the hell outa here or I'll smash your head in!"

I bolted and dashed upstairs. Hush, shush! Upon going to bed in the
anteroom, I started thinking: "What do I hear and what do I see? The
doctor's big, fat, and tall! Why did Goodman say the doctor's a little man?
Could he have lied? Impossible. He never tricked me. He always told the
truth. There's more here than meets the eye!"

A few days later, when I was eavesdropping at the door to the doctor's
study, I overheard a conversation he was having with the druggist.

"Doctor, I sent you a whole lot of patients this week, but you haven't
sent me even one."

"C'mon, Getsl! What about yesterday?"

"What happened yesterday, doc?"

"You've got a short memory! What's wrong? You've forgotten that yesterday I was a little man for your sake alone. I put thirty leeches on the patient just so you'd make a little money. Between you, me, and the lamppost, he didn't need leeches any more than you or I. All he had was an upset stomach. Honestly, Getsl, I was a little man yesterday for your sake alone!"

"Doc, you were, as you put it, a little man yesterday, whereas I was a little man yesterday and today for your sake. Between you, me, and the lamppost, did today's patient need a doctor? All he had was the sniffles, but I told him to consult you anyway. Well, if you wrote him a prescription, he'll be sick for at least a couple of weeks, and you'll look in on him twice a day."

"So what do you want, Getsl?"

"Doc, I've still got a whole bunch of leeches!"

"Don't worry, Getsl. Honestly, tomorrow I'll apply leeches to all my patients. Just don't worry."

"Aha! So that's the story!" I mused in bed. "As I can hear and see, being a little man doesn't just mean being a little man! You can be a big man and still be a little man."

I realized that being a little man involved sucking blood and fleecing people. Now I had an inkling of what it meant to be out in the world. Well, granted, I knew a little of the secret, but what good was it? I was no doctor, no druggist, I couldn't apply leeches. This wasn't my path. I had to find some other method of becoming a little man—there had to be a way. . . .

"Ha! This sure isn't complicated, it's very obvious! I really should work for Issar Choker! As sure as I'm a Jew! Issar Choker! Why, he's a little man too, a rich and happy person, isn't he?!"

I lay in bed, my brain teeming. The next day I promised the broker I'd pay him an even bigger fee within a couple of days, if he could palm me off on Issar Choker.

Issar Choker was one of the most powerful men in Hypocritia. All the townsfolk were terrified of him and they trembled the instant he opened his mouth. "Some man—that Issar. He's no fool!" Issar did no business personally, he never lifted a finger. Yet his home was a beehive: one man coming in, another going out—everybody and their uncle passing through. Now do you think that he was a great scholar, that he had a wonderful lineage? Not on your life! Issar didn't have even a smidgen of either!

He could barely pray, and his ancestors were all tailors—the worst thing you could be among Jews!

But I didn't know all that until much later. The truth is: I found out that he was a little man and that he did a whole lot better as a little man than others with their learning or their earning. The richest man in Hypocritia positively adored Issar: Issar this, Issar that! Issar, help me, Issar, I need your advice. Issar was his very soul, his right hand, his mainstay.

I never got to meet that moneybags. He may have been a great man, a gifted man, a sage and a scholar. But Issar was truly a soul, truly a little man.

I learned so much from Issar. He and he alone was my real rebbe. He opened my eyes and showed me how to become a little man. I was a moron, a full-fledged simpleton. But as it turned out, I wasn't a fool by nature. Starting in my childhood, I'd been abused and clobbered, I was an orphan and an outcast. I'd been raised on kicks, whippings, and punches. Well, how does the old saying go? "If you beat your breast, you'll hurt your chest." A lot of beating will leave you bleeding. I'm not joking when I tell you that any arm I saw looked like a stick or a whip. I was dazed, stunned, confused.

I was born in a small shtetl, and a provincial remains a provincial. Shtetl people are quite different from other human beings. They're not big or small, not smart or stupid, not good or bad, not fish or fowl. They're just your average Jews. To sum it up, you shouldn't be surprised that a numb-skull like me occasionally hit on the right idea and had an intelligent notion. In short, I was certainly a moron, a full-fledged idiot, but not by nature. I was simply neglected, confused. I wasn't missing any screws, but the screws weren't tight enough. That's the way I was. And that's why I was capable of learning, surmising, that's why I could grasp Issar's theories.

I won't spend much time on Issar, for he's been in the True World for many years now, and why should I tally his sins? I don't like talking about him. It's enough for you to know that I was his pupil, and my antics should tell you the kind of person he was. Let me explain his system, his outlook, which I made my own.

Issar had a crony, whom he poured out his heart to, and whenever he got a little tipsy he'd wear his heart on his sleeve and blurt out all his deepest feelings.

Once he came home with his crony, both of them cheerful and drunk as a lord, and they went into Issar's study. I heard their conversation since eavesdropping had long since become second nature for me.

"Listen, old pal! I did some smart work today. Or rather: I didn't work the way those morons thought I worked. Actually, I worked as much as you did, I only pretended to work—you catch my drift?"

"But you did get money, didn't you, Issar?"

"Haha! And how!"

"Tell me about it!"

"It's an old business. Yankl could have taken a stroll to Siberia—actually he's innocent. And he'd kept asking and asking me to help him out of his jam. You know me, my answer is always the same: 'We'll see. We'll see.' It's the same for me either way. If the guy wins, people think I saw, although I saw about as much as I can see my ears. I take a nice fat wad for myself. And if the guy loses, I don't lose my prestige and power. He thinks he's lost only because I wouldn't see. But if I'd seen, I would've certainly taken care of it. So the guy's got a complaint. Well, let him come and choke me, let him call me every name in the book—who cares? I haven't lost my reputation as a man with clout. The guy'll get over his anger and he'll come and ask me for another favor. And my answer'll be the same as ever: 'We'll see. We'll see.' Understand?

"Well, that was my answer when Yankl approached me: 'We'll see.' I could see about as well as a blind man at night. Don't let's kid ourselves about my clout. Still, Yankl thought that I saw and that I'd gotten the rich man to see. But I didn't let out a peep. Then I happened to learn that the whole business had worked out in Yankl's favor. So this morning yours truly went over to his place, I was breathless. 'Yankl,' I said. 'Get out the wine! I knocked myself out so you'd win. I just have to check with the secretary.'

"You should've seen the way Yankl and his wife threw their arms around me! 'We owe it all to you, Issar! Without your help, we'd be up the creek! We're gonna tell the whole world, Issar!' They gave me all sorts of good stuff, and I really cleaned up.

"Believe me, old pal, the truth'll get you nowhere, and you won't earn much by the sweat of your brow! Work your fingers to the bone and you'll starve to death ten times a day. In this life, by God, it's best to be a little man. A great mind counts for nothing. You have to be cunning. You may have to be a liar, a flatterer, a hypocrite—whatever it takes. What should you do? You gotta have money! Without money you're nothing! What's a pauper? Can you imagine how deeply the rich hate a pauper? They may talk to him once in a while and pretend to feel sorry for him. But they really can't stand him. They consider him irrelevant. When they see him, they feel a stab in their hearts. I don't have the words to describe it all. Money's the root of everything! If you've got money, you've got this world and the next. Having money means being a little man, and being a little man means being a flatterer, a hypocrite—whatever it takes."

"But, Issar. What about your rich man, the one who dotes on you? He's got money, yet he's a fine person."

"I don't wanna talk about him, old friend, do you understand? I don't wanna talk about him. So long as he's got my concession, I don't wanna talk about him."

"What are you saying, Issar? You've granted your rich man a concession?"

"Old pal, you're a lord, a schoolteacher. Let me explain. You have to understand that in this world everybody's only out for himself. A rich man has a lot of power. Everything comes to him. People doff their hats to him, even if they never get anything out of him. A rich man's got respect. And I, Issar, tell you, that you should value only his money. Do you understand? Only his money! He himself is second best. If you can't use a rich man, then he's worthless. You can ignore him totally. Someone who's shrewd and cunning has to do everything that can benefit him. I'll repeat it for you. Everybody's only out for himself. A rich man is very powerful, and a smart man has to do anything that's to his own benefit. So he has to know how to exploit the rich man. You think you're gonna get money out of him? Think again! You have to use him the way an actor uses his stage or a Gypsy uses his bear. You've bought a ticket—well, then, go into the theater and watch the fine acting. Or, if you pay me, I'll tell my bear to dance for you. Get it? I've granted my rich man a concession. You wanna see him? You wanna discuss something with him? I'll sell you a ticket. My rich man respects me, he's crazy about me! I've given him a concession. Is that enough for you? Do you understand now, old pal?"

Needless to say, Issar's theories were at first too subtle, and some of what he said was Greek to me. But I was a quick study. Having money means being a little man, and being a little man means being a flatterer, a hypocrite—whatever it takes. That was the secret I learned. But I didn't quite grasp what it meant to be a flatterer, a hypocrite.

I ought to add that back then I didn't understand what to do or not to do. Sins, for me, were: looking at the priest during his benediction; not sacrificing a rooster at Yom Kippur; not going to a river at Rosh Hashanah to dump my sins into the water; not believing that Elijah went around at Passover, sipping wine in each home; not believing that dead Jews prayed in the Grand Synagogue at night; not believing in the World of Chaos—that is, not believing that there are a lot of people who are actually ghosts, even though they do business, travel, buy and sell, but because of some defect in their prayer shawls they are never called up to read the Torah in the synagogue.

Sins, for me, were also: not believing in reincarnation, that is, not believing that a holy human soul could return as a black cat, a pig, a calf, a rooster, a stallion, or a canary; not believing that the Guardian Angel marched in ghosts like recruits when the Rabbi of Nopeople passed judgment; not believing that a shtreymel (the fur-edged hat worn by rabbis and Hasids on the Sabbath and on holidays) was holy and that Jews had worn shtreymels in Egypt, where God had rewarded them by helping them escape.

In short, those were what I regarded as sins. But since I was a flatterer, a hypocrite, a little man—those were not on my list. Fine, why not be a little man? You're rich and happy! No one dares to beat you. A beating hurts so awfully. When a tailor or his wife gives you a smack, you see stars. And when a cantor twists your ears, you practically faint. Or when you kowtow, putting on or taking off the galoshes of a man who sits there with arms akimbo, staring at the ceiling. How awful! So naturally I longed to be a little man! I wouldn't have to suffer any more, I'd be rich and happy. That was why I kept eavesdropping on Issar when he was talking to his friend. I understood him a lot better than I'd understood the heder teacher.

I served Issar for many years. I got polished and I understood and got to know what a little man has to know. For I listened carefully and I was a quick study. I started inspecting myself and I asked myself what Jacob asked Laban [Genesis 30:30]: "When shall I provide for my own house also?" Which means: "When am I gonna do something for number one?" I said to myself: "I'm practically a young man. 'It is not theory that counts, it is practice' [Aboth 1:17]. In other words: Don't waste time talking, go for it!"

I mulled and mused until I hit on a plan: "Damn it! I'm such a moron!

Issar himself says that everybody has to be out for his own good, and you have to grant a concession to a rich man so you can earn your kopeks. Damn it! Issar is also rich. So why not be his concessioner! I'll become Issar's heart and soul. Why go begging for milk if I've got a cash cow?"

To make a long story short, I began cajoling and flattering Issar and I found a thousand ways of fawning on him until I had him in my clutches, until I became his heart and soul. He was only human, after all. He loved being stroked and sucked up to, even though he knew how powerful flattery can be. For instance, he would tell someone: "You're wise, kind, pious, charitable, and you come from a wonderful family!" But he meant just the opposite: "You're stupid, nasty, crooked, stingy, and you come from a rotten family!" That seems to be the way of the world: everyone loves to be fooled.

However, that's easier said than done. It took me a long time to worm my way into Issar's good graces. Now you may wonder how a servant managed to do so. Well, please don't be offended, but you obviously don't know human nature. Most servants are honorable people, and most honorable people are servants.

When the townsfolk saw that I was in Issar's good graces, that I was his heart and soul, they started flattering me. When someone needed something from Issar (and who didn't?), then, aha!, that person would ask me to intercede—and he'd shower me with gifts and money. He was happy enough, figuring I'd put in a good word with Issar, while I knew that Issar would be as helpful as leeches on a corpse. Why should I care? Let the petitioner think whatever he thought and let him give me money.

In this way I collected thousands of rubles. Who knows? Eventually it might have added up to a sizable nest egg. But then all of a sudden, my luck ran out. Issar's rich man died, leaving Issar high and dry, which, needless to say, left me high and dry. People stopped coming to Issar, for he was no longer a concessioner and he no longer had a bear. And since Issar no longer had any power, then, obviously, neither did I.

I was still in Issar's good graces, but since he could no longer help me, I needed him like a hole in the head, and so I turned a deaf ear. That's what he himself had taught me, I had it straight from the horse's mouth.

I had my thousands of rubles, so why should I care about Issar? I wondered where I'd find another job, a place where I'd sort of be in command. It struck me that I should move to Foolsville, the home of a rich man of some renown. I'd grant him a concession.

On the way, I stopped off to see the Hasidic rebbe to whom Foolsville belonged. For if you want to grant a concession to a rich man, you first have to see the rebbe. Everything begins with him. That's what Issar had done in his time. I gave the rebbe a fat fee, he blessed me so I'd succeed, and I then rode into Foolsville. At that time I was in my early or late twenties, but I wasn't sure of my exact age, I never counted my years and I didn't know when I'd been born—what good was knowing?

I claimed to be a widower and I worshiped in a prayer shawl, for a young man isn't taken seriously—especially one in his late teens. I embellished my prayer shawl with a silver fringe, it glistened and sparkled. That kind of adornment, especially in those days, is the finest recommendation. That's what I'd heard from Issar Choker (may he rest in peace!). I also had money, which made it very easy for me to meet the VIPs of Foolsville. I told them I'd be starting a business here, but actually I kept my eyes peeled for my concession. Otherwise I was as useless as a hole in the head.

God helped me, I met the rich man. He was very simpleminded, he enjoyed doing stupid things, and he always wanted to know what was going on everywhere. It was a perfect fit—that was just the kind of person I needed.

To make a long story short, my business was a spectacular success. It wasn't very difficult for me to become the rich man's heart and soul. To sum it up: for some two years I was his concessioner, which brought me a nice income. You know that all the townsfolk doff their hats when they see him; rich and poor, old and young, everyone needs him. So you can see how well I did as his heart and soul.

I've already told you that it's not in my nature to speak ill of others. In this respect I go along with Issar, who said: "I don't wanna talk about my rich man." I mustn't confess on his behalf. He'll have time to confess on his own. We're talking about my confession to the Almighty:

Forgive me for the sin that I committed by oppressing my fellow man! When people saw how important I was, they figured me for a very powerful man. Anyone who had something on his mind, something to get off his chest, went straight to Yitsik-Avrom the Power Broker (that was my nickname, Rabbi, you know that). Raking in heaps of gold, I would reply, "We'll see. We'll see"—just as Issar replied. The petitioner assumed I'd help him, but after taking his money, I forgot all about him. Just another sucker!

Forgive me for acting callous to my fellow man! I fleeced paupers, widows, orphans. When a poor man bawled his eyes out in front of me, I'd turn a deaf ear. "What do I care about your tears?" I thought. "All I want is your money!" This means: "Jew, hand over your cash!" Or: "Dog, give me rubles, and go choke on your tears!"

Forgive me for doing evil. Doing evil is a lot easier than doing good. A cat can wreak havoc too. If you want to do good, you need wisdom and money. But doing evil is child's play. It doesn't take much wisdom, it doesn't cost any money. And in order to maintain my reputation, I deliberately did lots of evil. The townsfolk knew I was a force to be reckoned with and they were terrified of me.

Forgive me for the sin of bearing tales. I had to slander a lot of people, tell a lot of lies, get back at someone, while I myself remained the rich man's heart and soul, his concessioner.

Forgive me for the sin of pride. When I wanted to get rid of a decent man who was in my way or cheat an honest and intelligent man who had figured out my dishonestly, I would demonstrate my full power—that is, my arrogance, my chutzpah, my little man.

In short, I was a little man, which meant a good life for me. I married a girl with money and I was wealthy and respected. My concession provided me with a huge income. I become wealthy during the twenty-odd years I lived in Foolsville.

I've already said I wasn't a moron or a simpleton by nature, I'd just been abused and beaten down. I likewise have to point out that I wasn't cruel or evil by nature, I was led astray. Whenever I did something ghastly, my heart would bleed a little and I'd feel so depressed that I didn't know where to turn.

Issar, I recall, said that a little man shouldn't envy people like Goodman, authors of heretical books, God help us! You have to despise them, persecute them—they're worse than fire, they get under your skin with their truth. "Luckily," Issar would say, "the donkey has no horns, and luckily those scribblers are poor and needy, otherwise they'd give us no end of trouble! They'd be like bedbugs—impossible to stamp out!"

What Issar told me, needless to say, was like the word of God for me. I was very sorry that I had to despise Goodman, whom I really cared for, but I had to obey Issar. Otherwise I couldn't have been a little man, a concessioner, and I would have kept on enduring abuse and violence by the ton. I may have persecuted people like Goodman, but when I grew rich and no longer had to be afraid of suffering, I felt a pang in my heart. I thought about how decent and quiet he was—such a good person! And he had truly cared about me! He had never treated me like a servant. And despite his poverty, he was always cheerful and joyous.

Once his wife was in tears because Passover was around the corner, and they had nothing for the holiday. Goodman sent me out with books for the entire day—but I couldn't find any takers, people just made faces. That's why Goodman's dear wife was crying.

"Why the tears?" Goodman asked his wife. "We're better off than all the rich people. We're honest, we suffer for the truth. Suffering for the truth is a lot better and finer than being happy with lies. Don't worry, God has helped and He'll keep helping. I don't need two jackets and a fur coat, I can wear only one jacket at a time. The fur coat's also superfluous, by God. Summer's just around the corner, and the coat'll be eaten up by moths. Listen, Abraham. Take the coat and one jacket and pawn them or sell them so that we can buy matzohs for Passover."

I've never forgotten that episode. I saw that Goodman was happy without money. Apparently money couldn't buy happiness, which was based on something entirely different. After all, Goodman had said: "We're better off than all the rich people. We're honest." I've always remembered what he told my friend Jacobsohn. "Real suffering is cajoling and flattering people. The hypocrite, the flatterer must always be on the watch just like a thief."

I now saw how true his words were. Goodman understood intellectually that a hypocrite and a flatterer are as badly off as a thief, because they always have to be afraid and avoid getting caught, avoid detection. A secret life is never much fun.

I, however, sensed those things in my heart. Experience rather than logic told me that a dishonest person is badly off. He feels twisted, he feels a rock crushing his chest, his blood curdles, his head pounds, he burns and blazes. Yes, I now realized that true suffering was cajoling and flattering. I was rich but I wasn't happy!

My dreams were bitter and nasty, I saw myself holding a knife and slaughtering someone, I could hear moaning, groaning, rattling, dying, and the skirts of my coat were soaked in blood. I once dreamed that Goodman and his family were sitting together, peaceful and cheerful. When I approached him he ruefully shook his head. "Oh, Abraham!" he said gloomily. "You used to be a much finer person even though you were a bit simpleminded. Too bad, Abram! You've been led astray, you've been ruined. Shame on you! You've become a little man!"

I was so harshly tormented by dark thoughts this year that I got sick. I felt I wouldn't last long. So I quickly wrote down the story of my life to atone for my sins and I also made out my will.

I've amassed a fortune, about two hundred and thirty-five rubles, and I'm leaving fifty thousand each to my two little children. That's more than enough. When I was their age, I didn't have a kopek to my name. By the time they marry, some interest will have accrued. I'm also leaving fifty thousand rubles to my wife.

Please, Rabbi, send for Herr Goodman the instant I pass on. The two of you are to utilize my money as follows. You, Rabbi, are a decent and honorable man, which means you're very poor. If you wanted, you could be as rich as any rabbinical judge. Goodman is just as decent and honorable, by God, even though he doesn't wear a hat and he trims his beard. He has your precious character. Please, Rabbi, be kind to him, the two of you of will like each other, for Goodman likes everyone and he loves the Jewish people. He'll be very helpful to you in carrying out my wishes.

First of all, I want to set up a permanent fund of eighty-five thousand rubles to improve the local Talmud-Torah. The two of you will know what is needed. Herr Goodman is an expert in such matters. The most important thing is that the poor children should not be thrashed. Furthermore, the teacher should not provide every last interpretation of a biblical verse. Believe me, all those explanations merely scramble the brain.

Secondly, please set up a school for training craftsmen so that the poor apprentices won't suffer at the hands of tailors and their wives and they won't have to empty slop buckets. It's a pity that many orphaned apprentices wind up as cripples without a whole bone in their bodies. Why shouldn't we do something for these unhappy little children?

Thirdly, if any itinerant cantor shows up in Foolsville, please pay his expenses and send him packing immediately. A cantor is not an actor, he shouldn't wander through the world. If you're a cantor, stay at home and take care of your synagogue. If you're an entertainer, you can go on tour and sing in various theaters.

Beyond that, you should spend the money however Herr Goodman deems fit. I know that both of you are grand and wonderful people. You'll probably know what to do, and you don't have to answer to anyone else.

I am leaving you and Herr Goodman my entire mansion and acreage, with its annual income of five thousand rubles. Both of you are to live here and raise my little children.

You are to read this letter aloud to a gathering of all the rich townsfolk. It will be an expiation for my sins and it will serve them as a lesson. After that, please have my life story printed. Let the whole world know that money never buys happiness. You're happy only if you have a good heart and do good things. It's better to suffer so long as you're an honest person, rather than have all the finest things and be a little man.

Please give this letter to Mendele Moykher-Sforim, he knows all about publishing. Furthermore he travels throughout the Jewish Pale of Settlement, so he'll be able to distribute my story. Pay him decently for his troubles; after all, he's very poor.

WHEN THE RABBI finished reading Yitsik-Avrom's letter, I looked around the audience. These rich men were angry, so angry that they bit their lips. But they held their tongues. One rabbinical judge was so upset that he kept rubbing his mustache. But the other judges, remaining calm, said: "A Jew remains a Jew. 'Even the sins of Israel are as full of good deeds as a pomegranate.' Just look at what a Jewish heart he had! He sinned—an oversight. Now he's repented. For an entire year we will commit ourselves to studying a chapter of the Talmud daily and saying Kaddish for him daily without remuneration."

"Well, Mendele," the rabbi said to me. "First, tell me: who is this Herr Goodman in Hypocritia? Is he really an honest man? Do you know him?"

"Rabbi," I answered. "Goodman trims his beard, but he's an honest man."

"If he's honest," said the rabbi, "then I don't care if he trims his beard. You know the old adage, 'Better a Jew without a beard than a beard without a Jew.' Secondly, let me ask you a favor. Please go to Hypocritia right away and deliver this letter, you'll be paid handsomely. Ask Herr Goodman to come here immediately so we can start carrying out the dead man's last will and testament. And thirdly, my dear Mendele, please publish this life story and sell it throughout the Pale. Keep the price low so that people can afford it. I'll reward you nicely."

As I retrieved my candles from the shelf, we heard a voice from the street: "Charity delivereth from death!"—a verse [Proverbs 10:2] recited at funerals. The rabbi (long may he live!), the judges, the rich men, and

I went out and escorted Yitsik-Avrom the Power Broker to the cemetery. The rabbi had asked the Talmud-Torah boys to lead the way, reciting: "Justice precedes him and guides his paths."

After that I hurried over to harness my horse. By now the brats had pulled almost every last hair out of his tail, leaving perhaps forty. But that's neither here nor there.

I quickly started off for Hypocritia, which I hadn't laid eyes on for nearly two years. Upon arriving home, I was told that Goodman had long since moved away from Hypocritia, and no one knew his current where-abouts.

I had the manuscript printed as soon as possible, hoping that when Herr Goodman reads it, he'll immediately come to Foolsville. The rabbi is looking forward to his arrival so that they can improve the Talmud-Torah and do other good things.

Shem and Japheth on a Train (1890)*

1

FOOLSVILLE WAS RAISING a rumpus, a racket, a sky-high riot. No fires were burning, no outlaws attacking—God forbid! It was the normal may-hem of Jews in their train depot. They were dashing full speed ahead, dis-traught, distracted, laden with sacks, with bundles and packs; among them, women were fighting, more dead than alive, wrestling with their bag and baggage, with infants in their arms and whining children at their sides. It was one big rushing, shrieking, shoving, stomping on toes, bull-dozing in backs, in ribs, crawling on all fours, clambering up the ladders to the third-class cars—people risking their necks just to grab a seat in time.

And I, Mendele Moykher-Sforim, Mendele the Book Peddler, loaded down with my staples and supplies, girded my loins and raced and knelt and stooped and climbed together with my Jewish brethren, musing that this was business as usual—what with this being my first railroad trip and all. I was still a lord of the manor. But imagine my surprise. We Jews bus-

*The translation is based on M. Olgin's Yiddish version.

tle and jostle like crazy to scramble aboard, terrified that we may miss the departure—Heaven help us! Yet all the while we kowtow to the conductors, virtually praying to them: "Please take pity and let us travel!" The Gentile passengers, in contrast, keep strolling nonchalantly to and fro on the platform, with their hands clasped in back of them, and it's only when the bell rings a third time that they leisurely climb into the train. Why the difference?

With God's help the Jews survived the pushing and the hubbub and managed to struggle aboard with their goods and chattel. But now a new pandemonium began: the hunt for seats. Some could thank their lucky stars: they found seats immediately. Others—poor things!—went roaming and roving, unable to find a resting place. A woman with a broad belly, a long nose, and talking a blue streak, elbowed and shouldered her way in, shoving her parcels and packages ahead of her and falling down on them, stretching out full length, gasping, wriggling like a hogtied turkey in the marketplace before Passover: the instant you bring it home and unbind its legs, it lies on the ground, stretching out its wings and, with its head askew, its beak agape, it ogles every which way.

This woman was followed by another, who dragged in bedding and whole bales of rags while turning her head toward her offspring and hollering: "Faster! Faster!" Thanks to the good Lord, she settled next to me, squeezing and squashing in with her husband and children, surrounded by a wall of luggage.

There we sat in the train like the Jews mourning by the waters of Babylon, except that our rivers were rivers of sweat. I was flabbergasted by all the commotion and spectacle. I was cramped, squooshed in. It was horrible. There I sat, like a golem, too scared to budge and sweating like a pig. In the old days, when I used to travel all over the world with my horse and wagon, it hadn't been hard for me—God forbid!—to perch, hunched over, among my stacks of books. Not to mention sweat. Perspiration was always my inspiration. During the great summer heat in the Jewish month of Tamuz, when God draws the sun from its sheath, and everything burns and swelters, a driver sprawls face up in his wagon (as I do) and sweats. A man like that knows the value of a good sweat!

But now, on the train, sweat wasn't what it used to be. Plus, sitting all crushed up was awful, it sapped your strength. I began to wonder—go figure, maybe the nature of Jews had changed because of our sins, and I was no longer worthy of these privileges: the ability to be all hemmed in and the ability to sweat—two great gifts with which the good Lord has favored His nation of Israel.

Observing the way the conductor handled the passengers, and the way the passengers treated each other, I was deeply upset. It made me realize that it wasn't I, it wasn't my nature that had changed—God forbid! Then who or what had changed? It was quite simple: the manner of traveling had changed. You couldn't compare the ancient covered wagon with the modern railroad. In a wagon I'm my own man, I'm in full command, I'm lord of the manor and lord of the manner. If ever the wagon gets too crowded, then passengers' legs get woven together: yours, mine—what's the difference! And if things get too close for comfort, and you feel like herrings in a barrel—well, the choice is yours. You can stay seated in torment and torture; or if you want a little joy out of life, you can climb out—who's gonna stop you? You can stroll a bit—the whole earth is yours for the asking. The possibility of choosing for myself lessens my sufferings and helps me endure them. But the train is different: I am not my own boss, my will is not my own. I've been sold to the brass button, to the conductor, body and soul, kit and kaboodle. I feel like a convict, unable to get out of my cell for even an instant.

And the same holds true for sweat. Sweating of your own free will is not the same as sweating because you have to sweat.

There's another difference. A wagon is like a small colony with a few people, who, in the course of the trip, become a family. We ride slowly, very slowly, there's no hurry: "And the evening and the morning were the first day"—one day, two days, three days, and so on. There's enough time to look around, to view everything along the way. The sky is spread over us like a blue curtain, beautiful fields, panoramas of all sorts of grains and herbs, stretch out before our eyes. The wagon capsizes, you tumble into a ditch, but it's endurable. The earth, like a devoted mother, takes her children back to her bosom. You lie in her lap, get a good rest, and then you're back on your feet.

A train, on the other hand, is like a moving, flying metropolis with all its tumult and turmoil, with its inhabitants of various ranks and classes, with their skirmishes, rivalries, and competition. You fly, you crisscross the world without really looking at the beauty of nature, without knowing the places you whiz through.

The official in charge of signals emitted a blast that sounded like the ram's horn ushering in the Jewish New Year (*tekiyaaaaaa*), and the train lumbered off. The faces of the passengers changed, turning more cheerful. So long as they were moving, so long as the train was chugging along! The people began scrutinizing and interrogating each other: Where was the other man from? Where was he heading? What was his trade? This, that, and what not—as is the custom among Jews. Strangers became kinsmen, distant relatives became close relatives, and outsiders became insiders. They addressed each another by name as if they'd met before.

Khaim opened his knapsack, pulled out some schnapps, took a swig himself, then passed the bottle to Shmuel; Shmuel produced bread, onions, a whole array of goodies, and the crowd became lively, friendly, merry! Shmerl gave Anshl money for an in-law in Anshl's shtetl, and Ruven handed Shimen bills and letters for Levi, the shopkeeper in Spleenville—the entire carriage was transformed into a fair, a market. The children of Israel were hustling and huckstering, all of them talking at once, and the place was seething and boiling like a cauldron.

I likewise felt a hankering to do business and I was about to untie and peddle my stacks of books. But being stuck under mounds of other stuff, they were beyond reach. I was drenched in sweat for my efforts—and that was that! Dejected and discouraged, I perched on the edge of my seat, gazing at the passengers with whom I was packed in.

Opposite me, on a huge pillow from which feathers were floating, sat a gloomy, scrawny woman, all skin and bones, with a thin nose, hollow eyes, parched lips, and a pale, drawn face as shriveled as a baked apple. Since she'd come in, she hadn't had a moment's peace from her children. They'd been driving her up the wall with their questions, with their bickering and tattling. Three smaller children kept swapping places, climbing up to her, climbing down, poking her in the ribs, while a baby was dozing in her arms after wailing his lungs out. His bloodless tears still glistened on his cheeks, and his breathing was very faint and arduous. The woman's husband sat at my side: a tall, gaunt man, with a crooked back, a long, bumpy nose, and a goatee; his eyes were sad, and a vague, bitter smile flickered on his lips. To his right sat his older, marriageable daughter, pensive, doleful, sorrowful, and two younger girls.

I must confess before God and man that at first I absolutely hated my fellow passengers as though they had invaded my territory. And if truth be told, they wouldn't let me relax, so that I mentally cursed my cruel fate, which had thrown me together with such bizarre and annoying people. But after studying them, I had a change of heart, I viewed them in a new light. Their ragged clothes, their appearance, their bleak expressions indicated quite clearly that these were miserable souls who had endured enough, suffered enough in life, and my heart went out to them. The mother's resentful sighs every minute broke my heart, and I was deeply moved by the father's efforts to keep the older children from bothering me and crushing me.

But most of all I pitied the baby, who, after bawling his eyes out, was napping in his mother's arms, feeble and exhausted, no blood in his lips, no breath in his infantile chest—all these things were enough for me to picture the harsh and brutal life of this unhappy family. I imagined thousands of such forlorn and wretched families who suffer hunger and privation, bearing their burdens in meek silence. And my heart wept bitter tears. . . .

2

IN THE MIDST of my grim thoughts, one of the little boys burst into tears, begging his mother for food. And she calmed him with these words: "It's still broad daylight, Yankele! This is no time to eat. Wait a bit. Wait!"

"Shush, Yankele," the father joined in with a wry smile. "Shush, Yankele. Bismarck has prohibited eating . . ."

"Is your little boy sick, God forbid?" I asked the father in a pitying and loving tone. I was intent on conversing with him and learning what was wrong.

"He's not sick, thank goodness! He's as fit as a fiddle! And he's got an appetite like nobody's business! His little belly digests a king's ransom several times a day."

I was astonished: "And who's your Bismarck, who's prohibited a healthy boy like your son from eating?"

"What? You don't know who Bismarck is? Amazing!"

"So what if I don't? He must be a doctor in your area. Back in Foolsville we've got dozens of doctors and barber-surgeons like that, and if you follow their advice, you can quickly say farewell to this sinful world. There's an old adage in our shtetl: 'If you heed a doctor's prescription, you'll need a benediction.'"

The father and his family all laughed at my proverb. I smiled in delight and self-satisfaction. I was about to show off my wit by telling them jokes and stories about our healers, our physicians, and our horse doctors—

when I was interrupted by the conductor, who walked in to check the tickets.

Once he left safe and sane, the stowaways—thank the Lord—emerged from the hellish tortures of hiding under the seats: pillows were heaped, packs were shoved, sacks were piled, and a human shape was abruptly resurrected across from me. This traveler's getup was Gentile: no hat, old, patched-up trousers, a Polish farmer's coat made of coarse material and closed tight with brass hooks. His face was chalky white, his cheeks were hollow, the ends of his twirled mustache dangled like mouse tails. Getting back on his feet, he stretched his legs, coughed his fill, yawned his fill like someone waking up from sleep. The other passengers, big and little, peered amiably at him and greeted him, nodding their heads contentedly; and he responded in kind.

I was dumbfounded, I couldn't understand his connection with a poor Jewish family—Jewish, as they say, to the bone. Countless theories flashed through my mind, and all I could figure was that this must be that Bismarck whom my neighbor had mentioned. But then I realized it wasn't Bismarck—I was wrong! You see, the mother addressed him by his name and talked to him in a mishmash of Yiddish and Polish:

"Why are you standing, Mr. Przszenkszvirzitski? Why don't you take Itsik's seat, and Itsik'll squeeze in next to his father."

"Don't worry about me, Khaika darling. I'll put my dear Itsik on my lap. Your husband Moyshe's got little enough room as it is," replied the man with the nineteen-letter name in a hodgepodge of corrupt Polish and fractured German.

"Did you have a good nap under the seat, Mr. Japheth?" Moyshe asked with a friendly smile. "I taught you nicely, and you followed my instructions to the letter. You can thank your lucky stars! . . . At the next station it'll be my turn to lie under the seats."

"Me too, me too!" Yankele pleaded. "Put me in your lap, Mr. Japheth!" The boy climbed up next to his brother, and the man affectionately clasped them both in his arms.

I gaped and gawked and then peered wordlessly at Moyshe, hoping for an explanation: What was going on and what did it mean?

Catching my drift, Moyshe said: "That man is a Polish Gentile, he's from a small town somewhere in the province of Warsaw."

"Why do you call him Japheth?"

"Because his Polish name, Przszenkszvirzitski, is a jawbreaker.

Secondly, the name Japheth fits him, and in these times he fits the name like a glove."

"Your answer makes me want to ask more questions—I'm still in the dark. You're like those ancient exegetes whose commentaries left people more confused than ever. Please tell me your story, but not piecemeal or in patchwork and not out of whole cloth."

"Since you want to know, I'm Moyshe the tailor, and a tailor, you understand, uses his needle to turn pieces into whole cloth and into a garment. And when he tells a story, he mends and patches and sews one word to another. But for your sake, I'll do my best to talk coherently, as you wish. Oh, but I've forgotten my manners. Sholem-Aleikhem, peace be with you! And may I ask you your name, sir?"

3

MOYSHE THE TAILOR was by his very temperament one of the cheeriest of Jewish paupers. They don't let their poverty get to them, they don't become despondent and melancholy, they don't curse their bitter lot or the way of the world. They view everything as quite natural: their squalor, their misery, their indigence, their destitution. And they don't even venture to complain, they don't sinfully request a better life, they don't even fantasize about a little joy, a little pleasure. Earthly delights are not for the poor, they were created for the salt of the earth, for—how do they put it?—the cream of the crop. If a pauper suffers a hardship, a misfortune—so what? You keep a stiff upper lip and shush! When a wave surges toward the pauper through the ocean of distress in the dark world, he meekly bows his head. And if ever he describes his troubles and agonies, he sweetens the story with a bright idea, with a smile, and he laughs at himself.

"As I see," Moyshe went on, "you don't seem intent on becoming my in-law. So I don't have to impress you by tracing my family tree through my father and my grandfather all the way back to Abraham. And I don't need to give you a blow-by-blow description of my entire life since the day I was born. It'll be enough to tell you my recent history—its substance is quite old and it's been handed down through all the generations of Jacob's children. My story was sewn with broad stitches and with no trimmings or decorations. That being the case, let me begin.

"You should know that I come from Lithuania. In my youth I moved to Prussia. There I supported us as a tailor—me, my wife Khava, who's also from Lithuania, and our children, whom you see before you. So long as we were *Juden*, Jews, I worked peacefully and kept our heads above water. Granted, the designation *Juden* brought me no great honors—and no human rights either. We weren't on a par with counts and princes, but then again, we weren't accused of any great sins or crimes because we were *Juden*. People didn't scrutinize me, they let me live, they let me breathe freely, so to speak."

"What do you mean?" I exclaimed. "Are you saying you're no longer a *Jude*?"

"That's right! Today I'm no longer a *Jude*. In fact, there are no *Juden* left in the world." Moyshe the tailor laughed. "I guess you don't know what times we're living in."

"What do you mean, I don't know? Here's the little calendar I got printed with my own two hands. Just look." I blurted out in one breath: "Today is Wednesday, this week's portion of the Law is about Korah, who was punished for rebelling against Moses [Numbers 16:1–18;32], and it's been 5640 years since the Creation of the World." I pulled one of my small calendars from my breast pocket and dangled it under Moyshe's nose, making sure that everyone realized I was hawking calendars for the current year.

"But the Germans think differently," said Moyshe, calm and cool. "The Germans, who keep inventing new things, have reversed the clock, they've turned world history back several millennia, and we're now living in the days before the Flood. The Germans call a Jew Shem and a non-Jew Japheth. Noah's sons, Shem and Japheth, have been resurrected and they've brought along all the antediluvian customs: 'And the earth was filled with violence' [Genesis 6:11]—the world is overflowing with thievery and robbery. The non-Shems, the antisemites, blame all kinds of sins on the children of Shem and they hound and harass them, especially because the Shems want to eat and drink as the peers of everyone else. And Shem is also faulted for having children, for having offspring like any human being.

"At first these 'backsliders' were laughed at and regarded as lunatics. But they didn't lose heart, they propagated their lunacy every chance they got: in parliament, in church, at the tavern, at the bathhouse. And then gradually, very gradually, more and more lunatics joined the gang, until their madness became fashionable in the German nation and its leaders. Their chitchat circulated widely, making an impact on everyone. The plutocrats, the rulers, the authorities snatched up those ideas like precious stones. The blind masses began to shout and swear: 'So that's why the pike stinks! That's why we're so poor. Shem's children, those Jews, are sucking out our blood!'

"Things went from bad to worse with every passing day. Until the great leader—Bismarck is his name—hit the ceiling. He issued a decree stating that all of Shem's children who were not German citizens had to leave Germany and not show their faces there again!

"Thousands of families were left without food, without shelter. And we were strewn and scattered over the world like stray sheep. And my Yankele!" the tailor cried out with a bitter smirk. "Imagine his chutzpah! He refuses to obey the edicts of the great rulers. He's hungry! He yells for food! He's got a belly and he wants to stuff it! . . . Oh, you little brat!"

"Are you coming from Germany now?" My heart was bleeding for Moyshe and his poor children.

"It's been nine months since we left Germany," he replied. "And that's how old my baby is." He pointed at the child sleeping in his mother's arms. "The police devils showed up and said: 'Get thee out of thine land [Genesis 12:1]—Leave your home, leave the country.' My wife, Khava, was in the midst of giving birth to little Layzer—bless him! The bailiffs said: 'Leave, leave!' And I said: 'Congratulate me! My wife's had a boy—what luck!' But the bailiffs didn't feel that congratulations were in order. I begged, I implored: 'For God's sake, my wife is sick, the baby's scarcely breathing. For God's sake, have some pity and put off my expulsion for a few months until my wife's a little better, and the weather's a bit warmer.'

"But the bailiffs, showing incontrovertible evidence—strong hands and heavy clubs—convinced me that the good deed of expelling Jews is one of the best deeds, taking precedence over human life. Jews, even naked and barefoot in the midst of winter, even weak and sick and deathly ill, are not exempt from the good deed that the times have brought upon them. Seeing that pleas and prayers were useless against an iron-clad law, I picked up my stick and my knapsack, I took my naked and barefoot wife and children, kissed the mezuzah, and trudged through the heavy frost and the deep snow, leaving the town where I had lived since my youth until now, the time of my decline. Naturally the bailiffs escorted us with a guard of honor, making sure we didn't lose our way—God forbid! After all, it's no small matter: we Jews are the sons of kings and the grandsons of Abraham! . . ."

4

MOYSHE RESTED A bit, then resumed with a venomous grin: "And so the children of Moyshe the tailor wandered from land to land—one hundred twenty-seven countries. Our clothes wore out, our shoes decayed. We were practically naked, our pockets were empty, I didn't have a penny to my name! We pinned our hopes first on God, then on His Jews—bless their souls! We figured they'd feel sorry for us, they'd let me make an honest living again and not become a vagrant and beggar. But Jews have enough supplicants—panhandlers, that is—from all directions. Some come from Morocco, others from Persia and Midia, each one with his pedigree, with a diploma in begging. But the householders can't fill a bag that's full of holes. They've got enough paupers closer to home, and the local poor take priority over outsiders, according to Jewish law and Jewish justice. After all, the locals are our own people. In short, I've suffered enough, I've roamed enough, I've wandered enough with my family, trying to find a place, a home, so I could settle down and rest my weary bones. But my efforts have been useless, I've found nothing, and now I'm en route from Galicia."

His story sent shivers up and down my spine. I was so upset that I gazed at the floor without uttering a word. And as I sat there, miserable, lost in thought about the bitter quandary, the torment and poverty of my people, Layzer suddenly awoke and started wailing and bawling. He wept, and my heart wept with him. I heard anguish in his weeping, a dirge. About his dark fate, his harsh plight of being born to adversity. No sooner had he seen the light of day than he had faced ghastly destitution and a life of homeless wandering. He sounded as if he were cursing the world and the way it treated him. His life had been tarnished the very instant he'd first opened his eyes. The world wouldn't allow him to savor the slightest momentary pleasure, to lie with his mother for a mere few days—something even cattle can enjoy!

His mother now lulled him, caressed him, rocked him in her scrawny arms, and promised him good things to come, future delights. But Layzer turned a deaf ear. He hollered and lamented, as if quoting the prophets [Jeremiah 15:10]: "Woe is me, my mother, that thou hast borne me to see toil and trouble and wear away my years with vain hopes and promises of better times ahead."

His father likewise tried to appease him with gentle irony: "Put your finger in your mouth, Layzer, suck it, and keep quiet. Shush, Layzer, a Jew mustn't complain, mustn't shout, even if his stomach is empty, his tongue parched, his mouth is shriveled, and he hurts all over. Shush, you poor thing! A wild bear is coming, and he's going to gobble you up. A sooty man, a chimney sweep is going to grab you and throw you into his bag. Shush, shush, little Layzer!"

But Layzer, the little Jew, wept even louder in his screechy voice, kicking his legs, waving his fists, as if taking his father to task: "You pauper, you! You beggar! You toady! Why did you bring such a miserable creature like me into the world? I've suffered a new pain every hour of my life and you've brought me to a different house for every hair on my head!"

Moyshe was talking and little Layzer was bawling, each responding to the other. The mother was sighing, the girls were groaning—and my heart was bleeding, bleeding. But eventually the Pole took the baby in his arms, cuddling and hugging him—and Layzer calmed down. The more I learned about the dreadful predicament of this unhappy family, the more curious I was to hear the end of the tailor's story.

So I asked him: "Please tell me. Who is this Pole? And what's your connection with him?"

"This Pole is my pupil. Not in my work—I'm a tailor, and he's a cobbler. He's my pupil in 'Jewish studies.'" Seeing my astonishment, he went on: "Please be patient. Slow down, and with God's help, I'll clarify everything."

Moyshe's Story

BOTH OF US, the Pole, that is, and I, lived in the same German town for many years. Each of us plied his trade, and we lived in peace. On holidays we'd enjoy a beer together at the tavern, talking shop, discussing personal things—this, that, and the other. If either man had a problem, the other would help, give him support in a brotherly way. True, sometimes we'd debate religion. He defended his religion and I, naturally, defended mine. He cited evidence from his books, and I from our sacred tomes—if I may mention them in the same breath. He championed the pig and was annoyed that I refused to eat pork, which he praised to the skies. Pork, he would say, is delicious. And I would spit seven times, saying: "Ugh! What an ugly animal. A pig is a pig!"

We'd argue so loudly that our throats dried up. "Hey, innkeeper, two beers!" And that would end our dispute. We agreed to disagree and we remained friends. He admitted that Jewish foods like carrot stew and gefilte fish were quite delectable, and that Jewish women were fine. He'd tell me that it was all right with him if Jews went to Heaven. I, for my part, gave in a little: I declared pork legal for Gentiles and I granted pious Christians a section of the lower paradise. I even went so far as allowing them to live in this world so long as they permitted us to enjoy it with them. Finally: "More beer!" He crossed himself and drank, I recited the Jewish beverage blessing, and we each wished the other the best. That's how we lived for many years.

But when times became antediluvian again, human nature also changed. People were savage, they mistreated one another, those who were close grew apart, and chaos descended upon the earth. I took one look and—aha!—my friend had also changed. He was no longer the same. When I ran into him on the street, he wouldn't greet me, and when I greeted him, he wouldn't respond. At the tavern he sat off in a corner, drinking alone, while I sat in a different corner, drinking alone.

Once, upon entering the tavern, I spotted the Pole sitting with a whole gang of boozers. Trying to bait me, they started loudly cursing the Jews, but I pretended not to hear, as if it didn't concern me. When they saw I was ignoring them as if they were a pack of barking dogs, they got even nastier. Ranting and raving for all they were worth, they poured out their bile directly on me. Then, singing foul ditties, they stomped over to my table and, in their wild drunkenness, they bellowed in German: "Get the hell outa here, you goddamn Jew!" The hubbub brought over the innkeeper, who, with a genteel, ingratiating tone and a sweet-and-sour expression, kicked me out. I left, boiling mad.

Like the flea that entered Titus's ear and plagued him for seven years, the experience gnawed and gnawed at my brain. I couldn't forget and I kept arguing with God: "Lord of the Universe! According to the fourth of the Eighteen Blessings, You chose us from among all the nations. You love us, you dote on us. Why must I and the whole of Israel be so terribly shamed, humiliated? If that's Your attitude, we'd be a lot better off, a lot happier, if You didn't love us, if You hadn't chosen us from among all the nations. You say You pay back the evildoer by punishing his children, his grandchildren, his great-grandchildren, but that's small comfort. What good does it do me, Moyshe the tailor, the son of Your servant

Dvossye? I've barely lived, but I've suffered enough. I've been mistreated by every scum, by every bully. Some day, in the very distant future, will you remember me and reward my children's children's children's children for my trials and torments? On the other hand, why should the off-spring of today's criminals have to atone for the sins of their parents? It's better to judge them on the spot and get even immediately—and that'll be the end of it!

As it says in Job [19:4]: "Be it indeed that I have erred." Such were my sinful thoughts, and I frightened myself by indulging in them. Only the evil spirit could have turned me against God. Try as I might, I couldn't help it, for those thoughts haunted me, crept into my mind against my will.

Once, I was gloomily walking along. It was a very bad period, I could barely make ends meet, I didn't have a stitch of work, my prospects were dismal! I was in a horrible mood. And then who should come along but my ex-friend! Turning up his nose, he sneered at me and insolently stroked his mustache. By some impulse, as if prodded by a demon, I walked over and greeted him humbly.

"You can't go outdoors nowadays without bumping into those devils, those pests!" snapped "Japheth," taking potshots at both me and my people.

"Mr. Przszenkszvirzitski!" I pleaded. "Why are you avoiding me? What sin have I committed?"

"Who is it?" he shouted arrogantly, averting his head.

His curt retort made me realize how deep his hatred was—so deep that he could say to me, his former best friend, "Who are you? I don't know you."

Nevertheless I didn't give up. "What do you mean, Who am I? You don't know me? Me? Your true friend? Didn't we go way back? Let me ask you again: How have I sinned? What have I done to deserve this?"

"What sins?" he asks. "Hasn't your nation committed enough sins? You people are robbers, leeches, exploiters—!"

"Who've I robbed?" I broke in. "Who've I exploited? Tell me, tell me! C'mon! You of all people know how rich I am! If you search my home, what are you going to find? My entire furniture—if you can call it that—consists of an old bed, a broken table, and chairs that stay upright purely by some miracle. You know what poverty I live in. All we ever eat is a tiny pot of potatoes that my wife fries up—bless her! That's what I get for my hard and bitter drudgery. That's the reward for my labor. You know what a great life a workingman lives. Don't I labor day and night in the sweat of my brow?"

"I know, I know!" he fired back with scorn and hatred. "That's the whole point! You work day and night and you take away our jobs. You ruin us, you snatch the bread from our mouths."

"But I'm a tailor and you're a cobbler," I said. "I work with a needle and you work with an awl. I don't ruin anybody, no matter what you say, I don't harm anybody. I'm a skillful tailor, thank goodness. You yourself thanked me for the trousers I once made you. And I don't charge high prices like other tailors. No matter what you say—who do I harm? I harm myself—that's who! . . .

"Now listen," I continued with a very friendly smile. "Don't be a moron, for God's sake. Come over to my place. Khava'll fry up some potatoes for us the way she used to. Look! Your pants are torn, they've been serving you faithfully for three years. And my shoes are worn out, they need help. You can see very plainly that we need one another. It's better for people to live in peace and help their friends. I'm a tailor, so I'll patch your trousers, and you're a cobbler, so you can fix my shoes. It'll be good for both of us—God willing!"

He was stunned, dumbfounded. I could see that he didn't know where to turn. Taking advantage of his confusion, I went on in a kindly tone: "Frankly, you're not as stupid as you act, and you're not as bad as you sound. It's time you stopped being so foolish, so savage, so crazy. You know what? Tomorrow's Friday. Why don't you come over for Sabbath dinner, and I'll treat you to gefilte fish."

"I hate fish that's served by people who hate my pork!" he thundered, turning a fiery red.

"What do you mean?" I said, grasping the source of his hatred. "Is that what you're so worked up about? Pork? You're bothered because I observe my religion and won't eat what I'm not allowed to eat? That's why you despise me and persecute me? Damned if I understand what's become of you! Have you ever heard such lunacy? Tell me, are you feeling all right?"

By way of response, he punched me and dashed away.

I didn't run into him again. But later on I heard he'd participated in the pogrom of Stettin, where the rioters robbed and plundered and also burned down a synagogue.

. . .   .

5

WHILE MOYSHE THE tailor was telling me his story, his elder daughter was sighing and trembling feverishly. All at once she jumped up, chalk white, and went to the door, trying to get some fresh air. Her mother shook her head gloomily, with hot tears in her eyes. A dark cloud of melancholy passed over Moyshe's features, and he lapsed into silence. I gathered that he and his wife had endured greater sorrows than he'd told me about, sorrows involving their daughter.

When Moyshe pulled himself together a little and saw how curious I was, he started whispering to me. His daughter, it seems, had been engaged to a fine young man, a carpenter's assistant in their Prussian town. She had loved him with all her heart, and he had been crazy about her, too. "I, Moyshe the tailor, on the fiancée's side, agree to provide my daughter, Brayndl, with a dowry of two hundred marks in cash to be paid to the fiancé, Zelig, prior to the nuptials, so that he may open a workshop and buy tools." The wedding, as stipulated in the engagement contract, would take place in three months, once Zelig completed his training and received his master's certificate. The loving couple ardently looked forward to the happy day, proudly fantasizing about their beautiful home and, God willing, their future bliss together. But suddenly, the government issued the expulsion decree. Moyshe and his family went into exile, and the lovers were parted.

"This," said the father mournfully, "is a misfortune that I can't endure. I love my daughter more than anything in the world and I'm willing to give up my life for her. You can imagine how awful I feel seeing her so miserable, so pitiful and despondent. The world is a dark place for her without her fiancé!"

Now I understood why she'd kept sighing during her father's bitter story. My heart bled for the unlucky girl. I sat there, silent, pensive, unaware that I was humming "Lament, Zion," which we sing on the Ninth of Av to commemorate the destruction of the Temple: "Like a maiden clad in sackcloth and mourning her lover! . . ."

6

THE TRAIN HALTED at a small station. The Pole went out and returned a minute later with a clay pitcher full of cold water. He handed it to the poor daughter standing by the door, then to little Layzer and the other children, and they felt refreshed. I liked the Pole for doing that and I mentally thanked him. I was very anxious to learn more about him. How had he practically become a member of Moyshe's family after what had occurred between them?

When the train got rolling again, Moyshe waved his hand as if shooing away his melancholy and resumed telling me his story in his ironic style.

Moyshe's Story

WHAT I'M ABOUT to tell you took place in Galicia. One evening, as we were wandering, I happened to enter a vast, almost deserted, ramshackle tavern. A lamp was hanging in the middle of the ceiling, but its light didn't even reach the walls. I could make out human shapes in a dark corner; they were scuffling and hollering at the top of their lungs. A man and a woman were cursing and swearing, and a softer voice was begging: "Please have pity on me, you dear, sweet people! My hunger and my thirst got the better of me. They forced me to eat your bread and drink your beer without paying. You can kill me if you like, but I haven't got a penny to my name."

The others shouted more and more furiously and were about to yank off his hat and his coat. These were obviously the innkeeper and his wife, who were in a frenzy because the pauper couldn't pay his bill. As a Jew who's known hunger and the bitter taste of poverty, I decided to help the poor man out. First I tried kindness, I quoted the Bible: "'If a starveling steals a piece of bread, then it's not such a great crime.'" But since mild words and moralizing were useless, I paid for the unfortunate stranger's meal, and the yelling stopped. The poor man thanked me from the bottom of his heart.

When we emerged from the dark corner and looked at one another, we were taken aback. I recognized him—who do you think it was? My old friend Mr. Przszenkszvirzitski! He recognized me too. Tailor that I am, I looked at what he was wearing—and I nearly fainted. His clothes were ripped and ragged, his shoes old, worn, crooked, he had on a crumpled jacket and some sort of cap. He was all skin and bones, his face was green and sallow, bloated with hunger. We stood there for a few minutes, eyeing one another, speechless, in a trance. I was the first to break the

silence. My heart ached with pity for my unhappy friend. Taking his arm,
I asked:

"What's wrong? Why do you look so awful?"

Lowering his head to avoid my gaze, he quietly replied: "Bismarck
inflicted the expulsion decree on us Poles, too. He kicked us out of
Germany. And now I'm wandering around, begging for food."

"That's terrible," I murmured, shaking my head.

"Can you really feel sorry for me?" he asked sadly. "Can you forget my
hostility toward you?"

"Exile makes up for all sins," I said, holding his arm warmly and firmly.
"Let's forget the past."

"My sins are like heavy rocks on my heart. I'm in bad straits now, the
same as you, and I finally understand the harshness of the sins that the
sated inflict on the hungry, the citizen on the alien, the strong on the weak.
. . . I've learned a lot, a whole lot, in these bad times, starting recently,
with the incident at the tavern. If the same thing happened to those stupid, refined, and genteel idlers, they'd be the better and wiser for it, and
the world wouldn't be such an awful place. Moyshe, you're a good and
decent man, and I'm ashamed of myself."

"Well, a penitent is on a high level," I said lovingly. "Let's forget about
it, brother. It's a sin that's passed down from father to son in all generations. Sit with me, let's have a beer and let's be brothers again."

The evening we spent in the tavern was truly wonderful. We opened
up, we poured out our hearts, just as we had done in Germany over beer.
We recalled our past life, when we had worked quietly, and we described
everything we'd suffered during our Exile. I told him my troubles, and
he told me his. He said he'd been roaming and roving without finding a
stitch of work in this foreign country. People offered no work and no compassion in these times of bad, bad luck in all business. Competition was
high, faith and trust were low, and everyone was absorbed in his own
needs. My friend had depleted what little money he had, selling off his
possessions one by one. He was down and out with nothing but the old
and ragged clothes on his back. He had just spent his last penny and was
about to call it quits. I tried to cheer him up with beer after beer. For as
it says in Proverbs [31:6–7]: "Give strong drink unto him that is ready to
perish, and wine unto those of heavy hearts. Let him drink, and forget
his poverty, and remember his misery no more." In other words: treat a
lost man to some beer. My good deed warmed him, his old friendship for

me blazed up again, and he hugged and kissed me. I likewise did my share of toasting our new encounter. We boozed it up, drowning our sorrows a little, getting a bit tipsy, and talking for all we were worth, until the innkeeper came over and said: "Gentlemen, it's bedtime."

The night was radiant. The moon was shining, showing the world her entire face. The street was deserted, the inhabitants had been asleep for a long time. The town was hushed, all we could hear were our own footsteps and the barking of stray dogs. Upon reaching a corner, where we were to go our separate ways, I shook my friend's hand. It felt like ice and it was shivering.

"I'm staying down the street," I said. "Where are you heading?"

"Wherever my feet take me," he answered with a sigh.

"You don't have a place to stay?" I asked.

"Oh, my," he murmured. "As Jesus says [Luke 9:18]: 'Foxes have holes, and birds of the air have nests; but the Son of Man hath not where to lay his head.'"

"Don't you have any philanthropists? Where are your wealthy Christians?"

"We have no philanthropists, and our rich men have no compassion for a poor foreigner. Not every wealthy home is open to strangers and not everyone is privileged to cross the threshold."

"Listen," I replied, shaking my head. "'Exile,' which is a cherished prize in God's treasury, is something He presented only to His beloved nation Israel. 'Exile' belongs only to us Jews and not to you Christians. No other nation has the necessary strength to live in Exile. And once you've been granted the privilege of Exile, then, brother, your only remedy is Judaism!"

"What do you mean?" He was flabbergasted. "Am I supposed to become a Jew?"

"Don't be silly! The Jewish God doesn't need to enrich Himself with one more Jew. He's satisfied with the Jews who already exist. He's got enough Jewish paupers. He's busy feeding them and keeping them alive with great miracles. I absolutely don't mean that you should convert. Remain a Christian, but I suggest you get familiar with the Jewish way of life. You'll manage to get along somehow or other while carrying the yoke of Exile. I know that initially it'll be hard. But don't worry. In time you'll get used to suffering. You'll be trained by hardship, by torments and tortures.

"Do you think," I went on, "that the Jews were in this condition, with all its paraphernalia, when they originally appeared in the world? Not on your life! They were humiliated for many years, they suffered all kinds of anguish and agony, until they became what they are today. Their Exile has made them different from other nations, they have their own features and abilities, and it's put a special stamp on how they give and take charity. 'And what one nation in the earth is like Thy people, like Israel?' [II Samuel 7:23] What other nation besides the Jewish nation knows how to find out its needs, to keep body and soul together? What other nation has so many alms boxes and so many kinds of fraternal associations? Paupers go begging from door to door, making charity a duty. Householders give without asking who these beggars are or where they're from. They have no choice, they give and give, willy-nilly, to anyone who holds out a hand—no matter how healthy and able-bodied he may be. Moreover some benefactors, with a good will, invite beggars to meals, not only on a Sabbath or holiday, but also on a weekday. And they even treat their guests, as it is written, like members of the family. That's the effect of Exile with all its calamities and catastrophes, all its oppressions and persecutions. We know how to deal with this Godsend, and it's made us stronger than iron."

"YOU'RE SO RIGHT, Moyshe," I, Mendele, broke in with a sigh. The history of our livelihood is filled with miracles. From start to finish. From the manna we ate in the desert for forty years to the beggar's bread in today's Exile. And that's why every Jew has to recite the biblical passage about manna every morning after prayers, for the miracle of manna is an everyday occurrence. It fits his way of life and his soul. But that's neither here nor there. Please go on with your story."

"There's not much more to tell. Listening to my words, my friend gaped and gawked at me and he exclaimed: 'Tell me very clearly what I have to do. You've talked a lot, but I'm totally at sea!'

"'Take your time. I'll guide you in the rules of Exile, I'll teach you how to stay alive despite the worst hunger. I'll make you a member of my family, and you'll go wandering with us, until we find a place where we can settle and rest our weary bones. But steel yourself, my son! Take the Jewish sufferings upon yourself and don't forget what I, your mentor, teach you.'

"And henceforth, ever since he joined us and came under my wing—under my supervision, that is—I've been tutoring him in the laws of poverty. I've given him good lessons in the dark and horrible tragedy of Jewish life, I've taught him how to be satisfied with next to nothing, with little food and drink, how to resist his nasty belly, indeed punish it often with fasting till it shrivels up like an old, dry fig.

"I've initiated him into the secret of door-to-door panhandling, I've instructed him on how to submit to every fiasco, overcome every obstacle, obtain the barest necessities. I've taught him this, that, and the other, and my efforts—praise the Lord—have not been in vain. At first my disciple found it difficult to endure these bitter miseries and he wanted to kill himself. Even suicide would be better than this living death. But gradually he got used to the afflictions, he made great progress in his studies, reaching the highest level of penury, endurance, and resilience to all kinds of torture. He can now torment his body like a true-blue Jew. He knows how to live in Exile.

"He's a happy man," Moyshe ended his story with a smile. "He's happy, and I, as his teacher, am happy that I'm privileged to witness such things."

I looked at the Pole, who was cheerfully playing with little Layzer, imitating all kinds of birds and animals. He crowed like a rooster, mooed like a cow, neighed like a horse, croaked like a frog, growled like a bear. He was tender and delicate, he didn't make a racket, he didn't alarm the others. The children danced around him, merry and lively, Yankele jumping on one side, Itsikl prancing on the other side. Brayndl, the sad girl who'd lost her fiancé, smiled brightly and forgot about him for a while. The sorrowing mother put on a happy face as "a joyful mother of her children" [Psalms 113:9].

As for Moyshe, he beamed proudly, placed his hands on his belly, and winked at me: "Rejoice, oh my entrails, for I have lived to see Japheth in the tents of Shem, see him studying the laws of Exile with such great pleasure." And Moyshe repeated the Hebrew words that are recited when a Jew completes the reading of the Pentateuch. "Congratulations, Japheth, desire to study for your own sake and for your educator's sake, and let us both grow strong!"

I had a lot of other questions for Moyshe, but there was no time, the train was chugging into a large station. I had to say goodbye to Moyshe the tailor and his family.

Carrying out my bundles, I saw the Pole standing in a corner, whispering humbly and abjectly to the conductor, and sorrowfully handing him a silver coin. I instantly caught his drift, I grasped what the coin meant and what Moyshe's disciple was requesting. Gazing up at the sky, I exclaimed from the bottom of my heart:

"Lord of the Universe! Please grant us lots and lots of such disciples. Shem and Japheth will then be brothers, harmony will reign upon the earth, and peace will come to all Israel. Amen!"

MORDKHE SPECTOR (1858–1925)

*B*orn into a Hasidic family in Uman in the Kiev province, Spector lost his *father at four years of age. At fifteen the boy began writing directly in Yiddish, without the usual forays into Hebrew. Because of the pogroms of 1881, he moved to Mezhibuzh to prepare for the university, learn a trade, and leave Russia. The first few chapters of his second novel,* The Jewish Muzhik *(1894), with its quirky and episodic structure, dealt with the theme that eventually became central for the Zionist movement: the Jewish return to the soil. The tsarist government was erratic and self-contradictory in both encouraging Jews to become farmers and preventing them from doing so.*

Yiddish folk stories tended to describe peasants and physical characters in negative terms and intelligent, intellectual Jews in positive terms. Hasidic tales, however, sometimes offered sympathetic portraits of farmers and manual laborers. The Jewish Enlightenment took the next step, with Spector choosing his heroes among healthy Jews, both idealistic and practical. Jewish literature then introduced Jewish farmers and even Jewish cowboys and gauchos. Yitsik Rabon's various agricultural novels included The Jewish Cowboy *(in Yiddish, 1942); Alberto Gerchunoff wrote* The Jewish Gauchos of the Pampas *(in Spanish, 1910); and much Hebrew fiction, followed suit.*

Spector's many best-selling novels, often one-dimensional, usually non-experimental and penned in a lucid, simple, at times clumsy Yiddish, helped to prepare the ground for the classic Yiddish authors.

In 1921, Spector moved to New York, where he died in 1925.

From *The Jewish Muzhik* (1894)

The Town Is Up in Arms

SOMETHING INCREDIBLE HAPPENED in the town of Nezvink, something that had never happened since the Creation of the World. Sholem Roitman, one of the finest Jewish householders, had suddenly decided to up and sell his dry-goods store, his house, his furnishings, and all his earthly possessions and had bought a farm in the village of Stepkivke. No matter where you went and where you came, people were talking about nothing but Sholem Roitman:

"Wow! Who'd 've guessed? The finest Jew in town, with the finest seat at the eastern wall of the synagogue. He always led the procession at Simkhas-Torah. He was always called up on the Sabbath to read the biggest lesson from the Torah. And why not?"

Sholem was a decent Jew, well versed in the holy texts. He enjoyed being the first to make a charitable donation. Everyone liked him for his fine and quiet ways. He wouldn't have hurt a fly. So who would have expected him to do such a thing?

"Out of the blue he suddenly ups and sells his home, his dry-goods store, moves to the country, and becomes a Jewish muzhik! That would be all right for a crude ignoramus, a pauper, a tenant farmer, a tavern-keeper. They're fit for plowing and digging like a peasant. They used to be water carriers, porters, draymen—so they can till the soil. But how can this happen to a decent Jew like Sholem Roitman? How can such a fine man become a peasant? It's incomprehensible. He must have scrambled his brains, God forbid, he's lost his mind!"

One of the Jews sprang up: "C'mon! I've been saying that for a long time!"

"Now listen, friends!" A rather broad, gray-haired man pushed his way into the middle of the crowd. "To tell you the truth, I'd never have believed it. I kept thinking, 'What can possibly happen to a man? Who can understand it?' But then I saw him this past Sunday at the fair in our town. He drove up in his farm wagon and sold millet and potatoes, just like any muzhik. So now I believe that Sholem has gone crazy! I figured

he'd be ashamed to show his face in town. Believe me, friends, I shuddered when I saw him shopping with all the other peasants and buying a
week's supply of threads, needles, dried fish, oil, and all the other stuff a
peasant has to have. I was too embarrassed to look him in the eye—I felt
as if I'd stolen something from him. Sholem even said 'Good morning'
and tried to strike up a conversation with me. But I was ashamed—I don't
know why. So I just kept walking without answering him."

Another man burst out laughing. "There's nothing new about seeing
Sholem in the marketplace on Sunday—with a pair of oxen harnessed
to his big wagon. But what decent person would exchange even half a
word with the Jewish muzhik? He used to be a good, observant Jew, but
now he's turned everything upside down! I tell you it's as bad as converting to Christianity. So what decent Jew can deal with him?"

For a while the Jews of Nezvink kept seething, clamoring, talking about
Sholem Roitman, who was now nicknamed "the Jewish muzhik."

Sholem Roitman

HE WAS ONE of those many Jews in Ukraine and Podolye who spend
their entire lives in their stores, buying and selling while dreaming of
something very different. Seldom do they reveal their true selves. Unlike
them, Sholem Roitman didn't care to while away his existence and then
take his secret yearnings to the grave. He wanted to make them come true
in his lifetime. And to everyone's surprise, he showed them who he was.

Sholem was a studious Jew, immersed in the sacred books, which he
never abandoned. He loved his fellow Jews, especially ancient Jews, who
had lived thousands of years ago on their own soil, in the Holy Land,
where each Jew had his sheep, his camels, his vineyard.

When people saw him sitting outside his dry-goods store, they figured
he was on the lookout for customers. But actually he was thinking about
those ancient Jews, who had been peaceful farmers, eating their own
bread, which they made with their own hands—the product of the fields
that they plowed and sowed. As he sat there thinking, his heart swelled
with joy, and he was proud that those ancient Jews were his ancestors.

But when he returned to the present and looked around, he trembled
at the realization that the Jews in his shtetl were agents, shopowners, tavernkeepers, windbags playing the clown for the Polish landowner, fawning on the aristocrat just to grab another ruble, increase the commission

for brokering, or boost the interest rate on a loan. Comparing these Jews with the ancient ones, Sholem would clutch his head and wonder: "How did Jews get this way?"

Sholem knew the reasons very well, he was acquainted with the history of his people, and sometimes, during the long winter nights, he enjoyed telling his wife, Freyde, about Jewish history. Knitting a stocking by the warm oven, she loved hearing Sholem talk to her and tell her these things.

"I feel ashamed just speaking about it. Our enemies attack us nonstop because of our livelihoods and make all sorts of nasty accusations. But it's really all their fault. The Jews were driven out of their Holy Land and scattered throughout the world, among other nations, who looked askance at them as if they were spiders, and they wouldn't let Jews do any decent work. However, Jews need to eat too and they want to live as equals with all of God's creatures, but they were only allowed to deal in old rags."

Freyde sighed about the terrible wrongs that the Gentile nations had inflicted upon the Jews, the Chosen People. She was so upset that she lost two meshes in her knitting.

"Shush, don't sigh. Yom Kippur is past. The Ninth of Av is still a long ways off, and Simkhas-Torah is just around the corner. I hate it when people sigh! We Jews have been sighing for almost two thousand years now. I don't like the Ninth of Av, when we mourn the destruction of the Temple! I prefer action. Action can lead to something, sighs lead to nothing! Listen, Freyde, one of these days I'm going to get rid of the store. I don't want to be a storekeeper—I can't be a storekeeper! Do you hear?"

"Shush, not so loud. Are you starting again?"

At that moment their two little children, Khaim and Khava, came in, said, "Goodnight," to their parents, and were about to go to bed. But Sholem held them back and silently perched them on his knees. After hugging them for a long time, he released them: "Sweet dreams, children! And don't worry. So long as I'm alive, I'll never let you become storekeepers like your mama and papa!"

The children, at a loss as to what he meant, nevertheless walked out with a smile on their lips. They were certain their father had promised them a good thing.

Once the children had closed the door behind them, Sholem went on with his discourse. "Commerce! Commerce! After being driven out from all other countries, the Jews arrived in Poland, and since the Poles felt that buying and selling was beneath their dignity, they did it through the unfortunate and humiliated Jews. The bereft and miserable strangers had to obey. The Jews were forced to keep stores, run taverns, and the like."

Freyde was surprised. "What do you mean 'forced'?" she asked. "Only a knucklehead would force someone to take over a lucrative business like a store or a tavern."

"You're a woman, you don't understand! That was what happened in Poland long ago. The Jews behaved decently, they never got drunk and carried on like the Poles, and they saved up solid nest eggs. When confused aristocrats got a whiff of this, they started borrowing the cash, so that Jews eventually became moneylenders, brokers, cringing flatterers just to earn a pittance. . . . In time they got so used to their work that they now regard farming and artisanry as shameful. I'm a storekeeper myself, I hustle and bustle, even though I can't stand it because it's hard being an honest merchant. Dry goods aren't my cup of tea, I can't secretly trim off an inch from a yard of cloth the way most merchants do. I can't swear on the heads of my wife and children that I'm selling something at a loss. I can't butter up a landowner while letting him call me the most disgraceful names and still addressing him as 'Your Lordship.' I just can't, Freyde. I'm as proud to be a Jew as the aristocrat is to be a Pole. I can't let myself be trampled on while I kiss his whip like all the other Jews. I can't!"

Sholem would often complain like that to his wife, who would sigh softly because her husband said things you never heard from any other Jew. This calm, quiet woman, a devoted wife and mother, had once asked Sholem why he had gone into dry goods if he didn't like the business, and he had replied: "I don't know . . . It just happened . . ."

And indeed, Sholem really didn't know how he had become a businessman. By the time he and his wife had moved out from her parents' home, they already had two children. He was forced to do something. It made no sense going through their savings, which wouldn't last long anyway. So he went into dry goods because his wife had learned the business from her parents, and he plied his trade for all of six years. He got to be known as quiet and honest. He never hoodwinked anyone and he never stood outside his store to drag in customers by their coattails. Because of his integrity he barely made enough to cover his overhead. Watching his more prosperous competitors, he blamed no one but himself: "You have to love a business," he would frequently say, "and you can't be above cheating a little."

Sholem would often pour out his heart to the Talmud teacher Kalmen

Tepliker. Kalmen might have been the finest Talmud teacher in Nezvink, but he was sickly, he had a weak heart, which prevented him from teaching children. Since he had to earn a living, he gave writing lessons. He found that this was easier than teaching the Talmud. Sholem was very fond of him because he was learned and very decent. This elderly man had lost his wife, and his children were scattered around the world.

"Sholem, do you really believe," replied Kalmen, "that you're the only Jew who'd like to abandon his business and try his hand at calm and quiet farming? A lot—a whole lot—of Jews sit in their shops and dream about it, but not a single one of them is strong enough to go through with it and turn his thoughts into action. I've got the same dream, but God's punished me, I'm sickly, and a farmer has to be healthy."

Kalmen mused for an instant, then went on: "Oh, if I were healthy, I'd be the happiest man in the world! I'd exchange the finest store for a patch of soil and I'd till it myself. Just look at how beautiful the fields are. I envy every peasant who lives on his homestead and works his land. I know, I sense that many Jews share our dreams—all the wheelers and dealers, as our enemies call such Jews. Take my word for it, Sholem, every last Jew would love to swap his Jewish occupation for a plot of earth, where he'd live a calm and quiet life—the equal of everyone else. . . . But he doesn't know how to go about it. He won't even take a stab at it because he's scared of being laughed at. He's waiting for others to start farming, and then he'll imitate them. He doesn't want to be the first. And he's actually too embarrassed to expose his innermost thoughts."

"You'll see, Kalmen," said Sholem Roitman. "One of these days I'm going to be the first Jew in this area to turn his back on the town, on his store, on his home—lock, stock, and barrel. I'm going to get a farm and become a peasant. Our enlightened brethren never stop preaching that we Jews have to return to the soil. Yet these erudite gentlemen work their fingers to the bone and shell out their last kopek to send their kids to the Gentile high schools and universities. As a result, their kids become Goys, who are ashamed of their own parents. I want to show those Jews, I want to turn my children into Jewish farmers."

"Then what are you waiting for, Sholem? You're in the prime of life, these are your best years. This is something you can't put off till you're older. I know your Freyde won't oppose you, and your kids are still too young to have a say. At this point you can do anything you like. So why delay it any further?"

"I know, I know, and I'm already doing something about it . . . I'm getting my wife (bless her) used to the idea of moving to a farm and I'm looking to buy good soil, but I want to keep it a secret for now—everyone is going to laugh and make fun of me. So let them do it after I leave town."

Kalmen joyfully cried: "Then I'll live long enough to see a Jew like yourself give up hustling and bustling and become a farmer just like our ancestors on their own earth in the Holy Land!"

"Why shouldn't you live that long? Once I get properly settled, with God's help, you'll move in with us."

"Oh, come on! What am I going to do on a farm?" Kalmen waved him off and then pointed toward the cemetery. "That's where I'll be soon. What can a sickly person like me do on a farm? Live off you and be a burden on you?"

"Excuse me, Kalmen, but no one can predict the future. If you join us, you'll earn your livelihood."

A happy smile appeared on Kalmen's sickly face.

A Government Inspector Comes to Town

IN THOSE DAYS, the sheer mention of a government inspector threw the fear of God into every heart; and now an official from the county seat arrived in the town of Nezvink. Upon learning this, the Jews closed their shops early. They went to synagogue to recite late afternoon prayers and to hear the news. There was quite a ruckus about the official, who monopolized all conversations. Some Jews said he wanted to cut off their sidelocks and shorten their long caftans. Others said the government wanted to declare the town a county. Still others said that Moses Montefiore, that rich British Jew, wanted to buy all Russian Jews—a ruble for each man and half a ruble for each child and woman—and resettle them in the Holy Land. A few congregationists said that the government was planning to give the Jews land and money, thereby compelling them to become Christians, because Sophie, the wife of the first Count Potocki, had died and left a great deal of land and money for that purpose.

Only Sholem Roitman knew the real reason for the official's visit. Sholem was so distracted that he didn't go to synagogue for late afternoon prayers, even though, like all the other Jewish merchants, he had closed up earlier than usual. He went straight home. When Freyde served him tea, he said: "Zalmen will be dropping in soon. Please leave us alone, I have to talk to him about something important."

Freyde went back to her chores, Sholem shut the door behind her to muffle the yelling of the children. Then Kalmen arrived. Sholem greeted him in a very friendly fashion: "It's great that you've come. Before the inspector leaves, we've got to take care of everything. If not now, when? How long can I keep fooling myself? All my life I've thought about becoming a farmer, I hate shopkeeping and yet I've ended up as a businessman. How much longer will I think like a woman? I'm already thirty, the prime of life! What am I going to do?"

Kalmen kept silent while Sholem poured out his heart, releasing everything that had been gathering in him for years.

"What's there to talk about?" Kalmen said finally. "The government official has come to help the Jews who want to be farmers, and those who can't afford to buy land will get parcels for free. Now since you intend to use your own money and be your own boss, they'll certainly help you to settle wherever you like."

"It's time I stopped dreaming and started acting. If I remain a storekeeper any longer, I'll definitely wind up as a loan shark. And my children will likewise have to do all sorts of horrible things just to keep body and soul together. And whose fault will that be if not mine?"

A Jewish Woman

SHOLEM HEARD THE familiar footsteps coming toward the door and he felt even happier. Waking up as if from a good dream, he opened the door. Freyde came in with some knitting.

"The samovar is getting cold. Would you like some tea?"

"Tea wouldn't hurt. What do you say, Kalmen?" asked Sholem.

"Certainly," Kalmen nodded. "A glass of tea would be fine."

When Freyde brought the two glasses of tea, Sholem said to her: "It's good that you're here now, Freyde. Sit down. I want to tell you some news. I've discussed it with Kalmen and now I want to talk it over with you."

Kalmen drained his glass. "Well, I'll be saying goodnight. I wish you the best of luck."

When the visitor was gone, Sholem said to his wife: "Freyde, do you know what I'm going to tell you?"

"How should I know what you're going to tell me?" Freyde put the stocking and the knitting needles on the table. "Once you tell me, I'll know."

Sholem did not hold back. "Everything has to come to an end," he said. "I've often told you how much I hate the business world, but so far it's been all talk. Now I've decided that we should get rid of the store, and I'll become a farmer. I want to start the process tomorrow. You see, a county official arrived in town this week, and he says the government will make loans to any Jews who wish to take up farming, and we'll have years to pay them back. I don't want to be restricted to land that someone gives me—suppose I don't like it? Dealing with bureaucrats and red tape—that's not for me! I've made up my mind to be my own boss! For the money we'll get for the store, the house, and our furniture, we can buy a nice parcel. Listen, Freyde, there's one thing I'll ask the official. I'd like him to point out some good soil. And at the beginning I'd like to hire a few experienced farmhands who can show me the ropes. I'm sure of myself. People say that a Jew is capable of anything. So what do you say to my plan, Freyde?"

"Why ask me? You've often told me that a wife should do as her husband says. You don't have to ask me anything, Sholem. I know that whatever you think or do is totally for our benefit. So what can I tell you? You want to close the store and take up a new livelihood? Well, then God bless us and bring us good luck!"

"No, Freyde, this is not a new livelihood. It's a very demanding enterprise. I and you and our children—bless them—will have to work very hard. Now I and the children will get used to the drudgery, but what about you, Freyde? A farm can't operate without a housewife, you know."

Freyde was offended. "C'mon, Sholem. How can you talk such nonsense? I'm surprised at you. What do you call work? What do you call drudgery? What do you think I do now? Lounge around and twiddle my thumbs? What woman in the world labors as hard as a Jewish wife?" Freyde peered at her husband and sighed. "Just look at you! With the shop and all, do I have time to pay any attention to you? If I could pay more attention to you, like a wife to her husband, you'd look very different!"

"What's wrong with me, Freyde?" Sholem smiled. "What is there about me you don't care for? I look like everyone else—knock on wood—like a shopkeeper, a merchant, who has to keep wracking his brain. Listen, Freyde. With God's help we'll live on a farm, on our own field, under a vast sky, in free and fresh air, and then we and our children will be very different."

"May God grant us success in your new occupation, your new undertaking."

The Village of Stepkivke

THE VILLAGE OF Stepkivke was celebrating a major holiday: ten years had passed since Sholem Roitman and his family had moved from the town to the country. The anniversary came in the loveliest time, the harvest season, when the peasants cut down the grain and then mow the fresh and fragrant hay.

Peasants who were his friends or acquaintances were visiting Sholem, congratulating him and his family; during those ten years of drudgery their land had finally started yielding bumper crops.

Sholem couldn't sleep that night; he kept thinking about that past decade. The thoughts flashed through his mind like lightning. He recalled the misfortunes he had endured after giving up his store, selling his house, and moving to the farm. He remembered all the affliction and adversity he had suffered until he could finally enjoy his own green, fragrant hay, mown on his own field.

He had turned his life upside down, losing his friends, becoming a laughingstock, and all because he had traded his textiles, his merchandise, for black soil and a pair of oxen and a horse. Since he hadn't known how to plow or sow, things had started out badly. An old and seasoned peasant had taught him the ropes; many hands make light work. For a year or two, Sholem labored almost in vain, with the earth yielding little. He had gone through fire and water. During the third year, he did somewhat better. He had enough grain to supply the household for a year, and there was leftover grain to sell. He finally turned a profit. And Freyde also had some income from her work: she got milk, cheese, butter, wool, and meat from her cows and sheep, and she also made money raising geese, ducks, and chickens.

Nor were their children idle. They helped their mother and eventually they worked in the fields with their father. The whole family worked. The slightest thing brought in cash. Sholem grew richer each year. He bought additional acreage. His sheep, horses, and cattle kept multiplying, and the rubles piled up in his iron moneybox. His wife, Freyde, and the children, Khava and Khaim, were healthy, the harvest had brought in a lot of hay, and all his barns were bursting with grain, so that he needed more storage space.

Often Sholem would lie on fresh hay under the blue sky, musing about everything that had happened to him in the past ten years. He proudly told himself that he was doing well, that he had reached his goal: he had his land, his sheep and cows, just like his ancient forebears in the Holy Land.

When he looked at the forest, at the mountain, he felt he was in Jerusalem. There was the Cave of Machpelah, where our patriarchs are buried. A bit further on you could see the Wailing Wall, the sole survivor of the destruction of the Temple. And today he, Sholem, lived near Jerusalem. A month from now, when all the grain had been taken in from the fields, Sholem, with his wife and children, would make a pilgrimage to Jerusalem and bring the High Priest in the Temple a gift: a big pot of butter and a measure of new grain. Sholem would hear the Levites singing and playing in the Temple, and he would thank God for the rich harvest, praise Him with all his heart and soul.

Amid these sweet thoughts, Sholem dozed off.

Sholem was no more than a third of a mile from his home, which had several rooms and a thatched roof. The cottage, which faced the fields, was surrounded by a thorn thicket. On the side lay a long orchard containing all sorts of fruit trees and next to it a long stable for the cattle and horses and a barn for the grain. In the farmyard there were several sheaves of hay, straw, and stalks, plus unthreshed grain. You could see a wagon nearby as well as boards and logs, a wornout plow, and other farm utensils. Freyde and Khava had just completed their chores and were sitting outside, drinking tea. They were waiting for Sholem and Khaim.

But the son showed up alone, without his father. While he was putting away the scythe, his mother asked him: "Isn't Papa coming home tonight?"

"No. You're forgetting he likes to sleep in the field after the harvest."

"Did your teacher's boy mow a lot today?" his sister asked, as she served him a glass of tea. "I left early, so I can't tell."

"He's not made for this kind of work. He'll never become a farmer. We figured we could get some use out of him for cutting hay, but we were wrong. He picked up the scythe and swung it every which way until he finally injured his legs."

Khava and Khaim roared with laughter.

When Sholem had moved to the country, he had taken along a poor Jew, who could write well and do a decent job of studying and teaching the sacred texts. He was also a kosher slaughterer. The teacher had a boy the same age as Khaim. Sholem had grown fond of the teacher and had built him a small cottage on his own land, giving him everything he needed: Sholem wanted to turn him into a peasant. But it was no use. Leml (that was the boy's name) had been born under an unlucky star and wasn't good for anything. His father had barely managed to teach him how to pray. He was constantly depressed and confused, but the peasants all loved him and felt sorry for him. "God punished him!" said the Christians, and so did Sholem's family.

When Khava and Khaim laughed at Leml's farming, Freyde would say, "Children, you should never laugh at an unfortunate person! You're still young, you don't understand. Is it his fault that God made him that way?"

"But what good is Leml?" Khaim asked.

"It's amazing that God creates people like that," Khava remarked.

"C'mon, children. There's no telling why. We can't explain God's actions. Just look at that poor dullard, that dimwit Leml! He could marry a decent woman and have decent children, who might turn out to be very useful in the world. Are things like that very rare?"

That was how Sholem's family talked about Leml. Next they talked about the harvest, about how the neighbors, the Christian peasants, had gotten a good crop of hay. Freyde reminded the children that they shouldn't forget to bring the teacher a wagonload of the new hay for his cow. Khava said it was time to pick the sour cherries in the orchard, they were red by now.

So the mother and her children sat there, chatting, until the moon was at its zenith. Freyde said it was bedtime, the moon was already dropping . . .

But they didn't go inside all that soon for the night was unusually beautiful. Their spirits were buoyed by the good air and the fragrance of the newly harvested fields, and nobody wanted to turn in.

Sitting there, they again reminisced about everything they had experienced and suffered during those past ten years of living in the country. They remembered that when Sholem had thought about selling his business and becoming a simple farmer, several nasty people had been so angry that they had set fire to his store. But God had helped, and the fire had been promptly put out. Sholem had then decided to sell everything all the more quickly and carry out his plan to till the soil.

"Thank God that we moved to the country!" said Freyde. And they all blessed the good Lord.

YANKEV DINEZON (1856–1919)

Hailed or scorned far and wide as the creator of the Yiddish tearjerker—a wondrous field of endeavor—Yankev Dinezon was probably the most popular author of the Jewish Enlightenment, especially among women. Born into an Orthodox family in Poland, he nevertheless managed to study German and other secular subjects. He was known as a Hebrew writer by the time he published his first Yiddish novel—after which he was all but ignored by the Hebrew world.

As a vivid and detailed genre study of the life of shopkeepers, The Crisis depicts a theme that was current in the European bourgeois novel as practiced by, say, Charles Dickens, Honoré de Balzac, Gustav Freytag, and hundreds of others. What distinguishes treatments of Jewish petty bourgeois life is the profound concern with Jewish destiny—the negative attitude that the world of retail and wholesale trade is a vast comedown for Jews. While many shopkeepers in European fiction of the nineteenth century were ultimately fulfilled as tradesmen, their Jewish counterparts felt they were forced into commerce by antisemitism; so they yearned for the agricultural past—and then future—in the Holy Land (as in Mordkhe Spector's The Jewish Muzhik).

The Crisis (1905)

Chapters 1–3

IT WAS A hot summer day. The sun was burning and parching, and the air was like opium fumes.

In Hillel Abelman's dry-goods store the three salesclerks were standing around, idle. Their heads were heavy, their eyes kept closing, and now one clerk and now another kept trembling and dozing off. But they quickly woke up and peered around to make sure the boss hadn't noticed. They were embarrassed in front of one another and they felt as though they were standing on hot coals. If the boss had been absent, they'd have known what to do: they'd be playing dominoes or checkers, arguing, joking around. And if worst came to worst, they'd have taken turns slipping under a pack of merchandise to catch forty winks—what bliss. But recently, alas, the boss had been in the store continuously, sometimes even forgetting to go to lunch. A bit of work would have been bracing, but there was absolutely none to be had; and the heat was powerful, the air made you drowsy, it was hard to stay on your feet and keep your eyes open.

The middle of summer always brought a lull in wholesale textiles. Nevertheless, there were slight stirrings. Granted, provincial merchants and shopkeepers showed up only twice a year, for the semiannual seasons. However, individual town customers did a little buying. They didn't make you rich, but they got you through the long summer day, justifying the same salaries for the quiet times as for the high seasons.

But this year—God preserve us! Not a single kopek, even though the store was open all day. Not even a dog, as they say, stuck his nose in. If ever a tiny order did come in from a small-town small-scale merchant, the boss would take his ledger, peer inside, and say: "Just look! He's in such a hurry! That's a bit of chutzpah! He's behind in his payments. Eight hundred rubles is peanuts for him, and he doesn't want to pay the whole thousand!"

And his tone of voice always made it sound as if he were certain that the customer definitely wouldn't cough up the money. Nevertheless the boss opened the store every morning, they endured the sufferings, and each day dragged by like a year—whether they were completely idle or drudging away. Shopkeepers would sometimes try to get "interest-free loans" to tide them over, but this summer there were none to be had; and the boss sat in the cashier's booth as if business were bustling. He wrote and reckoned, getting lost in thought and gazing at the shelves of merchandise. Was he doing an inventory in his head? Or building a castle in the air? The devil only knew!

The assistants weren't the least bit despondent about the income lull: you didn't get rich from individual customers. The dry spell was bound to end. A new season would come, with new and old merchants, and they, the assistants, would be slaving away for their salaries. They also knew that their boss was wealthy enough to get by, and he was known among the dry-goods merchants as the most solid one. But it was still unpleasant for the assistants to be sitting or standing idly in the store, twiddling their thumbs. They were also tormented by the heat, by their drowsiness, and by the way the boss peered gloomily at one, then the other clerk.

Now the boss looked up, eyed them for a long time, and then suddenly asked: "What are you standing around for like a bunch of klutzes? Aren't you ashamed of yourselves?"

The assistants exchanged glances, as if wondering, "What does he want? Is there any work to be done?"

The boss lowered his eyes to his ledger again, and the assistants signaled one another, either smiling or whispering so the boss wouldn't hear.

The head clerk, Khaim Leyb Beylin, stood in the doorway, his hand cupping his eyes against the sun, and he scrutinized the street for a couple of minutes like a man looking around the desert and quoting Psalm 121: "From whence cometh my help?" And perhaps he was thinking: "It would be wonderful if a cloudlet appeared in the sky, bringing a little rain to cool us off a bit."

After a few minutes of scanning the street, the clerk abruptly stepped back inside as if preparing to respond to a customer. And indeed somebody promptly came in: a girl of eighteen or twenty stood in the middle of the shop, uncertain as to whom she should address. All three clerks surrounded her, and one of them asked, "May I be of service, Miss?" The second clerk began listing for her all the kinds of silk, satin, and calico they carried; and the third clerk quickly stationed himself between the counter and the shelves, ready to show her every last item—anything to avoid slacking.

The girl, however, was unresponsive and, upon seeing the cashier's booth, she faced it, took her hand out of her pocket, unrolled a crisp new hundred-ruble bill, and said: "Could you change this for me, please?"

Hillel Abelman, who was sitting in the booth, didn't catch on at first.

"Can't you change this for me?" the girl repeated and handed him the banknote.

Abelman gaped at her as if surprised that there was anybody in town who still had a hundred-ruble bill. "Whose daughter are you?" he asked.

"Are you afraid it might be counterfeit?" the girl retorted.

"God forbid!" replied Abelman. "I wish I had a hundred thousand such bills. But it doesn't hurt to know who your father is." What he meant was: It might come in handy if ever he'd need an "interest-free loan."

The girl told him who she was. He changed her bill, and she counted the money nimbly, like someone who knew how to deal with cash. Meanwhile the clerks stood in front of the door as if blocking it.

"Lovely calico—all the rage!" one clerk, who was about her age, said to her. "Woolens, Miss, silk, satin, foulard. At your service, Miss!"

"I've already heard it," said the girl, hurrying toward the door. But then another clerk cut her off and likewise ran through an inventory of everything she could buy here, and he moved so skillfully that she couldn't reach the door.

The girl asked them not to bother her: "I don't need anything. You saw that I didn't come here to buy."

"Not buy, Miss. But it won't hurt to look at our patterns. Then you can buy once you need something!" The clerk was trying to convince her, but he didn't mean to sell her anything, he just wanted to drive away his sleepiness.

"Velvl!" Beylin shouted at the clerk who had slipped in between the counter and the shelves. "Take down the roll of fashionable calico that they're using for frocks and blouses. The same kind you sold Madam Fainberg yesterday for two dresses and two blouses—one each for herself and for her daughter."

Velvl was perfectly aware that he hadn't set eyes yesterday on any Madam Fainberg, but this was simply a trick of the trade to entice a customer, particularly a stubborn girl who didn't even want to have a look. In one swoop Velvl sprang up on the counter and hauled down a roll of merchandise. The clerk standing nearby was already unrolling it and unfolding it to show what it would look like as a frock or a blouse.

The girl was apparently intrigued: "I'll just have a look, but I tell you in advance, I'm not buying anything."

"Just have a look," said Beilin. "That's all I want. It doesn't hurt to know what kind of textiles we carry. You'll buy when you need to."

Half embarrassed and as if doing them a favor, she stepped over to the table. From the way she twisted her lips, Beilin could tell that she didn't like the pattern. "Velvl, damn your hide!" he shouted. "Did I tell you to show us this pattern? I told you to show us the material Madam Fainberg bought for herself and her daughter. C'mon, why are you so stingy? Take down several pieces, we've got quite an assortment to choose from—knock on wood!"

"Why go to all that trouble?" said the girl. "I'm not buying anything."

"It's no trouble," answered Beilin. "All we want to do is show you. Our boss—bless him—pays us good salaries for our trouble. If you don't buy today, you'll buy another time. It's worth the trouble to let you know that the merchandise you get here you won't get in any other store, thank goodness."

Velvl had handed down item after item, and his colleague had unfolded each roll and held it up to the girl so adroitly that she finally became interested. The girl asked how much it cost per arshin [=28 inches], and how many arshins were needed for a dress, for a blouse. The clerk demonstrated his experience like a true dandy, who knows what people are wearing, how they're accessorizing, how much the extras cost, how much a tailor would charge, and which colors would go with blonde hair and which with brown hair.

"I can recommend this item for you, Miss. You'll be grateful, I tell you."

After the girl took a few samples to show her mother and her sister, Velvl stopped taking down the rolls, and the girl, thank goodness, left the establishment safe and sane.

The clerks had the job of returning the scattered textiles and putting the shelves back in order.

Abelman had watched the comedy wordlessly. The silence in the store was depressing, and he was glad that his dismal musings had been interrupted by the show. Indeed, his recent thoughts had been quite sad and grim. On the one hand, he heard daily that some shopkeeper, an acquaintance in his neighborhood, had declared bankruptcy. And on the other hand, he himself received protest after protest, as if all his customers had formed a pact not to pay him a single kopek this year.

Earlier, upon hearing that a neighboring shopkeeper had gone belly up, Abelman had said: "He was no businessman in the first place. A building can't stay up for long without a solid foundation. If things are quiet, then it'll keep standing on its own. But if there's a blast of wind, the building'll collapse. And if a building collapses, then normally people are bound to get hurt." Now, however, realizing that he too suddenly had trouble standing on a solid foundation, he focused his thoughts on himself rather than on others. He calculated and calculated, and the bottom line was that his foundation had been undermined during the past few years—not because of blows inflicted by his debtors but because of blows inflicted by Abelman himself.

These self-inflicted blows included what his children had cost him and were still costing him. He had married off two children in two years, and the weddings had cost him a fortune. The dowries weren't such a drain—"After all, that's what a man labors for, so he can give his daughter a nice dowry." And he had agreed to a dowry that was no larger than what he could and should give. But then there was a whole hu-ha about his daughters' wardrobes and furniture and all sorts of major and minor expenses, necessary and unnecessary, ten rubles here, a hundred rubles there, until the bill added up to twice the size of the dowry and it sprang a leak that was hard to plug.

If that had been the end of it, the whole thing might have been endurable. But his daughters were still costing him a pretty kopek today. One son-in-law, a physician without a practice, had become partners with another doctor and had sunk the entire dowry into a sanitarium. He had recently gotten a medical position at a Jewish hospital in a provincial town and was hoping to build up his own practice. But meanwhile Abelman had to contribute to his son-in-law's upkeep, which cost him quite a chunk every year.

His other son-in-law, who had a rich father, was a lumber dealer and had been doing quite well. But then the bottom had dropped out of the market, and the son-in-law was left without an income. He'd been smart enough to sell his business in time and come out with the cash. But as things stood, until he found another livelihood they couldn't just sit back and live on the principle; so Abelman had to support them in the meantime, and that cost money.

However, Abelman's only son cost him even more money and health. After doing well in high school and obtaining his diploma, he had been turned down by the university—he was a Jew, after all. So he took off to attend university in Switzerland, which didn't pose any problem. But then he got involved with a girl, the daughter of a Talmud teacher in some shtetl—and she just had to attend the university. Abelman's one and only son had married the girl according to the laws of Moses and Israel, then written to his parents asking for their blessing and, of course, for some money to be sent by return mail so he could live in the manner he was accustomed to as the only son of a big businessman. Abelman was afraid not to send money—what with today's children and all. So he sent it. And the son cost him enough: a thousand rubles a year wouldn't do. In fat years the father could manage; but now that he was deluged with protests, and the bank had reduced everyone's credit to rock bottom, it was unendurable, and Abelman faced a not very cheery future.

That was why he was so depressed, and it affected his entire business. Even the clerks, who were used to looking at the boss and deducing what expression to wear, felt his melancholy, especially when there was no work to do.

2

ABELMAN WAS IN the habit of napping for an hour every afternoon. Even at the height of the busy season, when things were booming, he would never skip or shorten his nap. "I'm no worse than an ordinary street paver," he'd say. "Even a laborer gets his hour for napping." But now, since the start of the economic crisis, he couldn't sleep—day or night.

"Why don't you catch forty winks?" his wife had once asked him.

"When there's a fire, you mustn't sleep," Abelman had replied. He didn't mean that a house or a store was on fire, God forbid. He meant that the entire business world was burning and that you had to keep awake constantly and be ready to save yourself before the flames reached you. Sparks were already flying in the shape of protested invoices. Merchants had to have water handy to put out the fire before it spread, before it was too late . . .

By "water," Abelman meant cash: he needed cash for the protested invoices and for his own invoices at the bank. And whenever he left his shop, he felt as if something would happen in his absence, something that might not otherwise occur. He didn't know how to explain it, but he couldn't spend an extra moment at home. No sooner was he done eating than he was drawn back to the shop.

The first morning had passed by somehow or other. Abelman's employees had even put on a show for him—to while away the time. Now he was back in his cashier's booth, peering at the long, high shelves filled with hundreds of rolls of textiles, and he didn't really know why he was peering at them. Was it that he didn't recognize his merchandise or that he wanted to count it up to make sure nothing was missing? No, he quite clearly recognized his merchandise. He hadn't become a dealer just today and he had always boasted that a mere glance was enough to tell him that something was missing from the many shelves. Now he was looking for his own merchandise—the textiles, that is, for which he had long since paid the manufacturer. But he couldn't find any.

"Oh my, what's the world coming to?" he wondered to himself. "You distribute your own merchandise among all the devils and demons, it's strewn and scattered among all the railroads and all the businesses, and in your own shop you keep watch over merchandise you haven't paid for, you tremble, you don't sleep at night, you're scared your creditor might take it away—God forbid!—the way you yourself took back unpaid merchandise."

And again the shop fell silent. Again the clerks stood around, not knowing what to do. But then they heard footsteps, and two local householders came in. One was a portly, elderly gentleman with a thick, whitish beard: Srol Epstein, the father-in-law of the government-licensed rabbi. The other visitor was a young man with restless eyes: Yudl Gintsig, a community representative. Abelman knew that they weren't customers, and that their visit would cost him a few rubles. But they were important persons, after all, and they had to be welcomed appropriately.

"Oh, it's so hot!" moaned Srol Epstein, doffing his hat and fanning himself with it. "If you go outdoors, you'll be burned to a crisp." He turned to one of the clerks: "Young man, please get me a chair. Can't you see that an elderly man is standing?"

The clerk brought over two chairs, and the visitors sat down. Epstein again turned to the clerk: "Don't you have a glass of cold water?"

"Velvl," Abelman said to his youngest employee, "get us a bottle of soda water and a couple of glasses."

"Let me explain," Epstein began as they waited for the refreshment. "The world's in bad shape, Mr. Abelman. I'm sure I don't have to tell you that. People are saying that the war—perish the thought—is going to drag on without an end. Just look at Japan now. Who knew anything about it? What a catastrophe! It wasn't even foreseen in the Torah!"

Meanwhile Velvl brought in the soda water, and Epstein began sipping it slowly and moaning: "Oh, good, good. Oh, good, good," until he drained it completely. Putting down his glass, he went on: "According to Psalms: 'As cold water to a thirsty soul, so is good news from a far country.'"

"You mean Proverbs [25:25]," Yudl Gintsig corrected him.

"Let it be Proverbs." Epstein didn't argue. "You know I'm no scholar. Listen, Yudl, you be the spokesman, I'm depleted."

"But you're older," replied Yudl.

"I'll forgo the honor of being older. You explain the matter to Mr. Hillel, while I rest and drink another glass of water. It's only noon, and the heat's awful already. I'm as thirsty as if I'd just left a bathhouse."

"Fine, if that's what you want, then I'll do the talking." Yudl began: "What do I care about Japan? I don't know the country and I don't want to know it. I'm not the least bit worried about Japan. We've got much bigger worries with the masses of poor Jews who are dropping like flies and starving to death. It's a bloodbath, Mr. Hillel, and it can't go on! We have to do something—at least distribute bread, at least distribute some cooked food. We're Jews after all, we're human beings. How can we just sit back and watch? Last night we had a meeting at our rabbi's house—bless him!—and we decided that each one of us should join the roster of monthly benefactors until the storm is over—'until the wrath be overpast,' as it says in Isaiah [26:20]. We need monthly donations to buy bread and monthly donations to expand the soup kitchen. The soup kitchen is our top priority—I hope there'll be enough bread. We'll also probably get a few hundred rubles from the kosher-meat tax—our rabbi's taking care of it. But we've got problems with the soup kitchen. We've been serving a hundred lunches a day for five kopeks each. But from now on we'll be serving at least five hundred lunches a day and for free to boot. Where is a pauper or an artisan without a stitch of work supposed to get five kopeks? In short, it's as clear as day. We're counting on your generosity and asking you for a monthly contribution to the bread list or a monthly contribution to the soup kitchen or both."

"Why don't you tell him the crucial point?" said Epstein.

Yudl looked at him. He had no idea what crucial point he was talking about.

"I mean my son-in-law, the crown rabbi. You see, Mr. Hillel, he wanted to ask you to the meeting and not reach any decisions without your approval. Our rabbi thinks the world of you and he says that a mind as fine as yours is a rarity. But to tell the truth, there was no real meeting. The poor and the starving Jews assembled on their own and came to our rabbi's home to tell him that they barely had the strength to stay on their feet, and mothers even brought their children who were fainting with hunger. I happened to be visiting my son-in-law, and Yudl came by in the end. And what do you think all those people were asking for? Bread, even dry bread, to keep body and soul together! I told them: 'Shush, friends. First of all, just let one person at a time speak, not all of you at once. Then we can find out what you want.'

"'Bread, bread, dry bread!' they suddenly all yelled again in unison, yelled to high heaven.

"'And secondly,' I told them, 'we'll summon the householders, have a meeting, and see what we can do and must do.' I felt I'd said what I could and what I should. But these are our fellow Jews, after all, and we can't hold a grudge. The poor things were starving and they raised a ruckus: 'Stop cramming your meetings down our throats! We know your meetings! We ask for bread, and you reply: "A meeting!"'

"Well, to make a long story short, our rabbi stood up—God bless him!—he took out ten rubles and said: 'Son-in-law, I'll donate ten rubles. Give according to the dictates of your heart! Yudl will probably also contribute. That will start the ball rolling—bread for the starving. Tomorrow, if you like, we'll summon the householders and we'll definitely do something.'

"Needless to say, we soon had thirty or forty rubles and we handed out vouchers that could be redeemed for bread at Avrom's bakery. We scheduled the meeting for today, but Yudl interfered. He's here now, and I can say it to his face: he killed the meeting. 'We don't need a meeting!' he shouted. 'How can a meeting enlighten us? Nobody's going to say we mustn't give bread to a hungry man. The point is: we have to have something to give.' And our rabbi agreed. We would draw up a list, go from house to house, and write down whatever each congregant could donate.

"We made the list immediately, and Yudl and I planned to start our canvassing the next morning. But it was impossible to go out this morning, it was too hot. So we've started now—you're the first, Mr. Hillel. Here's the list, please enter the figure yourself—first off, the monthly sum you pledge for the soup kitchen and secondly the monthly sum you pledge for bread."

"But I already contribute to Bread for the Indigent," said Mr. Hillel, "and my wife contributes to the soup kitchen—I'm not sure how much, five or six rubles a month. And now you want more?"

Yudl sprang in: "You say you contribute to Bread for the Indigent. That's as it should be. But this is Bread for the Starving—literally for the starving. Do you understand me? That's one thing. You also say your wife contributes to the soup kitchen. Well, according to Jewish law, a wife can replace her husband only for the benediction of the wine, but not with alms. Charity is a good deed that cannot be done on another person's behalf, everyone should give whatever he can. Don't haggle, Mr. Hillel, it won't help. Be the first person to sign our list and put yourself down for at least twenty-five rubles a month for bread and twenty-five a month for the soup kitchen."

"Why are you telling him how much to donate?" Epstein snapped at Yudl. "Maybe he wants to donate twice that sum!"

"Not even once that sum," said Hillel, waving them off. He was about to write down ten rubles.

But Epstein grabbed the list and wouldn't let Abelman write. "God help you! If you enter such a tiny amount, then the next donor will do the same. Don't you understand that the little householder copies the big one?"

Yudl now stuck his nose in: "We need your donation, but your firm, together with a large figure, is equally important to us. Nowadays a well-known firm plays a major role in business. Your firm, thank the Lord, is known to all the world—"

Before Yudl could finish, a bank courier walked in, clutching a sheaf of receipts—white, green, red, and brown. He handed Abelman two white ones and a brown one, then he opened his ledger and showed Abelman where to sign. Upon checking the brown receipt, Abelman blanched. His quill trembled, and he barely managed to scrawl a portion of his name.

"Beilin, do you hear? Minkin isn't paying either, God help us! He owes us eight hundred rubles. I hope he gets eight boils in his throat—that fat, childless numskull! He can go to hell! Has he suffered in the crisis too, that bandit! Does anyone owe him a kopek? No one's paying him, so he pays no one. When calamity makes the rounds, it's sure to knock at my door!"

"Just write him the nastiest letter you can! Tell him that if he doesn't cough up for the second invoice, you'll send him your lawyer and strip him of everything he owns—down to the teeth in his mouth. Have you ever heard such cruelty? He doesn't even have children to take care of, he doesn't help his relatives. He owns several houses and a whole slew of stores. Does he need to go bankrupt too? You can see what times we're living in and what happens when you shoot your load with a whole lot of philanthropy!"

"Calm down, Mr. Hillel!" Mr. Epstein tried to comfort him: "Don't make yourself miserable because of a monetary loss! How does the old saying go? When you chop wood, the chips will fly!"

"You say 'chips'? You call a rat like Minkin 'chips'? So where's the wood? The others aren't chips either—they're ripped-out pages, out-of-date calendars, total has-beens! And you go and do business, you travel to Moscow, to Lodz, you remain honest with the manufacturer, and you're an upstanding member of the congregation with a big donation, whether or not you can! Oh, what times are these, God in Heaven!"

Yudel put in his two kopeks: "Bite your tongue, Mr. Hillel. True, it's been a lean year, but there have also been good and fat years. And you don't lose out with the good Lord."

"I'm not denying we've had very different years," said Hillel. "But what good are they now? There were once seven fat cows too, and what became of them? Just check Exodus!"

"C'mon, you're not as badly off as you say!" said Yudl. "Your children are all married, thank goodness, and they've got decent spouses. I also see that your shelves—knock on wood!—are filled with textiles, may they increase! No matter how much a man has, he never has enough. As it is written in the Midrash [Ecclesiastes Rabbah 3:13]: 'If a man has a hundred ducats, he wants two hundred, and no man dies with even half his desires in his hands.' I don't feel sorry for you, Mr. Hillel. Your shop is worth more than my possessions and Mr. Epstein's possessions put together! Don't be a pauper! Sign the list and pledge a huge donation. Show the good Lord how deep your faith is. And when he tests you with some loss, then give to charity. If you do, I tell you, God will make up for your loss with an abundance of good things!"

Hillel calmed down a bit. It didn't at all suit him that an outsider should know about his loss, nor did it suit him that he had gotten so wrought up and displayed so much anguish. Even though Minkin's protest had upset him so deeply, he should have merely bitten his lip and held his tongue. Trying to gloss over his mistake, he forced himself to sound amiable: "Maybe you're right, Mr. Yudl. They say misery loves company. No one's doing well this year, but the man who can give alms is certainly better off than the man who has to receive them—God help us!"

"Listen to me, Mr. Hillel," said Epstein, poking in his nose. "We're householders and we'll remain householders, God willing! There are wicked and vicious men in the world—the hell with them! Put yourself down for a generous donation, and God Blessed Be He will help you so that you can continue giving charity as you have till now!"

And with a stifled heart, Mr. Abelman forced himself to sign the list, pledging monthly contributions to Bread for the Starving and to the soup kitchen. His hand was trembling because of his agony: the two visitors didn't notice, but he felt it very sharply.

3

"BEILIN, HAVE YOU written the letter to Minkin?" Abelman asked his clerk as soon as the visitors left.

"I'm writing it," replied Beilin.

"That fat, childless clod! I hope his life is as bad as his response!" Abelman muttered to himself. "It's tough only before you pull the stunt. Once you've done it, you can laugh your head off at the whole world and you don't have to answer a letter even if it's penned in blood! It's a waste of postage! But if you don't write, your heart aches!"

Now another Jew stepped into the store: Abo-Leyb Gingold, likewise a neighborhood wholesaler. "Hillel," he said. "Can you lend me two or three hundred rubles till tomorrow? I totally forgot that I have a five hundred-ruble payment due today, and I've already gotten a notice from the notary. I managed to shake out two hundred rubles from my cash register and I'm asking Sorkin for one hundred, so I'll need two hundred from you. But if you can, give me three hundred just in case Sorkin hasn't got it."

Abelman didn't say a word. Instead, he pulled over the cash box and removed a sheaf of protested invoices held together by a rubber band. Flaunting them to his visitor, he said: "This is all I've got! Not a plugged kopek in cash!"

"What are you showing me?" cried Abo-Leyb. "Nowadays that's nothing to write home about! Who doesn't have protested bills? Kidding aside, lend me the money, Hillel. I can't fool around with a notary."

"Maybe tomorrow," said Abelman. "I don't have any money today. Look, you can see I've got to fork over more than eight hundred rubles tomorrow, and I don't have a kopek to my name!"

"What good is tomorrow? Tomorrow I may be lending *you* money. I need the loan today, and that's that! Might your wife have it at home? Hand me a note, and I'll send it over to her."

"Is she my cashier?" exclaimed Abelman. "If only she had something stashed away. It would come in very handy for me now!"

"What awful times. If I can't borrow from you of all people, then it's the end of the world." Abo-Leyb sighed and hurried off to dig up money somewhere else.

Abelman knew very well that no businessman can get along without such loans. He himself ordinarily gave and got them without giving them a second thought. Furthermore he did have the three hundred rubles that Abo-Leyb needed. But Abelman said he had no money because Minkin's protest had upset his applecart: he currently had to discharge bills amounting to over two thousand rubles, and he had relied blindly on Minkin's four hundred fifty rubles. He had assumed that the money was already in the bank and that he, Abelman, could add enough to cover his invoices. But all at once no money was coming from Minkin, only a protest. Aside from the hole left in his heart by the damage, Abelman now had to cudgel his brain and figure out some way of digging up the four hundred fifty rubles he was lacking. Given the times and his situation, he was afraid to lend out what little cash he had left.

He felt sorry for his good friend, Abo-Leyb: how could Abelman turn him down if he had the cash? He justified his action: "As it is written: 'Charity beginneth at home.' These aren't the fat years."

Meanwhile Beilin completed the letter to Minkin and handed it over to his employer. Abelman read it and shrugged. "This isn't what I'd write to that crook!" he snapped. "'I have the honor to inform you—' Is that what you say to such a murderer? Write him? I'd rather stick spears into his fat belly! Why stand on ceremony? Don't pull any punches. Tell him that if he doesn't cough up for the second invoice, you'll kill him, you'll knock out his teeth. What a crook! I hope he dies a horrible death! Anyway, mail the letter." After reflecting for a moment, Abelman went on, "What a waste of postage. It's like pouring water into a sieve!"

At that moment, an aristocrat came in, a young man dressed to the nines, sporting a top hat, and with a portfolio under his arm. "Is this Mr. Abelman's establishment?" he asked a salesclerk in Russian.

"*Da,*" was the terse reply.

"Is the proprietor here?"

The clerk pointed at Abelman in the cashier's booth.

Turning toward the booth, the visitor doffed his top hat. "Do I have the honor of addressing Mr. Abelman in person?"

Abelman felt like taking off his own hat in deference to such an aristocrat. But upon hearing the man's Russian with its true-blue Yiddish flavor, Abelman told himself: "'The voice is the voice of Jacob.' so Esau's hands are not so scary. I mistook him for the license inspector."

"I'm Abelman!" he replied in Russian.

The man gingerly placed his top hat on the table, removed a business card from a notebook, and handed the card to Abelman. Beilin brought over a chair and offered it to the visitor. Abelman put on his glasses and read the card: "Naftal Terentyevitsh Tabakhov, Agent and Inspector for the Yakor Life Insurance Company."

Abelman didn't understand what connection the card had with him. He eyed his visitor as if asking: "Fine. Now that I know your pedigree, what do you want from my life?"

The visitor caught the hint and he replied: "Your policy is expiring tomorrow. At precisely twelve o'clock, you will no longer be insured by our firm. Originally Mr. Shikman underwrote your policy, but he is no longer on our staff. So I have taken the obligation upon myself: first of all, to notify you that your policy will become null and void tomorrow; and secondly—if you so wish—to extend your policy for another year at the same rate that you are paying currently."

"How come Shimkin's gone?" asked Abelman, ignoring the information.

"His fingers were a bit too light," the agent replied. "He embezzled several thousand rubles."

"Is he doing time?"

"Not on your life! He was smart enough to take French leave."

"If that's so, how can you say his fingers were too light? It's his feet that were too light!" Abelman himself didn't know why he was joking. Perhaps he considered the young man a jerk, a dandyish twit just aching to be made a little fun of.

"Well?" asked the agent.

Abelman lifted his head, gazed at the shelves of textiles surrounding him, and thought to himself: "The leeches, the bandits, the bankrupts should live so long till I own even a ruble's worth of this merchandise. Let the manufacturers shell out for the insurance!"

"Well?" asked the agent again.

"Well, it's not worth the money—trust me!" said Abelman. "I've been paying for so many years—paying and paying. Paying the guild, paying all kinds of taxes, paying interest! 'Jew! Cough up!' Where am I supposed to get it all from?"

"That is your choice, Mr. Abelman," said the agent, who had himself glanced at the surrounding textiles. "It is entirely your choice. But it is my duty to inform you: Your insurance policy will become null and void tomorrow, at twelve o'clock on the dot. You can renew your insurance today without the usual formalities. But after twelve o'clock tomorrow we will have to regard you as a new customer—that is, we will have to draw up a new estimate of your inventory, which will bring you unnecessary expenses. And there is something else you need to know: Because of the prevailing economic crisis, the company has circulated a memorandum cautioning us to be careful when underwriting policies. We are turning down many applicants and also greatly reducing our coverage in many cases. As for your merchandise, I will, at my own responsibility, insure it for a higher figure than before."

"Thank you for your heartfelt kindness," replied Abelman, "but you want to increase the coverage? Does that mean I'll have to pay higher premiums? Thanks, but no thanks. What must be must be. Do I have any choice? Sleeping peacefully at night is also worth something. But I'm not obligated to pay higher premiums. Don't make things worse than they were!"

"Well, so you want to renew your insurance policy with the same coverage and with the same conditions as before?" asked the agent. "Then please be so good as to sign this declaration of intent. If you like, you can pay now or else you can send the money to our office. But it must arrive *before* twelve o'clock tomorrow.'

"Beilin, do you recall how much we're insured for? I've forgotten how much coverage I have and what my premiums are."

"I can tell you," the agent broke in. "You are insured for forty thousand rubles—that is the extent of our risk. Your own risk comes to twenty-five thousand rubles. But if you like, I can raise your coverage to fifty thousand, which comes to an overall total of seventy-five thousand rubles, and that means your own risk will not go up by even one ruble."

Abelman finally made up his mind: "Thank you again. But nowadays we shouldn't be running up any unnecessary expenses. Let's stick to my old coverage." He signed the declaration of intent and forked over the sum that the agent calculated.

After giving Abelman a receipt for the annual premium, the agent shook his hand, saying: "Now, Mr. Abelman, you can sleep peacefully for another year."

"Yes, yes! Sleep peacefully," Abelman repeated. "I'd sleep peacefully if your firm could insure my invoices and discharge them. Fire is disastrous—God preserve us! But customers who don't pay their bills are even more disastrous. Can you tell me how to protect myself against them?"

"The best protection," said the agent, "is not to deal with clients who do not pay."

"But how do you know who's going to pay and who won't?"

"Get paid up front in cash and do not make loans." The agent was astounded that Mr. Abelman didn't grasp such simple advice.

"Fine. I'll do as you say." Abelman feigned an earnest expression. "But what if my customers won't buy for cash?"

"They will have to buy," countered the agent. "What else can they do? Are they going to go home empty-handed? Shut down their stores? What will they live on?"

"If I don't make loans, other merchants probably will, and so what will my obstinacy get me?"

"The merchants should all join forces," the agent advised, and he decided once and for all: "If a person has no cash, do not sell him even an inch of merchandise."

"It would be a good thing and certainly safer. But what if the other merchants don't go along with it?"

"Why wouldn't they go along with it?" The agent was surprised. "How could all the insurance companies bring about such an agreement—that is, this kind of unity—on various points that concern everyone equally? I believe that the issue of credit pertains to all merchants equally, because if a customer can't pay you, then he won't be able to pay a second or third creditor either."

"And that's where the shoe pinches!" Abelman snapped venomously. "First of all, merchants aren't humane, they're not even human. They begrudge one another the very air they breathe, they won't even converse with one another, none of them knows what the other is going through. And if they happen to be human, there are lots of reasons why it's hard to achieve cooperation among them. There are very few insurance companies—ten or twenty in the whole of Russia. But how many merchants do you think we have? As many as there are Jews in the world (may they increase). And because every Jew is a merchant, naturally or unnaturally, willingly or unwillingly, most of them become bunglers rather than merchants. . . .

"There are few people who know what business is all about, and even fewer who know how to run a business, who know how a business should progress and what not. There is no chaos in the world like the chaos you find, hands on, in the Jewish business world! Maybe it's not our fault. Maybe it's all due to our awful situation, our poverty, our ignorance, our lack of free choice. But it's not good. That's why everything explodes in Jewish life, everything goes up in smoke. And a merchant can thank his lucky stars if he drudges a whole lifetime and manages to get buried in his own shroud.

"Granted, you may see expensive headstones on the graves of merchants. But have you ever added up the unpaid debts they've left behind? Believe me, a merchant's shroud doesn't have as many threads as the number of unpaid debts he's racked up in his lifetime. Be that as it may, given the way business is conducted in the world, it can never lead to anything better and finer!"

Initially Abelman had meant to poke a little fun at the agent, but now he had poured out his bitter heart, forgetting that his visitor couldn't possibly understand him. Abelman hadn't even noticed that the agent was on pins and needles, aching to get away.

"Why are you saying these thing?" the visitor suddenly asked.

"Oh, just because! There's a pre-seasonal lull now, and if someone walks in, a shopkeeper just babbles some nonsense. Anyway, when are you bringing me the new policy?"

"In the next few days," replied the agent. "But your receipt is as good as a policy. It is the firm that pays, and not the policy. Good day!"

"Good day to you," Abelman responded and he stood there helpless and embarrassed. Why had he jabbered on like that? What had induced him to express the thoughts he had every evening, every night when he couldn't sleep? And whom had he opened up to? A mindless agent, who could do nothing but keep rubbing his top hat. "Fine! So I talked. Let it be!" Abelman said to himself. "But meanwhile I feel the noose around my neck getting tighter and tighter. Minkin's protest was bad enough, but now I've had to shell out a few hundred rubles for insurance! And how am I going to discharge my own debts the day after tomorrow?"

Abelman felt another depression coming on, driving him out of the shop. He quickly secured the cash box, took his cane, and told Beilin to lock up without him. He didn't feel well and he most likely wouldn't be back today.

Once the boss was gone, the clerks launched into a discussion. They were annoyed that the shop was insured for such a tiny sum, whereas, according to their expertise, the inventory was worth more than the estimate.

"A store is a thief," said Beilin. "In a store like this, there's more merchandise than people have on the surface. Do you have even the foggiest notion of what we have in the back? An old and poor merchant has a larger stock than a new and wealthy merchant."

"And more headaches and backaches!" remarked one of the younger clerks.

"Well, I wouldn't mind having the boss's invoices—even with all his headaches!" said Beilin. You can keep the merchandise. Protested bills are money too—if not today, then a year from now, and if not the face value, then fifty or even just forty kopeks on the ruble."

Meanwhile the boss was heading home, and as he walked, all sorts of things kept whirling in his head: Srol Epstein and his son-in-law—"bless our rabbi!" Epstein, sweating and sipping soda water, moaning: "Ah, ah, good! I'm so delighted!" Minikin and his protest, and Abelman's own anxiety: how would he manage to pay his own debts? He'd forgotten all about them! He was annoyed at the agent and his business card: "Naftal Terentyevitsh Tabakhov."

"Fine, 'Naftal' can come from 'Naftolle.' 'Naftal'—maybe 'Naftolle.' And you can figure out where 'Tabakhov' comes from, his father or his grandfather was named 'Tebekh'—'slaughterer.' But 'Terentyevitsh'? What's been Christianized? Just show me a kosher slaughterer named 'Terenti'! Too bad I didn't ask him about the synagogue and by what name his father was called up to read from the Torah. Is it proper to summon a Jew named 'Terenti'?"

The agent's business card had crept so deep into Abelman's brain that even when he was immersed in the late afternoon prayer at home, he felt as if he weren't reciting the Eighteen Benedictions, as if his tongue were speaking against his will: "Naftal Terentyevitsh, Naftal Terentyevitsh Tabakhov. . . ."

PART FOUR

Modernism:

Nineteenth Century

to the Present

*F*or Jewish writers in non-Jewish languages, "modernism" meant something very different than for Yiddish writers. European modernism involved drastic breaks with the past, rebellion against traditional values, a rejection of absolutes, experimentation in both language and subject matter—nervousness, agitation, shock. Jewish authors in Gentile languages frequently operated in a double bind: they wholeheartedly welcomed Jewish assimilation into Gentile culture; and yet they challenged, confronted, and undermined that very same culture. Arthur Schnitzler, a thoroughly assimilated Viennese physician, playwright, and storyteller, nevertheless introduced stream of consciousness into German literature (*Leutnant Gustl*, 1901). Gustave Kahn, a thoroughly assimilated French poet, brought free verse into French poetry—though one might find its predecessors in the free verse of the book of Psalms. The irony was that Jews had abandoned their traditional Jewish languages and rooted themselves in European languages in order to become members of European civilization; and yet modernist writers, many of whom were Jews, attempted to shatter the traditional structures and strictures of European languages.

For Yiddish writers, modernism signified, among so many other features, an at least partial and often total secularization of Jewish life: a partial, that is, nonlinguistic acceptance of European, especially Central and West European, culture.

Yiddish writers, usually fluent in several languages, took over genres, structures, attitudes, experiments from European literature, while trying to maintain a Jewish or more specifically Yiddish identity. This quest for identity was politicized by efforts to obtain full civil rights for Jews and by movements such as Zionism, which aimed at both an ancient and a modern Jewish image. The ultimate split between Yiddish and Hebrew further confused the search for a modern or else timeless feeling of Jewish selfhood.

A specifically Yiddish issue was the very use of the Yiddish language, its development and modernization, as Yiddish writers expanded its vocabulary—through new uses, new usages, and borrowings from other tongues.

And a both Yiddish and more broadly Jewish problem was how to deal, in literature, with the violence that bedeviled Jewish life, especially during the Fascist and Nazi era, when Christian Europe set out on the worst murder spree that the world had ever experienced. In trying to record this period, Yiddish stories, though technically fiction, barely differed from factual accounts. Indeed, the question of fact versus fiction in Yiddish literature has never been solved. It haunts all efforts at facing the past; it requires realism as the basic literary approach; and it ultimately works against Yiddish. For in trying to record the worst six years in Jewish history, some Yiddish authors, hoping to bring their message to a nonparochial audience, have turned to writing in major non-Jewish languages. Thus Elie Wiesel, who started out as a Yiddish writer, switched to French—a wise move perhaps since he otherwise might not have been discovered by a wider audience. Not only did the horrors defy description; they demanded a readership that broadly transcended Yiddish—the language of most of the victims.

YITSIK LEYBESH PERETZ *(1852–1915)*

*P*eretz *was born in the Polish city of Zamosc, still under Russian domi-*
nation at the time. His first book, published at age twenty-seven, was a col-
lection of Hebrew poems. Though he eventually became an amazingly
prolific story writer in Yiddish, he continued in Hebrew as well, becoming
a beacon for later authors in either language. Unwilling to focus on any
single theme, he dealt with an enormous variety of styles, sources, and gen-
res: secular Yiddish, Hasidic Yiddish, "folk" tales, fantasies, essays—and
even a few plays.

When Peretz—one of the greatest Jewish writers—died, a hundred thou-
sand mourners accompanied his coffin to the cemetery. Not a single Polish
newspaper mentioned his death.

On the Stagecoach *(1891)*

1

HE BLURTED OUT everything at once, in a single breath. Within a
minute I found out that his name was Khaim, that he was the son-in-law
of Yoyne of Hrubyeshov and the son of Berl of Konskievole, and that
Merenshteyn, the plutocrat of Lublin, was an uncle on his late mother's
side. Except that the uncle's household was practically goyish. He didn't
know whether they ate unkosher food, but they definitely didn't wâsh
their hands before a meal—he had seen it with his own two eyes!

They were, he said, very weird: they had long towels draped on their
stairs. And you had to ring a bell before entering their home. Painted
tablecloths were spread out inside . . . The place was like a prison, they
sneaked around like thieves. All in all, they were as quiet as deaf
mutes—God help us. His wife had a similar family in Warsaw, but he had
nothing to do with them, they were poor. "What use are they to me, huh?"

The Lublin uncle didn't follow God's commandments, but at least he was rich. Well, if you rub against a greasy person, some of the grease comes off on you. Where there's wood being chopped, there's chips. Where there's a banquet, there are leftovers. But those Warsaw relatives—they were paupers!

He was hoping he'd eventually get a job with his Lublin uncle. Business, he said, was bad. At present he was dealing in eggs. He bought them in the countryside and sent them to Lublin, from where they went to London . . . People said that in London the eggs were put in limekilns and out came chicks . . . "It has to be a lie. The Brits simply like eggs." But be that as it may, business was rotten . . .

Still, it was a lot better than dealing in grain. Grain was as dead as a doornail. He'd gotten into grain shortly after marrying. Since he'd been a novice, they'd given him a partner, a seasoned merchant, and the merchant had tricked him thoroughly and robbed him blind. . . .

2

IT WAS DARK inside the coach, I couldn't see Khaim's face, and even today I still don't know how he could tell I was Jewish. When he climbed in, I was dozing in a corner. I was awoken by his voice. I don't talk in my sleep. Did I let out a Jewish moan? Could he have felt that my moan and his were one and the same?

He also told me that his wife was from Warsaw and she still disliked Konskivole. "Actually, you know, she was born in Hrubyeshov, but she was brought up in Warsaw. She was an orphan living with that unkosher family!"

In Warsaw she dabbled in other things. She had a good grasp of Polish, she could read German notices fluently. She even said she could play—not a fiddle but some other strange instrument . . .

He suddenly grabbed my arm: "And who are you?"

There was no question of my catching any more sleep. Besides, I was getting interested in him. There might be material here: a young husband from a small town, a wife who'd been raised in Warsaw and disliked the small town . . . "Something could come of this," I mused, "I have to get the basic facts, then add something, and it'll turn into a novel. I really have to include some kind of robber, a convict, throw in a couple of bankruptcies, mix in a dragon, so I'll be interesting too."

I leaned toward my neighbor and told him my name.

"Aha," he said. "It's really you in the flesh. So please tell me: where does a man get the time and the patience to make up stories?"

"You can see for yourself!"

"How should I know? You must have inherited a bundle and you're living off the interest."

"God forbid! My parents are still alive—knock on wood!"

"Then you won the lottery!"

"Wrong again!"

"So explain."

I didn't know how to respond.

"Can you make a living like that?"

I replied with a genuinely Jewish reply: "Mmm!"

"And that's your entire livelihood—with no other source?"

"For now."

"Oh my! And, if you don't mind my asking, how much do you make?"

"Very little."

"So business is dead for you too?"

"Dying."

"Bad times," he sighed.

There were a few minutes of silence, but my neighbor couldn't hold back for long: "Please tell me, what good are those stories?" He apologized. "I don't mean to attack you, God forbid! When a Jew has to earn a living, he'll go to any lengths. No question about it. What won't a Jew do to earn money! Look at me: I couldn't take a Jewish wagon, so I'm traveling by coach. God only knows if I'm sitting on kosher cloth or not. Actually I mean the general public. What do they need stories for? What's the practical purpose? What are those books about?"

Instead of waiting for my response, he supplied his own answer: "It must be a fad—like hoop skirts. Women's stuff!"

"What about you?" I asked him. "You've never read a modern book?"

"I can admit it to you, I've peeked into them—this much." He measured off a fingertip: a nail and a little flesh. But it was too dark.

"Was it interesting for you?"

"For me? God forbid! It's my wife who reads that stuff. Look, this is what happened. It must've been five or six years—probably six years ago—probably one year after we got hitched. We were still living with her parents. Now one day my wife seemed under the weather. She wasn't exactly sick, God forbid! Just a bit out of sorts. I asked her what was wrong—" He interrupted himself. "Actually, I don't know why I'm bothering you with this stuff."

"No bother at all, my friend. Please go on."

My fellow passenger laughed. "Isn't that like holding a candle to the sun? You need my stories? You can't make up your own?"

"Go on, my friend, go on!"

"Apparently you write lies for other people, but for yourself you want the truth?"

It didn't occur to him that a writer might write the truth.

"Fine," he said, "okay."

3

"WELL," SAID MY neighbor, "there's nothing to be ashamed of. We had our own room in her parents' home. I was young and more indulgent about such stuff. So I asked her what was wrong, and she burst out crying. I felt awfully sorry for her. Aside from the fact that she's my wife—long may she live—she's also an orphan and an unhappy stranger here."

"What do you mean a 'stranger'?" I asked.

"You see, my late mother passed away a year or two before my wedding, and my late father never remarried. My late mother was modest and pious, and my father couldn't forget her. So my wife was the only woman in the house. My late father never had any time. He spent practically the entire week making the rounds of the countryside, peddling just about anything you might want—eggs, butter, clothes, hog's bristles, linen."

"And you?"

"I sat in the study house, poring over the holy texts . . . So when I asked her what was wrong, I figured she was scared being all alone in the house. But why the tears? She wasn't scared, she said, she was bored. Bored? What did she mean?

"She went about almost sleepwalking. Sometimes you'd talk to her and she didn't hear you. Sometimes she'd be lost in thought, staring into space, staring and staring . . . Sometimes her lips moved but no sound came out. Now what did she mean that she was bored? Female stuff! Women are a strange species. A man never gets bored. A man has no time to get bored. A man is either hungry or full. He's doing business or else he's at the study house—or else he's sleeping. If he does have a free moment, he smokes a pipe—But bored?"

"Don't forget," I said. "A woman doesn't study the Bible, she doesn't take part in community affairs, she doesn't have the Six Hundred and Thirteen Precepts that a man has to obey."

"That's the point! It quickly dawned on me that boredom was a kind of laziness, idleness, and it drives you crazy. Our sages knew that long ago in the Holy Spirit. You know what it says in the Talmud [Ksovut 59]: 'Idleness causes boredom.' According to the law, a woman shouldn't be idle. So I says to her: 'Do something!'

"And she says: 'I want to read!'

"'Read' was a strange word for me. I knew that for people who learned how to write, 'studying' meant 'reading' books and newspapers—Heaven help us! But I hadn't realized she was so educated—she talked even less to me than I talked to her! She's tall, but she always keeps her head down. Her lips were rigid, as if she were feeble-minded. She was quiet by nature, a sheep. And she always had a worried look, as if she'd lost a whole shipload of sour milk. She wanted, she said, to read. Read what? Polish, Russian—even Yiddish! So long as she could read something.

"But there wasn't so much as a trace of a modern book in Konskivole. I felt sorry for her, I couldn't say no. So I promised that the next time I visited my uncle in Lublin, I'd bring back some books.

"'You don't have any?' she asked.

"'Me? God forbid!'

"'Then what do you do at the study house all day?'

"'I study the holy texts.'

"'I want to study too,' she said.

"I pointed out to her that the Talmud was no storybook, it wasn't meant for women, and it even said that women shouldn't study the holy texts, and besides, the Talmud was written in the Holy Tongue.

"But it was no use! If the congregation had found out, they'd've stoned me—and they would've been right. Well, I won't keep you in suspense. To make a long story short, she pleaded and pleaded, crying her eyes out, until I finally caved. Every night I sat down with her and translated a page of the Talmud . . . But I knew how it would turn out."

"And how did it turn out?"

"Don't ask. I'd translate a page and add commentaries by various sages, I talked, and she—she dozed off night after night. Those texts weren't meant for a woman!

"But then I had a stroke of luck. When we had a huge blizzard that winter, a book peddler got stranded in our town. So I brought home a ton of books for my wife, a whole ton of storybooks . . . Now the tables were turned: she read to me, and I dozed off!

"And even today," he said, "I still don't know what good those storybooks are. They're worthless for men! Are your writings meant only for women?"

4

MEANWHILE THE DAY was dawning. In the dark coach my neighbor's face loomed up: long, thin, and sallow, with tired, bloodshot eyes. Apparently he was about to start his morning prayers. He wiped the misty windowpane. But I broke in: "Tell me, my friend. If you don't mind my asking, is your wife content now?"

"What do you mean, content?"

"She's no longer bored?"

"She's got a stall in the marketplace, where she sells salt and herring. She's nursing a baby, and she's got two more kids to wash and comb. She's busy all day blowing their noses."

He wiped the pane again, but I broke in once more: "Tell me, my friend. What does your wife look like?"

My neighbor straightened up, gave me a sidelong glance, looked me over from head to foot, and quizzed me sternly: "Why do you ask? Do you know my wife? Did you meet her in Warsaw?"

"Not at all. I was just wondering. If ever I run into her in Konskivole, I'll recognize her from your description."

"You'll recognize her?" His mind at ease, he smiled. "No problem. She's got a mole on the left side of her nose."

5

HE CLIMBED OUT of the coach and waved goodbye to me from a distance—rather coldly at that. He apparently figured that I knew his wife, that I was a member of her unkosher family!

Now I was alone, but there was no question of my sleeping any more, I was suffused with the morning freshness. The wind lifted the tails of my overcoat (a product of my literary life), and the cool air stole into all my limbs. I snuggled into my corner again. The sun began shining. I may have been traveling through a marvelous area, with the sunbeams perhaps gently kissing the green trees and the mountain peaks and perhaps gliding across a shiny blue river . . . But I didn't dare open the small window—a Jewish writer respects the cold. I began "making up a story," as my fellow passenger had phrased it. But my mind was elsewhere.

Two different worlds: a man's world and a woman's world. On the one side, a world of religious texts; and on the other, a world of storybooks that you purchase by the ton. If he reads to her, she dozes off, and if she reads to him, he dozes off. As if there weren't enough things dividing us! It's not enough that we're either French noses, British canes, German Jews, Jewish pigs from Lithuania, Jewish schnorers from Poland, or Palestinian beggars. It's not enough that every part of our body lies in a different stable and has its own sonorous nickname. And it's not enough that each part is subdivided into multiple segments: Hasids, anti-Hasids, Reform Jews. As if those things weren't enough, we're also divided into male and female—every single damp, cramped, filthy Jewish home has to be split into two different worlds. If he reads, she dozes off, and if she reads, he dozes off.

There had to be a way, I told myself, of bringing those two worlds together . . . That would be the duty of every Jewish writer. But Jewish writers have too many duties, as it is. We should at least earn enough to keep body and soul together.

My ruminations about a larger income were disrupted when the driver blew several sharp blasts on his horn. But I didn't get out. The coach was a bit warmer, the sun was becoming more generous.

I had a new companion now and, taking a good look at him in the bright morning, I even recognized him. An old acquaintance. We had ice-skated together as children and often played at baking bread; we had almost become good buddies. But then I had gone to the dark and dirty heder, and he to the bright and free Polish school. When I didn't know something at the heder, I was whipped, but if I could guess the meaning of a sage's question, I got my cheek pinched. Both hurt me. He, in contrast, got either a five-kopek coin or detention. I had to rack my brain over Talmudic passages, he had to pronounce Greek and Latin tongue-twisters.

But since we didn't live that far apart, we kept in touch. He secretly taught me how to read Polish and Russian and then he lent me books.

Later on, we dreamed up the wildest feats as we lay on the grassy river-bank. I wanted to invent things like a gunpowder that would shoot a mis-sile a thousand miles; he wanted to invent a balloon and then fly to the stars and establish a government among the people there. We felt dread-fully sorry for the miserable world: it had tumbled into quicksand — how could we pull it out? The world was a wagon with ungreased wheels and lazy horses, and the driver was fast asleep!

After that I got married, while he left for the university. We didn't cor-respond. In a roundabout way I heard that something had interfered with his getting an MD, so he had become a druggist in some tiny shtetl . . .

When the new passenger climbed into the coach, I practically whooped for joy. It gave me a warm feeling to see him. My arms spread out, my whole body leaned toward him. But I held back — held back with all my strength.

"Imagine that!" I thought to myself. "It's really Janek Polniewski, the son of our sequestrator." It was really my old friend. He had once had wide arms and had wanted to embrace the entire world, to hug and kiss it for all it was worth — except for the ugly warts, which had to be cut away. But nowadays you never can tell. Perhaps he had become an antisemite. It was quite possible. Perhaps we Jews were now the warts, and these had to be cut away from Europe's beautiful nose. He might size me up with a pair of cold eyes or embrace me, saying I wasn't like most Jews . . .

But I was wrong. Polniewski recognized me, flung his arms around me, and before I could even open my mouth, he asked me what I thought about that vile antisemitism. "It's," he said, speaking Polish of course, "it's a kind of cholera, an epidemic . . ."

"Some people say it's about politics."

"Don't you believe them," said Polniewski. "True politics doesn't make things up out of whole cloth. It relies only on hard facts. Antisemitism suppresses some facts and amplifies others. It can puff up any spark into an infernal fire, but it can never generate a new spark. It's human nature and not politics that spins the threads of history. Politics only twists and untwists those threads, ties them together and tangles them up! Antisemitism is a disease. Politics stands at its sickbed like a stupid quack who tries to prolong the illness.

"Politics," he went on, "exploits antisemitism. A rock flies through the air, and Bismarck's underassistant steers it toward a synagogue window. If he didn't, another window would shatter. Someone shakes a protesting fist, and someone else shoves a bent and bony Jewish back under it. If he didn't, other bones would crack."

"But the rock, the fist, the hatred—they exist on their own."

"Who dies in a physical epidemic? Frail children, old people, weak people. Who gets infected in a moral epidemic? Riffraff, degenerate aristocrats, and a few lunatics, who jump out and lead the sick in a wild dance! Only sound minds are immune."

"How many sound minds do we have?" I asked.

"How many? Very few, unfortunately."

We lapsed into a melancholy silence. I don't know what my neighbor was thinking. But I was thinking that even sound and strong minds can get infected. There are two recurring phases in history: sometimes the masses are led by the finest and wisest men, and sometimes the masses drag along the finest and wisest men. The leader of the masses is a Columbus seeking new happiness for human beings, taking them to a new world. But when bread and water grow short, the sailors mutiny and run the ship themselves! The first thing they do is kill someone—they have to devour meat and quench their lust for blood.

"And don't think," said Polniewski, interrupting my dismal thoughts, "that I'm patting myself on the back, that my sound mind is immune to the epidemic, that I'm an oak tree that doesn't budge in a storm. No, my friend, I'm no hero. I'd be like everyone else, the wind would have torn me like a rotten leaf from the Tree of Knowledge and swirled me around. I would have lived just like all the other rotten leaves, I would have thought that we were at a ball, that we were dancing because we enjoyed it, that the wind was our hired musician playing his pipe for us . . . I was saved by sheer chance. You see, I met a Jewish woman. Just listen."

I leaned toward my neighbor. His face was grimmer, more earnest. Placing his elbows on his knees, he propped his head on his arms.

"But don't think," he said, "that she was like the heroine of a novel, a woman with a steely character, a woman who breaks down barriers and roadblocks and then proudly goes her way. Don't even think that she was an 'exception,' an 'educated' woman with modern ideas, or some ideal type. No, she was an ordinary Jewish wife, one of the better ones—and one of the unhappy ones. Let me be frank: I fell in love with her. And whenever I hear or read a nasty generalization about Jews, I see her face, her sad, moist eyes, and I can hear her saying, 'Don't believe it, I'm not like that.'"

He fell to musing.

It was a very simple story, and, brought back from his thoughts, he began to tell it.

"We haven't corresponded all this time, you and I, and you don't know what's happened to me. I'll keep it brief, I'm only going as far as Lukowa.

"I began studying medicine, but I never finished. I put some of the blame on my friends, some on my teachers, but most of it on myself. I dropped out and became a druggist. I married, got the dowry, moved to a small town, and set up shop with pills, castor oil, and so forth. I did have some luck, though. The town wasn't so bad. My father-in-law was a decent man and he paid me the dowry soon after the wedding. My wife's name was Maria, and she was good and beautiful. I can see her now . . . She looks into the mirror and then awkwardly turns to me. Her golden curls refuse to submit to her despotic comb. They merrily tumble every which way. They rebel against being forced into a wreath—which was all the rage back then! She was so slender, and her eyes were so kind, so cheerful, so sky blue.

"The shop left us plenty of spare time. The town was poor, and if there's no doctor, then a druggist isn't much help. Our income was tiny, but we lived in paradise. We spent each summer day on our veranda, hand in hand, eye to eye, lip to lip.

"And why should we be interested in anything else? We had our livelihood, and where else were we to go? From our veranda we could see the entire town: the low, buckling cottages with high, broad, black wooden gables, which leaned tenderly over the women selling bagels or fruit at shabby stands in front of their homes. It was as if the gables were trying to shield the old, dry, shrunken faces from the sun.

"The town had once been prosperous: the lofts had been full of all kinds of grain and fruit. The marketplace had been jammed with wagons, farmers, and brokers. Now and then, among the gray coats and the coarse, white caftans, a big landowner would show up—or at least so we were told. But a highway was built and then a railroad, which bypassed the town, excluding it from the business world. The streets were empty now, the lofts were crammed with rotten onions and hunks of cheese—the sole legacy of the good years.

"You can't imagine how poor the town became. For every sack of rye lugged by a peasant there were ten buyers driving up the prices. But then they came to terms: either they put down a deposit or they joined forces.

But when it was time to pay, all ten merchants realized their pockets were empty. So they had to borrow money and pay interest.

"There were a hundred tailors for every pair of trousers, five hundred cobblers for every pair of shoes. I've never seen such poverty in all my life.

"We kept aloof from the town as much as possible; happy people are egoists. But across from our home we noticed a young wife of not more than eighteen or nineteen, at most twenty. We couldn't take our eyes off her. Nor could she take her eyes off us. It was a strange situation. She was very beautiful. Imagine: a lovely picture in a shabby frame under an ugly, crooked roof, like so many Jewish windows in a small shtetl. Imagine: a pair of sad, moist, dreamy eyes in an alabaster face—and under a hair-band!

"Oh, God! She looked so awful! She'd spend hours at the window, wringing her hands, choking back her tears, gazing sadly at us or at the stars. We saw that she was always alone (you Jewish men never have time for your wives), she was always troubled, melancholy. Her misery was inscribed in her pale face. She must have come here from another town, from a better, freer home. She apparently yearned to be far, far away, longing for a free life. She too wanted to live, to love and be loved . . . You can say what you like, but you Jewish men often wrong your daughters by selling them! Granted, in time they adjust to their situation, in time they forget . . . They're pious, they're decent, they're patient. But who can count the bitter tears that fall upon their humiliated faces until their eyes run dry? Who can reckon up their heartaches until they get used to a living death? And why do they deserve this treatment if they're good and pious?

"You should have seen her husband—a sallow little hunchback. I'd see him twice a day: he'd go out in the morning and come home at night. It was pitiful."

You'll understand that I couldn't respond. We were silent for a while until Polniewski started speaking again.

"One day the woman vanished. She didn't appear at the window all day long. We figured she was sick. That evening the sallow-faced husband came and asked us for a medicine.

"'What kind of medicine?'

"'I don't know,' he said. 'A medicine!'

"'Who is it for?'

"'You really have to know? For my wife.'

"'What's wrong with her?'

"'How should I know! She says she's got a pain in her heart.'

"That," said Polniewski, "was how we first got acquainted. To make a long story short: since I'd studied a little medicine, I went over to their home . . ."

Polniewski was embarrassed now. He searched his pockets for cigarettes, then for matches. Finally he opened his overnight bag and poked around in it for several minutes.

I was haunted by various thoughts. I now saw Polniewski in a different light. I was very bothered by his story. Who really knows another human being? Who can say what he's capable of? I wondered if I was dealing with a Christian polecat who sneaks into Jewish chicken coops. He was too interested in the fate of Jewish women, he was spending too much time looking for matches. This man was embarrassed in front of me. Why did he want "to make a long story short"? Why not tell me the whole story with all the details? Who can say what role he played if not the ancient role of the serpent in the Garden of Eden? What was it? Wouldn't his conscience let him talk? A fine business! Going after a Jewish wife—why not? Christians used to consider it a good deed to get a Jew baptized. Today they at least try to set a Jewish wife against her parents, against her husband, against her entire life, against her God.

It's called liberalism: you visit a prison, let in a billow of fresh air, a sheaf of sunlight, wake up the prisoner, hand him a piece of cake—and then you vanish . . . You don't have to see the prisoner grind his teeth when the rusty key turns back in the lock, when his face darkens, his air grows foul, his breathing spasmodic, when he tears out his hair and his flesh—and if he can still weep, he sheds bitter tears on his moldy, mouse-bitten crust of bran bread. . . .

Wake up the gloomy, drowsy, yearning heart of a Jewish wife, create a sweet, romantic atmosphere, kindle a new, wild, unfamiliar or long-forgotten emotion, kiss her and then—goodbye! Nail the door shut! Let her life be sour and bitter! . . . We've gulped down so much venom, rancor, hatred that when we're offered bread with salt, we're certain it's poisoned. Let the hand tremble with mercy, let tears of compassion gather in the eyes, let solace emerge on the lips. It's hard to believe. We too are infected, we too may be doomed. . . .

Meanwhile Polniewski had found his matches, and I reluctantly took a cigarette from him. We smoked, the coach filled up with blue smoke rings. I stared at them, followed them with my eyes, and thought to myself: "The good and the bad don't last any longer than smoke!"

"That's how we met," my Christian neighbor went on, "but we never developed a close friendship."

"Why not?" I asked in surprise.

"We continued looking at one another from a distance like the best of friends, but she couldn't come to us, and we couldn't go to her.

"That's all she'd 've needed! Our shtetl is profoundly devout. Aside from the barber-surgeon and the young tailor for women, all the Jewish men wear the traditional caftan. Except for that, I myself don't know what held us back. But that's not the issue. You see, I suffered the worst possible blow that a man can endure: my wife got very sick. Day after day I watched her dying, and there was no chance of recovery. She needed to go to Italy, but the pharmacy was bringing in very little, barely enough to feed us. As you know, even when a person is wasting away, he's still very hopeful, he doesn't believe he's really ill.

"You have to choke back your sorrow, bury it deep down in your heart. Your heart bleeds, but you have to smile and keep from frowning. Every bit of you dies every second, and you have to make plans together for the coming year, plans to expand the house, buy a piano."

His voice broke. "I don't have the strength to tell you everything and relive all those horrible moments . . . However, my misfortune brought me together with that Jewish woman, and we grew closer."

Lukowa appeared in the distance.

"We've got only a few minutes, but I can tell you that miserable as that woman was, she nevertheless had so much feeling, so much compassion for other people—I've never met anyone like her. And her emotions were so simple, natural, and unpretentious. She never budged from Maria's bedside. She got her husband to lend me money at a low interest rate. She was our nurse, our housekeeper, our cook, our staunchest friend. And when Maria died, it was harder to comfort our friend than me.

"By now I was convinced that hatred between nations is unnatural. But things are bad in the world. More ardent, more passionate, more miserable people try to protest, but the dishonest writers, the manipulative politicians blame all problems on the Jews. I very clearly saw that Jews aren't our enemies and that we can all live in peace."

Lukowa drew closer and closer, and I was afraid of the ending. Interrupting him, I asked: "What became of the Jewish woman?"

"I have no idea. I buried my wife, sold the pharmacy, said a tearful goodbye to the Jewish woman—and that was that! Today I live in Lukowa, and I'm no better off."

"Listen, what's the name of the shtetl you used to live in?"

"Konskevole."

"Was that woman tall and pale?"

"Yes!"

"Slender?"

"Yes! Do you know her?" he asked joyfully.

"Does she have a mole on the left side of her nose?"

Janek laughed. "A mole? What are you talking about?"

Perhaps I mixed it up. I asked: "Was the mole on the right side of her nose?"

"What kind of mole? What are you saying?"

"Maybe you didn't notice. Is her husband very pale?"

"Yes."

"Is his name Khaim?"

"I don't think so, or maybe it is. God only knows!"

"Is her name Khana?"

"Not at all. It's Sorre. I'm certain of that. It's Sorre! I used to call her Sarychna in Polish. I certainly wouldn't forget her name!"

I was a fool. Is there only one Jewish wife suffering that kind of existence?

Cabalists (Hebrew, *1891;* Yiddish, *1894*)

IN BAD TIMES even religious studying (which, as we Jews say, is the best merchandise) goes downhill.

At the Lashtshiv Yeshiva, the only people left were the director, Yankel the rebbe, and a single pupil, Lemekh (which also means "good-for-nothing" in Yiddish).

The rebbe was an old, scraggy man with a long, disheveled beard and old, snuffed eyes. His beloved pupil was young, equally scraggy, but tall and pale, with curly black sidelocks, feverish lips, a pointed, trembling Adam's apple, and black, burning eyes with dark circles around them.

Both men were in rags, no shirts, and with chests exposed. The yeshiva director could barely trudge along in a pair of peasant boots, while the cobbled shoes kept slipping off his pupil's naked feet.

That was all that remained of the famous yeshiva!

The impoverished shtetl kept sending them less and less food, inviting them to fewer and fewer meals. So the poor pupils had taken to their heels. But Yankl wanted to die here, and his pupil would place the potsherds on the corpse's eyes.

At times both suffered from hunger. If you don't eat much, you don't sleep much. And if you never sleep and never eat, you get—a hankering for the Cabala.

Make up your mind already! If you're gonna stay up all night and fast all day, you might as well get some use out of it! After all, starvation and mortification will open the doors to the world of secrets, spirits, and angels.

And so, they had been studying Cabala for a while.

And now they were sitting at the long table—just the two of them. For everyone else it was after lunch, for them it was before breakfast. But they were used to it. The yeshiva director was talking with glazed eyes; the pupil sat and listened with his head propped on both hands.

"This," said the rebbe, "has many levels. One man knows a bit of the melody, another knows half, still another knows the whole melody. Our rebbe—God rest his soul—knew the entire melody, plus an extra part! But I," he added dismally, "I was worthy of knowing only a teensy bit—this much." He measured the very tip of his bony finger. Then he went on:

"Some melodies require words—that's a very low level. There's a higher level—the kind of melody that sings itself, completely without words, a pure melody! But this melody still requires a voice, and lips to pass through. And lips, you understand, are material things. Now the voice may be of a nobler matter—but it's matter all the same! So fine, let's say that the voice is on the borderline between spirit and matter. Now be that as it may: the melody that's heard through a voice, that relies on the lips, is not yet pure, not fully pure, not genuinely spiritual! . . .

"The true melody sings itself without a voice. It sings itself inside you, in the heart, in the innards! And that is the actual meaning of King David's words [Psalms 35:10]: 'All my bones shall say, Lord, who is like unto Thee?' The melody must sing itself in the very marrow of your bones, that's where it has to be—the highest worship of God Blessed Be

He! That's not the melody of a flesh-and-blood creature, it wasn't composed by a human being! It's part of the melody with which God created the world; it's part of the soul that He endowed it with.

"That's what the heavenly hosts sing and that's what the rebbe sang (God rest his soul!)!"

The lesson was interrupted by a disheveled youth with a rope around his loins—a porter. He walked into the study house, put a bowl of grits and a chunk of bread on the table next to the rebbe, and said in a crude voice: "Tevel sends food to the yeshiva director!" He then turned around and, while leaving, added: "I'll come back for the bowl!"

Shaken from the celestial harmony by the porter's crude voice, the rebbe struggled to his feet and, dragging along his big boots, he trudged over to the washstand. On the way he kept talking, though with less ardor, and his pupil, staying in his place, gazed after him, his ears perked, his eyes dreamy and burning.

"However," said Yankl in a dismal voice, "I am not even privileged to know which level it's on, through what heavenly gate it passes. You see," he added with a smile. "I do know the necessary mortifications and numerological combinations, and perhaps I'll even reveal them to you today!"

The pupil's eyes almost popped out of his head. He kept his mouth open, eager to catch each word. But the rebbe paused. He washed and dried his hands, murmuring the blessing. Then he trudged back to the table and, with quivering lips, he recited the blessing over the bread.

His scrawny hands trembling, he lifted the bowl of grits. The warm steam shrouded his bony face. Then he put down the bowl, picked up the spoon in his right hand, and warmed his left hand on the bowl, while his tongue mashed the first bit of salted bread between his toothless gums.

After warming his face with his hands, he furrowed his brow, pursed his lean, blue lips, and started blowing. The pupil's eyes were glued to his teacher. And when the rebbe's trembling mouth approached the first spoonful of grits, something snapped in the pupil: he buried his face in his hands and crumpled together.

Several minutes later another boy walked in, carrying another bowl of grits and bread. "Yoysef sends breakfast for the pupil!" But the pupil didn't remove his hands from his face.

The rebbe put down his spoon and trudged over to his pupil. For a while he gazed at him with pride and love; then he wrapped his hand in his coattail and touched his pupil's shoulder. "You've been brought food," he wakened him with a friendly voice.

Slowly and sadly his pupil removed his hands from his face. And his face was paler, and his eyes, with their dark circles, burned more wildly. "I know, rebbe," he answered. "But I don't wish to eat today."

"Your fourth day of fasting?" the rebbe asked in surprise. "And without me?" he added reproachfully.

"It's a different kind of fast," the pupil replied. "It's a penitential fast."

"What are you talking about? You doing a penitential fast?"

"Yes, rebbe! A penitential fast . . . A moment ago, when you started eating, a sinful thought flashed through my mind . . . I broke the ninth commandment: 'Thou shalt not covet.'"

VERY LATE THAT same night, the pupil awakened the rebbe. They slept on facing benches in the study room.

"Rebbe! Rebbe!" the pupil cried in a feeble voice.

"What is it?" The rebbe woke up, terrified.

"I was just on the highest level!"

"What do you mean?" the rebbe asked drowsily.

"Something sang inside me!"

The rebbe sat up: "What do you mean? What do you mean?"

"I don't understand it myself, rebbe," the pupil replied in an even feebler voice. "I couldn't sleep, so I concentrated fully on your words. I absolutely had to know the melody. And I felt so miserable about not knowing the melody that I started crying. Everything was crying in me, all parts of me were crying in front of the good Lord!

"Meanwhile I was making the numerological combinations that you gave me . . . A miraculous thing: I wasn't reciting with my mouth, it was something inside me . . . all on its own! Suddenly, everything grew bright. I closed my eyes, and everything was bright, very bright, dazzling!"

"Go on!" The rebbe leaned toward him.

"The light made me feel so good, so airy . . . I felt so weightless, as if I could fly . . ."

"Go on! Go on!"

"I was cheerful, lively, full of laughter . . . Nothing stirred in my face, not even my lips—yet I was laughing . . . And I laughed so merrily, so heartily, so joyfully!"

"Go on! Go on! Yes, full of joy!"

"Then something hummed inside me, hummed like the beginning of a melody."

The rebbe leaped up from his bench and was instantly with his pupil: "Keep going! Keep going!"

"Then I heard a singing inside me!"

"What did you feel? What? What? Tell me!"

"I felt as if all my senses were blocked and closed, and something inside me was singing . . . Singing as it should be—completely without words, just like that . . ."

"How? How?"

"No, I can't . . . I knew it a second ago. Then the singing turned into . . . Turned into . . ."

"Turned into what? What?"

"A kind of playing . . . As if—forgive me for mentioning it in the same breath!—as if a fiddle were playing inside me, or as if Yoyne the fiddler were playing Sabbath hymns . . . at the rebbe's table! But the playing was finer, more delicate, more spiritual! And all of it without a voice, without the slightest trace of a voice—sheer spirituality!"

"You're so fortunate! So fortunate! So fortunate!"

"Now everything's gone!" the pupil said sadly. "My senses have opened up again. And I'm so tired, so tired, sooo tired! So that . . . Rebbe!" he suddenly yelled, clutching his heart. "Rebbe! I'm dying, let me confess my sins! They've come for me! The heavenly hosts need a little singer! An angel with white wings has come for me! Rebbe! Rebbe! Hear, O Israel! Hear . . . O . . . Is. . . ."

* * *

EVERY LAST JEW in the shtetl wished for such a death. But it was too little for the rebbe.

"After fasting just a few more days," sighed the rebbe, "he would have died an easy death—with the kiss of God!"

Stories *(1903)*

"SHE'S COMING TODAY," he thought to himself as he strolled along the banks of the Vistula.

And in his thoughts everything came alive: He was sitting on his bed in the dark, waiting. At every sound on the stairs, his heart began pounding, and he was surprised: Why? Was he in love with her?

There she was! Her light, buoyant steps. He stood up and lit the small table lamp. Meanwhile she paused at the door, catching her breath—those arduous stairs. She fixed her hair and peeped through the keyhole. Then, almost inaudibly, she tapped her finger on the door.

"Please come in," he said in Polish. And she opened the door and called out on the threshold: "Will you tell me a story?"

If not, she'd leave.

She didn't like *him*, she would say. In fact, she was scared of all Jews. But she loved his stories.

They had met accidentally in Warsaw's Saxon Garden, during a heavy downpour. She'd been standing under a tree, in a white blouse and without galoshes. The tree had barely protected her from the rain, and she had been peering through the sparse branches, peering up at the sky, frightened and desperate. He had walked over to her with his umbrella and offered his assistance. She had refused. He had pleaded sincerely and earnestly; she had given in and let him escort her. She had explained: There were so many bad people in the world! But his voice aroused her confidence. Encouraged, he had held out his arm. She had hesitantly slipped her arm into his and given him her address.

Walking several blocks (he'd had no money for a cab), he had learned that she was a seamstress (it was true, her fingers were full of pricks), and she had learned that he was a writer. Did he write poems? No, little stories. Ah, she loved stories. He could tell her his stories. Might he visit her? No, she had no father, and her mother was nasty. The girl's voice trembled slightly. That was all she needed, a visit from a stranger and—she gave him a sidelong glance, then finished wickedly and with a blush—a Jew, to boot.

"How do you know I'm a Jew?"

She could tell: his eyes, his hair, his accent, and finally his nose—ha ha ha! Her voice was altogether childlike, but there were creases in her forehead.

In the summer they would meet in the Saxon Garden. In the winter, she—though seldom—would drop in on him to hear a story. She would first leave a note with the janitor in the morning. Today he had gotten such a note. Her written Polish bristled with mistakes, but it was so childlike and sincere.

"Jew, prepare a beautiful story, a cheerful story about a princess. Life is so sad. And you mustn't touch me. It's not you I'm after. You're so ugly. If you touch me, I'll scream and run away. Do you hear?"

But he knew how to soften her: make the story sad. The prince and the princess encountered danger. The lovers were driven apart because of a terrible intrigue by treacherous people . . . If he wanted to, he threw the princess into a foreign dungeon and took the prince to a gallows. A false accusation. The listener then knelt before him, grabbed his hands, stroked his face, begged for mercy for the unfortunates. And for a kiss on his lips he did away with the danger and led the prince and the princess to the wedding canopy amid pomp and music.

Why did he do it? What good was her kiss?

He was sorry, and yet there was something that brought them together: they both yearned for happiness . . . Both had none and both wanted to delude themselves, at least for a while.

Two lost souls. Once he asked her: "Does your mother ever hit you?"

She blanched, and tears came to her eyes. "Don't ask. Just keep telling me your stories."

He stroked her brown hair and went on.

But today, walking along the river, he had no story to tell. His thoughts were unclear and unsteady, like the dark water dashing against the bank and ebbing, and his thoughts drifted up like the patchy fog.

What was tugging at his heart?

It dawned on him that he hadn't eaten all day.

There was some sort of hustle and bustle in his lodgings, and all at once a golden sun appeared, and he jumped out of bed and went outdoors without first having tea. The streets were likewise unusually tumultuous. The devil only knew why everyone was in such a hurry. He got poked in the ribs a few times. He barely made it down to the Vistula, where he usually strolled every morning. Now he felt faint. He touched his vest pocket. He had some change, so he went to the restaurant where he normally ate after his stroll. There he sat down at the window facing the Vistula.

The restaurant was empty at this time of day. The redheaded girl was dozing at the bar. His arrival woke her up, she greeted him drowsily, served him his order, and dozed off again. While eating, he mused that he had to have a story about a princess. She had to be sleeping on some mountain. A wizard or a witch was guarding her. Today the storyteller would put a serpent at her feet. The listener already had enough sleeping princesses. The serpent would make quite an impact. He thought about placing the princess on an extra-high mountain. He had never seen a high mountain. But he would tell her: "High, high . . ." And she would raise her dreamy eyes, and they would follow his finger aloft. Further down, at the feet of the princess, he would circle the mountain with a cloud. The cloud lingered there for an entire year. For beauty's sake, he would give the cloud a rosy lining. A summer day. There would be a burning edge. Down in the valley no one ever saw the princess, she was hidden by the cloud. That must be sorcery too. By contrast, the sky above the princess was forever clear. She lay between the cloud and the sky, and was guarded by the serpent!

He finished his meal. He would definitely find a prince on the way back. Meanwhile he had to pay his check. The redhead was asleep. He wanted to wake her up—in his usual way: make little pellets of bread and pitch them at her long nose. He would hit the mark one time in twenty, and she always woke up, terrified. "The gentleman constantly plays pranks!" she would say, irritated. "What did you have?" He would smile amiably. Tell her what he had had, and pay.

But today he couldn't pull it off. He threw and threw and he missed each time. Meanwhile he searched for a prince.

He pinched off another lump of bread and kneaded it, he made little pellets and forgot to aim. The prince was walking. He walked through forest after forest. And a crow he had once saved from certain death told him the secret of the princess . . . And the crow flew ahead, showing him the way. But he wouldn't let the prince reach his goal so quickly. For right after the story the listener would hurry away, and the storyteller would remain alone, alone with his unsteady nerves and fragmentary thoughts . . . He would send a wolf after the prince—he would kill the wolf. Next—a stream. He would uproot a tree, throw it on the water, and float across. Next he would put a mountain in the prince's way. So the crow would carry him on her wings—no, an eagle, the crow's uncle, would do it. Next he would simply get hungry. Banality must always intrude . . . A traveling prince can easily starve to death. The crow would fly ahead, looking for food. But they were very far from the nearest village. A long time wore by, and the crow didn't return. The sun was blazing; the prince was out in the open fields. He was languishing. If at least wheat or rye was growing here, then he, though a prince, would tear off a few stalks. But the only things growing here were bitter herbs, and the crow had warned him before flying away: "Do not touch them. These herbs are poisonous." The mountain where the princess was lying was close by, and the wizards had deliberately sown the poison herbs in order to kill anyone seeking her, and indeed, very many seekers had perished here . . .

And it was hard, very hard to wait for the crow. The prince was dying of hunger. His eyes were burning. Then a peasant girl walked by, holding a small loaf of bread. Fresh bread. The aroma filled the prince's nostrils . . .

"Peasant girl," he called feebly, "give me a little piece of bread."

"Pay me!" she tersely replied.

"I don't have any money . . ."

"No money, no food."

"I am a prince. I'll pay you as soon as I come home!"

"Look for the wind in the field . . . A debt written on water."

"I'm dying of hunger!"

"So what? Better you than me!" She walked a few steps, then came back. "You know what? I like you. Agree to marry me, and I'll give you some bread."

"I can't marry you, I'm in love with the princess!"

"Don't you want to eat?"

"I'm hungry!"

"Marry me and you'll eat your fill!"

The peasant girl dug in her heels—the prince, tortured by hunger, had to give in. He swore eternal fidelity to her. At that instant a hare scurried past. He caught it so it could be a witness. Then he grabbed a piece of bread and followed her to her village.

The redhead opened one eye and shut it, and the story went on:

By the time the crow returned, the prince was gone. The fresh bread had disagreed with him, and he lay sick in the village. When he recovered, he married the peasant girl. The prince couldn't plow or sow or reap; but he could read and write, so he became the village teacher. Their life together was peaceful. His wife would lovingly say, "Darling," and he would smile foolishly. But he kept the princess in his heart. Anything was possible! His wife operated the landowner's thresher and she could have an accident . . . He would watch for it . . . Of course he mustn't say anything aloud. And perhaps he didn't even know what he was thinking. The hope lurked silently in some dark nook of his heart, and he kept the secret to himself.

However, his wife didn't have an accident. Quite the contrary: she grew stronger and healthier each day; but he didn't. He grew old prematurely, either from the bad peasant fare or from longing, and when he realized that his beard was gray, his eyesight dim, and his forehead wrinkled, he tearfully revealed the secret of the princess to his pupils. They burst out laughing: the teacher had lost his mind! And yet . . .

He noticed that the light had changed: it was dark now. He glanced out the window; the weather had turned completely. A wet snow was falling. He felt a twinge in his heart. He quickly snatched a bread pellet, aimed it, and hit the target. The redhead woke up.

"Come on over, redhead. I'll tell you a story . . ."

"Who needs it!"

"A beautiful story, about peasant boys looking for a princess . . ."

"Stupid stuff!"

"It's not stupid. The princess is sleeping on a flowerbed on a mountain peak. The village teacher told them to look for her . . ."

"How wonderful!"

"Of course it's wonderful. The princess is beautiful, virtuous, intelligent."

"That's enough fun. Now pay your check and get going!"

"Certainly, certainly, but the children made wooden swords and wooden spears—"

The redhead yawned.

"Are you tired, redhead?"

"What awful weather!" Then she angrily added: "On a Jewish holiday the weather has to be bad."

"What holiday is today?"

"Their Easter . . ."

Passover! That explained the hustle and bustle in his building, the tumult in the street. He paid and hurried off.

He burst out laughing. The spirit of his grandfather or great-grandfather was lurking somewhere in his soul! The longing that overwhelmed him. Every man goes about with spirits in his heart.

The first year after he left home, he nearly went crazy with homesickness for the seder. The family he was lodging with had gone away for Passover, and he remained alone in all the rooms. Having nowhere to go, he turned in early, but he forgot to pull down the shades and the moonlight woke him up. His heart was pounding. For a long time he lay there, not knowing where he was. Then he remembered. Suddenly he leaped up, yanked the sheet off the bed, and wrapped it around himself like the traditional robe that his father wore at the seder. He then ran around the apartment, yelling out the entire Hagadah.

The following year, he was so afraid of getting homesick that he pawned a coat and went home for Passover. On the way he kept repeating that he would surrender, surrender completely. And he actually attended synagogue with his father, then took part in the seder, leaning on a cushion and asking the Four Questions. But when he came to the acronyms for the Ten Plagues visited upon the Egyptians, he exploded. He refused to dip his finger in the wine goblet. His tearful mother could barely calm him down. Then, when he was supposed to recite the Ten Plagues in detail, he hit the ceiling. And on the third day of Passover, he left without saying goodbye to his father. His mother was waiting outside the town.

He went up the stone steps from the riverbank.

He was sorry.

Why had he offended them?

He had said: "For the sake of Truth." Is there such a thing as Truth?

"We young people," he thought to himself, "have to suffer. Our sorrow is creative. It drives us to do new work, to create new forms. The sorrow of the older generation is barren, it pours itself out in useless tears if it doesn't turn to stone in the heart."

He walked through Krasinsky Park. The dairy stand was deserted. Latecomers were hurrying across the garden. He came to the small hillock that faced Nalewki Boulevard. He felt tired. But it was too early to go home. She wouldn't be coming for another hour. He sat down on a bench in front of the hillock.

The bottom part of the hillock was bare, virtually peeled. Further up there was grass with scattered thornbushes . . . Eventually small flowers would be growing on them. "I think so—a sapling on the side, a tree, lots of trees." Birds could sing in their branches. She loved to hear birds singing. She said that when she'd heard them singing a couple of times while she was sewing in her village, she couldn't hold back her tears . . . Her soul had been weeping, and so sweetly.

At times she spoke so wondrously . . . tugging on the long, white nails of her pricked fingers in her even whiter teeth, and she had such curious locutions . . . "Soul tears" . . . Where did she get them? Could she too be a hidden princess? Her mother—the laundress at the washtub—was no mother, she was a witch, guarding her, warding off any prince who might come and awaken her . . .

But none would come. The prince had to be pure of any sin . . .

A nanny with four little boys came hurrying by. The boys ran over to the hillock. Boys armed with swords and spears. "They're climbing the mountain!" The nanny was angry: it was time to go home. The parents would be worried. Today was Passover . . . The children paid no attention, they kept climbing. "To the princess."

"The four pupils of the village teacher . . ."

The sun was setting.

The rattling was heard in the garden. There was still time.

He closed his eyes and watched the boys, armed with wooden weapons, climb up toward the princess . . . A cloud hovered between the climbers and the princess, they didn't see her, but they believed in her. Should he let them reach her?

But now she tore through the cloud—the witch, riding toward them on a broomstick. She grabbed one boy by the arm. "Where are you going, little boy?"

"To the princess!"

"What do you want with the princess?"

"I want to awaken her!"

"Why?"

"I want to marry her!"

"Why do you want to marry her?"

"She's good, the teacher told us. She's smart and sweet. The teacher knows!"

"Of course. And you like good and sweet things?"

"Of course I do. Mama says I've got a sweet tooth!"

"In that case, my child, why climb the mountain on a wild-goose chase and get tired. You're an aristocratic child, after all."

"What business is it of yours?"

"I'm your aunt, you silly thing. Don't you recognize me? I'll give you very good things."

She waved her hand and, presto, a small basket fell down at the boy's feet as if from the sky. The basket was filled with very good and sweet things: almonds in their yellow husks, pressed figs, strands of raisins, fiery red oranges, chocolate, and things that the boy couldn't even name. And he cried out in sheer delight and knelt down in front of the sweet little basket.

Meanwhile the other three boys had gone further. All at once, they encountered a wizard, an old man with white eyebrows and a white beard, and with big, blue spectacles on his nose.

He heard the creaking of the park gates. He opened his eyes. The nanny and her charges had already disappeared. He hurried out. And the story kept weaving against the deserted boulevard.

The old man stopped one of the three children. "Where are you going, little boy?"

"I'm going to awaken the princess. I want to marry her."

"How come?"

"The teacher praises her—she's so smart."

"Do you want her to make you smart?"

"Of course! A person has to be smart. If you're smart, you can get respect and money."

"Really? You're already a little smart. But if you want to be smart, you can do it without the princess."

"How?"

"It's very simple. Here!" And the old man produced something from his breast pocket and handed it to the almost smart child: a fine, illustrated book, gilt-edged and bound in white leather. "Here," said the old man. "Sit down and read it. If you read just one page, you'll be smarter than your parents. If you read two pages, you'll be smarter than the entire village. And if you read half the book, you'll be as smart as three professors!"

The boy grabbed the book, sat down, and began reading.

Meanwhile the other two boys kept climbing. Suddenly the serpent blocked their path. One boy ran off, the other was paralyzed with fear.

However, the serpent caressed the boy's lips and asked him in a sincere and serpentine voice: "Where are you going, little boy?"

He said he was going to the princess, he wanted to awaken her and marry her because the teacher had said that she was so beautiful!

"Do you like beauty?"

"Of course!"

"Well, then, come with me. Do you see that crystal palace over there? It is inhabited by dolls. They wear velvet clothes and white silk slippers . . . They have cherry red lips and diamond eyes . . . You can choose any doll you like. The palace is nearby and the road is straight."

And the boy went ahead of the serpent.

"But what about the fourth boy? What do we do with him? Should we let him reach his goal? Too bad! He'll be the unhappiest one. He won't even have something he regrets, something he can reproach himself for."

Still, he had to do it for her sake! He would keep going, he would awaken her . . . And then?

Then—a wedding . . . Music, dancing . . . A honeymoon trip . . . A stroll through airborne gardens . . .

She'd close her eyes in sheer ecstasy. Deeply moved, she would let him draw her over, and he would seat her on his lap and wonder why he did it. She would put her hot cheek against his—he would feel her pure breath and he would kiss her and reproach himself: "Swine!" She would jump away, pale, frightened, weeping in a quavering voice, and he would throw himself at her feet and beg her to forgive him. In his heart he would call himself "Clown!" And she would not forgive him immediately, she would stay away for a long time . . .

Someone bumped into him, almost making him slip on the wet sidewalk.

THE STAIRS WERE dark, one kerosene lamp for two landings. He had no matches. His neighbor had a flashlight—but he wasn't envious: the neighbor had an ugly wife. Whenever he passed their door, he shuddered at the thought of running into her. Ugliness is the greatest sin. And if the lady of the house was ugly, then the maid was even uglier. Brrr . . . He shuddered—both cold and disgusted. He had forgotten that his spats were ragged, that he had stepped in puddles. At night he would cough and perhaps run a fever. The doctor would warn him again about consumption. "Serves me right!" Let him be consumptive—so long as something happened.

He halted, terror-stricken. In the corner of the stairs an image appeared, woven out of a pale glow.

A Passover table—a snow white tablecloth—red beakers—shiny plates—old but glittering silverware—candles in three pairs of old, high, wrought-silver holders . . . His mother standing there, blessing the candles. He saw her from behind, her gaunt back was trembling . . . She was crying—crying because of him! Where was he now?

"It's starting!" Angry at himself, he took several steps at once. He was grieved that he had run away. His mother would turn to him . . . What did she look like now? She had written him that she couldn't get a full night's sleep . . . She had recently sent him four pairs of socks: "Look, they'll keep your feet warm."

He opened his door with a trembling hand. "Oh, so what!" He shook off the snow. "I'm only human."

With firm steps he entered the room; with a firm hand he turned on the light. He was slightly afraid of the dark. "What poverty!"—he was looking around his room. Cobwebs. But on the other hand (he smiled bitterly), not a crumb of leavened bread. Someone would invite him tomorrow. He would go to the Reform temple . . . A teacher he knew . . .

He sat down on the bed. The lamp smoked a little. He wanted to go and fix it, but then he forgot why he was getting to his feet. He sat back down. Pulled in his legs. His eyes alighted on the small piece of mirror on the wall. He took it down, gazed at his reflection.

"I'm nowhere as ugly as she says!" He smiled and rehung the mirror. "A bit dark like a Tartar. But what eyes . . ."

He was proud of his eyes. Few women could resist them. Whenever he got intimate with a woman, she would kiss his eyes. His lips were too fleshy . . . They kissed too hastily, they were too dangerous. Back home—

He interrupted his own thoughts: What was going on at home? Had his father returned from synagogue? He could hear his father's "Happy Holiday!"—his mother's response. It didn't sound cheerful. Alas—only one child, and he wasn't joining them.

He tried to focus on something else. But without success. The seder haunted him. This was already his fifth year away from home!

He stood up and went over to the window. The wet courtyard cast trembling reflections of the small holiday flames in the windows. Latecomers hurried across. He didn't want to raise his eyes to the windows. But he had to. He slowly raised them. Halfway up, his eyes fixed on something. Another image:

A seder table. A large seder table—crystal and golden tableware. Was it a family? No. It had to be several families. Women in strange clothes—very old costumes! Men in white, embroidered ruffs under their traditional robes . . . Ornamental gold crowns on their prayer shawls . . . Gold-embroidered skullcaps . . . Where were they in the service? A soft recitative . . .

Suddenly there was a knock at the front door.

The men, the women shivered—paralyzed with fear. A young girl fainted—a young woman threw her arms around her husband, choking back her tears . . . What could it be?

"Open up in the name of the law!" someone shouted from outside.

A blood libel! It had to be that!

"Hurry! Look under the table!" cried the eldest man. They bent down. Horrible! A dead child! They all froze.

The front door burst. And the eldest commanded in a firm if stifled voice: "Cut him into pieces!"

They did that. The front door was broken down. Heavy footsteps—the clanging of weapons.

"Everyone put a piece on your plate." They did that. The visitors were already knocking on the dining-room door.

"Eat it!"

The dead child was eaten up. The door was broken down—policemen and soldiers. They searched the apartment. A wild-goose chase. They left angrily. And all the people in the apartment shouted furiously:

"Pour out Thy wrath upon the heathen that know Thee not!" [Jeremiah 10:25]

It began to drizzle. The image blurred.

"Not for me," he mused. "It would take a stronger pen."

He stretched out on the bed and closed his eyes.

"I've lost my strength." He was drained by his moods.

There were easier images.

The seder in the home of the Baal-Shem-Tov . . . No, not in his home. In the home of a rich Jew, who received a sudden visit from the Baal-Shem-Tov. The host was an anti-Hasid, and the Baal-Shem-Tov had to beg him for an invitation. He had done so in synagogue, after prayers.

"I want to help you," he had said.

The rich man had then asked his rabbi if one could invite a Hasid to the seder, include him for the blessings. The rabbi told him not to offend the Hasid.

And the Baal-Shem-Tov sat at the Passover table. They were in the midst of reading the Hagadah when suddenly the Baal-Shem-Tov ordered them to bring in one more Hagadah text plus a Passover robe, a belt, and a skullcap. They laughed. He exclaimed: "Do what I say!" First he had barely begged his way in, and now he was giving orders. The host looked—the Baal-Shem-Tov's eyes were ablaze. The host was terrified. They brought the items the guest had demanded and they put them in front of him. The Baal-Shem-Tov then kicked something under the table and said: "Jantek, stand up!" And a pale young Christian boy emerged from under the table. Not a drop of blood in his face. A corpse with closed eyes. His throat was cut! They all gaped in fright.

"Jantek, open your eyes!" Jantek obeyed. "Jantek, put on the robe, the belt, and the skullcap." Jantek obeyed. The Baal-Shem-Tov handed him a chair. Jantek sat down in the robe and the skullcap. "Open the Hagadah and recite. Everyone—recite!" The trembling Jews recited the text and Jantek did so too.

Suddenly the door was broken down. The surprise visitors were looking for the dead body that had been planted there. But after searching high and low and finding nothing, they left empty-handed, disgruntled . . .

The Baal-Shem-Tov then said to the resurrected corpse: "Jantek, close your eyes. Go to the Jewish graveyard, and bury yourself. Since you had the privilege of wearing a Jewish prayer robe and reciting Hebrew, you have the right to be buried in a Jewish graveyard. And when you meet Father Abraham, tell him—"

A soft tapping on the door.

"Come in."

"Do you have a story for me?"

"All kinds, all kinds. . . ."

Hear, O Israel, or The Bassist (1920)

ONE BRIGHT AND beautiful day, a boy, a poor adolescent, showed up in Tomashov, a small Polish shtetl on the Austrian border. Nobody knew where he was from, nobody knew where he spent his days and nights.

From time to time he would ask for food, and as it is written: "To him who holdeth out his hand will be given." Especially since he asked for nothing: not a kopek, not food, just a piece of dry bread. As it is written: "One doth not inquire into motives of him who asketh for food." You don't question him about the whys and wherefores—every living soul has the right to eat.

However, the townsfolk noticed that there was something strange about him. His eyes seemed to be staring far, far away and never saw what was happening under his nose. He continuously moved his earlobes (the way other people move their eyebrows) as if he were catching voices from the air—even though the air was as still as before the blowing of the ram's horn at Rosh Hashanah. And because he could see and hear so far, his mind was always elsewhere. If anyone addressed him, he would tremble as if he'd been awoken from the beyond. And when replying, he'd say either yes or no; otherwise he'd get all tangled up in his words as if in a net, beads of sweat would emerge on his forehead, and he'd be unable to untangle himself.

If ever a householder or a housewife hired the boy as a messenger, he'd vanish for several days, then return with a scrambled reply—not because he was lazy, Heaven preserve us, but because his mind was elsewhere.

"Did you find So-and-So?" (the person he'd been sent to).

"Not till today."

"And before today?"

It turned out that he'd come upon a tiny mouse en route. The mouse had squealed, probably because it couldn't find its way home. Next something or other, a bird, had called to him from above, and he'd followed it, so he hadn't reached his destination till today. And he'd been given a message but he'd failed to grasp it or he'd forgotten it—and so it came out topsy-turvy. He smiled naively and held out his scraggy hand for a piece of bread—he hadn't eaten all those days.

In a poor shtetl, where there's no business during the long, idle summer days, the householders sit at their windows, yawning, peering at the marketplace, waiting for something to happen, something to latch on to. If a householder then spotted the poor boy, the stranger, he'd call him over. The boy had nothing to do, all the flies had been caught by now. So the householder could interrogate him.

"C'mon in, boy."

The boy merely shook his head: he didn't want to go in.

"Why not?"

"Just because," said the boy.

The householder laughed and didn't hesitate. He stepped out and sat down on the stoop.

"What's your name, boy?"

"What's my name?" he repeated. "Avrom! I think it's Avrom. Yes—Avrom!"

"You're not sure?"

He was never sure. How could anyone be sure? A lot of things only appeared to be what they were.

The householder gasped for air: "What about your last name?"

The boy didn't have the foggiest notion. He naively asked whether a person needed a last name.

The householder said: "Certainly, there are lots of Avroms, we might confuse them with one another."

"So what?"

"And whose boy are you?"

"My father's."

"And what's your father's name?"

"His name is Father."

"And where does your father live?"

"The same place yours lives!" And he pointed at the sky.

"A fine thing!" The householder smiled and then asked: "And you don't have any other father?"

"No."

"Do you have a mother?"

"Do I need one?"

The householder roared with laughter. And the boy asked: "May I leave?"

"Soon, soon!" said the householder in sheer delight. "And where do you come from, you sage?"

"From the village."

"And what's the name of the village? Where's it located?"

The boy didn't know.

"Is it far from here?"

He had walked and walked and walked . . .

And the boy kept reiterating the word "walked" until his lips got dry, and so he finished: "And walked."

"How many days and how many nights?"

He hadn't counted.

It then occurred to the householder to ask: "Do you know how to pray?"

Pray? The householder had to explain the word "pray," and he talked a blue streak until the boy finally caught on: "praying" meant "talking to Father."

"Yes, yes!" said the householder, laughing so hard that he practically had kittens.

The boy knew "Hear, O Israel, the Lord our God, the Lord is one."

"Who taught it to you?"

The boy said that while going from the village to the forest and into the town, he'd encountered a very old man. The old man had told the boy who his father was and had taught him how to talk to his father and recite "Hear, O Israel." And even though the boy didn't know what he was saying to his father, the old man told him that his father understood and enjoyed the boy's words.

"And when do you talk to your father?"

"Twice a day." And he played while talking.

"You play? What do you play?"

"Whatever." In the village countryside he'd played on reeds and blades of grass. Then he'd been taught how to carve a wooden fife, so he'd play on the wooden fife. In the town he'd been given a clay fife, so he played it . . .

"What if you were given, say, a fiddle?"

The boy's eyes shone: oh, how badly he wanted a fiddle, like the ones played by the town musicians! Especially a huge, huge instrument that you carried on a strap. Oh, how he'd play . . .

"You fool!" The town householder continued his mock interrogation. "Maybe someone'll buy you an instrument like that. But first show what you can do!"

The boy took out a clay fife from his shirt and he fifed. As he fifed, a tumult developed in the sky. Flocks of birds came flying and they circled overhead, and the boy looked up at them and smiled and then put back his fife.

But the householder hadn't looked up and hadn't seen anything. When his wife heard the fife, she came out, followed by the maid. Two couples approached the window and peered out. The householder wanted to flaunt his keen mind, so he went on questioning the boy.

"And what did you live on in the forest?"

He'd lived on mushrooms.

Hah, he must've been a mushroom maven! "And what did you live on in the village?"

Whatever he'd been given.

"Who gave you something?"

A peasant, a peasant woman, even the priest and the innkeeper . . .

"And what did they give you?" The householder held his breath: now the cat would come out of the bag.

The boy answered naively that they had given him cabbage and borsht and meat and bread. But he'd eaten only the bread—he'd thrown the rest of the food to the birds.

"And why only bread?"

Bread was all he liked, he disliked any other food.

The old man in the forest had also asked him what he ate, and when the boy had told him that all he ate was bread, the old man had said that was why he liked the boy, and that was why he taught him how to talk to his father. And the boy liked the old man so much, so much . . . And he recited "Hear, O Israel" so earnestly because the old man had told him to . . .

The householder wouldn't let the boy go; he asked him: "What if the old man told you to steal?"

He'd steal.

"What if he told you to murder someone."

He'd murder . . . But the old man wouldn't tell him to do that, he was a good person.

"But just suppose he came and told you to kill someone."

He'd kill.

"And you wouldn't be afraid of your father?"

Why should he be afraid?

"Afraid he'd punish you."

This was the first time the boy's face lit up in a dazzling smile: "You're fooling. A father doesn't punish."

Meanwhile who should come knocking but the synagogue knocker (the man who summons Jews to synagogue)! So the householder dashed off to recite the late afternoon prayer and to boast about his clever interrogation.

Naturally this would have provided grist for the shtetl's mill, but something else happened. The congregation had a band: two fiddles, a flute, a clarinet, and cymbals (or potlids, as they are known in other places)—plus, as is customary, a bass fiddle. It was a poor band, which played at Jewish pre-wedding celebrations and weddings, earned a few kopeks at Purim and Hanukkah, and sometimes, if other bands were busy, these klezmers would perform at a nobleman's ball—though they didn't display any great skill.

Now this is what happened. One winter dawn, the musicians were trudging home from a ball. They had drunk a lot but, as was customary, hadn't been allowed to eat, except perhaps a piece of bread. They straggled along, half singing or humming, half swearing; and the bassist, lugging the heaviest instrument, plodded after them, barely managing to pull his feet out of the snow. He was old and weak. He called and hollered and begged his friends not to run out on him. But it didn't make a dent. The musicians were too scattered, and they were snapping and cursing; in the middle of the road they were arguing about money. And, as we have said, they were a bit tipsy . . .

Meanwhile the weather began turning: a stiff wind was blowing, and new snow was falling. The musicians walked faster; partly sobered, they hurried on and, arriving in town, each man headed for his cottage and collapsed on his bed like a corpse. But they didn't get much sleep: the bassist hadn't shown up, and his wife was rushing around to all the klezmers, shouting and yanking them out of their beds: "Where's my husband? Where's my husband?"

Their minds numb with liquor and fatigue, they came to and they grasped what she was screaming. They shuddered. Then they dashed out to look for the bassist. You couldn't tell the hills from the dales, everything was covered with a smooth, white shroud, with fresh, innocent snow. It was a wild-goose chase . . .

They returned empty-handed. But they clung to the hope that the bassist had had enough sense to seek refuge in some hamlet.

A day passed and then another. The frost had receded, the snow was half-melted. It was Friday. In honor of the Sabbath, the Jews went to the bathhouse. They asked one another about the bassist, but nobody had any news. Suddenly a peasant drove into the middle of the marketplace: he was carrying the frozen bassist. The Jews grabbed the body and buried it before the housewives could bless the Sabbath candles. They were afraid the Gentile officials might dissect and inspect the corpse. They barely managed to finish up before the Sabbath began.

The next morning the widow refused to let them take out the Torah at the synagogue. The bassist had left her with five tiny children. When the Sabbath was over, a meeting was held, and the klezmers were summoned. Since the congregation had no funds, it wanted them to play without a bass and pay the widow. Not on your life! A band without a bass is no band. It might work at Jewish festivities, if the community agreed, but without a bass fiddle no aristocrat would stick out a leg for dancing. The rabbi argued that a Jewish life was more valuable than a band and an aristocratic dance. To which the klezmers retorted that please don't be offended but the rabbi was no expert in music. Whereupon someone yelled: "What chutzpah!"

Meanwhile the householder, our interrogator, who had so intelligently cross-examined the boy, pounded on the table: "Shush, gentlemen!" He had an idea. He knew a boy who wanted a bass and could definitely play. He could marry the widow. The wolf would be sated, and the goat would be saved, and it wouldn't cost the community a plugged kopek.

The householder may have been joking, but the congregation and the rabbi on one side and the klezmers on the other side grabbed at the suggestion like a drowning man snatching at a straw. The widow likewise agreed, so did the boy Avrom, and the wedding took place that very same month. That was how Avrom unexpectedly got a wife, five little children, and a bass fiddle with a bow all at the same time.

He lived harmoniously with his wife, never setting foot inside the house and spending each night outside the door. He wandered about for days on end unless there was some celebration in the shtetl or the nobleman was hosting a ball. If Avrom got hungry, he'd tap on the window, and his wife would hand him a piece of bread. Then he'd vanish until he felt hungry again. When neighbors asked her about the peaceful household, she'd laugh: It couldn't be better! What did an old woman want anyhow? He never ate, he never drank, he never said an unkind word to her, and she herself would always settle accounts with the musicians, who paid her his share . . . So what did she lack?

Nor did Avrom seem to lack anything either. Initially he'd had problems with the other musicians because he never caught on to their melody, he played solely for himself. And if they stopped playing, Avrom would nonchalantly keep going as if accompanying some other band playing far, far away, a band that no one heard but him. In time, however, the klezmers got used to him. They knew what to do in an aristocrat's home: when the music was about to end, one of the klezmers would grab Avrom's bow. But at Jewish weddings, they deliberately let him continue, and the spectators laughed their heads off, especially during the wedding banquet.

The community was certainly content with Avrom. He would sit there, quiet and tidy, his face toward the wall, his back toward the audience, to avoid seeing any women. Nor would he eat anything at a wedding: he always brought along his own piece of bread, and people didn't even spot him eating. Furthermore they used him for an entire year as the synagogue knocker. For Avrom was in the habit of reciting "Hear, O Israel" three times a day on the bass: at sunrise, at sundown, and at midnight prayers . . . At dawn and at dusk he would do it in a meadow by the river, and at midnight in the marketplace. The notes from his bass would flow through the silent midnight and pass into the houses through doors and windows, pass into all hearts. And the sounds were filled with so much earnest devotion and simplicity that if someone failed to hear the synagogue knocker, then he'd be awakened by the bass, by its "boo-boo-boo-boooo." And Jews would willy-nilly arise from their beds for worship, light candles, and hurry to synagogue for the midnight prayer.

At an aristocratic ball a nobleman would sometimes leave his noblewoman in mid-dance, hurry over to Avrom, and tear out a sidelock because he hadn't joined in the melody correctly. At Jewish festivities the spectators would laugh; and for an entire year they would sigh as they got out of bed at midnight: "The poor guy's a simpleton. But there's something about his playing, there must be something. . . ."

Others said: "A mute soul, poor thing. He wants to talk to the Creator but he has no other language."

* * *

ONE DAY A major wedding took place in Tomashov—the kind of wedding that comes once in a blue moon. Imagine! The leader of the Lublin community and the Rabbi of Cracow would become in-laws, and Tomashov lay dead center between them!

Now the Lublin leader wanted to delight the Cracow rabbi with a wedding that would show the rabbi just whom he was dealing with. To pay for the wedding, the Lublin leader had a keg of ducats rolled up from the cellar. He then sent caterers to Tomashov to prepare a royal feast, as befits

a wealthy leader of the Lublin congregation when he has the honor of
becoming in-laws with the Rabbi of Cracow.

Arriving in Tomashov, the first thing the caterers did was seek out a
location for the wedding. After all, there would be guests from Lublin,
from Cracow—and even Tomashov! There would be rich men, prominent householders, Jews with eminent ancestries, scholars, rabbis, judges.
And three bands would be playing: one from Lublin, one from
Cracow—and the Tomashov klezmers would also do them proud.

On the edge of town, right next to the Vistula, there was a huge shed,
where commercial lumber was dried over the winter and then floated
downstream to Danzig. The caterers rented the shed, which was the size
of Noah's ark. They covered the outside with all sorts of paintings and
decorated the inside like a tabernacle, with expensive curtains and
embroideries. Then, from one corner of the ark to the other, they set up
separate tables for men and for women, and they lined the walls with
sconces and Japanese lanterns. The ark had enough space for forty
minyans, and there were special doors for women, for waiters, for
klezmers, while the enormous central entrance, with the ornamental
Torah crown painted high overhead, was reserved for the Rabbi of
Cracow and other prestigious Jews.

The wedding day came. Guests were still pouring in and they were put
up at the homes of various congregants, who considered it the greatest
honor to give up their finest chambers. And when the company sat down
for the banquet, the candles blazed in large Sabbath holders on the tables
and in sconces and Japanese lanterns on the walls, and the women's ear-
rings and headbands and bodices glittered and glistened. And the shed
was filled with the radiance of the Torah: Talmudists from Cracow and
Lublin, with Tomashov Talmudists in the middle, and the Rabbi of
Cracow at their head.

Strings of waiters carried enormous platters of fish, and the clattering
of silver knives and forks mingled with the cheerful murmuring of the
women at their own tables. But all the noise was drowned out by a Torah
debate at the table of the Rabbi of Cracow. Then the music broke in—a
freylekhs (a merry, marchlike tune). Three bands at once, the music reverberated, the candle flames on the tables and on the walls trembled with
joy. The Rabbi of Cracow leaned back and listened in sheer delight: after
all, he was a big music maven.

Next, the bands launched into a lively Walachian tune, virtually drifting across, barely hinting at a transition . . . The music flowed and glided. A Cracow fiddle played, it practically spoke words, opened all hearts and poured in . . . And the three bands accompanied the fiddle softly and neatly. It sounded like a rolling river, a Vistula gushing and shimmering, silently rocking, swishing, quivering in honor of the bride and groom, in honor of the Rabbi of Cracow and the cherished guests. And above the water, a bird—wonder of wonders!—flew around and around, singing, and its song was so sweet, so enchanting and mournful—a hushed lament, another lament, and, in their midst, cheerful, joyful, sublime cries, and then another lament—it was a happy occasion, but in our Exile we mustn't forget that the Shekhina, the Divine Presence, is also in Exile—and then another shout of delight.

This was a unique wedding, with a gathering of Talmudic scholars headed by the Rabbi of Cracow (a Lublin cantor had arranged the music), and the bands were suddenly swept away, all the instruments resounded—louder and louder, higher and higher, as if the delighted musicians were ascending from level to level, and there was noise and dancing and brightness—

And suddenly everything halted, as if all strings and all instruments had burst. It was still, but in the stillness the company heard: "Boo-boo-boooo . . ." Only Avrom kept playing, all eyes were on his back. Everyone was still, no one so much as batted an eyelash. Avrom's hand was the only thing that was moving, as it drew the bow back and forth: "Boo-boo-boo-boooo."

The other klezmers were playing a trick on him to entertain the audience, but this time it didn't work. . . .

The klezmers peered at the spectators, waiting for them to burst out laughing. Instead, the spectators gazed at Avrom and then at the Rabbi of Cracow. Nobody would laugh in his presence. Their faces wrinkled, their lips twisted, their eyes smirked. But the spectators were looking at the rabbi, waiting, and the rabbi sat there, leaning back, with his shtreymel [fur hat] on the arm of his easy chair. His eyelids were down: goodness, had the Rabbi of Cracow dozed off?

And the bassist kept playing: "Boo-boo-boo-boooo . . ."

The crowd grew uneasy.

All eyes then shifted from the rabbi to the central entrance. A commotion, footsteps could be heard outside. Waiters hurried over, pushed back the door, and yelled in terror: "No, no! There's going to be a paupers' dinner for you . . ."

Apparently the beggars wanted to come in. The Rabbi of Cracow opened his eyes and was about to say something: perhaps he wanted to let in the poor or whatever.

At that same instant an old man appeared in the doorway. With his tattered hat and his disheveled gray beard and sidelocks, he looked like an ordinary beggar. But his eyes and his gestures showed royal grandeur. The awestruck caterers cringed willy-nilly before his gaze. He waved his hand, and they made way for him willy-nilly. The old man, in the most beggarly rags, yet with regal eyes and gestures, came in, followed by a flock of paupers; he halted in the center of the shed, and the entire flock of paupers halted behind him. The wedding guests were stunned and speechless, and so was the Rabbi of Cracow. But Avrom went on with what he was doing; and people could see that his bent back was trembling as he drew the bow to and fro. And the bass moaned poignantly and earnestly: "Boo-boo-boooo-booo . . ."

After a while the old king in beggar's clothes opened his lips. The guests at the front tables leaned forward, while those in back jumped up soundlessly and stood on tiptoe. They were drawn to his lips like a magnet, they hung on his every word.

And the old man uttered a single word: "Midnight!"

Then he went on: "Rabbi of Cracow, Avrom performs for midnight prayers, and if you don't believe me, Rabbi of Cracow, you will hear for yourself. You will have the privilege of hearing Avrom play for midnight prayers, and the only reason why you and the leader of the Lublin congregation are becoming in-laws is that Tomashov lies halfway between your homes. And for your sake everyone will hear it, but not as you will! After all, you're a music maven . . ."

"Boo-boo-boooo-booo," Avrom played for himself—and the audience was mute, dazed, spellbound. And the old beggar lifted his right hand and motioned toward the ceiling, and the ceiling split in two, half to the right, half to the left, like the wings of a tabernacle.

And the sky appeared, the sparkling, starry heavens. And the moon silently drifted across the opening, silently sailed away. And once it was gone, the old beggar waved his hand again, and now the heavens split, and endless, quivering, self-generated light soared across the universe, and in the throbbing radiance the wedding guests could hear singing and playing: the good Lord and His heavenly hosts were reciting the midnight prayer. Angelic choirs were singing, angelic bands were playing, and they were all performing the same melody, and Avrom's bass blended with it and drifted with it in the hymn of brightness, which swayed and rolled and throbbed in the heights—

And the wedding guests shuddered . . .

The old man motioned a third time, and the heavens closed. The music stopped, and tiny stars twinkled and floated and trembled in sad and silent delight.

The old man motioned yet again, and the two halves of the roof of the shed connected and fused together. The audience sat petrified, scarcely breathing, and they again heard Avrom's bass: "Boo-boo-boooo-boooo . . ."

All at once the bow and the bass slipped from Avrom's hands. He stood up, turned to the wedding company, and began: "Hear, O Israel!" And he recited, using the same melody that he had played in Heaven. And when he was done, he fainted. The old man caught him as he fell.

"Take him to the hospital!" he ordered the waiters, who then carried him away.

"Rabbi of Cracow," the old man said. "You haven't come to a wedding, you've come to a funeral. Avrom has been called to the good Lord and His angelic hosts, they needed a bass." And the old man vanished with all the beggars.

And so that was that.

Two days later Avrom the bassist died in the synagogue. His funeral was attended by the Rabbi of Cracow and all the wedding guests.

They say that the old man was the renowned scholar Leyb Soress.

It's quite possible.

S. ANSKY
(SHLOYME-ZANVL RAPOPORT)
(*1863–1920*)

*B*est known today for his supernatural drama The Dybbuk, Ansky (born in Vitebsk, Russia, the birthplace of Marc Chagall) kept reinventing himself. He started out in Hebrew, soon shifted to Yiddish, then Russian dur-

ing a thoroughly assimilationist phase. Next, profoundly affected by Russia's lethal antisemitism, he returned to Yiddish — but wrote a vast number of stories, poems, memoirs, novellas, and so on, in Yiddish and/or Russian. An avid folklorist who imitated, in Yiddish, the Russian return to the "folk" as the wellspring of the national soul, Ansky headed the famous Jewish Ethnographic Expedition (1912–14), which scoured Eastern Europe for Yiddish folk tales, poems, songs — until the outbreak of the Great War. Ansky died in 1920, a few short months before The Dybbuk *had its world premiere in Warsaw.*

Mendel the Turk *(1892)*

1

DURING SUMMER AND autumn of 1877, when the Russo-Turkish War was going full blast, I found myself in a far-flung Lithuanian shtetl, supporting myself as a tutor and leading a very solitary life.

One day around noon, as I was coming home from a lesson, an amazing sight made me halt at my door. In the courtyard, an unfamiliar young man, wearing a yarmulke but no coat, was peering through my window: with his upper body inside my room and his arms propped on the table, he was absorbed in the Russian newspaper lying there. The instant I stopped, he trembled, raised his head, quickly pulled himself out through the window, and stood there, confused and very embarrassed.

"Oh! No hard feelings, please!" he stammered with a guilty smile. "I didn't touch anything of yours, God forbid! I happened to be passing when I noticed your gazette in the distance, and some word caught my eye. I couldn't resist temptation, I went over . . . The window was open . . ."

I calmed his fears and handed him the newspaper.

"Thank you! Thank you so much!" he replied cordially but not yet fully at ease.

"Something aroused my interest . . . something important!"

"What aroused your interest? What were you reading?"

"What aroused my interest? How can a gazette arouse interest today? What does a gazette write about today? War, politics, of course!"

"You're interested in politics?"

The young man gave me a probing look, then lowered his eyes. "Well," he murmured vaguely, then promptly added: "What do you mean—am I interested in politics? Who isn't interested in politics? In normal periods, of course, it's not worth your time dealing with politics. But today, things are different, there's a war on. Today, politics are crucial!"

The young man intrigued me, so I invited him in.

"With the greatest of pleasure," he answered, "but this isn't a good time. The kids are about to return from lunch."

Now it dawned on me who he was. Across the courtyard from my window there was an old hovel serving as a heder, and from morning till late at night it emitted a hubbub of children's voices. I often saw skinny, raggedy little boys scurrying around the courtyard like frightened mice. But I never got to see the teacher. I don't know why, but I pictured him as an old man with a nasty face. However, the melámed standing in front of me was a young man in his late twenties, with noble features and a short black beard. The deep, pensive gaze of his large black eyes lent him a very serious expression. His velvet skullcap, long curly sidelocks, and short beard made a fitting black frame for his face.

After musing a while, he said: "If you're not busy tonight, I'll drop by. I must admit, for some time now I've been longing to converse with someone like you . . . Please, tell me, do you read the gazette every day, every single day?"

"Yes, every day."

He eyed me with a look of profound envy. "Of course!" he sighed. "That kind of reading makes sense, it's got substance."

"And you? What do you read?"

"What do I read? It's catch-as-catch-can—I don't read. Every other week I happen to get hold of that Hebrew newspaper *Halevanon*. Does that give you an inkling? The rest of the time I have to content myself with the bulletins posted around the marketplace, with chance information from some individual or other, with my own conclusions . . . But that's not a reliable foundation."

I invited him over for that same evening.

2

LATE AT NIGHT, the teacher came by, apparently straight from the heder. He now wore a long coat and a velvet cap.

"Good evening," he greeted me, halting in the middle of the room without extending his hand.

I offered him a chair. He sat down slowly, then peered around the room, his eyes finally resting on my bookcase. It instantly struck him that these were not traditional Jewish texts, and he gaped at them in amazement.

"Are they all goyish books?"

"Pretty much. They're Russian, German . . ."

"Really?" he asked vaguely. "What's in them? What do they deal with? Goyish laws and grammar?"

Not surprised by his question, I explained that books in Russian and other languages were not just about laws and grammar, they also contained stories, poems, science, philosophy.

"No kidding! Filosoofya? There are also Russian books about filosoofya?" Flabbergasted, he eyed the bookcase more attentively.

But then, more at ease, he smirked derisively. "Let's see now—filosoofya. What's it all about? The fact is that if those books contain any profound wisdom and inquiry, they must get them from the Talmud or Moses Maimonides." His tone of voice changed. "Look, politics is a totally different matter, politics is a special kind of wisdom, it's got its own rules and it deals with all the nations in the world. Take Bismarck, for instance— what a mind! A genius! Naturally, Disraeli is grander and deeper. But that's no surprise—after all, he's a Jew."

For a while he sat there in silence, pensively gazing at the glass of tea that I had placed before him, apparently without his noticing it. "Listen," he exclaimed suddenly and resolutely, pushing away the tea as if desiring a clear space in front of him. "I want to discuss the war with you, but discuss it in a proper way."

He sat more firmly on his chair, propped both arms on the table, and began speaking slowly and earnestly:

"Everything in the world has its foundation, its substance, its sublime essence. In order to correctly understand an object, you have to find its foundation, its essence. Needless to say, a war also has its essence, which everything revolves around. Please explain to me, and I'll listen, I'm all ears: What is the substance, the essence of the current war?"

But then he suddenly held up his hands as if to delay my response. "Wait a bit, please! Wait! I said, 'essence,' but first we have to clarify just what an 'essence' is, what it's all about. What does the 'essence of the current war' mean? It means the reason why the war broke out and why it's being fought. And just what does the reason consist of? Now we come to the heart of the matter. Pick up a newspaper, any newspaper at all, and start reading. What will you find? You'll find a single word: 'Slavs.' The 'Russian' is something like a holy redeemer, he's sacrificing his own life and spilling torrents of blood in order to free his brothers, the Slavs, from the Turkish yoke.

"So I say: All well and good! What more could you ask for? But then scoundrels, insolent reprobates claim that the Russian doesn't give a tinker's damn about the Slavs. So then what is he after? It's quite simple: the Russian wants to grab the two bodies of water flanking Turkey, the Bosphorus and the Dardanelles, and saving the Slavs is merely a pretext . . .

"And do you think that's all? Not in the least. You see, there's a third viewpoint that says neither the Russian nor the Turk has the foggiest clue. The British are pulling the wool over their eyes, they've sicced them on each other, making them tear each other to shreds like fighting cocks. And once the Russian and the Turk are both lying on the ground, exhausted, England will come and finish the job. So I ask you: Which side do we believe? Naturally, you have to have a good head on your shoulders. In order to choose the right path, you have to be objective. And here we've come to my request."

"Namely?"

"It's quite simple. Tell me the history of the relationship between the Russian and the Turk from the very start . . ."

"From the very start." That wasn't as simple as my guest assumed, for he was unaware that Russia had already fought several wars with Turkey. Nevertheless I told him about the kind of state that Turkey used to be, about the way its interests had clashed with Russia's interests, and so on. My guest listened very hard. He sat there, keeping his head down, but now and then giving me a sharp and serious look. When I was done, he sat motionless for a while as if thoroughly digesting my words.

"I must tell you, you've opened my eyes," he murmured with a tranquil face but with inner rapture. "You've opened my eyes. Now I can see the world unfolding before me, I can see a path, a road, I can think of brand-new theories . . ."

Suddenly he calmed down entirely, took a lump of sugar, dipped it in the cold tea, recited a blessing, and started drinking. Upon draining the glass, he thanked me and resumed our conversation.

"As I've gathered from your comments, you favor the theory that the Russian is concerned about his Slavs—the Bulgarians and the Serbians. Frankly, I don't find it plausible, it sounds pretty farfetched, I can't imagine the Russian risking his neck for anyone!"

Before I could reply, he quickly added: "But never mind, let's assume you're right for argument's sake. It's not essential. If I catch your drift, you feel that the Russian will win. Now that, you see, is one thing I don't get. Do you truly believe the Russian will prevail?"

"I'm convinced of it."

"Well, listen to what I have to say," the teacher stated in a very self-assured voice. "Naturally you know all the ins and outs of war and politics a lot, a whole lot better than I do. Well, call me stupid, call me arrogant, but I can assure you—the Turk will be the winner! It's as clear as day for me. Just wait a week, and another week, and you'll see that I'm right."

And, as if fearing that I might prove him wrong, he swiftly buttoned his coat, said goodnight, and left. At the door he scornfully threw in, almost to himself: "Oh sure! The Russian will be the winner! And against whom? The Turk!"

3

THE NEXT MORNING, when I was having my tea, who should walk in but my landlord, one of those unfortunate husbands who spend their lives being henpecked. An old, scraggy Jew, quiet and downhearted, he felt like a stranger in his own home. His third wife, who was much younger than he, was the energetic and despotic ruler of the household. Whenever she went shopping, she first locked everything up, not because of her husband but because of the maid (the couple had no children). Often the wife forgot to leave a few lumps of sugar for her husband's tea and sometimes she neglected to give him a couple of kopeks for his snuff, without which he would flop around like a slaughtered goose. She was usually surly with him and she yelled at him just the way she yelled at the maid. It was only on the Sabbath and on holy days that she showed him any respect at all since she needed him to recite the blessing over the wine, usher out the Sabbath, and what not.

All day long the old man wandered through the house or went to the synagogue. Initially he avoided me or, if our paths crossed, he hurriedly moved aside with a frightened look. But little by little he got used to me and he even started coming to my room to sip a glass of tea or borrow a few kopeks for snuff. However, he would diplomatically conceal the reason for his visit; before requesting a loan, he would ask me all sorts of circuitous questions: Had I already paid the rent, a ruble — information that concerned him only theoretically, since his wife kept him away from all financial matters.

This time he again used a pretext to drop in on me: he was looking for the copper ladle. I was fully aware that what he really wanted was a glass of tea. The ladle was presumably in its normal place, on the water barrel in the kitchen; but he needed some kind of excuse. I shrugged silently to indicate that I didn't know the whereabouts of the ladle either, and then I casually said: "Would you care to join me in a glass of tea, Mr. Ber?"

"Huh? What?" the old man mumbled, pretending he hadn't heard me.

"I asked whether you'd care to join me just this once for a glass of tea in my room."

"Tea?" the old man responded in surprise, as if he'd only just noticed that I was sitting by the samovar. "No! Thank you!" he categorically refused. "I don't feel like it! I just had some tea!"

That was part of the ritual. Now I had to urge him, coax him.

"I can never get you to have a glass of tea with me." I was hurt. "Isn't my tea kosher enough, God forbid?"

"What are you talking about? You're a God-fearing Jew!" the old man cried in alarm. "Not kosher? What do you mean, not kosher? What's gotten into you? I simply don't feel like it, I just had some tea. But, if you insist, pour me a glass, and I'll force myself . . ."

Everything went according to ritual, and the old man sat down at the table.

"Tell me, Mr. Ber," I asked, "what sort of person is the young man who teaches across the courtyard?"

"Who? Mendel the Turk?" my guest blurted out, putting down his glass and gaping at me. "What do you mean, what sort of person? He's just an ordinary person, a young man. A pious young man, a Hasid . . . A scholar . . . If you will, even a sage, a savant."

"What did you call him, the Turk? Is that some kind of family name?"

"Family, shmamily!" The old man grinned. It's his nickname at the synagogue. So what can I tell you? That's what I call him too."

"How did he get that nickname?"

"How did he get that nickname? A good question. He simply got it. You know Russia's at war with Turkey. You do read the gazette. Well, Mendel's sided with the Turk, so he's nicknamed 'the Turk.' If he'd sided with the Russian, he'd 've been nicknamed 'the Russian.' What could be simpler?"

The old man gave me a triumphant look and went back to his tea. When I refilled his glass, he pushed it aside and continued: "You talk about Mendel and what sort of person he is. The whole town's in an uproar! What are people talking about? Mendel. Actually, they're not talking, they're feuding, they're fighting like mad, they're at war—and about what? About 'the Turk' and 'the Russian.'"

"Where are they fighting?" I asked.

The old man gawked at me in disbelief. "What do you mean, where? At the synagogue, of course. Where else can you fight? Now you're a modern Jew, you don't go to synagogue every shabbes. But if you went, you'd get a load of what's going on there. Everyone, I tell you, everyone, young and old—they're all in a rage! When the 'Turks' and the 'Russians' get together, a whole new war erupts, a real war, like the one fought by King Gog of Magog."

The old man talked so heatedly about the war between the Jewish Turks and the Jewish Russians that I wanted to know which side he was on. "What about you, Mr. Ber?" I asked. "Are you rooting for the Turks or for the Russians?"

"Me?" He was startled. "Ha ha! Do you honestly imagine I'd get mixed up in stuff like that? What kind of moron do you think I am? I just listen to them prattle—it goes in one ear and out the other."

"C'mon, Mr. Ber, don't change the subject! Tell me the truth," I insisted. I saw that he wanted to express his opinion but was too embarrassed.

The old man abruptly grew somber and, leaning toward me, he whispered in a mysterious tone of voice: "Ishmael [the Muslim] is a savage, but he's better than Esau." Then, as if confiding a state secret, he added: "If Ishmael wins, the Messiah is sure to come."

"You're a God-fearing Jew, Mr. Ber!" I exclaimed. "But what does the Messiah have to do with Ishmael's victory?"

"Ha! Don't interrogate me!" he shouted. "They're talking, Jews are talking. They know what they're talking about . . . Jews are talking—I don't mean you or me . . ."

He began murmuring incoherently. I didn't interfere, and he gradually calmed down.

"Last night," I said, "your 'Mendel the Turk' came by here."

"Mendel? In your room?" He eyed me incredulously as though asking about my connection with the pious Hasidic teacher. But he caught himself, like someone having a brilliant idea.

"Aha! Well, well! I get it!" he said mysteriously, wagging his long, bony finger. "You know what I think? He didn't come for your sake, he was after the gazette you've been reading. Yes, yes, yes! Count on it! I know him!" Then the old man shouted ecstatically: "Ah! What a clever guy! He never misses a trick! He's Mendel the Turk all right!"

I confirmed the old man's assumption: "That's precisely why he visited me."

"So you see I'm no fool! Well, it's obvious. Why else would he visit you? He wants to grill you about what it says in the newspaper! And that's how he pieces together his politics, bit by bit . . . Ha ha! Like a hen! She picks and picks, groat by groat, until her craw is full—and then she lays an egg!" The old man ended his embryological revelation.

"And you know what?" he continued in a mysterious tone. "I'm afraid to say it out loud, but ever since Mendel got excited about politics, he seems less diligent about the holy texts. Why, he used to spend all night studying at the synagogue. But now . . . Now he wanders around hunting for a newspaper . . . Yes! Yes! Yes!" the old man ended fervently, and he even pushed me slightly as if declaring that he would brook no excuses. Since I had no intention of defending Mendel against that terrible suspicion, the old man calmed down and started on his third glass of tea.

Upon draining it, he thanked me and stood up. Suddenly his face was wreathed in twinkling smiles, and with childlike naïveté he said: "Ha ha! I have to confess, I was dying for a cup of tea. My missus went shopping and she forgot to leave me some sugar."

What a diplomat the old man was! He was practically a Bismarck or even a Disraeli!

4

THE FOLLOWING SABBATH I attended late afternoon prayers at the Great Synagogue in order to personally witness the war of Gog and Magog between the Jewish "Turks" and the Jewish "Russians."

It was twilight. Evening shadows were already gathering on the high walls of the synagogue, blurring all contours in an uncanny tableau. Several hundred men were standing and silently reciting the Eighteen Benedictions, rocking to and fro, murmuring softly. They were like a young grove swaying and rustling in the breeze. And the nebulous, mystical tones and sounds evoked memories of my long-past childhood.

I pictured the old synagogue in my native shtetl and the Sabbath twilights . . .

Late afternoon prayers are over, and the synagogue is growing darker and darker, eerier and eerier. The elderly Jews scatter through the synagogue. Dreamy and wistful, tranquil and content, with their hands behind their backs, they slowly shuffle back and forth, humming a Hasidic tune to themselves. Still absorbed in their thoughts, they sit down on the benches, and a conversation begins, as dreamy and eerie as the evening: one man tells a Hasidic tale, another describes an event, which takes on an eerie character. They all listen very attentively, and when the speaker is done, everyone remains hushed, spellbound, no one wants to break the enchanted silence.

Everyday life, with its bustling and worrying, is now very remote. Everyone feels mellow and dreamy. Imperceptibly they start humming the familiar melody to themselves, "Bim-bam-bom," each man putting in his own dream . . . But now someone hastily comes to, as if awakening from sleep, and heartily pleads: "Zorekh! Say something!"

The request is so warm and earnest that Zorekh wouldn't even think of refusing. Remaining in his seat, he softly croons a Hasidic air. He croons the traditional prayers of Rosh Hashanah and Yom Kippur. Gradually the singing grows louder, stronger as the worshipers join in one by one, and the old, small, low synagogue resounds on and on with the severe and splendid, the infinitely mournful pleading of the melodies of the Days of Awe.

Evening has set in. The synagogue is dark. A few stars are in the sky—and the singing doesn't stop. No one wants to start the evening prayer, which ushers in everyday life. No one is in any hurry to return to the everyday world with its prosaic anxieties.

Those are happy moments for the children, too. The twilight and the presence of their elders create a special mood, high spirits. Some boys quietly snuggle with their fathers, listening to their tales. Others form a close group and tell their own stories, which are just as fantastic and terrifying—stories about demons and highwaymen. The livelier boys take advantage of the darkness to play pranks. They play hide-and-seek, they make a "bomb" out of a twisted towel and throw it at the beadle or even at a congregant—whichever! For now, such mischief goes unpunished. "Boys will be boys, let 'em play!" Those are the thoughts of the mellow worshiper. And feeling a need to pour out his mellow mood on someone, he grabs a particularly mischievous boy, pulls him between his legs, and without even checking who his prisoner is and without interrupting the song, he paternally strokes the boy's head. The boy is amazed, dumbstruck by the stranger's unexpected tenderness. With a joyfully throbbing heart, a deeply blissful smile, the boy responds to the loving caresses, the warm affection, and the adult's hand moves more slowly, mildly, gently.

Unforgettable hours, unforgettable devotion! . . .

But here, in the Grand Synagogue, things were very different. The tempest of war had blasted its way in, destroying the hushed and dreamy tenderness of a Sabbath twilight.

5

FOLLOWING LATE AFTERNOON prayers, the men scattered throughout the synagogue, launching into animated and jittery discussions. Everybody was talking at once. Spirited yells resounded: "Shush! Quiet!" And the commotion gradually died down. At the center of the synagogue, a large group gathered around two or three men, who were speaking. The others, curious, jostling, cupping their ears with their hands, listened closely.

An elderly Jew of medium height, with broad shoulders, astute, gray eyes, and a trimmed, snuff-stained mustache, stood at the midpoint of the cluster, speaking with calm self-assurance. He gestured, while firmly holding a pinch of snuff between two fingers.

"C'mon! C'mon! What are you so worked up about? C'mon! So we didn't take Plevna! So what? Who says you have to win victory after victory in a war? If we didn't take Plevna this time, we'll take it a week from now."

"Mikhl," shouted a tall man with a red beard and a red neck. "You say the Russians'll take Plevna? Huh? Can you guarantee it? You're crazy! What are they gonna take it with? You've forgotten that the Russians have sacrificed half their army, trying to take Plevna."

"Just wait!" a skinny young man broke in, craning his long neck toward the group. "Why not ask the exact opposite? You ask, 'What'll the Russians take Plevna with?' And I ask, 'What'll the Turks hold on to it with?' You're forgetting that every Russian attack is costly for the Turks too."

"But that is the poioioint! Coooostly!" Those words, coming from the other side, were chanted in Talmudic singsong by a young man with a goatee. "No bullet will reach Pleeeevna. They can shoot where they like, they can shoot at the sky—it won't matter. And frooom Plevna—"

"You with the beard—shut your mouth and keep it shut!" yelled an older man. "Creep! He's gotta stick his nose in too. I'll smack you so hard you'll forget about all Plevnas!" The angry man was the goateed man's father.

The goateed son quickly slipped away.

"Have you ever seen such a creep? He has to stick his nose in too! He's an expert too. Plevna!" The father was beside himself.

"Well. And what about you, genius? Do you know what Plevna is?" The red-bearded man pounced on him. "Plevna is a rock fortress, the walls are vertical and they're three versts high. Halfway up there's a deep hollow space, a kind of nest, and that's where the city of Plevna is located. How do you think anyone's gonna reach it? Who's gonna take a fortress like that?"

"They'll take it all right!" exclaimed a fat man who had imperiously shoved his way into the group. His face had money written all over it, and he had a wide satin sash around his huge belly. "You jerk! What are you blabbing about? 'Fortress!' 'Hollow!' Your Plevna isn't worth a plugged kopek. You're all talk! Plevna-Shmevna!"

"I guess Khaim-Isser had a good Sabbath pudding today—that's why he's so bossy!" said an old man with an ironic smirk, a long gray beard, and intelligent eyes. "What does he need politics for? All he has to do is yell, kick—and he's the winner . . ."

"Well, and what about you?" cried Khaim-Isser loudly but less aggressively. "Where do you stand? Do you agree with them that Plevna won't be taken?"

"Huh? Where do I stand? I think that in order to discuss war, you have to know what it says in the papers. You can learn a thing or two from Mendel. Who knows more about politics? And all he does is sit on the side and recite psalms," the old man concluded, slightly ironic.

Mendel! Now I remembered him and I looked around. He sat a long way off, hunched over a Psalter, swiftly devouring the verses. At first you might have figured he was uninterested in what was going on in the synagogue. But on closer inspection I realized that he was like a hunter lurking in his lair, that he was following every single word.

By now, Mikhl, the man with the trimmed mustache, was at the center of the group. Loudly asserting himself, he spoke in a tone of bitter reproach:

"Honestly, as it says in the Bible, 'Eyes have they but they cannot see, ears have they but they cannot hear.' How can you fail to see, how can you fail to understand that the Turk has one foot in the grave? You keep harping on Plevna. Don't you realize that Plevna will be conquered in the end, if not by fire, then by hunger? Just have a good look. During the four or five months since the Russians crossed the Danube, they've stormed all the fortresses, captured tens of thousands of Turks, and marched halfway across Turkey—are all those things meaningless for you? What other signs and wonders do you need? A month ago you were cheering, 'The Shipka Pass! Suleiman Pasha! The great hero Suleiman Pasha!' But then it turned out that the real hero isn't Suleiman, it's General Gurko. Now you're cheering, 'Plevna! Osman Pasha!' And so what are you gonna be cheering when they march into Plevna. . .?"

"I won't have to cheer then! I'm cheering now!" yelled the man with the red beard. "I'm cheering that you're lying through your teeth! That's what I'm cheering!" He then dashed toward Mendel and rebuked him harshly: "Honestly, Mendel. It's a sin! What are you acting so stupid for? Why are you sitting on the side, reading psalms like an old lady? Come on over! C'mon! You can at least hear a man who's got the chutzpah to tell lies in a holy place."

"Mendel! Mendel! Come on!" The shouts rang from all sides. "You've read enough psalms!"

Mendel plainly did not much feel like joining the debate. Nevertheless he stood up, put away the Psalter, and called over a boy: "Velvel! Hurry to the marketplace and check whether a new bulletin has been posted."

The boy dashed off. Mendel slowly joined the group and turned to Mikhl with an ironic smirk. "I can hear you from far away, you've been raising a rumpus, uprooting mountains and devastating whole countries. In less than a minute you've ground the poor Turk into dust and scattered the dust over the seven seas."

"And you, miracleworker," Mikhl retorted, "have you come to gather the dust and knead it into a golem?" Then he struck a more earnest tone. "Well, tell me! Do you really believe that the Turk doesn't have one foot in the grave? You just don't understand—"

"C'mon already! What are you talking about?" Mendel broke in, bitterly agitated. "You claim that Plevna is surrounded. You have to be blind not to see that it's not Plevna that's surrounded—it's the entire Russian army." Mendel swiftly appealed to the congregants encircling them and hanging on his every word. "Do you want to know exactly how things stand? I'll make it clear to you. The entire Russian army and all its generals are now in Turkey between the Danube and Plevna. And Osman Pasha is sitting in Plevna with a hundred thousand soldiers who are blocking the Russian advance. Suleiman Pasha is on the left—"

"He was beaten by Gurko!" someone called out.

"Shh! Quiet!" Mikhl sternly shushed him.

"Suleiman Pasha is on the left with a powerful army, and Mohammed Ali is on the right with an even bigger army . . . Now listen carefully. The Russian army is beleaguered on three sides. It can't advance, it refuses to retreat. The summer is over, it's starting to rain. The Russian army is exhausted, starving, far from home, in a strange country. How is it all going to end?"

He looked quizzically at his audience, then went on, self-confident. "There are two possibilities. Either fresh Turkish reinforcements will surround the Russians, grab the Danube, and capture the entire Russian army and its generals. Or else Osman Pasha will form an alliance with Suleiman Pasha and Mohammed Ali, then they'll strike the Russians on all three sides, crush them, and kick them out of Turkey within two days."

Mendel's cogent speech and the clear picture he drew had a strong impact on his audience. Mikhl was heckled several times. He had been standing there, quiet and alert, his eyes glued to Mendel. "Are you done?" asked Mikhl.

"Done," Mendel replied curtly.

Mikhl was disappointed. "Too bad, too bad you were done so soon." He picked up the snuff box from the pulpit, tapped the box with two fingers, opened it, and took a large pinch. Then he closed the box and returned it to the pulpit, slowly and calmly. "Yes, it's too bad you were done so soon. You could've carried on a lot longer. You've kicked the Russians out of Turkey—that alone is worth something. But why did you stop? Why, for instance, didn't you bring the Turks to Russia? Why didn't you have them occupy a few Russian towns, say, Petersburg and Moscow? It wouldn't have been hard to do, would it, here in the synagogue?" He finished, laughing.

"The Turk swore an oath never to set foot on Russian soil!" someone jeered.

"My friend," Mendel turned to Mikhl calmly but with relentless irony. "You know the Turk is a brutal savage. If he had a heart, he'd be freeing other nations from the yokes of their oppressors. Don't worry, he'd certainly find somebody to free. Well, Poland, for example. Huh? Are you gonna tell me that Poland isn't suffering as much as Bulgaria? But what can we do with Ishmael, that savage? He feels no pity for anyone, he doesn't free anyone, and all he wants is to be left alone . . ."

Khaim-Issar piped up: "Are you saying you don't believe the Russian will free the Bulgarian from the Turkish yoke?"

"What do you mean, I don't believe?" Mendel eyed him in amazement. "Am I a heretic, God forbid? Do I refuse to believe that the Russians are going to free other nations? Who would be a more suitable redeemer than Russky the Thief? The role fits him like a glove."

There was resounding laughter.

"Well put!"

"Right on target!"

"Russky the Messiah!"

"Shush, I've heard these wisecracks," Mikhl shouted impatiently. "I'm fed up with them! Let me ask you: Why did the Russians start the war?"

"You want me to tell you, so I'll tell you," Mendel answered. "Russia and Turkey are eternal enemies. This isn't the first time they've fought each other. Russia has waged lots of wars with Turkey and captured lots of Turkish cities. The ultimate Russian goal is Constantinople. In short, Russia wants to wipe out the Turkish state and annex most of Turkey. . . ."

I listened carefully: Mendel was repeating almost verbatim everything I had told him about the relationship between Russia and Turkey.

Mikhl listened impatiently. But in the end, he lost his self-control and angrily yelled: "You moron! You idiot! Your comments are so stupid that they turn my stomach!" He swiftly faced the audience: "Listen, men! Russia occupies a territory of ten thousand versts by ten thousand—that's one sixth of the globe. Russia has treasures that no other country possesses. So how can you believe that Russia would spill torrents of blood just to grab a bit of the Turkish desert?"

"Gershen!" Mendel addressed an elderly man who looked wealthy. "They say you've got thirty thousand rubles to your name. Is that true?"

Gershen was thrown off-kilter by the unexpected question, especially because it touched on a delicate matter. But at the same time he was pleased that his wealth had been confirmed in public. Realizing that Mendel had not asked at random, but was about to score a point against Mikhl, Gershen stroked his beard and, with an arch smile, he answered leisurely: "Thirty thousand rubles, you say? Well, let me calculate . . . Let's assume it's true . . . What of it?"

"Yet you maintain your business all the same. Do you go to your shop every day? I've also heard that you've signed a huge contract to build some meat markets. Apparently you still don't have enough, you want more."

"And how!" exclaimed Gershen with a contented laugh.

"Did you hear that, Mikhl?" said Mendel, turning toward his opponent. "He says: 'I have little, I want more.' Do you know what 'more' means? 'More' means 'everything.' You say: 'One sixth of the globe.' And why not all six sixths? Haven't there been seven emperors starting with Nimrod? Not one of them, it seems, was satisfied with his share—not Nimrod, not Sennacherib, not Nebuchadnezzar, not Alexander the Great. And believe me, the Russian isn't satisfied either with his sixth of the globe. But if you like, I'll tell you that he's not really after the 'Turkish desert,' as you put it. He needs the Turkish seas, the Bosphorus and the Dardanelles."

"Are you saying the Russian is fighting the entire war purely for plunder and the Turk is a saint?" shouted a tall, scrawny man with an ascetic face and eyes blazing with anger. "What's really going on? Are you fooling yourself or do you take us for a pack of morons? What do you think we do? Sit behind the stove, know nothing, hear nothing about how the unhappy Bulgarians are suffering under the Turk—that savage, that barbarian!—may his name and remembrance be blotted out! The Turk destroys cities, burns down villages, slaughters thousands of people, rapes women . . . Your hair stands on end, the blood freezes in your veins when you hear about his atrocities! And now a bandit like you comes along, you side with the Turk and make him out to be an innocent lamb? You deserve to be drawn and quartered!"

"Only a robber, a killer could side with the Turk!" an agitated young man shouted. And jumping on a bench, he shouted hysterically across the entire synagogue: "Listen, everyone! As sure as I'm a Jew, as sure as today is Shabbes throughout the world, I swear to you that the instant the army starts recruiting again, I'm going to volunteer! Without any examination! I'll abandon my wife and children and go to war! And if I get killed, I'll be martyred for the greater glory of God!"

The hysterical shouting triggered a frenzy among all the congregants. It was as if a dam had burst. There was an indescribable hue and cry. Everyone was yelling. The "Russians" pounced on the "Turks," cursing and berating them. The "Turks" defended themselves, likewise cursing and screaming. Mendel tried to speak but they didn't let him.

It was late at night. The synagogue was dark. The pale moonlight, seeping in through the dusty windows, mournfully illuminated the grotesque rioting of dozens of agitated men. The beadle, a short, gloomy manikin, trudged from one congregant to the next, respectfully tugging at their coattails and repeating in a voice that begged for pity: "It's time for the evening prayer, it's time!"

But nobody paid him any heed. Who could think of praying at a time like this?

Suddenly the door flew open, and Velvl, whom Mendel had sent to the marketplace for the latest bulletins, came bursting in like a bomb. "A bulletin! A bulletin!" he shouted breathlessly.

The congregation instantly fell silent. Everyone turned to the messenger.

"Oh, a battle! . . . Lasted three days . . . Gurko . . ." Velvl could barely speak.

Mikhl pounced on him impatiently: "Talk! Did they take Plevna?"

"No! Plevna wasn't taken! . . . They took Hubniak and some other city! . . . Two thousand Russians killed! That's what it said: two thousand. And Turks — maybe ten times that number! The bulletin said: Countless!"

The news was shattering! Mendel, pale, wrought up, wide-eyed, devoured Velvl's every word. All at once Mendel stood up, glared at the congregants with passionate fury, and shouted hysterically: "Murderers! May the innocent blood fall on your heads!"

And he dashed out of the synagogue.

For several minutes a tense silence filled the synagogue. As if crushed by the weight of a terrible sin, the "Russians" and the "Turks" lowered their heads and scattered in all directions.

One man muttered to himself: "I don't see why he's the only one who's right. Who can tell who's more to blame?"

And as if in response to the tense mood, the mournful chanting of the weekday evening prayer rose from the pulpit: "And He, Merciful One, will forgive our sins and keep us from destruction . . ."

The "Three-Day Battle," which Velvl had learned about from the posted bulletins, ended with the Russian occupation of Gorni-Dubniak and Tellish. This meant that Plevna was totally blockaded and cut off from the rest of the Turkish army. Now, there was no one, aside from the Jewish "Turks," who didn't doubt that Osman Pasha had no choice but to surrender. The newspapers assured their readers that Plevna had no food left, so that the beleaguered army would have to capitulate. Everyone suspensefully waited for the fall of Plevna, which would bring peace or at least an armistice.

But things didn't move all that fast. Days wore by, weeks, the whole month of October—and Plevna still held out. And Osman Pasha repelled the most powerful Russian assault. The suspenseful waiting gradually turned into a doubting. Pessimistic voices were heard. Everyone started thinking of Plevna as an invincible fortress, and Osman Pasha acquired the reputation of a brilliant military leader.

6

AFTER HIS FIRST visit, Mendel dropped by from time to time, but now our conversations were brief and to the point. Noticing that I didn't root for the Turkish side and that I wasn't fervent about politics, he never debated with me. He merely asked me if there were any important items in the newspaper or if I could clear up some political issue for him.

Several days after the Russians took the fortress of Kars (November 6), Mendel walked in, uttering a dry "Good evening." He came over to me at my table and, glaring with cold, almost hostile eyes, he said with strained courtesy: "I've been told you're acquainted with a number of aristocrats in town. Could you get a Turkish gazette from any of them?"

"A Turkish gazette?" I was astonished. "What are you talking about? And why do you need it?"

"I need it . . ."

"Take off your coat, have a seat."

"No thank you, I don't have time," he replied coldly; then, with restrained impatience, he added: "How can I get a Turkish gazette?"

"I don't know what to tell you." I said. "What would a Turkish gazette be doing here? Who would have one?"

"What do you mean?" He was amazed. "There must be some local aristocrats who are interested in politics."

"Even so, why would they need a Turkish gazette?" I was still perplexed.

"At least to get the Turkish viewpoint!" he shouted, deeply agitated.

"Don't you understand?" I said. "It's impossible to get a Turkish newspaper here! And even if, for argument's sake, you could get one, who could read it here? Who knows Turkish?"

"What do you mean, Who knows Turkish?" He was amazed again. "I figured all the aristocrats know Turkish. I was sure you knew Turkish, too. I was told you know German and French, so I assumed you know Turkish." All at once he energetically yelled: "No! You can say what you like, but without a Turkish gazette, we'll never know the truth!"

"What truth? About what?"

"About Kars! 'The Russians have taken Kars!' Do you think the Russians pulled it off so easily? Maybe someone betrayed the Turks. Somebody helped the Russians—maybe the British . . . But I don't understand how Osman Pasha could have allowed it!"

"For God's sake, Mendel!" I exclaimed. "What are you talking about? Where is Kars and where is Plevna? They're at opposite ends of the Turkish empire! And besides, how could Osman Pasha have helped? He's completely beleaguered and he's stuck in Plevna."

"Huh! 'Beleaguered!' 'Stuck!'" Mendel repeated in annoyance. "What kind of drivel are you handing me? How do you know that Osman Pasha isn't beleaguering the Russian army and preventing it from budging?"

I didn't reply. But after a while I calmly asked him: "Tell me, Mendel, why are you such an enemy of Russia?"

Mendel wasn't surprised by my question. But he didn't answer right away. He sat down and calmly stated: "To tell you the truth, I don't see why I should be such a great friend of Russia. The good things I've received from Russia—I could donate them to ten monasteries! But if you like, I'm no enemy of Russia."

"What do mean, you're no enemy? You want the Turk to defeat Russia!"

"Now look. This is an entirely different issue. It's got nothing to do with hate or love. If I felt that Russia was in the right, I would defend it tooth and nail, the way I've sided with the Turk . . . It's a question of justice. Torrents of blood are being spilled—so how can anyone think about hate and love?"

"But don't you feel some kind of closeness to the Russian nation," I retorted, "some kind of sympathy with the people you've lived with since your birth?"

"Live with? Who do I live with? The Russians? Where do I live with them? Not on your life! And just who am I close to, who am I friends with? The peasant whose life starts in a pigsty and ends in a tavern? Or with the nobleman who thinks only about a good dinner, an elegant suit, and—pardon my saying so—a beautiful woman? What connection do I have with him?

"On the other hand," he added with a smile, "I can quite understand that they don't have much respect for me. Just what kind of person am I really? I don't eat pork, my name is Mendel, not Ivan, plus I have side-locks and a long caftan. Needless to say, I'm a savage in their eyes, or some kind of animal."

He smirked bitterly and ended our conversation with a wave of his hand.

7

ON NOVEMBER 28, Plevna finally fell. Osman Pasha and his entire army of forty thousand men were taken prisoner. After reading the bulletins that morning, I hurried home. I wanted to see Mendel's reaction. I don't know why, but I was certain he already knew.

I was wrong. Mendel didn't know. He was deeply engrossed in teaching. He and two of his six pupils were gesticulating and swaying back and forth as they chanted a Talmudic passage in a singsong of profound despair. The other four pupils, swaying over their open Talmuds, listened in silence. The subject was thorny and intricate, far beyond the grasp of these children. They were worn out, terrified, and their eyes were filled with fearful dejection. Mendel was even more exhausted. His waxy, sallow face was covered with sweat. He was working with all his strength, with his hands, his voice, his eyes, his entire body, straining to elucidate the complex problem for his pupils. But it was all in vain. The children, dizzy from their own yelling and straining, had lost their ability to understand anything at all. They mechanically parroted Mendel's words, shouting them with passionate desperation.

I had visited Mendel's heder several times, so he wasn't surprised to see me. He suddenly stopped yelling, took a deep breath, used his arm to wipe the sweat off his shirt (as usual he wasn't wearing a coat), and he asked me in a faint voice: "Any news?"

I didn't have the courage to stun the exhausted teacher with the devastating news, so I shook my head vaguely. Mendel was satisfied with my response. He took another deep breath, opening his mouth wide, and spoke bitterly: "They've sapped me dry! They refuse to understand! I might as well lie down and die!"

Returning to his pupils and swaying to and fro, he cried out in a Talmudic chant: "Agaaaaain! Our raaaaabbis teeeach . . ."

Less than ten minutes after my arrival, Mikhl entered the heder. This "Russian," who had been Mendel's most vehement political opponent at the synagogue, had recently also become his best friend. Both teachers were followers of the same Hasidic rebbe, they had a lot of common interests and often visited one another. So Mendel thought nothing of Mikhl's presence now. But I instantly knew why he was here. He even seemed to wink at me, hinting that I should hold my tongue.

He shuffled in slowly and quietly with a dismal expression. Murmuring, "Good morning," he sat down in a chair, but then promptly stood up, went over to the table, and peered into an open Talmud. "Aha! So that's where you are!" he exclaimed sympathetically. "A well-known passage. It's a quagmire, I wouldn't wish it on my worst enemy. A year ago I spent a week on it with my morons, till I finally crawled out!"

"The subject is not so difficult," said Mendel. "If only they made a little effort, they would grasp it. But forget it! They refuse! I'm totally drained because of these idiots."

"C'mon, you're exaggerating. It's a difficult passage. I've seen elderly men with good minds sweating over it . . . It's sort of like Plevna, hard to capture." Mikhl chuckled good-naturedly.

Mendel also smiled. "Nevertheless we'll conquer this passage faster than the Russians'll conquer Plevna," he said confidently.

"Uh-oh! My friend, you're sadly mistaken," Mikhl added amiably. "Plevna's been taken!"

"Oh, sure!" Mendel snapped sarcastically.

"No, it's really been taken. Yesterday," Mikhl went on earnestly and looked boldly at Mendel.

Mendel shuddered under that look. But he still didn't believe Mikhl. "What? What are you talking about?" he exclaimed nervously.

Mikhl produced his snuff box, opened it leisurely, took out a pinch, whiffed it thoroughly, wiped his nose with his handkerchief, and turned to Mendel. "No, my friend. I'm not babbling. I specifically came here to announce the good news. Plevna has been taken—and not simply taken! Osman Pasha and his entire army are prisoners of war. That's the long and short of it!"

Mendel was shaken by "the long and short of it." He looked at me as if seeking help. "What's he saying? What's he talking about?" he asked me.

All I could do was confirm what Mikhl had told him.

"What do you mean?" Mendel was all the more astonished. "You know about it, too? Why didn't you say something? . . . How'd you find out? From the newspaper?"

"No. There was a bulletin."

"Where? In the marketplace?"

And Mendel jumped to his feet, ready to dash over to the marketplace and read the bulletin.

"No, no! Don't go!" Mikhl stopped him. "I didn't mind spending two kopeks to make you happy with the good news." And he handed Mendel a folded gray poster with the bulletin printed on it. Then he went over to a small shelf where, among some old, ragged holy volumes, he found a thin notebook filled with small, curved lines of dense handwriting—his rebbe's thoughts. Mikhl settled at the window and buried himself in the manuscript as if he'd forgotten all about Mendel and Plevna.

Mendel said to his pupils: "Study this subject on your own for now and try to understand it."

The pupils, happy about my and especially Mikhl's visit, which interrupted the class—at least for a while—were extremely interested in the news about Plevna. Pretending to stick their noses in their Talmuds, they strenuously hung on every word of our conversation and quietly discussed it among themselves. From the few words I myself caught, and from their expressions, I saw that these children likewise were divided into "Russians" and "Turks" and now, under Talmudic cover, the "Russians" were celebrating their victory over the "Turks."

Mendel nervously unfolded the poster and focused hard since he read Russian slowly and arduously. He pored over every phrase as if trying not only to comprehend it but to delve into its deepest meaning. Several times he seemed about to speak, but then he held back and returned to the poster.

When he was done reading, he sat there, pensive, his head lowered, his brow furrowed, as if he were struggling to recall something. His face grew calmer with every passing moment. Then he suddenly lifted his head and, with gaping eyes, he looked at Mikhl, at me, at the bulletin — and he shuddered profoundly as if he'd been unexpectedly awakened from sleep. But then a new look appeared in his eyes, a grim, earnest, almost ascetic expression. It was as if he had experienced an enormous upheaval in those few minutes, had thrown off a nightmare, had found the solution to a difficult problem.

Meanwhile Mikhl sat there for half an hour, absorbed in the mystical text. Figuring that Mendel had managed to read the bulletin and mull it over, Mikhl slowly closed and returned the notebook, took a chair, put it opposite Mendel, sat down, and, scrutinizing his opponent, he said, cold and calm, harsh and cruel: "So tell me, Mendel, what do you think of all this?"

Mendel didn't answer right away. He peered at Mikhl with the same cold, calm eyes and replied in the same tone of voice: "What about you, Mikhl? What do you think?"

Mikhl had not expected this composure, this response. He was surprised at Mendel's obstinate self-control. "You're crazy!" he shouted angrily. "A man has to be crazy to talk the way you talk! Plevna has fallen and Osman Pasha has surrendered — isn't that enough for you? What kind of signs and wonders do you need? Do you want the sky to collapse?"

Mikhl's shouting had no impact on his friend.

"Stop making a racket," Mendel said tranquilly. "One could think it wasn't General Skobelev who captured Plevna, it was you, with your strength and wisdom . . . What do you want me to say? Do you want me to admit that you were totally right and I was wrong?"

"Yes," Mikhl snapped, "that's what I want!"

"Well, then, I'll spell it out for you," Mendel said resolutely. "I admit nothing!"

"So what did I say?" Mikhl shouted. "I said that you're totally crazy!"

"If you'll just pay attention and hear me out, you yourself will admit that I'm not crazy. Think back. What have I been arguing all this time?"

"You've argued—"

"Wait!" Mendel broke in. "Let me state my arguments myself. First of all, I argued that the Turks were in the right and the Russians were in the wrong. So what does the Russian victory prove? That the Russians are right? Is the victor always in the right? Don't we know that just the opposite may be true? Doesn't it say in *Berakhot,* the very first tractate of the Talmud, that the wicked thrive and the righteous suffer? . . ."

Mikhl tried to cut in: "But you kept shouting—"

"Let me talk!" cried Mendel. "I know what I kept shouting. I kept shouting that the Turk was stronger than the Russian, and I'm sticking to my opinion. The Russian has won, you say? So what does that prove? Does the stronger side always win? We often see that the weaker side defeats the stronger. A tiny little fly lodged in Titus' brain and defeated him. Delilah defeated Samson . . ."

"David and Goliath," one of the pupils suddenly tossed in. Deeply embarrassed, the boy hid his face. The other children burst out laughing and one of them quoted, softly and sternly: "'He who shows up a teacher is deserving of death!'"

"Children, don't butt in—it's none of your business. Do your assignment." After rebuking them calmly and not sternly, Mendel turned back to Mikhl. "I made only one mistake: I assumed that the Turk would win. I admit I was wrong."

"Aha! So you do admit it!"

"Now look!" Mendel added. "You made the same mistake."

"Who, me?" Mikhl was astonished. "What mistake?"

"My mistake wasn't that I assured you the Turk would win. It was that I acted on the information in the gazette and the bulletins . . . And you made the same mistake. We both scurried around like a chicken without its head, looking for news, data. But all we could gather from the gazette and the bulletins was what had already happened, not what was going to happen. The gazette couldn't give us the essence of the events, their true reasons and deeper meanings. Not on your life! Because neither the gazettes nor Bismarck nor Disraeli with all their complex political theories have the foggiest clue about the sources, the root causes of all developments . . ."

And with a cold challenge in his eyes, he glared at me as if I were the representative of the gazettes and the advocate of complex political theories.

Mikhl listened carefully to Mendel while trying to get a word in edge-wise. But Mendel kept talking: "If we really wanted to penetrate to the heart of the war, with its events and victories, the gazettes and the bulletins wouldn't be much help. We'd have to consult the holy *Zohar* and other religious texts . . ."

All at once Mendel lapsed into pensive silence and his face took on a mystical!y cast.

Mikhl was confused by those last words and didn't know how to respond. He produced his snuff box, quickly opened it, took out a full pinch, and hastily inhaled it. The snuff calmed him down and cleared his mind. "Maybe . . . you're right . . . But that's a different issue," he muttered, almost to himself. After a brief silence, he added: "A couple of days ago, a young man gave me an interpretation of the opening words of the Bible: 'In the beginning God created. . . .' By rearranging the Hebrew letters and calculating their numerological values, he'd come up with: 'In the days of Tsar Alexander, the Turk will fall into the net of stronger Russia.'"

"Huh? Can you repeat that?" said Mendel.

Mikhl repeated the phrase, and Mendel jotted it down.

For a while the two teachers said nothing. Mikhl finally struggled to his feet. "Are you coming to the meeting tonight?" he asked.

"Of course," Mendel replied. "We have to talk about sending alms to the Holy Land. It would be shameful if we couldn't raise a few rubles."

"Of course, shameful!" Mikhl agreed with a sigh. Nodding toward Mendel and myself, he left.

Mendel's eyes followed Mikhl all the way to the door, then he went back to the table and exclaimed resolutely, almost solemnly: "Well, children, now we have to return to our passage as is customary. It's not hard to grasp, just give it your all."

With both hands Mendel gently, almost tenderly stroked the dear gray, crumpled pages. Sighing deeply, he launched into his Talmudic chant: "Our rabbis teach us . . ."

Upon regaining my room, I found the old landlord all wrought up. He was trudging haplessly from one corner to the other, unable to settle down. When I entered, he threw himself at me and shouted: "Is it true? Is it really true?"

I was amazed. "What are you talking about?"

"Did the Russians really capture . . . that town—what's it called? I forget its name . . ."

"Plevna?"

"Yes, yes! Plevna! Was it really captured?"

"It was really captured!"

"*Oyoyoy!*" he cried in despair. "What's next?"

"They're going to make peace."

"Peace?" he called out, shaken. "And that's all?"

"That's all!"

For a while the old man gaped at me in terror. Gradually calming down, he turned to leave, then said in a despondent voice: "How do you like my missus? She went to the store and she didn't even leave me enough money for a pinch of snuff. I've been flopping around all morning like a slaughtered goose . . ."

I lent him the two kopeks for a pinch of snuff, and that made him forget all about the historic event that had thrown him into such turmoil.

MY ACQUAINTANCESHIP WITH Mendel came to an abrupt end. He stopped dropping by, and whenever I ran into him, he avoided me. I soon moved to a different room, and then several months later I left town for good.

The Starveling (*1892*)

A Sketch

1

I WAS TWENTY at the time and residing in some Byelorussian town far, far from home. I hadn't had any relationship with my fanatically religious parents for quite a while; in fact, I had broken completely with the entire Jewish world. I lived like a free bird, giving private lessons while preparing for the university entrance exams.

All in all, I wasn't so badly off. I had my small circle of close friends, with whom I spent hours discussing and debating. My mind was teeming with ideas and issues, and my soul believed in a radiant future. I did go hungry now and then, but it wasn't so awful.

One morning in May, the cheerful sunbeams were pouring through the window of my small room and flashing on my face. I awoke, opened my eyes, and, squinting because of the dazzling rays, I lay motionless for several minutes. I had a slight headache, but I didn't try to drift off again. I got up and began dressing.

It was eight a.m. Hearing a heated exchange in the next room, I automatically eavesdropped and from the first few words I caught the overall drift: my landlady was scolding her son, Grishka, a coachman. He had gone out with his droshky last night and had now come home drunk and penniless. An old story.

I finished dressing, then washed my face and my hands. My headache had eased a bit, but now I felt a gnawing in my belly. It dawned on me that I hadn't had a bite to eat since yesterday morning after spending my last three kopeks on bread for tea. Then I'd stayed at the library most of the day. Upon coming home in the evening, I'd been about to light my lamp and resume studying when I'd noticed there was no kerosene left. Deeply annoyed, I'd gone to bed.

It was awful! I'd been starving that whole month. I had no pupils; still, I'd managed to just barely squeeze by somehow or other. But now all wellsprings were dry. I had no bread, no tea, no sugar. More precisely: I had enough tea and sugar for one last cup. I pulled out my desk drawer and found a few tea leaves.

Something had to be done. Should I go to the grocery store and ask for bread and sugar on credit? Hmm! That old Jewish woman was sitting there. I didn't like her. She always gazed at me with such mournful, accusing eyes. She knew perfectly well that I was Jewish, but she pretended she didn't know, and she addressed me in Russian as "Sir," though probably cursing me under her breath. So it made no sense asking her for credit. Not only would she refuse but she'd insult me into the bargain. Forget it!

Well, I might ask my landlady to lend me a chunk of bread and a few lumps of sugar. But how could I go about it? I couldn't approach her straight out, it wouldn't do, I had to hit on some ruse. This was my plan: I'd pretend to go to the grocery, then come back and tell her that it was shut and that I didn't feel like going any farther. I would then casually add: "Please cut me a few slices of your bread, Vlasyevna, and I'll pay you back next time I go shopping. And please throw in a few lumps of sugar." Excellent!

I went next door. My landlady, a tall, skinny, elderly woman, was busy at the stove. On a bench under the holy icons sat her ten-year-old daughter Peklusha, calmly munching a piece of bread. Her drunken son Grishka, a boy of eighteen or so, was sprawled on the bed, mumbling in his sleep.

"Did we wake you?" the landlady asked me. "That goddamn moron could wake the dead!"

"What's wrong?"

"He's what's wrong! Get a load of him!" she answered, pointing toward the bed. "He drove around all night, practically killed the horses, and all he brought home was a lousy twenty kopeks!"

"M . . . , M . . . , Manka . . . ," stuttered Grishka.

"I'll bash his head in!" Vlasyevna shrieked, grabbing the poker. But then she promptly put it down and went on in despair: "Oh, all my troubles! A drunkard at his age! I'm doomed, and so are my poor fatherless children!" Calming down, she continued in a normal tone: "I'm going to the bazaar" (she sold pots there). "If you leave, take Peklusha outside and lock up. Slip the key under the eaves. He can lie here alone!" she snapped, glaring at Grishka.

"Okay. But did you notice," I asked, "whether the grocery woman was in her shop?"

"Why? Is she sick? Why shouldn't she be there? That Jew bitch. She's there from five a.m. on. The hell with her!"

I knew that my landlady didn't much care for the grocery woman, so I pretended not to hear her foul response, which I really didn't need. I took my cap and, as I left, I nonchalantly said: "I'm getting some bread and sugar."

"Go on, go on! The samovar is boiling."

I stepped outdoors, sauntered along, then turned at the corner, passing right by the grocery. It was open, of course. The woman sat on a crate near the door. She gave me her usual pitying look. Avoiding her, I walked to the corner, then doubled back.

"The samovar's boiling—it's horrible!" said Peklusha when I returned. "And Mama's gone to the bazaar."

"I've lost the battle!" I mused with a sour smile.

I went into my room and rummaged through the desk drawer, looking for buried treasure. I did find a lump of sugar, thank the Lord! "But is it worth dragging in the samovar? I really want to eat!"

Nevertheless I lugged the big-bellied samovar to my room, used up my last few tea leaves, and then picked up a book. "I'll drink my tea," I mused, "finish with Peklusha, and then go dig up money somewhere in town—thirty kopeks should do the trick."

That was exactly what I needed for bread, tea, sugar, and kerosene. If I got that much, I wouldn't have a care in the world.

I drank the first glass with sugar, and the rest without. The flood of boiling tea dulled my hunger pangs slightly, and I tried to forget by reading the very interesting articles in the new journal I had borrowed from the library last night.

The clock next door struck eleven. I began tutoring Peklusha. She was my only pupil—pro bono, of course. But I was very pleased with her. She was unusually bright. I liked hearing her solve problems quickly and skillfully in her high-pitched voice while her small, birdlike face livened up and her fingers drummed rapidly on the table.

Today's lesson was brief. I was tormented by hunger. I felt it in my stomach, in all parts of me. My mind was numb, my heartbeat was faint, the tea was still drying in my mouth.

I had to go. Where? I didn't know. I checked off a mental list of all my friends: most were starving too, and I couldn't possibly approach the wealthier ones . . .

A thought flashed through my mind: "Why not try Aunt Bashe?" But I had just washed my hands of her. I had a few relatives in town, all of them religious, indeed, fanatical Jews, with whom I had nothing in common and with whom I never socialized. Aunt Bashe wasn't quite like them—she even had a son attending the Russian gymnasium. Still, during those whole two years I had visited her only once. She had been very warm and friendly, but I couldn't let myself go back, I had no desire to return to my old milieu, stir up old memories. So how could I suddenly ask my aunt for a favor?

"I'll go to Alyosha!" I decided.

2

ALYOSHA ROGOV, A gymnasium student, was a member of our little circle. We all liked this quiet, taciturn, self-effacing boy, though none of us was especially close to him. Living with his parents, he was fully provided for and never suffered our hardships, but he was too tactful to offer us help.

It was the wrong time to drop by: the Rogovs had just sat down to lunch. I knew they'd invite me to join them, but I felt queasy, it was physically impossible for me to do so. A starveling at a table with strangers, and dozens of eyes peering at you! All those people would instantly notice how starved I was.

Anxious to leave right away, I told Alyosha that I needed a German dictionary and that I was in a great hurry.

"Just wait a bit till I finish lunch," he replied in his soft, effeminate voice. "The dictionary's somewhere in my room, under a pile of books."

So I had to wait. Alyosha's elderly father, Andrei Stepanovitsh, came into the dining room. His hair was gray, but his frame was solid. He had a medical degree, but being wealthy, he didn't bother much with his practice. The townsfolk regarded him as an eccentric. At times he'd spend three or four hours with a patient, chatting about the most diverse topics. He seldom took a cab, preferring to walk. He avoided rich patients on principle and was very popular among the poor. He was always very cordial to Alyosha's friends, but with a touch of irony.

Rogov silently shook my hand and, sitting down, he asked: "Won't you join us?"

"No thanks, I'm not hungry," I replied in a staccato tone and I sensed I was turning red.

"Have you had lunch?" Then, "Sit down!" he added, his eyes drilling into me.

If he hadn't peered at me like that, I might have sat down at the table. But now I couldn't: I felt the old man could tell merely by looking at my face and my dry lips that I was starving. I lied again. "No, thanks. I just had lunch."

He gave me a fleeting glance and didn't say another word.

Lunch was served. I hadn't eaten for several weeks, and the smell of the hot food slammed into my face, it was painful. My head whirled, and I felt drawn to the table. I could have kicked myself for so resolutely turning down the invitation. Why had I done it? I could have said offhandedly: "Thank you, I'd be delighted to have lunch with you," and sat down at the table.

"We haven't seen Miltsin for quite a spell— he hasn't come by for two weeks. Do you know how he's doing?" asked the host, wiping his lips with a napkin.

His question abruptly changed my mood. I even forgot all about my hunger, and deep down I was glad I hadn't joined them for lunch. "Miltsin? I don't know," I hurriedly replied. "I haven't seen him myself in a dog's age."

Miltsin, a mutual friend of mine and Alyosha's, had been expelled from the gymnasium for some peccadillo. He now gave private lessons and read a lot. He was not a dunce, but neither of us could stand him because of his utter tactlessness. Miltsin would invade your privacy at the drop of a hat, he'd think nothing of going to a friend's room during his absence, devouring his last piece of bread, and taking along a necessary book, often even clothes. And if you ran into him and asked: "Why d'you remove it without my permission?" his response was always the same: "Philistine! Bourgeois!"—the nastiest invectives you could hurl in our little circle. How many times had we refused to shake his hand and categorically told him we wanted nothing more to do with him! It never sank in. A day or two later he was back as if nothing had happened. A while ago he had started visiting the Rogovs once a week, arriving just before lunch and then lingering on for the meal. I was extremely annoyed; it struck me as the ugliest mooching.

And now, during lunch, old Rogov was talking to me about Miltsin. Why had he remembered him at this very moment? If I'd had lunch with them, Rogov would have thought: "Is this guy too going to show up for lunch every week?"

I went to Alyosha's room. He soon followed me there. Upon locating the dictionary, he handed it to me.

"Could you lend me thirty kopeks?" I casually asked as I was leaving.

"I've only got twenty on me," he calmly replied. "But I can get another ten from my father."

"Never mind!" I quickly said. "Twenty's fine."

3

I WENT HOME in a rare state of exuberance. My mind conjured up a wonderful scene: a boiling samovar on the table, fresh bread and herring, with me eating, drinking, and reading. Suddenly I spotted Isakov. He dashed by without recognizing me. I called out. He halted, looked around hastily, and was delighted to see me. "You're just the man I'm looking for!" he cried. "I figured you'd be in the library."

"What's wrong?"

"Do you have any money?"

"So that's it!" I burst out laughing.

"Tell me quickly. Don't beat around the bush—I don't have time," he snapped half-fretfully. "It's disgraceful. Honestly, I can't dig up a single kopek anywhere."

"How much do you need?" I asked wryly.

"Give me whatever you have."

"I don't have a kopek," I replied, digging in my heels.

"It's awful!" he shrieked in despair. "Help me drum up some money."

I regretted lying. If Isakov was so relentless, there must have been a real emergency. And how could I join him in raising money if I had some cash in my pocket? "Actually, I've got twenty kopeks," I said reluctantly. "But I need it very badly."

Gaping at me, he shouted: "Stop playing the fool!"

"What do you need it for?"

"A whole family is starving to death, they've got one foot in the grave," he answered, deeply upset. "Two of them are sick!"

"I'm starving to death myself," I said, smiling awkwardly. But feeling the sheer clumsiness of my response and my smile, I reddened in confusion.

Isakov, who was lost in thought, didn't notice. "Don't worry, you won't die," he said, adding: "The tragedies we witness! Today I was tutoring at a merchant's home when all at once I heard shouts and yells from the next room. The mistress of the house was carrying on like a lunatic, chewing out her maid. When she saw me, she beamed and, pointing at the maid, she shrieked: 'What do you say to this slut? We've got little children here, and she lets in a girl whose entire family is down with typhus! It's unbearable. What a nasty piece of work!'

"After hearing it all, I completed the lesson, and upon leaving I saw a little girl emerging from the house. She was about eight, scrawny, barefoot, with a thin pigtail, and wearing just a flimsy dress. She could barely walk, and her head was drooping. I figured this had to be the girl the merchant's wife had kicked out. I followed her, caught up, and looked into her face. It broke my heart! Her little face was sallow, greenish, bloodless, with an expression of dull suffering.

"'Where are you going, little girl? Home?' I asked.

"She murmured: 'Home.'

"'Which of you is sick?' I wanted to have a clear notion of who she was.

"'My mama and my brother.'

"'Where's your papa?'

"'Why, he's dead.' She sounded surprised I didn't know.

"I asked her why she'd gone to the large house.

"'Our aunt is there and she gives me bread. But now the mistress threw me out.' The girl almost burst into tears.

"'Don't you have any bread at home?

"'No . . . Mama's not eating, she only wants to drink. Sienka too. And Kalka and Dunka keep yelling for bread and crying. It's horrible at night. Mama's feverish and delirious and she keeps shouting.'

"I accompanied the little girl to the edge of town, behind St. Nicholas's Church. There I spotted an ancient, rotting, ramshackle hovel. Upon stepping inside, I was hit full force by a putrid, suffocating stench. I looked around: the floor was made of dirt, and two posts at the center propped up the tumbledown roof. There wasn't a single chair in the shack, just two long benches, while an upturned barrel served as a table. Plank cots hugged the walls next to a decrepit stove. In one corner there was a swarthy board, an icon. That was all.

"An elderly woman lay on one cot, her face burning, her skin parched, shiny, her lips black. She kept silently lifting and dropping her arm in what looked like an unconscious movement. Right next to her lay a boy of about fifteen. He was tossing and turning, and he begged for water. Two tiny children huddled under the planks! Oh, God!"

Isakov broke off. He was upset. Tears glowed in his eyes. His emotions infected me.

"Where should we go?" he said. "We have to buy bread, tea, sugar, and milk for the twenty kopeks. I've already brought them my samovar and a piece of bread that I had. But I haven't had tea and sugar for two days now. My cupboard's empty. I've only got one lesson today, but I was paid an advance two months ago. . . ."

Isakov took me to the hovel. He hadn't exaggerated. The scene made my skin crawl.

"Why don't you stay here," I suggested. "I'll rush over to Dr. Rogov and bring him back."

4

I FOUND ROGOV in his study, he was leafing through the latest issue of a medical journal. I must have been running very fast because when I arrived, my head reeled, I saw black spots in front of my eyes, and I had to lean against the wall to avoid collapsing.

Rogov came over and anxiously asked: "What's wrong?"

Sitting down, I recovered somewhat. "Nothing's wrong . . . I ran too fast. I'm worn out. My head aches . . . But it doesn't matter . . . I've come here for a different reason." I told him all about the miserable family.

He sat there, one arm propped on the table, his face turned in my direction, and his intelligent, penetrating gaze focused on me.

When I was done, he calmly said, "Okay, I'll go with you." Still peering into my eyes, he added: "Is this the first time you've encountered anything like this?"

"Yes!" I blurted out.

"I see these things every day—I've been seeing them for thirty years," he continued sorrowfully. "And do you know where you can find these conditions mostly? Among the destitute Jews in the crowded suburb. Have you ever been there?"

"No . . ."

He eyed me in amazement. "Why have you never been interested in having a look there? You're Jewish, after all."

It was odd. I never hid being Jewish. Nevertheless, whenever someone reminded me of it, I would redden in confusion as if I were embarrassed. Not because I was ashamed of my Jewish background, but I found its mere mention unpleasant.

Rogov's question struck me as very bizarre and a bit tactless. So I dryly answered: "I don't see what my being a Jew has to do with it. I don't distinguish between Russians and Jews. And just because I was born a Jew doesn't mean I have to live among them. Every man has the right—" Suddenly my stomach cramped up. I doubled over in pain, unable to complete my sentence.

"What's the matter?" Rogov was frightened. He came over, took my pulse, pulled up one eyelid and studied my eye. I apologized profoundly. I felt like a guilty schoolboy. It was a disagreeable situation. With an agitated shrug, he said: "God only knows what's wrong! Why, you're sick yourself. It's impossible to live the way you do."

I was terrified that Rogov would now humiliate me by proclaiming I was hungry. I wanted to crawl into a hole and die. "Andrei Stepanovitsh!" I shouted, almost in despair. "Don't worry! I swear to you, I'm as fit as a fiddle. We'll talk about it some other time. Just let me take you to the sick family."

Without answering, he donned his hat, took his thick cane, and we left. Contrary to his usual custom, he hailed a cab—apparently for my sake. He held his tongue throughout the ride, which pleased me no end, because the merciless jolting over the cobblestones was agonizing for my empty stomach and I wouldn't have been able to converse.

When we arrived, Rogov entered the shack, greeted Isakov, silently examined the family members, and questioned the little girl. We learned that her mother did the laundry in various homes and that she'd been lying there unconscious for five days now after a long spell of forcing herself to work. The brother had been lying in bed for three days already, and no one came to them because no one was left in the neighborhood, which had burned down just recently.

"Well," said Rogov, "the patients have to be hospitalized, I'll take care of it immediately. But what about them?" He pointed at the younger tots, who were huddled in a corner, gaping at us in wonder, in almost mystical terror.

"Don't worry about them," Isakov said quickly. "We'll arrange something."

"Where are you going to arrange it?" Rogov asked curiously.

"Don't worry, we'll arrange something!" Isakov exclaimed even more firmly.

When Rogov was gone, Isakov and I tried to figure out what we could arrange for the children.

"One of us'll have to stay with them," I suggested.

"No, we can't leave them here," Isakov objected. "We have to get them away from this hovel. I'd take them in, but I can't look after them."

I had a gratifying idea: "Let's bring them to Anushka."

"You're right! Anushka! That would be best." Isakov was delighted. "But we'll have to ask her first. She lives with her parents. Go and see her, and I'll wait here."

5

ANUSHKA PAVLOVA WAS the daughter of an ex-official who was a drunkard. A former pupil of Isakov's, she was a member of our little circle. Thin, edgy, and wide-eyed, with an endless reservoir of kindness, Anushka was studying to teach in a village school.

When I found her, she was alone, sewing something. She welcomed me with a bright, childlike smile. "I was about to visit you. I wanted to borrow the latest issue of the journal. The librarian said you had it."

"It's at home. I'll bring it by tomorrow," I replied. "But now I've got something important to discuss with you." I told her about the sick family. She listened silently, her expression alternating between horror and deep pain.

"What about the children? How can they stay there?" she asked tearfully. "Why didn't you bring them here?" she then added reproachfully.

"Well, you live with your parents," I explained. "So we had to ask you first."

"That's true. I totally forgot." Anushka looked gloomy, anguished. "You know what? We'll bring them to Isakov's home, and I'll take care of them, I'll bring everything that's necessary." She was already at the cupboard, pulling out rolls, tea, sugar, preserves. "Wrap these up. Here's a kerchief," she said quickly, stepping into the next room.

While wrapping the food, I felt my hunger. Without thinking, I broke off a bit of a roll and was about to chow down. But then it hit me: "You're stealing bread from hungry children." I swiftly put back the piece of roll. Meanwhile Anusha returned with a pillow, clothing, and linen. "You're gonna lug all that to Isakov?" I asked in surprise.

"Not so loud," she whispered nervously. "Mama's next door. She'll hear us and she'll start cross-examining us!"

In the past I'd often asked Anushka for food when I'd been hungry, and I'd never felt any qualms about it. But now I was incapable of telling her I was hungry. The request was on the tip of my tongue: "Actually, why don't you give me something to eat too?" But the phrase kept sticking in my craw. Indeed, it was only the word "actually" that wouldn't get through. It would have looked as if I'd come to solicit bread for hungry people but "actually" wanted to feed my own hunger in the process. No, I couldn't ask Anushka either! And unfortunately, she didn't think of offering me something to eat.

We left. Anushka walked swiftly, while I, carrying the packages, barely kept up with her. Upon reaching the corner, I was too exhausted to go on. My head was spinning, my heart was pounding furiously.

"What's wrong?" asked Anushka.

"Nothing. I've got a headache," I replied, continuing.

"You poor thing," she said, as she usually did at such times. She then added: "Are we taking the children straight to Isakov?"

"No," I answered in a faint voice. "I want to go home. I can barely walk . . ."

"What's wrong with you?" she asked, more concerned now. She halted and peered into my face. "Are you sick?"

Not wanting to scare her, I retorted: "Don't be silly! I'm perfectly fine! C'mon, let's walk faster."

When we arrived, the patients were gone. They had already been hospitalized. Anushka and Isakov took away the children, and I headed home.

6

IT WAS AROUND nine p.m. I trudged slowly. I was horribly worn out. All I could think of was dragging myself to my room and lying down.

"Stop!" I suddenly heard a shout behind me. Someone slapped me on the back. I turned and saw Miltsin. He was dressed all in new clothes and looked glamorous.

"Good evening!" he cried, grabbing my hand. "It's been ages, damn you!"

"What a dandy!" I was amazed. "Did you strike it rich or something?"

"Did I ever, pal!" he cheerfully replied. "I'm earning a whole forty rubles for tutoring, and lunch is included for one of the lessons. And what a lunch!" he added ecstatically. "Three courses!"

Rather upset, I dryly shot back: "Well, good . . ."

"Why don't you come by tomorrow, pal?"

"Like hell I will!" I snapped, trying to move on.

"Wait!" He grabbed my sleeve. "I want to drop by your place and get the new issue of the journal. I heard you had it."

"I have it, but not for you . . ."

"Stop nagging me," he replied phlegmatically. "I'll pick it up tomorrow."

I was getting angrier and angrier. "If memory serves me: before you got rich, you free-loaded off Isakov for a couple of months!" I was choking back my rage.

"So?"

"It wouldn't hurt if you gave him two or three of your pupils."

"Dammit, I didn't realize he had no work! If he'd come and told me, I might've—"

"Might've!" I mimicked. I wanted to insult him but couldn't get the words out, my throat tightened up on me. I turned and tried to leave.

"You moralist!" Miltsin shouted. "Shake my hand, say goodbye properly! Why don't you give Isakov some of your pupils? Okay, so don't shake my hand. Go to hell! You philistine—I don't want to know you. But I'll pick up the journal anyway!"

I reached home more dead than alive. My conversation with Miltsin had left me terribly agitated. I could barely undress and climb into bed. Then I was unable to fall asleep. My head was roaring, I heard the blood rushing through my arteries, my heart beat spasmodically. For a while my mind was a blank. Suddenly I panicked: I thought I saw a huge spider dangling from the ceiling, hovering over my nose. I covered my face with my hands. Then I felt someone gazing through the window. I opened my eyes wide, but I saw nothing. I grew more and more frightened even though I was certain nobody was there. Struggling to my feet, I lit a match. This calmed me a bit. Lying down, I thought of my dead mother—I don't know why. Suddenly I felt pain and anxiety. Tears were streaming down my cheeks. I let them flow. I felt a sweet feebleness, my chest was lighter. Gradually my weeping turned into moaning. I couldn't control myself.

I sobbed involuntarily. All I could think in my fear was: "If the landlady hears me, she'll get scared, she'll come in, and there'll be a big commotion." Pulling myself together, I stood up, had a sip of water, rinsed my throat, wet my forehead, and dragged myself back to bed. I now lay calmly, without thoughts or feelings. I was just dozing off when for some reason I awoke and lay on and on with open eyes.

All at once, amazingly vivid images of my childhood started passing before my eyes: I saw myself with my family, in the Jewish elementary school, at the synagogue. How warm and loving were those scenes! I was overwhelmed by coldness, by an oppressive sense of solitude and homelessness. It struck me that all my friends and acquaintances—Isakov, Anushka, Rogov—were alien, distant, and as irrelevant to me as I was to them. I no longer felt sorry for the laundress and her hungry children, I pitied only myself. The hunger ached in my stomach and I had a similar anguish in my soul: I was likewise starving for intimacy and affection, for people who were near and dear. I wept, not knowing which hunger, the physical or the spiritual one, was a greater torment. It wasn't until dawn that I fell into a deep sleep.

7

I AWOKE VERY late. My head and all parts of me were very heavy. For a while I lay motionless, waiting for the clock to strike. It struck eleven. I was fully aware of my critical state, but it didn't bother me. I didn't even muse about digging up money; it seemed petty, trivial.

I dressed, washed, and went to my landlady's room. Peklusha was there all alone. "The samovar is boiling, boiling!" she cried out upon seeing me.

"I'm not having any tea, dear," I said faintly and feebly. "And we're not having a lesson either . . ."

She gaped at me in surprise and was about to ask me something, but I returned to my room. I picked up the journal and started leafing through it. Then I put it down apathetically.

"I ought to go somewhere . . . Visit the sick laundress . . . Visit Isakov . . . Yes, I really have to . . ."

I left, but I didn't go on my visit. I was exhausted, I needed rest. I'd visit her next. But first I'd head for the library.

The reading room was a cherished home for our circle. We went there not to read but to relax. The silence of the vast room with its high ceiling, the walls covered with books, and the friendly smile of the elderly librarian had a remarkably soothing effect on us.

There was no one in the reading room. I saw down at the window and picked up a newspaper. After mechanically scanning a few headlines, I discarded the paper and picked up a second one, a third—but I couldn't focus. I tried a journal—but nothing registered: within minutes, the letters somersaulted before my eyes, and my heart pounded furiously. I put the journal aside and gazed aimlessly through the window. A profound gloom took hold of me. I wanted to cry.

I sat on and on like that, immobile. My hunger pangs slowly grew sharper: something was gnawing and wrenching in my stomach; my throat tightened convulsively. I couldn't find a comfortable position. I felt a languishing desire: "Eat! Eat! Eat!" At least let me munch on a piece of stale bread, let me feel my teeth chewing, let me feel breath in my mouth.

I pulled off a few petals from the flowers on the sill and began chewing them. But they tasted bitter, so I spit them out. I grabbed a glass of water and started drinking, but it nauseated me. I sat down, doubled over, bit my lips bloody, and shut my eyes. The pains eased a bit.

The clock struck.

"I'm going to eat lunch at the Rogovs!" I decided without thinking about it. I stood up. But Isakov walked in at that very moment.

"I'm just been to the hospital," he announced. "The woman's better, thank God. Anuskha's with the kids. She wanted to bring them to her house, but her mother wouldn't hear of it."

"I'm hungry," I murmured,

"Me too!" he responded, laughing freely. "I haven't had tea today. Oh, well, that's unimportant. We really ought to discuss Laskin."

Both of us were tutoring Laskin, an unhappy creature with a great thirst for knowledge but no aptitude. He was a martyr who also tortured the two of us.

"Let him become a bookbinder, a locksmith, a tailor—but he ought to leave education alone!" I shouted. "He's already made my life miserable with his doleful and sorrowful physiognomy!"

"He's not going to apprentice himself to an artisan."

"Well, then, you prepare him for the gymnasium," I snapped fiercely.

Isakov laughed perfunctorily. "There's no way he can prepare for the gymnasium. Algebra's gonna be the death of him, it'll break his heart. Actually," Isakov recalled, "there's a seven-ruble lesson for you. And just imagine, Miltsin's offered it. He came to me specifically. He was all dandied up and he said he had millions of rubles' worth of tutoring and a lunch worth ten thousand rubles . . ."

"He had a pang of conscience," I replied, telling Isakov about my encounter with Miltsin the previous day.

"Well, fine." Isakov smiled amiably. "So take the lesson."

"Why are you giving it away? You're the one he offered it to."

"I've already got a pupil and you've got none. Besides, I don't have the time. I'd like to give my pupil away," he added, laughing, "but I was paid two months in advance."

"I don't want any pupils from Miltsin. I'd be in his debt forever," I answered, irritated and tearful. By now I was so weak that the slightest fuss brought tears to my eyes.

Isakov started talking about Anushka, but then he saw my mind was somewhere else. "You're not listening," he exclaimed in surprise.

"I'm hungry," I muttered.

Isakov eyed me. "You don't look so good," he agreed in a blank tone. Then he tried to comfort me: "Hey, once I get some cash, we'll party like there's no tomorrow!" And he left.

How bizarre! Isakov was a sensitive man, always willing to help someone in trouble. Nevertheless, when I, his closest friend, was starving to death, he didn't catch on.

I don't believe I stayed in the library much longer. But I don't recall where I went. My thoughts were tangled, my emotions hazy. I only felt I was growing more and more feeble . . .

8

SOME WONDROUS SINGING woke me up. But before opening my eyes, I noticed something soft under my head—a pillow, no doubt. I wasn't surprised, even though I hadn't had a pillow for months. I felt fine and calm. Lazily I opened my eyes—only to find myself in a thoroughly unfamiliar room. It was nighttime, but the door was ajar, letting in a glimmer of light. The singing that had roused me was glorious, extraordinary. At first I couldn't tell what language it was in. Somewhere on the other side of the wall a woman was crooning, almost praying, very quietly, mournfully, poignantly, yet gently, lovingly. Then I knew: it was the prayer usually sung by women at the close of the Sabbath: "God of Abraham, of Isaac, and of Jacob. . . ." I recognized the voice: Aunt Bashe. I wasn't surprised, I didn't even ask how I'd come here. I was calm and contented like after an illness, and my aunt's singing was tender and lyrical.

"Auntie!"

"Coming," she replied hurriedly. A moment later she entered, carrying a lamp.

"*Oyoyoy!* Yosel," the old lady gently rebuked me, shaking her head. "What a scare you gave us!" Her eyes were radiant with goodness, her smile affectionate.

"What happened? I don't remember a thing!" I said, bursting into laughter as if at a hilarious joke.

"What happened? You dropped by unexpectedly. Then you began mumbling incoherently. Suddenly you turned pale and you fainted. It took the doctor a whole hour to revive you . . . Then you fell asleep."

"I don't remember anything."

"He's alive!" Shouts came from the next room. "He's resurrected!" And who should appear in the doorway but Anushka, Alyosha, Rogov, and another friend of ours, a seminary student. I was astonished at the sight of these unexpected guests, and my mellow and peaceful mood instantly changed. I was upset and frightened, annoyed that my comrades had found me. I recalled my aunt's praying and I now understood why she had crooned so softly. I was irked that my friends might have heard her. I wanted to get away from here as fast as possible.

Sitting up in bed, I asked: "How did you all get here?"

"His father was here," said my aunt, pointing at Rogov. I was peeved by her bad accent in Russian and her singsong intonation.

"You have no idea what went on here—God help us!" said Alyosha. "They sent for my father, and that's how we found out. We've been here all day. Your aunt served us tea and all kinds of Jewish treats."

"Treats!" my aunt snapped. "They didn't even want to eat a tiny piece of fish." And she left the room.

"Your aunt's a dear, a darling." Anushka beamed. "It's been only a few hours, but I'm madly in love with her."

"My father's well acquainted with her," Alyosha exclaimed. "He says she's a very intelligent and interesting lady. He sometimes spends whole evenings with her here—he calls her 'sweetheart.'"

Suddenly all my anger and vexation were gone. I felt as if I didn't have a care in the world. Turning toward the door, I called out cheerfully and unabashedly: "Auntie! Why are you letting me starve? Hand over your gefilte fish!"

"I'm coming! I'm coming!" I heard her hasty and exuberant steps.

Anonymous Folktales

From *The Destruction of Galicia* (1920)

THAT EVENING, AFTER completing our work, we were enjoying a glass of tea when an old man showed up: the town cantor, lank and scraggy, with soft, young, sparkling eyes. He was here to request aid. The amount he asked for was so minuscule and so equitable that I instantly agreed. I asked whether he knew any Hasidic stories. Livening up, he enthusiastically launched into tale after tale. And what a storyteller he was! Filled with rapture, teeming with marvelous details like a true poet. Each tale he recounted was a work of art! I felt sad that I couldn't write them down word for word. Characteristically, all his stories were about the Messiah. Later on, I concluded that elderly Jews throughout Galicia were deeply interested in the figure of the Messiah. I can recall only one of the cantor's stories.

* * *

"WHEN RABBI YISROEL of Rezhin was in prison, his Hasids and his relatives moved heaven and earth for his release. And when he was set free, the joy was inconceivable. They had banquets, they danced and sang. But one of his Hasids, Motele, who had always been devoted heart and soul to the rebbe, neither danced nor sang. He sat there gloomily, refusing to speak to anyone.

"People urged him: 'C'mon! It's a wonderful celebration. The rebbe is out of prison, and you're not happy, you're mournful! How come?'

"'I faithfully believed that our rebbe was the Messiah, and I told myself: "Let the blister burst! Let it burst!" But the blister hasn't burst. The Messiah hasn't come. The rebbe was set free, and now we're right back where we started. So how can I be happy?'"

* * *

DURING MY PREWAR ethnographic research, I had noticed that so many Jewish folk songs and folktales are full of grief and lament—"So they began to weep and wail," "Woe and sorrow," and so on. And Russian folk songs likewise say, "He shed a torrent of tears" . . . "Bathed in tears." I had always seen this as mere grandiloquence. But now, in Galicia, I realized that such sorrow is true to life. I saw people "shedding torrents of tears." There are moments when tears come streaming on their own, almost unnoticed, as surrogates for words. They flow as easily as words, and they keep pouring when words have lost all strength and there is no one to talk to.

When the musician stopped, and I asked him to sit down with us, the cantor recalled a legend about a melody:

"A JEW CAME to consult the Rebbe of Ruzhin. So the rebbe crooned 'Elijah the Prophet' set to a non-Jewish tune and asked his visitor to memorize it. The visitor didn't understand why, but he obeyed the rebbe and learned the melody by heart. Fifteen years later, while traveling at night, the man had to pass through a forest haunted by demons. Walking along, he suddenly saw that he was accompanied by a short Gentile with a pipe. The Jew was terrified. The Gentile asked him where he was going and the Jew replied, 'To the next town.' The Gentile then said, 'I'm going there too.' The Gentile took the Jew's arm and said, 'Sing something for me.' The Jew was even more terrified. But he remembered 'Elijah the Prophet' with the non-Jewish melody, which he had been taught by the Rebbe of Ruzhin, and he began to sing it. And he kept singing until they reached the town, and there the Gentile vanished."

UNDER THE IMPACT of what I had seen and heard at the rebbe's court in Sadagura, I recalled a story about the Rebbe of Ruzhin:

BECAUSE OF A defamation, the rebbe, as we know, was arrested for supposedly ordering or allowing the murder of two Jewish informers. But even though he was ultimately released, the authorities continued to persecute him. He fled to Austria, and the Russian government tried to extradite him. With great efforts and with the help of Metternich, he convinced the Austrian government not to send him back.

This was the basis of the legend about a gigantic struggle between the rebbe and Nicholas I [1796–1855, a ruthlessly antisemitic despot]. It was said that the tsar nurtured a fierce personal enmity toward the rebbe and persecuted him relentlessly. The government ministers, who were very amazed, once asked Nicholas: "Why are you persecuting the Rebbe of Ruzhin? Is it suitable for a great monarch like yourself to devote his life to chasing a despicable Yid?"

Nicholas jumped up and angrily shouted: "What do you mean, 'a despicable Yid'? I spend my life twisting the world one way, and he twists it the other way. And I can't get the better of him!"

The rebbe used to say: "I was born on the same day as he was, but three hours later—and I can't get at him. If I'd been born just fifteen minutes earlier, I could defeat him."

He would not reveal himself as a tsadik and mount his Hasidic throne so long as Nicholas was tsar: "It's him or me!"

There was a tumult in all the heavenly palaces, and it was decided that Nicholas should be dethroned. But then the tsar's guardian angel spoke up:

"What's going on? There's no law and no judge here—this is anarchy! If both men wanted to mount the imperial throne, then we could discuss which should yield to the other. But Nicholas—long may he live—is already emperor. So how can he be deposed?"

The celestial tribunal ruled that Nicholas should remain in power and that the Rebbe of Ruzhin should submit and reveal himself. But to make it up to him, the tribunal allowed him to go through all the celestial palaces and take whatever he liked. And when he walked through the Palace of Music, he took along the most beautiful melody.

NICHOLAS I HAS long since died and decayed, but the war between him and his antagonist is still raging. He has stretched out his dead hand through three generations of tsars. He has destroyed the Rebbe of Ruzhin's court, profaned his synagogue, and flung his bones from his grave.

Dead hands commit worse crimes than living hands.

SHOLOM ALEICHEM *(1859–1916)*

Born Sholom Rabinovitch in Poltava, Ukraine, he became, among other things, a government rabbi. Initially writing in Hebrew, he switched to Yiddish—still a daring move in 1883. Mainly a humorist, Sholom Aleichem was much harsher and nastier than his warm-and-fuzzy reputation in the English-speaking world. He produced a monumental corpus of mostly comical stories, novels, dramas, and memoirs. With his highly sensitive ear for colloquial speech, he created an enormous human comedy of Jewish characters, the most famous being Tevye the Dairyman.

The 1905 massacres of Russian Jews drove Sholom Aleichem and his family out of Russia, and he ultimately settled in New York. He is buried in New Jersey.

Seventy-five Thousand (A Pack of Tsoris)

(1902; publ. 1920)

YOU SAY "TSORIS"? For you, everything is "tsoris"! . . . It seems to me that ever since God created the world and ever since Jews became a nation, such a pack of tsoris has not been heard, seen, or even dreamed of! If you've got the time, please gather round and listen carefully, and I'll tell you the whole story from A to Z, with every last trimming and every last trapping—the story of the seventy-five thousand. I feel squeezed, crushed, a fire is burning in me, I must, I *must* unburden myself! . . . You do understand, don't you?

There's only one thing I ask of you: If I bog down or if I go off on a tangent, tell me where I was. You see, ever since I got the news about the jackpot, that is, the seventy-five thousand, my head's been buzzing (may you be spared!), and so I sometimes forget what I'm talking about. . . . You do understand, don't you? Tell me, do you happen to have seventy-five thousand on you—damn it, I mean, do you happen to have a cigarette on you?

So anyhow, where was I? Oh, that's right, the seventy-five thousand. . . . This past May 1, just as I'm standing before you, I won the seventy-five thousand. Now on the face of it, what's the big deal? Are there so few people who've won money? Didn't a tsarist soldier, I hear, just recently rack up two hundred thousand rubles? And then there's that poor, young bookkeeper who won forty thousand rubles. Shush, fine, good, not another word about it, all right already . . . Granted, the big jackpots get worldwide attention, we were the envy of one hundred thirty-six million people. You do understand, don't you? But the fact is, no two winnings are alike. This jackpot story is very bizarre, it's a concatenated story, a story of a story, and a story inside a story, and a story about a story. You see, you really have to make a strenuous effort and hear the entire story if you want to understand what happened.

First of all, I have to introduce myself. Now I'm not going to brag that I'm a great scholar, a great magnate, a great philosopher. I simply am, as you can see, an ordinary Jew—that is, a Jewish householder, with my own home, with a good name and a bit of prestige in my shtetl. You do understand, don't you?

True, I once had money, a whole lot of money. What's a whole lot? Brodsky certainly has a lot more. So what? I had several thousand rubles, but God, as you put it, led me into temptation, and, you understand, I longed to strike it rich. So I dealt in bread in the hungry provinces and I lost my shirt, as they say. You do want a little luck—that's all. Now do you think I was the least bit crestfallen—God forbid!—when I lost that money? You obviously don't know me. You see, for a guy like me, money is about as important as—what should I say?—as the ashes of this cigarette. It's got no importance whatsoever!

Oh, by all means! Money is a good thing. But fight for it, put my life on the line?—forget it! It's only bad when you don't have what you need, when you don't have the appropriate position, when I can't donate to charity what I'd like to donate. When I see them asking householders for a small contribution for a good cause, but they skip my house—believe you me: I could die on the spot! You do understand, don't you? I'd rather get cussed out by my wife when there's no money for the Sabbath than turn down a beggar if there's spare change jingling in my pocket. You do understand, don't you? That's the kind of lunatic I am. Does anyone happen to have any spare change—dammit, I mean a light for my cigarette?

So anyhow, where was I? Oh, that's right. Well, I lost my shirt, you see. And when I lost my shirt, I say to my wife one fine morning: "Listen, Ziporah," I say, "listen. We're cleaned out!"

So she says: "What do you mean, we're cleaned out?"

So I say to her: "We haven't got a kopek!"

So being a woman and all, she yelled and screamed: "Oh, how awful, how horrible, how terrible! Oh, how ghastly! Yankev-Yosl, what are you talking about? Where's your money?"

"Shush, shush," I say. "What are you carrying on about? Where is it written that it's my money? 'The Lord giveth and the Lord taketh away.' Or how do the Gentiles put it, 'Mikita never had a penny to his name and he never will!' Where is it written that Yankev-Yosl should have a four-room apartment and keep two maids and get all dolled up on the Sabbath? Why? I ask you. There are Jews who are starving to death—so what if they are? It won't kill them! I tell you: if you always had to choose between taking this path and taking that path, the whole universe would collapse."

I said similar things and voiced similar arguments, and so finally she—my missus, that is—saw the light. You do understand, don't you?

You ought to know that my wife is very special, and I don't need to be the least bit ashamed of her. She understands well enough—you don't have to keep arguing and arguing. She soon stopped yelling and screaming. Instead she poured out her heart to me: maybe this was a godsend—God is a father, after all. He'd do right by us.

And I didn't do a lot of thinking. I rented out my apartment, we moved to a single room with a kitchen, and we got rid of the maids—if you'll pardon my saying so. My missus—long may she live—rolled up her sleeves and bent over a hot stove. And I called myself up to read from the Torah. I was in fifth place—not a very honorable number: "Reb Jankev-Yosl the Pauper please come up and make your donation!" I branded myself—how would you put it?—a poor man. Now what do you mean "poor"? There are, as you can imagine, much poorer people than me. Say what you like: I've got my own home, plus an apartment from which I derive an income. The fly in the ointment is that there are four weeks in a month. A month should have no more than two weeks. That way I might get through with my expenses. But this way there are two more weeks till the next month, and that's not good, you understand.

Still, what can you do? How do you put it? You get used to tsoris. I tell you, there's nothing better or more calming than poverty. You're rid of all annoyances, you understand: paying, lending, borrowing, running around—the world of chaos. But there's a God in the world, and He says: "What good is it, Yankev-Yosl, to lead a life that's calm and without tsoris? You've got a lottery ticket? Here's seventy-five thousand rubles, go and suffer!" You do understand, don't you? . . . Do you happen to have a ticket on you?—dammit, I mean a cigarette!

So anyhow, where was I? Oh, that's right, I was talking about the lottery ticket. So a Jew has a ticket and hauls in seventy-five thousand rubles? Just hold your horses! To begin with: how come a Jew's got a ticket? In order to redeem it for cash. C'mon, Yankev-Yosl, you fool! Take the ticket to a bank and pick up your booty!

Let me explain. First of all, there are no banks in our shtetl. Secondly, a bank—who needs it? Can't a bank go belly-up if it wants to? The world isn't lawless, no one's grabbing it out of my hands, and who needs my ticket anyway? You do understand, don't you? That's what I was thinking, or maybe I wasn't thinking—I simply made up my mind. You see, I had a tenant in my apartment, a young man, a pawnbroker, a very fine young man, who piously studied the sacred books, a decent young man. Why shouldn't I leave the ticket with him? Let him give me two hundred rubles for it, I'd gladly take the money and run—why not?

So I went to my tenant—Birnboim was his name—and I say to him: "Mr. Birnboim, would you give me two hundred rubles for my ticket?"

So he says: "I'll give you two hundred rubles for your ticket."

So I say: "How much interest are you gonna charge me?"

So he says: "How much interest should I charge you?"

So I say: "How should I know how much interest you should charge me? Charge me what a bank would charge."

So he says: "I'll charge you what a bank would charge."

In short, we agreed on the interest rate, and I gave him the ticket for five months and took the two hundred rubles. You do understand, don't you? C'mon, Yankev-Yosl, you fool! Get a receipt indicating that you've pawned such-and-such a lottery ticket in such-and-such a series with such-and-such a number! No. Instead, he—Birnboim, that is—has me sign an IOU stating that he's lent me two hundred rubles for a period of five months against such-and-such a lottery ticket with such-and-such a number in such-and-such a series; and if I don't pay him back the two hundred rubles within the stipulated time, then such-and-such a lottery ticket with such-and-such a number in such-and-such a series will become his lottery ticket, and I'll forfeit all claim to it. . . . You do understand, don't you?

What was I thinking? I was thinking: "What's there to worry about? It can go either way. Either I'll redeem the ticket on the due date, and that'll be fine and dandy—or else I'll pay him the five months' interest, and he'll extend my loan—why shouldn't he extend it? What does he care so long as I pay the interest?" You do understand, don't you?

And so it was. The due date came, and I didn't redeem the ticket. The five months were followed by another five months, and little by little two years and five months passed by. Needless to say, I kept paying him the interest. That is: sometimes I paid him and sometimes I didn't—why should I worry? Was he going to sell my ticket? He was not going to sell my ticket! Why should he sell my ticket? That's what I was thinking, or maybe I wasn't thinking . . . Meanwhile it was a bad time for me, there was no business. All the weeks in a month were too many. You work your butt off—what else can you do? And you've got tsoris like there's no tomorrow . . . Until this last spring . . .

This last spring, close to Passover, God sent a little deal my way. I bought several wagonloads of millet. The price of millet skyrocketed. So I sold the millet and made a bundle, thank goodness. You can imagine what a great Passover I had. I outdid Brodsky—he couldn't have held a candle to me! Wow! A man doesn't owe a single kopek and he's got a few hundred rubles tucked away. Who can beat that? You do understand, don't you?

So, Yankev-Yosl, you fool, take two hundred rubles to Birnboim and redeem the lottery ticket! No. I figured: "Don't I have time? Birnboim isn't going to skedaddle with the ticket. I'll have time enough to redeem the ticket after Passover. Or if not, then I'll pay whatever interest is due and I'll get a receipt for the ticket." That's what I was thinking, or maybe I wasn't thinking. You do understand, don't you?

So I went and spent the money on sacks of grain, and I stored the sacks in a granary. Then God worked a miracle. Somebody smashed the granary lock. It was just before Passover, the night of April 30—and the lottery drawing was to be held the next day, May 1. My sacks were heisted, and I lost my shirt.

"Ziporah," I say to my wife. "You know what? We're cleaned out again."

"What do you mean," she says, "we're cleaned out?"

"We don't," I say, "have even one sack left."

"What are you talking about?" she says. "What's become of the sacks?"

"They were carried off," I say, "from the granary last night."

So she began to yell and scream, just like a woman. So I say to her: "Shush, shush, Ziporah! Stop shouting! You're not God's only child! Let's say our apartment burned down, and we got out stark naked like on the day we were born—would you be better off?"

"That's a comfort!" she says. "And the sacks get stolen to boot?"

"What's one," I say, "got to do with the other? Mark my words—the sacks'll turn up again."

"How," she says, "are they gonna turn up again? The robbers are gonna throw the stolen sacks at your feet or your name isn't Yankev-Yosl! You think they've got nothing better to do?"

"Ugh!" I say. "You're a fool! A human being can't fathom the ways of God."

And that's the way it was. The sacks were gone, they had vanished clean off the face of the earth. Who'd bring them back? And what sacks? I dashed around like a lunatic, I went to the police, I searched high and low, every nook and cranny, every mousehole. But no mice, no dice! It was a wild-goose chase, a needle in a haystack! You do understand, don't you?

I was screwed, my heart was sober, my mouth was dry, my soul was dark and desolate. I was standing in the marketplace, by the labor exchange, near the pharmacy, and an idea flashed through my mind. It was around noon. "Wait! This is judgment day! May 1. The drawing's today. A problem for God? We've got a great and a powerful God! If He wants to, He can bring happiness to me and my entire family. . . ."

Then I remembered the stolen sacks, which made me forget that it was May 1, that I had a lottery ticket, and again I started looking for the sacks: there had to be some trace of them. And I searched all day and all night—till it was the morning of May 2. I had a one-track mind, I hadn't eaten for twenty-four hours, it was already one p.m., I felt despondent—you do understand, don't you?

Then, when I arrived home, my wife pounced on me: "Maybe you can wash your hands and have a bite? Maybe you've had your fill of the sacks? I've had it up to here with your sacks! The hell with the sacks! Do we have to kill ourselves because of the sacks? With the sacks, without the sacks—what's the difference! What a nice business with the sacks! Sacks-sacks! Sacks-sacks!"

"You know what, Ziporah?" I say to her. "Maybe there's been enough sacks already. My head's sacking enough already. And now you come and pour salt in my wounds: 'Sacks-sacks! Sacks-sacks!'"

You do understand, don't you? Do you happen to have another sack on you?—dammit, I mean another cigarette?

So anyhow, where was I? Oh, right, I was talking about the sacks. Well, the sacks were gone forever. What could I do? You can't spit out your soul. I washed and sat down at the table. Why and what for? I couldn't swallow a single morsel.

"What's wrong, Yankev-Yosl?" asked my wife (long may she live). "What's gotten your goat?"

"I haven't a clue," I said, leaving the table in the middle of the meal and stretching out on the sofa. As I lay there, the gazette came from the post office. Pick it up, Jankev-Yosl, you fool, and take a look. Today is May 2. Maybe your ticket won something? Who? What? For all I knew it could be May 2 or June 22 or the first of Dismember! And you can ask me till you're blue in the face! You do understand, don't you?

I picked up the gazette and began reading, of course, from the very start. In short I lay there and took in all sorts of news: shootings, hangings, stabbings, killings, Brits and Boers—it all went in one ear and out the other. Who cares about the Brits, who cares about the Boers—when all my sacks had been heisted? The hell with all Brits and all Boers—just find me my sacks! That's what I was thinking, or maybe I wasn't thinking. I turned the first page of the gazette, then the second, then the third—I take a look: "Drawing!"

All at once, a thought flashed through my mind: maybe I'd won five hundred rubles? That would make up for my sacks and make my wish come true. I ran down the five hundred list—no dice. I tried the thousand list—no dice. Five thousand, eight thousand, ten thousand—no dice at all! And so on and so forth until I came to the seventy-five-thousand prize. And when I came to the seventy-five-thousand prize, something hit me in the eye and banged into my head: series 2289, number 12! I could have sworn it was my ticket number! How could a shlimazl like me have ever hit such a jackpot? I took a good hard look at the figures. Lord of the Universe! It *was* my number.

I wanted to stand up—but I couldn't. I was chained to the sofa. I wanted to yell, "Ziporah!" But I couldn't. My tongue was suddenly chained to my palate. I gathered all my strength, stood up, went over to the table, and peered into my ledger. Yes, as sure as I'm a Jew: series 2289, number 12!

"Ziporah!" I say to my wife, and my arms were shaking and my teeth were chattering. "You know what? We've found the stolen sacks!"

She looked at me like I was crazy: "What are you talking about? Do you know what you're talking about?"

"I tell you," I say to her. "God's returned our sacks a thousand-fold and with interest. Our ticket's won," I say to her, "we've hit the jackpot. A bucket of cash!"

"Are you serious, Yankev-Yosl, or are you kidding me?"

"What do you mean, kidding?" I say. "I'm dead serious! Congratulate us! We've won money!"

"How much have we won?" she says, gazing right into my eyes as if saying: "Aha! You're lying, but you're not gonna get away with it!"

"Gimme a for instance—how much do you figure we've won?"

"I have no idea," she says. "Maybe a few hundred rubles?"

"Why not," I say, "a few thousand rubles?"

"What do you mean by a few thousand?" she says. "Five? Six? Maybe as much as seven?"

"You can't," I say, "imagine more?"

"Ten thousand?" she says.

"Use your imagination," I say. "Try a bit more!"

"Fifteen thousand?"

"More!"

"Twenty? Twenty-five?"

"More!"

"Yankev-Yosl," she says, "tell me. Stop torturing me!"

"Ziporah!" I say, taking her hand and squeezing it. "We've won a bonanza! We've won a windfall! More money than you've ever dreamed of!"

"So tell me already, tell me! How much have we won, Yankev-Yosl? I'm on pins and needles!"

"We've won," I say, "a mint, a fortune, a treasure trove—seventy-five thousand rubles! Do you hear, Ziporah? Seventy-five thousand!"

"Blessed are you, God!" she says. She jumped up and scurried every which way, wringing her hands. Praised be your name, oh Lord, for looking at us for once and bringing us good fortune! Thank you, God, oh, thank you!

"Are you sure you read right, Yankev-Yosl? You're not mistaken—God forbid!—are you? Sanctified are you, oh, Lord, merciful father, kind and devoted! Our entire family will be blissful, friends will be delighted, enemies will be furious. Goodness! So much money—knock on wood! How much did you say, Yankev-Yosl? Seventy-five thousand?"

"Seventy-five thousand!" I say. "Hand me my caftan, Ziporah, and let's go!"

"Where do you want to go?"

"What do you mean, where? I have to go to Birnboim. He's got my ticket, I pawned it . . . And I don't have any receipt."

When she heard that, she—my missus, that is—turned all shades of green. Grabbing my hands, she exclaimed: "For the love of God, Yankev-Yosl, don't go right away. Think about what you're doing, where you're going, and how to talk to him. Don't forget, it's seventy-five thousand rubles!"

"Just like a woman!" I say. "So it's seventy-five thousand—big deal! I wasn't born yesterday!"

"Listen to me, Yankev-Yosl," she says. "Think it over first, discuss it with a friend, don't go to Birnboim right away—I won't let you!"

To make a long story short, you know that when a woman digs in her heels, she gets her way. We summoned a friend and told him the whole story. After hearing us out, he said she was right—my missus, that is—because seventy-five thousand is no chicken feed. Meanwhile Birnboim had the ticket and I had no receipt. Money is a temptation, anything's possible, and if a bad thought were to enter his mind—well, it's seventy-five thousand!

You do understand, don't you? What can I say? They got me so depressed that I started worrying too and thinking goodness only knows what! Just what was I to do? In the end we decided that I was to take two hundred rubles (money was promptly available: when you've won seventy thousand rubles, your credit rating shoots up) and I was also to take along a person who'd remain outside Birnboim's door. I'd have a little chat with Birnboim, pay off my debt and the accrued interest, and get back my lottery ticket. It would work one way or the other. Either he'd return the ticket—which was certainly good; or he'd refuse, in which case I'd at least have a witness. You do understand, don't you?

"It'll work," I mused, "only if he hasn't heard that the ticket is worth seventy-five thousand. But what if he's got a newspaper too and he's seen the winning number? And what if he says something like what that famous woman with the broken pot said: 'First of all, I returned your ticket long ago. Secondly, your number isn't the winning number. And thirdly, I never got your ticket in the first place!' You do understand, don't you? Unless God has performed a miracle, and Birnboim hasn't heard about the jackpot yet!"

"Don't forget, Yankev-Yosl, it's no chicken feed. You're going for seventy-five thousand! Your face shouldn't reveal the slightest clue, the slightest hint of seventy-five thousand. And whatever happens, don't forget that life is worth more than seventy-five thousand times seventy-five thousand!"

That's what my missus said—may she be healthy. Taking hold of both my hands, she told me to give her my word, my sacred word of honor, that I would keep calm . . . Calm? Do you understand? Try and keep calm while my heart was boiling in me, my mind thrashing about—and I couldn't forgive myself: "What, Yankev-Yosl, what, you fool! Give away a lottery ticket worth seventy-five thousand to Birnboim, a perfect stranger? And you don't even get a receipt, and he doesn't even dip his pen into ink?" You do understand, don't you? Do you happen to have a pen on you?—dammit, I mean a cigarette.

So anyhow, where was I? Oh yes, Birnboim. "It'll be a fine thing," I thought to myself, "if Birnboim's already gone through the gazette long since and found out about the seventy-five thousand just like me, maybe even sooner than me, and I go to him and I say:

"'Good day, Mr. Birnboim.'

"'Good day. What can I do for you?'

"'Where is my ticket, sir?'

"'What ticket?'

"'Ticket series 2289, number 12, which I left with you as collateral.' And he looks at me like an idiot."

Those were the thoughts flitting through my mind, and my chest felt tight, I was choking, gasping for air, for breath! So what finally happened? I went to see Birnboim. Where was Birnboim? He was asleep . . . Asleep? Why, that was a sign that he didn't have the foggiest notion. The Lord be praised! Upon entering his apartment, I found his wife, Feygele, in the kitchen. The place was filled with smoke and heat and mire.

"Welcome, Yankev-Yosl," she said, inviting me in and offering me the seat at the very head of the table. She then asked me how come they'd seen so little of me.

"How should I know why you've seen so little of me? I wish I knew myself!" And, gazing deep into her eyes, I thought: "Does she know or doesn't she know? She doesn't seem to know. Or maybe she does know? . . ."

"How've you been doing, Yankev-Yosl?"

"How should I be doing?" I said. "Maybe you've heard about my tsoris?"

"What tsoris?"

"Goodness," I say, "you mean you haven't heard about the theft of my sacks?"

"Oh, those tsoris?" she says. "Why, that's yesterday's news. I figured you had some real news."

"News? Could she mean the seventy-five thousand?" Those were my thoughts, as I gazed deep into her eyes. But I couldn't read her mind, it was a blank slate!

"Would you like a glass of tea, Yankev-Yosl? I'll fan the fire under the samovar until my husband gets up."

"A glass of tea? With pleasure, why not?" And my heart dropped, I was choking, gasping for air, my mouth was dry, the apartment was hot, I was sweating buckets, and she—Feygele, that is—was talking to me, but she might as well have been talking to the wall! For my head was in the alcove where Birnboim was lying fast asleep and snoring like there was no tomorrow. You do understand, don't you?

"Why aren't you drinking?" she says—Feygele, that is.

"I'm drinking, aren't I?" I say, stirring and stirring.

"You're just been stirring," she says, "for an hour now, but you haven't drunk a drop."

"Thank you," I say, "but I don't drink cold tea—I mean hot tea. I'd rather," I say, "let the tea stand a while and get really hot, I mean really cold—that is, it really warms up, I mean cools off . . ."

"You seem very confused, Yankev-Yosl," she says. "You're so confused that you don't know what you're saying. Are you so confused because your sacks were stolen? God will help, the sacks will turn up. I've heard that there's some clues. Hey, my husband's stirring, he's getting up, here he comes!"

In walked my old pal, drowsy and sporting a silk skullcap. Rubbing his eyes, he eyed me askance. "How are you, Yankev-Yosl?"

My first thought was: "Does he know? Or doesn't he know? He doesn't seem to know. But maybe he does?" I say: "How should I be? You've heard about my bad luck with the sacks?"

"The story's got a beard. Tell us something we don't know. Feygele, have you got a little jam? I just woke up and I've got a bad taste in my mouth," says Birnboim, making a face.

"Well, if he wants jam, it's a sign he hasn't got a clue." Those were my thoughts, and I began to chat with him about only goodness knows what, it was totally incoherent. My stomach was heaving, I was choking, I felt like I was about to kick the bucket, I was ready to collapse, I was ready to yell out: "Help! Jews! Seventy-five thousand!" You do understand, don't you? But then God took pity, and I launched into a conversation about interest.

"Mr. Birnboim, I can give you a little interest—that is, I can pay off the interest I owe you on the ticket."

"Ah, with pleasure, what an honor!" he says, tasting a spoonful of jam.

"How much do I owe you," I say, "I mean interest?"

"Do you want to know," he says, "the exact amount or do you want to pay me money?"

"No," I say, "I mean, that is, I want to pay it off!"

"Feygele," he says, "c'mon, hand me the ledger."

Upon hearing that, I came back from the grave. "The poor guy doesn't have the foggiest clue!"

After paying him the interest, I say to him: "If you don't mind, Mr. Birnboim, please record in your ledger that you received the interest from me on my lottery ticket, series 2289, number 12."

"Record it, Feygele, lottery ticket, series 2289, number 12."

"He doesn't have the slightest inkling!" I thought to myself and I began chatting about lottery tickets and how it wasn't worth having a ticket and paying interest on it, and what would happen with the ticket.

"Why do you say so?" he says, eying me askance. A knife slashed through my heart. I didn't like the way he eyed me—you do understand, don't you? But then I pulled myself together, and I say: "You understand, Mr. Birnboim, I'm saying that because I've got nothing but expenses with that ticket. You ought to charge me lower interest now. After all, we're old acquaintances, as you say, and close neighbors."

"No," he says. "Anything but that. We'll keep the same interest, or else pay me the principal and pawn your ticket somewhere else."

"Right now?" I say, my heart pounding like a hammer—Bang, bang, bang! Bang, bang, bang!

"Right away!" he says.

"Well, then take your money!" I say, laying out my two hundred-ruble notes—and my heart practically leaped from my chest.

"Take the money," he says to Feygele, and then he leaned over toward his glass of tea and ate a spoonful of jam. After that spoonful he had another spoonful, and after that spoonful he had another and still another. I wanted to get my hands on my ticket, and all he did was gulp down jam! Every minute, every second cost me some health and some life's blood! But you shouldn't be a swine. If a guy likes jam—then bon appétit! It's not nice rushing him. You may be in agony, but you have to wait till he's done with his jam. You do understand, don't you? Do you happen to have a little jam on you—dammit, I mean a cigarette?

So anyhow, where was I? My old pal was eating jam. After finishing his jam and wiping his lips, he says to me: "Yankev-Yosl, I've taken your money, you've paid the interest, and now you want your ticket back?"

"Absolutely," I say pretending to be cool but practically fainting with delight.

"There's only one problem," he says, "I can't give you the ticket today."

When he spoke those words, I felt a knife slashing my heart. I'd been in seventh heaven, but now I suddenly came crashing to the ground—I don't know how I managed to keep on my legs.

"What's wrong, Mr. Birnboim? Why can't you give me my ticket today?"

"Because," he said, "I don't have it here."

"What do you mean," I say, "you don't have it here?"

"It's in the bank," he says to me.

Upon hearing that, I breathed a little easier, and I began thinking.

"What are you thinking about?" he says.

"Nothing," I say. "I'm just standing here and trying to figure out what we should do."

"It's very simple," he says. "I'll go downtown tomorrow and bring you the ticket."

"Fine!" I say, and then I say goodbye and head for the door—but then I came back. "Goodness, Mr. Birnboim, what kind of businessman am I? I've paid you the principal. I've paid off the interest, and you've still got the ticket. So at least give me a receipt!"

"What do you need a receipt for?" he says. "You can't trust me for two hundred rubles without a receipt?"

"Maybe you're right," I say and head for the door, but then I came back once more. "No," I say to him. "It's not right, it's not good business. If you leave a lottery ticket with someone, you need a receipt . . . Please do as I say, Mr. Birnboim and give me a receipt. Why shouldn't you give me a receipt?"

Suddenly Birnboim got up, went behind the curtain of his alcove, and called over Feygele.

"Mr. Birnboim!" I cry out. "I know why you're calling over Feygele. You wanna tell her to send the servant out to get the newspaper. Today's May 2, and you wanna see whether the ticket's won anything. Why waste your time? I'll tell you the news: my ticket, thank the Lord, has won big time!"

Birnbaum's face turned every shade of green. "Really?" he says. "Praise the Lord! How much did it win?"

"It won," says I, "a nice tidy sum—may it happen to all Jews. And that's why I want a receipt from you—you do understand, don't you?"

"I tell you," he says. "let the good Lord help you with your two hundred ten thousand. I'm happy for you—believe me!—with all my heart! But how much did the ticket win? Why are you scared of telling me?"

"Mr. Birnboim," I say. "The ticket's won. Why waste our breath arguing? It's won seventy-five thousand rubles, and you've got my ticket. I've paid off the interest, I've paid off the principal—give me my ticket! You say you don't have the ticket, it's in the bank? Then give me a receipt, and that'll be that!"

"What do you need it for?" His eyes suddenly flipped over and his face turned a fiery red.

I could see that his mood was anything but cheerful. I took him aside, grabbed his arms, and said: "My dear friend! Take pity on me and on you, tell me what you want. We'll get through this. Don't torture me, I can barely stand up! Tell me how much you want and give me a receipt for the ticket. It may sound crazy, but I'm not leaving without a receipt—it's a question of seventy-five thousand rubles!"

"What can I tell you?" he says, his eyes ablaze. "People have to trust one another. You have to take people at their word!"

"Who cares," I say, "about people? Let's be people ourselves. Listen to me, Birnboim. For the love of God—tell me what you want! We don't want to become laughingstocks, we don't want any scandals!"

"Only people!" he says. "I'll do whatever people say I should do!"

I saw I was getting nowhere fast, so I opened the front door and summoned my man—that is, my witness. "Zaidl, you can go now!" Zaidl took to his heels and shouted all over town that Yankev-Yosl's ticket had won seventy-five thousand rubles and that Birnboim had the ticket and refused to hand it back! You do understand, don't you? That was all I needed. In less than half an hour, Birnboim's apartment was mobbed, the street was inundated. There was a tumult, a hubbub, a hurly-burly: "Ticket . . . Yankev-Yosl . . . Birnboim . . . Seventy-five thousand." People took up my cause. Some were pounding on the table, others swore they'd clobber him soundly, break every bone in his body, smash his home to bits—and they weren't joking! Until we agreed to consult our plutocrat and accept his judgment fully. And so all of us, the entire congregation, went to see the plutocrat.

OUR PLUTOCRAT, YOU ought to know, is a quiet man, very friendly and decent. And basically he doesn't like to arbitrate disputes. But then the entire congregation came tumbling in, shouting "Help!"—otherwise they'd tear the place apart. He had no choice, he was forced to deal with the mess! And we had to agree in writing that we would fully abide by his decision. Poor Birnboim had to sign the ticket over to the judge, who decreed that tomorrow or the day after, God willing, we'd all go downtown and get the ticket from the bank, and I would pay Birnboim whatever the judge decreed. You do understand, don't you?

Now you probably think that that was that, don't you? Not by a long shot! This is where the mess really gets going. Understand that I had a partner for my ticket. Where have you seen a Jew with a lottery ticket all to himself? Who was my partner? My partner was my very own brother. Henekh was his name, and he lived in a small shtetl not so far away. And it was through him that I gave this Birnboim the ticket as collateral. No, I mean the other way around. He, my brother, gave this Birnboim this collateral through me. You do understand, don't you? But there's a whole story behind that, and I have to tell it to you very accurately, so that you'll understand.

Now just where was I? I was talking about my brother Henekh. Well, I've got my very own brother (long life to him), and so what can I tell you? It's not easy talking about your own brother. How do you put it? "Blow your nose and smear your face!" You shouldn't air your dirty linen in public. But between you, me, and the lamppost, we don't really get along. You do understand, don't you? I hope that what I did for him won't be held against me. I can boast that I helped him stand on his own two feet. First God, then I made him a mentsh. I don't have to toot my own horn—you do understand, don't you?

You see, he sent me a lottery ticket and asked me to sell it or pawn it—to get two hundred rubles for it and send him the money—I could do that, couldn't I? Oh, why should he worry about the ticket? Why bother? Think about it, insure it, pay interest on it—so why should he care? And with God's help—the ticket won. Who banged his head against Birnboim's wall? Who practically had a heart attack until we figured out a solution? And finally, when something came of it, what did that brother of mine argue? "Who asked you to get lovey-dovey with my ticket?"

Have you ever heard the likes of that? How do you like that kind of response from a crude individual? Naturally it made me hit the ceiling and it cut me to the quick: "Well, if that's the kind of crude person you are, who says the ticket is yours?"

"So then whose ticket," he says, "is it?"

"Whose ticket?" I say. "Whosesoever it is. Meanwhile we have to rescue it from someone else's clutches. Because it's no chicken feed," I say. "It's seventy-five thousand rubles!" You do understand, don't you?

Well, what would I get out of it? Did I need the aggravation? Did I need to have my table pounded on? My chairs smashed? The world says you can't make a rabbi's hat out of a sow's tail! And that, I guess, is as true as can be. . . . So I made up my mind: why fight with my brother? We were the envy of 136 million people, and in the end the two of us were at each other's throats—brothers! My ticket, your ticket—who cares? First we had to safeguard the ticket. That, I figured, was a wee bit more crucial. Huh? What was that? It's not so?

Well, try arguing with a crude person! I mean my brother Henekh, that's who I mean—and I hope God won't punish me for saying that! For if Henekh had told me what was bothering him, if he'd told me that this was no run-of-the-mill ticket, that there was a fly in the ointment, I'd've known what to do. But when did my brother tell me about the fly? Long, long after the ticket had been signed over to the plutocrat, and the examining magistrate had issued an injunction and grabbed this ticket from the bank, and each of us had been individually interrogated—that is, the magistrate summoned us and told us to make an effort and testify in detail about the ticket:

How had this ticket, he asked, come into my possession? And what was Birnboim's part in the affair? "And what," he says, "does the plutocrat have to do with it?" What a mess! You do understand, don't you? What did the examining magistrate have to do with it? And why did he have to hear all these stories? And now listen: that was where the fly in the ointment came in. It was the kind of fly that you couldn't avoid—you can choke on a fly like that! You want to know what the fly in the ointment was? It was some sort of monk, a priest. You do understand, don't you? A monk, a priest who lived in the same shtetl as Henekh, who had been doing business with him for lots and lots of years, with nothing in writing, borrowing money and selling his wares, and they got along like peaches and cream. You do understand, don't you? . . .

Now one day, something happened (according to the priest—so go take his holy word). My brother went to him and said: "Father, I need a noninterest loan, a couple of hundred rubles. It's market day for me."

The priest replied: "Where should I get it from? I don't have a kopek to my name."

"That's no excuse!" says my brother. "I gotta have two hundred rubles—it's a matter of life and death!"

"What a strange person you are," says the priest. "I told you I haven't got a kopek to my name. If you like, I can lend you a lottery ticket, a winner, which you can redeem for cash."

You do understand, don't you? It was actually the ticket that eventually won seventy-five thousand rubles. That's what happened, according to the priest—so go take his holy word. But then, when the ticket won, the priest came dashing over to my brother, and he says to him, he says: "The ticket's won a nice tidy sum, thank the Lord."

So my brother says to him: "Yes, I heard it's won some money."

So the priest says: "So what are we going to do?"

So my brother says: "So what should we do?"

To make a long story short: they discussed, disputed, dissented, disagreed. They had nothing in black and white, no document—you do understand, don't you? My brother at least had a ticket—but what did the priest have? Nothing but grief. So they finally settled: he—the priest, that is—asked my brother for at least several thousand rubles.

So take the money, you crude person, Henekh, my brother, stuff his mouth with several thousand rubles, and stop quarreling! But my brother argued: "Why should he get anything? The ticket's mine, after all. I swear by all that's holy that I bought it from him three years ago!"

Now it would've gone smoothly if it hadn't been for our dear Jews—long life to them! Our shtetl per se is a good shtetl. Maybe you've heard of it? Slanderville? Well, as it says in the Bible [I Samuel 25:25]: "As his name is so is he"—the name says it all! It's a town of backbiters and badmouthers—may they all be burned alive on a summer day!

So anyhow, what can I tell you? Off they went to the priest, and they enlightened him, saying he stood to make a bundle, he should drop everything, go to the big city, and head straight for the district attorney, and testify that Jews had cheated him out of a lottery ticket, that the ticket had won seventy-five thousand rubles, and that the Jews refused to give him back the ticket. You do understand, don't you? So anyhow, what can I tell you? The priest didn't waste a second, he did everything he had to, and more than he had to, and the district attorney's office took out an injunction and grabbed the ticket, and thereby hangs a tail, and it's no laughing matter! Here was the next calamity—wasn't that enough?! And here was the fly in the ointment—a priest! Eventually my brother promised him ten thousand rubles, then fifteen thousand. The priest changed his mind. They confused him so thoroughly, you understand, that he himself didn't know what he wanted. And that's the story of the fly in the ointment—you do understand, don't you? . . .

So anyhow, where was I? Oh, that's right. I was talking about the fly in the ointment. God granted us a real fly—you can imagine! We couldn't force it down and we couldn't spit it out! Between the devil and the deep blue sea—it was stuck in our craw. But there is a God in the world, a great God—how do you put it? With one hand He assails, with the other He heals. People were found—pals, in-laws, friends, and simply ordinary people. They mediated, they arbitrated, they adjudicated from all sides—to and fro, back and forth, between my brother and the priest, between the priest and my brother, between me and Birnboim and between Birnboim and me, between the two of us and my brother, and between the three of us and the priest. A hustling and bustling, a hurrying, a scurrying, a flurrying! To make a long story short: after loads of struggling, we just barely managed to come to terms. What kind of terms? How good were the terms? Don't ask—at least we came to terms. How do you put it: you can cook injustice for supper.

Or as my brother put it when he and the priest were brought face to face: "Your Holiness, let's share according to the decision of a third party."

To which the priest said: "Let's share! But you, Henekh, are a thief!"

"*L'khaim*, Father. To your health!" said my brother, handing him a glass, and we each took a glass and we all drank up and hugged and kissed. Everything was just fine and dandy, we were all satisfied . . . Satisfied! How could we be satisfied if each of us had at some point almost held the seventy-five thousand and then watched it carried off by the wind? Dammit! You want to know how? Here's a simple calculation. So forget it, no one says I didn't have the seventy-five thousand—serves me right! But I ask you: What would, say, my brother've done if I hadn't wired him that our ticket had won seventy-five thousand? Do you know what anyone else would've done in my place? He'd 've held his tongue and not let out a peep! Why should I bother about my brother? Why should I worry about Henekh? I could've told him I'd sold the ticket! I could've said I'd pawned it with Birnboim and failed to redeem it in time—after all, Birnboim had my promissory note describing my collateral as a ticket with such a serial number and stating that if I didn't redeem it by such-and-such a date, then such-and-such a ticket with such-and-such a number—you do understand, don't you? Not on your life! It never even crossed my mind—let me be free of all evil! Because as you see me here,

I'm the sort of man who doesn't give a tinker's damn about money! Just what is money anyway? Cash is trash, so long as God helps—as my wife says—so long as you've got your health and everything else you need. Well, but it was annoying all the same—seventy-five thousand rubles is no chicken feed! You do understand, don't you?

Now take Birnboim, for instance. Why, Birnboim is as innocent as a newborn lamb. The poor man actually let the seventy-five thousand slip through his fingers. After all, he's an honest young man, as honest as the day is long, and he wouldn't want to profit from someone else's lottery ticket. He just wanted to ask people what people would say. You do understand, don't you? There would be no hitches, because he had an IOU, which said that if I didn't redeem the ticket by the deadline, then such-and-such a ticket in such-and-such a series—you do understand, don't you? And this ticket up and won the seventy-five thousand! Doesn't that—I ask you—curdle your blood? So there were two unhappy souls in the world, and each had practically thrown away seventy-five thousand rubles. Huh? Isn't that so?

The third unhappy soul was my poor brother Henekh. He simply went around like a mugging victim, like a slaughtered chicken. You had to desperately pity him for getting so little money out of the deal! After all, he's accustomed to hitting the jackpot every year, maybe even twice a year, and always raking in seventy-five thousand rubles—not a kopek less! So he went around, yelling: "What do they want from me? Why are they robbing me? I'm supposed to shell out to all of them? Give to the priest, shell out to my brother, shell out to Birnboim—they want to leave me penniless!" You do understand, don't you?

The fourth soul, the priest, was truly an unhappy priest! He swore—and you'd have to take his holy word—that he didn't understand why these Jews were getting part of the money. "Fine," he says, "Henekh may be a shark and he may go to synagogue, but we're from the same shtetl, and he's good pal. But the entire Jewish congregation?" he says. "What does the congregation have to do with my ticket!"

You do understand, don't you? Just try talking to a Gentile priest, try teaching him the meaning of honesty. On the one side, there was the pal who could have taken all the money and no one would have been the wiser, and on the other side there was the young man who was as honest as the day is long and who had my note stating that such-and-such a ticket in such-and-such a series—you do understand, don't you? Did he have a hidden agenda—I mean Birnboim? Was he asking for money? Did he have any demands? God forbid! All he wanted was for us to ask people *what people would say!* A person who was in love with people—a humane human—you do understand, don't you?

Basically, you see, four people had each won a share of seventy-five thousand rubles and four people had each lost seventy-five thousand rubles—four miserable, beaten people. But they had managed to come to terms, and that was that! Maybe it was a godsend. And what was left to do now? Now we had to get our shares—that is, all four of us had to go to the bank, get the ticket to pick up the jackpot, give each person his share, wish one another mazeltov, and seal the bargain with a drink. Wasn't that so? Take it easy, take your time, hold your horses. First of all, the ticket had been sealed by the investigating magistrate, so it had to be released. But the priest refused to have it released till he was guaranteed his share. You do understand, don't you? How could we guarantee him his share? We had to transfer the ticket from the plutocrat's account to my brother Henekh and the priest. But the plutocrat wouldn't hear of it. You see, he—the plutocrat, that is—argued and he was right:

"What's my connection with some else's lottery ticket? How can I transfer a seventy-five-thousand-ruble ticket if it's enjoined and I don't know who the rightful owner is? It used to belong to Birnboim and Yankev-Yosl, but today I hear that it belongs to Henekh and the priest. And later on, new owners are going to come out of the woodwork, new Henekhs and new priests. What if each of them demands seventy-five thousand from me? C'mon! Where am I going to dig up all that money? I'm no Rothschild, you know!"

You do understand, don't you? Now a whole free-for-all began with lawyers. And lawyers are like doctors: if one says something, then the next one says the opposite. They take your money and they give you advice, each one a different piece of advice. One lawyer says that the plutocrat could transfer the lottery ticket to anybody he wanted to. A second lawyer says that the plutocrat absolutely mustn't hand over the ticket. But then along comes a third lawyer and he says that the plutocrat *must*, otherwise he'll be in a lot of trouble! Along comes a fourth lawyer and he says it would be best if the plutocrat simply abrogated all responsibility for the ticket and everything will be just fine and dandy. But then along comes yet another lawyer and he says: Not for all the tea in China! Because if he—the plutocrat, that is—severed his link to the ticket, the ticket would be left dangling in the air, and he'd be up to his ears in trouble. And along comes still another lawyer and he says that if the plutocrat doesn't abrogate responsibility for the ticket, then he'd really be in trouble. Then along comes a new lawyer, and he pronounces a new verdict: Whether the plutocrat keeps the ticket or gives it up—it doesn't matter, he'll be in trouble either way. You do understand, don't you?

It struck me that the plutocrat already had more than his share of trouble. For besides the fact that everyone kept yelling away at him, the poor man—the plutocrat, that is—had to come to town every week and dash from one lawyer to the next, forking over money and begging for mercy and for advice on how to get rid of this white elephant! It was a pity, I tell you, a crying shame, a scandal! They take a person, a quiet, honest man, who wouldn't harm a fly, and they saddle him with a white elephant, bamboozle him—and he manages to hold on! And do you know why? And who? And how come he gets saddled with a white elephant? It's because people went out of their way to help a fellow man—you do understand, don't you? Now do you happen to have a white elephant on you? Dammit! I mean another cigarette.

So anyhow, where was I? Oh, that's right. I was talking about the white elephant they saddled our plutocrat with. And would you like to hear what happened with the white elephant? Nothing! A white elephant is a white elephant! At this point it was still dangling in the air. Every week the plutocrat came hopping into town, consulting with lawyers. The lawyers took money and gave advice. One lawyer said this, a second one said that, and a third—needless to say—said neither this nor that but the other way around. God alone knew how it would end, for no human mind could imagine the outcome, and if it came to a trial—God forbid!—no one could guess the verdict. You do understand, don't you?

Meanwhile who was ready to bite the dust? Yankev-Yosl, that's who! The whole town—what am I saying, the whole town? The whole world put in their two cents. Everyone pointed at me: "There goes the seventy-five-thousand-ruble man." I was cut out of business, I didn't have a kopek to my name—it was worse than before. My wife was too embarrassed to go to market: people nicknamed her "Mrs. Nouveau Plutocrat."

In synagogue that Sabbath, I was the sixth man called on to read from the Torah (the sixth is a great honor!)—and for charitable donations. They'd drawn up a list of how I was to spend the seventy-five thousand rubles: how much I *had* to give the town, how much I *should* distribute to poor relatives, and what I would do with the rest. One man said I'd probably become a moneylender, another claimed I'd go back to dealing in bread, a third one demonstrated that the best thing for me would be an office. If I had an office, they said, I'd do the most lucrative business, for what office in town had a startup capital of seventy-five thousand? Cash—they figured—cold, hard cash. That's what they figured. You do understand, don't you?

You see, the Jews in our shtetl are all big nonbelievers: nobody believes that anyone has more than twenty-five rubles to his name. Our shtetl, you must know, is a proper shtetl—the devil hasn't carried it off! It's the kind of shtetl people ask for. There are enough idlers with nothing to do, so they wander from group to group, talking about everybody and their uncle. If you don't have a business of your own, then you talk about someone else's. They gather outside the pharmacy—the so-called shlock exchange—and they speculate about other people's business dealings. They're worried that someone might be in the black, and if someone else is in the red, then they rejoice, it makes them feel good.

So you understand what a dark cloud passed over the shtetl when they heard about the seventy-five thousand? As of that day, tongues were busy wagging from dawn till dusk. People made nasty cracks and quips, they jeered at one another, they tormented one another, they asked one another snide questions: "Why didn't you win the seventy-five thousand? You could really use the money!"

"Why didn't *you*? You need it a lot more than I do."

To spite everyone else, some mathematician calculated that I was the richest man in town. "It's a simple calculation," he said. I'd won seventy-five thousand, my apartment was worth about six or seven thousand—that came to some eighty-five thousand, which was not that far from one hundred thousand. And if a man had a hundred thousand, you could say he had two hundred thousand, because if you estimated that a man had two hundred thousand, then he didn't have one hundred thousand either! So I must have had two hundred thousand. In other words, I was the richest man in town. Were there richer men than me? The answer was: How could you tell? Who had dug in their pockets and counted their money? They could be insolvent. You do understand, don't you?

It cut a lot of people to their very marrows. The poor devils couldn't stand the fact that all at once a run-of-the-mill Jew had up and won seventy-five thousand rubles without so much as lifting a finger. There's a man in our shtetl, a rich and stingy bachelor, and the scamps sent him a messenger to bring the good news that Yankev-Yosl had won seventy-five thousand rubles. The man got so sick—it shouldn't happen to you!—that they thought he was a goner. People truly pitied him. For several days he went around in a horrible state. But then, after hearing about my brother Henekh and the fly in the ointment, the bachelor felt slightly better. "The priest oughta get it all! Why should a Jew have so much money?"

You do understand, don't you? Now you may think your relatives would be glad for your sake. Well, you've got another think coming! They'd be happy to drown you in a spoonful of water! You can assume that if I'd gotten the seventy-five thousand, they would have sung a different tune. Everyone would have gotten something—my relatives and outsiders. But since things turned out the way they did, they sang an altogether different tune. Well, the family could sew themselves new moneybags. As for my brother Henekh, he's a real philanthropist (may he enjoy good health!). If he starts handing out cash donations, then you'll really get an eyeful! Apparently he allotted between sixty-five and seventy-two rubles for his poor sister's wedding and he bestowed a cool hundred on his father: let the old man—his father, that is—realize that his son had won the seventy-five thousand. You do understand, don't you?

So much for the local relatives. Those who lived far away simply came pouring in from all over the world, one with these tsoris, another with those tsoris. Many of them began arranging matches and weddings on my account. A few got divorced, hoping for better marriages. Now those were at least kinsfolk. How do you put it? Blood is messier than water. You do understand, don't you? But when it comes to strangers, perfect strangers, why should I feel obligated? What responsibilities do I have? For whose sins? You see, if I've got an enemy anywhere, I only wish he'd win seventy-five thousand rubles! You can take my word for it: I couldn't endure all the mazeltovs, all the accompanying smiles, all the flattery! People I didn't know from Adam came to me for advice:

"We heard about you, Yankev-Yosl," they'd say. "We heard long ago that you're an intelligent man. Please don't think," they'd say, "that we have any ulterior motive now that God has granted you the seventy-five thousand—heaven forbid! We've simply come to you," they'd say, "for an old-fashioned heart-to-heart."

You do understand, don't you? Someone came to me from some

strange town—I've forgotten its name, it's in some faraway country, where even my grandfather's grandmother has never been to. The door opens, and suddenly in walks a man and puts down his bags.

"How do you do?"

"How do you do? Where are you from?"

"From Byelorussia. Are you Mr. Yankev-Yosl?"

"That's me, Yankev-Yosl. What's the good word?"

"Are you the Yankev-Yosl who won the seventy-five thousand? I come here for you—that is, I happened to be in the neighborhood when I heard about the seventy-five thousand. So I figured, why not just go there for a day? I want to see the winner with my own two eyes, the lucky man who won seventy-five thousand! It's no chicken feed—it's seventy-five thousand!"

You do understand, don't you? Try telling each single person the whole story about Birnboim, who wants people, about a brother named Henekh, about the fly in the ointment, about a white elephant, about lawyers, and about spirits and demons! You see, I longed for the happy years before the seventy-five thousand, the years that were better and certainly more peaceful than now, after the seventy-five thousand! I'll tell you the truth: I'm not sure of my life now. Recently I went to the city and to the lawyers there, and one of them enticed me to his home for a glass of tea. So I went to his home, it was nighttime, and I found another man there, a Jew with a fine beard and all, and he was poring over a holy book. He greeted me, stood up to smoke a cigarette, put out the lamp, and we remained in the dark . . . You do understand, don't you? Now if it weren't so late and you didn't have to get going, I'd tell you this story too, by God! And there's another story sitting on this one, and still another on that one. How do you put it? There's a pustula on a blister, and a blister on a boil. You do understand, don't you?

So anyhow, where was I? Oh, that's right. I was talking about the end of the story. An end, you think? We've got time, there's no hurry, we're only at the start. What am I saying? A start? The start hasn't even started yet. And whose fault is it? Mine? Why say it's my fault? Why me? How should I know? I'm only human, you know, I'm only flesh and blood. But what good is that when bad luck comes your way? Why is it my fault if I . . . Oh, never mind! You mustn't grab the fish before the noodles—wait! It's the other way around: you mustn't grab the noodles before the fish. Let me tell you the entire story slowly, without hurrying, from the very start—that is, not from the first start, but from the last start—that is, from the start that you think is the end.

In any case, if you recall, we arduously and painfully agreed to share the jackpot with God's help, whereby each one of us was to get part of the money. Easier said than done, of course. We did enough haggling, enough hollering at each person in turn. The priest argued: Why should Birnboim and I—the two of us, that is—get any money? And my brother Henekh claimed that I should rely on his sense of justice and on his goodwill and on his intelligence. And my friend—Birnboim, that is—shouted that he didn't want anything, all he wanted was people, he wanted to hear what people would say. You do understand, don't you? Brokers stuck their noses into our business—three at a time, laboring, dividing, with no end in sight.

We finally agreed, if you recall—now what did we agree? We agreed that the four of us should go to the big city, take out the ticket, get the bit of cash, and divvy it up: here's yours, here's mine, and hail and farewell! Well, talk is cheap. There has to be a ticket. But what if there's no ticket? How can there be no ticket? A ticket existed. But if you recall, where was the ticket? Locked up in some bank, under someone else's name, and, if you recall, it—the ticket, that is—was, I'm sorry to say, under an injunction. So just trying getting your hands on such a ticket!

What should we do? First off, if you recall, we had to finish the whole business—terminate it for now, and then we could see what we had to do. You do understand, don't you? Now who should finish the whole business? The priest, of course. But, if you recall, the priest said that we first had to give him a power of attorney—that is, transfer the ticket to his name. Then he'd terminate the whole business. And wasn't he right, after all? Now who was to transfer the ticket to his name so he could terminate the whole business? Our plutocrat, of course.

So we went to our plutocrat and asked him to please transfer the ticket so we could terminate the whole business. But the plutocrat had the same old argument, if you recall, and he was right: "Why come to me?" he says. "Why've you burdened me with someone else's business?"

To which we countered: "You're right, of course. But what can we do if we can't terminate the whole business without you?"

So he says: "So what? Is that my fault? You can terminate your business or not terminate your business—but what business is it of mine?"

You do understand, don't you? By the way, do you happen to have a business on you? Dammit! I mean a cigarette.

So anyhow, where was I? Oh, that's right. I was talking about terminating the whole business. Well, take this advice, take that advice—we decided to go to court. And to go to court you need to consult a lawyer. And to consult a lawyer, you have to go to the city. And so it started all over again: What lawyer should we consult? One person says we have to consult this lawyer, someone else says we have to consult that lawyer. So we consulted both lawyers—what choice did we have? And this lawyer says the very opposite of what that lawyer says. And the third lawyer just fizzles out. Things looked bad—so we went to a fourth lawyer.

Now do I have to tell you what lawyers are like? Lawyers and doctors are the same kind of plague. They were created solely in order to contradict one another. When one of them says something, another says the exact opposite—it's like the Aramaic translation of the Bible, if you'll excuse my mentioning them in the same breath. I've got a friend, and he says: "Just what is the Aramaic translation all about? It's about being contrary. If the Hebrew says 'sayeth,' then the Aramaic says 'says.'" And just try doing something about it! You do understand, don't you?

When one lawyer says that all four of us should sue the bank and the plutocrat for refusing to hand over the ticket, it sounds like a useful idea, right? But then along comes the other lawyer and he says that only two of us should sue, me and Birnboim, and we should only sue the plutocrat for refusing to order the bank to hand over the ticket. Well, that didn't sound so bad, did it now? But then the third lawyer told me: What was my connection with the bank? Did the bank know me? Had the bank ever had any dealings with me? Birnboim alone should sue, and he should sue only the plutocrat, not the bank, for why was it the bank's fault that he, Birnboim, had recently told the bank to transfer the ticket from his account to the plutocrat's account? Well, that sounds reasonable enough, doesn't it? But now along came another lawyer and he claimed that neither I nor Birnboim should sue: you see, the suing should be done by the priest and my brother Henekh. Well, that made sense too, didn't it?

But then along came yet another lawyer and he hit on yet another idea: there was, he said, no need to sue. How, he said, did the bank get a lottery ticket in the plutocrat's name? Birnboim had brought it in. And where had Birnboim gotten the ticket? From Yankev-Yosl—from me, that is. And where had I gotten it? From my brother—Henekh, that is. And where had my brother Henekh gotten it? He'd borrowed it—I mean bought it from the priest. Henekh said "bought," the priest said "borrowed"—what difference did it make, what was done was done! The priest, said the lawyer, should ask my brother Henekh for the ticket, my brother Henekh should ask me, I should ask Birnboim, and Birnboim should ask—whom? Birnboim should ask the bank. But didn't the bank argue that it didn't know Birnboim, it only knew the plutocrat? So Birnboim should ask the plutocrat, and the plutocrat should ask the bank.

Well, but wasn't the plutocrat afraid to do that? What if he were sued? The lawyer had an answer for everything. Birnboim should give the plutocrat a note, a receipt, I should give Birnboim a receipt, my brother Henekh should give me a receipt, and the priest should give my brother Henekh a receipt. So how do you like that idea? What could be fairer than that?

But then along came another lawyer, a true sage, and he asked a boggling question. How did we know, he said, that the ticket stopped with the priest? For all we knew, some creature might be hiding in some attic and he might get up tomorrow and show up with documents and witnesses and claim: "The ticket is mine! For goodness sake, where is my ticket?" And what would happen next? He might demand not just a ticket but seventy-five thousand rubles! And who would he demand it from? The plutocrat, that was who! But didn't the plutocrat have a receipt from Birnboim, and didn't Birnboim have a receipt from me, and I from my brother Henekh, and my brother Henekh from the priest? Let the plutocrat go, said the lawyer, and sue Birnboim, Birnboim me, I my brother Henekh, and my brother Henekh the priest—the very same story as "The Song of the Kid" that we sing at the Passover seder:

> The kitty ate the kid,
> The puppy bit the kitty,
> The stick beat the puppy,
> The fire burned the stick,
> The water quenched the fire,
> The ox drank the water,
> The slaughterer slaughtered the ox.

You do understand, don't you? So the situation was bleak again. What should we do? We had to consult a different lawyer—someone on the level of Copernicus—and from him to a higher lawyer, the "Golden

Sage." What good was it—we didn't skip a single lawyer, and these lawyers lawyered our heads so thoroughly that no matter where we were, no matter what we were doing, all we heard was "Lawyer!" and "Lawyer!" and "Lawyer!" Do you happen to have a lawyer on you? Dammit! I mean a cigarette!

So anyhow, where was I? Oh, that's right. I was talking about the lawyers. Well, God helped and the lawyers hit on a solution—they were lawyers, after all. What was the solution? This was the solution! Me and Birnboim—just the two of us—should be the first, before anyone else, to draw up and notarize an affidavit disclaiming any connection, any tie whatsoever, with the lottery ticket, etc., etc., and that the aforesaid lottery ticket was sent to me by my brother Henekh, who got it—purchased it, that is—from the priest in order to have it pawned, and that I had pawned it with Birnboim for two hundred rubles, which was the truth, the sacred, the sacrosanct truth and nothing but the truth. It was simple and straight-forward, with no tricks, no ploys, no hidden motives—what could be better than the truth? Yet no one had hit on this before, you do understand, don't you?

But hold your horses, it wasn't over. Do you honestly believe that the two of us—me and Birnboim—would take a beating like that? What about our shares? What would we do if we were then told, "You can kiss my butt!"? Should we rely on my brother's sense of justice and the priest's assurances? So what if we signed the affidavit and drank to one another's health? It meant nothing. A sheet of paper costs a kopek, and you can drink to one another's health every day—so long as you have a little schnapps.

What were the two of us—me and Birnboim—after? A guarantee—they should guarantee our shares, what was coming to us. You do understand, don't you? And now the real circus began. "Guarantees? Why should they get guarantees? It's bad enough for them to get money for nothing, and now they want guarantees in the bargain!"

It really shook us up. "How can you? Is that how you repay our honesty? It's enough that we're doing you this big favor—after all, we could get the whole seventy-five thousand, and nobody would care two hoots about it! And now you're making more demands?!"

"You expect us to thank you and pinch your cheeks?" That's what my brother Henekh said.

I was so annoyed. Then one word led to another, bangety-bang, which is normal between brothers. To make a long story short, they finally agreed—they'd give us a guarantee. IOUs? An IOU is a left-handed monkey wrench. A promissory note is a waste of paper. Well, then what? Cold cash. As my granny used to say (God rest her soul): "The best milk product is a piece of meat." But where can you get cash nowadays, when nobody has any cash? Money's available, a whole lot, but only among the Rothschilds.

"That's a bunch of empty words!" says Birnboim. "I'm not signing anything till I get a guarantee!"

"What kind of guarantee?"

"Any guarantee you like, so long as it's a guarantee. I'm not going to have the world laugh its head off at me and say that Yankev-Yosl is a fool!" You do understand, don't you?

But that wasn't enough. My pal—Birnboim, that is—began harping on the same old story: "People!" Since, he said, he was supposed to sign something, a receipt, and forever at that, he wanted us all to rely solely on people—whatever people would say—that would be.

"People again?" I say. "I thought we were done with that! What good are people?"

"Please understand," says Birnboim. "I want us to ask people. Maybe people will say that I've got nothing coming to me—why should I take money for nothing?"

You do understand, don't you? I'm yelling "guarantee" and he's arguing about people. "We'll get our guarantee afterwards. But first we have to ask people!"

"Stop carrying on about people," I say. "My head's peopled with all your people! We'd be better off," I say, "talking about a guarantee. A guarantee is much more crucial."

So anyhow, where was I? Oh, that's right. I was talking about a guarantee. Well, as you can imagine, we were guaranteed, we were tied to one another, as was proper, we signed any number of documents, had them notarized too, submitted them in the appropriate places, and we started going to lawyers, filling out documents, this document, that document, constantly hopping into the big city, paying expenses, paying for rooms, sleeping with bedbugs (so long as it was a "hotel"—an inn wasn't good enough!), eating fried roaches (so long as they were called "roasts"—stews weren't good enough!), sweating like in a steambath, broiling in the sun, walking the streets, going deaf, dumb, and blind from the banging and pounding and hullabaloo. And why endure all that? Something to boast about: seventy-five thousand rubles! Come what may, let's be done with it all!

As my wife says (long life to her!): "A copper kopek in the hand is worth more than a gold ruble in your dreams. Your seventy-five thousand," she says, "has already left seventy-five thousand holes in my heart. Thanks for the great honor, but no thanks," she says. "Who needs it?"

"Oh," I say, "you're just a woman, and a woman is a woman." That's what I said to her, but deep down I felt she was right. What good was the jackpot? I couldn't take it to market. All I could buy would be gratuitous enemies. One man would simply envy me, another would resent my good luck and worry that I might take money: "How come Yankev-Yosl gets so much money?" You do understand, don't you? You can imagine: enough blood has been drained until you finally hear the good news that everything's been resolved, the case is closed! And your eyes have done enough bulging until you're finally lucky enough to see the ticket!

But do you think we got to see the ticket that soon? Hold your horses—where's the fire? First we had to let a specific length of time pass—that is, a month—to allow anyone to appeal the court's decision. I don't know whether I had even one good night's sleep all that month. I kept having such wild and confused dreams—you do understand, don't you?—that I often woke up in the middle of the night, hollering in a strange voice: "Ziporah, I'm flying!"

"Where are you flying to?" she says to me. "How are you flying? Spit three times and tell me what you dreamed."

"I dreamed," I say, "a wonderful dream. I dreamed I had wings and I was flying, and weird beasts were flying after me, all kinds of bizarre creatures, snakes and lizards, trying to rip me to shreds."

That was one time. Another time I dreamed I was sitting on a sack, a big, inflated sack made of red rubber, and "75,000" was scrawled in big numbers on the side. It was on a summer day, a Sabbath—you do understand, don't you? All the townsfolk, men and women, were strolling about and now and then they halted and ogled me, goggled at me. All at once—boooom! We heard an explosion. The rubber sack had burst, and I was falling, falling, and shouting: "Ziporah! Burst!"

"God help us! Who? Who burst? I hope my enemies burst!" That's what my wife said as she woke me up and interpreted my dream favorably, as women usually do.

So anyhow, where was I? Oh, that's right. I was talking about getting the lottery ticket. Well, when we were about to go and pick up the ticket, a new debate broke out. As it says in the Bible [Exodus 10:8]: "Who are they that shall go?" Who, that is, would perform that task? Everybody trusts himself completely, but no one is obligated to trust anyone else — it was too big a temptation, it was seventy-five thousand rubles! You do understand, don't you? It was decided that I didn't trust you and you didn't trust me — so let's all of us go together.

Now what did "all of us together" mean? It meant some ten people. And how had it gotten to be ten people? Just figure it out and you'll see. I'm one, Birnboim makes two, the priest makes three, my brother Henekh makes four, three lawyers (one for the priest, one for my brother, a Tarashts lawyer, and one for me and Birnboim, a Tsherkask lawyer), which already makes seven people (knock on wood!). And then there were the three brokers, who had given their all to making us reach an agreement — which made exactly ten, the right number for a quorum at synagogue.

At first it was a bit unpleasant. My brother Henekh fought tooth and nail against the idea of sending so many people — a whole gang! "It would be enough," he says, "if just two of us went" — he and the priest. Apparently he didn't much care for the fact that nobody wanted to rely on his sense of justice and the priest's assurance. But his antagonism was, you can imagine, as useful as a hole in the head, because everyone had his own claim and everyone was right. For instance, I proved I had to go since I was a brother — not because of honor but because one brother can cheat the other brother, and what would I do after that? Take him to court? He was my own brother, after all!

And my pal Birnboim argued that if a man won't trust his own brother, then he, a perfect stranger, couldn't rely on miracles in regard to honesty. He was isolated enough as it was. And you couldn't say he was altogether wrong. And we couldn't exclude the three lawyers because, they said, we would have to write and write and write.

The brokers were left, and they said that they had to go along, and all three of them at that, because they had been through the mill — that is, they were experienced. They had, they said, gone to a good school. They had taken the course at the Yehupets stock exchange, so they knew a thing or two about the commission, the "brokerage." It was like a matchmaker's fee, which, they said, was paid right after the signing of the engagement contract — you do understand, don't you?

We did agree on one thing: we at least shouldn't all go together, we should go one by one. But since each of us wanted to be the first, we all reached the bank at the crack of dawn and we cooled our heels for quite a while until the doors opened, and we went in to get the ticket. Well, I'll spare you the details of what a bank is all about. A bank hates to rush, it's got plenty of time. What does the bank care about lottery tickets, Yankev-Yosl, seventy-five thousand rubles, priests, Henekhs, Birnboims, brokers, who want to earn a little money—poor things—and simply people in general? What does the bank care? Not a tinker's damn. One employee is smoking a cigarette, a second one is chitchatting, a third is sipping a glass of tea, another is sharpening a pencil, yet another is reading a newspaper—sticking his nose deep, deep inside and never even looking up, come hell or high water!

We walked about, we yawned, we coughed, we were longing to get it over with—but the bookkeeper wasn't here. Once the bookkeeper arrived, the cashier wasn't here. Once the cashier arrived, the manager wasn't here. Where was the manager? He was still asleep. The owner of the bank, you see, was fast asleep. What did he care about tickets, Yankev-Yosl, seventy-five thousand rubles, priests, Henekhs, Birnboims, brokers, who want to earn a little money—poor things—and simply people in general? What kind of salary was this manager pulling down? Six thousand rubles, no doubt, and maybe eight, and why not an even ten? Did the poor man really drudge? I would have done his job for half his salary—what am I saying?, for a third—and I'd have worked harder than him and more honestly!

I stood there, thinking, or maybe I wasn't thinking—you do understand, don't you? Meanwhile the manager showed up. The instant he walked in, we all pounced on him together. Terrified, he waved us off. So only the lawyers—all three lawyers—and the priest went up to him and handed him the documents. You do understand, don't you? The manager then locked himself in his office with the paperwork, and we waited and waited, waited and waited, on and on, until at long last the manager came out with a fat landowner, stood there with his backside (pardon my French) toward us, and talked and talked. What did he care about tickets, Yankev-Yosl, seventy-five thousand rubles, priests, Henekhs, Birnboims, brokers, who want to earn a little money—poor things—and simply people in general? Suddenly he turned his face toward us and said in Russian: "Your documents are ready. Go to the cashier." Couldn't he have said so earlier?—You do understand, don't you?

Grabbing the documents, we dashed over to the cashier and handed him the documents. We assumed that now everything was wrapped up. Not on your life! It hadn't even started! The cashier was busy, he was counting money, banknotes, hundred-ruble bills, five hundred-ruble bills like so much chicken feed, and gold, gold, whole piles, a full desktop! How much money was there? *Veyz-mir*, if I'd had only a tenth of it, I'd have thumbed my nose at the lottery ticket! I stood there, thinking, or maybe I wasn't thinking.

Meanwhile the cashier kept counting and counting the gold—if only he'd dart a single glance our way! What did he care about tickets, Yankev-Yosl, seventy-five thousand rubles, priests, Henekhs, Birnboims, brokers, who want to earn a little money—poor things—and simply people in general? The gold flew through his hands, flew with the sweetest of sounds, the sound of gold. A "golden sound"—you do understand, don't you?

So anyhow, where was I? Oh, that's right. I was talking about a little gold. When the cashier was done counting, he lifted his glasses and peered at us. He took our documents and leafed through them as if counting banknotes, hundred-ruble bills, with a bizarre cracking of his fingers. Next he opened the desk drawer and produced a rather large packet. He removed an envelope, tore it open, and pulled out the ticket—the actual ticket, and he asked: "Who's taking it?"

Ten pairs of hands whipped out!

"No!" exclaimed the cashier. "I can't give the ticket to so many hands. Pick someone in your crew."

And so—you do understand, don't you?—we picked someone in our crew: the eldest of the three lawyers. The eldest of the three lawyers slowly took hold of the ticket with both his hands the way you carry a baby to his circumcision. He showed the ticket first to the priest, then to my brother Henekh, then to me and to Birnboim, the two of us, so we could see whether this was the right ticket or not.

The priest said he'd recognized it even from a distance, when the cashier had been holding it—there was, said the priest, a good sign on it. What sort of sign? He'd rather not say. And my brother Henekh swore by all that's holy that if he were awakened at two a. m., he'd recognize the ticket at first glance! You do understand, don't you? And I and Birnboim, the two of us, didn't exactly recognize the ticket—why should I fib? We just had a good look at the series with the number 12—that was the main point, wasn't it?

From there we headed straight for the government bank in order to cash in the ticket, to get our hands on the goods—the seventy-five thousand. We all went together, and on foot, even though it was all uphill. The eldest of the lawyers held the ticket high, clutching it with both hands so he wouldn't lose it—God forbid!—and so nobody should think he might pull a fast one and switch the ticket—Heaven forbid! You never can tell! Such an unlucky ticket!—You do understand, don't you? And there were no longer ten of us—by now we had enough people for more than two synagogue quorums. And where did we pick up so many people?—God help us! Let me tell you.

First of all, some had attached themselves to us by sheer accident— friends from my shtetl, who happened to be in the big city that day, and when they saw us taking the lottery ticket to the government bank in order to get the seventy-five thousand, they joined us, hoping to get a look when we picked up our winnings, because that's not something you see every day.

In short, as you can imagine, we had a fine retinue and then a friendly welcome at the government bank. The corporal guarding the entrance was initially terrified at seeing so many Jews with a Christian priest in their midst—God help us! Nevertheless he received us very cordially, inviting us to step inside one by one.

We carried our ticket to the appropriate place, and when we said what we were after, they led us to a teller with a bald head as shiny-white as a dairy plate, and we handed him our ticket, and then said something to him—I don't know what. The bald teller sitting on the other side of the bars looked up, glared at us through his glasses, and continued whatever he was doing. He was holding a sharp penknife—you do understand, don't you?—and he was scraping inside a book, scraping and scraping, never stopping. He was scraping, and we were standing there in agony, watching him scraping, and everyone else was standing there, scrutinizing us from head to toe, and he, the bald teller, wouldn't stop scraping, and all around us tellers were sitting at desks, counting money. And what do you think the money was like? It was like chaff, like dung! Gold—heaps of it! Your mind whirled, your ears rang with the "golden sound," your eyes were dazzled by the glow!

"Who thought it up?" I wondered. "This money, which humiliates people, drives them crazy, makes them want to devour one another alive? There's no brother, no sister, no father, no child, no neighbor, no friend—nothing has any value, only money and money and money." I stood there, thinking, or maybe I wasn't thinking—you do understand, don't you? And he, the teller, wouldn't stop scraping. What did he care about tickets, Yankev-Yosl, seventy-five thousand rubles, priests, Henekhs, Birnboims, brokers, who want to earn a little money—poor things—and simply people in general?

But sooner or later, everything comes to an end. God took pity, the teller stopped scraping, closed the sharp penknife, slipped it into his vest pocket, drew out a pure white handkerchief, and blew his nose thoroughly, as was proper. Then he picked up the ticket the way you pick up an ordinary sheet of paper for a kopek; he opened some ledger, some kind of chronicle and looked—looked in the book, looked at the ticket, looked at the ticket, and looked in the book.

"I guess this genius is worried the ticket might be counterfeit." Those were my thoughts. "Scrape, scrape!" I thought to myself. "Smell, smell! The ticket's genuine, dammit, it's not counterfeit!"

Suddenly he took the ticket and practically threw it in our faces—and I remember his words as clearly as if it had been yesterday: "Who told you that this ticket won the seventy-five thousand?"

You do understand, don't you? Who told us? How do you like that for a question?

"What do you mean," we said, "who told us? The ticket told us that it won the seventy-five thousand! Series 2289, number 12!"

"Yes, he said very gravely. "That's true. Series 2289, number 12 did win the seventy-five thousand. But your ticket is series 2298, number 12. A teensy-weensy mistake. A very minor oversight."

Now how do you like that? So what can I tell you? The instant he said those words, we were all dumbfounded. We figured: either he was nuts or we were crazy or else we were dreaming. And we gaped at one another. Only then did we bother to look at the ticket. Yes! As sure as we were Jews! Series 2298, number 12! You do understand, don't you?

What more should I tell you, my dear friend? I'm incapable of transmitting even one tenth of what happened, you're incapable of writing it down, and no one could be capable of imagining the scene, the spectacle occurring at that bank, where we stood speechless, gawking at one another. Our faces were marked—what can I tell you? Those were no human faces—you do understand, don't you? Those were animals, beasts in human guise, wild creatures pretending to be men. If any of them could've torn another to shreds, he'd have done so with his eyes, with his gape!

What had happened? What was done to you? You dreamed a dream about seventy-five thousand rubles? So is that any reason to kill yourself? Does life have no value outside of money? Lunatics—you do understand, don't you? No one, I tell you, got me so annoyed as my pal—Birnboim, that is. The others at least justified themselves and blamed everyone else. The priest put the entire blame on my brother Henekh, and my brother Henekh said you could ask him till you were blue in the face—he had never even dreamed of seventy-five thousand rubles, and he wouldn't have had a clue if I—Yankev-Yosl, that is—hadn't sent him a telegram congratulating him. You do understand, don't you?

"Brother of mine, you certainly," he said, "did a good job of reading the paper!"

"Why didn't you look?" I ask.

"You," he says, "were the brains behind this! You," he says, "were in charge!"

Have you ever heard of such a thing? Earlier, with seventy-five thousand rubles in the offing, he wanted to deny me totally. And now, when everything had fizzled out, I was in charge. You do understand, don't you? Fine with me! I, Yankev-Yosl, the scapegoat, would take the blame for everything. I assume full responsibility! And where were your eyes, you morons? All of you saw all the documents and receipts and affidavits at least nineteen times, and all of you saw the figures: series 2298, number 12—and the winner was series 2289, number 12. Why didn't it ever cross your minds to have a look? You would have seen the 9 standing before the 8. And when you had the ticket in your hands, would it have hurt you to recheck the tables in the newspaper and see which series won the seventy-five thousand: series 2298 or 2289? Listen, you weren't too lazy to go to the bank—the whole bunch of you, right? You thought you'd be getting money? You do understand, don't you?

But, I tell you, nobody got me so furious as my pal—Birnboim, that is. You should have seen him standing on the side, like a total stranger, as if he had absolutely no connection to all this. It was only now that he decided to leave no stone unturned. People! People! He wanted to rely on people! And now he stood there, a pure and innocent little lamb! It turned my stomach—you do understand, don't you? I made up my mind:

let me at least ease my heart after the anguish he'd caused me on May 2. If you'll recall, I'd been standing before him, begging him — like dealing with a highway robber — to give me the ticket.

"Mr. Birnboim!" I exclaimed. "Now you've got time to rely on people. There are people here in the bank — a whole lot of people, God help us! Why are you so quiet? You don't want people anymore? Are you done with people?"

The people — you do understand, don't you? — stood around us in sheer delight. Why the delight? I can't say. Was it because I was reminding my pal Birnboim about people? Or did these people enjoy the fact that the seventy-five thousand had fizzled out?

I can tell you, and I'll swear it on a stack of Bibles, that I no longer cared about the money — let it go up in smoke! The only thing that bothered me was that when people had thought I'd have seventy-five thousand rubles, they had addressed Yankev-Yosl as Mr. Yankev-Yosl; and now, when they learned he didn't have a — pardon my French — damn kopek to his name, his name was mud. Did I insult your fathers or your mothers? How did I sin? Seventy-five thousand, yes — seventy-five thousand, no. What difference did it make?

Listen to what I have to say, Mr. Sholom Aleichem. You can boast about your fellow Jews and about the entire world. But honestly, it's a disgusting world and a false world and a misguided world and a stupid world! Now tell me the truth. Doesn't my seventy-five thousand make your ears ring and your mind whirl and your hat fall off?

Please forgive me for talking your head off. Stay well — you do understand, don't you? — and may God grant us better business.

ALEXANDER KAPEL (*1878–1958*)

Born in Byelorussia, Alexander Kapel lived in many different places and studied at various foreign universities. He published his first book, a collection of stories and sketches, in Warsaw in 1911. After going abroad, he eventually returned to Russia, where he witnessed the Revolution. In 1922 he moved to New York; as earlier in Europe, he was always deeply involved in the Yiddish theater, writing criticism under his pseudonym A. Mokdoyne

(Alexander of Macedonia). The story "Vifil Doyert a Pogrom?" from Ertseylungen un skitsen *(Warsaw, 1911) is unusual in its thrust. Rather than focusing on the actual pogrom itself, it details the various tensions and traditions, including economic factors, that lead to a pogrom.*

How Long Does a Pogrom Last? *(1911)*

Conversation

YOU HAVE A simplistic picture of a pogrom. A well-off and respected shopkeeper lives a proud and happy life. All at once, angels of destruction pop out of nowhere and within minutes they destroy everything, wipe out everything. No, my friend, a pogrom is Death coming after a long-drawn-out illness. Death, you understand, rarely strikes a fresh and healthy person out of the blue: "Hand over your soul—don't argue!" No. He creeps into you little by little, never hurries—why hurry? After all, he's the only possessor of your soul. Sooner or later, your soul is his. So he tortures a person for a long time before taking his soul . . .

I started sensing the pogrom ten years ago, when I became a shopkeeper. The first time I entered my shop, I felt the pogrom in every fiber of my being. It was a few days after my wedding. Previously I was no shopkeeper, nor were any of my ancestors. My father was a kosher slaughterer, and I was a rich, clean, middle-class boy, always in a white collar, polished boots, and with a neat part in my hair. I ate and drank leisurely, read the newspaper every day, read a book. In short, I was no shopkeeper.

But then I got engaged to a shopkeeper, an orphan girl. Her inventory was worth seven or eight hundred rubles, and that was the dowry she gave me. During our engagement, I never so much as stuck my nose in her shop, I was no expert in regard to merchandise. Khanna, my bride, told us that her holdings were worth seven or eight hundred rubles, and my father and I believed her. We even privately asked other shopkeepers, experts, but could we learn anything concrete? Everyone knew that an engagement was in the offing. Enemies smirked and said that Khanna's stock was worth no more than five hundred. In contrast, friends (I don't mean real friends, a shopkeeper has no friends; I mean shopkeepers in some other line) felt sorry for the orphan and said that her inventory was worth eight or nine thousand. So why waste time: my father and I believed her, and I never set foot in the shop until after the wedding.

In fact, I didn't get there until three days later, and quite casually at that. Khanna was in the habit of sitting there, but she was very restless. She asked me to spend some time with her in the shop. Not because we were chasing rubles — no, that was one thing you couldn't say about me; I hadn't yet acquired a taste for profits, nor did Khanna give them a second thought back then. She still wore her silk wedding dress, her gold rings, eardrops, and bracelets, and her white wedding slippers, and she still gave off a scent of cologne which she'd sprayed on herself before the ceremony. I wore a black frock coat and a white necktie. Newlyweds are so happy! Can they keep their minds on a shop, on sales? Anything but! We felt like going to the shop — but only to be alone, nibble on something, eat some candy, smoke a good cigarette. We were happy that no one bothered us, we entertained each other. No Jewish customers came, and if one did happen to show up, it was only to congratulate us and apologize for missing the wedding . . . No one had the heart to ask for a herring or for kerosene from two happy people, from a bride in a silk dress and white slippers.

As we sat there, quiet and happy, like a pair of doves, in walked a Gentile, Khvedko the drunkard. He veered straight toward the herring barrel and, after a lot of rummaging, he yanked out a herring.

"How much?" he snapped.

Knanna's face promptly took on its workday expression. "Three kopeks," she replied, cold and grumpy.

Khvedko scrutinized the herring from all sides like a true expert. Then, peering at Khanna, he said: "It's as worthless as you."

Poor Khanna turned crimson, and I was boiling.

"Two kopeks," Khvedko haggled.

Khanna couldn't stand it. "Don't try to cheat me!"

"Who're you cursing at, you dirty Yid? You've got the goods and I've got the cash!"

I reeled, and my heart wept for Khanna.

"Two kopeks," said Khvedko as if he hadn't heard her price.

"Give him the herring and let him go to hell!" I muttered with downcast eyes.

"Shush, he understands Yiddish," she whispered, terrified. She had barely spoken when Khvedko swung the herring, hitting her face, hitting her dress, hitting her shoes, her white kidskin shoes. . . .

"Take that, Yids! And go to hell!" he shouted furiously, and stormed out of the shop.

Khanna and I stood there, thunderstruck, not saying a word. She quietly wiped her face, her dress, her shoes, and tears, large, warm tears, ran from her eyes, and she softly said to herself: "An indelible stain! An indelible stain!" My heart shrank in agony, it wept blood tears of pity for Khanna, for myself, for our sweet, quiet happiness, which Khvedko had trampled underfoot.

And that, my friend, was the beginning of the pogrom that destroyed my shop.

FOR A WHOLE week, I was simply too scared to enter the shop. But on Sunday, which was market day, I promised Khanna I'd come and help her. I put away my Sabbath apparel, pulled on my shopkeeper's clothes, reeled off my prayers for the first time in my life, gulped down a glass of tea, wiped my boots with a rag instead of polishing them as I liked doing, and rushed off to the shop.

Khanna had opened up at the crack of dawn. She was no longer a bride, she was a shopkeeper again. Wearing a dirty apron, she handled the herrings, the kerosene, the oil. Her face was earnest, anxious, no trace of joy, of happiness . . . Shoppers walked in, walked out. Khanna worked as coldly as a machine, flashing a smile only at good customers. In free moments, she acquainted me with the merchandise, told me each name, each price, introduced me to the barrel of oil, the barrel of herrings, the barrel of kerosene—all the best and finest things in the shop. I let her teach me.

That afternoon, the shop was packed with customers. I was helping Khanna: handing out purchases, taking in money; and, as if through a dense fog, it drifted toward me—a passion for profit, for buying and selling. I vaguely started feeling that this merchandise was mine. It cost me money, and you have to earn a living. And a warmth flowed through my body—I zealously, eagerly handed over purchases, took in money . . .

In the evening, a whole mass of Gentiles suddenly poured into the shop. There must been twenty of them, all yelling in unison: "Tobacco, makhorka!"

I spotted Khvedko in the crowd.

Khanna went over to the tobacco shelf.

"How much?" asked one man, removing a package of makhorka.

"Six kopeks," answered Khanna.

"Huh!" They were all surprised.

"How much is the excise . . . ?" asked another man, and I saw him pocketing a pack of makhorka.

"Khanna," I muttered, "keep an eye on our guests and watch what they grab."

Khanna nodded at me and bit her lip.

"This is a phony excise stamp," said Khvedko, "a Yid forgery!" And he stuck a pack of makhorka into his shirt.

"That ain't tobacco, that's wood shavings," said yet another man, tearing open a pack of makhorka and pouring it out on the floor.

Everyone laughed, but Khanna and I were trembling.

"Do you sell vodka too?" a young peasant giggled as he stuffed tobacco into his pocket.

They all laughed and kept stuffing tobacco into their pockets and their shirts.

"Let's go!" someone shouted, and they all crowded toward the door.

I couldn't help myself: "Where's the money for the tobacco?" I asked.

"What tobacco?" Khvedko jumped up.

"Shush!" Khanna whispered to me.

And I, half-paralyzed, replied: "The tobacco in your pockets!"

"Are you calling me a robber?" yelled Khvedko, dashing toward me with a clenched fist.

"Khvedko, old friend!" Khanna begged. "Khvedko, old friend. Don't! He doesn't understand, he's not a shopkeeper!"

Khvedko calmed down, and they all shuffled out.

I was boiling. "They must've walked off with twenty packs of tobacco!"

"I hope they choke to death on the smoke," Khanna coldly replied.

"Is our property up for grabs?" I hollered. "What is this?"

"So it's finally hit you that Jews are in exile," Khanna said coldly.

Late that night, a Gentile woman came tearing in. She was out of breath. "Gimme a pound of tobacco. And step on it!"

"All we've got is half a pound," replied Khanna. She handed it over, and the woman scurried away.

I waited for Khanna to put it on the woman's tab since she hadn't paid. But nothing happened!

"What is this?" I asked.

"It's for the town clerk," she replied.

"And no money?"

"You expect him to pay?"

"Why not? What's so special about him?"

"He's a clerk—he's bosom buddies with the excisemen."

"Is our property up for grabs?" I hollered.

"So it's finally hit you that Jews are in exile," Khanna said coldly.

Little by little, I became a shopkeeper heart and soul. I took off my white collar, I soiled my suit, my hands, and even my face. Take two baths a day, polish my boots?—why bother? I secluded myself in the shop and fell madly in love with profits. Khanna explained that this was the right time for us to get on a solid footing. Later on, our kids would be growing, we'd have to pay their school fees, rent a bigger apartment, and we'd be unable to put by a ruble.

I understood and I became a shopkeeper with every fiber of my being. Every article of merchandise grew as dear and precious to me as a child. Whenever a good customer came in, I would shake with delight and jump up to the shelves with trembling arms and legs. On the other hand, every stolen pack of tobacco caused me pain, made my blood boil, made me sick.

One day, the clerk came sauntering in. He shook Khanna's hand and asked who I was. Upon hearing that I was her husband, he reproached her for not inviting him to the wedding.

"Why, sir," she replied. "I knew you wouldn't come."

"C'mon," he said. "You still have to invite a friend, and if you don't, you should at least send your friend something from the wedding."

Khanna laughed. "Among Jews it's customary for a friend to send a gift to the bride and groom."

"Among us, it's the other way around." The clerk was lying his head off. "Gimme a thousand cigarettes and send me an invite."

"I don't have a thousand. All I've got is five hundred."

"Don't tell me that! Look for the rest now!"

Khanna looked and she gave him a wedding present of one thousand cigarettes.

When the clerk was gone, I grabbed my head. "A thousand cigarettes, a thousand cigarettes!"

"He's still not satisfied," replied Khanna. "Just wait. We should've given him a package of Popov's tea."

"What for?" I shouted. "I'm not gonna stock cigarettes anymore. The hell with cigarettes!"

"You think he needs cigarettes? If we don't have cigarettes, then he'll find something else to latch on to. We've got a few cans of paint."

"I won't stock paint anymore either. The hell with paint!"

"You think he needs paint? If we don't have paint, then he'll find something else. I'm wearing a silk kerchief, and he can claim it's for sale."

"Is our property up for grabs?"

"So it's finally hit you that Jews are in exile," Khanna said coldly.

And she was right: our clerk wasn't satisfied with the wedding present. A few days later, his maid showed up with a whole list. I looked at it, and it wrenched my heart. But I started putting the items together: tea, sugar, sardines, cocoa, candles—the best and finest of everything. Khanna wasn't in the shop, so I placed it all in a basket and wrote out a bill. As the woman started heading toward the door, I asked her: "What about the money?"

"I ain't got none. It's for my boss."

"For who?" I acted naive.

"For the clerk!"

I was so angry I shook like a leaf.

"No, my dear," I said. "Go to your boss and ask him for money." I poured the groceries out of the basket.

When Khanna found out what had happened, she practically tore my eyes out. "You idiot! What've you done? He's gonna get back at us—he'll put us through the wringer!"

"I'm not stocking any more cigarettes or paint. The hell with it!"

"You idiot! God damn it! You're gonna make yourself miserable!" Khanna kept repeating it over and over.

We instantly started getting rid of the contraband, we hid the paint cans, we stored the cigarettes with a neighbor—but I kept one pack for myself since the license was in Khanna's name. And we waited, trembling, waited for the clerk and the exciseman. Meanwhile Khanna ran around, bribing and cajoling the police officials, the village constable, even the commissioner, regaling each of them—and she bullied me every time: "Just look at what you've done, you idiot!"

Finally, the clerk and the exciseman came and they scoured every nook and cranny, even Khanna's pockets. Then they started frisking me, and they found the cigarette pack that I had held on to.

"My husband smokes, for God's sake, he smokes," she argued tearfully, "he's not the shopkeeper!"

But she was wasting her breath. They lodged an official report—it was an awful mess! To make matters worse, Khanna was about to give birth. "No one's gonna lock me up—not on your life! They're not gonna nail up my shop!"

We tried to get advice, tried to deal with the clerk, hired people, go-betweens, we smoothed everything over. But one fourth of the shop was gone. The shelves grew vacant, and the barrels empty.

To top it all off, the clerk buddied up to us even more once the affair was settled. He kept dropping in and he more frequently took anything he liked. And at every visit he would tell us that the case was signed and sealed.

The police and the constable likewise got chummier with us. Even Khvedko got a whiff of things and often came by.

And time wore on and it brought us three children, brought Khanna various illnesses, brought me worry, anxiety, agony, and pushed me closer to old age . . . Khanna took care of the children and I myself became the shopkeeper. I was old, dirty, harried, despondent—and I had to deal end-lessly with doctors and druggists: one child had the measles, another chicken pox, still another whooping cough. In short, I was up to my ears in worries.

I was devoted to the shop with all my soul. The entire world, my entire life were confined to my small, cramped shop. Cold and calm, I watched Khvedko stealing, the clerk taking, I watched people robbing me and I was not enthusiastic, and they grabbed whatever they could.

And many years wore by.

The court case was long forgotten. But then the bloodsuckers began talking politics with me.

"You're rebelling, you Jewboys," the clerk snapped and pocketed tea, sugar, cigarettes.

"The Yids are disturbing the peace everywhere," said the village con-stable and seized a big can of sardines.

"The Jews are against the tsar—I know it," complained Khvedko and helped himself to makhorka.

And the police officials did likewise, and so did the drunkards.

And the longer it went on, the worse it got.

ORGANIZATIONS FORMED IN the town, there were incidents, episodes, red flags, songs, guns—the devil only knows what got into the young folk. But I wasn't the least bit interested. I was a Jew with five kids, my mind was bogged down in school fees, rent, license fees, money, doctors, druggists, hardships, adversities, afflictions. And it all came from whatever I earned at that awful shop, which had ten owners besides me: a Khvedko, a clerk, and a whole gang of bastards! So when did I have time to even think about organizations? Forget it! There was no room in my life for anything but the shop. I had kids, but I never saw them except on the Sabbath. The shop was my life's blood. The shelves, the barrels were my only friends. The good barrel of herrings paid the school fees, the barrel of kerosene paid the doctors, this shelf paid the rent, this one paid for bread, this one for clothes, that one for the license, that one for a prescription—in short, each shelf and each barrel gave me something, kept me afloat, kept me and my wife and kids from starving. All parts of the shop helped me as best they could—those dear, good, wonderful friends!

"I know everything," Khvedko complained, "your rubberlushonary orgizayshuns—they're all here." And he threatened me.

"You're a rubberlushonary too—all Jews are rubberlushonaries, I know it!" said the clerk, and he mentioned a town where there had been a pogrom . . .

And then came the end of my pogrom.

I was hiding in a hole, but I could see very clearly. The ax shattered the barrel of oil—gone was the school fee! The ax shattered the barrel of herrings and they were trampled underfoot—gone was the rent! A shelf was ransacked—gone was our food! The second shelf—gone was my license fee! The third shelf—gone was everything else, everything! And finally, Khvedko smashed his club into Khanna's head—gone was the mother of my little children! Gone was my life, gone was everything!

LAMED SHAPIRO (*1878–1948*)

*O*bssessed *like so many Jewish artists, historians, and other intellectuals with the Ukrainian pogroms, Shapiro, who was born in Ukraine, devoted his early stories to those sweeping massacres that had such a devastating impact on Jewish life. In 1906, he settled in the United States, where he* *kept somewhat broadening his themes and refining his language, spending far more time on his craft than is perhaps common among Yiddish writers. His memoir,* The Writer Goes to School *(1944), details the linguistic and aesthetic problems he faced in helping to create a modern literary Yiddish.*

The Cross *(1909)*

1

HOW SHALL I describe him? A giant of a man, huge bulk, broad shoulders, but not stout. Indeed he was gaunt. His countenance dark, sunburned, with high cheekbones and black eyes. His hair was completely gray, yet made him seem youthful—thick, shaggy, a bit curly. A child's smile on his lips contrasted with an old man's tiny wrinkles around his eyes.

Then I saw his wide forehead. It was marked with a sharply cut brown cross, a shallow wound—two knife cuts, crossing each other.

We met on the roof of a railroad car racing along on the East Coast of the United States. Since the two of us were tramping across the country, we decided to team up until we got fed up with each other's company. I knew he was a Russian Jew, like myself; I asked no further questions. No passports are necessary for the kind of life we lead.

That summer we saw almost every state in the Union. During the day we usually walked, cutting across forests, bathing in rivers we found on the way. We got food from the farmers. Some we were given and some we stole—chickens, geese, ducks, which we roasted over a campfire in a forest or on the prairie. But some days we had no choice; we had to make do with gooseberries we picked in the woods.

We slept wherever we happened to be at nightfall—out in the open fields or under a tree in a grove. On dark nights we sometimes "hopped" a train, climbing on top of a railroad car to hitch a ride. As the train sped along, a stiff wind blasted into our faces, carrying smoke from the locomotive, fumes and puffs dappled with great sparks. The prairie glided and rambled around us, breathing deeply, speakingly softly and quickly, with sundry sounds in many tongues. Distant galaxies sparkled over our heads, and thoughts drifted across our minds—such strange thoughts, as wild and free as the voices of the prairie. They seemed disconnected, and yet they seemed intertwined, linked and chained together. In the cars beneath us people were sitting or lying, many people whose paths were marked out and whose thoughts were closed off. They knew where they were coming from and where they were going; they told these things to one another, yawned and went to bed, unaware that two untrammeled "birds" were perched above them, resting briefly from their travels. Travels from where to where? At dawn we jumped to the ground, stole a chicken or fished with makeshift poles.

ONE DAY IN late August I was lying naked on the sandy bank of a deep, narrow river, drying myself in the sun. My friend was still in the water, as noisy as a gang of schoolboys. Then he climbed up the bank, fresh and glistening from head to foot; the brown cross on his forehead stood out sharply. For a while we lay wordlessly on the sand side by side. I wanted yet did not want to ask him about that mark on his forehead. Still I finally asked that question.

He lifted his head from the sand, eyed me curiously and a bit derisively. "You won't be frightened. . . ? I've been an outsider for years now."

"Tell me," I said.

2

MY FATHER DIED when I was only a few months old. From the things I heard about him I gathered he was someone special, a man from a different world. I carry his image — a fantasy image — in my mind because, as I've said, he was *someone special*. But that's not what I want to talk about.

My mother was a tall, thin woman with broad shoulders, with a cold and gloomy nature. She ran a store. She fed me, paid my school fees and often beat me because I didn't turn out the way she wanted.

What did she want? I'm not quite sure. She probably wasn't quite sure either. She had fought with my father all the time. When he died she was only thirty-two, but she refused all marriage offers.

"No, after him there's no other. I don't need anyone — and how can I take a stepfather for my child?"

She never remarried. I had to be my father's replacement, but without his faults. He had been completely impractical; she said he was too hot-headed. In any case, she used to beat me relentlessly. Once when I was about twelve she hit me with the iron rod she used to bar her store shutter on the inside. I was so furious that I hit her back. She froze, her face blanched; she gaped at me. She never beat me again.

The atmosphere in our home became even colder and tenser than before. Six months later I went out into the world.

It would take me too long to tell you everything, and it wouldn't be all that interesting, so let me get to the main point. Fifteen years later I was living in a large city in southern Russia. I was a medical student and survived by giving private lessons. I had brought my mother there, but she was not dependent on me. She lived with me but supported herself by peddling old clothes in the marketplace. She wasn't ashamed of her work, but she was contemptuous of the other junk dealers: Who were they compared to her?

She was as cold to me as ever, at least outwardly, and I was just as cold to her. I think I even hated her a little. Beyond that she didn't concern me. I lived in an entirely separate world.

3

IT WAS A trivial matter: we had to remake the world—first Russia, then the rest of the planet. Meanwhile, we were still working on Russia.

All of Russia was feverish with agitation. Group after group, the masses were being sucked into the torrent; over their heads their individual heroic deeds would blaze with the burning red fire of rockets. One person after another, of high birth and low, fell in the struggle. The old order responded; it responded well—with such things as pogroms. The pogroms made no special impact on me. We had a term: *counterrevolution*; it explained everything very precisely. Of course, I had never experienced a pogrom, but our city would have its turn.

I was on the local committee of a political party, but that was too little for me. A thought as sharp as a knife was cutting deep into my brain, slowly but surely. What it was I didn't really know. I didn't want to know. But I felt as if my muscles were getting stiff, more cramped. Then one day—I didn't know why—my grip broke the arm of a chair in the home I was tutoring in. I froze, bewildered. Another time one of my pupils asked me in astonishment, "Who's Minna?" and I realized I had inadvertently said her name, *Minna*. I also realized that even though it was a random thought, Minna was a girl I knew, her image constantly in my thoughts.

I would hear the sound of her name, *Minna,* feel that strange sense of significance that was always in the air when Minna was present.

There were four other men and one girl in our committee. I didn't remember the eyes of the men, but Minna's eyes were blue, light blue. Yet at certain moments they would darken, get darker, until they were black and deep as an abyss. Her hair was black, her figure average, lovely; and there was something slow and serious in her movements.

She seldom joined in the debates at our meetings. In two or three terse phrases she would make a suggestion or state an opinion. She would then remain silent and attentive, narrowing her myopic eyes. Very often, after heatedly debating an issue, cleansing it, ridding it of all misunderstandings, we were amazed to see that we had reached the same conclusion that Minna had already formulated in her two or three terse phrases.

All we knew about her was that she was the daughter of a high Russian official of high position. Once we passed through the door of our underground cell each of us shed his personal life, like an overcoat in the vestibule.

4

NOW THE CLOUD of a pogrom was looming over our city. Strange sounds were audible, soft, sharp sounds, like the hissing of a snake. People went about with their ears atuned, with quick, sidelong glances. They twitched their noses as if sensing a suspicious smell, quietly, grimly.

One hot afternoon our committee had an emergency session in Minna's apartment, which was the meeting place of our underground cell. It wasn't a long meeting: just brief discussions, no debates, and a resolution. We were to organize some kind of self-defense as fast as possible. Several times during the meeting I caught Minna gazing at me and, when the other members began filing out one by one, she signaled to me to stay.

I stopped in my tracks, my hat on my head, my back and my hands leaning against a table. Minna, with her head lowered and her arms on her chest, was pacing up and down. We both remained silent. Then she raised her head, paused and looked right at me. She was pale, very pale, but her eyes were deep black, as only Minna's eyes could be.

I felt cold. All at once, as if illuminated by a strong, sudden burst of fire, I saw the light. I had to be one of the "rockets" that light up the path of the revolution—and pay the price.

Minna was the first to understand. She had seen it on my face even before it became clear to me. How had she known?

"Have you made your decision?" she asked after a while, her voice choked.

"Yes," I replied, calmly and firmly, feeling as if I had made my decision that very instant.

She gazed at me for a while, then began pacing up and down again. In a few minutes she was as calm and serious as ever.

"We're sure to meet again," she said, shaking my hand.

Walking back to my home, to my mother, I felt my whole body vibrating. I thought how strange a person's destiny was, his path in life probably very short, going from a woman he almost hated to a woman he was starting to love.

Before stepping inside my apartment, I glanced around at the city. The sun was setting, and a translucent golden veil of peace was draping its soft folds over the streets and houses. How lovely our city was.

5

WE WERE TOO late. The pogrom erupted that very night, suddenly, like an exploding mine, and in my own neighborhood.

The first screams came to me confused, in a hazy dream. Then it dawned on me what was happening. I jumped out of bed, lit a lamp and threw on my clothes. At that moment my mother sat up in her bed, looking at me strangely. Her look gave me chills. It was cold and ironic, as if the pogrom were aimed at me and not her. I stood there for a moment, half dressed, eyeing her in bewilderment, and all those minutes the house was shaking, as if in the eye of a storm.

Then the windows shattered, one door burst open after another. Like a foaming wave, with disconnected shrieks and cries, a gang of pogromists crashed into the house.

I'm a strong man, but before that night, I had never had to fight seriously, angrily. I had never known real anger before that night, anger that intoxicates you like wine; real anger boiling up deep in your blood, seething through your body, crashing into your head, sweeping away all thoughts. And when the pogromists—every variety, young, old, with homemade weapons or none at all—when they jumped on me, I defended myself coldly. Yet I was dazed. I didn't seem to understand what they wanted from me. But suddenly something minor happened—I think someone smashed my writing implements on the floor. An intense heat burned through my body; my mind was whirling; my arm flew up, of its own accord. I confronted a short Christian of indeterminate age. His face was gaunt, bloodless, with a bristly red moustache and small, beady eyes full of icy brutality. I think I bashed my fist into that ugly face, and I couldn't help bellowing like a raging bull. Then everything was spinning, around me and inside me, whirling fast and hot, as I felt a bizarre pleasure.

I don't know how long it went on. My fury and my pleasure grew as my strength encountered resistance and overcame it. At the same time, something reached me from far away, an annoying, monotonous voice like the buzzing of a mosquito, and disjointed Russian words: "Don't . . . don't . . . tie . . . tie . . . tie. . . ."

Their resistance to me grew swiftly, more swiftly than my strength, on all sides, over me, under me. Then it suddenly solidified around my body, like a stone membrane. My pleasure vanished. And fury, sheer infernal fury, burned my chest and dried my throat. Little by little my fury cooled, froze, and remained on my heart like a sharp, heavy chunk of ice. I came to.

I was lying on the floor, tied up, almost wrapped, in rope, covered with wounds, bleeding. The short Christian was dancing around me, the one with the piercing eyes. But his face was horribly bloody and altered. And there was blood on the faces of the others crowding around me.

They picked me up from the floor like a sack and tied me to the foot of my mother's bed.

My mother! This was the first time I had remembered she was there. She had jumped off the bed, obviously to help me. Now they dragged her back to the bed I was tied to.

I almost didn't recognize her. She was wearing a nightshirt on her broad, gaunt frame. Her hair was wildly tousled, her eyes flashing, her teeth clenched, and she was mute. They hurled her into the bed opposite me.

6

IMAGINE A SINGLE gray hair torn from a head. It is nothing, absolutely nothing. Two hairs? A clump of hair, torn out at one time, many clumps of long, gray hair. Forget it—nothing, nothing at all.

When you break bones they crack. But when you break twigs, dry wood, goodness knows what else, it all cracks, a "natural phenomenon."

Imagine two old, shrunken breasts. Flesh, matter consisting of certain elements. Just ask a chemist. And if they're your mother's breasts, two chaste breasts that once nursed you, that you've never seen bared since childhood. And dirty fingers rip them to shreds before your eyes.

Tell me, please. What does nature, what does the universe know about filth and shame? There are no such things in the universe as filth and shame.

Oh, certainly. Never, not ever, has a human body, the fine body of a man or woman, been spit at like that and humiliated. But what should I care. After all you can be sure: there are no such things in nature as filth and shame.

A year passed, two, ten, one hundred and two hundred. How is it possible? How can it be that I could live that long? Can a human being really live that long?

Mother! Scream! Scream! Damn you, what do you think? That you're back in the days when you used to beat me so brutally, so silently! Just one scream! Just one scream! Oh, God!

Years upon years . . .

Can you see the bloody face, the first human face I saw when my life began? A severe, gloomy face, the first face I ever saw in my life. The woman with that face used to beat me, and I hated her. I still hate her even now, even more than before, and my hatred chokes me, strangles me. For why, if it wasn't out of hatred, did I gaze so eagerly as the face changed from minute to minute? Why didn't I shut my eyes? Why did they bulge so painfully, with such burning curiosity? Good, dear people, poke out my eyes! What do you care? One slash with a knife and they'll ooze out, bubbles of liquid, these two accursed globes of liquid that I should not have. Goddamnit! You're laughing! You're happy people, very happy, but poke them out, what do you care?

Years and years.

7

THE SHORT CHRISTIAN said: "The old bitch still don't wanna scream. Let me at her!"

It took a while, but then I heard a sound. It was a groan, a sob, a shriek—everything at once, and words in the shriek. Although the voice was hoarse and totally changed, the words echoed in my ears, clear and sharp, like the slow, distinct peals of a bell: "Oh, my son!"

For the first time in her life.

The sweat rained from my forehead and filled my eyes. I wrenched my body with all my strength, and the rope cut deeper into my flesh. God took pity on me for a while: my head whirled and I blacked out. But I had time to hear laughter all around me.

I came to for a moment. Again the short Christian was speaking: "That's enough. Let her die slowly, right before his eyes. And I'll make the sign of the cross on him to save his kikey soul from hell."

I felt two deep cuts in my forehead, one crossing the other, and again I heard laughter. A warm, narrow trickle ran from my forehead, down my nose and into my mouth.

I blacked out again.

8

TOTAL BLACKNESS. TOTAL silence. Nothing coming from the outside, no fixed point on the inside. Only a disquiet, a deep disquiet and a tremendous effort to find some sort of fixed point.

A word came wandering into this world of chaos: "What?" Then three times: "What? What? What? . . ." Then twenty times: "What. . . ." The word grew, it spread out and multiplied. It became: "What is here? What is around? . . . What is myself, and what is outside myself?" Suddenly, a sharp brightness and intense pain in my head. Three words stuck in my brain like a long, thin needle reaching from one ear to the other: "Oh, my son!"

I recovered my wits.

It was night. The lamp had gone out, or else *they* had put it out before leaving. I was still tied to the bed. I felt a wound on my forehead, burning intensely, making me forget all the other wounds. All kinds of noise came from the city. The city was shrieking in the night, a dull shriek with sudden, sharper outbursts from time to time, like a distant blaze. Near me, on the bed, something was writhing in the darkness.

"Mother!"

Silence.

"Mother?"

No answer. My voice couldn't reach that far, reach that world of agony haunted by her strict, harsh ghost. "Oh, my son," she had called to me.

Yes, her son. Every drop of blood she was losing flowed along invisible paths into my veins, igniting an infernal fire. "Oh, my son!" A heavy hammer went up and down, slow and incessant, falling on my head each time. Whole worlds collapsed in ruins.

9

"WHAT'S THAT ON your forehead?"

"It's supposed to save my soul from the suffering of hell," I replied.

They shook their heads and began to disperse. I became nervous, "Wait," I said. "I'll explain it to you."

They shook their heads again and vanished.

"I am the Lord God who took you out of Egypt."

"Thou shalt have no other gods but me."

"I am a jealous and vengeful God, and I demand of you: 'Be something.'"

The gusts of the tempest stormed over the shaken masses. The bodies, enslaved, shook as if being whipped. But the dark, gaunt faces and the feverish black eyes ignited with the crimson fire that crowned the head of the mountain.

"Oh, my son!" she said. Those were her very words: "Oh, my son."

DAYBREAK. MY HEAD was swollen and empty, like a barrel. I should have fled. Yes, fled, but—aha—the ropes. You can find some device. There has to be some device, some . . . kind of . . . device. . . .

I strained to put my thoughts into some kind of order. An iron nail. In the footboard of the bed I was tied to was a twisted nail with a broad head. What was a nail doing there? It didn't matter. With the nail you can . . . what can you do with the nail?

I twisted and struggled until I managed to push one of the ropes onto the nail. Then I started rubbing the rope across the sharp iron head of nail.

Hours dragged by, and my head grew numb. I barely knew what I was doing. But I kept on working, as precise and obstinate as a machine. Eventually the ropes yielded slightly. A little more effort and, bit my bit, torn, frayed ropes were lying at my feet. Shattered fragments of gods were lying at my feet.

10

I LEANED OVER the bed. There was definitely something there, feverish, bearing no resemblance to a human being. The moaning was already so faint that my ear could barely catch it. I softly murmured, "Mother. . . ." My breath reached the raw wound that had once been a face, and I repeated, "Mother."

A stirring ruffled over the wound, and something opened. I peered hard; it was an eye. One eye; the other had run out. The remaining eye was blood-soaked, but still glowing, like an ember.

Did it recognize me? I don't know, but I felt it did. I felt it was looking at me with a question and a severe demand. "Yes, yes, it will be all right," I said, loud and earnest, not really knowing what I was talking about.

Then I looked around the room. Among the pieces of shattered furniture I spotted a broken table leg, thick, cylindrical, well turned. It would be just right.

I picked it up. With all my strength I swung it down upon the glowing eye. The bloody something twitched a single time, then remained motionless as a stone. The glowing eye was gone.

I heard a short sob, followed by a strange bellow that was immediately stifled. It was something unwilled, I assure you. And the voice was so alien that I still am not certain it was mine.

When I went outside the sun was setting, the ancient sun, which had spun its golden orb over this place a thousand years ago. Who says a thousand years are more than twenty-four hours? I was a thousand years old.

11

THEN CAME THE darkest days of my life, as the city suffered through a state of fever. Fire, slaughter. Bloody fighting, shooting in the streets. The Jews had organized a self-defense under the very blaze of the pogrom.

What did I do? I don't know. I found myself now in the ranks of the defense organization, now in the mobs of pogromists. I felt like a leaf wafted by the storm. The cross burned on my forehead. The words "Oh, my son" echoed in my ears.

If I'm not mistaken, I once ran into *my* Christian, the one that belonged to me alone. I felt as if I could grab him and drop him into my pocket. He turned pale, unable to move, but I didn't grab him. He aroused nothing in me. I simply patted his back and winked at him cheerfully. I didn't notice whether it inspired more courage in him.

ANOTHER EPISODE REMAINS in my memory.

An old Jew was running down the street chased by a young Christian, about sixteen years old, with an ax in his hand. The boy caught up with the old man and, with one stroke, he split his skull. As the old man fell, the boy pushed the split head together with his boot.

Instantly, gun in hand, a young Jew darted up, a pale young man, with a gaunt face and glasses. They ran, and I ran after them. The young Jew shot, but missed. The Christian left the broad, open street and ran into a courtyard. My foot got caught in something, and I fell.

By the time I ran into the courtyard, the Christian was standing in a corner, his back to a fence. His childlike face was green, his gray eyes gaped and bulged, his teeth chattered in a rapid rhythm. The young Jew stood right in front of him, with the gun in his raised hand, but his face was even paler than before. He stared at the wild terror of young flesh and blood, stared for some time. Then he put the gun to his own head, and fired.

The last light of reason vanished from the Christian's eyes. He sat down beside the body twitching at his feet, rose. Then, with an insane shriek, he leaped over the corpse and ran out of the courtyard.

A wild laugh erupted from inside my throat. My foot rose, of its own accord, and kicked the bloody carcass, lying twisted on the ground like a trampled worm.

12

IT WENT ON for days and nights; I don't know how long.

One evening, I stood at a door, knocking in a special way, a sign indicating I was a friend. What kind of signal was it? What was its purpose; how did I know it? I didn't ask myself those questions, just as you don't ask such questions in a dream. The door opened, and I saw Minna.

Lightning flashed in my brain; for a moment I was terror-stricken. I realized now where I was and what I was going to do, and calmed down instantly.

She didn't recognize me right away. Then she shuddered, grabbed my hand and pulled me into the room. I let myself down into a chair. She looked at my head, at my forehead where the cross burned, and she said nothing. Then, in a hushed voice, she spoke:

"Tell me everything."

I told her. I told her willingly and calmly—everything. Told of my mother's agony, with shameful details. Her face turned from red to yellow. When I was through, I bowed to her with a pleasant smile. She barely noticed; she buried her face in her hands. When she looked up again it was covered with tears, real tears. I swear it: wet, soft, and—I'd bet anything—warm tears! She knelt before me and took my hand, as my smile broadened. This time she noticed, quickly stood up, and began pacing up and down the room, glancing at me nervously. I kept on sitting and smiling—very pleasantly, I thought.

Finally, she resorted to what she considered an extreme measure. She sat down on the chair across from me and asked softly: "What about your decision?"

My decision? What decision? . . . Wait a moment . . . Yes, years ago, many years ago, I made a decision, a very important one, but—about what? . . . And suddenly I remembered.

I burst out laughing. I laughed in her face. But soon I became serious again, and looked into her eyes. She had turned as white as linen, and she leaped up from the chair. I stood up slowly and calmly.

I raped her.

She struggled, as my mother had struggled. But what use was her strength against the man with the cross on his forehead? Her face alternately changed in fright from blazing redness to corpselike pallor. She didn't scream. She bit her lower lip, chewed it, swallowed the blood. And I did my work, with all the humiliating touches. It took a long time.

Then I strangled her, quickly and tempestuously. I dug my fingers, long, bony fingers, into her white throat. She turned red, blue, and then black. It was over.

I collapsed on a chair, falling asleep almost that very instant, as if sinking into deep water—no dreams.

13

WHEN I AWOKE I noticed that the tallow candle on the table had not grown much shorter. I probably hadn't slept for more than fifteen minutes, but I was fresh, alert and calm.

. . .   .

THAT MOAN, "Oh, my son!" still haunts me today, but from that day on it became softer, more maternal. My mother's soul had found its rest.

Our secret meeting place was furnished comfortably, almost elegantly, to avert any suspicion. I went into the bathroom and washed my head and my hands. The mirror showed me that I was gray. And at last I saw the cross that I had felt all that time. The wound no longer hurt; it merely itched slightly.

At first I wanted to take a knife and cut a swath off my forehead, in order to erase the cross. Then I changed my mind. Let it stay: "A frontlet between thine eyes." Ha! Is this the kind of "frontlet" that our dear, old God meant?

14

I NOW OWED nothing to anyone, nor did I want to pay anything. I left our city that same night. Two days later I crossed the German border and set sail for America.

The ocean embraced me with its endless vastness, with strong winds, with its sharp, salty breath. It talked to me about wonderful things. It spoke out loud, it spoke silently. I listened to it with joy and amazement, and I have no words to express what it told me.

SOON AFTER I arrived in America I began to wander across the country, and the prairie began to translate into its language what the ocean had said to me. Oh, the nights and days on the prairie!

I'VE BEEN WANDERING for three years. And I feel like a newborn child, feel that I'm strong enough now. Soon I'll return to civilization. And then . . .

I GAVE HIM a sidelong glance, but he had stopped speaking. He had clearly forgotten me.

And I, an outsider for years, mused: "A generation of iron men will come, and they will rebuild what we have allowed to be destroyed."

DOVID BERGELSON *(1884–1952)*

*B*orn in Ukraine, Bergelson, starting with his early—and sometimes best—fiction, was one of the most delicate, refined, and polished Yiddish authors. His lyrical and melancholy tales and novels deal with the mournful decay of the shtetl. Bergelson spent part of the 1920s in Berlin, which had a tiny but active Yiddish world that was terminated in 1933, when a plurality of the German electorate voted the Nazi dictatorship into office. Bergelson had traveled widely, even visiting and writing about the United States. His blind faith in the Soviet regime led him back to Russia, where he produced a vast, politically correct oeuvre. In 1952, however, Bergelson, like most Soviet Yiddish artists, was labeled a "cosmopolitan" and murdered in a wave of Soviet antisemitism, one of whose main targets was Yiddish culture.

Two Roads *(1922)*

TWO ROADS LEAD from the town, a wide road and a narrow one.

The wide road runs along the green fields all the way to the horizon. Somewhere near a mountain, this road reaches the highway that leads from one county seat to the next. And the road is chopped off so abruptly by the highway, so sadly as if it were dissatisfied with something and were lamenting:

"Just look how small I am, I can't lead anywhere anymore."

The narrow road separates from the wide road immediately, by the town's wooden gate, and veers off to the left, toward the overgrown peasant cottages. Together with these cottages it rises, together with these cottages it slopes into the depths, as though afraid that, by leaving the cottages and remaining all alone, amid valleys and mountains, it will go astray and never find its own beginning. The road finally reaches the tiny Kozlov River, where the peasant cottages end, and from there the road, all alone, alas, has to climb up the small mountain.

If you ride some three miles along this narrow road, you go down into a silent green valley; if you then continue up the mountain, you come to a small, lonesome wood, and no one knows who owns that solitary wood, for which a Polish landowner has been fighting with obstinate neighboring peasants for years now. From up there you can look down at the village in the valley, the sunken brick factory, which smokes day and night like a limekiln. And higher up, on the mountain, you can see the big, always noisy paved highway, which leads far into the distance, to the large commercial town.

Business wagons roll to and fro, encounter one another, pass one another, and head in opposite directions, dashing along, gloomy and earnest, as if they were also thinking about their homes somewhere far away, in various towns and shtetls, thinking about that noisy corner of the business world, to which their minds are dragging them.

The wheels clatter endlessly over the stones, and an echo of that clattering is born between heaven and earth, a pure, naive, a childlike echo, that soon wafts across vast fields and even enters the small, lonesome wood, causing a barely perceptible rustling.

And if a breeze puffs from anywhere, it also comes whisking into the small wood, and it charges so fearfully through the trees as if bringing them gloomy greetings from those scurrying merchants:

"Yes, yes, the merchants are still driving . . . They're driving out there, on the highway."

Then the entire forest shivers and becomes melancholy. Trees bow their heads low and worship as they rock toward a distant corner of the sky. Who knows? Perhaps they're praying for the merchants, sighing and praying:

"It's time, time the merchants stopped dashing around!"

But the wagons keep dashing, and they keep sending the clattering of their wheels far away. Foreign and unfamiliar, they emerge from one end of the horizon, carry their drowsy, noisy secret across, and finally vanish on the other end of the horizon. Then new wagons appear, likewise foreign and unfamiliar, and they keep up the noise. Dismal skies peer down at the wagons and stay silent, and the surrounding air is so accustomed to all this and to the empty story that hovers there day and night:

"The story of an old, gray merchant who didn't have the strength to do business and therefore prayed for death . . ."

There are cottages somewhere along the highway, small lonesome cottages scattered so far apart that one cottage doesn't know where the next is located.

In the summer, when everything is green and overgrown, and only the uneasy paved road stretches with its lead-colored stones like a severe and ordinary ribbon and resounds with its usual monotonous noise, a couple from the city may turn up in one of those lonesome cottages for a month and spend entire days wandering around the green fields, valleys, and mountains. They lead such a calm, quiet, and isolated life here; they forget all about the big and distant city, and they get ideas, big ones.

Who knows? Perhaps they wish to remain here forever and be able to stroll here forever with slow, mythically huge steps, so that they can reach the distant, distant end of the horizon in just a few paces.

They sometimes come to this highway at twilight and stand nearby, leaning against the trees. The highway hums; the business wagons roll to and fro, encounter one another, swerve by one another, and vanish together with the secret of their eternal restlessness. One end of the horizon releases them, the other end swallows them up. The couple is then overcome with sadness, and a melancholy peers out at them from every rolling wagon and from the dark twilight air. They stand and stand there, watching silently, and they themselves do not know why their eyes watch so pensively and why neither person can say a word to the other.

Without a Name (*1922*)

MY FRIEND, A writer, told me the following story:

I'M OFTEN GLOOMY, I'm drawn from one place to the next and I keep wandering. I have a lot of friends but I don't know where they are. I know only one or two things about some of their lives. I have a fiancée, but I don't know her name. This isn't fiction, it's fact. Imagine this:

You go through a bad time. You find yourself in a big, strange city, where you've come to look up your close friend. That's why you've been traveling for almost twenty-four hours. But when you arrive at your friend's apartment, it's closed up. You ring and ring the janitor's bell, and he finally comes out with a full, chewing mouth, and he quickly answers you between chews:

"The tenants are in the country."

"What about the subtenant?"

"Out of town."

"Where?"

"Who knows!"

And turning his back on you, he swallows, yells at a strange, unclean dog nestling in the courtyard, blows his nose thoroughly, wipes his hands on his trousers, and goes off, vanishes in the black hole of the strange entranceway—and all this takes place in late summer, one evening, in the first young glow of the electric street lamps, which have just been lit. You stand there a while, facing the row of stores, you simply stand there—what's the hurry? You don't know anyone else anyway in this big teeming city. Besides, the evening is cool, almost like autumn. A lot of strangers are walking here. Every cozy fire draws you. Every lit window peers at you, strangely calm, as if to say: "You jerk—have I taken anything from you, God forbid! I've got my own stuff."

You turn into a second street, a third, a darker and more silent one, and everywhere the same strangers.

At the corner, a double trolley whizzes past you. It swerves by with a quick, terrified jangle, with a shrill, violent screech of the back tires. You can see that the second car, an open summer car, is brightly lit. It's packed with strangers in fine summer clothes. A lot of women are sitting there in white frocks and hats of different colors. Someone, if I remember correctly, is holding a bouquet of flowers. A hundred strange human lives, brightly lit, have whizzed by very close to you, luring you, drawing you, exciting you—and fleeing. And once again you walk alone through the external noise and the strange internal calm.

Lit windows of multistoried buildings peer at you again like eyes in the still night, which snuggles against them, calling you and driving you . . . In a moment like this you're ready to cling to anyone who doesn't push you away. Why not go to any housemaid sitting alone and humming to herself on a chair by the small courtyard door? Why not, for instance, marry her and go off to America with her? . . . The only reason you don't do it is because you've still got time; you want to think about it. At a moment like this you're ready to mount any clean marble stairs, ring the buzzer by a polished door with a small, shiny brass nameplate, and think to yourself that it's time. It's time that your wife lived here, and that you, a tired man, went in to her, sat down at the table with the boiling samovar, and said to her: "Good evening."

If you don't do these things, it's only because people still aren't well-bred and are still scared of everyone else; they're still capable of raising a rumpus . . .

And I really experienced a moment like this in that big city, where I came to look up my friend. The next day I fled that city, which stirred up so many emotions in me. I fled as if fleeing an enemy . . . But now comes the story I want to tell you:

THE NEXT EVENING I was wandering all alone through a tiny, empty train station, where I'd arrived to look up my friend's parents. But when I arrived at their house at twilight, I found it closed up. I walked all the way around it, I peered through the windows; I saw that it was empty, and all the while I remembered that *I* was peering.

"I'm a jerk, I'm really a jerk—what am I doing here?"

Next door, however, everything was brightly lit and very cheerful. They were celebrating a wedding, klezmers were playing, guests were dancing, and lamps were flickering, flaring and flickering. I went over. The bridegroom's rich mother was dancing with her daughter, a young girl, and the daughter's cousin, a student, danced toward them in sheer ecstasy, in deep gratitude toward her aunt, who was dancing. They were all jostling and looking, and no one cared that I, a stranger, was looking too. No one minded in the least that I too wanted to see her with my own eyes, see how skillfully this dignified aunt was dancing.

At first no one understood. "Where did *he* pop up from?"

But then it soon turned out that someone here knew who I was. The bride had heard so much about me from her cousin, my friend Misha, whom I was looking for. I had to come in, she said, I had to sit right there, by the head of the table, next to her and the groom. She had a lot of roses—an aristocratic family had sent her roses, and she wanted to tell me a lot about herself and about her cousin, my friend Misha. She would tell me where he was, but for now I ought to have something to eat and drink. This was her bridegroom—already her husband, so to speak.

What? He didn't know who I was? That was what she asked the groom. And the groom answered: Right. Why should he know?

He amiably shook my hand and told me that he was "interested." Back in his shtetl there were also Zionists.

I sat alone, as a stranger, by the head of the table, with the refreshments that had been set before me, and I smoked a lot of cigarettes. I looked at that young, brown-haired girl who, like all the other girls, was wearing white; but she wasn't dancing. Why didn't she go and dance even once? She sat, like me, all alone, huddling in a corner, refusing to let our eyes meet. Whenever I looked at her, she turned away, she preferred gazing at her empty side rather than letting our eyes meet. Smiling and cheerful, clutching a half-drained glass of wine, her father kept coming over to her. He was good-looking too. He asked her something, but she remained as gloomy as before. Finally, however, I sat quite close to her, I sat on the next chair.

"I think I saw you at the station at twilight. When I arrived on the train, I saw you there."

To keep from alarming her, I added: "You were standing there in that white frock, without a coat."

Oh, right. She'd been standing there, she said. She'd gone to the station to pick up some guests, in-laws. But no one, aside from me, had arrived on the evening train. She hadn't known whether I was an in-law or not; she had stood there, waiting.

And once again she hid her eyes from me. A bit later she was standing outside with me, by the door. She stood there, leaning against the wall, her arms at her sides, and once again she hid her eyes from me. I stood there, thinking: "What, for instance, could I now tell her about?"

And suddenly, her voice trembled, it was so rich—that voice of hers, so deep, and yet it trembled so. She'd like, she said, to take a walk. Then she faltered:

If I didn't mind, of course. She was only afraid of the vacant spot opposite us. A cow might be lying there, chewing her cud. We could circle around it.

The air was silent, and we walked. Her head bowed even lower.

She wanted to tell me something, it was so hard for her to keep it to herself—the thing she wanted to tell me. She lived nearby with her father, by a small train station, and her life was gloomy. All the people living by the small train stations all around here led gloomy lives. She had no mother. She had an older sister, Esther. She read a lot of books—Esther did. Her father would always bring her the books week after week from the library at the large station nearby. Now Esther had gotten married—she had married a dry-goods storekeeper from a nearby shtetl. She didn't love him, but other people had said that he was not without his good points.

He had always appreciated her, he admitted that she was way above him, and he said that for her sake he was willing to break away from his mother and open his own store. Before the wedding the girl herself had told Esther: "Esther, think it over. Maybe you shouldn't . . ."

But Esther had said, "It's all the same," she had said; "I've made up my mind. It's like cutting off my hand!" she had said.

Now the girl was living alone, alone with her father, and she was reading the same books that Esther used to read. Her father would bring them to her from the library at the nearby station. She would read these books all day long, and in them she found the marks and notes that Esther had left. After reading she couldn't always sleep at night and she was very pensive. And now she wanted to ask me: "Honestly? Is life worth living? . . . No, I absolutely don't think it is."

"When I'm old and gray," I said, "I'll lie in bed and I'll work my toothless mouth and mumble, 'I want one more spring . . . One more spring.'"

And suddenly I began telling her a lot about myself:

"Once I gave five rubles to some beggar who was lying in the dirt. He had no legs at all—that beggar; they'd been chopped off, way above the knees. I watched him as he put the five rubles in his mouth and crawled away. I figured he would buy himself a coffin, but instead he went and bought himself a new blue shirt—he wanted happiness."

But no, that wasn't what I told her about.

"Once, when I was a child, on a winter evening, I was wrapped up in a lot of kerchiefs and taken somewhere. When I was put down on the floor again and unwrapped from the kerchiefs, I saw that I was at a wedding in a large, very brightly lit synagogue. I wasn't even four years old at the time and I didn't realize that today was preceded by yesterday. When I was unwrapped, I looked down at myself and started peering at my small, black velvet suit and my small, white kidskin shoes. I really liked them—those small, white kidskin shoes. But when I looked around, I saw the bride and groom next to me on one side and the Holy Ark on the other side, and I suddenly began shaking on my legs and dancing. For the first time in my life I began dancing."

But perhaps that wasn't what I started to tell her about either, perhaps it was something else. We walked along the railroad tracks—which were empty twenty-four hours a day—until we reached the edge of the small, dense woods; I was still talking incessantly. And as we doubled back, we saw that the day was already dawning and that we were holding hands, squeezing them firmly—we had confided our hands to one another. In the house, the tired klezmers were still playing. Suddenly she focused her eyes on mine, allowing me to look into her eyes for a whole instant. I saw that the day was dawning in those eyes too.

But then we went back to the tracks, to the place where they vanished at the edge of the small, dense woods. We again had a lot to talk about, a lot.

When we doubled back a second time, everything, everything had been worked out: I would hurry to the tiny train station where she lived and I would move into the small Christian house across the road from her because it was all the same to me where I lived. For the time being, we would say nothing to anyone. Suddenly she nestled against me and peered into my eyes.

"Meanwhile," she said, "meanwhile you'll write me—won't you?"

By now the klezmers had stopped playing in the house.

The in-laws were having tea before going their separate ways. They were all talking at once, they were laughing cheerfully, and the sun was coming up. Perhaps they were laughing cheerfully because the sun was coming up. The bride was still wearing the long, white, fingerless gloves, she said something to me with a smile, but my mind was elsewhere, and I asked her:

"What?"

Together with many others I stood on the steps outside the house, not far from the simple wagon waiting with the Christian driver, and I watched my girl cheerfully saying goodbye to everyone and tying a kerchief around her head in a simple rustic manner.

"Just write 'us,' simple letters," she whispered as we said goodbye, "'we're simple people."

And her father was already sitting at the front of the wagon and waiting for her.

I was excited and all the while I kept thinking there was something else I had to do—I had to hurry for the wagon was about to take off.

When the wagon took off, I dashed after it and made the driver stop. I was holding a lot of roses, which the bride had given me at my arrival. I gave them to the girl and I saw them smiling—her and her father. But when the wagon took off, I instantly felt that this wasn't what I had to do. I tried to remember, but I couldn't. I said goodbye to the bride and went to the train station. A long train was standing there, with its locomotive pointing in the direction I had to travel. It had to leave. It started right away. I stood in an almost empty third-class car, I peered through the window and heard the wheels clanging faster and faster. And suddenly I remembered what I had to do: I didn't know her name, I should have asked her:

"What's your name?"

I should have asked her.

The Deaf Man *(1906)*

1

IN EARLY AUTUMN, something happened again between Mendl, Vovve Bik's [Bull's] tall, handsome boy, and Esther, the deaf man's twenty-two-year-old girl, who was a cook in Bik's home. Tongues were wagging at the market stalls and at the large bolting mill, where the deaf man stuck his clogged ears everywhere, suspiciously eying each person who smirked nearby; and yet for a time the deaf man failed to catch a word.

Mendl was still cheerfully joking around with the young grain dealers, who brought wheat to the mill, and he would poke his elbow in their sides.

"Listen, you, do you know what Max Nordau says?"

But as usual he actually meant: "Do you know how many kopeks there are in a ruble?"

You couldn't tell just by looking at him.

He had come here from the county seat not so long ago and, hanging around the courtyard of the mill, he had looked at his reflection in his shiny boots. He kept stopping the young miller, Schultz, and motioning to him.

"How do you like my new boots, huh?"

And Schultz, the serious German, never grew bored with kneeling in awe and stroking the new boots on Mendl's legs.

Schultz yearned so deeply for the shiny boots, and his steel-hard envy grew from day to day. And he wasn't too lazy to pull off one of those boots and try it on for size.

The deaf man saw all this secretly through the window on the top floor of the mill, where he was working by the hoisting jack, and he kept looking around to make sure no one was watching him.

Esther brought Mendl food from town every day. Then Schultz and Mendl watched her leaving the courtyard; Mendl smiled, silent and pensive, and Schultz, the miller, motioned toward Esther's back and tickled Mendl in an ugly place. And workers somewhere in the mill saw that, and they swiftly clustered at all the windows:

"C'mon, lemme look!"

The broad-shouldered deaf man with the tense, frightened face felt sharply prodded and he so ardently wanted to know what the workers were laughing about. But he was awfully deaf and he was ashamed in front of everyone and in front of himself; he couldn't look anyone in the eye and he kept thinking about Mendl and Schultz's joint sin with a pregnant peasant girl from the nearby village of Ribnitse.

They had then sent her away for a while.

After that the deaf man had run into Yósele Babtsis, the haggard and unshakable mill overseer, who had yelled and yelled into one of his deaf ears; the deaf man had caught only one word in ten, but he had kept nodding:

Yes, yes, he heard.

He had a timid habit of nodding at people and reassuring them:

Yes, what did they think? That he couldn't hear?

For two weeks his deaf mind had retained those few words he'd caught from Yósele, and it was only afterwards that he began to understand the whole story:

A story of two dismissed mill workers, who wanted to beat up Mendl; and in the dark evenings they hung around there, near Bik's home; and these two workers, it seemed, had noticed something . . . The deaf man still didn't know what these workers had noticed, and he had stopped Yósele near the mill and gestured:

"What does this really mean—this story about Mendl and Esther?"

His heart had pounded so strongly in his broad chest. And he had breathed with long heavy breaths. He had felt ashamed in front of Yósele.

"She's in love with him," Yósele had yelled into his deaf ear. "She, Esther, is in love with him, Bik's boy."

"She's in love with him?" he asked Yósele softly.

He thought that the haggard and unshakable Yósele was joking, so he opened his mouth and laughed.

"Ha ha ha . . ."

No voice could be heard from him, only a strange, wild roaring from his wide-open mouth. His lead-colored eyes were so wry and bizarre. It was only then, when he realized Yósele was in earnest, that he began to talk in his deaf, incoherent way, making elaborate grimaces with a round, bent hand and violently tearing single words from his broad and powerful chest.

She should ask him, the deaf man . . . He knew them thoroughly—Bik and his son . . . It was child's play. He'd been working in the mill for twenty years now.

And let Yósele talk—he knew, didn't he?

Yósele nodded, and his face was nasty.

He knew. Why shouldn't he know?

And he, the deaf man, so ardently desired to find out what people were saying—healthy people who weren't deaf. He walked along, gesturing to himself.

If two big and deaf ears hadn't been hanging on both sides of his big head like two rags, he could have caught a word here, caught a word there.

He planned to go to his daughter eventually, find her in Bik's kitchen, and tell her a necessary thing or two. But at this very moment, the awful accident occurred. It seemed to be his fate.

2

THE LATE AUTUMN days were short and plaintive. Foolish twilight skies made faces and wept, gazing at the wet, black earth as if lamenting a dying man:

"How awful . . . What's become of you? . . ."

And there, at Bik's mill, in the lonesome valley outside the town, the electric lights were burning day and night, shining in the depths of the gray fog, winking like weary yellow eyes at the nearby town, which had lapsed into autumn:

"We're grinding flour, we're grinding flour."

The four-story mill was swathed in the damp fog. Calm and wistful, the mill chanted its ancient, monotonous roar, shaking together with its forty workers. Amid the roaring and the tumult, the workers labored mechanically, earnestly, mutely like the machines and the wheels turning all around them, and the workers never talked, never thought, as if the huge, wheat-packed sheds were located in their brains, robbing them of their minds.

"The sheds are so fully packed with wheat . . . Do we have any choice? The mill has to grind!"

At rare moments the mill suddenly trembled, cutting through with an oracular voice:

"Stop! . . . Stop! . . ."

But no one responded, and it was as if the oracular voice were remote and forlorn, straying into this alien, unfamiliar world, seeking something and unable to find it.

With bare feet and a dusty and indifferent face, the deaf man was sitting in the loaded hoisting jack, descending from the fourth floor. Someone hurrying by noticed something amiss in the hoisting jack and began shouting wildly and dreadfully:

"Turn it off! Turn it off!"

Something tore off in the deaf man's heart, gushing into his brain and flashing there with a terrified thought:

"The rope . . . The rope has snapped!"

With nervous haste he grabbed hold of the one remaining rope. He wondered:

Would he really plunge down from this height?

But at the same time he was hurled aside. He felt himself falling, and yet it was as if someone were pitying him and were whispering into one of his deaf ears:

"Too late . . . Too late . . ."

Never had the deaf man heard such a faint voice; terrified he closed his big, lead-colored eyes.

Later on, when he reopened his eyes, he found himself surrounded by many dusty workers, who were leaning over him and yelling into his deaf ears: "Where? Where does it hurt?"

With a deathly pale face, he lay on the floor, too weak to point to his injured shoulder blade and higher, on the side.

Then he was carried to his tiny cottage in the narrow lane where the small synagogue was located. The old-clothes man and his wife, who lived in two rooms of the cottage, refused to allow the workers to leave the deaf man in their space. So they put him in the old wooden bed in the kitchen.

IN HIS NASTY mind, two-faced Yósele Babtsis still came out with little flattering jokes.

He scratched himself disparagingly right in front of Mendl and downplayed the deaf man's accident:

A great mishap . . . But the devil won't take the deaf man so soon.

Next he visited the deaf man in his kitchen and yelled into his deaf ears:

What was it? Had he thought he'd make it safe and sound out of Bik's paws?

And what good was this two-faced flattery of Yósele's?

Bik had already suspected him of an ugly theft. Once, in winter, Bik had even thrown him down the stone steps of the mill, hurled him so forcefully that he, the haggard Yósele, was scared to death; he had grabbed his bleeding, pointed nose and sobbed like a woman.

"Oh! . . . My head! He's killed me, my head . . ."

Perhaps he too was already fed up with his life of flattery and wanted to be more decent and truthful, but he was unable to change and he at least found it necessary to say a kind word to the deaf man.

It would be all right, absolutely all right. He simply needed to stay in bed for a time and keep his rib and his shoulder blade thoroughly warm.

But the deaf man didn't catch on to those jokes and he mournfully nodded:

Fine, fine, he would stay in bed.

He didn't seem to think on his own—not about life and not about death. He lay in bed with a pale and indifferent face, haunted by a gloomy thought:

"Fallen . . . Fallen from the fourth floor."

He didn't seem to care whether he'd ever get up again.

Once, Esther came by, fresh and slender, in a new black autumn jacket and with earnest eyes that were newer and blacker. She stood at his bed for a while, astonished and lackadaisical, even holding a finger on her chin and pensively sympathizing: "This is a fine thing, a fine thing."

She leaned over, apparently trying to shout something into his deaf ear, but she couldn't hold back, she loudly burst into tears. She buried her head deeper and deeper in the rags by his chest, sobbing and crying. It was unclear whom she was grieving for: the fallen and bedridden deaf man or herself, or her secret and unknown misfortune—as on that dark autumn night when the two dismissed workers had hung around near Bik's home and noticed something.

The deaf man gazed at her with his big, lead-colored eyes, trying to say something crucial, very crucial. Vague and shapeless, the words hovered in his mind for a long time:

No, she should keep her head screwed on right!

He had already opened his mouth and bent an arm. But Esther stood up and began buttoning her autumn jacket. She nodded slowly and gloomily, sighed mournfully, and even clucked her tongue in despair as if the clucking were meant to say: "He's a father, after all . . . God help us . . . and she'll listen to his advice."

AFTER THAT, THE rain poured down day and night, regular and, for no reason, obstinate, as if someone had asked the rain to stop, and it refused to listen, and it kept repeating out of spite:

"I want to . . . I want to . . . I want to . . ."

Foul autumn tears ran down the wet, colorless panes, winding slowly and lazily and finally sinking into the wet, bent kitchen walls.

Who needed those tears?

Everything around was so sullen and angry, even the bent and shabby stove, which peered into the deaf man's face day and night.

It was so silent all around that the deaf man was surprised that he sometimes caught the whirring of the old-clothes man's sewing machine.

He spent silent and melancholy hours sitting on the bed, his legs dangling, his eyes beseeching the old-clothes man's wife, who kept coming into the kitchen and fussing over the wet wood in the stove.

What he wanted to ask her was very trivial, and yet his pale and worn-out face twisted like a beggar's face.

If she could have only yelled a few words into his deaf ear, he could have heard how much deafer he'd become.

But the woman was such an accursed serpent. She kept passing his bed, even grazing his dangling legs, but never so much as deigning to glance at him. She was so nasty, this scraggy woman, and he couldn't get her attention even with his face twisted like a beggar's.

Now if he had stuck out a leg and blocked her passage, she would have trembled in fear and surprise.

Just look: he was still alive—the deaf man!

He resented her and he glared at her and muttered angrily. That was how he had glared at his wife, Leah. She would defiantly go to bed fully dressed, and he would grab the bowl of food from the table and hurl it to the floor.

Esther again dropped by and she argued and argued with the woman in front of him, and he lay in bed, hearing nothing and again thinking those earnest and crucial words that he needed to say to Esther. The words circled in his deaf mind for a long time and finally came out soft and silly, and not as he had thought:

"Oh, you see, if your mother were alive . . ."

He tried to sound hard and tough, but his eyes then looked ashamed in front of himself and in front of her, his slender and agitated daughter, who couldn't remember her long-deceased mother's face. She looked at him so amazed as if asking:

What good was she now—her deceased mother in the old graveyard?

She took a piece of butter pastry from her bag and handed it to him. He tasted the pastry, enjoying its delicious flavor, and inspected it. "Bik knows a good thing. . . ."

And suddenly the thought that had been haunting him for a long time took shape in the necessary words: "It wasn't nice . . . what the two workers saw at night. . . ."

And what else? He didn't trust them, didn't trust Bik or his son. He absolutely refused to trust them.

3

DURING THE FIRST frosts, the pain in his side and in his shoulder blade weakened. The kitchen windows were blasted by snow, and the wood grew wetter in that woman's stove. The deaf man was cold, so he arduously pulled on his boots, slipped into his padded cotton jacket, belted himself tightly with the red belt, and put on the threadbare lambskin cap over his deaf ears.

The old-clothes man's wife was surprised:

Where was he going, the deaf man, where?

To synagogue, he told her softly and mournfully. To warm up . . . to synagogue.

Her mouth quickly formed something. Maybe she was scolding him. He didn't know and he went on out.

At the small synagogue, Yósele, the overseer, found him by the hot stove and yelled at him: "Bik! . . . Bik!"

He yelled something about the way Bik had unfairly dismissed him, Yósele then yelled something about him, the deaf man:

Yes, yes, the deaf man ought to take Bik to court. . . .

To court? The deaf man was surprised.

He didn't understand. He raised his hand and said, "Bik," then lowered his hand almost to the synagogue floor, and talked about himself:

Bik was so big, he was so big, and he, the deaf man, was so small . . . very small. The big man was sure to beat the small man.

Yósele fell to thinking as he furrowed his brow and took hold of his beard. And the deaf man assumed that he had said something wise and deep. He therefore likewise fell to thinking and he added:

Bik ought to leave him, the deaf man, in peace.

However, he didn't really mean himself and Bik, he was actually alluding to Esther and Bik's tall, dark son; the deaf man wanted to ask Yósele something, but he didn't know what.

The evening was cold and snowy. Lost in thought, he was going to see Esther, to tell her something crucial; it was on his mind all the way there, and he even rehearsed his opening words.

"A man has to know . . . a man has to understand . . ."

But when he opened the outside door to Bik's kitchen, he saw Mendl, tall and agile, suddenly dashing from a corner of the room and slamming the white door that led to the other rooms. The deaf man was frightened, his heart pounded wildly, and he again lost the necessary words. And his deaf mind wandered, suspicious:

"Mendl is a nasty guy . . . just a nasty guy!"

But Esther was already sitting next to him, pushing a baked potato into his hand and yelling at him:

Notte had been there, Notte the marriage broker.

And the deaf man's face lit up, and his lead-colored eyes smiled, and he asked somewhat cheerfully: "Really and truly? . . . You're not fooling me?"

She yelled something at him: "It was about Yoyl . . . Pinne the dyer's son."

The deaf man bit off a piece of the hot potato and kept it in his mouth. His broad face twisted as if asking for pity: "But that's an awful match . . ."

She yelled into his deaf ear: "Yoyl is a rat . . . a rat from Odessa."

Chewing the potato, the blind man nodded in agreement.

"Yes, yes, a rat . . . Definitely a rat."

4

IT WAS A frosty night.

The deaf man dreamed that he was standing at the highest window of the mill, gazing down into the courtyard, and watching Mendl chase the peasant girl who cleaned the office. The terrified girl was scurrying away, slipping on the vast stretch of ice. Mendl would grab her now, now. And there, off to the side, stood Schultz, the miller, holding his belly, laughing and shouting: "Grab her! . . . Grab, grab! . . ."

And suddenly, he, the deaf man, saw that Mendl was no longer chasing the peasant girl who cleaned the office, Mendl was chasing Esther. The deaf man shuddered, Esther fled, holding out her arms and yelling in fear. If the father hadn't been deaf, he would have heard a heart-rending shriek.

After that, the old-clothes man's nasty and scraggy wife kept cursing the deaf man all morning:

The hell with him! Did you get a load of him—bellowing at night?

She even went over to him and pulled at his sleeve:

Huh, why had he bellowed last night?

He shrugged in surprise:

He had bellowed? He hadn't bellowed at all.

He didn't remember the dream, didn't remember Mendl or the peasant girl. Pulling on the old boots, he examined them from all sides, he figured he ought to smear them with a greasy substance, and he went out to the small synagogue. There he sat and sat by the hot stove, musing that

he, the deaf man, liked warmth, he also liked a fish head, fresh, hot challah, and a piece of fat meat, the same fat meat that Bik had once eaten
in front of him.

"Bik knows what's good!"

The small synagogue gradually filled up, Jews were milling about, chatting. How come they weren't praying? More people kept arriving by the
minute; they were hurrying around, joining the crowd, and the crowd
swallowed them up and grew bigger, bigger. The deaf man peered with
his lead-colored eyes and noticed: the faces of the newcomers were terrified, their mouths were gaping and their eyes were gawking fearfully.
He seemed to be asking the men who were already there: "Really?
Honestly?" The men who were already there nodded, and the newcomers halted, petrified and dejected, and went "tsk-tsk-tsk."

"What a pity! . . ."

They seemed to be looking at him. Clusters of people were whispering and eying him askance, and he wandered near them and stuck his
deaf head in everywhere. They drew closer to him. Someone pointed at
him, and he looked around and thought about his clothing: Anything was
possible, maybe his trousers weren't buttoned right. People came over and
yelled into his ear that he should go to Vovve Bik, and he gaped at them
and didn't understand: What good would it do the crowd if he went to
Vovve Bik? A respectable-looking congregant came over and yelled into
his ear, telling him to go to Bik. And the deaf man pointed at his own
chest: "I? I should go?"

He didn't understand, but he would go to Bik anyway, he shrugged and
went.

But when he reached Bik's home, there were a lot of people in front
of it. They seemed to be the same people he had left at the small synagogue. They pushed their way into Bik's rooms, from his rooms into the
kitchen, and he, the deaf man, pushed his way in together with them. He
didn't want to push, he didn't know why he was pushing, but he kept
pushing anyhow.

The kitchen was already mobbed, it was dark, he felt dizzy, everything
was trembling and quaking swiftly like the sieves at Bik's mill. The
kitchen, the people were trembling and quaking, and so was the plank
bed with the constrained and blue corpse, to which the deaf man finally
pushed his way through. He recognized the corpse within a second:

"Yes, it's Esther, it's definitely Esther."

He wasn't even surprised. In fact, it was as if he'd already stood by this very same bed with the very same corpse. It had been long ago, long, long ago, but it had really happened. The very same people had stood about, and it had been a melancholy winter morning like today.

Someone pulled at his sleeve and pointed at the ceiling. The deaf man looked: A rope was still dangling from the hook. Now he understood that she'd hanged herself, and he wanted to ask, "Why?" But he didn't ask, he glanced at the old woman standing by the head of the corpse. She was making a face, that old woman, she was hunched over, she opened her toothless mouth, closed her eyes, turned away her head, and made a face. She was crying, apparently, in a heart-rending voice, but he was deaf and he couldn't hear. He also made a face, he also wanted to cry, but couldn't. A commotion developed, the crowd was driven apart, the old beadle of the burial society yelled from the door: "C'mon, enough, enough, good-bye and good luck!"

The kitchen emptied out. They tried to make the deaf man leave, but he refused. They pulled him by his shoulders, but he glared harshly as he clutched the plank bed with both hands. They pulled him violently, and he dragged along the plank bed with the corpse. They got tired of pulling him, so they left him alone. He then spotted someone in the kitchen doorway and he recalled his dream, the courtyard of the mill, Mendl, the peasant girl, and Esther. He let go of the bed and ran off somewhere. But then he promptly forgot where he was planning to run. He dashed into the street and ran swiftly, with all his strength. His boots dug deep, deep into the windswept snow, and he breathed heavily, he felt his life draining, and he kept running.

5

IT WAS SO strange and wild.

At Bik's home they had forgotten to lock up the cow in the stable, and they found her at dawn by the gates of the property: her tail had been slashed off. With Bik at their head, they all left the house and they drove the cow into the courtyard, surrounded her, peered at her, exchanged looks of surprise:

"What does this mean?"

A sharp instrument had chopped off the tail at its very root. Blood was still dripping from the wound. Lowering her head, the cow stood, melancholy and unhappy, amid the crowd, her big, cowish eyes glistened sadly, and she appeared to be thinking:

"Just look! My tail is gone forever and ever, and I feel so awful, so awful . . ."

For several days in a row, the people in Bik's household were wracking their brains:

"Who could have done it?"

They again looked askance at Yósele, the dismissed overseer, and they suspected the two workers who wanted to beat up Mendl, they even summoned both men before the village constable, and he interrogated them. It was only after two weeks that they speculated:

"Listen, you think the deaf man did it?"

Someone just mentioned it casually, and they all jumped at the idea. It was so bizarre, and they found it hard to blame the tall, broad-shouldered deaf man with the belted undershirt and the lambskin cap pulled down over his indifferent, melancholy face. And yet they believed it, they were surprised and didn't understand, yet they believed it:

"Could it be the deaf man? He's always had a screw loose."

Once the old-clothes man's scraggy wife had gotten angry at the deaf man, and he'd flung a boot at her head. Then he'd grabbed her beds, chairs, and table and hurled them outside.

All the Jews had come running, they had peered from far away, too scared to get any closer. One person told the next:

"The deaf man's 'passions' rose to his head."

The old-clothes man's scraggy wife was hovering nearby; she banged her fists against her forehead and bawled out of her narrow and strident throat: "Just look—he's inflicting a pogrom on me . . . a pogrom!"

And the men stood and watched. A few able-bodied and kind-hearted boys were ready to pounce on the deaf man, but the old clothesman's wife had enemies, and they glared at her nastily and whispered behind her back: "Forget it, forget it, she's gotten back at him enough!"

And there, by the cottage, the deaf man hurled something else while cursing, choking, moaning.

"G-g-goddamn!"

He was summoned to the constable and interrogated.

"Do you know her—Bik's cow?"

The deaf man caught hold of the word "Bik" and couldn't forget it. "Yes, yes, Vovve Bik."

The constable was soon fed up and he wanted to get rid of him as fast as possible—this tall and broad-shouldered creature who gaped at him with bulging eyes and kept heavily jabbering a single name. But the deaf man refused to leave, he kept creeping closer and closer to the constable and even waved his hand at him.

"Vovve Bik . . . Oh . . ."

He wanted to tell the constable something about a bolting mill that kept shaking, about a plank bed with a corpse, and about a hook with a rope—he wanted to tell him but he couldn't. At his very first thought of Bik he got all tangled up as if in a net and he didn't have the strength to tear loose.

The constable finally pushed him out and locked the door, and the deaf man stood there for a long time and, God only knew why—he kept binding and rebinding his underpants. A town Jew passed by, and the deaf man forgot about his underpants and shuffled toward him, even holding out his hand, and he started telling him what he had wanted to tell the constable:

"Oh! . . . Bik! . . ."

The Jew was frightened and, with his heart pounding in terror, he dashed away, and the deaf man shuffled on toward the town, holding out his hand to everyone he ran into. People were scared and they stepped aside to let him go by, and he would halt each time, holding out his hand and unable to complete a sentence:

"Oh! . . . Bik! . . ."

In his squeezed brain each thought, it seemed, began with those same words, but no one cared to listen, so he remained with those words, as if that thought were waiting and hoping for someone: here he'd be coming—the man who would want to hear him out, and the deaf man would release the first few words and expose all the thoughts in his deaf and squeezed brain.

Slowly he trudged to the small synagogue, opened the door, and stuck his deaf head inside. There was no one to be seen, and so he sat down by the hot stove. The room was still and calm. The windows were covered with dull frost, the lecterns were deserted like the gravestones of martyrs, facing the eastern wall to catch a glimpse of the Almighty.

Somewhere across from the hot stove a Jew, a beggar, was snoring: he had trudged here on foot from faraway and was snoring soundly, napping by day and dreaming about lots and lots of single kopeks.

And the deaf man sat melancholy by the stove and didn't hear and didn't even know that a man was sleeping there, across from the stove. The deaf man's brain was squeezed, cold, and it feebly and hazily remembered dismal things: an injured shoulder blade, a plank bed, a corpse, an iron hook with a rope tied to it. And an unfinished thought hovered over everything:

"Bik! . . . Oh! . . ."

In walked Yósele the overseer, he took off his sheepskin coat and sat down by the stove, next to the deaf man. He stroked his pointed beard slowly and dreamily. And he seemed to be thinking his ever nasty thoughts. Thoughts about a Jew burdened with lots of children and without a job. However, Yósele had a soul that was touched at times by total strangers and their business. He yelled something into the deaf man's clogged ear, and the deaf man leaned over with his squeezed brain and nodded:

"Died? . . . What else? Certainly, died."

He wanted to say something but Yósele laughed. His upper lip with its trimmed mustache twisted up, exposing yellow, smoke-stained teeth. Yósele yelled again, and the deaf man peered into his eyes. His face was melancholy, the leaden eyes were petrified and gaping, but they managed to catch occasional words from Yósele and to inform the deaf man's squeezed brain:

"Bik is a bastard . . . a rich bastard, that's all!"

The deaf man thought that Yósele was teasing him, and he resented it. But he promptly forgot that he resented it and what he resented, and he remembered Bik's whitewashed home with its high roof, the acacias growing apart from each other in front of the windows, and the pure blue fence, which looked as if it had just been painted.

The windowpanes, covered with frost flowers, darkened. Men were entering the small synagogue, so the deaf man slowly went out, slipping his hands into his sleeves and trudging along. He trudged slowly, his head drooping, but then he forgot where he was going, he didn't feel he was going, he couldn't tell whether it was summer or winter. A few youngsters left off skating for a while and scurried after him. They yelled something at him, but he didn't hear. He trudged between two rows of wooden shops but paid them no heed. People turned away from him, but he didn't notice them. A sleigh came along. The peasant driving it was cold and he was too lazy to grab the reins and swerve. He shouted: "Watch it!" But the deaf man didn't hear. The sleigh shaft crashed into his broad, hunched back, his hand touched the injury, he didn't look around, he kept on trudging.

He stopped in Bik's dark vestibule and didn't know where to go. The right-hand door, which led to the dining room, was locked, hard and firm, as if from the inside. The left-hand door, which led to the kitchen, was ajar; a long, narrow strip of light shone through the crack, lying motionless across the floor of the dark vestibule. The deaf man stood in the opposite corner and was likewise motionless. Someone hurried by with a lamp and was terrified upon noticing a pair of worn boots. There was a ruckus, and the entire household was already standing around the deaf man. Bik was yelling something in one of his deaf ears, but the deaf man couldn't hear him and he thought:

"Bik is a bastard . . . A rich bastard . . . That's all!"

Trudging back to his cottage and standing by the stove, near the old-clothes man, the deaf man kept thinking that same thought.

Now he remembered that he had been in Bik's home and had seen him up close.

And he also remembered that he himself was a deaf porter, who had once had a wife named Leah and a daughter named Esther.

He made a face and pointed at his own chest:

Food—his heart felt heavy.

And the old-clothes man calmly sat near him, holding a dirty child in his lap and stroking the child's filthy head. The dealer's voice was slovenly and monotonous like a woman's voice. He had no beard. The few sparse hairs on his chin and on his upper lip quivered, and he rocked while talking. His mouth opened in a wide yawn, and he then stood up and yelled into the deaf man's ear: "He can afford to pay—that Bik . . ."

The filthy child made a face, opened its small, toothless mouth, and went on a crying jag; but the old-clothes man didn't hear it, he was still yelling into the deaf man's ear: "Bik can go to hell!"

The dealer's wife came hurrying in from the street, she grabbed hold of the weeping child in her cold, scraggy hands, and shouted through her narrow throat: "He can pay through the nose for that sort of business— that Bik . . . But he knew who he was dealing with!"

She grabbed the deaf man's hand and she yelled: "You deaf dummy! . . . Cat got your tongue?"

But the deaf man's thoughts were tangled up again. He gazed into the woman's face and never stirred.

A neighbor, a tailor with a soft, bright beard entered the cottage, peered at the deaf man for a long time, and pulled at his sleeve.

"Deaf man, do you know what today is?"

He was such a soft and kindly man, that young tailor with the long, soft beard. He wanted to see how confused the deaf man was, and his own heart was pounding so fast, and his face, his noble face, was already crimson, and his eyes were ashamed, sparkling and ashamed; Who could say? Perhaps he had done something stupid.

But the deaf man didn't know who was pulling at his sleeve, didn't know why it was being pulled, didn't know if today was a Sabbath or a weekday for the person pulling him. Stooped and with concealed hands, he left the cottage, headed somewhere and didn't know where, hovered near the small synagogue and near the stalls in the marketplace, and all at once he found himself in Bik's home again. Bik stood facing him and he yelled into his raglike ear:

"What do you want, deaf man?"

The front door was opened, and the deaf man was shown out. He again slipped his hands into his sleeves and silently obeyed.

6

THE FOGGY WINTER nights yawned and gave birth to short, frosty days. Actually, these were no days, these were dark, cold, dangerous twilights.

It kept snowing hard.

At the crack of dawn the old-clothes man wrapped himself up in his sheepskin coat and his wife's scarf, hurried to the marketplace, and quickly returned, covered with snow, his nose blue. He rubbed his frozen ears with rigid fingertips and he told his wife about three frozen corpses that had been found near a buried village.

"Oh, and what else? Some Jews set out to a fair and they barely managed to drag themselves back—more dead than alive."

He was so glad that he had stored a lot of fuel; he held a piece of cloth near the hot stove, peered at the frosty windows, and in his joy he even joked around with the deaf man: "Have a seat, deaf man . . . Can you hear what I'm saying?"

But the deaf man didn't hear, and he focused on what he was doing: he put on his short, thick undershirt, firmly belted his loins, pulled the cap down over his ears. Then he glanced at the old-clothes man's wife and pulled at her jacket:

Let her see he was going . . . He was going to the mill . . . to Bik at the mill . . .

"Go . . . Go to hell! . . . I hope you don't make it!"

And he nodded his head: "Yes, yes, to Bik at the mill!"

He trudged slowly through the town, then turned left and kept on toward the lonesome valley, where the blizzard mixed with smoke as it circled the mill.

The mill watchman, who was packed in fur, spotted the deaf man, stationed himself at the entrance, and refused to let him in. He began to struggle, they practically crippled each other. Finally the constable was summoned, and he turned the deaf man over to two peasants.

After that, the night was hushed, frosty, and covered with stars.

At dawn a sleigh filled with drowsing Jews was silently driving toward some fair in the next shtetl. The air was so still all around. The peasant cemetery was drowsing to the right; and Vovve Bik's white home with its long orchard was sleeping to the left. And over everything, a pure dawn sky with fading stars, twinkling at one another, telling tales about the secrets of the night.

Their heads sinking, these Jews nodded off with a pious thought:

"God willing, let's have a good fair . . ."

Suddenly: a snort from a terrified horse, the sleigh skidding to the side, a terrified shout from the peasant driver: "Whoa!"

The passengers woke up in panic, their hearts racing.

"What's wrong?"

The peasant was already standing by his horse, cursing it obscenely.

"Goddamn it! You nearly ran over somebody! . . ."

The Jews clambered down from the sleigh, hurried over to the peasant, bent down, and recognized the deaf man:

He lay there, his twisted body in his padded jacket, his lambskin cap pulled over his ears, and he gripped an ax in his clenched right fist.

He was still warm, so they put him in the sleigh and brought him home. Did they have any choice?

The Jews heading for the fair were unhappy, they looked at the pale eastern sky and yammered:

"We'll miss the fair, as sure as I'm a Jew!"

. . .   .

THE TOWNSFOLK LAUNCHED into their interpretations:

"So what else is new? The deaf man decided to kill Bik!"

Soon a witness turned up, scaring Bik even more.

So what had the witness seen? Late one night he'd been walking past Bik's home when he'd seen a man trying to climb the high fence, climbing and scrambling back. The witness had panicked and run away.

And furthermore: didn't everyone know that the old-clothes man always found the deaf man's door locked in the morning?

Bik soon hired an able-bodied watchman, who kept banging the fence all night. The half-frozen deaf man was sick for two weeks, flat on his back like a clod in the damp kitchen.

Someone took pity on him and called the doctor, a young, calm, kindly doctor with a thin mustache and intelligent black eyes. The calm and kindly doctor sat by the deaf man for a long time, gazing on and on at the indifferent face and listening on and on to the old-clothes woman's story as it emerged from her narrow and strident throat. Everything the doctor saw and heard appeared to strike him as terribly important and interesting. That was why he sat there quietly, pensively, and respectfully.

And two days later he came again, that same calm, young doctor with the same short mustache and intelligent black eyes, and again he sat on and on at the deaf man's bedside.

He gazed into the deaf man's face and also thought about something.

The deaf man gazed into the doctor's face and also thought about something.

And yet neither understood the other. They were so different and worlds apart—these two creatures gazing right into one another's eyes.

Finally the deaf man reflected and recovered on his own, without the least bit of help, and he couldn't think about anyone else.

It was so strange.

He was perhaps even sounder and stronger than before the illness, and yet an unpleasant failing remained:

He stopped sleeping at night.

Tall, broad-shouldered, and indifferent, he wandered about the room, hushed like the still and dark nights.

The nights were so dark and long, and they shrouded the whole dreaming world in their gloomy depths, lulling everything that lived and thought, except for him, the sole pulse of the world, and he didn't dare rest, he didn't dare even think about resting.

He paced up and down the small room, like a restless pendulum, bearing all the sorrow and melancholy of the sleepers. He wasn't tired and he didn't think about resting. If anyone had grabbed his arm and made him halt, he would have torn loose without looking and he would have continued pacing.

Sometimes the old-clothes woman's child woke up in the middle of the night, moaning and then crying.

The woman sat up with a very sleepy face, raised her sleeping head, and tried to calm the child: "So go to sleep, go to sleep."

Her voice was so raucous, and when she heard the deaf man pacing in the next room, she cursed him: "Goddamn him! The hell with him!"

But the deaf man didn't hear and he kept pacing. His footsteps were so hard and solid, and the night was so silent, and slowly and silently it swallowed the hard and solid footsteps and waited for more of them. And they came soon, more hard footsteps, and they banged like a hammer in a drowsy brain. Perhaps because the night was silent and no one but the deaf man was pacing, it was as if the deaf man would be walking forever and ever, and as if the night would endure forever and ever. The old-clothes woman was terrified at that thought, she pulled the covers over her head and fell asleep with an old, familiar childhood fear . . . Everything inside her was already sleeping, but her sleeping brain was haunted by a fragmented, raucous curse:

"Goddamn him! . . . The hell with him! . . ."

One pale night, when the old-clothes man woke up, he didn't hear the deaf man's footsteps and he simply wondered: "Maybe the devil's taken him?"

The deaf man was lying in his bed, and he began hammering his feet against the foot of the bed. He wasn't sleepy and he didn't know whether there had been a day before this night and whether there would be anything after this night.

Something peered in through the window. The deaf man got to his knees and peered back through the window. A cow was standing there, a miserable and melancholy creature, peering into the room. Then he recognized the cow.

"Vovve Bik's cow . . ."

He grabbed the ax and hurried outdoors. A cow was standing there, pulling wet straw from the low roof and slowly, slowly chewing it, dully and evenly. The cow saw him and she moved away from the thatching. He followed her slowly, nonchalantly. The darkness was silent and empty, a damp wind blew through the pale night, playing all kinds of tricks. At a nearby hunched cottage the wind plucked a few straw halms off the roof and scattered them across the dingy, dirty snow. Then that damp wind grabbed the trees in front of a wealthy house, banging their tops against the iron roof.

Somewhere in the next street a merchant, returning from a trip at this late hour, was pounding on the door of his sleeping home. A pack of dogs behind a nearby cottage peered amiably at each other's faces and cajolingly wagged their tails. One dog scurried away from the rest and dashed toward the cow and the deaf man, and then all the other dogs followed suit. The cow broke into a run. The deaf man hurled the ax at her back and raced after her. The wind forgot the treetops and pursued the group. The cow, the dogs, and the deaf man melted into the pale darkness, speeding across ditches, hollows, and dungheaps.

EARLY IN THE morning some Jews found the deaf man's corpse and next to him the slaughtered cow belonging to Pessi, the dairywoman.

Pessi wept so bitterly:

The Jews ought to tell her why it was her fault that . . .

She couldn't go on, her heart ached so badly that she choked on her sobs. And the Jews stood there, pensive and silent.

DOVID PINSKY *(1872–1959)*

Born in Russia and supposedly one of the earliest Yiddish writers to join the Socialist movement, Pinsky reached New York in 1899. There he launched into a prolific career, writing mostly political dramas, stories, and novels that were generally realistic in style and often tragic in content. Before

Isaac Bashevis Singer, Pinsky was probably the most widely translated Yiddish author. A Labor-Zionist, he moved to Israel in 1949; he lived and wrote there until his death in 1959. The following story was written in 1893.

In the Madhouse *(1893; publ. 1910)*

THEY SAID I was crazy, and they pointed their fingers at me. They asked me how I felt, and they admitted that I looked awful, that I was as yellow as wax, that I ought to see a doctor. I know they're referring to my mind, but I don't care. Why bother? I thank them for the advice and I go my way. Or else I halt and peer into the advice giver's eyes with an ironic smile until he grows flustered or terrified and dashes off. And then I laugh, I laugh! It's a lot of fun. I enjoy putting idlers in an unpleasant situation.

Bastards! . . . They drive me crazy and they ease their consciences.

They used to laugh at my old, yellow hat, which took on a few more colors and split in a few places. They used to laugh at my old, torn trousers, in which the holes revealed my dirty black shirt and my bare, filthy skin. They used to look at me and laugh and pity me. "Simply crazy, an awful pity!"

And I'd hit the ceiling! "What do you care?" I'd yell. "Why d'you pity me? Why don't you care about your workers, why don't you pity your machine operators, your drivers, your coal haulers. Their skin also shows through their torn and ragged trousers, and they don't have a shirt to cover their skin!"

"Those are paupers," they stammer, "they don't have any money, that's why they go around like that. But you! . . ."

"Me? . . . Am I rich? . . . On what? With what? Because my father built up a capital from other people's labor?"

"Listen!" they broke in. "You're really crazy! You're—"

I couldn't hear any more. I grabbed my head. I squeezed my temples and I ran and ran . . . I didn't dare stop. I felt my blood starting to boil, my heart wanted to burst, and my hands itched. Another minute—and he'd have gone away minus his nose, minus his eyes. No! They'd have carried off a corpse! I'd have tugged, pinched, torn, bitten nonstop, and my heart would have screamed wildly . . . It was better to flee.

. . .   .

I AM RICH. My father employed hundreds of workers, who could barely drag their feet, barely stay conscious, and he grew richer from day to day even though he lost a lot at cards and squandered a lot on feasts. And when he was about to declare bankruptcy in his exuberance, he fired over half his workers, who had nothing to eat the next day. Was I going to make use of his money? . . . Does that money belong to me? . . . We are rich! They are the real owners—the bitter, unhappy, gloomy, hungry paupers! My father's money really belongs to them! I have to give them every penny that comes my way from my father—even if you kill me, murder me, and call me "crazy" a hundred times a day!

Crazy? Ha ha ha! I often heard them saying: "He talks like a human being but the poor guy is crazy." Ha ha ha! They couldn't make me forget the calm and bitter truth for even a moment. I'd laugh my head off in that man's swinish face . . . I'd hold my sides . . . He'd get flustered, terrified . . . Ha ha ha!

I WAS ANGRY and I'm still angry today at the paupers. They also thought I was a little crazy. They didn't throw it up at me, God forbid. But I could tell by their conduct, their behavior toward me, I could hear pity and sympathy in their kind, friendly voices. It just about killed me! "My poor brothers! I'm not crazy, believe me. Why do you insult me?" Tears would come to my eyes, my body would shudder. They'd try to calm me, and in every word of theirs I'd hear pity for a lunatic!

"Brothers!" I'd continue, bitter, desperate. "Have you grown so accustomed to being machines that you think I'm crazy?"

They'd swear they understood me, but I didn't believe it then or now. They tricked me, they comforted me . . .

I ponder and I smile . . . Ha! Once they understand me, how happy we'll be—they and I! . . .

CHILDREN DIDN'T RUN after me, they didn't throw rocks at me. But from their curious looks and smiles, from the way they shivered, from the way they avoided me and stepped aside, I knew that they too regarded me as crazy. I was so angry that I wept, that my heart ached. Oh, how badly

I wanted them to understand my heart, my mind! How I wanted to explain everything that occurred between me and their fathers!

"Children, come to me!"

"Children, I don't bite, I don't harm anyone!"

"Children, I have life, genuine life! I carry it in every limb, in every bit of my marrow!"

"Children, come to me, I'll give it to you in lovely little stories. You need it, you're only just starting to live.

"Children!"

But it was no use my talking. The children were scared of me.

THE ONLY PERSON who understood me was *she*, and *she* was my solace.

My darling, my sweetheart, how I long for you. Grune, beloved, now I can see you. Ahh! I feel I could smash through these walls and run to you—otherwise . . . Otherwise my heart will burst, blow up! . . . I'll do it! I'll push out the windowpane! I'll shatter it!

No, wait! Quiet, quiet . . . The guard is passing with his stick . . . Quiet, quiet, good boy . . .

Ha! I'm tied up! They tied me up. Ohhh, Grune, darling! I feel like crying, Grune darling. I feel sick, Grune darling!

Ahh, Grune! She understood me! She didn't think I was crazy! Ah, no, no, no. Not at all! She quarreled about me with everybody. "You're the crazy ones!" she used to reply on my behalf.

Grune! Darling!

She was a seamstress. She drudged for her relatives, but she herself didn't have a shirt to her name. I was annoyed when I looked at her. I wanted her to go about in a whole frock, in a white shirt. She'd laugh at me: "You're such an egoist!"

Once I brought her some money so she could buy some linen for shirts, but she threw me out.

"You're an awful egoist!" she snapped.

I never spoke another word about it to her. But whenever I saw her ragged dress and her dirty black shirt, I felt as if someone had plunged knives into my heart.

Maybe I really am an egoist. But I have no choice. She's stronger than me. I was scared of her. Even when she'd offer to wash my shirt. I couldn't say no. When I tried, she'd scold me!

Oh my, what a sharp tongue she has! Ten lawyers couldn't outtalk her—ohh, Grune! Will we ever meet again? Oh, yes, yes! I'll even burst out of chains! That's the way it is! Ohh, ohh, ohh!

Keep quiet, quiet.

EVERYONE, INCLUDING HER, said she wasn't beautiful.

"How can you love me?" she'd say. "I'm not beautiful."

I laughed at her fears. Not beautiful? She stopped teasing me.

But she'd list all her defects: "Thick lips, big eyes, a long nose."

She was wrong! It wasn't true! Nothing of the kind! I would have noticed. I couldn't take my eyes off her. I know that Miss Chatskelevitsh used to walk past me, as sickening as a frog, as something repulsive . . . I would hide! Yet poets can't praise her beauty enough, and people shout that she is the most beautiful girl in town. But everything is in reverse with them! Their wealth is other people's drudgery, and I—I'm the crazy one! . . .

I COULDN'T BE a craftsman, my hands didn't work right. If I try to hammer in a nail, it gets twisted, its head coils, and the nail lies on its side. I beg it: "C'mon, friend, get into the wall, get into the plank!" But the nail won't budge. I lose my temper. I practically want to bite its head off. But the nail won't budge! I had pockets full of nails and I kept hammering at random—to no avail! The nail won't budge . . . even today.

Thread a needle—you could chop my hands off but I can't! It's as if the thread were toying with me, defying me. "Just look," says the tailor, and the thread instantly slips into the needle's eye. But I can't and can't and can't! . . .

"You're useless," every craftsman said. He should have stuck a knife in my heart. I've already wanted to chop my own head off . . . I was with a carpenter. I tried to aim the ax here, but it wandered far away. I tried to aim there—and it wound up God knows where. I wanted to try, but they pulled the ax out of my hands.

I cursed myself and my hands. A big laggard—and totally useless! And all the while I had to eat at my father's table, which was paid for by the drudgery of hungry workers—blood money!

I started thinking about putting an end to it. I pictured a rope hanging from the ceiling. I already had a rope. When I made the noose, I felt an urge to go to her, look at her, sit next to her. I'm a real egoist! I imagined saying goodbye to her. And I felt that it was hard for me to be without her . . . I felt so gloomy, so empty, so desolate. I threw down the rope and dashed off to see her, scurrying as if I'd been poisoned.

"Grune, you know what?" I said to her. "I already made a noose, but you won't let me . . ."

"What?" she cried, her eyes bulging.

"Put an end to it," I stammered.

"Have you gone crazy?"

"I eat and I eat . . ."

"Have you lost your mind?"

"I'm useless for any craft."

She glared angrily at me. "You're a moron!" she said, dwelling on each word.

"But Grune—"

"If you want to, you can. You can dig ditches, carry rocks, clean streets . . . You can find work! Put an end to it indeed—!"

I didn't let her finish. I felt a huge strength inside me, and my small, childlike hands looked big enough to do the hardest work.

"Yes, Grune!" I shouted. "That's what's going to happen! And I won't show myself to you until I start earning a living!"

And I dashed out. I only noticed her nodding, she agreed with me. But she was still angry! . . .

I RAN, I RACED straight to the greasy spoon. It was lunchtime. Workers were eating. I stood at the door, watching them eat their wretched meal of rotten cabbage. I planned to ask all of them about finding work. I must have looked bad because everyone paused and stared at me. A tattered laborer came over to me and, with his dirty, swollen, callused hand, he gave me nine individual kopeks, enough for a meat dish. I was amazed, flustered.

"No," I stammered, refusing the money. "No, I mustn't . . . I'm not hungry . . . Thank you . . ."

Suddenly I threw my arms around him and kissed him.

"Give me, brother, give me! Give me the kopeks that you've labored for so bloodily! Give them to me! I'll put them in a case and wear them over my heart forever! No! Give them to me, and I'll run through the streets and show your kopeks to all the leeches, all the bloodsuckers, all the parasites who are known as philanthropists! Give me your kopeks, I'll use them to gore out their eyes!"

I snatched the coins from his hand and ran away.

Behind me someone yelled: "Ah, the crazy man!" But I kept running, running.

A bit later I wondered whether my tattered benefactor also regarded me as crazy. I ran back . . .

He did look at me as if I were crazy.

"No," I told him, "no, a lie, a lie . . . I'm not crazy . . . Believe me . . . A lie . . . I'm sane. We'll be friends, huh? You'll understand me . . . Yes, you'll understand me . . . Just tell me—what do you do?"

"I do odd jobs," he replied, "I'm no craftsman."

A light went on in my brain. I felt a tickling in my chest.

"Tell me what you do. Can I do it?"

"Yeah, why not? Anyone can do what I do."

I almost hopped with joy.

He was a porter for masons, he carried bricks, sand, water.

I became a porter too.

When I received my first pay, I flew to her breathlessly.

"Grune, here it is!" I yelled and I threw my arms around her.

"Now you're a real human being," she murmured, patting my head, and her big, kind, intelligent eyes expressed love, a deep ardent love.

"You see? And you wanted to kill yourself." She reproached me so sweetly.

My heart skipped a beat. I was happy, I laughed and I rubbed my hands . . . I sat down across from her, took hold of her hands, and described what had happened.

When I was done, she exclaimed, "Let me meet him."

Holding her hand and smiling happily, I broke into a run.

"You're both crazy!" people yelled after us, but we just squeezed one another's hands.

Ha ha ha! Ohh, Grune, I can still picture you! My darling! . . .

"Why don't we all live together?" I asked her.

"No," she replied, "we mustn't. I want to live with my family. But the two of you can live together . . . You should be brothers, brothers forever!"

Ohh, Grune . . .

We followed her suggestion. We were brothers. Lived together, worked together, ate together, shared every scrap of food. After work she would come by, or we would drop in on her, and I was happy, blissfully happy . . .

Initially my parents gave me no peace. They wanted to drag me back home by force. But I dug in my heels. Until they gave up on me, and I could breathe easy . . . Our tiny garret seemed like the biggest mansion. Large and wide. A paradise! She would tidy it up for the Sabbath! A celebration! Sheer delight! . . .

Luck was with me! I constantly had work and I started helping my father's poorest workers. These paupers didn't want to take any money . . . Poor, kind, simple men . . . I was only giving them what was theirs! They wanted to give me money too! And they refused to take anything . . . So I secretly left them money at their doorways . . .

I was happy!

NOW I WAS working with my friend one terribly hot day. The sun scorched us, burned us. We were pouring asphalt. My friend began feeling sick, he fainted. He was carried home. I stayed with him instead of going back to work. That evening he felt worse, and we didn't have a single kopek between us. So I hurried over to our boss, an old, tall, potbellied Jew with dubious sidelocks and a long overcoat.

"The worker who got sick today," I said, "is feeling awful, and he doesn't have a kopek to his name. He needs a doctor. Can you give him an advance? — he'll work it off."

"I don't give advances," the long overcoat replied and tried to leave.

I blocked his path.

"First of all, we worked half a day. And in any case we'll work off the advance. He's critically ill, have some pity . . . *I'll* work it off!"

"I told you, I don't give advances!" the potbelly snapped.

I saw red, my heart pounded, a rock appeared in my hand — I don't know how.

"Damn you!" I shouted in a strange voice.

Unfortunately the rock flew by. I pounced on the potbelly . . . I yelled, foamed at the mouth, spit, roared, bit, tore, choked, scratched. They could barely pull me off him . . . I was dragged to the police station. My father got me out. He told them I was crazy. He slipped them a banknote.

THE NEXT DAY I hurried home. My friend lay on the floor, he was covered with a black cloth. She was kneeling at his side, crying . . . The room was filled with workers from the neighborhood . . . All of them sad . . . I thought I'd go crazy . . . I threw myself on the floor, ripped out my hair, bit my hands, laughed and cried . . .

"Where've you been?" she asked me. "Where'd you disappear to? He could've been saved. You should've called a doctor right away!"

"We got here late . . . too late," the neighbors explained. "We did bring a doctor—he couldn't help!"

I didn't listen, I ran to the boss . . . A death for a death! Luckily for him the bastard spotted me and had me captured. I just had time to hurl a rock at him. It hit him! It hit his fat belly! . . . Ha ha ha! . . . It boomed like a drum, like a kettledrum! . . . He doubled up in pain and groaned loudly. . . . Ha ha ha! . . . It was music to my ears!

But I was arrested. An iron hand clutched my left shoulder—and the boss survived! I won't forgive myself! I'm a rat! A good-for-nothing! My father brought me here, to the madhouse . . . I yelled that I wasn't crazy . . . I should be tried and judged! . . . I deserve to be hanged, shot, drowned . . . Such a good-for-nothing! . . . Ohh! . . .

BUT WHY WON'T they let Grune in to see me? . . . Why don't they let Grune see me? . . .

I. M. VAYSENBERG *(1881–1938)*

A factory worker in a small Polish town, Vaysenberg started publishing Yiddish fiction in 1904. In contrast with other sometimes nostalgic and idealized tales about shtetl life, he described harshness and brutality, especially in his novella The Shtetl *(1909), which, in its raw class consciousness, depicts the failure of a strike. Vaysenberg also managed to draw gross humor from his roughshod characters, as in the following story — an example of the delight he took in portraying bullies, laborers, good-for-nothings rather than scholars and other virtuous Jews. In his later years, Vaysenberg turned to mystical themes.*

A Father and His Sons *(1911)*

SHLOYME THE NUMBSKULL — that was what his wife, Khanna-Leah, nicknamed him, because on every Friday evening, while Jews were off to synagogue, he and his two sons would wedge the pot of carrot stew between their legs and all three men would dig in with wooden ladles. Their faces red and flushed like the faces of Turks, they would stuff their guts, ladle in, ladle out, until not a smidgen was left for Khanna-Leah's Sabbath breakfast. Sundays at the crack of dawn, that very same Shloyme the Numbskull, without even washing his hands according to the pre-scribed ritual, would grab his sack and his stick and march into the coun-tryside together with his younger son, Moyshe the Brute. As for Pinkhes, the older boy, the father was too scared to bother him. Like a real sol-dier — his mother even called him Soldier Boy — Pinkhes was stretched out on his cot, which was made up of noodle boards on chairs, with troughs serving as pillows. The boy's snoring filled the tiny cottage with its gray walls, as he lay there, his nostrils pointing at the ceiling and his bare elbows flung under his head.

"Let 'm sleep," Shloyme cautioned his younger son as if saying, "The hell with him!" Tiptoeing and putting a finger on his lips, he whispered: "Let's get outa here and go to the village. You can have his share. . . ."

And with their sticks in their hands and their sacks slung over their shoulders, her two breadwinners snuck away so quietly that Khanna-Leah, lying there with her head and its white nightcap buried in the pillow, didn't even hear the creaking of the door.

The room grew quiet. The pale dawn shone into the cottage, whiten-ing the walls. Shloyme and his son were now footloose and fancy free.

"Look, Pa!" Moyshe the Brute held up a maimed bare foot while hop-ping on the other. "Look! It got ripped on a stone!" He displayed a raw, red gash on a black, muddy sole.

"Go to hell!" his father exclaimed, eying him from the side. "I can't count on you guys for nothin'. That's whatcha get for runnin' around day an' night!"

Moyshe the Brute tightened his belt and marched alongside his pa, feeling that he himself and not Pinkhes was his pa's right-hand man. His vest pocket contained a thimble, needles—an apprentice's equipment— while his pa's bag contained a master's equipment: a measuring tape, a piece of chalk, and a pair of scissors. Moyshe envied him. He would catch on by observing his pa—then he would set out all alone on a Sunday morning, hurry to the village by himself so his family wouldn't know what had become of him. His ma would scurry around hysterically, wringing her hands: God only knew—maybe her son had drowned or maybe devils had dragged him to a forest and married him off to a calf. Who could tell? And he, Moyshe the Brute, would spend a whole week in the village, eating roast potatoes with sour milk, and he wouldn't catch a glimpse of the shtetl until Friday evening. The Sabbath candles would be shining in all windows, he'd be sweaty and dusty, and the women would admire him for being such a good breadwinner. And he'd drop in on his ma, put down his sack, and hand her a whole five rubles plus a gift. "Here you are, Ma!" he'd say to her "I earned this and I'm givin' it to you."

And he pictured what a Sabbath that would be! His ma would thrust dish after dish at him, and he would act quiet and refined, and not eat much.

Moyshe the Brute's eyes glowed with sheer delight, and he peered at the sandy road, as he and his father emerged on the hill behind the town, where the green field and the distant blue forest spread far, far away.

Moyshe gazed eastward, toward the sunrise, where the sky was ablaze with all kinds of streaks—fiery red and brownish red. Then, puffing out his cheeks, he asked his pa whether the village they were going to had burned down during the night.

"You lunkhead!" said the father. "Can't you see the sun's coming up?"

And Moyshe looked again and saw that the sun was actually behind a vast, azure cloud bank, the light rays pointing across the heavens like long horns—Moyshe realized his father was right . . .

The boy saw how early in the day it was . . . Far off, in the low-lying field of the valley, stood a pair of oxen and a peasant with a broad straw hat, his shirt dangling over his pants. A nightly hush still lay upon all the surroundings, and a dark calm hovered beyond the distant blue forest, so that the oxen and the peasant seemed mysterious as if spirited there randomly out of the clear blue sky.

But in the air before the huge, blue cloud bank spreading from the east between sky and earth a single, tiny bird fluttered straight up, shrilly twittering to welcome the dawn, dipping its wings in and out of the clouds, filling the air with its sweet playfulness. And a sweetness diffused in the morning air as the bird soared higher and higher, becoming a black dot, vanishing in the cloud. And its twittering faded as if coming from across the vast world. Later on, two hours from now, Moyshe and his pa would be beyond that vast world. The bird was certainly peering down at the distant cottages with their thatched roofs, white walls, and small, single windows facing the sandy road. The bird most certainly saw them, and he, Moyshe, would be there later on.

"How good," he mused, "that'll be . . ." His pa would then slip into the innkeeper's prayer shawl and prayer thongs and say his prayers at the innkeeper's window, and he, Moyshe, would likewise pray. And the innkeeper would then serve them a snack, a bowl of pot cheese and a chunk of black bread—if that didn't beat all!

His pa, deliberately brushing against Moyshe, interrupted his thoughts.

"Listen, Moyshe, didn'tsha hear Ma sort o' groan before?"

"Groan?" Moyshe the Brute gaped at his father, his mouth half open, his lips puffy.

"Didn' ya hear her groan?"

"What d'ya mean, groan?"

"Get atta here, you jerk!" He shoved Moyshe away, and with a sidelong glance, he added: "You just don' get it!"

Moyshe acted stupid. He knew his old man would soon be hosting a circumcision, Khanna-Leah would be squeezing another kid from her guts any day now. But why should Moyshe care? Let the old man think that Moyshe didn't understand such business . . .

And so, flimflamming one another, they hoofed it to the village all the faster.

"Shake a leg," the father told his son. "I'm older 'n you, and look, you can eat my dust, thank the Lord!"

The father took longer and longer strides, his coattails flapping against his boots. By the time he briefly halted to pull his boots off on the grass, Moyshe was still limping along, favoring his injured foot, too far behind to catch up, until they disappeared way beyond the fields. . . .

. . .   .

IT WAS ONLY now that Khanna-Leah awoke. The first thing she saw as she raised her head was that the other bed was long since empty. And then, when she looked at the window and saw how high the sun was in the blue sky, she pictured her two breadwinners slogging barefoot across the fields, their caps askew over their foreheads, their faces excited, and she pictured him, the old man, with his boots slung over his shoulder. She looked at her son on the cot, he was snoring away, with his healthy red face, his lips puffing up, his nostrils rising. He was like a steam engine throttling full blast.

The mother thought to herself: "Oh, Lord, what've you inflicted on me?"

But when she gazed at his two closed eyes, she mused, a bit more calmly, that it was good that the ogre slept at times . . . And now she felt it was good for the whole world that the ogre was asleep.

For this was what Pinkhes did once he got up in the morning: He'd stuff rolls into both his pockets and—forward march! Off he'd go to his gang in the square, to his pigeons. Or else he'd grab a horse in the market, in broad daylight—no matter who it belonged to. And he'd gallop down to the river to bathe the horse all day or to the meadow behind the watermill to pasture the horse all day. And if someone came looking for the horse or if a couple of boys came running and pointing—"There he is! That's him!"—Pinkhes would keep an eye on the other side of the meadow. At the first hint of trouble, the first sign of an onslaught, Pinkhes would jump on the horse and, hellbent for leather, he'd dash along a back road behind the Christian cemetery, straight to the highway. There he was as free as a bird—and just try and catch him on his mount. If he felt like it, he'd return the horse to where he'd found it—even after the whole shtetl had lost all hope of recovering it, and agitated people were gathering in all corners and shouting that Pinkhes had stolen a horse.

One day, however, he played a really nasty prank. He spotted a peasant girl among other peasants. They'd just taken the first sprouts in their gardens to the priest, who'd splashed holy water on the plants so they'd have a good harvest. Pinkhes grabbed the girl's sprouts and gave her a few hard smacks to boot. People said: "Aha!" Now he'd really get it, he wasn't long for this world. And his father flew at him for molesting peasant girls in the street. But Pinkhes shot back, saying that his father had forgotten what he'd done as a boy, before marrying. That was the son's retort, and the two of them locked horns, like goats facing one another on a plank. But Pinkhes knew how to make up with his father. He couldn't care less about his mother, but he didn't want to feud with his pa.

Once, with God's help, a merry-go-round with some conjurors had come wandering into town. It gave Pinkhes a new lease on life. And the instant the carnival boss, the whole gang of Gentile girls, and the dark girl, who looked like a Gypsy with braids—the instant they hoisted the central pole in the middle of the marketplace, Pinkhes lent them a hand. He helped them pull up the rope, attach the canvas, and hitch the wooden horses to the colored carriages. That Sunday, the peasants came to the shtetl from the surrounding parishes, the men in caps with shiny vizors and white collars, the women in white kerchiefs. And the merry-go-round lurched into motion.

Pinkhes was already in the carnival boss's good books. If he'd joined the carnival, the boss might have let him marry one of the girls. Who could say?—he might have become a respectable man, a conjuror with his own carnival, he could have been on his own by now. But his heart wasn't in it, even though the boss had urged him, and the oldest girl, with black hair and crimson lips, seemed to have winked at him and gazed right into his eyes, trying to bring him around. Nevertheless Pinkhes took his father to the marketplace to show him how greatly the boss admired him.

Shloyme gaped at the circular canvas tent with the red flag at its very tip and the huge crowd of Jews, guys and girls and women mingling with peasant guys and girls from the surrounding countryside. He gawked at the middle booth with its velvet hangings and its multitude of beads and at the battery of brass trumpets with their mouths gaping straight at the markeplace. Taking in all these sights, Shloyme felt exuberant, even more so than his son: to think that such wonders could be found in a carnival. And he looked forward to stunts right here in the shtetl—and what stunts!

And he asked his son: "What kind of stunts are they gonna do?"

"Wooden horses are gonna gallop on their own. If you pay six pennies," the son tersely replied, "you can mount a horse, and if you pay four pennies, you can ride in a carriage."

Shloyme couldn't believe his ears: ride a carriage or mount a wooden horse? And when he pushed his way through the crowd and saw the horses saddled and harnessed to the carriages and the carriages followed by more horses, his eyes and his mouth opened wide.

"And," his son boasted, "I helped them put all this up. You think it was easy? If you like, Pa, you can ride a horse for free. You can bet on it—for free!"

Shloyme the Numbskull's face lit up and his eyes glowed at the sight of the velvet hangings and the multitude of beads. "Wait, we'll see." Peering at his son, he stroked his beard.

And the instant the polished brass trumpets blasted away—*Tatatarrrra! Tatatarrrra!*—Shloyme, unable to hold back, started bawling the marching tune, which he learned on the spot and in which he still sings the Sabbath hymns today, so that his wife hollers: "How can a man be so shameless and sing the same tune day and night!" But why should Shloyme care? Why should he worry? The trumpets blasted, *Tatatarrrra!*, and he chimed in. And he puffed up his throat as if he wanted to change it into a trumpet. And the carousel with its horses and carriages and tent roof—everything was whirling and spinning, and the flushed faces and sparkling eyes of young peasants, male and female, dazzled the onlookers. Shloyme couldn't stand it any longer—he lovingly ogled his dear son. And when the carousel halted, Pinkhes grabbed his pa and plunked him on a horse. He winked at the boss's wife, indicating that this was his father, and he clambered to the top of the tent, where he turned the crank and drove the entire carousel.

Shloyme's eyes blazed up at all the girls and wives standing around and seeing the prestige he'd gained from his son. He whistled at him: "Pinkhes! Let's go!"

A bell jingled on the velvet canopy with its multitude of embroidered white and blue beads. The passengers grabbed their tickets, the men got on the horses, the women stepped into the carriages, and the trumpets blasted: *Tatatarrrra!* And Shloyme the Numbskull began to soar, he and the entire carousel, everything whirled and reeled.

But among all the flushed faces, his flushed face was the only Jewish face. A gang of Jewish boys standing around the chain started banging sticks or plying whips. Next they decided to prod Shloyme's horse. The turmoil and the raucous laughter came from all sides: "Giddiyap! Giddiyap!" And the boys kept banging and whipping. Shloyme grew dizzy, his beard flew apart like a disheveled broom, his eyes flashed and sparkled, the boys thrashed and flogged his horse. And suddenly just look: Shloyme was chasing a Gentile girl. She was sitting in a carriage in front of him, and he was on a horse behind her. The tails of her kerchief with its aigrettes were soaring over her head, and he, with his beard flying apart, looked as if he were chasing her nonstop, and it didn't help that the boys kept yelling and heckling and whistling. Shloyme kept chasing the peasant girl—until his son got so dizzy that he threw up on his father's head, disgorging just about everything he'd eaten for the past ten years, pouring it over his father's face and beard. Next Pinkhes fell down—right into the peasant girl's carriage. The bell jingled, and the carousel screeched to a halt.

Father and son scurried off across the marketplace with their tails between their legs. And the gang of kids dashed after them in utter turmoil. The boys were as agitated as bees: Shloyme the Numbskull had chased a Gentile girl! But Jews were unconcerned about the misdeed. They figured it had something to do with the carousel. In fact, the delighted merchants stood at their thresholds, smirking into their beards as they watched Shloyme scooting along with flying coattails like old Ashmedai, the king of demons—followed by his son and the gang of kids, like a flock of birds.

Khanna-Leah came scampering with outspread arms to rescue her husband and her son. Goodness only knew what theft they'd been caught red-handed at—and as she quickly dragged them into the house, she learned that old Ashmedai had actually ridden the carousel. Shaking her head, she eyed him with pity: how can a father act like such a jerk?

Shloyme felt that she was right, he had been a jerk—so he blamed it on their son. But there was no way she could get at Pinkhes, she saw that he was growing worse and worse by the day—and as of this moment she gave up on her son, she figured no good would ever come of him.

And now, as she watched him lying on the makeshift cot, with his sleeves rolled up, she clearly saw the soldier in his face—and she thanked and praised the Lord that this ogre was asleep, and that the world could be happy that Pinkhes was slumbering away.

Khanna-Leah got up, threw on her kerchief, and went next door to get a live coal so she could start a fire. Her neighbor gave her a few live coals, and the two women started chatting away. Khanna-Leah poured her heart out: her sons were making her miserable. The neighbor asked how she was getting on with the new child, and Khanna-Leah replied that she was expecting it any moment now.

Actually, she regretted the whole business. After Moyshe the Brute, she had vowed never to have another baby. She recalled how difficult the delivery had been. A pair of her husband's trousers had been hanging on the wall opposite her, she had told him to remove them and she had cursed the living daylights out of him. But in the end, she'd let herself be tricked again.

Her neighbor comforted her: God would grant her an easy delivery this time. And they fell to talking about how a woman requires special protection when she gives birth.

And Khanna-Leah, Heaven preserve us, told about a third baby she'd had—between Pinkhes and Moyshe, and this newborn had been the size of a six-month-old—may he rest in peace.

Her neighbor had her own tale to tell—about Tsheytl the nightcap maker. One Sabbath evening she'd been sitting by a lamp, sewing a nightcap. All at once, Tsheytl saw a woman with undone hair racing past the window and holding a baby to her breast. It was Yutte's daughter-in-law—God help us.

Khanna-Leah spit three times and went home.

When Pinkhes got up, she asked him to take the mezuzas to the scribe and have him check them. She had prepared diapers, shirts, and a clean sheet to hang as a curtain over the bed. And when she turned in at night, she would have a Bible at her head—not the Yiddish version for women, but Shloyme's Hebrew Bible.

And what do you think? That very same night, a few neighbors were attending her, and at around three a.m. they knocked on the midwife's door.

Khanna-Leah gave birth to a boy, who came into the world with a shock of black hair.

There was a good reason why Shloyme, walking outside the town, had wondered if she was already groaning. He looked forward to a merry Sabbath. He'd come home, God willing, and his Khanna-Leah would've finished by then and she'd be safe and sound.

Khanna-Leah lay in bed like a countess. A sheet hanging from a rope suspended from a beam was covered with amulets. And if she needed something from time to time, she would stick her nightcapped head through the curtain. Her face was purified, her voice softer and tenderer than before. She had only one thing in mind: to shield the baby, to keep him from enduring what had happened to that other baby and what her neighbor had told her about—God forbid. The new mother was determined that she wouldn't let go of the child, wouldn't let him out of her arms. Even while sleeping she'd hold on to him with all her might, lie on him with her entire body like a devoted mother.

And now it was Thursday night. Khanna-Leah fell asleep, her mind full of pleasant thoughts. Shloyme would come home tomorrow and he'd see what kind of boy she'd have for him—without his knowledge. Their third surviving child.

And she slept.

And she dreamed about the Queen of Sheba herself, with her bare breasts, long, undone braids, and her roundish frock, a crinoline of Turkish calico in a pattern of dots and flowers. The queen was squeezing in through the half-open window, squeezing and squeezing—such a fat, heavy woman. Khanna-Leah panicked, and choking back her shrieks, she hugged the baby tight, and the baby didn't need any other Queen of Sheba than the one he had.

THE DAY WAS barely dawning, the blue air seeped in through the windows. Shloyme tapped gently on the door, and Pinkhes, blending with the grayness of the night and the young daybreak seeping into the cottage, jumped down from his makeshift bed and opened the door. Shloyme tiptoed in, followed by Moyshe. The father hadn't caught a wink of sleep in the village and he was coming here together with the day. And now, when he spotted the curtain above the bed, his eyes glistened softly. Tugging on Pinkhes's sleeve, he murmured: "A boy or a girl?"

"A boy," answered Pinkhes.

"A boy?" Shloyme's face was wreathed in smiles.

Moyshe joined in with a jig. "We're gonna celebrate, and I'm gonna have a whole basket of peas!"

"Shut up, you bastard!" His father jabbed him. "Ma's asleep!"

"Shut up, damn it!" Pinkhes exclaimed, supporting his father.

"Did she just fall asleep?" the father asked.

"No, she's been sleeping all night," Pinkhes replied.

"All night?" Shloyme's heart skipped a beat. Slowly and quietly he stole over to her bed. "Khanna-Leah, Khanna-Leah," he called gently, almost to himself, as if he didn't want his voice to go too far. "Khanna-Leah."

Khanna-Leah went on sleeping.

"Lemme wake her, Pa!" Moyshe the Brute said gruffly.

"Shut up, you bastard!" Shloyme snapped. "You'll scare her! . . . Khanna-Leah, Khanna-Leah!"

"Huhhhh?" A long, drawn-out grunt came from behind the curtain.

"Khanna-Leah, where's the baby?"

"My God! The baby!" she cried, waking up.

The horrified father yanked the curtain apart. Both sons were petrified, and their glassy eyes bulged at the curtain.

"My God! The baby!" cried the mother and she lifted the baby up by one hand like a dead gosling. His head dangled. Gaping in terror, she grabbed the baby's face and started tearing away at it.

"Goddamn you to hell!" roared Shloyme, his hands forming a "blessing" over her. The baby had stopped breathing; its body was as cold as a chunk of dough. "You bitch!" Shloyme hollered. "You already killed one son of mine!" With a lowered head, he stepped away from the curtain.

Khanna-Leah kept yelling, and so did the two sons. Shloyme, robust and clumsy, loped up and down the room like a bear hunter, glaring at the curtain.

A few women from the neighborhood came hurrying over and they learned that the baby was dead.

And now Khanna-Leah launched into a lament. "What a calamity! The Queen of Sheba came crawling in through the window. She had fat teats and she smothered the baby with her teats."

"Teats!" shouted Shloyme. "It would take much fatter teats than even yours! Go to the rabbi—quick! A divorce! God damn you to hell!"

"Shloyme, darling, what d'you want?" She tried to weep. But it didn't work. Their two sons were huddling in a corner, thanking the Lord that none of this was their fault.

Later on, when a member of the burial society came for the baby, the mother had to make the bed, pull down the curtain, and accompany the father to the rabbi.

"Dear Rabbi!" Shloyme pled, furious and fervent. "She's made me miserable, she killed two sons of mine! Two sons!"

"If you please, woman," the rabbi asked, "what do you have to say for yourself?"

"Two sons—it's awful!" She wept with maternal pathos.

"What do you want from her, Shloyme?" the rabbi argued. "She's a woman! She certainly wanted them to live!"

Pinkhes burst into the rabbi's home after thundering away at the door.

"Pa, go home!" Next Moyshe the Brute came lumbering in, bellowing: "Ma!"

The terrified rabbi thrust out his arms, warding off Pinkhes.

"You're gonna divorce my ma?" Pinkhes pounded his fist on the table. "Go home or I'll beat the hell outa you!"

"Didya hear that, Rabbi! That's the thanks I get for bringing up my kids!" After pointing at Pinkhes and at the mother's belly, Shloyme dashed out, slamming the door behind him.

"And you, Ma." Pinkhes removed a coin from his pocket. "Go home and fix some supper!"

To avoid running into people who knew her, Khanna-Leah went home along a fence through a back street. She had endured enough shame. All the way, Moyshe kept nagging her to use the cauldron, not the smaller pot, and to fill it up with potatoes, because he hadn't eaten since leaving the village. And so Khanna-Leah came home.

The following Friday, Shloyme, together with the two sons—like bulls—was once again sitting with the pot of carrot stew between his legs. All three men were clutching ladles, and their faces were flushed like the faces of Turks. And Khanna-Leah was once again berating them for not leaving anything for Sabbath breakfast.

Friday night, however, when the Sabbath candles were burning, and Shloyme and his two sons were sitting at the table, crooning "Sons and sons of sons," Khanna-Leah was gazing with radiant eyes at her two sons. She didn't know why, but for some reason she cared more for Pinkhes now. And she herself didn't feel a tear rolling down her cheek and dropping into her bean soup. But Shloyme was glaring vengefully at her: Let her rot in hell! The bitch! With four sons like these he could have conquered the world. Fed up with looking at her, he motioned to his sons, and all three men started bawling the words of a Sabbath hymn to the marching tune of the carousel!

FRADEL SHTOK *(1890–after 1942)*

Fradel Shtok (also spelled Stock) was born in the East Galician town of Skalle (German and Polish Skala, then part of the Austro-Hungarian

Empire and later part of interwar Poland). She was one of the few Yiddish women authors in the early twentieth century. Arriving in the United States at seventeen, she began writing poems and stories. Indeed, she was one of the first poets to develop the sonnet form in Yiddish. When her book of stories, published in 1919 and titled simply Gezamelte Ertsaylungen (Collected Stories), *was badly received, she switched to English, but with no greater success. The lexicon of modern Yiddish literature* (Leksikon Fun der Nayer Yidisher Literatur) *claims that she died in a mental hospital around 1930. However, the Abe Cahan Archive at the YIVO Institute for Jewish Research, New York, contains a letter she sent Cahan on October 20, 1942, along with a new story, which was then published in the* Jewish Daily Forward *on November 19, 1942. No further information about Fradel Shtok has come to light.*

The settings in her sole book of Yiddish genre stories alternate between her native shtetl and New York—a typical dichotomy in Yiddish literature.

The Archbishop *(1919)*

WHILE THE TOWNSFOLK knew that an archbishop was coming, no one in Skalle made a big fuss about the news. It was only when pine gates were set up at the entrance that people began talking about it in the street.

Mótkele the Redhead, whose brother was a big cheese at the town hall, explained: "Do they really have a clue? They think archbishops are a dime a dozen! Imagine how long it takes to climb that high! First you gotta study for the priesthood—you're not born a priest. Then you become a canon, then a supreme canon, then an elder, which he knows and which he's already forgotten—Ah, a blessed man. And then you become a bishop. And it's not till a long, long time later that you become an archbishop."

Why was an archbishop coming to Skalle? Nobody knew for certain. One person said that an archbishop visited Skalle only once every fifty years. Another person said that an archbishop came by only when the Christians were about to build a church. Henekh the Marriage Broker, who was standing nearby, glanced at the old Catholic church. He figured it wouldn't be such a bad idea: the town really needed a new church. He spit superstitiously, but he secretly mused: "A new church.

The town'll become more genteel, more civilized." For Henekh knew how many matches had been nipped in the bud purely because Skalle was uncivilized.

In short, the idea kept growing on Henekh, and so he tried to convince everyone that it was a fact, that it couldn't be truer. And the Jews started believing him, because if Henekh wanted to talk you into something, he did so hands down.

Alter asked: "Well, so what's gonna happen with the town clock? What's the town gonna look at?"

The fact of the matter was that Alter wanted to get rid of the town clock. His home was next to the Polish church, and being a usurer, he had nothing to do. So he spent all day looking at the town clock, but by now he was totally sick of looking at it. He felt that if it hadn't been for the clock, he could have eaten one meal after another—only the clock didn't allow it. For instance, when he drank his cup of cocoa in the morning and the dial face said eight, it seemed to him that the hands would be approaching twelve, which was the reason he wasn't hungry and couldn't finish his lunch so soon.

Meanwhile a few other people were worried, because their own timepieces kept pace with the town clock, and if it were removed, their own timepieces would have nothing to keep pace with. And if all the clocks in town stopped working, how would they know? Without a clock, you can kick the bucket and not know when.

Now Shloyme the Deaf Man pointed out that it would bring good luck and prosperity for Skalle if a new church was "construcked."

"Prosperity from a church, Shloyme? Please explain."

Avrom the Chatterbox was delighted that he had tripped up Shloyme.

The deaf man didn't like getting tripped up, especially by Avrom. So he snapped: "Goo aargue with yourseelf!" (Shloyme drawled because he came from a different region). He looked at Henekh and addressed him, but he actually meant Avrom. Whyy in the world didn't hee geet it? A goyish miind! "Wheen you construck a chuurch, you doo need engineers—aarchitecks, that is. Plus woorkers. They'll bring in the woorkers from other towns, peasants from the four corners of the world'll come to our fairs. Doo youu geet it noow—goyish mind?"

He meant Avrom, but he said all that stuff to Henekh, who caught the drift and held his tongue.

In short, the Jews looked forward to the arrival of the archbishop as they did to the coming of the Messiah (if you'll forgive my mentioning them in the same breath). Bórekh promised Sluk the dowry after the archbishop's visit. And when Henekh had to pay tuition for his son, he begged Shloyme to wait until after the visit—God bless us!

A bit later it was rumored that the town rabbi would welcome the archbishop with a Torah scroll. A few curious men pounced on the beadle, Shloyme Perets, in the street and asked him whether it was true. Shloyme winked his blind eye (which could spot a bad coin faster than a seeing eye) and he snuffled: "How should I know?"

"They're putting up a gate at the beginning of the street and another gate right by the pharmacy, and Dvoyre is standing there."

Alter's daughter Godel asked him: "What's Dvoyre doing by the pharmacy? Tell her to come home for lunch."

Godel explained that Dvoyre was standing there with her friend Shayndl, they were watching the construction of the gate.

"If she's with Shayndl, that's fine. Shayndl is a decent girl." And he went home.

By now, though, Dvoyre was standing without Shayndl, as she was watching the construction. And she didn't even give Lutsuk a second thought. Well, when Lutsuk came out alone, he came out alone—was it her fault? Was it her fault that the gate was being constructed by the pharmacy? And if he greeted her and doffed his hat, shouldn't she respond?

"It's too bad," said Lutsuk. "So many young pine trees shattered!"

"Yes, too bad." Shouldn't she have responded?

When Lutsuk looked at her, she looked away.

She stood there for a minute, then fled. She felt as if the entire marketplace could see that she yearned for the Christian.

She then had an urge to go to the wineshops. There she counted the young trees, one, two, three, four, five. "So many young pine trees shattered!"

A Gentile was walking home in a new straw hat with a peacock feather. He was strumming a mandolin and singing a Ukrainian folksong: "Hey there under the mountain." And the feather's greenish-blue eye sang along.

Dvoyre felt alien among the trees, with the Gentile who was walking home all alone to his village, but she wasn't afraid. She had an urge to go back to the marketplace, to the shops, with their Jewish merchandise.

. . .   .

THE DAYS WORE by and the weeks wore by, and Dvoyre lived through her days and nights with the words: "So many young pine trees shattered!"

She felt it was sinful to think about the Gentile. In her depression she helped her mother, Brayne, darn socks. Her mother didn't have a clue, but she wouldn't let Godel do anything spiteful to Dvoyre.

Alter, as usual, stood at the window, gazing at the town clock, intent on what he wanted from life. At eleven, for instance, the roast wasn't ready as yet, but it *was* ready by twelve noon. He argued that with God's help couldn't he live to see the roast done a bit earlier today?

His wife Brayne replied that everything required a little effort, otherwise . . .

Alter caught the hint and he broke in: You couldn't see any steam on her, the fat wasn't oozing from her double chin. And as corpses ate, that's what they looked like—was she listening or not?

Of course she was listening, and she replied that he ought to set his mind on more important things, there was a marriageable girl in the house—the mother groaned that her world was so dark and wretched.

Alter was at a loss to reply, but he didn't want to be tripped up. So he exclaimed: "What can I do? She's turned down Mayer Zisi. How come, girl, how come? Who can we talk to, who?"

Dvoyre was used to all this, she was used to hearing Mayer Zisi's name no matter where she happened to be. He was a good man, a fine man, Mayer Zisi with his big Adam's apple and his hammered shoulders.

She was used to seeing her mother shake her head:

She didn't want to? Didn't want to? She had something to boast about—a girl was a precious thing. Mayer Zisi had a problem, a boy had a problem—oh, sure! It was a reasonable thing, it couldn't be more reasonable! . . . A reasonable dowry here, a reasonable dowry there, a reasonable legacy at death—God forbid! Our own cousins—what could be more reasonable?

But Dvoyre was already used to it.

It was harvest time. The reaped wheat and rye lay in stacks in the fields, and people walked across the hayfields to go swimming in the river, and the swimming and the summer sunsets gave Dvoyre a tan. Lutsuk's voice haunted her everywhere—on the paths, among the stacks of wheat and rye, far, far, reaching all the way to the mill. And she was ashamed to undress in front of his voice, which followed her, burning her back, echoing her footsteps—wasn't her gait beautiful, wasn't it graceful! Peered into her eyes, from all mirrors, beautiful eyes, Dvoyre? Undo her braid, long hair, Dvoyre? No, short hair, a short braid wasn't beautiful, smear salves in her hair, soak it in the juice of yellow flowers, then the braid will grow, grow, grow. And can you sing, Dvoyre? Sing, softer, softer, don't squeal, it's not appropriate for a Jewish girl. Just a sigh, very soft, shh, keep it to yourself.

So many young pine trees shattered! . . .

The Gentile was walking home all alone to his village, strumming his mandolin so beautifully and singing: "Hey there under the mountain."

Become a Christian and die!

Next Tuesday morning Moyshe-Yoyne beat the drum, telling the merchants to close their shops. Anyone who failed to do so would be fined. The Jews realized that *he* was coming today.

That morning, Alter had yelled at Godye, warning him not to go and look, for it was rumored that military personnel would be present, and he might get crushed. Later on, during the big commotion, Alter ran into him and he shouted: "Go home! A Jew mustn't look at him! I'm going to synagogue."

But later on, they bumped into one another where a Jew mustn't look.

The marketplace was mobbed. Well, now everyone had seen that it was no simple matter. Yugan, the school principal, hadn't gone to spend the day getting drunk in Móyshele's tavern. At the crack of dawn, when the rooster had crowed, Yugan had sneaked in for no more than one drink.

The peasants, who had driven in from the surrounding countryside, were all in their Sunday best, and you could have said that their heads had swelled because of the great honor done to their town.

Dvoyre was standing near Hanzel's shop, gazing at the ring of spectators formed by the policemen. They were under the command of Commissioner Prakavitsh, who was riding his horse, with his fearful police mustache flying apart and with a pine sprig in his lapel. And Moyshe-Yoyne the Drunkard, who had hung up his drum, reeled after him, shouting: "Keep back! Keep back!"

Dvoyre, upon seeing the throng of Christian strangers in her Jewish marketplace, felt like a householder visited by unknown guests, who turn everything upside down, who bring along alien things and linger for a while.

She was looking forward to their returning to their lairs, their cottages, their fields. This was not their place.

Nobody knew why the police had formed the spectators into a ring. A jokester swore that the ring was meant to keep the pigs from going through.

It was getting late, and Yugan the school principal was still hurrying around, drenched in sweat.

Everyone was now looking at the priests, fat and skinny, tall and short, their bodies indicating the kinds of brains they had, fat or skinny.

But noisiest of all was the canon, who was the local priest and who had the face of a yearling heifer. His own cook said that he was an honest priest.

Suddenly the crowd began to stir and mill, to hustle and bustle. Someone announced that he was arriving.

Who was arriving? Apparently the archbishop—no, it was the town rabbi. They were going out to receive the archbishop right there, there. "Cut it out, stop shoving, you—I mean, Alter."

"Who is it, who is it, Mottye, can you see him? The archbishop—I mean the rabbi?"

"Ah, ah, if you'll forgive my mentioning them in the same breath. What crap! An ox has a long tongue, but he can't blow a ram's horn!"

"What business is it of yours?"

"Shush! There you have it! Jews have found a time to fight. Shush, quiet, they're singing. Who's singing, what's singing? Are you deaf or something? The beadle's singing. There's the rabbi, he's walking with a minyan and he's got a Torah scroll. Itsik and Velvel are holding him by his arms. The beadle is singing. Shloyme Perets with his blind eye? What is the beadle singing? The imperial anthem, he's singing the imperial anthem."

"Alter, now then! Lemme have a look!"

Alter didn't retreat from the box he was standing on. He stayed there, and even though he recognized Shloyme's voice, he pretended not to hear, then he answered deliberately, harried, dazed by the noise: "What's the big deal? Huh? An archbishop? Ain't you never seen no archbishop before?"

A minute later, however, Alter himself was so dumbfounded that he gave Shloyme a tiny space on the box. "Stand there, slowly, don't tread on my foot. Wow! Wow! The rabbi's coming!"

Dvoyre came running over. "Papa, let me stand on your box!"

He let her climb up, and she watched.

The rabbi with the beautiful beard was walking under a canopy, escorted by two fine congregants. He was carrying a Torah scroll. Four young men in silk caftans bore the four poles of the canopy over the Torah.

The archbishop stood facing them—an old, gray priest sporting a high, square hat and escorted by priests who were holding crosses and wearing lace robes with expensive silver embroidery. Two priests in strange high, angular hats and white stoles were carrying the statue of Jesus.

As the rabbi approached the archbishop, both groups halted.

The Torah versus Jesus.

The marketplace grew so still you could have heard a fly soaring past. There were as many people as grains of sand on the earth, and they all suddenly hushed up.

Shh.

The archbishop bowed his head to the Torah.

"OH, JEWS! I can't stand it! The Messiah is coming!"

"Did you get a load of that? He bowed his head!"

"Of course, how could he not? The Torah is older, we're older."

Dvoyre stood there as if in a dream.

If they walk across an iron bridge, they'll fall in, and if we walk across a cobweb, we won't fall in.

She peered at the old, bent rabbi holding the Torah. Its old velvet mantle was embroidered with gold, and both the velvet and the gold had faded long since. But noble and respectable like an old, rich woman, with a silk cloth, her genteel and aristocratic nature lying in the creases in her face, lying in the dust of the velvet folds.

"Dvoyre, why don't you want Mayer Zisi, why don't you?"

THE GLAD TIDINGS spread throughout the town: He had bowed his head, he had bowed his head.

And, as she hurried home, those words hurried after her: "Of course, how could he not? The Torah is older, we're older."

HERSH DOVID NOMBERG *(1876–1927)*

A prolific and best-selling storyteller, Nomberg, who was born near Warsaw, also wrote poems and articles. His fiction, thoroughly modern in tone, deals chiefly with the outsiders of the Jewish world—artists, dreamers, intellectuals, many of whom are so assimilated as to shed every last Jewish feature of their background. He devoted the last few decades of his life to his journalism.

In the Mountains *(1922)*

WHENEVER A CONVERSATION turns to youth and health, I picture Sonya, with her full, fleshy body. She was a young painter I met in Munich several years ago. Looking at her, no one would have dreamed that she was a member of the artistic tribe. A full, curving, rosy face, a solid, powerful body, very lively, vibrant eyes—in short, a strong, muscular woman with scarcely any girlish weakness. Where in the world did she get all the softness and dreaminess that she expressed with her paintbrush? This was an enigma for many people. Her entire being was ruled by a single tone that darkened all others: her health, her exuberant youth, her highly developed body overflowing with energy.

It was only as I got to know her that I saw specific lines in her face, lines that marked her individuality: raw, wild features—especially when she spoke. At such times, a bestial savagery might flash across her face. And in the angular corners of her splendid forehead I found a deep, native intelligence.

This creature was no older than twenty, yet she was exceptionally talented. Her professors praised her. With a loving freshness she painted nature: cows, herds of sheep, the tranquil sea and the southern sky (her father was a Jewish landowner in southern Russia).

She was free in her ways, candid, sometimes brutally so, and she loved all kinds of sports, movement, light, and joy. Within two weeks of meeting her, I was head over heels in love, and she cared for me too—at least more than for any of her other acquaintances. Neither of us took our relationship too seriously. We made few demands on each other, and we lived happily. She didn't like tenderness or affection, she refused to be passive, even in love. She apparently knew nothing about quiet yearnings, tremulous feelings—passion would pounce on her like a whirlwind. Now and then, as we were strolling along, she might take hold of my hand, squeeze it, and snuggle against me like a child. Or else I might be sitting in her home late at night, and she would grow agitated, and that savagery would flash across her face. She would then jump up and ask me to leave.

"Well, get going. And don't come tomorrow," she snapped.

Before I left she would kiss me instead of responding to my protest, and push me toward the door: "Well, I'll drop by your place if I feel like it. Now get going—fast!"

Around that period I also saw a great deal of a friend of mine, a Jewish student from Russia, who was semiassimilated in Germany. His name was Schwarzwald [black forest]. He was smart, very smart, but he had a weak, poetic character. And he was poor, lonely, uprooted. A broken man. I tried to paint him, I worked hard on his portrait, but I failed to catch the "keynote" in his features, the quintessence that intrigued me. His face was gaunt and sickly, with hollow cheeks, bulging lips, and a long aquiline nose that wasn't ugly or typical per se, yet seemed to poke out extraneously from all that scrawniness. And yet there was something very likable about his face, something appealing—and that I ultimately failed to capture or depict. The lines in his jowls and in the creases by his mouth gave him a submissive, a helpless, hopeless look. . . . No, that wasn't quite it. That expression actually lay in his deep, gray, mournful eyes. The lines in his face contained something else—a holiness? No, it wasn't that either. It was more like a stillness, a calmness—the calmness of a dead face. All he had to do was close his eyes and slightly lower his head—and any trace of life, of motion would vanish, and you would assume that he was dead. He generally appeared to be kneaded out of sorrow. Yet even these sufferings were no longer alive, they lay dead and frozen in his face. Nonetheless, no shadow of bitterness, no sign of rancor or sarcasm could be found in his features!

I told Sonya about him, and she came to observe him, as if he were an

Indian from America. She arrived while I was painting him, and she instantly began to scrutinize him from up close, full-front, and in profile—without standing on ceremony and certainly without saying a word to him. I was totally embarrassed. I didn't know Schwarzwald very well, but I knew his innate pride, which he managed to nurture despite his kind heart. Sonya, however, soon realized what she was doing and she started apologizing to him: "Please forgive me, Herr Schwarzwald, for taking the liberty of examining you like this. It's in our nature. Nothing exists for us except line and color. Isn't that true?"

I noticed that she had made an impression on my friend. It didn't even occur to him to feel offended, and he answered amiably: "It's true. Of course."

"And you know, I'm always arguing with him." She pointed at me. "He says that seeing line and color isn't enough, you have to feel the soul of a thing. Is that so? I've never seen any soul, I don't know what that is. How am I supposed to feel it? What do you think, Herr Schwarzwald? He's told me that you're smart and that you have clear thoughts about art."

"Ah!" Schwarzwald exclaimed. "I'm no artist, I'm a student of philosophy. When it comes to art, I can only philosophize. And for an artist, philosophizing is superfluous."

"I like that, and that's exactly what I say! I don't want to know anything, I want to see and paint. See and paint, that's all."

I disagreed. "An artist has to have a heart, feelings. You have to relate to the thing you're painting. You have to have a spiritual outlook. . . ."

And so we launched into our usual argument.

Schwarzwald held his tongue. Rather than listening, he looked at the young painter who was so deeply in love with lines and colors. In the end, he sided with her.

"You're doubly wrong," he turned to me. "First of all for even arguing. Leave that to us philosophers. You artists should stick to painting. Secondly, seeing a thing, seeing it artistically, means seeing it with your heart, with feelings, with a spiritual outlook, with anything you wish. You're arguing about words."

The three of us now began viewing my work. Neither of us liked it. I least of all. The next day I started from scratch—and again I failed to complete the portrait. I tried him in yet a different pose, but nothing came of my efforts.

. . .   .

SONYA WOULD OFTEN drop by while I was working. Schwarzwald would often join me in visiting her and he would spend the evening with us. And tedious evenings they were. They dragged along, slow and sad, leaving me unsatisfied, with some sort of profound and unknown anxiety. Schwarzwald would sit there in silence. We were ashamed to talk— what should we talk about? Philosophy? Our ideas didn't interest him, he had already heard them a thousand times. Chitchat? That was impossible: his presence cast a pall on us. His entire being emanated a hopelessness, a dreadful melancholy from worlds that had been destroyed long ago. When he was here, it seemed as if we could talk about only one thing: death.

And during those tedious evenings, I peered at his face, studying every last line, every last crease, every quiver, every mien, every glance. And very soon, a terrible secret was exposed: the poor man absolutely worshiped Sonya, he devoured her with his eyes, he was in love with her, madly in love, with the full force of his hopelessness! Whenever she spoke or drew closer to him, a bizarre change came over his face. It was as if the frozen sufferings in his face had melted and come alive. They were telling horrible, heartrending stories, and they were pleading, pleading . . . Oh, how repulsive his face became at such moments! How helpless, how weak and sickly, how pitiful and foolish. Often I couldn't stand it, and I covered my eyes with my hands. As for Sonya—she was bored. By the end of such an evening she felt sad, tired, apathetic, yet she didn't try to find a way of breaking off with him. Quite the contrary: she kept inviting him over, and was annoyed if he didn't show up for a day or two.

"Tell me," she said after he left, "what does a person like that live for?"

I held my tongue, but she kept nagging me as if it were *my* fault and *my* life.

"He believes in nothing, loves nothing, hopes for nothing. Nothing, absolutely nothing, matters to him! Nothing interests him, no books, no people, no art—nothing. Just how does he live? Tell me, please."

"He lives because he lives. What do I live for? What do you live for?"

"I? I love art!"

She uttered those words with such pride and self-assurance that she could have won over the greatest skeptic. The artist in her was speaking and making her eyes sparkle.

"And maybe he does love someone. You never know," I tersely remarked.

She caught my hint, and instead of an answer, a contented smile played on her lips. That was her way of terminating a conversation, and her special smile spread over her entire face, revealing the deep and boundless happiness of a woman in love with herself.

And thus time wore by, evening after evening.

She was bored by him and yet she fawned on him. She kept complaining to me about that depressing "Black Shadow" (her nickname for him) and yet she kept inviting him back and never stopped teasing him. She would play with his hand, ask him to touch her arm muscles and see how strong she was. And she would stand stiffly against him in her youthful freshness and thrust out her breasts. The poor man obeyed her like a child.

I was still working on his portrait even though I felt it would come to nothing. I was fed up with the project—but then Sonya dropped by in a white fur hat above her rosy face. Clutching and clanging her ice skates, she brought in the freshness and beauty of a frosty but sunny winter's day, which she so closely resembled. Schwarzwald stood up, went over, and greeted her, boldly and cheerfully, which was contrary to his nature. This was one of the sickly but vibrant moments that he had from time to time, like the sudden flaring of a candle. He grew agile, merry—a new man.

"How's the portrait going?" Sonya asked.

"It's not getting anywhere," I replied.

"Let me take a stab at it. Sit down, Schwarzwald."

She pulled off her coat, grabbed a pencil, and drew a few lines. But she soon got fed up and put down the drawing.

"It's not for me," she said.

"No, sketch me, please," Schwarzwald pleaded. "You have to sketch me. I'm sure you'll succeed, you and no one else."

"How do you know?" she asked bluntly.

"I know, I'm sure. I feel it, I really do. Sketch me."

Pleading, coaxing—that wasn't like Schwarzwald. And it was strange, it was uncomfortable hearing him use that tone of voice.

"Leave me alone," said Sonya, "I can't sketch such faces."

"Why not?"

"Because they're not beautiful."

Schwarzwald was caught off-guard by her curt retort, which could hardly have been news for him. How often had I heard him talking scornfully about his own clumsy appearance! Now he turned pale, his mood changed abruptly, he brooded quietly. And the frozen sufferings lay dead in his face.

We all felt bad; and when Schwarzwald said goodbye, Sonya asked him to drop in on her tomorrow, be sure to drop in, and she looked at him with flirtatious eyes, as if everything were in apple-pie order.

A god left Mount Olympus and came to wake me up:
Get up, you shameful sleeper, you who are drunk on life—wake up!
Where is your youth?—Forgotten.
Where is your happiness?—Gone.
Where is your hope?—Dead.
Get up, get up! You've dreamed a dreadful dream.
I've come from a distant land, you mournful man! From a land where the wellspring of life splashed and gurgled in generations past. I'm from the land of everlasting beauty—to wake you up: get up!

A new day is born in the east, a new radiance is spread out on valleys and mountains, meadows and forests, and with golden edges the clouds drift across the sky, to announce glad tidings to the world and to you. The dreadful dream has disappeared—wake up!

The morning air is redolent with fresh scents, soft winds stir, waking every leaf, every blade of grass: Wake up! Get up! Pure voices of clear bells tremble in the air, and the new radiance grows brighter and brighter, and the sun tears up its purple veil and emerges fresh and young and newly born. Wake up, you sleeper, wake up your good and evil feelings, wake up your hopes—the time has come. Get up!
What is waking up in me?—Your sleepy youth.
Why is my blood rushing in me?—It yearns for love and happiness.
What dazzles my eyes?—Your awakened hope.
Get up!

The black veil is torn from your eyes, and driven away is the city of death, I pour life and pleasure into your limbs, I—the god of love!
Get up!

That poem, written in German hexameters, was titled "Resurrection." Schwarzwald brought it over and handed it to me with a bashful look.

"Here, read it," he said, "if it doesn't bore you."

I read it through and then eyed him uncertainly.

"Well, why are you looking at me like that? Do you like the poem?"

"Yeah, sure. It's classical, which suits a philosopher. But if you don't mind my asking—are you, so to speak, in love? You are, aren't you?"

Slightly embarrassed, he said with a smile: "What if I am? Does it matter?"

"Not in the least."

He paced back and forth through the room. It was obvious that he wanted to talk to me about something. He was in one of his cheery moods, his eyes sparkled. And suddenly he turned to me.

"You do know who it is?"

"Of course. In any case, she's worth it."

"Are you a sincere person? You don't lie?"

"Don't worry."

"If that's so, then I want you to tell me the truth. Are you jealous? I want to know."

"Nonsense, Schwarzwald! I wouldn't dream of it! I can assure you, I'm not jealous. My relationship with Sonya is very casual. For one thing, we're both as free as a bird. And besides—how can I put it . . ."

I very nearly said that I could rely entirely on Sonya's healthy instinct. But I caught myself and didn't complete my sentence. He didn't notice. He wanted to pour his heart out to me:

"You're a decent person. I really like you. And you know, I'm in love, head over heels in love. I've never felt like this before. I can't think about anything but her, I can't talk about anything but her. I can't live without thinking about her. Otherwise my blood won't beat in my veins. . . . You'll probably say I'm stupid or crazy. But you don't understand, you can't understand. You don't know what this apathy is like, this dead existence, without interests, without joys, without delights, without hope, without happiness. . . . Am I fooling myself? Good! All I want to do is fool myself. I want to have my illusions. I can't stand my apathy anymore, it won't bring me a long life. . . ."

He soon left me to go home. His face was agitated, a sickly fire glimmered in his eyes, and he seemed like a man who was losing his mind.

"Hey, you oughta be congratulated on your new victory," I told Sonya that very same day. "Schwarzwald is dying of love. Read this."

I handed her the poem that Schwarzwald had given me. She read it and then said she didn't like it.

"Well, so you've conquered another heart. Be proud," I rebuked her.

"Could you possibly be jealous? I believe I'm still free."

"Bite your tongue. Me, jealous? Of whom?"

She burst out laughing, then asked: "Is he truly in love with me? You really think so?"

"He's dying of love for you."

She didn't respond, but a smile played on her lips—her smile.

IN THE MIDST of the loveliest winter, Sonya had the bright idea of going for a hike in the mountains, and she took me and Schwarzwald along. We dressed like tourists, in warm, light clothes. Sonya wore white: a knitted jacket, which made her fresh body even more attractive, and a white fur hat perched coquettishly on her head. Schwarzwald and I put on short, warm jackets and thick, hobnailed boots, knee-length stockings, and Tyrolian caps with a feather on the side. Frankly, his playful clothing didn't quite harmonize with Schwarzwald's figure, but he enjoyed it like a child. As I've already mentioned, a change had recently come over him, and at times he grew cheerful and excited. At other times, however, he lapsed into such a deep depression that he seemed like a mournful lunatic.

We left Munich after midnight and reached Kufstein by dawn. Kufstein, a small town in the northern Tyrol, right by the Bavarian border, is encircled by mountains. The Bavarian highlands stretch out on one side, while, on the other, lies the huge range called the "Emperor Mountains," which stand as sentinels in front of the gigantic Alps. We relaxed at a restaurant for an hour or two, until daylight. Then we hoisted up our backpacks, took our long sticks, and went outdoors.

The town was shrouded in a deep fog, and we couldn't even see the houses on the other side of the marketplace. This was no ordinary fog, it was a dense, ominous cloud that had come down into the valley and was lurking and pressing on everything and on us as well. People were walking through the cloud like shadows and seemed to be making strange motions. At times, they got lost and turned up again, swimming in from the gray ocean. We could detect no trace of the newly risen sun. And despite the fog, the air was frosty and the ground slippery, and we hadn't gotten enough sleep. So we huddled together like a frightened herd, grabbing one another's shoulders to keep from slipping. We walked quietly, wordlessly, and deep down we regretted that we'd gone along with Sonya's crazy idea of heading to the mountains in midwinter. And even Sonya, always cheerful, always energetic, walked mutely, like a sinner—and indeed she must have felt sinful, especially in regard to me. If only we could have been alone; but she had insisted that Schwarzwald join us.

Despite the fog we managed to reach the mountain and start hiking up; we trudged slowly for quite a while, sleepy and lost in thought. By the time we reached an altitude of some six or seven thousand feet, we noticed that the fog had dissipated. The air was clear, transparent, though we could see nothing around us. We were encompassed by trees. The road cut deep through the frozen snow flanking it, and we could see only a few yards ahead of us because the road curved and twisted, constantly zigzagging like most mountain trails.

"Well, how do you feel, dear madam?" I asked Sonya with no small amount of bitterness.

"Just fine and dandy, dear sir," she replied coldly. "Schwarzwald? Where are you?" she turned to my friend, who kept lagging behind us.

"Coming!" he shouted from the distance and began running to catch up with us.

There's nothing more annoying in a mountain hike than having to keep changing speed. It tires you out very quickly. I warned him, but he answered as if he were a veteran hiker: "Don't worry! I won't get tired."

And at that moment he looked younger and fresher, his voice sounded powerful and self-confident. "The god of Mount Olympus woke him, got him up . . ." I mused.

As we advanced, we started noticing splotches of light in the shadows of the trees that were traced out in the snow. We looked up, and through the interwoven branches we caught patches of blue sky. All three of us suddenly grew cheerful. For a while now our bodies had not felt the cold, our movements kept us warm, and we began striding more boldly. Our path kept snaking in and out—and it was covered by the same trodden snow as below and flanked by the same frozen snow, on and on. At times the splotches of light and the patches of blue sky vanished altogether. We had already been hiking for an hour. The climb to the very top of the mountain normally took four or five hours—unless you stopped to rest at an inn. And if you did, it would take much longer—a boring prospect.

But now our path wound out of the forest, and we were suddenly inundated by a warm, bright radiance: a lustrous crystal whiteness struck our eyes from all sides. We had unexpectedly been transported to a new, white, luminous world. We looked up: the sky was clear and cloudless, gleaming and dazzling like polished glass, and we were in a universe of snow. The snow glittered everywhere—around us, below, above, from abysses, from the deep plains, from the towering peaks that circled us completely. Our eyes were bathed in the illumination as if in a wellspring of pleasure, so intense that it brought pain and tears. We stood there in sheer surprise and delight.

Our path now led to the very edge of the mountain, and all our surroundings were revealed for miles and miles. At the foot of the mountain, the Inn River, a gray narrow strip against the white, snowy background, wound through the valley, its other side hemmed in by enormous mountains. In a corner of the valley, we spotted the cottages in Kufstein, heaped together and as tiny as houses of cards. A thin mist hovered above them, grazing the opposite mountain. This was the fog that had lurked over the town at our departure.

And around us loomed the mountains, various heights, various shapes, squeezed together or clambering atop one another. Some were terrifying with their rugged lines, some were soft and delicate like a woman's beautiful breasts. And everything was covered with snow and flooded with light, glittering and glistening. Off to the side we glimpsed a small cluster of mountains with three high, wild tips pointing at the sky. Having shaken off their snow, they bared their gray, naked, craggy bodies, and they recalled sleeping giants, evil monsters who would kill us all if they weren't fettered to their places by a mightier power. . . . We recognized the Wild Emperor—a name that conjured up a horde of dreadful popular legends.

"Oh, how beautiful!" we exclaimed, almost in unison.

Schwarzwald nearly wept in ecstasy. His eyes moistened, his gaunt, sickly features shone with pleasure, like the face of a saint.

"Yes, my friends!" he blurted out. "It's worth living and suffering for a hundred years just to look at this for a brief moment. Look at the chasm:

imagine jumping off and dying down there and being buried in white snow like everything else around us!"

We looked where he was pointing and we saw a profound chasm, from which we were separated by the flank of frozen snow. In the depths something was rushing and surging—a mountain stream that we couldn't see. All we spotted was a wispy haze oozing slowly from the fissures and caverns.

The sun was overhead by now. It was twelve noon. The path barely rose here, it ran straight, leading to a second rise. We walked calmly, plunging our long sticks into the snow and hardly exchanging a word.

Sonya likewise remained silent. But her eyes betrayed the impact made on her by the vista. The cheerful energy had left her face, and, perhaps for the first time ever, I noticed a deep, secret yearning in her eyes, a tender melancholy. Suddenly she turned to Schwarzwald and offered him her arm. They walked along together, I behind them. Half an hour later we arrived at an inn halfway up the mountain. After laying out our frozen stockings to dry, we relaxed, drank several glasses of mulled wine, and chatted with the customers, who kept coming in from the top or the valley. The beautiful, heroic Tyroleans greeted us like good friends and they spoke to us in their dialect, which we barely understood. Each man plainly felt it was his duty to gaze at Sonya for a while and tell her how beautiful she was.

"A strong girl," one of them whispered to me, winking his eye and nodding with his patriarchal blond beard.

Sonya took this very good-naturedly and smiled, merely smiled.

"WELL, FORWARD MARCH!" Sonya exclaimed, standing up. We likewise got to our feet and prepared to continue our hike.

A bright, cheerful sun shone overhead again, we were intoxicated by the shiny whiteness, we felt no fatigue even after hours of marching. Our legs moved virtually on their own; we inhaled the fresh, light, pure, crystalline mountain air and every breath we took brought us an unknown pleasure. Once more we spotted the three peaks of the Wild Emperor, the chasms, valleys, and plains—all covered with the virginal snow. The Wild Emperor's craggy ridge was smoking, and a tiny little cloudlet was drifting very slowly, a helpless creature clambering awkwardly to a hidden nest in some crevice. The higher we climbed, the more peaks heaved into view, new areas, new valleys and plains, and far, far away, the Alps shimmered in the lucid air, leaning against the heavens. At times their silhouettes stood out sharply, at times they looked like a throng of sunlit clouds slowly inching along. The Valley of the Inn, the river itself, the town, and its surroundings—they all disappeared. We felt torn away from the gray, workaday world that we had abandoned—three people alone amid cliffs and clouds and mountains and snow. Our unusual liveliness tried to find an outlet, and so we began to sing, to run, to yell. And the echoes answered us from all sides.

Of the three of us, Schwarzwald was the most intoxicated. His euphoria took the wildest forms. He shouted with a voice coming from deep inside him, provoking echoes, he sang and ran incessantly. His face was flushed, his eyes sparkled like those of a lunatic. He acted freely with Sonya, like a brother, clutched her hand, straightened her hat, and never left her side for even a moment. Sonya carried on with him, and only rarely did she glance at me, as if to say, "Just look at what love is really all about! This is how I want to be loved . . . like this . . ."

As we advanced, other hikers passed us on the way down or caught up with us from below. But since the road kept veering off, we were soon alone once more. All at once, we heard bizarre shouts that seemed to be coming from off to the side. "Sliding through! Watch out below!" The echoes responded from all around us, and before we even knew what was happening, something came hurtling down the crooked path, a small sled mounted by a red-faced man who was all sweaty from the breakneck speed . . . He barely had time to swerve by means of the cord he was gripping. The sled crashed into the wall of snow, the man tumbled off and flipped over several times. Then he stood up as if nothing had happened and he spoke to us, half reproachful, half smiling: "Ya gotta get out of the way. I did shout! Didn't you hear me?"

We apologized and asked if he had hurt himself. He explained that there was absolutely nothing dangerous about taking a spill. At worst, you keep rolling till you hit the bend in the road and then you stand up unscathed. This is a special kind of Alpine sport, it's called *rodeln*, tobogganing. We'd heard about it, but this was the first time we'd witnessed it, and we'd been alarmed at seeing the sled come blasting along. The tobogganist sat down on his sled, which coasted off and soon vanished. But soon more sleds came dashing toward us, and we got out of their way. They flashed by, leaving us dizzy. Some were ridden by couples. A healthy, rosy girl in a Tyrolean costume had her arms wrapped around a man, who sat in front of her, steering the toboggan. The girl leaned back to keep her balance, occasionally digging her feet into the snow in order to slow down. We didn't have enough time to enjoy this cheerful, happy vision, which promptly disappeared, and from higher up we again heard shouts: "Coming through! Watch out below!"

"Why don't we toboggan back down!" Sonya suddenly turned to me.

"You're not afraid?" I asked her.

"Are you joking?"

"What if you take a spill?"

"I'll get up again."

I praised her for her courage, and she enjoyed the compliment. With a loving glance, she squeezed my hand and said: "I have to return to my escort. I'm sure the Black Shadow misses me. He's so interesting today. Are you jealous?"

"Nope."

"Should we all ride one toboggan—the three of us?"

"If you like."

"Great." She squeezed my hand again and went back to Schwarzwald.

Now we were overtaken by another hiker, a tall, brawny Tyrolean with a blond beard on his patriarchal face—the same man who had whispered to me, "A strong girl." He slackened his pace upon reaching us, and, as we finished our climb to the top, we talked about the mountains, about avalanches, about mountain life. He was proud of his countryside and its natural beauty. He told us that a club he belonged to was having a private party at the next inn, and there'd be no room to spend the night, we'd have to toboggan down to the lower inn. He assured us that there was absolutely nothing dangerous about it. We couldn't possibly get lost. We'd be constantly flanked by the two walls. There was only one place where the snow was low and the road ran along the brink of a ravine, so that an inexperienced tobogganist would have to be careful. He advised us to walk rather than coast that stretch because an accident had occurred there several years ago.

We reached the mentioned place very quickly. The Tyrolean scraped the snow away from the wall, and we saw a stone bearing the carved name of the unfortunate man who had fallen over the cliff here and the date on which it had happened.

We peered down; the plunge was so deep that we felt dizzy. We were overcome with an instinctive fear; even the distant glare of the white snow barely reached us. Closer to us there were crags sticking out everywhere. This area was marked on our maps as the Devil's Cavern, a dreadful white abyss that was almost inaccessible. Some trail led to it from the other side of the mountain, the Tyrolean informed us, but that trail was now lost in the snow. You could reach it in the summertime, but the cavern was murky even in broad daylight.

"How deep is it here?" one of us asked. Instead of answering, the Tyrolean grabbed a handful of snow, made a snowball, and hurled it into the depths. He listened hard, and several seconds passed before we heard the bang.

"Nearly seven hundred feet," he said.

We started feeling a bit cold. An icy, cutting wind began to blow, the sky was dull, the air dark. Even in its brightest glow the sun had virtually begun trembling with terror. From far away we heard strange noises, as if trees were being chopped down in the forest. At times we thought a storm was brewing, with thunder rolling over the mountain. Soon the sky was entirely overcast, and the wind blasted pieces of frozen snow into our faces. An avalanche was cascading down the Wild Emperor, and the wind was bringing us a flood of snow that glutted the sky.

"It won't take long," the Tyrolean comforted us. "No avalanche'll hit here." But he did teach us how to escape if we encountered one. "This is what you do." He raised his hands and stretched his legs as high as he could. "You swim like this," he demonstrated, "you swim out of the snow."

After giving us this advice, he moved on. We soon lost sight of him. We were nervous, afraid of being buried alive by an avalanche. How horrible it must be to slowly suffocate under the white mass! A long, ghastly death. There are lost tourists who die in agony like that, over a whole twenty-four hours. And why had the Tyrolean left us? we wondered. He must have wanted to save himself, knowing we couldn't keep up with him! "Swim like this," we mentally repeated. And the snow, which had only just enchanted us with its clarity, delighting our eyes and cheering our souls, overwhelming us—that same snow now looked like a gray, chaotic, appalling mass, created only to destroy.

But our fear was short-lived. The avalanche was gone. Less than ten minutes had worn by, and we again had a pure sky overhead, shining like polished glass, and warm rays were pouring from the sun. The snow glittered and dazzled, and we felt twice as cheerful as before. We were euphoric. We sat down on the snowy road and bawled out some song in our loud voices. Isolated from the lower world, we had shaken off its chains. Schwarzwald started using the familiar form with us, and we both took liberties with Sonya. We kissed her, groped her from both sides, like satyrs assaulting a captured nymph in a Rubens painting. She tore herself out of our hands, dragging us along, and suddenly she threw herself into the snow, laughing so raucously that the air boomed around us.

The craggy ridge of the Wild Emperor was still smoking, the cloud grew bigger and bigger, lower and lower, till it lay on the mountaintops that loomed underneath us when we reached our destination—an inn over eight thousand feet high. By now, the thick cloud was at our feet, blanketing all the peaks, the plains, the chasms. But the mountains above us glimmered in their white cloaks, illuminated by the loving sheen of the evening sun.

WE HAD ALREADY rested and eaten, and a sweet weariness flowed through our limbs—like everything else around us, this fatigue was different. Instead of making us sleepy, it kept us awake, made us hear and see and move. However, a great change came over Schwarzwald. He lapsed into his deep depression, sat at the table not saying a word, his head propped on his arm, his eyes gaping gloomily. We left him there and went outdoors to watch the sun go down.

The cloud hovering below us began to redden. Purple stripes emerged wherever the sun could shine through. Soon the purple turned a fiery crimson, and the dense mass seemed to be blazing away. Closer to us the cloud was dark and coated in pale violet. The temperature plummeted. The changes all came unusually fast. On top of the cloud there was a kaleidoscope of colors, altering from minute to minute, darkening and brightening. There were pale shadows of pink, red, purple, and violet, flitting back and forth, darting about, displacing one another. The sun drew closer, dipping into the cloud as if trying to bathe in the sea of colors. The surrounding mountains stood out, earnest, silent witnesses to a sacred ritual. Their tips were still brightly lit and they appeared to be admiring the cloud that was raised in their crevices, coming out into the world, spreading, and then settling down, and was now about to swallow the sun.

Soon the final sunbeams vanished, but the mountain peaks were still sparkling and glistening. The cloud suddenly darkened, and in the very place where the sun had gone down a fire was still burning as if on fiery coals.

The two of us were standing together in silence, Sonya and I, her head resting on my shoulder. The twilight was gloomy and frosty, the colors were snuffed out, and the cloud was turning grayish black. Only the very tops of the mountains were covered with rosy shadows. Right in back of us was the round peak of our mountain. When we turned around, we couldn't believe our eyes. The peak was draped in a mantel of color that we couldn't capture in mere words. It was a kind of pink blending with violet, soft and frail, like the hues that we see only in dreams. And further and further, as far as the eye could reach, the Alpine peaks glowed in the dusk. They were like a choir crooning a soft melody that trembled in the somber air and melted into it.

Sonya nestled against me; I felt her breasts squeezing into my body; she slung her arm around my neck and kissed me. Hikers were standing next to us: it never occurred to them to smirk, nor were we at all embarrassed. Our posture was as simple and lucid as the whole beautiful world around us. All at once we spotted Schwarzwald. He stood there gawking at us, and his aquiline nose stuck way out. He was shivering in the cold . . . Oh, how awful his face was! People only look like that the last time you see them, before death blesses them with its tranquility. I left Sonya and walked over to him.

"Are you cold?" I asked.

He remained silent.

"We'll get warm down below. There's no place to sleep here."

"Yeah," he muttered vaguely.

We took two sleds, one for him and one for Sonya and me. She was cheerful, she kept slapping me on the back, laughing and playing. She joked around with Schwarzwald and kept calling him "Black Shadow."

"Black Shadow, aren't you scared?"

"I don't know."

"You've become a boring fool."

He didn't reply, but she wouldn't let up. She was too elated, her mind was swirling with impressions, and now she was about to go on a toboggan ride in the middle of the night, to shoot down the mountain with me like the Tyrolean girls with their boyfriends. She wanted to talk to Schwarzwald, tease him.

"Are you cold, Schwarzwald?" she asked.

"A little."

"And what are you gonna do if you spill?"

He kept silent again.

She was already sitting behind me on the sled. I turned and put my hand on her mouth. "Shush! Enough!" I whispered to her. She burst into raucous laughter.

"Let's go," I ordered. "Schwarzwald, don't stick too close to us. If we tumble off, stop, otherwise you'll crash into us. Well, one, two, three—go!"

Sonya hugged me tight from behind, and our toboggan slowly began to slide.

"Be careful!" I shouted at Schwarzwald. "When the road bears right, brake with your left foot, and when it bears left, brake with your right foot."

"And if you spill, don't forget to pick yourself up!" Sonya yelled.

The night was already pitch-black. The sky was dark and studded with shiny stars. The mountains were swathed in gray mantles and they seemed to be dozing inside them. But the stars twinkled, merry and cheerful, and they were virtually following us on our ride. At first we moved slowly and gingerly, constantly braking with our feet. Little by little, we got used to it. For a minute we let the sled go, and it gained momentum. We suddenly felt warm. And all at once, at the first curve in the road—bang! Our sled crashed into the wall of snow, knocked us off, and went dashing along on its own—and it didn't stop until it hit the next bend. We rolled over a few times in the snow, I on Sonya, she on me. And before we even had time to laugh and convince ourselves that we were unhurt—bang again! Schwarzwald crashed into us, flipped over, and the three of us went rolling over one another in the snow. Sonya was the first to get up, and she burst into raucous, healthy laughter.

Soon we were back on our sleds—and we had another spill. But we very quickly learned how to brake properly, and our trip proceeded, cheerful and happy. Every so often we had to wait for Schwarzwald, who kept lagging behind.

"Hey, hey!" we shouted at him from far away. "Where are you?"

"Here!" his distant voice replied, but we still couldn't see him.

Sonya and I changed places. She wanted to steer, and so I threw my arms around her waist and she let the sled whiz downward with a tremendous momentum. The road kept twisting and we heedlessly soared along one curve after another. We hadn't heard Schwarzwald in back of us for some time. Suddenly I remembered the Devil's Cavern, and so, using my leg, I brought the sled to a stop.

"We have to take this stretch on foot," I said.

But then it turned out that we had already raced past the Devil's Cavern. We hadn't realized how fast we'd been speeding. Forty minutes later we reached the lower inn safe and sound. We got off and waited for Schwarzwald.

"Hey, hey! Hey, hey!" we yelled. "Schwarzwald! Schwarzwald!"

No response came. Only echoes from all sides, and the stars twinkled overhead.

"Schwarzwald! Where are you?!" I started yelling louder, and my voice trembled. I sensed that something awful had happened. A fear was gnawing at me.

We doubled back to look for him.

It took a long time, and we felt more afraid at each step. We were afraid to talk, to draw closer together. We had long since stopped shouting, "Schwarzwald!" His name had acquired a terrible ring, leaving our nerves raw. We walked along separately, each with his dread, searching silently. In the end we found his sled in the middle of the road. Schwarzwald was nowhere to be seen.

Again we started calling, shouting, searching—but it was no use!

"What can have happened?" Sonya asked, and her trembling voice sounded harsh and agitated . . .

"I'm scared he fell off," I said.

"Fell off?" She grabbed her head and began yelling wildly: "Help! Help! Help!"

I began yelling too, and our surroundings reverberated with our voices. Even the mountains seemed to be trembling with us.

I tried striking one match after another, but the wind kept blowing out the flames, and my hands kept shaking. It was such a crazy idea—strike a match to light up a six hundred-foot chasm. I leaned over and very nearly fell in myself, and Sonya kept yelling and yelling.

People came from higher up. They had heard our shouts and had sled-
ded down with a lantern. Soon it was obvious what had happened. One
part of the wall of snow was pushed out. That was where he had fallen
off. It was impossible to rescue him. There was no way of peering down
at night — nor would it have helped. After falling from that great a height
he would have been dead on impact.

AND SO OUR friend died in the mountains!

We arrived down below, at the inn, frozen, dead tired, and shattered.
We had been unable to leave the place where the accident had occurred.
It was as if the still warm corpse of that poor man were lying near us, and
all we had to do was hold out our hands and touch him. And why not?
Who could tell? Perhaps he was still alive and calling for help? We kept
walking there, back and forth. We very nearly froze to death ourselves.
Eventually our survival instinct made us go down to the inn, where we
rented a room for the night. Sonya kept her clothes on. She merely sat
on the bed, with her head on my shoulder. I thought she had fallen asleep
like that. But then all at once she began sobbing and weeping, loud and
hard, and tears as big as raindrops rolled down from her eyes. She cried
for a long time, and her crying was as fresh and healthy as her laughter,
her talking, her entire being. That's how happy people cry when they try
to wash some kind of unhappiness from their souls. She fell asleep with
her head on my shoulder. I laid her out on the bed and then went outdoors.

The night was frosty. It was filled with an endless hush. The white
world was sleeping and it contained a young life that had just been blotted out.

A wild longing drew me there, to the edge of the cliff, where the depths
seemed to promise peace and happiness. I felt that if I went there I would
never come back, and so I halted, lost in thought. From the sky above the
stars beckoned and they told me that throughout their eternities it was all
the same to them — joy and sorrow, happiness and misery, life and death.

And all the way back to Munich we kept talking about him. It was so
strange that only two of us were sitting there instead of the three that had
come. We talked, and I finally told Sonya what I felt: He hadn't fallen
off, as the newspapers claimed. He had jumped.

"And do you think he really loved me?" she asked. And her face lit up with that contented, that happy smile of hers.

Oh, that smile!

YUDL ROSENBERG (1860–1935)

Rosenberg was born in Poland and trained as a rabbi. In 1912, he immigrated to Canada after starting to publish a number of works, including a series of Yiddish folk books.

The Golem, the legendary manmade creature of Jewish folklore, was supposedly created by Rabbi Levi in medieval Prague to fight the enemies of the Jews. However, like Dr. Frankenstein's monster (who was probably suggested by the Golem fantasy), the creature proved more powerful than his creator, at times turning against the rabbi and the Jews. Some of the Golem's excesses were amusing in that he overdid the tasks that the rabbi ordered him to perform, once nearly causing a flash flood in the rabbi's home. At other times, though unable to reason clearly, he helped Rabbi Levi and the Jews by foiling and even overpowering their enemies.

In Russia, starting in the 1890s and continuing for decades, there was increased persecution of Jews: pogroms, local violence, the tsar's refusal to grant Jews full civil rights, and so forth. One excuse for the persecution was the blood libel—the falsehood that Jews killed Christian children in order to have blood for baking matzos at Passover. A popular Yiddish-Hebrew pamphlet by Yudl Rosenberg containing a hagiographic biography of Rabbi Levi and a number of Golem tales was first published in 1904 in response to Russian antisemitism—specifically the blood libel. Rosenberg then put out an expanded edition in 1907. Detailing the Golem's humorous, serious, helpful, and at times destructive feats, and the ultimate Jewish victory, the pamphlet ends on an optimistic note (see the complete translation in my collection Great Tales of Jewish Fantasy and the Occult).*

---

*(New York: Overlook Press, 1976, 1987).

From The Golem, or The Miraculous Deeds of Rabbi Liva (1904)

Foreword

DEAR READERS! I am giving you a rare and precious treasure, which has hitherto been lying in a library for three hundred years. Jews have always been thinking and talking about this treasure, and some have actually come to deny the whole story, claiming that Rabbi Liva never even created a golem, that the tale is fictitious, a mere legend. The truth of the matter is that when the great scholar Rabbi Ezekiel Landau was rabbi of Prague, he did, in fact, confirm that the golem was lying in the attic of the old great synagogue. The day he found the golem, the rabbi fasted and took his ablutions in the ritual bath. Then, donning his prayer shawl and phylacteries, he asked ten of his disciples to recite psalms for him in the synagogue, whereupon he mounted to the attic of the old great synagogue.

The rabbi lingered there for a long while and then returned in great terror, saying that from now on he would reinforce Rabbi Liva's decree forbidding anyone from venturing to go up there. Thus it once again became known that the story of the golem is true.

But then several decades went by, and a number of people once again began saying that the story is merely a legend. This happens, of course, because there is no precise account of the whole story in Jewish history books. But truth will out. And thus you see that the entire story was written down by Rabbi Liva's son-in-law, that great scholar Rabbi Isaac (a true priest, blessed be the memory of that righteous man). However, the manuscript lay hidden for so many years in the great library of Mainz, where so many of Rabbi Liva's writings can be found. I had to devote a great deal of labor and expense to having this manuscript printed. And thus I hope that every intelligent person will be grateful to me for my work, and I am certain that every Jew will soon give this valuable treasure a place on his bookshelf.

—Yudl Rosenberg

How Rabbi Liva Created the Golem

RABBI LIVA DIRECTED a dream question to determine how to wage war against the priest, his antagonist. And the answer came out alphabetically in Hebrew: "Ah, By Clay Destroy Evil Forces, Golem, Help Israel: Justice!" The rabbi said that the ten words formed such a combination that it had the power to create a golem at any time. He then revealed the secret to me, his son-in-law, Isaac ben Sampson Ha-Cohen, and to his fore-most pupil, Jacob ben Khaim-Sassoon Ha-Levi. It was the secret of what he had to do, and he told us he would need our help because I was born under the sign of fire, and the pupil Jacob ben Khaim-Sassoon Ha-Levi, was born under the sign of water, and Rabbi Liva himself was born under the sign of air, and the creation of the golem would require all four elements: fire, air, water, and earth. He also told us to keep the matter secret, and informed us seven days ahead of time how we were to act.

In the Jewish year 5340, in the month of Adar [corresponding to February 1580 in the Christian calendar], all three of us walked out of the city early one morning until we reached the shores of the Moldau River.

There, on a clay bank, we measured out a man three cubits long, and we drew his face in the earth, and his arms and legs, the way a man lies on his back. Then, all three of us stood at the feet of the reclining golem, with our faces to his face, and the rabbi commanded me to circle the golem seven times from the right side to the head, from the head to the left side, and then back to the feet, and he told me the formula to speak as I circled the golem seven times. And when I had done the rabbi's bidding, the golem turned as red as fire. Next, the rabbi commanded his pupil Jacob Sassoon to do the same as I had done, but he revealed different formulas to him. This time, the fiery redness was extinguished, and a vapor arose from the supine figure, which had grown nails and hair. Now, the rabbi walked around the golem seven times with the Torah scrolls, like the circular procession in synagogue at New Year's, and then, in conclusion, all three of us together recited the verse: "And the Lord God formed man of the dust of the ground, and breathed into his nostrils the breath of life; and man became a living soul."

And now the golem opened his eyes and peered at us in amazement. Rabbi Liva shouted in Hebrew: "Stand on your feet!"

The golem stood up and we dressed him in the garments that we had brought along, the clothes befitting a beadle in a rabbinical household. And at six o'clock in the morning, we started home, four men. On the way, Rabbi Liva said to the golem:

"You have to know that we created you so that you would protect the Jews from harm. Your name is Joseph, and you will be my beadle. You must do everything I command, even if it means jumping into fire or water, until you've carried out my orders precisely."

The golem was unable to speak. But he could hear very well, even from far away.

The rabbi then told us he had named the golem Joseph because he had given him the spirit of Joseph Sheday, who was half man and half demon, and who had helped the Talmudic sages in times of great trouble.

Back home, the rabbi told the household, in regard to the golem, that he had met a mute pauper in the street, a great simpleton, and that he had felt sorry for him and taken him home to help out the beadles. But the rabbi strictly forbade anyone else from ever giving him any orders.

The golem always sat in a corner of the rabbi's courtroom, with his hands folded behind his head, just like a golem, who thinks about nothing at all, and so people started calling him "Joseph the Golem," and a few nicknamed him "Joseph the Mute."

The Golem Carries Water at Passover

RABBI LIVA'S WIFE Pearl, may she rest in peace, was unable to contain herself, and on the day before Passover Eve, she broke her husband's prohibition against giving orders to the golem. She asked him to bring some water from the river and fill up the two kegs standing in a special, festive room. Joseph promptly grabbed the two buckets and hurried down to the banks. But no one watched as he poured the water into the kegs. Joseph the Golem kept bringing back more and more water until the room was flooded up to the threshold. And when the water began pouring into the other rooms through chinks and cracks, the people saw what was happening and raised such a hue and cry that the rabbi, upon hearing it, came running in terror. He now saw what was going on and he smiled at his wife:

"Dear me! You've certainly got yourself a fine water carrier for Passover!"

Then he hurried over to the golem, took the two buckets away from him, and led him back to his place.

From then on, the rabbi's wife took care not to give the golem any orders. The whole incident gave rise to a proverb in Prague: "You know as much about watchmaking as Joseph the Golem about carrying water."

Joseph the Golem Goes Fishing at New Year's

THE KIND OF help that Pearl, the rabbi's wife, got from Joseph the Golem's water-carrying for Passover was the kind that the rabbi got himself when he sent Joseph fishing at Rosh Hashanah [New Year's]. The incident took place several years after the golem was created.

There was a shortage of fish for Rosh Hashanah because of great winds and a cold wave. It was the morning of the day before New Year's, and there wasn't even a minnow in all Prague. Since it is a good deed to have fish on Rosh Hashanah, Rabbi Liva was extremely upset, and so he made up his mind to order the golem to go fishing.

Rabbi Liva told him to bring a net and then go to the river outside the town and catch fish. Since the rabbi's wife didn't have a small bag to give him, she handed him a large sack instead, for holding the fish he would catch. Joseph the Golem paid no heed to the bad weather. He grabbed the equipment and dashed over to the river to catch fish.

Meanwhile, someone brought the rabbi a present, one scant fish from a village near Prague. As a result, they were less concerned about Joseph and his fishing, and they forgot all about him, because on New Year's Eve Jews are usually busy with other matters. Twilight was coming on, and it was time to go to synagogue for evening prayers. The rabbi needed Joseph for something and asked where he was. He was told that the golem hadn't returned from the river yet, and everyone assumed that he still hadn't caught anything and didn't want to come back empty-handed. But since Rabbi Liva needed him urgently, he sent out the other beadle, Abraham-Khaym, to call him home. And in case he hadn't caught any fish and refused to come back, then Abraham-Khaym was to tell him that the rabbi said to forget about the fish and just come home right away.

Abraham-Khaym the beadle left for the river immediately. He arrived at the top of the riverbank and shouted down to Joseph the Golem that it was time to go home. Joseph held up the sack and pointed out that he only had to net a few more fish to fill it up. He motioned that he couldn't start back until the sack was full. Abraham-Khaym shouted down that the rabbi had ordered him to forget about the fish and just return home right away, because the rabbi needed him. The golem, upon hearing these words, grabbed the sack and dumped all the fish back into the river. He slung the net and the sack over his shoulders and ran home. When Abraham-Khaym the beadle returned, he told them what a fine thing Joseph had done! Everyone had a good laugh and Rabbi Liva told us in secret that he now realized the golem was good only for saving Jews from misfortune but not for helping them with good deeds.

What Rabbi Liva Used the Golem For

RABBI LIVA USED the golem only for saving Jews from misfortune, and with his help he performed a number of miracles. Most of all, he used him to fight against the Blood Libel which hung over Jews in those times and caused them great difficulties. Whenever the rabbi had to send him to a dangerous place and didn't want him to be seen, he gave him an amulet to make him invisible.

Around Passover, the rabbi would have Joseph the Golem put on a disguise. He gave him Christian clothing to wear, and a rope around his waist. He looked just like the Christian porters.

Rabbi Liva told him to spend each night wandering up and down the streets of the Jewish quarter, and if he saw anyone carrying something or transporting it in a wagon, he should hurry over and see what it was. And if he saw that it was something for bringing a Blood Accusation against the Jews, he was to tie up the man and the object and lug them over to the police at city hall to have the man arrested.

Rabbi Liva's First Miracle with the Golem

THERE WAS A wealthy Jew living in Prague, a community leader named Mordecai Mayzel, who lent money on interest. A Christian butcher owed him five thousand crowns, and Mordecai Mayzel was dunning him to repay the debt.

The slaughterhouse was outside the city, and the butcher always drove the meat into town through the Jewish section. Being unable to pay back the money, he decided to bring a Blood Accusation upon Mr. Mayzel, which would keep the moneylender so busy he would forget about the butcher. A few days before Passover, one of the butcher's neighbors lost a child and it was buried in the Christian graveyard. That same night, the butcher dug up the dead child and killed a hog, taking out its innards. Next, he cut the child's throat to make it look as if the poor thing had been slaughtered, stuffed the corpse into the dead hog, and then drove to town in the middle of the night to plant it somewhere in Mordecai Mayzel's home. He was driving down the street, and just as he stopped not far from Mr. Mayzel's house, along came Joseph the Golem. He ran up to the wagon and, upon seeing what it was, he took his rope and tied the butcher and the hog to the wagon. The butcher was a strong man; he fought and struggled with the golem and tried to break loose. But Joseph wounded him several times and finally overpowered him, for the golem's strength was greater than natural force. Joseph climbed into the wagon and drove off to city hall.

Upon his arrival, a great hubbub began in the courtyard, policemen came, and other people, but meanwhile Joseph the Golem slipped out of the crowd and returned unmolested to patrol the Jewish streets.

In the courtyard of city hall, they lit torches and saw before them the butcher, bloody and maimed. Upon seeking further, they found the dead child in the belly of the hog. Since it was wrapped in a Jewish prayer shawl, the butcher couldn't worm his way out, he had to confess everything he had planned to do to Mordecai Mayzel. When they asked him who had brought him here against his will, he replied that it had been a mute Christian, who was more like a devil than a human being. The butcher was locked up and sentenced to several years in prison. No one in town knew who that mute Christian could be, and the enemies of the Jews were stricken with fear.

But Tadeus, the renowned priest, knew very well who was behind it, and he began spreading a story that Rabbi Liva was a magician. He hated the rabbi more than ever, and bent his entire heart and soul on a war against Rabbi Liva and all the Jews of Prague.

FISHL BIMKO (1890–1965)

Born in Poland, Bimko began a fruitful career—writing mainly fiction and drama—which he continued after moving to the United States in 1921. This story was originally published in Vaysenberg's Yidishe Zamlbikher

(Yiddish Collections, 1920). A thoroughly rewritten, extremely Christo-
logical version was published in Bimko's selected works (vol. 10, 1947).
Yiddish authors who dealt with Christian themes weren't thinking about
converting; they simply wanted to expand the repertoire of Yiddish literary
themes.

The Encounter (1920)

THE SUN WAS shining. A mild summer day was in the offing. But since it was still early, the air was balmy and dewy—refreshing, exhilarating. The heavens were high, three times higher than on an ordinary day. And the sun, hovering over small, pale, wispy clouds that were foaming and waning, filled the countryside with light, a torrent of magical light.

There was a grove of pines that had just washed their tops in the morning dew, and their lofty, slender trunks were swaying almost imperceptibly. They looked like a blue web or a blue mist sharply dividing sky and earth, hanging like a blue hem behind the heavenly curtain.

Beyond the grove, the eyes could grasp and absorb all the colors sparkling in the evenly stretching fields, filling each piece with the color of its crop—here a narrow ribbon of rye, a yellow span of richly blossoming lupinus, and there buckwheat flowering white, and next to it green, towering corn, its leaves fanning out like palm fronds—and it all looked wondrous, so wondrous. The sunshine was pouring down, imbuing everything with the dear, sweet chirping of birds, and the morning resonated on all sides in the pure, blue air.

A silent, delicate breeze wafted through the area, sending wisps of clouds across the sky. The breeze puffed along the heads of the stalks, and strips of light and shadow skimmed through the rye, which rocked with a tender and intoxicating swishing, like the capricious rolling of large streams. Suddenly a whole billow swept from one corner of the field to the other.

From there it dashed over to a distant hillock, to a pile of cottages in a tiny hamlet, which peered bizarrely at the entire calm, silent, beautiful countryside, peered like a young housewife, peered at the surrounding properties, at the windmill on the hillock: and the windmill spread its two remaining wings high into the air, while the surrounding fields, clad in

royal garments, supplied rye for grinding and baking and linen for clothing. The hamlet was a tiny, wordless housewife.

Today, however, the sun seemed peculiar, and the hamlet was nervous
as the shadows of wispy clouds slipped across the rye fields. Last night a
storm had erupted, and this morning, when the peasants stepped outside
in their nightshirts, odd-looking, foreign soldiers marched in. Their brass
helmets reflected the sun so intensely that they blinded anyone who
glanced at them.

THE COUNTRYSIDE WAS hushed and tense, the wide river seemed to
shrink between its banks, and the grove was quiet and astonished as it
watched the commotion among the cottages: foreign faces and helmets
glittering and blazing.

Softly, softly the countryside held its breath.

Then, around a woodland trail, the chirping of a bird and the overall
tranquility were briefly interrupted. Two cavalrymen came trotting along,
craning their necks, ogling the hamlet. They were soon followed by more
soldiers.

"Halt!" one of them cried, staring straight ahead, not turning toward
the others.

The riders halted, virtually concealed by the blue outskirts of the grove.
They stood there, tense and stiff, as if surprised by what they had found.
They gazed at the hamlet, listened to it, listened to the soft noise, like the
plashing of a water mill.

An instant went by. The riders wanted to retreat, for one soldier, the
first, was already patting his horse's neck and digging his spurs into the
horse's belly to make the creature turn around—when suddenly a wild
shot rang out, then more and more in quick succession.

The gunfire sounded like moans, the stalks in the fields shuddered,
and the grove submitted obediently, gaping and gawking like an intelligent entity.

BY THE TIME the sun rose higher, two cavalrymen were lying on the
ground after tumbling from their mounts behind the trees. Soldiers could
be heard roaming the hamlet as before; helmets were shining and glistening in the sun, and at times they looked like a moving row of blazing

torches. The muffled sound, like the plashing of a distant water mill, could still be heard; but there was silence behind the trees, where the two horsemen were lying.

It seemed like a meaningless coincidence, like a sudden, unexpected, momentary event. They had just been alive, those two riders, trotting along on their horses; and now they were lying behind the trees, opposite one another, some fifteen yards apart, their arms flung out, their heads shaven. They looked as if they were sleeping. One of them was sprawled faceup, his knee pointing at the sky; the other soldier was clutching grass in his clenched fist—who could say why? The grove was hushed, no one appeared, no hooves resounded. The other horsemen had long since galloped away. Nothing stirred. Only a hare broke the utter silence. Scurrying by, it paused on its hind legs, perking up its ears, gazing at the scene. The hare was confused, unable to orient itself after the mayhem, and scared even more by the two faces. Then it scampered far away, into the dense underbrush, leaving only a faint rustle in the air. The birds were still hushed after the brief turmoil. It was as if the world had sunk into an eternal silence.

THE SUN HAD already passed into the west and was now glowing on the other side of the grove, on the still area between the trees and the hamlet—an area turned red by the sunset. A few elderly peasants, with pipes in their mouths and spades on their shoulders, came down the hillock. Later on, when everything was calm again, a peasant woman, who happened to be in the grove during the shooting, trudged by the two corpses—young, fresh bodies, with full, clean-shaven faces. Upon reaching her home, she bitterly lamented the fate of the two soldiers. And now that the enemy had vanished, the peasants were going to the grove with their spades. No one had told them to do so; they viewed it as a sacred duty toward two unfortunate human beings.

The dark melancholy of nightfall blended with the sun's last, fiery rays as they swept across the grove. The treetops were kindled by the red sky, which blazed as if after a worldwide infamy. With the countryside shrouded in fear, the crimson west was as pensive as an old man who had thought a great deal about the world. The entire horizon was dipped in bloody fire. But despite the terror that had seized hold of the earth, four wordless, solemn peasants with coppery faces ignored what was happening around them. They stood there, opposite one another, diligently shoveling the soil until they had dug two graves side by side. Then they lowered the two cavalrymen into the earth and covered them with two fresh mounds of sand. Next they made a single cross out of a branch and thrust it into the ground at the head of the graves.

By the time the peasants left the grove, they were surrounded by a deep night. With faint sighs coming from their hearts, they felt they had done something crucial, and they went home, calm and silent.

The night was pitch-black, no star lit up the sky. Death hovered over the small area, spreading its dark wing over the young, fresh hamlet—and everything was snuffed and was left in the darkness as if in a profound mystery.

AVROM ZAK (*1891–1980*)

Born in Russian Poland, Zak lived in Warsaw. In 1908, he began a career of prolific publishing and editing. He was drafted into the tsarist army in 1913, sent to the front in 1914, and wounded near the San River. When the German army invaded Poland in 1939, he fled to Soviet-occupied Grodno, where, along with thousands of other Jewish refugees, he was arrested and imprisoned. In 1941 he was released and in 1946 he was repatriated to Poland. He moved to Paris two years later and settled in Buenos Aires in 1952.

A Wounded Man (*1923*)

"ZH — ZH — ZHI — I — K . . ."

Something burned quickly. The spade was torn from my hand . . .

It was burning!

A warm, red liquid was gushing—

A bullet—

I knelt instinctively.

My hand! An electric current flashed through my hand, which ignited like a searing flame.

My entire hand was black, covered with a shiny liquid . . . Where had it hit? I didn't know. My entire hand was dripping, my entire hand was electrified . . .

My voice quavered into the darkness:

"Orrr-derrr-ly!"

But no one heard me in that inferno, no one appeared.

A thought whipped through my mind:

"Go back!"

I was confused and agitated. I dashed wildly across the gloomy fields. At first my sound hand dragged along my rifle. I remembered a strict order: wounded men must not abandon their rifles. But when the burning in my hand grew worse, and my nerves were shattered, I lifted the rifle into the air, then, cursing furiously, I flung it into the darkness! —

I felt as if I'd thrown my rifle into the face of the embodiment of evil, the red devil, who had devised this cruel, this bloody game — — — —

— — — — — — —

How awful was the burning, how agonizing the pain.

"Orrr-derrr-ly!"

Not a living soul.

Dark. Gloom. Where was there a path here?

I didn't have the strength to keep running. I collapsed in a small dale.

The blood wouldn't stop flowing. How could I stem it? . . . A dark thought drilled into my brain. I remembered that I had a roll of gauze in a special pocket. I managed to pull it out, but I couldn't unroll it with only one hand. It was sewn together solidly—a closed ball.

And the blood gushed . . . Now I could tell where I'd been wounded: in the very center of my palm.

No. I didn't dare stay put. With trembling legs I broke into a run and scurried across the fields . . .

Someone appeared to be sitting next to a tree: a man! I held out my roll of gauze and, with a cheery glimmer of hope, I said: "Hey, buddy! Tear it open and bandage my hand!"

I got near him, then backed off, horrified: a terrible mistake—he was dead. He leaned against the tree like a living person. He seemed to have suffered his final tortures clutching the tree like someone near and dear, like his mother, and then he'd frozen— — — — — — — — —

Dug-up stretches. My feet went up, went down. I stumbled over a rifle, over ripped barbed wire.

I stumbled over something soft amid bushes.

Brrrr . . . A dead body . . . I clenched my teeth convulsively and scampered on like a lunatic.

What about the gushing blood?

"Orrr-derrr-ly!"

Lifeless fields. Dark. Not a glint. Not a living soul. But rifle bullets whizzed behind me—a sign that I wasn't so far from the front lines.

Several buildings stuck out in the darkness: maybe I'd find someone there?

I turned every which way, peered around—walls smashed by grenades, ruins with piles of black bricks. I recognized one building: a few days ago we'd been lying there under a tremendous cannonade. The enemy battery had kept up a hailstorm of heavy pieces of metal, scattering them on all sides . . . We had come here along a narrow trail. Just where was it?

Finally found it. Heaved a sign of relief and started walking along the grassy trail.

"Who's there?"

A voice! A human voice!

"I'm wounded," I replied, scanning the darkness.

I barely detected the shadowy blur of a human being right by a thick tree trunk. I moved closer—a soldier with a walkytalky.

"Bandage me up, buddy," I said in a broken voice, giving him my gauze.

"I'd do a bad job of it. Go straight from here, then turn left. You'll find a reserve squadron. Ask the orderly."

"Thanks, buddy!"

A bit cheerier, I set out.

I halted at a glow coming from the ground.

Trenches! I was there!

I headed toward the glow. Through the opening of a trench I saw an officer lying on straw and reading a newspaper by candlelight.

"Orderly!"

A short little soldier with a cross on his sleeve emerged from another trench.

"Who is it?" he asked softly.

"I'm wounded."

"Where's your gauze?"

I gave it to him.

He started unrolling it while I knelt down. As I breathed, a heavy moan escaped my chattering teeth. . . .

"Where's your wound?" he asked, fixing his flashlight on me.

A shudder ran through my body: a red hand. In the very center of my palm—a thick, black, cold splotch of coagulated blood . . .

"Hurry! Bandage it up! I can't stand the sight of it!"

The orderly started bandaging my hand slowly and gingerly.

"You're lucky!" he comforted me. "The bullet could've hit some other part of your body . . ."

"Yeah, luck! A hole in my hand . . ."

The orderly more or less finished bandaging my perforated hand and then pointed into the distance.

"You see that fire and, further on, that second fire? That's where you have to go."

I could make out two tiny, widely separated fires; they were low field lanterns marking the route from the front lines to the rear.

The orderly returned to his trench, and I rested a while, recovering a little. I was safer here. Few normal bullets could get this far. Only bullets shot by an extremely forceful powder charge. But by then they're powerless and they drop to the ground. The front was all of three kilometers away.

I knelt, looked at my bandaged hand, and mused: "Just what's happened? How's it gonna end?" For whole days and weeks I'd been tortured by one thought: "What's gonna happen? How's it gonna end?" Whether I was awake or asleep, it pierced my very marrow, it ruthlessly tore through my fitful sleep in fields, in barns . . . I was tormented by the incomprehensible situation, by the nightmarish enigma . . . And now . . . Now, in one instant, a bullet, faster than a thought, had brought me the solution . . . And how easily it could have been different, different, more dismal . . . The soldier wearing a sky blue coat in the enemy's trench could have easily, by some fluke, shifted his rifle a bit to the left, a bit higher, just as he had happened to turn it toward the right. And then, then—the bullet wouldn't have struck my hand, it would have hit some other part of me . . .

The clamor of loud voices came from the front lines.

Shush—they were yelling: "Hurray!" . . . The real game was starting. Things were close together there . . . The rattling of the rifles and the machine guns grew denser and more passionate, and the batteries on both sides flung heavy grenades at one another. With bizarre and ghastly howls they sliced through the air, sounding powerful enough to destroy the whole world.

A few platoon commanders and some curious soldiers crawled out of the trenches.

"It's begun."

"Can you hear them? They're yelling: 'Hurray! Hurray!'"

"Who's yelling? Our guys or theirs?"

And they all pricked up their ears.

I looked at my hand and thought to myself: "If it weren't for the bullet, I'd be among them now, and the bullets and grenades would be hailing down on me too, and I too would hear the order: 'With your bayonets pointing ahead!'"

Some grenades fell very close by.

"Into the trenches!"

The men all scurried back into the trenches.

"And you, the wounded man!" an officer shouted. "Run straight back!"

I got to my feet and dashed off.

There, there, to the fire.

Grenades howling through the air egged me on: "Faster! Faster!"

I still wasn't walking on a trail. Fields and meadows. Torn up, pitted, shredded.

I was already at the first field lantern.

A bit further the tremendously forceful artillery roared like terrible thunder. With every shot the ground trembled under my feet. I was dazed: Where was I?

"Who's there?" I heard a voice—a homey Russian voice.

A battery was buried here with its cannons. Each cannon was covered on all sides. Every few minutes there were eight deafening booms one after the other.

The soldier showed me where to go.

I was already at the second lantern.

A short while later—a river. The San. I turned this way, that way—and found a pontoon bridge.

I started across.

Right on the bank—trenches. Sappers were lying there.

"Where's the medical station?" I asked.

"Not too far on the other side."

On the bridge two sappers were fixing damage caused by a grenade.

I walked along the pontoon and gazed into the water—a fantastic black mirror. Waves spilled over waves, and an enigmatic boom rose from the depths. It resembled the quaking of a huge and sturdy giant. What was tormenting the giant? What was tormenting him in his chest? Couldn't he stand the corpses in his depths? Was he tormented by the gory banks of his bed?

The pontoon almost swayed with the quaking of the river—I felt it . . .

I clambered up the opposite bank and walked along a path.

I caught up with two silhouettes moving ahead of me. Wounded men. One held on to the other's arm. One with a bandaged hand, the other a bandaged head. He was shaking and he had to be led. His mouth was agape, and moans came from between his teeth . . .

"Take his other arm, buddy!" said the wounded man.

I did it.

And so the three of us, like fused shadows, trudged slowly through the darkness. We trudged wordlessly. No one spoke. We were from different regions. But in our misery we had become blood brothers. We were coming from the same hell . . . The same death was fanning about us . . . The same hard metal had opened each man's body and poured the same hot blood into it.

We trudged in silence, struck dumb by the agonizing pain. . . .

The man with the head wound began wobbling and stumbling. His bandaged head couldn't stay erect. We held him tighter and we dragged along even slower.

A GLOW FROM a window.

We approached—a movement of people.

The medical station.

We entered—it was crammed with wounded men. Some were sprawled on the floor. Orderlies lugged seriously wounded men on stretchers. Medics were bandaging the wounds. The air was filled with ghastly moans and sighs. Dark faces, thoroughly tormented. Their creases concealed a frozen horror of death. In other faces the teeth were clenched in unbearable pain . . . White gauze shone forth. In other men the gauze was bloodstained: the blood had soaked through. . . .

An orderly came over to me, looked at my hand, and decided that the bandage was good. He made a gauze sling for me, looped it around my neck, and I slipped in my arm.

They took down my data, and I went outside.

I was tortured by an awful thirst.

I stopped a hurrying Sister of Mercy: "A little boiling water."

She took me to some barn where a few orderlies were sitting.

She poured some lukewarm water from a teapot: "Drink!"

I took out some sugar—a round, black ball—from my ammunition sack . . .

Sugar from the front lines? . . . It had been with me in damp holes.

I tossed it away . . . The others all burst out laughing, and with a friendly smile the nun handed me a lump of sugar.

"Thank you, thank you, Sister!"

The orderlies helped me take off my cartridge belt—the two bullet straps and all the ammunition.

I felt a bit relieved and I stepped back outdoors.

I was surrounded: officers, junior officers, the Russian Orthodox chaplain with his gray curls and his crucifix on his chest.

They were all curious. They plied me with questions. They did the same with a few other wounded men.

"What's been happening there?"

Each wounded man told whatever he knew, whatever he'd experienced, and how he'd been hit by a bullet.

A junior officer comforted me: "Don't worry. In a couple of weeks your hand will've healed up and you'll get back to the front."

"Cheery prospects," I thought to myself . . .

The pandemonium on the other side of the river wouldn't stop. From time to time the firing blazed up with fresh intensity.

Field grenades began exploding nearby, pouring out shrapnel. One, a second, a third. The men grew nervous. On one side flames swept up. A whole village was burning. A fearful and fantastic brightness soared toward the sky.

Orders came to move back the medical station. And the unit transport, too. A stampede. They began harnessing the animals. Horses were neighing. One command drowned out the other. People scurried through the darkness from place to place. A squad of mounted Circassians in their tall fur hats turned up from nowhere like strange spirits, galloped off, and vanished in the night.

Faster! Faster! People were shoving one another, and shrapnel kept bursting in the air.

Together with a big group of wounded men we trudged along a path and headed into the dark. There was a village five or six kilometers away. That was the location of our division hospital. We had to get there. . . .

YANKEV KREPLAK *(1885–1945)*

*B*orn in Russian Poland, Kreplak wrote short stories and children's books. *Fleeing Russian conscription, he came to the Unites States in 1915. Barrack and War (1927) is a collection of stories about life in the tsarist army and the special difficulties endured by Jews.*

From a Letter

FROM BARRACK AND WAR (1927)

YOU'VE ASKED ME, darling, why I don't tell you about my life in the barrack. "You never write me a single word," you say, "about your experiences"—and you complain that "it's hard, it's tough not knowing what's happening to someone we're close to in this strange and unfamiliar world."

It's true that I've avoided writing to you. I felt that your knowing nothing was better than knowing the truth.

But you now demand, you insist that I tell you about my gray daily life in the Russian barrack somewhere in Finland.

Fine, I'll do so.

But don't think, darling, that this is easy. I can't tell whether you'll gain a proper notion, a clear portrayal of this life. I'm going to recount it because I'd like you to picture it. I believe that it's impossible for an outsider to grasp, or rather, to feel something that one should actually go through, endure oneself.

Still, I'll try to describe a day, a single day out of more than three years, which should have been the happiest time of my life (my life alone?). These are the best years of youth and manhood! But I have to spend them in darkness, in hatred, in deep spiritual suffering.

Each day resembles the next—like drops of water: monotonous, lackluster. My days drip by and vanish in desolate sand. I'll describe only one day, and if I succeed, you'll know about all my other days as well. If you see other soldiers, you'll see me, and if you see me, you'll see all the others too.

But don't forget for even a minute that there's a difference, a big difference: don't forget that I'm a Jew in a Russian barrack after the revolutionary years of 1903–06.

Don't expect a precise delineation—it's out of the question. Don't think that the barrack is as simple a place as it might seem. As fate would have it, the authorities have brought together men from every part of the great Russian empire. Men of diverse faiths, tongues, nationalities. A lot of them aren't merely different from one another, they're remote and alien.

They may all be living under one roof, eating the same grub from the army's same copper cauldron, they may all endure the same troubles and suffer all the hardships of military life, but they are still foreign to one another. They even understand woes and joys quite differently. At times it strikes me as horrible that people living in the same land should be so alien, so hostile, and even so opposed to one another.

In the barrack you'll find everything: the cunning and bustling city and the ignorant and superstitious village, the dense wilderness and the spoiled public, terrible fanaticism and complete heresy, hooliganism and bizarre purity. One soldier has an intricate, complicated past, another soldier has a naive, childlike past. Some of the men have gone through the momentous years and some have lived in utter unawareness.

And they have all been herded together in this tangle and covered with this uniform. Everything has to be gray and covered. The better soldiers have to be lonesome and withdrawn. They conceal their thoughts and feelings deep inside themselves. And if a man keeps his emotions buried, then they'll eventually become dull and numb . . . The better soldier turns thoroughly gray—all uniform.

I've seen men who, without being noticed, have lost the spiritual goods that they brought to the army. Some try to get rid of those goods as soon as possible, others barely have them in the first place. And a few of these soldiers have human blood on their consciences. Actually, it takes a miracle, a real miracle, to awaken a man's soul in a barrack, but it's been known to happen.

We are spending our best years here, and later on we will scatter. We'll stop thinking about one another, we'll forget about one another. Coercion has brought us together, our freedom will drive us apart.

It's difficult making an outsider feel this kind of life. At times it's an unpleasant job. I'll simply pull a thread here, a thread there from the tangle: I'll draw only a few hints on the paper, a few spots and strokes. Think your way in, read between the lines, and perhaps you'll feel what I, the Jewish soldier and ardent pacifist, am experiencing in the Russian barrack.

If I sound ugly and cynical, you can rest assured that reality is even uglier and more cynical. Don't think that I exaggerate, that I'm making things blacker than they are. Quite the contrary: there are things I can't and I won't write about. At times I myself don't know, I can't analyze. But there's one thing I do know: here in the barrack, lives are cramped, chained, fettered—the young lives of young men.

You can understand how thoroughly repulsive I, as an ardent pacifist, find the barrack—this training ground for war. This dreadful notion haunts me even though, as you know, the political horizon is quiet and we ourselves are living better than other soldiers—certainly better than other Jewish soldiers, and yet I can't shake my feelings.

Strangely enough, the word "war" is seldom used. The men never talk about why they are here. The concept of war seems remote and alien just as the concept of death is remote and alien for a young person.

Yet every second round the clock is geared to learning the tricks of war, mastering the ways of bloodshed, getting habituated to all those things. So do you think the soldiers don't feel it too?

They do feel it. And the thought of war drives them down into the farthest depths of their consciousness. But if a rumor arises, if the blood red fire of war shimmers on the horizon—my God! How tragic the reflection in the eyes of most of the soldiers!

The men are horribly homesick. Both Christians and Jews. Like convicts, but with greater yearning, the soldiers count the months, the days, the hours till they can go home.

For the soldiers, the barrack is a prison. The hard, tormenting life is quite palpable. The men become bitter, vindictive, and insolent out of despair and longing. They live on flimsy expectations, on all kinds of rumors, on the wild hope that they will fall ill or break an arm, a leg—and be released from the army. . . .

The soldier's entire training, from drilling to language, centers on military discipline—the supreme utterance of human degradation. Military discipline is a brutal process that gradually crushes even the freest soul. First, they kill the human being in the soldier. He has to lose his sense of self, his confidence, his human value from the very outset. Though an adult, he has to start from scratch, relearn how to walk, how to talk, how to hold himself, how to acquire new habits, a new language, a new bearing. His earlier life of freedom is viciously torn out by the roots. At the same time a deep terror is planted in his heart—to make him the most obedient creature on earth.

He is subjugated to a whole pyramid of superiors, all of whom he has to salute. I've brought up this minor annoyance because it's so ridiculous. At first it's funny: straighten up, raise your hand to your vizor, and gape at the officer. But after a thousand times, the salute becomes ingrained. A man can't endure doing unnecessary things. And if he's forced to perform nonsense over and over, he eventually finds meaning in it. Constant saluting actually makes a soldier feel that the officer is more important. Veterans have told me that even after they left the army and were back in civilian clothes, it still took them a long time to stop wanting to salute when they encountered an officer in the street.

The soldier who suffers most is the Jew, especially the ordinary Jew. Naturally other ethnic groups suffer too: Poles especially, Muslims—all the so-called aliens. But the simple Jewish soldier from the Pale of Settlement falls into a Christian ocean for the first time and drowns in scorn and derision. He suffers most from the junior officers and from the anti-Jewish soldiers.

Certainly the source of this hatred is to be found among the brass, but the Jewish soldier rarely sees them—perhaps at a parade, at a review. However, he does see the ordinary soldiers day and night, and they embitter and poison his life.

If the Jewish soldier did not take part in the revolutionary movement, then he's doomed. He fails to understand the gratuitous hatred that inundates him.

And even though I know the source of today's antisemitism, even though I'm not religious, even though I'm used to dealing with Christians, even though I can hold my own and I'm better prepared to adjust to the barrack, I nevertheless sometimes feel I'm suffocating.

Just listen to this recent incident. As you'll see, it was an exception. But you can picture what I experienced.

I was at the guardhouse, waiting my turn to go to my post. It was a wintry midnight. The room was overheated, the ceiling lamp was smoking, the only window was smashed. The white Finnish night peered in. The room was hot and close. Too many soldiers for such a tiny space. We were in full gear. Our mouths were dry because of the heat and the crowding. We could barely keep our eyes open, but we weren't allowed to sleep. So the soldiers swapped yarns.

I don't know how it happened, but we began talking about the disturbances in earlier years, and one story led to another. One man, who had a Polish accent, talked a great deal and he told us this story:

"IT WAS A SUMMER day in the time of the disturbances, when Jews were said to have tossed bombs into churches. I was alone, plowing my field. My huge dog, which could tear up a man, was next to me. He started gazing at the road. So did I. Far in the distance I saw the Jewish community's scribe driving in his britzka. So I left my plow and went over to the road.

"'Good day!' I said.

"'Good day!'

"'Anything new in town?' I asked.

"'It's begun!' he replied, gesturing, and he drove on.

"'So,' I thought to myself, 'it's begun. Where can I find a Jew now?'

"Then I saw my dog gazing at the road again. Far in the distance I saw a Jewish vagabond. They wander like that, from town to town. I thought to myself: 'A godsend!' And I stood there, waiting by the road. The Yid seemed to notice something. He halted, then turned and hurried away.

"I dashed after the vagabond, siccing my dog on him. My dog sunk its teeth into the man's coattails, and I dragged him over to my field. He was all in rags and he was trembling with fear. I looked at him and I said: 'It won't help!' I unhitched my horse, grabbed my whip, and exclaimed,

'Hitch yourself to my plow!' He pretended he didn't understand. I lashed him, and he yelled in his Yid language, 'Help! Help!'"

When the storyteller mimicked the Jew's cries for help, the soldiers smirked. One man was so delighted, he even neighed like a horse.

"I hitched him to my plow." The soldier was warmed up by the laughter. "At first he pulled, then he refused to go on. I tore off his rags and whipped his naked body. He collapsed. I got scared. He wasn't breathing, so I dragged him over to the ditch—it was filled with water—and I dunked his head. I could hear him gulping . . ."

"You goddamn bastard!" I yelled at the soldier. "You're lying through your teeth! You may have wanted to do that—you should've met me outside and not in this guardhouse! I'd 've knocked out the rest of your rotten teeth!" I turned to the others, who had lapsed into silence. "You can be witnesses! I'll turn him over to the higher officers for torturing and drowning a Jewish beggar!"

"He didn't drown!" the soldier swore. "I let go of him right away!"

"No, you drowned him! I'm sure of it!" I insisted, certain that the whole story was a lie, a wild boasting. I wanted to frighten him.

"How could I've drowned him?" he asked the other soldiers. "All I got was two weeks in jail . . ."

NOW I REALIZED his story was true. I tried to punch him, but the others held me back. Then the conversation turned to pogroms. I managed to arouse the consciences of the Russian soldiers. He was the only Pole and I was the only Jew. The Russians were particularly struck that the victim had been a Jewish beggar—such a Jew wouldn't have bothered them. They began cursing the Pole and calming me down.

Petrushin, a Gentile from Yekaterinoslav, started talking about the pogrom that had occurred there. He had been so fine—nothing like this Pole. He'd been standing at his window and he'd seen the pogromists torturing a Jewish girl. He'd been unable to watch and he'd turned away.

"Petrushin," I asked. "Why didn't you help her?"

I knew what he'd answer and I was right:

"They'd 've killed me!"

These are the kind of men I'm forced to live with: the Pole and Petrushin. I have to eat with them, sleep with them, delight with them, sometimes defend them, and worst of all, suffer with them. . . .

YOYSEF TENENBOIM (1887–1961)

Tenenboim, who was born in Austro-Hungarian Poland, served as a physician in the Austrian army during World War I. Moving to the United States in 1920, he published both fiction and medical articles. In the following story, he drew on his military experience in World War I.

Hear, O Israel (1926)

IT WAS A WINTER day in a dense Carpathian forest. A whimsical storm was toying with snowflakes, scattering them like feathers from a ripped featherbed. A cold wind was blasting. The trees were struggling to escape. Their branches were playing the wind's death march. The roads were snowy, and the trails buried. The front lines were cut off from the living world.

Nevertheless the front didn't rest. The soldiers were caught in a bitter clash. Their teeth sank into the jagged clods of ice, their nails clawed the frozen rocks. The enemy—and the angry elements—refused to surrender.

The cannon kept booming, the bullets kept flying—competing with the whirlwind to see who could whistle the loudest. Masses of soldiers were falling, rolling in the snow like dungheaps. It was a boring, meaningless fight—a fight for snow.

My medical station was filled with the wounded: Hungarians, Slovaks, Romanians, Germans, and Jews. Each man moaned in his native tongue, each man prayed to or cursed his own saints. A Babel of languages—a microcosm of the old Austro-Hungarian Empire. And some of the wounded were enemies. They had been fighting on our right flank, and my medical station was the closest one for their mangled bodies.

. . .   .

I WAS BANDAGING one enemy soldier, a junior officer with a shattered leg. The leg was dangling like a torn-off sleeve without lining. He was an intelligent warrior, a true hero. He was in great pain but he never moaned. I felt sorry for him. I offered him some liquor.

"Cheers, comrade! You'll soon be transferred to the army hospital, where they'll amputate your leg. Hmmm. You'll have one less leg, but at least you'll be healthy!"

The officer sighed like an expert and drained the flask. Then he spit!

"Oh, that goddamn Jew! . . ."

The compliment was aimed at his neighbor, a Jew who had only a light skull wound but was bellowing louder than anyone else: "Hear, O Israel, the Lord our God, the Lord is one!" He kept shouting those words over and over! "Hear, O Israel! . . ."

"Goddamn Jew! I could strangle him!" The officer tried to get up without his leg.

"Hear, O Israel, Hear—!"

"Shut up, you bastard!" He forgot his military discipline. "Shut up! Have some pity—gag him! Stuff that filthy mouth!" He felt for his empty holster. "Jew, Jew! Stop tormenting me!"

My interest was aroused. "What's wrong? Don't you like the Jewish prayer?"

"One. . . !" The Jew was virtually chanting a hymn—in spite of the officer.

The officer trembled. He was choking on his own curses. The creases in his forehead were filled with sadness. His eyes were wandering in an enormous void, in an abyss of terror.

I regretted my anger. I reminded the unfortunate "cantor" that he wasn't in synagogue, that I didn't need a prayer leader in my medical station. Fine, so the chief surgeon was an antisemite! What could the Jewish soldier do? He went down half an octave.

I turned to the junior officer. "Don't be angry, comrade!"

He looked at me as if seeing me for the first time. He inspected me like a slaughterer scrutinizing a cow. He hesitated. Rigid beads of sweat emerged on his forehead.

I tried to raise his spirits: "Do you need anything, comrade?"

"I committed a crime. I killed a Jew!"

"Killed a Jew? Well, war is war! You can't look at the enemy's penis!"

"I killed a Jew!" His voice was now as hard as steel. His face was a mask of despair and relentlessness. His tongue struggled like a fenced-in colt—it bit through the bridle.

He then told me how he had killed a Jew.

"IT WAS . . . IN the Russian-Polish mud. Our army was pursuing the shattered Russian divisions. The enemy was dynamiting the bridges and the roads. We lost contact with him, no information. I was ordered to reconnoiter the surrounding forests. A patrol accompanied me.

"I was an expert in recognizance." A touch of bragging colored his monotonous introduction. "I was a detective in civilian clothes. I also spoke a little Polish and I knew how to shake important data out of the local population. I set out with great confidence.

"Near the forest I found a tavern. An old Jew was sitting inside, swaying over a large sacred tome, chanting some sort of prayer. I asked him: 'Jew! Have you heard anything about the enemy?'

"'No, there's no enemy hereabouts. The Russkies have been swallowed up by the earth. Am I sure? Ha ha! I was just in the forest a short while ago. There was no trace of them.'"

"I shook him: 'Are you telling the truth, Jew?'

"'Am I telling the truth? On my word of honor! As sure as this is the truth!' He pointed at the faded, yellow pages of his holy book.

"'Your holy book is full of holes!' We taunted the Jew, but we believed him. And so we entered the forest unconcerned. We didn't expect any surprises. We wanted to reach the other side as fast as possible. We hoped that once there we'd learn more about where the enemy was hiding.

"We marched in a serried column, two by two, like geese." He was getting sarcastic. "Our rifles were swinging on our backs. Everything was very casual, as if we were picking strawberries. And we were bawling a hit song. We felt at ease in the dense forest as if we were hunting rabbits. What a fool I was! A goddamn fool!" He virtually pounced on himself. His wounded leg reminded him that he couldn't stand on his own. His eyes bulged with pain. His sharp mouth twisted like the beak of a predatory bird. His words were muffled as if he were talking through a sieve.

"There were fifteen of us. Fifteen of us marched into the forest—and only two of us came back. In the middle of the forest we encountered the enemy rear guard. They appeared to be waiting for us. We had no time to defend ourselves. We stepped right into their machine-gun fire, and—all that was left of my division was a heap of bones! My comrades! My dear comrades—they had trusted me so blindly."

THE MEDICAL STATION was hushed. The patients had stopped moaning and they were swallowing their sighs. They pricked up their ears. The front had likewise calmed down. Only a few stray bullets sounded like the blowing of the ram's horn before Ne'ila [the last Yom Kippur prayer]. The unfortunate officer was musing. His mind was wandering across the Polish mud. His eyes were seeking the thirteen comrades he had led to slaughter; he was trying to justify himself, he was begging them to forgive him.

"The Jew! The Judas!" Remembering that I was Jewish, my medical lieutenant bit his tongue. He tried extricating himself: "I mean the traitor! He deserved to be buried alive—I mean buried!"

"Bur . . . Bur . . ." The junior officer trembled.

"Bur." After a while he tried to straighten out his confused thoughts. His voice was hoarse, choking. His words fell hard. They were as heavy as lead. He continued his story:

"THERE WERE FIFTEEN of us. Only two of us managed to drag ourselves out of the forest. Both of us were wounded.

"We trudged back into the tavern. The Jew was gone.

"'Where is the Judas?'

"No one replied.

"I started beating the old woman and kicking the children. The children screamed, the woman held her tongue.

"I struck their heads with my rifle butt: 'Where's that Yid traitor?'

"'Ha ha! He's with the Russians.'

"I whirled around. An aristocrat with a twirled mustache and his trousers over his boots was standing there, offering me a cigarette.

"'You're looking for the Jew? Huh? You're wasting your time. The Yid's with the Russians. He went to them for his blood money, your lordship.'

"'With the Russians? With the—?' I was boiling! I dragged the woman and the bloodstained children over to the wall.

"'Stand there and suffer!' I began loading my rifle. "The Jew traitor is gonna get his reward!' I aimed at the terrified children.

"A shriek—and the Yid, who'd been hiding, was at my feet, licking my boots, cajoling me like a trodden snake.

"'So you made a deal, Yid? You traded soldiers' fresh blood for moldy rubles, huh?'

"No response. Just eyes—glassy eyes!

"My fury was growing like ocean billows.

"'Answer me, you Judas!' I started beating him.

"His lips trembled, but he said nothing. He wouldn't talk. He had nothing to say. My fury was boundless. I snatched his beard and dragged him outdoors the way you drag a corpse. In the garden I handed him a shovel:

"'Dig, Jew!'

"The Jew obeyed! He glanced at me like a whipped dog but didn't stop digging. He knew he was digging his own grave. I buried him in the grave. The children stood there, quaking. They were too scared to weep. My rifle butt had shattered bones.

"A mound went up on the grave. The old woman, who had fainted, came to. She saw what had happened. She hurled both her arms at the sky. She yelled in a pitiful voice:

"'Hear, O Israel!'"

The wounded Jew launched into a crying jag.

"Hear, O Israel!" the junior officer repeated in a Gentile accent.

"Hear, O—"

TWILIGHT FILLED THE room. A tongue of flame darted from the stove. A red glow played pranks on the killer's face. The dead Jew cast a long shadow. We all held our breath.

"The sleigh!"

"The sleigh!" Some life was restored to the exhausted and bloodless hearts. "The sleigh is here!"

They could hear the distant snorting of horses and the horse language used by the driver. The medical sleigh was coming to transfer the wounded to the army hospital.

"The sleigh! The sleigh!" The men who hadn't given up hope of living moaned, laughed, cheered, and rejoiced.

The killer didn't hear the sleigh. Overcome by deep sorrow, he was looking for sympathy. He then talked to himself:

"I confessed my awful crime. The aristocrat! The goddamn aristocrat.

They caught him a few days later and they strung him up. He confessed before his death: He'd been spying for the Russians! The Jew had been innocent. His tongue had been paralyzed with fear.

"Hear, O Israel!

"Hear, O Israel!" The snowstorm blasted the echo of the departing sleigh.

"Hear, O Israel . . ." A Jewish cantor and a Gentile chorister. "Heeeeear, Ooooooooooo, Iiiiizzz-raaaaael."

A REMARK AND an apology:

I have to say that once his confession was printed, I regretted it. Why open old wounds? I crossed out the murderer's nationality. All nationalities will repudiate him. During the war they were all the same: brutal, inhuman, primitive, bestial. Today they're the purest saints. Fine, why put on a flawed prayer shawl? Why recall one nation and omit another?

I also haven't mentioned the junior officer's name. He was no exception. He was a link in a horrible chain. And what does a link know about where the chain is dragging? Mention his name? Today he may be a father with children who dream about their father's heroism and who envy him for having had the right to kill people. He may even be a beadle in a church. A sermonizer. A judge of good deeds.

Why remember that he buried a Jew alive? Have few Jews been murdered during the war and since the war?

He confessed! Fine, I forgive him.

YESHUE PERLE (*1888–1940s*)

Born in Radom, Poland, Perle moved to Warsaw, where he wrote mainly fiction. This tale was first published in Vaysenberg's Yidishe Zamlbikher *(Yiddish Collections, 1920). Although harking back to a tradition of stories involving miraculous rescues of doomed Jews, it was obviously prompted by the Russian persecutions of Jews, the pogroms and expulsions, during World War I. In 1939, Perle moved to Lwów, where he was murdered during the German occupation.*

A Legend *(1920)*

YEARS WILL PASS, and generations will fade, like the foam on waves and like storms in the steppe. And the world will forget those who died with a curse on their lips and those who died murmuring a blessing. And the world will also forget those who grew old when young and those who went mad when old. The earth will smooth over, and the farmer will come with his plow: he will cut into the soil, then manure it, turn it over, until the fields are covered with stretches of bright, golden grain, and the barns will fill up again. Sheep and cattle will graze in the fresh pastures, joyfully praising God for the beautiful world.

But somewhere by a far-flung path, a lonesome poplar will stand with bare, scorched branches, and it will be able to tell us about skies that blazed day and night, about curses hurled at those skies. Somewhere in some field, trodden and plowed, we will see the mound of a brother's grave, which reminds us of mothers' tears and of sleepless nights, of unheard sighs and of bedtime prayers that children recited for their fathers, who were in the vast fields. And somewhere, an old, ruinous syn-agogue will croon a song of grief and sorrow, a dirge that has been weav-ing for generations, that, like innocent bloodshed, never rests.

There will come a time when only a few old people will remain of today's younger generation, and somewhere there will be a Jewish grand-mother, and when the sun, mute and miserable, is dying on a Sabbath eve, she will gather all her grandchildren, seat them by the stove, and say to them:

"Come, my dear children! Put your heads together and dream a dream. Grandma's going to tell you a story, and if tears come to your eyes, wipe them away and hold your tongue."

The grandmother will fall silent, as silent as the final breath of the Sabbath in a Jewish home, and this is how she will begin:

ONCE UPON A time there was a king, who lived near us. This king was the richest and smartest man in the world. He had sheep and cattle and all sorts of precious things. His subjects loved him very much, and he loved them. Other kings hated him for this and they secretly tried to figure out a way of getting his wealth. The smart king sensed their hatred, which left him feeling very sad and unable to sleep at night. So one day he called for a meeting of lords and other noblemen and told them how heavy his heart was.

The aristocrats mused, and the prime minister said:

"Your majesty! The thoughts you are nursing have been on our minds for a long time, and your dreams are our dreams. Our neighbors are about to invade us and wipe us from the face of the earth. And so our advice is: Sharpen the swords and the spears and be ready for combat."

This advice pleased the king, and he sent out his heralds to the four corners of his kingdom, ordering his subjects to be ready. And so, children, there was a great turmoil in the world, for the neighboring kings learned about this king's orders; they got up early and marched out with their armies.

And when the subjects woke up, they saw that the entire world was blazing. Towns and villages, fields and forests, orchards and vineyards, castles and palaces—everything was on fire. All water turned into blood, and every house into a mountain of ashes.

IN THOSE TIMES Jews in Crown Poland led harsh lives, harsh beyond all measure and all description. Jewish blood was spilled everywhere—north and south, east and west. For that smart young king and our king failed to come to terms. Our king was so infuriated that he tormented Jews. They were driven from one place to the next, and flocks of starving, naked refugees trudged along on cold winter nights, through deep mud, in the greatest frosts, their flesh shriveling: feeble, crippled, old people, pregnant women, babes in arms. Souls descended to the earth, and before they even managed to see the light of day, they had already passed on to the next world.

Now when that kingdom's army left a town, and our army marched back in, the wailing and shrieking rose all the way to heaven, for Gentiles came and they bore false witness, claiming that the Jews had been friendly with the enemy, that they had welcomed and regaled him. So the soldiers broke into the Jewish homes, destroyed all the furnishings, and slaughtered the inhabitants. The survivors plodded along deserted roads, ashamed before God's Heaven and God's earth. Homeless children wandered on the sides of the roads, asking every passerby: "Have you seen them? Have you heard them? My father sat studying the Talmud, my mother is a saint! Do you know what's become of them?"

AND IN THE town where your grandma was born, this is what happened:

One of the townsmen was a rich, learned, and hospitable Jew. He had three sons-in-law, who were as beautiful as gold—the Shekhina, the Divine Presence, rested upon them. They lived with their parents-in-law and day and night they assiduously studied the sacred texts and served the Almighty. Their parents-in-law felt such great pride and joy, and their wives, who were beautiful and virtuous like our holy Matriarchs, blessed the hour and the minute when God had bestowed such wonderful husbands on them. For these men seldom went out, except during fine weather, when they would spend an hour a day in the garden, which their father-in-law had planted for them.

All the mothers in town wished that their own sons would grow up no better and no worse than those three men and that their daughters would find such wonderful husbands.

Years and years flowed by. The world had no contact with these Jews, and they had no contact with the world. Until the dark turmoil came.

The armies that already occupied half of Crown Poland did not neglect our town. One lovely morning a rider came galloping on a white horse and he blew his trumpet east and west, north and south: "Let it herewith be known to all of you, young and old, that we are occupying this town and that we are now in charge!"

The town was filled with a deathly hush. Jews closed their shops and locked themselves in their homes. They were too scared to go out—they might run into a foreign soldier who'd want to speak with them. They knew that Jews in other places had been strung up just for talking with the enemy.

Time passed; no one knew what was happening in the great world, and the great world knew nothing about us. Until one night the noises of horses and wagons penetrated the closed doors and shutters, and no one could make heads or tails of it. But at dawn, when the sky was starting to turn blue, dust whirled up on the highway, and a new horseman galloped in, this time one of ours, and he too blew his trumpet in all directions: "Let it herewith be known to all of you, young and old, that we have retaken the town!"

The rabbi and his whole congregation went to greet the military commander with bread and salt, and out came klezmers with flutes and fiddles. Clutching the Torah, the rabbi gave a sermon hoping for peace in the world and for the realization of the prophet's words: "The wolf will lie down with the lamb."

But our enemies couldn't endure it. They turned to a Gentile gardener, who had spent years working for the rich Jew, and they sent the gardener to denounce him to the military commander, who was an aristocrat. The commander asked the gardener what he wanted, and the gardener said: "Your Lordship! If you promise not to expose me and to assure my life, I'll tell you what happened when the enemy arrived."

The commander promised not to expose him and to assure his life. The gardener crossed himself and then told the commander that during the foreign occupation one of our foot soldiers, who'd had not time to escape, had been hidden in the rich Jew's home for a day and a night. That morning, when the enemy had ridden past, the Jews had betrayed the foot soldier to the foreign horsemen!

"Are you telling me the truth?" the commander asked the gardener.

"The truth—as sure as there's a God in Heaven!"

The commander was furious and he sent out his soldiers to arrest all the men they would find in that house. They lost no time and they dashed over. The rich man happened to be away at that moment; however, his three sons-in-law were sitting there, studying the holy texts. The soldiers didn't ask who or what—they burst in and ordered them to come along. The three young men—poor things!—didn't understand what it was all about, they merely stood there, gaping. The soldiers assumed that these men were resisting orders, so they blew up and started beating and dragging them.

When the three wives saw what was happening, they wrung their hands and threw themselves at the feet of the barbaric soldiers: "Good people, where are you taking them and why?"

But it was no use, the three Jews were hauled off and brought to the commander. Scrutinizing them, he laughed, and when they failed to answer his questions (they didn't speak his language), he cursed and he spit into their faces. When the day waned and the night came, the commander ordered his men to take the three prisoners to the forest.

And here, children, there were three big trees—ancient oaks. The three Jews, poor things, realized their time had come, they recited their final confession in the silence and they bade farewell to the world. But they still didn't grasp what was happening—unless it was simply part of the war.

It didn't take long: a drum was beaten, soldiers yelled, there was a commotion. But when the first Jew was strung up, the rope snapped. And when they strung him up again, he again fell to the ground—and this went on, until he finally died. The second Jew's face glowed like the sun and his eyes shone like the stars, for he was the handsomest and most intelligent of the three. And when they came to the youngest, he closed his eyes, for his sorrow was great and his shame even greater. When he was strung up, he was calm and as white as alabaster. Not a single wrinkle, not a single hint of terror could be found in his face.

When the town soon learned about the three Jews, a great moaning and wailing arose. Young and old tore their clothes in mourning and poured ashes on their heads. Faces were grief-stricken, mouths were shut. People gazed but didn't know what they were seeing, they heard but didn't know what they were hearing. And the world was as silent as someone about to take his last breath. No breeze, no rustling of leaves—everything was petrified in the great sorrow that had struck the world.

Risking their lives, the despondent mother and her three daughters stole out to get the bodies of the martyrs. Since the night was as dark as the Egyptian darkness, the four women lost their way. But then all at once they saw something glowing in the distant forest, as if the moon were shining forth. As they drew closer, they saw the three corpses lying there—as white as doves, as pure as the wings of angels, and the forest was so radiant that they could see every leaf and every blade of grass.

The women collapsed and they sobbed bitterly, and all the trees in the forest, all the echoes and the night, joined their grief. After weeping their hearts out, the women wrapped the three victims in sheets and carried them back to town. A large throng of Jews headed by the rabbi had formed outside the synagogue. The eulogies were delivered, and the finest congregants brought the three dead Jews to the graveyard.

A DAY WORE by, then two and three. They came into the world gray and tearful and they departed in the same mood as if bearing the anguish of the recent disaster and the torment of the entire year. Every household was still talking about the incident; people wandered about as if in the World of Ghosts, their faces devastated, their eyes moist. But that wasn't the end of it. For it's the way of the world: one tragedy brings the next, and now a new affliction came.

The worthiest Jews in town were ordered to gather in the synagogue at sunset because the commander had to tell them some important news. Their faces grew darker, their eyes more tearful, because even though nothing was said, everyone sensed that a new curse hung over all heads—the commander certainly had nothing good in store for the Jews. They wandered about all day, asking one another: "Do you know? Do you know?" But who could have known?

They could scarcely wait for nightfall when all the worthy householders arrived at the synagogue, as the commander wished. They lit candles and all the chandeliers in honor of the commander. Perhaps this welcome would soften his heart. Then they waited with anxious faces, and when the synagogue was full, the commander's messenger entered, and the entire congregation rose and silently welcomed him. The messenger stepped up to the platform and said:

"Be it known to you Jews that we have hanged three of your brethren for killing one of our foot soldiers although we do not know why they did so. These Jews were informers, who also revealed our plans to the enemy. They spoke illegal words and did illegal deeds. I have therefore been ordered to inform you that inasmuch as you know that all my words are the pure truth, you have a sacred duty: you are to sign a document stating that our judgment was carried out with your approval and that it was just. Toward that end we give you a day and a night. And if you fail to carry out our order in that time, we will decapitate the eldest man in every tenth Jewish home."

A ghastly hush filled the synagogue, and every last Jew shuddered. But then suddenly a cooing emerged from behind the Holy Ark—it sounded like a dove: "Jews! If you sign the document, you will be signing a lie, and your name will be wiped out from God's earth, and the eternal light, which guides your steps, will be snuffed because you will inflict with your own hands a curse upon the whole of Israel!"

Suddenly a lamenting broke out in the synagogue: the walls and the menoras and the chandeliers were weeping, and so were the stags and lions, the flutes and fiddles, which were carved and painted on the eastern wall. And the curtain of the Holy Ark kept weeping as if the Shekhina, the Divine Presence, were trembling and weeping too.

A heavy night fell upon the town. No one slept in any home, no one even dreamed of shutting an eye. The synagogue was packed all night long, with Jews going in and out. They kept reciting psalms and prayers until dawn. The rabbi himself stood at the lectern, reciting one biblical verse after another, which the congregation kept repeating, until sunrise. At dawn, a fast was imposed, and the Jews read a passage from Exodus [32:11] beginning: "Lord, why doth Thy wroth wax hot against Thy people? . . ." Then they silently dispersed, each with an aching heart and with deep faith in the Lord.

The day wore by very slowly. Every hour felt like a year. But the weather was beautiful: the sun was shining and the snow was glittering, as clear and white as the souls of the three martyrs. But the day seemed motionless, as if night would never fall. However, when the fast ended, the night came, and the Jews recited their evening prayers. The rabbi, together with a quorum of elderly householders, went to the commander's mansion. They were accompanied by the entire town, and thousands of voices blessed them, thousands of eyes gazed at the heavens and begged for mercy. Children hurried along, wishing them success, and newlyweds gave their wedding presents to the poor.

And so the rabbi and the ten worthies reached the military commander's quarters, where they were told to wait since the commander was still asleep. They waited an hour, two hours, three, while the enormous throng stood outside, praying to the blue sky.

After sleeping his fill, the commander appeared before his visitors: "Have you come to sign the document? Good! The document will be brought in immediately."

But now our God-fearing rabbi, with his gray beard hanging down to his belt, stepped forward and said:

"Your Lordship! Your power is vast, you have influence with the royal court, which has sent you here. That is why every person is obliged to obey you and carry out all your orders. But look! Our hair is gray—not from weeping and not, God forbid, from sinning, not from old age and not from living peacefully. This is the grayness of wanderers who yearn for their homes, this is the sorrow of our martyred sons and daughters.

"Without the least sense of guilt you have taken three of our finest children, three young lives without a single flaw in their souls. And if you don't believe me, Your Lordship, then listen! The most sacred things that have remained from our former grandeur are our holy books and the dream of our Holy Land. My lips have never sworn a false oath and will never swear one. But if those three Jews were guilty, then may the good Lord, who took our forebears out of Egypt, forget us completely, and may He annul the great hope nurtured by our fathers, by us ourselves, and by our children, the hope of returning to our Holy Land. Your power, Your Lordship, is vast—decapitate us one after another. But we cannot sign our approval, for neither you nor your judgment is just."

The furious commander stamped his foot and yelled: "Shut up!"

But the rabbi couldn't shut up. He retorted: "No, great lord, I will not shut up, even if you have my tongue ripped out. And if I shut up, then these honest and pious men will not shut up. And if you have their tongues ripped out, then the spilled blood will not shut up. For you should know that innocent blood lives forever, and no matter where you are, no matter where you go, you will keep hearing the blood call for justice and punishment."

That was what our rabbi said. Whereupon the wicked commander grew even more furious. He ordered his men to tie up the rabbi and the ten householders and throw them in prison. Then he locked himself up in his private study and ground his teeth: "You goddamn Jews! You goddamn Jews!"

When the crowd of Jews saw that no one was coming out, they were overwhelmed with grief and fear. The night was growing darker and darker, and they didn't know what to do. It was a night of agony and anguish, of shame and despondency, for the householders prepared for martyrdom: each man said farewell to his wife and children and murmured his confession. The children cried out, "Daddy, why are you leaving us?" And the wives exclaimed that the world was about to end—"May God take pity and turn the world upside down once and for all!" But nothing helped—neither weeping nor shouting.

All night long, the rabbi's wife and the wives of the ten congregants wandered around the prison walls, tearing their clothes. And their weeping echoed across the dark town and their wailing ascended to the Creator.

Three fearful days and nights dragged by. Each evening the commander sent a messenger to the Jewish prisoners, asking whether they were ready to sign the document. But all eleven Jews shook their heads.

And on the fourth day, when they would be taken to the forest and decapitated, the entire town poured into the streets. Black was the sky and loud the lamentation. The Jews lay on the bare earth, tearing out their hair. But it was no use, and the day was already waning.

And now God worked His great miracle.

At dusk a horseman came galloping in and he announced that powerful enemy forces were heading this way. Then, as night was falling, the first enemy outrider showed up. By now the military commander and his men had retreated, abandoning everything—even the execution sites and the ten bound Jews.

And that was what happened! Oh, my dear grandchildren, where can I find the strength to tell you everything that occurred? The whole town of Jews burst into tears—this time out of joy. And they hugged and kissed and danced and they congratulated one another: "Mazeltov!"

And when the rabbi and the ten worthies appeared in the street, the joy was so great that even some Gentiles wept. Thousands of voices wished the worthies peace, thousands of blessings were heaped upon their heads.

However, God also paid the wicked commander his due. Three days later they found his corpse in the field—all his limbs were cut off. They tried to bury him, but the earth disgorged him, they flung him into the river, but the water tossed him out. And so the new commander had his body thrown to the dogs. But even the vicious dogs refused to devour him. And so his remains lay about.

Yes, children, that was what happened.

IN A GENERATION or two, on a Sabbath evening, a grandmother will be sitting, and if we still croon "God of Abraham," or if we've forgotten it long since, she will recite the story of our people. And her amazed grandchildren, with their fingers in their mouths and pure tears in their eyes, will listen in hushed reverence for a Jewish congregation and recall those Jews with the rabbi at their head. And they will listen to their grandmother's story, and they will cherish those Jews even beyond the grave.

And that's the story that will some day be told. But meanwhile the legend is being woven.

H. LEIVICK (*1888–1962*)

H. Leivick (pseudonym for Leivick Halper) was best known for his vast array of poems and essays and for his wide repertoire of plays, especially his international hit The Golem *(1920). Although he never wrote any prose fiction, his oeuvre includes a number of verse narratives like the one I've chosen here—a rich genre in Yiddish literature.*

Born near Minsk, the radical youth was arrested and then sentenced to four years of hard labor and permanent exile in Siberia. After his release he managed to reach New York in 1913, where he published prolifically while supporting himself as a paper hanger. He died in 1962.

He, *in which Jesus appears amid the dreadful Jewish sufferings, was written—like so many other works by Leivick—in response to the horrible Russian pogroms both before, during, and after World War I. The Christological substance of this sketchy expressionistic tale is not so unusual among Yiddish authors who, in critically treating New Testament figures, emphasize their Jewishness, particularly their agony as Jews. A prime example is Sholem Asch's novel* The Nazarene.

He (*1918*)

He walks into my place, an unexpected guest,
Sits down and says:
"They've provided me with everything that's available—
But isn't dearth my true dream?
They've built temples for me—
But isn't the cellar my true home?
They've adorned my forehead with diamonds—
But aren't thorns my true reward?"

I reply:
"You didn't want them to provide you forever—

But still they've provided you with everything.
Cellar insects gorge themselves on your skin—
And still everyone has built temples for you.
The wreath of thorns is your true reward,
And yet your crown is studded with diamonds."

He keeps still for a while and then says:
"They've spread my fame among all nations,
They've sown my glory
Over all seas and all lands.
All armies pronounce my name with joy,
And everyone kneels before me and kisses the hem of my robe."

I reply:
"They've spread your fame among all nations—
That's fine, let it be.
They've sown your glory
Over all seas and all lands—
That's fine, let it be."

He keeps still for a while and then he says:
"The whites of my eyes are bloodshot
From lack of sleep—I don't know since when.
What happened to me long, so long ago
Might not perhaps have happened otherwise.
There's only one thing that I want—to taste the taste of sleep,
The taste of sleep and nothing more.
I seek a threshold as my pillow,
A solid threshold, nothing more."

Now a hysterical grin flits over his lips,
A crippled hope is kindled in his eyes.
His fingers with their long, sharp nails
Start silently convulsing.
He pulls himself together, pulls his fingers together,
Cranes his drawn-in neck,
And I hear him gurgling down,
his gullet choking.

. . .   .

I think to myself:
"What does he want of me—
This epileptic?"

He keeps still for a while and then says:
"My Father—God in Heaven—is still my Father,
And my mother still denies her motherhood
And claims even today that she's a virgin.
You've no idea how sickening my memory of her:
When I was dying of my tortures,
She kissed me with her hot and lustful lips,
As if she'd been my bride and not my mother.
That single memory—that's all, that's all that I remember.
The touch of her lips bewildered, darkened everything,
Tore everything out from my memory.
Just tell me: how can I forgive her for my sorrow,
For not remembering anything but her lips?
And every day since then
I've shunned her threshold and I've begged her:
'Go and confess in all the streets, just tell about
All the nine months of heavy pregnancy,
All the distress and agony of birth,
Remind me of my first shrieks and first nursing,
And how you reared and nurtured me.
Tell the whole truth!' Do you know what she answers?
She answers nothing. She sits there, wrapped in black,
Her hands crossed on her bosom,
Her eyes raised upward piously,
She smiles her calm Madonna smile.
And if she does stir from her place
And turns her eyes upon me—
Do you know what she does? She kneels
And bows, she bows to each of my legs in turn,
And clasps my shoes and kisses them
And whispers feverishly: 'My Lord, my Lord, my Lord.'
You can't know how much lust screams from her whisper!
With all my strength I stifle all my hatred,

Prevent my foot from rising up, my shoe
From smashing that Madonna head on the floor!
And yet she is my mother—don't you know?
And yet I am a son, her son, and not a Lord.
I leave her and I flee,
And the next day, I come again,
And every day the same!"

I keep still for a while and then say:
"Tomorrow you'll be back.
And every day the same—
It will go on forever."

He replies:
"It can't go on forever,
For often things get worse:
When she, all shuddering with lust,
Kneels at my feet,
A whirlwind sweeps inside me,
As if someone had hurled some red-hot lead
Into the blood of my limbs.
The whirlwind rises to my throat,
And if I cannot swallow it right away,
As I've just done (you noticed it),
Then my entire body leaps aloft,
It leaps and then it promptly falls.
I can't escape. The hot whirlwind
Has swept up through my throat,
Seizing my tongue, my teeth, and suddenly
Exploding in a white and sticky foam,
Boiling upon my lips.
I'm flung upon the ground, I lie with eyes turned in,
And everything keeps growing darker, darker, darker.
And when I open up my eyes again, I see
(Oh, Father, Father, God in Heaven,
My eyes are all-seeing,
My ears are all-hearing,
Oh, Father, Father, God in Heaven),

I see myself upon the floor, on cushions
With silk and gold and silver embroideries,
Myself inside a ring of giant candelabras
With blazing candles sputtering tallow,
And over all the candles incense fumes
In curling, swirling, wafting cloudlets.
At first I can see nothing through the smoke.
Then suddenly a whitish female body
Emerges from all kinds of thin and colored veils,
Her hair all tossed over her shoulders,
Her eyes wide, glowing, feverish,
Her lips wide-open, drunken, but not sated.
She holds a beaker filled with wine,
A symbol of the Redeemer's spilled blood.
I lie there, gaping, curious and amazed.
And now she lifts the beaker to her lips,
And, gulp after gulp in thirsty ecstasy,
She drains the beaker to the dregs.
And then she stretches out her hand—
Do you know what she does?—
She dances, dances, dances,
Her pious eyes so eagerly peering at the incense.
The thin veils, just like airy feathers,
They spread and float apart and fully expose
Her nakedness, and then close up again.
And then the dance turns noisier and noisier
Around the ring of candles, around my body.
She drops upon the floor, gets up again,
Her hands are clasped around her neck,
Her hair and veils waft up, waft up,
It seems as if within another moment
Her hot breath will blaze up and seize her head, her hair,
And curl into the curls and swirls of incense.
Now all the veils drop from her body,
And she, all naked, naked, naked,
Grows dizzier, and more absorbed in dancing,
Her lips keep singing, stammering, murmuring:
"My Lord, my Lord, my Lord!"

(Oh, Father, Father, God in Heaven,
The white flesh is no longer white,
The slender neck's no longer slender,
The hot mouth is no longer hot,
The red wine is no longer red.
Oh, Father, Father, God in Heaven.)

I utter just one word:
"Bizarre!"

He interrupts and says:
"Words are no longer words.
In the beginning, the very beginning, was the word.
But now the word no longer is the word —
It's just a shard
That's placed upon a corpse's eye.
And who is as haunted as I
By the reek of a corpse?
And imagine if I don't run to you,
How would the night come to an end tonight?
Just look, there is a hammer in my bosom,
And if the hammer is too light,
I have a knife, just look.
You've no idea how I've been lured these years
By painful thoughts of matricide.
I've often stretched my hands out,
Ready to slash her naked white Madonna throat
In one swoop.
You just don't know, alas, you just don't know
What it means
To be the God of human beings,
To be the joy of kneeling, praying worshipers,
To be conveyed aloft, over everyone else,
Yet feel alone and miserable,
Incapable of carrying out, of satisfying
The painful thought of matricide.
And yet a day like that must come,
It has to come — the end must come."

. . .   .

I hold my tongue, I only think:
"The man conveyed aloft, over everyone else, the son of God,
Carries around a hammer and a knife
And nurtures murderous thoughts
Deep in his heart."

For the first time, he laughs, then says:
"I do repeat:
You've never been a God of human beings,
You've never been Jesus,
You've never hung on any cross.
No hands have ever been drawn to you,
And no one but myself, it seems, has ever pounded
His forehead on your threshold,
You've never smelled the smell of blood,
You've never tasted blood,
You've never walked across uncovered bodies
Or touched craned necks.
I seem to be the very first person
To come and pound his forehead on your threshold,
And the first person to expose before your eyes
A blood-stained knife,
The bits of marrow from a battered head,
Still dangling from my hammer.
The world is gorged now with pogroms,
With slaughter, with a death commandment—
Why should I be an exception?
Why shouldn't I fulfill the death commandment
Like everybody else?
(Oh, Father, Father—God in Heaven,
I haven't washed the knife as yet,
I haven't cleansed the hammer as yet.
The corpse has not cooled off as yet.
Oh, Father, Father—God in Heaven!)
Why do you jump, why do you shake, why do you run?
Why do you gape at me like that?
A man reserved, restrained like you,

With such a sharp and lucid mind —
And all at once you're terrified?
Throttle your voice, be stiller, stiller, stiller.
Why do you fill your throat with your fingers?
My knife is sharpened just for my near and dear,
And you — what are you? Just a stranger.
Don't you surmise that when I utter 'knife,'
The throat's been slashed long since,
And when I utter 'hammer,'
The marrow's been crushed out long since.
And when I say: 'The word's a word no more' —
That means the end has come, the end has come."

LEON KOBRIN *(1873–1946)*

*K*obrin was born in the Russian town of Vitebsk, the birthplace of S.
Ansky and Marc Chagall. Educated in Russian, Kobrin had scant knowledge of Yiddish and its literature. But after immigrating to the United States
in the early 1890s, he learned Yiddish and began writing for Yiddish newspapers. Strongly influenced by Russian and French authors, he wrote daring, realistic tales and dramas. Supposedly, Kobrin was the first Yiddish
writer to deal with carnal themes and one of the earliest to depict the hardships of Jewish life on New York's Lower East Side. He was known primar-
ily for his roughly fifty plays, which used to be highly popular but are now
largely forgotten. The story that I've included here comes from his collection The Tenement (1918). It was written in Brooklyn in 1914.

Apartment No. Four *(1914; publ. 1918)*

A BIT LATER, she hurried out of the front room, her thick, black hair
lying tangled and disheveled down her shoulders. Her face was burning,
and her eyes had the mute, frozen sorrow of a wounded animal. Her
entire body was shaking. Her jacket was violently ripped in several places.

The right sleeve was almost totally yanked off, and the exposed white skin showed the fresh, red marks left by squeezing fingers. It was obvious that she had been in a desperate struggle. . . .

Mabel, who was lying on the sofa with a cigarette between her lips, said, "Mazeltov," and upon seeing what she, Mrs. Drabkin, looked like, Mabel exclaimed, "Aha!" and burst out laughing.

Mrs. Gutman likewise peered at Mrs. Drabkin with laughing eyes and murmured, "My, oh my!" Grabbing a chair, she blocked Mrs. Drabkin's way and cried out: "You did yourself proud. Have a seat! Rest a little!"

Mrs. Drabkin couldn't feel her own despair as she pushed Mrs. Gutman and her chair away, dashed over to the door, and grabbed the knob.

But the door was locked. Mrs. Drabkin rattled and rattled it, harder and more desperately, but she failed to notice that the key was in the keyhole—all she had to do was turn it. In her confusion she forgot that she could also get out through the kitchen.

She wanted to shout, "Let me out of here!", but her voice was choking on tears. She covered her burning face with her hands, her body bent way over, and her shoulders trembled.

"She's ashamed, my, oh my!" Mrs. Gutman exclaimed with her naive and motherly smile. "Putting on airs, poor thing! She'll get used to it eventually, with God's help."

Mabel laughed even louder. "I'll lay odds on it!" she cried, rolling off the sofa.

Benny strutted in, looking like a victorious hero come home from war. Mabel threw her arms around him, burying her face in his shoulder, laughing and almost dancing.

Feeling Benny behind her, Mrs. Drabkin desperately rattled the door again, and when her hand bumped into the key, it dawned on her that it was there. She jerked it, opened the door so quickly that the key clattered to the floor, and she rushed out.

Behind Apartment No. Four they heard a baby crying. Mrs. Drabkin squirmed: "Oh, my baby!" Clutching her head with both hands, she ran into the apartment.

IN THE SEMIDARKNESS of the next room, her baby, a blond, curly-haired girl, was sitting in a cradle between a bed and a bureau. The baby was holding both her little fists to her nose and wailing pitifully.

Mrs. Drabkin picked up the baby and talked without hearing what she was saying: "This is so awful! This is horrible! My darling! My dearest! Your mama feels so awful! Your mama feels so terrible!" Repeating those words more desperately, she now could hear her own laments: "Damn it! What's happened to me? What filth! Someone's cast a spell over me! Damn it! Damn it! Damn it!"

She ran from room to room, from the bedroom to the dining room, from there to the kitchen, and then back to the bedroom, and though her hungry baby was wailing in her arms, all that the mother heard was the desperate shrieks of her own heart and soul.

But eventually she realized that the baby was crying, that she was hungry. The mother mechanically undid her jacket, which was now missing a few buttons, and she began suckling the baby. All at once she noticed a red mark left by those fingers; she shuddered as if she'd seen the mark of Cain, and she covered it with her jacket.

Her innate modesty and piety, which had been fighting with that awakened passion and which were now extraordinarily acute, prevented her from slipping her breast into the mouth of her pure and innocent baby.

She carried the bawling child into the kitchen. There was a saucepan of milk in the icebox. She took out the saucepan and placed it on the burning stove. The stove also held a big cauldron filled with laundry, which she did every Monday. The kitchen was piled high with soapy, steamy wash.

The baby was still bawling. She started calming her down, mechanically rocking her in her arms, crooning, her voice now full of tears.

When the milk in the saucepan was warm, the mother poured it into a bottle and gave it to the child. With a deep sigh the child grabbed hold of the bottle.

Next, with the child in her arms, the mother sat down on a chair in a corner of the dining room and, urgently needing to pour out her despair to a living soul, she started talking to the baby, who pushed the bottle into her little mouth.

"My darling baby . . . something awful has happened to me—I wish the earth would swallow me up! . . . If your pious granny—bless her— knew about it, if your pious grandpa—bless him—knew about it—God help us!—they'd sentence me to death! I'd sentence me to death myself! A pious woman! A pious daughter! From such a pious family! And now look at me! I deserve to be punished, I deserve it! I shouldn't have played with fire! I shouldn't have gone to where I musn't go! I shouldn't have touched their filthy cash! I should've said right away, I should have said."

She broke off; she suddenly remembered the five dollars she'd gotten from Mrs. Gutman, the "filthy cash"—and she fiercely tore the money out of her pocket and wanted to rip it up. But then her tortured eyes halted on an alms box attached to a doorjamb across the hall. She slowly got to her feet, put the child in the cradle, and moved toward the alms box. Raising both arms toward the ceiling, she peered upward with ecstatic eyes, and whispered:

"Lord of the Universe, you know my heart, you can see into it! I'm guilty, of course I'm guilty! I should've run away from them—oh, God!—but I didn't run away! My thoughts were sinful, the pain is so horrible—I'm a married woman! But God, this isn't what I wanted! She pounced on me like a killer! I didn't have the strength to put up a fight!"

She burst into agonized tears.

"Oh, God, I can't anymore! Is that how I'm supposed to rear my baby? I don't want to enjoy the five dollars—let decent Jews enjoy the money for your name's sake! Those five dollars will turn out badly for me! Forgive me, God, forgive me!" Bursting into a passionate lament, she stuffed the five-dollar bill into the alms box.

A BIT LATER she changed into a different jacket and sat down on the bed, near the cradle, in the semidarkness of the bedroom. Her mood had abruptly shifted from frenzy to powerless confusion. She sat there like a corpse, with bewildered eyes, and trembled from time to time.

In her thoughts she had unwillingly rehashed the struggle, the helplessness, the terror, the turmoil she had suffered behind Apartment No. Three. It was as if she could still feel his strong arms around her body, his hot breath on her face, as if she could still see his fiery eyes before her, still hear his wild words—and she felt so defenseless, so defenseless.

"Oh, God, oh God! How awful! How awful!" she moaned.

She sensed that if he now came to her again, she would have even less strength to keep him at bay.

She was going crazy, she was losing her mind, she wanted to kill herself, she wanted to jump out the window like that redheaded neighbor. Oh, God! How could she still be thinking about him now that she'd sworn an oath to her baby, now that she'd repented?

Oh, God! They'd bewitched her, mesmerized her, cast an evil spell on her! They'd slaughtered her, slaughtered her without a knife!

And she tried to mentally summon all the ugly men, the old ones, the crippled ones she'd seen—she wanted to frighten herself. But he kept replacing them in her mind—*he*, Benny, with his young, slender body. He was the only one she saw, the only one she could see!

Oh, God! If only her husband had been different! He would've cracked her head open, he would have butchered her—for his own sake, for his baby and for her!

She threw herself across the bed and dug her face into the pillows.

THE HUGE TENEMENT was now silent, as only a tenement can be silent. Here and there a door was slammed. Someone was climbing the stairs, someone was leaving the stairs. But the normal ruckus, the normal racket had stopped.

Suddenly a gramophone started playing on the fifth floor: a cantor and his choristers crooning "Kol Nidre," the prayer recited on the eve of Yom Kippur, the Day of Atonement. And their voices wafted down, poured down from the sky, holy and heartfelt and celestial.

Mrs. Drabkin tossed about and then sat up in her bed. She listened to the prayer. And the familiar melody painfully conjured up her old home, her native shtetl, with an earnest, fearful Yom Kippur mood, and all the familiar figures rose up in front of her, the pious Jews in white smocks, and her father in white and her mother in white, and the men were all standing in the synagogue among the burning Yom Kippur candles, swaying to the rhythm of the prayer, weeping, beating their breasts, while the familiar melody chanted by the cantor and his choristers wafted over them.

And now it suddenly dawned on her that Rosh Hashanah, New Year's, was only a month away.

"Oh, God, save me!" she whispered, beating her breast and curling up, and the solemn melody of "Kol Nidre" was still pouring down.

Beyond the door a white petticoat was hanging in the semidark room, and suddenly it didn't look like a petticoat, it was as if Mrs. Drabkin's mother were standing there in a white winding sheet, gaping at her with dreadful eyes and whispering to her, whispering. Mrs. Drabkin shuddered and turned her head. But the whispering remained. She heard it clearly, it came from beyond the door, from the other room or from the kitchen or even from under the bed. She started shaking with both cold and heat.

The gramophone stopped, but the whispering was still audible. She felt as if someone were whispering her name.

Trembling, she got out of bed, shuffled over to the petticoat, and tore it down. But the whispering didn't stop.

Suddenly Mrs. Drabkin saw Benny in the next room: he was whispering to her, asking if she was alone, calling to her. Terror-stricken she cried out and hugged the wall while gaping at him. He dragged her out of the bedroom, smiled at her, and said: "C'mon, I wanna show you the dress I brought you! C'mon you know I love you so much, darling, and soon your monkey'll be back from his peddling. C'mon, darling!"

And he grabbed her in his strong arms.

She struggled, biting his hand and emitting wild sounds like a wounded animal. He shrieked, gave up, and lifted his hand over her as if to hit her. But then he released her and burst out laughing. She dashed into the kitchen, he ran after her.

"Whatta ya runnin' away for? I kin catch you!" he said. "And this is how I am! If you've kissed me once, then you'll kiss me a third time, and a hundredth time!"

"It's a lie!" she yelled. "I never kissed you, you rat!"

She moved closer to the stove, and he rushed toward her.

"I'm gonna jump out the window!" she cried.

"So what!" he retorted.

"I'll kill myself!"

"So what!"

"I'll scream for help and tell everyone what you are!"

"So what!"

"You rat! Get outa here!"

"So what!"

And he pulled her over.

And suddenly, she somehow found the strength: she shoved him away so violently that his head practically smashed into the wall. And before he could come to, she picked up the huge cauldron of laundry and poured the boiling water over him. He screamed horribly and fell to the floor, twisting and writhing like a snake. She started yelling too, and the baby in the cradle woke up and also started wailing.

And all the noise was wrapped in steam, like in a bathhouse.

Men, women, and children instantly came running in. Some were neighbors and some came from the street. And Mrs. Gutman and Mabel also rushed in.

"Benny!" shrieked Mrs. Gutman.

Mabel started crying loudly and ran back out.

"Call an ambulance! Call a cop!" someone shouted.

Several people hurried out.

All at once, Mrs. Drabkin's desperate, almost hysterical yammering could be heard amid the bedlam:

"Jews! Jewish women! Listen. Mrs. Gutman—damn her! She's . . . she's—damn her! She . . . runs a brothel in this building. She leads girls astray. She makes decent Jewish girls miserable. That rat kicking the bucket over there was her partner! It's because of him that redheaded Brokhe jumped out the window. He destroyed her. He pounced on me. I begged him to stop. 'Leave me alone!'—until I dumped the cauldron of boiling water on him!"

She couldn't go on, she was out of breath. She broke into a savage, wordless howling like a fatally wounded animal.

The onlookers almost rioted. A confused Mrs. Gutman hurried away from the door.

A policeman showed up, then an ambulance.

A while later, they carried Benny out on a stretcher—or rather, they carried out a heap of feebly moaning cotton. The heap of cotton was thrust into the ambulance. The street in front of the building was mobbed. Two detectives led Mrs. Gutman and Mabel out from Apartment No. Three. The crowd, who knew everything by now, booed and hissed them. Then Mrs. Drabkin, accompanied by a policeman and by a neighbor carrying her child, emerged from Apartment No. Four.

They were gone. The street was still yelling and shrieking.

SARAH SMITH (1888–?)

At fifteen, after growing up in an Orthodox Jewish home in Budapest, Sarah Bronshteyn moved to the United States with her parents. In 1908, while working in a sweatshop, she began publishing stories in the

Forward *and eventually became a journalist for several Yiddish organs.
Under a pseudonym, she produced reportage as well as realistic short stories and novels serialized in newspapers. One of the earliest female
authors in modern Yiddish literature, Smith described the dreadful conditions of both Jewish and Gentile immigrant life in New York. Her
depiction of a mad housewife in her novel* The Woman in Chains *actually harks back to the Haskala, which focused heavily on the Jewish
treatment of women, especially amid poverty and spiritual deprivation.
One pungent example is Y. L. Peretz's tale, "A Woman's Fury."*
However, the family that Smith describes in her novel is completely
devoid of Jewish religion and Jewish, particularly Yiddish, culture; their
very names, like the author's family name, are non-Jewish. As a result,
Smith creates a more "universal" secular world that might be real for all
assimilating immigrants.*

The Woman in Chains *(1919)*

Chapters 1–2

Chapter 1
The First Bell

SHE HASTILY PUT down the little baby. With one hand she tenderly
tucked her in, while her other hand clutched the thick envelope that the
mailman had just given her.

When her four-year-old boy grabbed at the envelope, she held it higher.
Whereupon he burst into tears. "Gimme, gimme the stamps!" he
whined.

Frieda Gilbert's hands shook violently, and her heart pounded. Her
face turned pale with intense curiosity, which she tried to control. With
a mother's patience, she carefully tore off the stamps and handed them
to her boy. At last he was satisfied.

And now she quickly ripped open the thick package. The densely written pages released a sheet of gray paper:

*See my collection, *The Shtetl* (Woodstock, NY: Overlook Press, 1989).

My dear Frieda Sherman-Gilbert,

It took me quite a while to recall who Frieda Gilbert was. You see? I still remember you as the very charming Miss Sherman.

But once I remembered, I promptly read your manuscript. This time I was not neglectful. I did not shove it into some desk drawer as I do other submissions, which have to wait several months before I respond (I am ashamed).

I am very sorry, but I am forced to return your story. The idea and the material are very, very good, but the story lacks life! It lacks a real moving and stirring life.

And I do not understand, my very dear Frieda. What have you been doing these past five years since we last met? You, who had such a sharp mind, such a clear view of life, you, who could speak so interestingly—you have written something that is full of lifeless people, who put us to sleep.

Listen, my dear, I am deeply disappointed. In those years when I often conversed with you, I was certain that some day, with your clear view of life, you would write something really good. But where is that clear view today? Has the great happiness of your married life destroyed your sharp view?

I know nothing about you now, but if you have time, and you are not lazy, rewrite the story, do so a few times. And I am certain that your past sharpness of mind is bound to reveal itself.

But if you are in terrible need of money, send the manuscript back to me, and I will revise the story and have my journal buy it from you for a decent fee.

Do not hold back, write me a detailed letter about yourself and your current life.

Your old friend,
Harald L. Wellman

Frieda gazed soberly at the thick packet of densely written pages, which she had taken out of the envelope. Her lips whispered: "I knew it."

And rereading the letter, she laughed tersely and bitterly—for instance, when he wrote: "What have you been doing these past five years since we last met?"

"God Almighty, what have I been doing?" Frieda thought to herself so caustically. "I've cooked breakfast, lunch, and supper, done the dishes, darned socks, washed diapers, sewn dresses, bathed the children, nursed them through serious illnesses, cleaned the apartment, rarely satisfied a husband who's full of himself, controlled my nerves until they hardened into steel, until I forgot everything! Oh, my dear friend! If I described everything I've done in these past five years, then you'd truly see life, moving life, life as it really is!"

The baby on the couch burst into choking sobs, and when the terrified mother dashed over, she found that the baby had stuffed a good piece of blanket into her mouth.

Frieda calmed the little girl, glanced at her son playing with the stamps, again picked up the gray letter and lapsed back into her thoughts.

Reluctantly she compared what the past five years had done for her with what they had done for friends and acquaintances.

For example: her old friend Wellman. When Frieda had been the secretary of N. the editor, Wellman had been a very neglected, misunderstood writer. He'd been derided for his bizarre ideas, his threadbare clothes, and his stories. Frieda had greatly respected him and pitied him, and a warm friendship had developed between the older man and the young girl. Later on, Wellman had written an important work that had been enthusiastically received by a publisher. Wellman had gained renown and was now editor in chief of a very fine journal.

What about others?

Helen Relnik, once Frieda's best friend, was now a very popular author. As for the artist M., everyone had laughed at him, and Frieda had lent him a dollar every week until payday, sometimes buying him a coffee and feeling very sorry for him. But now his drawings appeared in the finest magazines!

And other and still other successful friends floated in front of Frieda's eyes. They appeared to be teasing her: "What've you accomplished? What, you smart girl?"

And Frieda was terrified. She was unfamiliar with those rebellious emotions, which she had suppressed for such a long, long time. She seemed to hear a bell summoning her, and she trembled.

Chapter 2
The Truth and the Mask

LATE THAT NIGHT, after getting back her manuscript, Frieda, lost in thought, still sat at the kitchen table, propping her head on her arms.

She was exhausted, she felt as if she could still hear the pitiful weeping of her baby girl, who, cranky all that day, was now teething. Both children and her husband were asleep, and she could hear his heavy breathing all the way into the kitchen.

A freshly written letter, its ink still wet, lay on the clean tablecloth. And Frieda gazed at the letter with cold, probing eyes. Indeed, her whole mood was cold and probing. During the past few years of hard labor—the same labor, day in, day out—Frieda had learned to forget about her "nerves," forget about her moods. She had learned how to be as precise as a clock and always on the job.

And the naked truth was described in the letter that lay in front of her:

Dear, Honored Friend,

Would you like to know why my story lacks life? Let me tell you why. You see, I too lack life, my golden expectations of married life have not come true, and everything that used to live in me is now dead. If hard labor and a great, great deal of trouble constitute life, then I have lived. But such themes do not make for a good story, and something that is unpleasant to read would not hold my readers' interest.

And as it seems, I am now incapable of writing about anything else—for instance, love. After five years of marriage, love is so alien to me that I often feel it is purely an illusion in the minds of daydreaming girls.

Please forgive me, but I clearly remember your sympathy with the oppressed, and that is why I will be very open with you and also talk about very commonplace things.

You would like to know what I've been doing these past five years, then listen:

I've done nothing that distinguishes me from an average woman. I married, I got a bit lost in the first flame of passion, what we normally call love, and my son was born within a very short time.

I cannot say that those times included many happy hours, and they were hours at the most. I lived in a three-room tenement apartment, and I myself made the fire in the stove, my white hands with their manicured nails got smeared with coal and ashes, I often got sick, and I did all the washing, ironing, cleaning, and cooking.

But I was hopeful that when the baby grew a bit older, I would leave him with my mother and develop myself, prepare myself for the career that my heart had always yearned for—and at that time my husband was my best friend, my dearest comrade. We dreamed together and planned together.

But then everything changed. For example:

Now I no longer live in a tenement where my hands get smeared with coal and ashes. No. Now I live in an "apartment building," where everything is silly finery and falsehood on the outside, but on the inside we freeze next to the cold steam pipes. Most of the wives buy their husbands' dinners at the delicatessen store, they smear their cheeks with false colors, tell a pack of lies, and are very often worshiped by their husbands. As for me, I cook good food every day, and all I get for it is an occasional muttering from my husband but seldom a nice, friendly word.

He too has changed just like our apartment. Now he's a businessman with very great responsibilities. I and the two children are a heavy burden on him, and if something goes wrong in his business, I nearly always have to pay the price. I work very hard, the children are seldom healthy, doctors cost a fortune, and this, naturally, angers my husband. I've got no money, just what he gives me, and he gives me little since business is bad. I try not to think, because I'm terrified of my own thoughts. And on some evenings, when I'm exhausted from washing diapers and I can't straighten my back, and at such a time, when I recall what I wanted to be and what I've become, I feel like — I feel like . . .

And it was at such a desperate moment that I wrote that story. My purpose was to make a little money — I so much want to have my own money, several dollars a month to do as I like! Do you understand, dear friend? If you do, then help me. I am sending you my story again.

Best wishes,
Frieda Gilbert

She reread the text a fourth time, burst into bitter laughter, slowly and grimly ripped up the letter, and wearily folded her hands in her lap.

Somewhere faraway a clock struck two. This awoke her to reality. Before she had time to sleep on one side, the child would ask for food, crying with those sick sobs, which Frieda was still unable to get used to.

Swiftly and businesslike, she resumed writing:

Dear, Honored Friend,

I deeply apologize for burdening you with my foolish story. I wrote it under the spell of an inspired moment, when I wanted to be a writer instead of a happy wife and mother.

I assure you that I am very happy and I thank you greatly for your interest.

Frieda Gilbert

And she mailed the second letter.

SHOLEM ASCH (*1880–1957*)

Sholem Asch became world-famous for his enormous output of plays, stories, and mammoth novels—often shallow, yet thrilling, exciting, absorbing blockbusters that depicted the panorama of Jewish life as if it were a department store for shopperholics. As exemplified in the story below, he dealt with taboo themes, such as raw sex, lesbianism, Christianity. Indeed, in 1923, the Broadway premiere of Asch's infamous play God of Vengeance, *about a Jewish brothel like the one in this story, was raided by the New York City Police.*

Asch, who was born and bred in Poland, moved to New York in 1914. There he wrote about the Old World and the New. In 1955 he settled in Israel, where he died two years later.

The Story of Beautiful Marie (*1921*)

THE GIRLS WERE still walking about, hoping for "guests." It was already late at night. The shops were long since closed, not even a shadow appeared outdoors. But the girls still didn't go to bed, they had slept all day. And now footsteps from another street resounded in the dead of night. Near the monument with the merman—an eternal reminder that someone had been saved here—a shadow flitted out: maybe a john was coming? But the steps were in unison, and the shadow of the sleeping merman didn't stir from its place. . . .

It was a lovely Sabbath night around Passover, the spring air was young and fresh and bracing. The sky was so deep blue and starry that strolling was a real treat. Everything was fragrant, and the girls felt newly born. One girl was whistling, another was singing and winking coquettishly as if a crowd of boys were standing in front of her. The night, as if holding its breath, was so still that the singing echoed through the distant streets and over the rooftops. The high and narrow houses in Warsaw's Old City stood there in silence. The upper stories were concealed in black patches of night, and the fragments of gray doors, illuminated by the lonesome street lights, were even more deeply hushed and mysterious. . . .

A soft, light drizzle began, a spring drizzle, each drop seeking an open mouth in the earth, making it happy, while the drops falling on stones and brick buildings spread their freshness, their summery balm through the air. The sprinkling made the little street cozy and delightful. The girls took shelter under the eaves, singing and talking and cursing at each other. Soon one girl stepped out into the rain. "I'll grow some more," she said. Then her friends joined her. The second girl, recalling what she'd done during such rain in her shtetl, pulled off her spats, shoes, and stockings and jumped around in the puddles. The other girls followed suit. They undid their wet hair and chased one another through the drizzle. And, forgetting where they were and what they were, they acted like children—playing, laughing, singing, whistling, splashing water at one another. But then suddenly they heard the nightwatchman rattling his stick. Their boss, the owner of the "house," was afraid they'd break loose, so he called them "home."

The girls noisily flocked indoors. One of them went over to her john, grabbed him by the hair, and pulled him off the couch: "Wanna marry me?"

"Shove it!"

The second girl went over to her john and patted him on the back: "What a guy! What a guy!"

The room was dark and sad. Young men lay on the beds, rolling cigarettes and trading loud obscenities. Only a flimsy partition stood between each cubicle and the big main room, and sometimes they'd hear the voice of an unseen person who was probably busy with something else in one of those many alcoves. However, the instant the gang of girls stormed into the room, the talking broke off. They threw themselves into the arms of their kept fiancés, whom they supported because these young men had promised to marry them. The girls put their hands over the mouths of their husbands-to-be. The atmosphere turned cheery. The guy who was with the girl from Vlotslavka set out some beer. There was also the "wild guy": he'd burst in, choose a hooker, fork over his ruble—and do nothing . . . They didn't know who he was—maybe a crazy Litvak wearing spectacles. And his clothes were absolutely pathetic. He would come at night, sit down, and ask them stupid questions. Sometimes he'd kiss and caress a girl for all he was worth, hiding his face and asking the girl to close her eyes like a chaste bride . . . And sometimes he wouldn't even do that.

Tonight the "crazy Litvak" had brought along a book of stories. They figured the book was about Beautiful Marie, and they were so thrilled that they gathered around him to hear him read! But he launched into a story about a hooker who was in a hospital and subsequently went insane and roamed the streets. The listeners were bored with the story. The fat redhead, whose father, a butcher in Koshevnits, was searching for her, soon dozed off as if she'd been listening to a Talmudic debate. So Khanele went over to the Litvak, snatched his book, bopped him on the nose, and took him in her arms: "C'mon, dance with me!"

The boss came in from the other room and asked the "fiancés" to go home, it was getting late. The boys left. The "crazy Litvak" begged the boss to let him stay, he didn't want to go home, his place was bleak and empty, and he was scared of his four blank walls. But the boss wouldn't hear of it. The johns were now all gone. The girls stretched out on the sofas and waited eagerly for Golde, the boss's daughter, to come and read them the story of Beautiful Marie.

The boss, who long ago had been one of the "fiancés," had married a hooker and opened up his own house. The couple led a very respectable life together: he had become a solid citizen—even sponsored a Torah scroll at the synagogue where he prayed; and his wife could always be counted on for a donation. They had a daughter named Golde, who had grown up in the house. They guarded her like a precious stone to make sure she remained "pure." But they had no cause for concern. The filth she was constantly surrounded by didn't have the slightest impact on her. She had grown accustomed to this life as a child and she saw it not as iniquity but as a livelihood . . . Anyone who needed it could have it. She got her three square meals a day with her parents—and the life below did not offend her. It was only when her father had ordered her to remain in their private apartment and not go downstairs that she had felt drawn there, either because she missed some of the girls or because her curiosity was piqued by the thought of the forbidden.

Sometimes, when her father was fast asleep, she would steal down to the "house." The girls really loved her. They talked about matches that she had been offered, about her getting engaged and married. And they would look with great interest and pleasure whenever her full, girlish face blushed at the slightest movement in an "occupied" cubicle.

The girl who waited most impatiently for her every night was Manke. And all the girls comforted themselves with the thought that nowadays even the respectable daughters were no better—the only difference being that the hookers sinned for their profession and the respectable daughters for their pleasure. And as soon as these hookers got husbands, they would become respectable once again, just like the boss's wife. They would run respectable households and have daughters who would blush at the slightest inducement, like Golde. However, they resented Golde's blushes and they wished with all their hearts that some guy would come along and get rid of her rosy cheeks. But Manke was different. Manke adored Golde precisely because of her freshness and girlishness, and she loved to hug her and snuggle against her full, rosy breasts.

Manke did not hope to get married. She was a hooker because that's the way she was. She had chosen the first man she had ever given herself to. He had promised her nothing. Nor had her mother been any better. Her mother had given birth to her in a hospital. Her legacy was reflected in Manke's face. She had a weak body and thin bones, but she was skillful, and everything about her hinted at hidden lust. A cunning lock of hair dangling down her forehead, a pair of high, colored stockings, a short underskirt and a reddish blouse cut in military fashion with a tassel . . . If she beckoned with her curl, then lust would dash into your very bones, your entire body would tremble—and you'd feel a need to wallow in mud because it was filthy . . .

Manke had two beds in her cubicle. She charged a ruble for doing it on one bed. That was her business, she had to pay the boss three rubles a day. The second bed was for her to sleep alone on. She wouldn't have serviced a john on this bed for even a hundred rubles. This was her home. Manke was still young enough to think about the future. She'd been here since the age of twelve. She was doing quite nicely, she had her lovely wardrobe, her basket of linen, and she went to the café every evening. Fat Itta, the butcher's daughter from Tempovke, would cry in her sleep and sometimes wake up like a lunatic because she had dreamed about her dead mother. She was cursed for the night. If she, Manke, had dreamed about her own mother, would she have wept? Quite the opposite: she would have wanted to see what her mother looked like.

Golde's face appeared in the window. She opened the window, and her wet hair billowed through. A soft breeze wafted through the house, and the girls woke up . . . In the silence a light hand tapped on the door.

Manke quietly went to the door and opened it with a pounding heart as if she were expecting her bridegroom. Golde came stealing in. She was wearing only a nightgown and was wrapped in a shawl. The fresh springtime fragrance spread by the rain lingered in her hair. Manke hugged her passionately and kissed her fresh lips. She led her to the couch, sat down next to her, and peered deep into her eyes. She showed Golde her own wet hair, told her about how she and the others had run through the rain. Then she cuddled with Golde and bared Golde's breasts—and kissed her, and had her snuggle against her own breasts . . . She kissed her full, cool hands, and her face nestled against Golde's full throat.

Manke wanted to take her into her cubicle so that they could spend the night together. But the other girls wouldn't hear of it. They settled around her. One girl loosened Golde's hair, a second girl kissed her bare neck and asked her to read them the story of Beautiful Marie—the part about the dark young man imprisoning her in his dungeon.

Golde knew how to read and she loved storybooks. And whenever she visited the girls, she had to read that same story to them—and each time they would settle around her calmly and listen impatiently, not as if they were hearing the story for the first time, but as if the heroine were a close relative of theirs. Golde had lost all interest in the story—she had been reading it to them for three years now. But the girls refused to listen to any other story. One of them had already brought over the lamp and the storybook, *The Secret Murderers*. They jostled one another, trying to get closer to Golde, and they lapsed into silence.

Golde began reading about the Dark Murderer, who was mortally in love with Beautiful Marie, "who had eyes like stars and a face like the moon." The Dark Murderer had kidnapped her the night before she was to wed her Robert, and the abductor had thrown her into his dungeon, and he had stood before her and poured out all his torrid love and tried to make her forget her Robert, who was now the Dark Murderer's prisoner, and Beautiful Marie only had to say a single word, "yes," and she would make the Dark Murderer happy and make herself happy and she would become the queen of the Secret Murderers. But Beautiful Marie refused to break her promise to take Robert's hand in marriage until death did they part. The Dark Murderer then saw that kindness would get him nowhere, so he whistled, and fifty of his bandits came running in "with black eyes in their foreheads" and "with sharpened spears in their hands."

"'Surrender!' he cried."

"Go to hell! Go to hell!" the highly agitated girls muttered in the silence.

The doors of the occupied cubicles opened, and girls dressed only in nightshirts left their sleeping johns, tiptoed over to Golde, and listened to her in the silence.

He ordered her to be stripped naked as God had created her and he ordered them to bring in Robert all tied up so that he might watch with his own eyes as her beauteous body was possessed by the Dark Murderer and then carved up into mincemeat.

Wretched Robert begged his bride not to let the murderer cut short her youth. And Beautiful Marie replied: "I will be true to our profound love as long as our stars shine in the heavens."

"Ah, Beautiful Marie," murmured the girls.

The Dark Murderer then ordered four servants to pull off her nightgown and to prepare the spears. But the instant her young body was exposed, the Dark Murderer was bedazzled by its glorious beauty.

"Halt!" he cried to the murderers with their spears. "Leave me alone with her!"

Within a minute, everyone else left the dungeon, and Beautiful Marie remained alone with the Dark Murderer.

Dropping to his knees in front of her, he cried:

"Beautiful Marie. Your beauteous body has ignited the flame of love in my heart, and your innocent young blood, which I will shed with my own hand, cannot extinguish the infernal fire of love that blazes in my heart. Only your lips and your gentle kisses can extinguish the flames. Look! I am the king of the Dark Murderers, my hands can break iron—and only a woman's love is stronger than iron. My hands shed the blood of men and steal their wealth—but they cannot steal a woman's love . . . Beautiful Marie! Like a powerless child, I, the king of the Dark Murderers, lie at your feet and beg you for mercy! I will lie at your feet like a dog! I will pamper you and spoil you!"

"You dirty bastard! Go to hell!" the girls muttered.

To which Beautiful Marie replied:
"King of the Dark Bandits! I am in your hands. Do with me as you will. But do not ask me to be dishonorable. I gave my promise to my dearly beloved Robert, and I must remain his until death do us part. . . ."

"That's tellin' 'im!" muttered the girls.

The Dark Murderer then threw himself upon her beauteous body. Beautiful Marie screamed, "Help!" But her shouts were lost in the wild forest. She tried biting the ropes binding her hands. But her efforts were futile! The ropes were too strong for her delicate teeth.

The room was hushed. The girls held their breath, waiting for what came next.

She bit the murderer's finger, she sank her teeth into his heart. . . .

"That's tellin' 'im! That's tellin' 'im!" the girls shouted.

Soon the weak female body was lying like a bound sacrificial victim under the murderer's hands.

"Oh, God! Oh, God!" the girls wept loudly.

But then suddenly the door flew open, and constables with drawn swords came bursting in and grabbed the bandit.

"Aaaah!"
The room was still. Golde stopped reading and gazed at the closed door of the cubicle: What was going on there? . . . The girls chatted about the story. Manke walked stiffly back and forth across the room, showing

her colored stockings and her short underskirt, and she beckoned with her curl and kept talking to herself: "Guy! Guy! Guy!"

The boss's daughter sneaked behind the partition of a closed cubicle and peered through a crack.

Crimson spots blossomed on her cheeks, her bosom heaved, and her breath was so deep and warm that her hands trembled and moved.

Manke noticed it. She hurried over to her, sank her thin, dry lips into the daughter's cheeks, and sucked out her blood through her full mouth. . . .

Outside the window the opposite wall was starting to turn gray.

Y. Y. SINGER (1893–1943)

Y.Y. Singer (I. J. Singer in English) was the older brother of Isaac Bashevis Singer. He was born into a Hasidic home near Warsaw. Starting out as a painter, he eventually chose literature instead; and after writing plays and publishing stories in various journals and anthologies, he came out with a volume of stories in 1922: Pearls, *from which "Magda" is taken. Despite early successes, he stopped writing fiction in 1927, but returned to it in 1931 at Abraham Cahan's urging. In fact, Cahan serialized Singer's novel* Yoshe Kalb *in the* Forward. *Settling in the United States in 1933, Singer continued publishing stories, novels, and memoirs about Jewish life in both Europe and America. He died in 1943.*

Magda (1917; publ. 1922)

ONCE, WHEN WOJCIECH Pietrzak of Dombrowka had a severe coughing fit, he found traces of blood in his phlegm. But he didn't go to the doctor and he didn't go to the healer and his herbs.

"No wife, no son," he mused. "Let His heavenly will be done!"

He climbed up on the broad oven, dried some tobacco, smoked his pipe, and coughed. Meanwhile his only daughter, Magda, pulled on his boots and went out to the field, where she swung the masculine scythe,

pushed the plow, hitched the horse, and dickered with the Jewish peddlers. She also spun linen and cooked for herself, for her sick father, and
for the cattle and the poultry.

Magda was in her early twenties, she was strong, ruddy, hardened, with
broad shoulders. Starting in childhood, she had been forced to tend geese
and pigs, cows and horses. And she herself had to tongue-lash a boy who
had let his cattle into her fields. She herself had to haul up buckets of water
from the deep well and water all their livestock. And she often had to ride
home on the nag without a bridle, just clutching the thick mane. She had
never had any brothers to stick up for her and she grew up so strong, big,
and tough that the whole of Dombrowka was afraid of her. If ever Magda
grabbed a cow that was poaching in Wojciech's grain, nothing could move
her to release it until the owner paid a ransom of one ruble.

"No, no," the villagers would say, "Magda won't release it, she'll hold
on to the cow until it croaks—so you'll pay through the nose."

Magda was usually quiet, silent, obedient. Her father mistreated her,
perhaps because she never asked him for help, she always relied on herself. It wounded his self-esteem, and he thought to himself: "You can do
everything yourself, so try the impossible!"

Perhaps because she was so busy and never had time to join him in driving to town or to neighbors, she couldn't show people what a fine daughter he had.

He wanted to hear people say: "She talks with a squeal—Wojciech's
daughter. She says 'Papa' just like an aristocrat's daughter, and she's so
delicate that you have to help her into a wagon."

In any case, he mistreated her and, indifferent, he watched the girl,
who was occupied from the morning star to the evening star with men's
and women's chores.

And Magda had good reason to complain about her father. She saw
that whenever a farmer reached old age, his daughter's fiancé would be
brought to the farm. They would drive to the scribe in town and the property would be transferred to the bridegroom. Then they drove to church,
got married, and the couple would move up to the stove. The old farmer
might fix a yoke, patch a fur, unhitch the horse, while the young couple
came from the tavern on Sunday. Next they'd be rocking the old farmer's
grandchild. That was the way of the world. Magda knew it, but she never
spoke. She worked and ate. That was all.

Farmers would often come to her father: "Wojciech, you're sinning.

Boys in the village keep urging: 'Go to Wojciech with some liquor.' Wojciech, don't be so stubborn — the girl needs a boy. She needs her own potatoes, her own parlor. And the farm'll look different. The girl shouldn't work like a dog — it's pitiful!"

But Wojciech would bang his pipe on the oven and dig in his heels. "I don't want to, I'm sick, I'll be useless to them. They'll hang a beggar's bag on me and send me to church to go begging."

The father often ran out of tobacco. Magda would have to drop everything, mount Lolek, ride over to Leybush's store, buy a measure of dried tobacco, and bring it home. And sometimes Wojciech would recall the good old days, when his wife had been alive: he'd give her a good thrashing with some rope, and he now made Magda pay off her mother's debt.

Magda knew perfectly well that it was time she got beaten by a husband instead of her father. But she was a quiet, silent person, so she simply wept hard, as her mother had done; then, wiping her tears with a corner of her apron, she went off to the field. She cupped her eyes with her hand, gazed across the area, and shook her head.

"Everything perishes, Jesus, Mary, everything."

But more than anything, Magda's heart bled for Lolek — taken in hand by Wojciech. Lolek, who was one of his horses, was known far and wide in Dombrowka and miles around. Magda loved Lolek with all the love that nestled in her strong peasant heart, which had no one to share it with.

At the age of one, Lolek was the darling of all the jades and their owners. He was a shiny, velvety bay with a smooth, narrow, skin-colored blaze down his long, proud head. He was supple, slender, with a broad, strong neck and powerful hindquarters, which swayed flexibly on a pair of thin, nicely shaped legs. His eyes were smart and impudent, his ears stiff and belligerent, his nostrils wide and quivering, his mane thick, and he had snow white circles around his hooves. Thoroughly aware of his own beauty, haughty about his great successes with the mares in his surroundings, he was not content merely with digging holes in the ground and foaming at every minor thing. But he liked having fun — teasing a gelding or baring his white teeth and licking a person's ear or nose.

Magda saw her father sizing Lolek up as if planning to sell him. Hot blood filled her angry face, and it felt as if the skin were ready to burst, as if the blood would wash her face.

Many farmers dropped by and talked about Lolek: "Wojciech, you've got a horse that'll outdo all the aristocrats' horses in the area."

Wojciech would prick up his long, thin ears with their sharp edges, a sickly smile would stretch out his scraggy face, and he would mutter: "You can use him, neighbor. Just fork over a couple of rubles."

The farmers would answer: "We'll come to terms, Wojciech."

And Magda would go into the stable, wrap her linen-covered head in Lolek's mane, and rebel against her father: "Lolek's so young, so young, he's barely a year old, you mustn't, I don't want you to."

She dreamed that Lolek would grow big and strong like the count's horse, Kseni. And why not? After all, Kseni was Lolek's sire. Magda remembered it clearly. It had taken place two summers ago, on a Sunday. They hadn't yet sold Lolek's dam, and so Magda had chained her front legs and pastured her at the edge of a meadow bordering on the count's vast fields. The dam was a passable mare, but a peasant creature, small in stature, with a heavy gait, a short head, and a chestnut mane dangling over her eyes.

Magda just lay on the grass, unaware of anything—and all at once, the count's Kseni leaped over the fence and made a beeline for the shackled mare. The count's boys wanted to drive Kseni away, but he was neighing and kicking. The mare was frightened, barely able to stand on her shackled legs, and the boys yelled: "Hey, hey, Magda, hey, hey!"

Afterwards Magda led the mare home by her mane.

In the course of time, the mare grew fatter and lazier. She gave birth to a colt that was more beautiful than any horse in the count's stables.

"Yes, like Kseni," Magda would dream, watching him grow from day to day. "Maybe he'll even outgrow him."

She watched over him, spent nights in his stall, exercised him, took him everywhere with his dam: Let Lolek gain a little more weight, and then, when he'd get bigger and raise his tail upon hearing the distant neighing of a mare, Magda would dash after him, clutch his mane, and drag him away with all her strength so that he wouldn't start too early. The boys would laugh—split their sides laughing: "Hey, hey, Magda, hey, hey!"

But she paid them no heed. She figured she would keep him for two years and she didn't think about anything. But her father didn't have God in his heart and he offered Lolek to all the farmers: "Three rubles, neighbors."

The first time, she tried to stop him and, lowering her head, she murmured: "I don't want him to, Father, he's barely a year old."

But Wojciech angrily banged his pipe on the oven. "I'll show you what you want and don't want. I'm the boss here, I'm the boss—everything belongs to me so long as I can manage to breathe. I don't want to leave anything after I die, let the bastard die with me!"

Magda didn't say another word. She knew how obstinate he was. She knew he even refused to yield to the count. The count's administrator had visited them a number of times: "Wojciech, the whole town's laughing. Give the count Lolek and he'll give you a couple of acres on the edge—Wojciech, the count doesn't want a peasant to have Kseni's offspring. He'll grab him away from you."

But the old man dug in his heels. "We've constantly argued about property lines, the count refused to let me enter his estate. Tell him he's dealing with Wojciech Pietrzak."

She knew how pigheaded he was, and with a heavy heart she did anything he ordered her to do.

The farmers used to remember his comments and repeat them to one another, and the boys practically tore their arms out as they dragged their neighing mares to Wojciech's stable.

"Magda, get out there!" Wojciech would shout from the oven when he heard the neighing of a horse who'd seen Lolek's head through the stall bars. "Magda, get out there and don't charge less than three rubles!"

Magda lazily dragged her thick legs, jingled the keys, and listened to the wild neighing of Lolek and the writhing mare.

Magda jingled the keys and muttered: "Three rubles, not a kopek less."

And the boys stood on the other side of the fence, ogled from under their skewed visors, and yelled: "Hey, hey, Magda, hey, hey!"

Wojciech grabbed his heart more and more often, peered at his handkerchief, and banged his pipe on the oven. "Magda, I need tobacco! Magda, you're not feeding me! Magda, you're trying to poison me! Magda, get out to the stable and don't take less than three rubles!"

Wojciech was angry. He sensed the presence of death. He saw that everything around him was healthy, fresh, everything was normal, as it had been before he got sick, when he was everywhere, applying his brains and brawn everywhere. He couldn't stand being sick, he bit everyone's head off. He was especially furious at Lolek, and so he often told Magda to open the stable. Lolek didn't know Wojciech. Magda was his sole trainer. Sometimes Lolek tried to play with Wojciech's ear or tug at a curl on his sheepskin collar. Lolek would let Magda ride him or curry his belly or clean the bits of sticky fodder from his wild nostrils. And Wojciech would angrily bang his pipe, get furious at Magda and at the aristocrat's bastard. And grabbing his sick heart, he spit out blood and gall. "Cough! Cough! Cough! My own horse is driving me away! Cough! Cough! Cough! Magda's in charge. Magda."

She was busy all day long with male and female chores. Her father told her to cook different leaves in water. At the slightest rustle he thought someone was bringing a mare. And he never let Magda sit for even a moment: "Get out there, Magda, get out there!"

Then Gypsies moved into the village. Some of them passed their fence and, with their black eyeballs shining in their milky whites, they softly murmured to themselves. Magda didn't speak a word of the Gypsy language, but she did understand that the Gypsies might take a liking to Lolek and cut through the iron bars of the stall. So she spent every night in the stable.

During the day, she had no time to think. But at dusk, lying in the stable and smelling the fresh manure with a horse's healthy foam, she'd feel the blood rising within her and she'd dream about young, booted boys at the fair, boys with harmonicas under light-colored mustaches. And she'd conceal her linen-covered head in Lolek's black mane, throw both arms around his powerful, excited neck, and cover his skin-colored blaze with passionate kisses.

Lolek, happily enjoying Magda's tenderness, would stick out a supple tongue and lick her red hands. He'd peer into her eyes with his intelligent, impudent gaze, and his shiny, supple neck would sway like the neck of someone who knows his masculine value. Magda would slip her fingers into his thick mane, and Lolek would emit puffs of healthy air through his wild, mobile nostrils, and Magda would grow redder and redder.

Days wore by in Dombrowka, years wore by. Wojciech kept grabbing his heart more and more often, spitting into his red handkerchief, and only bits were left of his once big and healthy lungs. And Magda's arms, legs, and bosom grew thicker and thicker, her cheeks grew softer and redder, her eyes smaller and narrower. Farmers were already charging five rubles for Lolek's offspring, but Lolek himself stood in his stall, weak and sad. Now nobody wanted to bring him a mare, and his owner lay on the oven, angry at the horse and at Magda. Wojciech still believed that a mare was neighing at the gate, and, though no one heard him, he muttered: "Magda, get out to the stable, don't take less than three rubles."

Magda still led Lolek out to the meadows, trying to grab his mane to keep him from visiting the feeding mares in the old way, free of charge. However, Lolek was old and skinny. His dried-out spine bent his proud back, his knees buckled, one lip dangled from his mouth, and his ribs stuck out like hoops. He tried to neigh in a young voice and grimace with his earlier pride, but the mares were no longer afraid of him. Young shepherds struck his legs with lowly swine whips. And because he also played tricks, poking fun at a gelding and closing his teeth on an ear, the farmers refused to tolerate him on the shared meadow and they made up nasty things about him.

"He's crazy—that Lolek! He shouldn't be allowed to mingle with healthy horses!"

Magda still kept caressing him every night, kept drenching his mane with tears, kissing his blaze and hugging him. But he turned away from her, and Magda would then curl up in the hay and peer at him with guilty eyes.

She jingled the keys frequently and opened the stall.

Winter came to Dombrowka. Thick snow covered the fields and the indifferent thatched roofs. Farmers sat calmly by burning stoves, inhaling the pungent odors from the barrels of sauerkraut and fried pork scraps, lazily yawning their hearts out and delighting in tales of terror. And no one would have touched the snow in the village except Wojciech, who lay belly-down on the stove; and every time he coughed, dust balls and bits of soot flew up, covering the ceiling. Magda had harnessed Lolek to a sleigh and brought back the priest. Neighbors came in, bared their heads and, filled with an awkward fear of death, each one held the prayers in his mouth, ready to chant them.

After several days of Wojciech's groaning and coughing, the priest's dull carriage turned up in the village. Wojciech was now lying in bed, wearing a white shirt and gazing calmly with his dark eyes. He was so close to dying that he didn't even think of getting angry at the living. He merely gaped in surprise at the burning yellow candles and at the both cruel and clumsy faces of the visitors surrounding him.

The crowd recited biblical verses, and the priest thundered in his bass: "Beat your breast, Wojciech!"

Wojciech kept clutching his sunken chest until he could no longer lift his hand. Magda and the neighbors knelt down and prayed on and on for his soul.

Magda didn't cry, she behaved like a son: she ordered a coffin and came to terms with the priest. She then took out the old, dried boots, which Wojciech hadn't worn in a while; after thoroughly smearing them with grease, she washed his white coat.

That Sunday, they hitched Lolek to the sleigh and heaved in a yellow coffin with a tin cross. The mourners trudged through the snowy fields and woods, baring their heads under the falling white spangles. They trudged lazily and earnestly, concealing their fear of the power of death, which roamed across roofs and chimneys, swooping down wherever it wished. And they crooned psalm after psalm.

Magda kept silent. She watched them lower the coffin into the snowy grave, watched them pulling out the ropes, watched them filling the grave with hard soil. Then she and the mourners went straight home, she had drinks with each neighbor in turn and was content to hear them praise her: "Just like a son, not at all like a woman."

The snow covered any final trace of Wojciech. A frost turned the naked lindens and poplars into spears. The warm huts frequently squeezed out a bit of steam through the narrow, slightly open doors. Farmers hitched their horses to their wagons, the women put on flowery kerchiefs and tied pig's feet into long ropes, and they all set out for the Christmas fair in the nearby townlet.

Magda, the owner of ten acres, her own house, and a stable, plus several cows and swine, began to feel her sound condition. She had been freed from her father's yoke and she was now in charge of her work. She relished her freedom with all the might of a long-standing but now liberated meekness. She took down her father's red fur coat and put it on. Then she tied some money in a kerchief, which she slipped into her bosom. After harnessing Lolek to the sleigh, she rode to the fair for the first time. The frost made her cheeks glow red, the sleigh scraped over the snow, and she was happy: "Ten acres of land and a household!"

And, wandering through the fair, buying and selling, she saw what she wanted herself. She slipped her hand into her bosom whenever she felt like it, she counted, calculated, and each farmer held out a hand to close the deal: "Let's shake on it, c'mon! It's not appropriate for a lady like you to haggle this way!"

Later, at the tavern, people were drinking, dancing, and Magda drove with a boy who was holding her fast to keep her from rolling off the narrow sleigh. The boy drove quickly, outspeeding everyone else. A pair of folded boots was slung over his shoulder, a harmonica moved to and fro under his mustache. He was driving so fast that farmers avoided him. The sleigh bell jingled, and the boy held her so firmly that she screamed: "Oh, Jesus, Jesus—you're gonna smash my ribs!"

Next they attended church, then they went dancing, and women said embarrassing things to her, and then she was alone with the boy, and he wanted her to drink liquor, and she didn't want to, so he forced it down her throat. And the world grew dark. His hands were so strong, and she pummeled him for fun.

"Hey, woman, where ya goin'?"

A whip cracked, Lolek reared, capsizing the sleigh, and Magda lay in the snow, entangled between people and vehicles.

The snow cooled her warm dreams; she waited for a while, waited for a boy to lean over her, slip his arms around her waist, and pick her up: "That's a woman for you!"

The smart alecs laughed, and one of them, a semi-peasant, semi-idler in a city coat and a red embroidered scarf, winked his eye and yelled like a conjuror driving boys away with a leather whip: "Hey, hey, hey! Tell Lolek! He'll lift you up!"

"Ha ha ha!" A solid laughter boomed like the bursting of dry vats!

Magda turned the sleigh right side up and drove to the marketplace.

She spent the whole day trudging through the mob of people and animals. She visited the tables, she wanted to buy something. Earlier she had felt good and free, knowing she could slip her hand into her bosom at any time; but now she wanted someone to escort her through the market, pick this and that, even haggle with her, not let her buy everything, even take her from table to table, argue with the merchants, inspect the items, and keep telling her to stand there: "Try it on, Magda, see if it fits you."

She trudged through the sea of particolored beads and kerchiefs, peered at everything, and she was angry at the saleswomen, who didn't take her for a girl, who called her "Ma'am" as if she were married.

Later on, she was approached by an elderly farmer, a friend of her father's; the man took her to the tavern and bought her a drink. Here she also saw the boy in the outgrown city coat and the red scarf, and he kept poking fun nonstop at her and Lolek.

When the crowd had swallowed a bit more, they started playing their harmonicas, and the guys and the girls began rocking to and fro, as if provoking one another. Farmers also approached Magda, slipping their arms around her waist and stamping their heels. But all these men were older, and the women dashed over to them and tore out their hair: "Uh-oh, little man! I'll teach you to babble away at women, you old dog!"

The boy with the red scarf was everywhere. He darted from corner to corner, scooting right and left, like a bird among seeds, winking and flashing his hungry eyes. He played strange tricks. A farmer filled up his glass and was about to drink—but the boy grabbed it, drained it, and bowed like a clown. Apparently unwilling, the boy provoked a farm girl and touched his brow with one finger, like a veteran drummer. The farmers didn't quite understand what sort of prankster he was, and they glared and glowered at him. But he knew what he was doing. He went over to Magda, held his head in his hands, and slyly yelled: "Hey, hey, Magda!"

And the farmers forgot about everything and they laughed so hard that they cried. "What a clown! He's killing me!"

Later on, a farmer offered to swap his horse for Lolek. The boy was standing in the distance, and no one even thought of laughing. But the boy was back within a second, twisting every which way and winking his hungry eyes.

"Don't do it! Aside from the fact that he doesn't work, you'll have to give him your female!"

The merrymakers were so amused that they fell upon one another. There was also a town drunkard, a drifter, whom Wojciech had never allowed on his field so he wouldn't steal potatoes. And this drunkard was now so delighted by the joke that he hurried over to Magda and rubbed his gray, prickly chin across her face. But she bashed him so hard in the teeth that he spun around several times. And the merrymakers were so ecstatic that they grabbed their knees and doubled over in their mirth.

"Oh, is she ever gonna cut him up! Oh boy!"

Magda sat down in a corner and gaped. The tavern was full—chockful of guys and girls. She knew a whole bunch of them—how big they'd become! Magda could remember running into them while pasturing geese on the meadow—and now they were dealing with men, pulling on their shoulders, shouting: "You've guzzled enough!"

And the women grabbed a sip themselves.

And there were others, who'd emerged just a short time ago, they were swaying back and forth, tossing their skirts, dealing with their fiancés, and gnawing on long pieces of candy.

"They got engaged, got married," Magda was amazed, "but when, where?" And where had Magda been? She'd never attended any wedding in the village, never visited a fair, never gone to the tavern on a Sunday. She'd done nothing but drudge away for the old cougher from sunrise to sunset. She'd slept in the stable like a dog in a kennel, jingled the keys. And boys had stood on the other side of the fence, chuckling up their sleeves, and winking from under their skewed visors: "Ha ha, Magda, ha ha ha!"

She no longer heard the farmer who wanted to swap his horse, no longer heard the elderly women yelling at the boy in the red scarf: "Aren't you ashamed of yourself, you drunkard? God'll punish you for the way you're treating the orphan girl!"

Magda dashed out of the tavern, removed the bag of oats from Lolek's head, and drove home.

Lolek hadn't had a good day either. He too had tried to love and had been whipped. He was wild, angry, and he trotted nervously.

Evening fell in the wintry hush. Magda, swaying to and fro, was all alone in the rocking sleigh. She listened to the cheerful, drunken shouts of the young people who'd come out to the fields. The sleigh rocked past the straight lines of the spearlike poplars, grinding the frozen snow.

Magda sat with her head on her bosom, thinking about her lonely cottage, which stood solitary among white, snowy fields, about the coming Yuletide holidays, about the long, long winter nights, and about the wide, loose bed.

The sleigh skidded to the side as if someone were missing, someone to provide balance with his weight, and Magda gazed at Lolek's shadow gliding over the white snow. The sleigh entered the dark forest. In the distance the final drunken shouts faded over the snowy tops of the pines, arousing fearful echoes and vanishing forever among the tall, mute trees.

AVROM REYZEN (*1875–1953*)

Born in White Russia, Reyzen settled in New York after the outbreak of World War I. In wistful, delicate, lyrical sketches, stories, and poems, he created a vast spectrum of Jewish types—mainly those struggling with the dark side of life in both Eastern Europe and America, and with the spiritual deprivation caused by drudgery and poverty.

The Jew Who Destroyed the Temple *(1917)*

IN THE SMALL village in the Catskills where I was vacationing, I had a neighbor, an American citizen named Henry Rosen. His house was next door to my hotel. He's resided in the village for years and years, makes a good living, and has plenty of time to chat.

Of course, he won't chat with just anyone. He's proud to be an American, he's practically memorized the entire United States Constitution, knows the names of all the senators and all the honorable congressmen of the Republic, and calls them "honorable" even behind their backs.

He thinks the world of America, naturally, and he won't allow anyone to knock his country's institutions. Luckily, it's still easier for him to speak Yiddish than English. Which is why he spoke Yiddish with me. But if we were talking somewhere outside, and a real American happened to wander by, Henry Rosen would break off and greet the man in pure English: "Howw doo yoo doo, Mr. Nelson? Verry niice daay. But maaybee it will raain laater." Having said his piece and gotten a "yes" or "maybe" from the real American, he would turn back to me, revert to Yiddish, and explain who Mr. Nelson was and how they had gotten friendly. He told me that he generally gets on very well with Americans. "They're *fine* people"—and then he whispered into my ear: "Better than us Jews!"

Now one might think that Henry Rosen is an antisemite, God forbid! But we would have to defend him against such an accusation. In point of fact he's really very fond of Jews. Nevertheless, for all his fondness, he's also the first to see their faults.

Their biggest fault is that they're so slow in getting Americanized.

"So very slow," he sighs, and you can really feel how hard he takes it.

I asked him for an example because I felt that the Jews in this little village were actually *over*-Americanized.

And so he told me the story of the temple:

Several dozen Jewish families had settled in the village and they realized they had to find some sort of place for what modern Jews call a "divine service." They may not have been all that religious—but what would the Gentiles think? *They*, the Christians, had their church, and the Jews had to have one too. Of course, Henry Rosen didn't mean a shul like in the old country, he meant a little temple, something fancy: instead of a khazen, a cantor, instead of a rebbe, a rabbi, and so on.

Money was no object; after all, the Jews weren't exactly paupers. They purchased a small lot from an upright American, who, upon hearing that it was to be used for a Jewish church, let them have it at a low price.

And so they built a lovely little temple.

On the outside it looked almost like *theirs*, like a real American church. And on the inside it was just like a synagogue. But Rosen called it a temple, something he remembered from the Jewish upper classes in the big European cities.

"What's the difference between a temple and a shul?" Henry Rosen asked me and then supplied the answer himself:

"In a shul everyone prays together, out loud. But in a temple the praying is left to the cantor, the congregation remains silent, and if someone doesn't want to rely on the cantor, then he prays along, but very, very quietly, so as not to make a racket."

And that's how it went for a number of years. People simply didn't have the chutzpah to open their mouths during "divine services." What would the Christians think? It was a temple, after all.

But not for long.

One fine summer day, a Jew with a real beard moved into the village—one of those real European Jews. He opened up a stationery store and settled down as a resident.

"He wasn't a citizen, just a resident, do you see? And I saw that this Jew wouldn't be to our credit. Never mind the beard—after all, real Yankees also have beards, even though their beards are more . . . genteel. But this new Jew came into the temple even though he didn't have the foggiest notion of the difference between a temple and a shul. The cantor started off, and the greenhorn began chanting along as though he were back in Poland somewhere. I nearly fainted—he was murdering the temple.

"So I went up to him after the service and remarked genteelly, in Yiddish:

"'Mister,' I says to him, 'this is a temple, and not a *bes-medresh*, a study house. It's not customary to pray out loud here.'

"So he smirks and answers: 'Well, this is America, and if you can turn a shul into a church, then you can certainly turn a temple into a study house.'

"And just try and stop him! He was too powerful. The moment he began bawling his old country chant, someone else joined in, and then a third man, and a fourth. At first they were a bit cautious and quiet, but then they grew louder and louder. And as the liturgy progressed, the noise soared up into a wail, like in a regular study house. And toward the end, even the cantor forgot that he was using a modern style and he switched back to his shtetl ways, with the old melody.

"There's no more temple now. They *davven*, pray, like in the old country, they bawl and rock and sway, and when the service is over, they actually spit—just as they've always done!"

The First Photograph *(1920)*

THE HOUSE, WHICH didn't have rich furnishings, finally acquired a mirror. But the mirror couldn't be trusted. If you peered into it from time to time, it made your face rounder and bigger, so that all the family members, who, by nature, had skinny bodies and longish faces, didn't look so hot. It was also unfortunate that the reflection was greenish. That was why no one relied on the mirror's opinion, and it lost its reputation for truthfulness the very first week, when it was hung on the wall.

The mother, who set no store whatsoever by beauty, even though she was only thirty-eight, would seldom turn to the mirror. And if she did, it was not to check whether she was beautiful, but, quite the contrary, to see whether she was awfully ugly—especially on Fridays, after the baking of the challah, when she was covered with soot. The mirror may not have been truthful, but it did reflect certain colors accurately. Granted, it did turn white into green. But when the mother looked black with soot, the mirror showed the truth. It reflected black accurately. And, moving away from the mirror, the mother would heave a sigh: "*Oy vey iz mir,* I'm as black as soot."

The father certainly set no store by beauty, and if ever he glanced into the mirror, it was to check his beard, not his face. And indeed, his beard was accurately reflected. His black hair did come out black, but the few gray streaks were yellowish. The first time he saw this, he was so surprised that he called to his wife: "Look, I could swear there were yellow spots in my beard."

His wife peered at his beard like a *maven*, but finding no yellow whatsoever, she calmed his fears. "Your hair's turning gray, not yellow."

Gray didn't bother him, it was about time! He was almost forty-five.

More than all the others, Zelde, the eighteen-year-old daughter, wanted to find the essence of her face in the mirror. She wanted to find out whether she was beautiful. But the mirror didn't want to tell her the truth either. All she could see was that she had black eyes, black hair, but she had no inkling of what her face looked like, because she knew that the mirror was untruthful.

No one in the household imposed his expertise on anyone else. Of if somebody did, it was in moments of anger, and Zelde couldn't bank on such opinions. If, for instance, her younger brother was fighting with her, he would call her a "freak." This terrified Zelde, who thought she really was a freak. But then when he tried to make up, she wouldn't forgive him until he took back that word: "You're no freak, I was only fooling."

Well, she may not have been a freak, but was she beautiful? How could she know?

Leybe the tailor lived across the street, and one evening, Itsik, his assistant, had actually told her that she was a fine girl. Now first of all, fine was not beautiful, and secondly, he may have been untruthful too. No, you couldn't get the truth from a guy like Itsik any more than you could from their mirror.

There was something she could do, however. She could go to the town photographer and have her picture taken. If he did her portrait, it would be as genuine as gold. And she hoped that her father would approve.

Her father refused once and then twice: "Who needs it? It's a waste of a ruble."

But the third time, her mother interceded: "Who knows? It might come in handy for a marriage proposal. Before they meet, we can send a picture."

If it might help in a proposal, then that settled it. She was already nineteen. Just recently, Groynem the matchmaker had asked him: "She's already nineteen, isn't she?"

THE YOUNG PHOTOGRAPHER, who came from the city and always dressed like a bridegroom, both on weekdays and on the Sabbath, welcomed Zelde with great respect. He addressed her as *bárishnya*, Russian for "milady," and he wove other Russian words into their Yiddish conversation—words that Zelde took as signs of esteem: "Please," he said in Russian, "don't move, that's right, a little smile, *spasíbo* [thank you]!"

During the week in which her three portraits were being prepared, Zelde went around in a daze, full of expectation. She was virtually waiting for herself, for her second birth. She had been born for the first time nineteen years ago, and now she was being reborn . . . fully grown. What would she look like? She didn't want to see herself in the untruthful mirror, she wanted to hold herself in front of her eyes and finally see who she was.

The scheduled time came at last. With a pounding heart, she went to pick up the three portraits. She clutched the ruble and the twenty-five kopeks in her hand and felt as if she were buying three Zeldes.

When the photographer saw her entering his shop, he cried out, "*Otlítchno* [Excellent]!" She caught his drift. It meant that the Zeldes had come out accurately. He handed her one of them. She took hold of it and was promptly dazzled by a distant, alien beauty. She exclaimed feebly and with inward agitation: "This is me?"

"*Konyéshno* [Certainly]!" The photographer smiled. "Very accurate. Even the two dimples. Everything came out right."

Only now did she learn who she was. She hadn't known herself at all. She was beautiful. And what a good person! . . . Her goodness lit up her face. No, with a picture like this you couldn't fare badly. With a picture like this, you couldn't stay at home, waiting for a bridegroom.

Now the world was open to her! Even America!

At first her father wouldn't hear of it, her mother wept—to have her move so far away.

But a year wore by, and no proposals were offered. At twenty, a girl was practically an old maid. Maybe she *should* go to America. The world was on the move, she could strike it rich, she could marry there.

She left two of her portraits with the family and packed one for herself. Her cousin, Uncle Beynesh's daughter, urged Zelde to give her a portrait as a keepsake. But Zelde couldn't part with herself.

"You're silly," her cousin coaxed her. "America's got better photographers."

Zelde yielded and, after a long, hard look at her last portrait, she presented it to her cousin as a keepsake.

IN AMERICA, ZELDE had to work in a sweatshop, and at first she couldn't get used to it. It wasn't so much the work as the overall atmosphere. She felt alien, insecure. But soon she settled in and she forgot that there was any other world than the shop and her rented room and an occasional movie for a nickel.

The small mirror she acquired in America was certainly a truthful mirror with polished glass. But she didn't trust it. She felt she ought to be photographed. In a picture she looked so beautiful, and she remembered her first picture, the one she had left at home.

She now got photographed by a well-known photographer and she ordered a total of six pictures. She'd send four to her family, give one to her best friend, and keep one for herself.

The pictures were ready sooner than she'd expected. The photographer handed them to her in an envelope.

With trembling hands she took out one picture, a second, a third. After studying them all, she finally paid.

But in America, photographers do things very differently. Instead of dimples, the pictures bring out creases, and instead of looking good, a face looks earnest, nasty.

She expressed her opinion to her friend: "In our shtetl the photographs are more beautiful, more accurate."

Her friend smiled. "What are you talking about? The picture's wonderful, it's you to a T. You don't look nasty, you look earnest, lost in thought. It's very accurate."

"No!" Zelde argued. "That's not me! If you saw my first photograph from three years ago, I look totally different."

She hid the new photographs in her trunk and decided not to send these pictures home. She'd have other ones taken, by a different photographer. She wanted to send her family accurate pictures, like those first ones.

Six months later Zelde got phographed again. Since she was working in a union shop and receiving higher wages, she could afford to order an entire dozen pictures for four dollars. They should only be like the first ones!

What a disappointment, what a heartache. Even these new pictures were unlike those first ones, the ones she'd gotten in her shtetl. It was obvious that American photographers didn't know what they were doing.

And she longed for her first photograph, for the portrait with the two dimples, the kind face.

No! They didn't know what they were doing. She'd have to go back to her shtetl if she ever wanted to get accurate photographs.

DER NISTER *(1884–1950)*

*P*inkhes Kahanovitsh, who was born in Berdichev, Ukraine, changed his name to Der Nister (the Hidden Man, the Cabalist). A mystical writer, he was one of the few Yiddish authors to depict a lyrical if macabre world of demons in inscrutable allegories. His melodic and ironic prose quivers with internal rhymes and subtle rhythms. Influenced by the Cabala and by its handmaiden — a wealth of dense Hasidic tales — Der Nister created a unique style. After spending 1921–26 in Berlin's intensely dynamic Yiddish colony, he settled in the Soviet Union. Abandoning his mysticism, he yielded to the demands of Socialist Realism with prosaic stories and also with a fascinating two-volume saga, The Mashber Family (1939; 1948). Despite his aesthetic allegiance to the Soviet state, he was arrested in 1949 and died in a prison hospital one year later. The story translated below is probably his most opaque.

Beheaded *(1922)*

"WHAT SHOULD WE do? Crown him?"

"Whose head is next?"

"Certainly not his!"

"His head really hurts . . ."

And with a stiffly bent and scrawny finger bone, it struck the middle of the forehead. And the scalp-and-skull pan flew up like the lid of a box, opened up, and his Comedian, his headache, came out — a dandy, Comedianly elegant, and from his breast pocket a handkerchief stuck out, white and perfumed, and he quickly pulled it out and hurriedly squeezed it, and he applied it to his temples and to his dim and closed eyes, moistened them and perfumed them, and his headache abated . . .

"How do you feel, Adam?" the Comedian asked.

"Better. But it would be even better if I hadn't seen you."

And it was night now and almost midnight, and the room where Adam was to be found now filled up with light, with lamps hanging from the middle of the ceiling; and his Comedian did not come out alone, he came out with his implements, with a bedsheet spread on the ground and with his hocus-pocus wand for his magic tricks. The sheet was already spread on the ground, and the Comedian, a wandering dervish, was sitting on it, in a linen morning robe and with a saucer for alms, with his feet tucked in and his wand nearby.

"What is it?"

"I want to talk to you about crowns: about how crowns turn into thorns."

"Don't bother, we've already talked."

"And finally how thorns stop being thorns."

"We know it ourselves."

"And if a head is only—it wants to hurt—made, then that is its vocation and its sole justification."

"Very nice!"

"And if *your* head is justified, and I loyally serve it, and my function is important, and I perform it as I should."

"That's appreciated!"

"And if you count up and draw up the account, what will remain in your world besides that and besides me? Nothing!"

"My good luck and ill fortune: just what do you want?"

"Put a little something in my saucer . . . Support your poor dervish, he wanders through your land and through your towns and he can tell you a lot about your estates; converse with him."

"So I converse with him. Well? . . ."

"RECENTLY I WAS in one of your cities, in one of your Baghdads, on a market day and at a mammoth fair. And people were hustling and bustling on and on, and when the dickering was done and the fair had faded, the people gathered in bevies and bunches. They talked about you, about the lord of the land: He was well, they said, and good, and they ought to placate him.

"'With what?'

"And all the small grouplets merged into a huge group. And after lots of speaking and speechifying, they decided to commemorate you with a monument. And they promptly started collecting money. And the wealthy forked over each in turn, and the well-to-do made do with hard and tiny copper coins. But then a fakir, a semimadman with damaged eyes, produced a sick and mangy monkey from his lap, and a second and similar fakir gave up his daily take.

"I saw: the poverty of the poor and the disgrace of the rich—so I turned to the throng and started dissuading; the matter was no matter, and the whole business was refuted and irrelevant . . . 'I know our lord,' I said, 'and in his lifetime, I'm certain, he won't agree to a monument. He's a coward by nature, at night he never goes out alone, and the monument must constantly—by day and by night—remain outside, and our lord won't allow that, I'm certain, at all.'"

And I dissuaded the crowd and I returned the monkey to the first fakir and his daily take to the second fakir; and that brought a sigh of relief from the rich, and the well-to-do were cheery and chipper, and the throng dispersed, and the square was soon deserted, and your subjects were good subjects, and your compatriots were freed of a debt . . . And I remained alone with myself, and I and myself scrutinized one another after the throng's dispersal, and we both were delighted, and we stayed in the square, on and on, to ponder it all, and we sat on a rock and we spent the evening pondering . . . Yes, Adam!"

"That's a lie, Comedian!"

"Why a lie?"

"Because my subjects know that I demand nothing from them, and they're not so evil or so stupid, and you're maligning them for nothing."

"God forbid, and yet . . ."

And now the dervish leaped up from sitting on the spread-out sheet, and again as before, and again dressed up like a Comedian, he stood and again with his handkerchief he gracefully moistened Adam's temples and perfumed them, and his headache abated and it spoke to him thus:

"And now, Adam, I want to talk to you again about crowning—that is, crowning not myself but others . . . I mean your Master . . . And midnight's coming soon, and your Master will come to you, here, in this room, with his hard evidence, and you can already feel your great reverence, and your fear and your awe are expressed on your face, and you'll drive me back into your head, and through your eye slits I'll watch out for what's happening, and I'll have to see, and hush and listen and not say a word and be a witness, a silent one, and not disturb the whole kit and caboodle and not interfere . . ."

"Comedian!"

"Permit me."

And so the Comedian went to a wall, holding his wand, waving it in the air, halted at the wall, at its side, and left the rest of the wall to Adam, to the only watcher, and then, and standing ready for a few moments, and the upper half of the wall now moved and disappeared and the lower half remained, and through the vanished upper half a person appeared, his appearance disguised: tall and wiry, wearing yellow and in a yellow jacket, and holding some kind of vessel, holding it to his ear, and the vessel was covered by a small tablecloth, and from time to time, with his other hand, his free hand, he kept covering the mouth of the vessel . . .

He had heard that the Master must come here, so he had brought him a soul to mend.

"A soul?" asked the Comedian.

"Yes."

"And what's wrong with the soul?"

"No firmness in its legs, its knees are buckling, and it is feeble on its feet." And the person added: "The soul was born sound, with all its limbs as they should be, and also with legs without flaws, but the soul has no strength to stand on its legs, says the soul, and it constantly and continuously needs a stay and a support."

"Well?"

"And so he treated himself for a time, doctored and healered himself and visited lots of treatment centers. But nothing helped. And now he's heard about the Master, and about Adam. He's heard that Adam has the same illness, and so the soul has come here to join Adam in turning to the Master."

"Show the soul."

And now the person pulled off the tablecloth, and from the pot and from inside it, like an eraser, and springing up, a second Adam, like a twin, came forth and jumped to the floor and, right in front of Adam, face to face, he halted.

"What's here?" Adam turned to the others, looked them over, looked at them, considered them and admired them, and turned mainly to the first one, to his Comedian: "What's here?"

"Don't be afraid, it's nothing. It's another patient and a colleague for your illness, and he who brought him here is like me to you, merely a servant . . . Look at him."

And Adam looked at the person who'd brought the patient, and Adam saw: It was true, the person and his servant looked just like one another, and the patient and he himself repeated one another, and for him it was unclear what was happening there, and what in front of his eyes had occurred got mixed up in his brain and blurred—what did it denote and what did it connote, just who was this twin and what was this din?

"What's here?"

"Don't be afraid, and we're not alone, and people (see!) like you are many, and people (see!) like us are not rare and not scarce."

And Adam looked and he saw: The walls of his room were slowly deteriorating and disintegrating, and his room turned into a vast hall, and the hall became huge and already it resembled a field, a wide field, and the field was full and filled with people. And the people consisted only of Adams and only of servants, and they were all mixed, and the crowd consisted only of two kinds altogether . . . And the Adams looked very earnest, very tired and pale, and the servants had servant smiles on their lips . . . And a large light illuminated everyone, and the hour was late and midnight close by. And suddenly—and everyone's eyes turned upward, and a murmuring passed through the crowd, and in everyone's eyes and in everyone's murmurs: "The Master, the Master"—was sensed . . . And suddenly and over all the heads, halting high and in the air, the Master did appear . . . And all the Adams saw him and were frightened, couldn't stay on their feet, and they fell to the ground. And the servants likewise saw the Master, and saw that their own Masters, the Adams, had fallen to their knees, but the servants remained on their feet and glared scornfully at their own Masters . . . And on their lips the smiles grew big, grew bigger, grew large and larger, grew into great laughter, and the servants laughed and laughed, and the servants held their sides: "Blockheads and knuckleheads! . . ."

"Comedians!" yelled Adam in a strange voice, terrified and horrified. And his eyes widened and they looked like empty, wild, and gaping glasses. And suddenly he remembered and he slapped his forehead, and his scalp-and-skull pan unbolted as if from a narrow lock. And then, turning to his nearby Comedian, he commanded and demanded and pointed to his head, his opened head.

"Get in!"

And the Comedian obeyed, and the Comedian was aghast at his Master's order, and he climbed into his head and closed the lid. . . .

And the field was no longer a field, and the many people disappeared from the field, and the walls reappeared as before, and the room became a room again, and only the person who had brought the patient was standing with the patient, standing and waiting for Adam's word.

"Into the vessel!" Adam then ordered.

And the second Adam jumped into the vessel; the servant then covered the pot with his tablecloth, and he turned his back on Adam, turned his back as if nothing had happened, silently went through the vanished wall. And the wall turned back to its earlier square, and the room regained its appearance, and Adam was already alone, but very expended and exhausted by what had occurred. And he settled on a chair and heaved a deep sigh about what he had gone through. He wiped his forehead with his hand, and his hand grew wet with icy sweat. . . .

As he calmed down, he saw: The time was midnight; warm and weary, the shine shone down from the ceiling lamps, a stillness, a midnight quietness, hovered in the room and in the corners, and the walls, after what had occurred, were waiting for something else, for something and anything that would now be recurring. . . .

And the wall across from where Adam was sitting opened gradually and shifted aside . . . A vast, straight field emerged, and in the vast and silent field a path appeared, a path, and far on the horizon you could see the Master arriving, and in front of him, a long distance ahead, a group of disciples, with bread and with wine in their hands, came toward Adam, and they put down the bread and put down the wine. And silently toward the horizon, they waited for the Master and for his arrival. And the Master came closer, and the Master came over, and the disciples made way so he could sit at the head of the table, the disciples made way silently and respectfully and stood at the sides of the table. And the Master raised his arms and his eyes and he blessed the table and the bread and the wine:

"A blessing on the table, a blessing on the bread and the wine and on all of you, disciples. . . . Eat the bread and drink the wine and think about our new disciple: we are going toward him and coming, and today he will crown himself on our goods and our fate."

And the disciples ate, and the disciples tasted the wine, and while eating they pondered the Master's words and thought about the new and not-yet-seen disciple.

And while the Master was waiting next to his disciples, waiting for them to eat, Adam felt dizziness in his eyes . . . The field did not stay, and the

wall that had opened was now back in place . . . Softly . . . but on the door
to the room a gentle tapping could be heard.

"Come in," said Adam.

And saying those words, Adam felt a great responsibility for saying them,
and he felt that what was from the other side had to come here soon and
cross his threshold. And he stood up from his place and his chair, and he
turned his face and his body toward the door, and turning and staying
respectfully, looking expectantly through his door . . . And the door
opened up, and the Master left first, and after him the field disciples
emerged and entered, and Adam took the chair and gave it to the Master,
and the Master sat down, and the others clustered around him. . . .

How long did the initial minutes last? Adam didn't know and didn't
reckon; and the minutes dragged on and dragged on, and they lasted and
lasted for such a long time, and the room filled up with a silence, and the
Master sat and the disciples stood, and the Master's words had not yet
been spoken, but soon they were heard:

"You're in the act of crowning, Adam, and so are we, and we now have
to be in the square of the beheaded—look!" The Master turned to all the
people surrounding him. And Adam's whole room disappeared all at
once, with the ceiling and with light and the walls and the corners all
around. And the Master and the attendants all found themselves in a
large, wild place . . . And they saw: Across the entire breadth of the place
a lofty wall towered up toward the sky. And the wall was clay and was deaf,
and some kind of light ladder twisted upward like a curling vine, and the
rungs and the steps were of human heads and skulls, and those levels
were few, and between the sky and the highest height of the wall there
was a gap, a very great gap . . .

And the place was deserted, and no one came, and an emptiness dominated its sides, and if anyone did come he was stricken with fear, and
whoever was weak kept very far away from the limits, and whoever was
stronger stayed closer to the limits, but all were terrified, and they turned
away, turned away . . . Especially if someone saw the wall, saw how high
and broad it was, and much more, and if someone saw the distant ladder
and what its rungs and its steps were made of . . . They walked away . . .

But once in every generation someone did go across the limits, and
once every so often someone, a risk-taker, did walk over to the wall. And
a site was waiting for him, a court-and-judgment site, with a block and a
headsman near the block, and prepared with a large sword. And that

risk-taker was prepared, and the risk-taker laid his head on the block, and the headsman chopped it off, chopped it off . . . And when the head was chopped off, the headsman handed it to the beheaded man, and he took his head and climbed up the ladder, and the ladder grew one head higher, and the ladder gained another rung . . .

And the Master and his attendants walked across that place, toward the site of judging and beheading, and the headsman was already standing, prepared. And the Master was the first to put away the head, and then he took it and climbed the ladder with it, and the Master was followed by all his disciples, and each in turn did the same, and Adam was the very last one, and Adam's head became the last and the highest rung.

And when they were done, the Master gathered all and sundry, and a great bright light shone in the place of his face, and the faces of the disciples were likewise lit up by light. So he gathered them all and he placed them around the site of judgment, placed them around and said to them:

"Disciples and crowned men! Since you'll be heading home without your heads, your nearest and dearest will stand around you, and weep for your appearance and for your fate, and your Comedians will appear before you, and they will provoke you and delight in your defeat and say: 'Men of the mind, where did you lose your heads?' And you will grow flustered, and shameful and shamed you will point to light from your heads. And they'll laugh and poke fun at you, and they'll hold their bellies, and — 'Comedians!' — they will say to you, 'How will you get by without your heads, and on whose rope of counsel have you set out, and not listened to you, and even called us Comedians! . . . And what good will it do you when the wind seesaws your heads on that wall, and — luck will be yours! — someone's feet will tread on you in order to hang another head over yours? . . .' And that's what they'll say to you. Listen! Let your near and dear weep their eyes out, and your near and dear grieve, and if you remain with the Comedians, have them tell you the tale of the bridge and the Universe Bridge."

And this is the tale he told:

The Master's Tale

ONCE UPON A time a bridge spanned a river from shore to shore. A bridge like any bridge, it let people and shipments, horses and wagons cross itself and cross the river — day and night, summer and winter, rain or snow, in every weather and every air. The bridge served and never complained, and it never argued with anyone. If it had a hole, the hole was fixed, and if a board or a beam was used, it was always new, and it did its work and did its job: linking a shore with a shore, bringing people together with people, and at its post both day and night, honestly and honorably earning its bridge-bread and its upkeep. . . .

But many years wore by, and the river beneath the bridge started drying out, and the stream and the running water were dotted with islands and willows, and the shores spread and were covered with reeds and the shores pushed so deep into the river. And one day an imp settled in the reeds, and by now the bridge was old, and the bridge often moaned and it groaned about its task, and when wagons with huge loads rolled across, the bridge would buckle and shudder. And from time to time, during great floods that heralded the spring, the bridge couldn't hold, and half was torn off, and one day the current carried off the whole bridge . . . The men would chase after the bridge, catch it, keep it ashore, safe from the flood, and then bring it home and tie it to its shores, and put it back in its place for its service and its age.

And the bridge moaned and groaned and seesawed and broke under loads, but it had no choice, it did its job, and no one paid heed to its inability, and no one was concerned about its age and its incapacity. And who should care and who should be concerned? . . . Only the imp. . . .

Now one night, when the bridge was all alone, one still and starry night, when the shores were asleep, when there were no drivers and no walkers and no links between the shores, and the river was calm, and the sky and the stars were mirrored in the nightly bottom of the river, the imp would leave the reeds, go on the bridge or under it, and sit down and converse with the bridge. And the bridge would tell the imp about its daily tribulations, and the imp would hear it out and agree with its complaint, and the bridge would ask the imp for advice, and the imp would have only one piece of advice:

"You fool, why do you hold out? What will you get out of the horses' hooves? And, old fool, what do you owe anybody? . . ."

And the bridge would mull and muse, and it would gaze at the river and the sky in the river, and they were silent and they didn't join the conversation, and only fish in the river and stars in the sky—and sometimes a fish would dart, and sometimes a star would twinkle—and they replied and retorted and allowed the old bridge to succeed with the imp's advice.

And the bridge lapsed into a deep melancholy, and the bridge did its job unwillingly and reluctantly, and often and very often it suffered misfortunes: a horse broke a leg, a man fell through a hole—and they fixed the bridge too frequently, and fixing never helped, and the fix wouldn't last.

"Bridge, collapse!" the imp kept advising.

"But that could cause a misfortune!"

"And why should you care? And what good does it do you if there's no misfortune? What do you gain and what do you lose?"

"C'mon, imp. And what will other bridges say?"

"Ha ha!"

And it was night. Radiant stars shone from one side of the shore, from under a mountain, and from the mountain and from a path you could see a Wanderer coming down to the river. The bridge waited for him, and when he came down and set one foot on the bridge and was about to step on the bridge, the Wanderer suddenly heard a voice down from the bridge or up out of the reeds—the Wanderer heard it:

"Halt!"

"Who? What?" The Wanderer was terrified and he pulled his foot back to the shore.

"I the bridge to you the Wanderer. I have to ask you something."

"What?"

"I'm old and worn down, and no purpose comforts me."

"And who led you to think so?"

"The imp in the reeds and my very own bones."

"My legs are swollen up to my belly, and the swelling will soon reach my heart . . ."

"And so?"

"And my legs see no purpose either."

"And yet?"

"And yet you're a bridge, and you must know the tale of the Universe Bridge."

And the Wanderer entered the bridge, and when he'd crossed it halfway, he took off his backpack, sat down, and told the tale:

The Tale of the Universe Bridge

THE UNIVERSE BRIDGE, which leads from the deepest abysses to the highest heavenly palaces (together with the other things that the Lord

God had no time for), was created on Friday evening, at twilight. . . . Nor did He deal with it for long, nor did He speak to it for long, nor did He clarify its calling. He then left it alone and went away—and the Lord God set out to meet the Sabbath.

And during the first night, the Universe Bridge remained alone, absorbed in its imaginings, and silently and in the dark it pondered its form and its volume, its makeup and where in the world it was. The bridge saw its own legs in the abyss and its head in a radiant heavenly palace. And the palace was filled with a holy hush, and in that palace a door led to some other space, and the door was shut. And that night, on the other side of the door, the Lord God and His Sabbath celebrated after the week and the world weariness. . . .

And the bridge was very content with its legs, and its legs were not superfluous, for its legs cooled it and wet it, and slippery wetness, and [*hipl*] and strange reptiles swarmed to them. So the bridge didn't feel good about them. Nor did it think good things about them, and thinking led to discontent, and discontent led to complaints; complaints that no one asked the bridge, complaints that no one gave it a choice, complaints that right after creating the bridge the Lord God hurried away from it and didn't linger with it . . . And as the bridge felt these complaints, Satan came to the bridge on a first nocturnal visit:

He had nothing to do, it was night and it was Sabbath, and the Lord God was now in His highest palace, and He left them—Satan and the Universe Bridge with its legs—down in the abysses . . . He didn't care: wetness and reptiles were swarming—let them, it was ugly and slippery—let it be ugly. He was resting now.

"Yes," the Universe Bridge agreed. "And why did no one ask?"

"Yes, why did no one ask? And why were all created things created for their own sake, and you for others and for their sake: so that people could step on you and walk across you?"

And Satan made its calling clear to the Universe Bridge: and he showed it from its earliest generations, then the later ones and still later ones, and then stopped with many and all the generations of walkers, as all walkers [*hipl*] bring much wetness and slipperiness to the bridge, and lots of soiling and befouling, and—going up and clambering up and coming halfway and peering down—they suddenly turned their heads, broke off and broke up, and with turned heads and with the slipperiness they'd brought, they fell back into the abyss . . . And the Universe Bridge saw all that, and it felt sick, and it hated its job, and it was disgusted, and it had more complaints. And now Satan moved closer to the bridge and whispered into its ear:

"You're insulted, bridge!"

"So what!"

"Collapse!"

"And what will happen?"

"You'll fall down, and the Lord God won't hear you, because the Lord God is now occupied in His final heavenly palace. And if you fall down, we'll establish our kingdom down below, we'll rule it together. And if there's a bridge, the height won't unite with the depth, and no one will stand upright, so that no one will clamber and tumble. Only the length will unite with the breadth, and everyone will walk on you light and easy, and right to where they wish to walk, and they will arrive. And the action is justified because even the abyss is just, and why serve the Lord God if we can be lords ourselves . . . And just rest here. . . ."

And the Universe Bridge heard Satan out and it fell to thinking, and a nasty thought crossed its mind, and it looked at Satan, at the inciter, and Satan turned away and left the bridge to its thinking. And the Universe Bridge waited and doubted, deliberated and meditated, and then, pondering, the bridge came to no conclusion. . . .

Now an icy shudder ran through its length and through its body, and the bridge shivered and trembled, and from concluding yes and from concluding no, it shook off only a bit of the bridge and shook off what had been put into the abyss.

At that moment, the light of the bridge's celestial palace, where the bridge's head was—the light went dark. And the Lord God emerged through the door of the next palace; and, resting and astonished, the Lord God looked at the Universe Bridge, looked and said nothing, looked and then returned to the Sabbath peace and quiet . . . And Satan did not turn back from turning away from the Universe Bridge, and angry and discontented, and insulted by his lack of success on his first visit, he vanished from the Universe Bridge's sight, and he went back to where he had come from. . . .

It was already dawn, and the day of Sabbath arrived, and the day of Sabbath also went by peacefully, and that night, when the light was lit in the Universe Bridge's palace, the atmosphere wasn't like yesterday, like the Sabbath, it seemed weak, like the ushering out of the Sabbath. And soon after the light appeared, the good Lord appeared at the threshold.

"Good evening," He said to the Universe Bridge.

And the Universe Bridge felt sinful and diminished, and the piece that was in the abyss yesterday left it, and while the bridge felt no darkness and no wetness from the abyss — its crown and the light from its head were dark and slightly rotten.

"Good evening!" the bridge returned the Lord God's blessing and, embarrassed, lowered its eyes and . . .

THE WANDERER ADDED to his tale: "And because of that piece of the Universe Bridge, all bridges now have to suffer, and the length and the breadth are occupied by Satan, and he's posted his imps at all bridges, and bridges are talked out of their calling; and a search began for the broken-off piece in order to affix it to the Universe Bridge, and the search has been going on and on, and the legs of the searchers are swollen from walking; and for the sin of the head of the Universe Bridge and for the diminishing of its light a lot of heads must be beheaded, so that the light from those heads may fill the light of the celestial palace . . ."

AND "DISCIPLES," ADDED the Master, "that's what you'll tell your Comedians when they come to you and give you grief, when they harass you and ask about your heads."

And the Master grew mute and he then left the group, and the place with the wall and the ladder disappeared, and the field reopened then, the field from which the Master and the disciples had originally come and shown themselves . . . And the Master was already far, and, going back, he leaned somewhere against the horizon, and the light from his head looked like a pale and fainting cluster, and the disciples halted, and with the light by their heads they had bread and wine in their hands — and they brought them into the world and where the Master led them. They walked and they faded and Adam gazed after them a while, until they had fully vanished from view . . . And then, Adam turned away from gazing after them, and with his own light too he headed home.

And when Adam came home and looked around his room, he found it as it had been yesterday and last night: he alone now lay in his bed, and in place of his head just a light lit the room. Near and dear stood around his bed, shook their heads at him, and wept for his appearance and his

luck, and he looked at them, and he pitied their weeping and their pitiful faces, and when they left him at last and went their ways, and he
remained alone with the light of his head, and when the Comedian then
appeared, and as if having wept, he was prepared to serve him further,
and, with his hand already in his pocket, to remove the handkerchief, to
relieve his headache—Adam's face was wreathed in smiles, he waved his
hand and did not let him come too close and "superfluous," he said, "you
can see, and don't make an effort . . ."

"What do you mean?" the Comedian feigned ignorance and naïveté.

"You can see for yourself, your service is not required, I've been
beheaded, and you can go and serve somebody else . . ."

And when the Comedian began as the Master had foretold: "Huh?
What do you mean?" and "Man of the Mind, why did you lose your head?"

"And so on and so forth." Adam's face was wreathed in smiles. He alone
was calm and he calmed the Comedian. He wouldn't let him draw near
or speak at all, he simply told him to sit and he told the Comedian what
the Master had told Adam.

SHLOYME GILBERT *(1885–1940s)*

*B*orn near *Warsaw, Gilbert lived in Otwock and Warsaw, where he was
murdered during the German occupation.*

Canary *(1922)*

A SMOOTH FACE with a pointed mustache, bright blue eyes, and a small
cap with a shiny visor over a mischievous sidelock. People call him
"Canary" and they know him only in the summer.

When you enter Canary's home, you're promptly inundated by a twittering of birds. The walls are hung with small cages containing all kinds
of birds, up and down, up and down, and they chirp and trill and whistle. The windowpanes are covered with green leaves and branches from
potted plants, and there are jars of water, in which small goldfish silently

swim around. We may be in the throes of winter, when the world is dark and closed off in cold and damp, but in Canary's home you're reminded of summer days, of high blue skies.

All winter long, Canary never goes anywhere. He's lazy. He lies in bed, fully dressed, or he sits at the table, dozing, his head between his fists. From time to time he gets up and puts a few seeds in the cages.

Now and then he ventures outdoors, but he quickly returns, paces to and fro, warms his ears with his hands, and curses the winter with its cold and its damp!

During the winter he develops a thick, dirty forelock and a wild beard, and he gets yellow, swollen cheeks like a man who's been in prison for a long time.

His wife, a full, pale woman, supports them by taking in laundry. They started fighting right after the wedding. She wanted him to get a job, and he kept telling her that thousands of people were unemployed, great wars were being fought, and soon the world would be a different place.

When she nagged him harder, he got a job in a factory, but it didn't last very long. Within a couple of days, he came home, gloomy and broken. He collapsed on the bed, fully dressed, and lay there a day and a night. He didn't go back.

His wife saw that the situation was bad, but she couldn't tear herself away from his mustache and his childlike blue eyes. She sighed quietly and started taking in laundry.

IN THE SUMMER, Canary revives. He raises and catches pigeons. He spends whole days in gardens, meadows, and forests.

Canary keeps busy with his pigeons on the roof. The cage is in the attic, near the small window, through which he chases them out and takes them back in. He himself gets to the attic through the second small window. Often he brings along colleagues.

Canary holds a long switch with a white ribbon at the tip and he uses the switch to drive out the pigeons. The pigeons don't feel like flying away. When he drives them off the roof, they soar over the building, circle several times, and then return and perch on the other side of the roof. He reaches them with his long switch and drives them away. The pigeons rise again, circle and circle aloft, over the building, yet they don't feel like flying away. Canary waves his switch, yelling and calling the pigeons all sorts of nicknames.

"Matke is as lazy as a cat!

"Black Devil destroys all of them!

"Hey, Cavalier! Take the Coquette!"

The local kids lend him their support. They stand there, peering up, holding two fingers in their mouths and whistling. The pigeons keep flying higher, getting further and further from the building. They form a long line and then whirl in a circle.

A second circle of pigeons forms over a distant building. The two circles intersect in the blue depth and virtually close ranks. The kids stand on the roof and stare, motionless. Canary keeps bending over, whispering something, and pointing. A few pigeons sheer out of one circle and join the other, while all the pigeons shriek.

One circle comes closer. Canary puts down the switch on the roof. All the kids sit down and gaze up silently. The pigeons whirl, whirl over the building, and then perch on the roof.

Canary warily creeps over, coos, whistles, and pours out birdseed. The pigeons peck the seed and draw closer. Canary captures the new pigeons one by one and slips them through the roof window into the cages. He gives his own pigeons free rein on the roof.

Now Canary gets to his feet, pulls up his pants, and says something to the kids, while motioning toward the circle that's still visible on the edge of the sky. He hands out cigarettes. The kids settle down comfortably on the roof and smoke, and Canary tells stories about his pigeons, pointing now at one, now at another. The pigeons silently stroll across the roof, puffing out and letting in their downy throats, sparkling in golden hues, peering with bright, round eyes, and cooing.

Once the kids have finished their cigarettes, and Canary has told his fill of stories, they all stand up, stretch, and yawn into the blue sky.

Canary waves his long switch at the pigeons, herding them together. The pigeons hop, jostle, and the frontmost step through the window. When the last pigeon is inside, Canary covers the window with mesh. He then puts away the switch, and he and his visitors crawl in through the other window, leaving the roof empty and silent.

. . .   .

CANARY GOES INTO gardens. The owners know him. He sits on the grass, carves a whistle from a green twig, and tells stories about birds.

Once, he says, he was looking for a particular species of bird. He walked into a dense forest. He went deep inside, the air was chockful of twittering and whistling, but he didn't hear the bird he was looking for. Still, he knew that it was to be found in the forest. He began whistling like the bird, spread his net, and hid in the thickets.

The bird responded. The bird was already flying around him, seeking and responding, seeking and responding! A smart bird! When he saw Canary in the bushes, his efforts became useless. . . .

Canary starts whistling like a bird. He listens and then asks the gardener whether he heard it.

Canary stretches out on the grass, his hands under his head, and he warbles and whistles. He hears a response, a kind of whistling, but still very faint, barely audible. Canary's face shines brightly, and the blue sky glows in his eyes.

He runs to the end of the garden, spreads the net, hides in the bushes, and whistles and warbles. When he catches the bird, he hurries over to the gardener. The bird twists its neck, half-closes one eye, peers at Canary, and opens its little beak.

Canary strokes its head, looks at it, and purses his lips, almost kissing its beak.

Canary tells stories about fish. He catches fish without a rod, without a net, with his bare hands. He doesn't like a huge body of roaring water, the fish are timid there. He goes to a tiny village pond: the fish are silent there.

He goes to such a village pond at night, when the fish are asleep. The pond is black, silent. It sleeps, its edges covered with plants and grasses.

He pulls off his boots, hikes up his pants, and cautiously steps into the water. He hears the splash of an awakened fish, and silent circles form in the water. Canary holds his breath. He halts and he feels the breath of the fish on his legs. They lie, fast asleep, on the bottom of the pond.

He pulls up his sleeve, thrusts his naked arm deep into the water, and takes out a fish. The fish pulls in, pushes out its watery mouth. Its glassy, yellow eyes bulge and gape in terror.

The fish yells, Canary feels sorry for it, and releases it into the water.

He gets out of the pond cautiously so as not to frighten the fish.

. . .   .

CANARY GOES OUT at daybreak to pick mushrooms and berries. He walks alone through the forest, stepping on a soft bed of forest soil.

A huge, red sun has just risen, and it shines through the branches, warming the fresh, cool dawn. The yellow needles that have poured down from the trees are still damp and soft, and the grass is still full of dewdrops.

Canary walks gingerly. Poisonous toadstools grow everywhere. They stand brash and high, shrieking with their flaming colors—yellow, red. The safe mushrooms are rare, they hide modestly and they barely peer out.

Canary holds every good mushroom in his hand and muses in sheer delight: "It grew overnight, a piece of meat, real meat for a meal."

Sometimes a squirrel leaps from tree to tree. The small yellow creature, with its long bushy tail, pauses for a while, raises its little head, and peers with its sharp, glassy eyes: "What are you doing in my forest kingdom?"

The squirrel leaps up a tree. It halts halfway up, peers down sharply, and, deciding that a human being spells danger, the squirrel dashes higher, screeching and dryly whistling.

Canary stands there, looking up and laughing.

CANARY PICKS BERRIES. A patch of the forest is covered with small bushes, and round blueberries hang under the small green leaves. From time to time Canary pops a berry into his mouth, and each time, as if it were a novelty, he laps up the sweet juice.

He stretches out on the ground for a long time, staring at the forest around him. Golden spots of sunlight shine here and there on the brown floor of the forest. The air is hot and still, and the young and old forest smells of strength and freshness.

Canary lies there, sweetly absorbed in a single thought: "How big and strong and beautiful the forest is!"

His wife always complains to him: "Other men bring back whole baskets of mushrooms and berries, while you spend entire days in the forest and you bring back nothing! What kind of fun are you having there? In that time you could earn enough to buy real meat!"

Canary replies: "This is better than meat, it's tasty and it's easy to digest. The forest is so big! If only summer lasted forever!"

During the summer Canary combs his full head of hair, and the blue sky is mirrored in his eyes.

When winds begin to blow, and clouds appear in the broad, deep sky, Canary becomes wistful. Silently he looks at the yellow leaves falling from the trees. He walks to and fro and asks fiercely: "What good is winter with its cold and damp?"

Later on, when the whole sky is gray and overcast, Canary goes home, plops down, and lowers his head between his fists.

YOYNE ROSENFELD *(1880–1944)*

Born in Volhynia, Russia, Yoyne Rosenfeld, orphaned at twelve, endured a miserable adolescence. Eventually he worked as a turner, but in his mid-twenties, encouraged by Peretz, he started devoting himself entirely to writing. He then produced short stories and also a novel In the Quiet *(1912) about the world of poor and harried laborers. In 1921 he arrived in New York, where he contributed regularly to Yiddish periodicals. His oeuvre included stories, novels, sketches, plays, and autobiography. His themes were death, violence, eroticism, futility, anxiety, insanity, obsession, irrationality— always with a profound sense of isolation. He was probably the first Yiddish writer to deal at length with the seamy side of the human psyche.*

Miss Bertha *(1924)*

SHE WAS ACCEPTED as one of their own—a guest like any guest, that is, even though her brothers were the owners of the Sunshine Boardinghouse. In fact, she was even closer than the others because she, although a sister of the owners, acted like a boarder: she ate with the guests and spent time with the guests. Most of all, they could bad-mouth the owners right in front of her, as if she were one of those people who, for their twenty-two bucks a week, wanted to devour the entire farm, people who think that, no matter how much they eat and whatever they eat, it's not very much and not enough for the money they pay. To such people she was a jewel. They bad-mouthed the owners, but it couldn't really be counted as bad-mouthing because they were talking in front of a relative of the people they were discussing.

Miss Bertha was truly faithful and devoted to everyone. Her loyalty to the boarders went so far that she was extremely patient with mothers who were here in the country with children (for the children's sake). Each mother wanted her child to eat and drink as much as she, the mother, wanted a child to consume and far more than the child wanted, since this was the country, after all.

"Miss Bertha, what can I do with my children? They won't eat and they won't drink."

And sometimes a mother might be sitting on the grass with her child, trying to force a glass of milk down his little throat. All at once Miss Bertha happened to be passing, and the mother would turn to her and plead: "Miss Bertha? Maybe he'll drink if it comes from you, Miss Bertha?"

The mother who stopped her might not be entirely to blame for stopping her. Miss Bertha always walked as if she were not walking for her own sake. She always seemed to be walking sort of from one person to the next. And whenever somebody stopped her, she would always linger and spend as much time with that person as if she had been planning to spend it. In case a mother with a child stopped her, Miss Bertha would commit herself to the child as if she had come here specifically to see the child and take over the mother's job.

Yes indeed. You can be that faithful and devoted to strangers only if the business establishment isn't your own, if it belongs to your relatives, and you enjoy all the comforts together with all the strangers who pay money for their comforts. Her brothers didn't saddle her with the task of watching and tending the guests and making sure they were happy. Quite the contrary: the brothers were only doing their duty, doing what had to be done for people who were paying such-and-such. The brothers were doing no more and no less than had to be done, and they were doing as much as other boardinghouse owners did for their own boarders, who were paying as much money as the brothers' boarders . . . Beyond that they didn't give a damn about anyone. But she, Miss Bertha, did give a damn about everyone. She was truly faithful to every single person and wanted everyone to be happy.

Whenever new boarders, male or female, arrived, Miss Bertha would welcome them so kindly, as if they'd been invited as personal guests and not boarders. She received each new vacationer as heartily as if she'd been looking forward to his arrival for a long time. During the first few hours she wouldn't leave the newcomer's side, and during those hours she'd introduce him all around, stopping each and every person who happened to pass by: "May I present Mr. . . . Allow me to present Miss. . . ."

There were also reclusive people who, out of vanity or what not, kept aloof from the other boarders. Bertha took it personally. She was concerned about the other guests: they might feel insulted. She was particularly offended by one distinguished personality, who was vain and reclusive. The brothers had gone to a lot of trouble to get him here, to use him as a drawing card. Unfortunately, he did more harm than good. Everyone disliked him, and no one was glad he was here. Miss Bertha stuck to him like a burr. No matter where he went, she turned up, and her complaint was always the same: "All alone! Always alone! Constantly alone. Aren't you fed up?"

And if she encountered a girl or young woman, she'd drag her over to him, eventually gathering a whole crowd. And, like it or not, he had to spend time with the craftily assembled throng so long as Miss Bertha remained at the center. But the instant she left, the crowd started thinning out—until he was all alone again.

Often a girl showed up from the big, tumultuous city, ready to spend a couple of weeks resting and recovering from a whole year's labor, ready for a holiday, relaxation, food, mountains, trees, grass—and mainly a holiday from herself. She wanted to spend a holiday with strangers, to play a role, to act as if her life were one long holiday, to bag a guy who was looking for a girl who was as she imagined herself to be.

However, after a few days (a significant amount of time in a brief vacation), a few fruitless days, such a girl becomes gloomy, apathetic, and she starts talking about leaving early. But along comes Miss Bertha and she sticks to the girl and she, Miss Bertha, does everything she possibly can to keep the girl from yawning: she drags her over to a couple of guys and girls, and the girl then stays for the rest of her vacation.

Every season, a few boarders of either sex, some guys and some girls, stick close to her, Miss Bertha, becoming her messengers, her adjutants, and satisfying her whims. Not her own personal whims, mind you, but other people's whims—her own whim being to take care of other people and keep them from getting bored. Now these aren't just random guests, they've been coming here for years and they're good friends with the boardinghouse owners and with Miss Bertha, their sister. And when these old-timers get together, then nobody yawns. They yank a girl into their circle and deafen her with their singing, and sometimes a girl who arrives with her nose in the air and claims that she doesn't speak any Yiddish is pulled into the group and becomes a plain Yiddish maydel and joins in when they sing Yiddish ditties, so that eventually she leaves the country in a cheerful frame of mind . . .

Yes, indeed, they catered to all sorts of people, including some who were very happy. There were couples who led a happy life, but others could see through their mutual happiness, could tell that these two were sinners, that they weren't really husband and wife, which was the only reason why they were so happy . . . Miss Bertha had nothing against such people, even though she herself was a quite modest and innocent girl. She felt that if others did what she thought one shouldn't do, then let them, because they might have a different opinion. She, the modest and decent girl, sometimes justified such things, which others, who were nowhere as respectable as she, regarded as immoral.

Such was the case with two boys who arrived with a girl. During the first few days, no one knew what connection the two boys had with the girl and with one another. And when people learned that the two boys had no separate connection with one another and that they and the girl lived together, the boarders caught the drift, and tongues wagged. Miss Bertha was alone in defending the three — even though she found it more unpleasant than anyone else. But she generally couldn't imagine that people were capable of doing mean things, and so she felt that no matter what mean things people might do, there was nothing mean about this situation.

The girl who was living with the two boys confided in Miss Bertha. She explained that she loved both of them and both were in love with her, and that they had had no other choice, and so they had decided to live together as a threesome. Miss Bertha justified it: What else could you really do in such a case, where both boys loved the girl, and she loved them both? What other solution could there be but the one the trio had hit on? Miss Bertha was only amazed that the two boys weren't jealous of each other. She was deeply interested in this issue and so she asked the prominent man who was vacationing there whether it was possible for two boys to love the same girl and live with her and not be jealous of one another? The prominent man said that it was out of the question; if both boys were in love with her or just one of them, then that one couldn't tolerate the second one.

Miss Bertha knew that the prominent man was right, for she felt the same way. But before hearing the prominent man's opinion, she had mused that the situation might not be what she figured: perhaps the girl who was living with the two boys only thought that both were in love with her. Otherwise, she wouldn't have done things she was doing. If that was so, people should open her eyes, point out that two boys couldn't possibly be in love with her and live with her and not be jealous of one another. And Miss Bertha told her so. And the very next morning the three of them got up and drove away instead of staying out the week they had meant to stay. And several days later someone conveyed their best wishes to Miss Bertha: he, that "someone," had seen them at a different boardinghouse in the area. And Miss Bertha was furious at herself for compelling the threesome to move to a different boardinghouse.

"WHO'RE YOU LOOKING for?"

Whenever Miss Bertha saw a boy or a girl wandering around, she knew that the boy or the girl was looking for somebody, and that it was her, Miss Bertha's, business. That is, she was very interested in their finding one another, and so she went looking for the person that this person was looking for. She lurched around like a golem, filled with, charged with other people's business, eager to find the person that this person was looking for. Her longish face, her pointed chin, and her sheeplike eyes expressed so much naïveté, and seeing her roaming about among trees and meadows, you might have assumed that a simpleton was sticking his nose into simple people's sins and passions.

Miss Bertha asked people she encountered right and left:

"Have you seen Mr. . . . ?" (And she uttered a name.) "Have you run into Miss . . . ?" (And she uttered a name.)

And as she looked and asked, someone kept popping up from the side or behind her, the prominent personality, and with a tone and an expression as if he had been looking for her, he asked: "Bertha, dear, whom are you looking for?"

And she didn't know what to say, for it now dawned on her that she didn't know whom she was looking for, and she felt embarrassed in front of this man and she moved away from him, while he called and shouted after her: "Bertha, dear!"

She hurried away and joined a cheerful group; she was always welcome everywhere because she never bothered anyone. You could get away with anything just as you could if she hadn't been present or if she'd been just anyone. And if ever a boy wanted to flirt with her just for the heck of it, she didn't resist, but neither did she flirt back . . . She was both the target of his flirting and an onlooker, as if she hadn't been what she was with that boy, as if she'd been, for herself, the same person that she was for him . . . He shouldn't have taken liberties, and so she was tranquil and indifferent. Lack of tranquility was all she could feel for the girl who was standing far away and shouting and calling her name: "Berthaaaa!"

EVENINGS, WHEN ALL the young and not so young got together in the boardinghouse casino to talk and dance, Miss Bertha was among them, likewise talking and dancing, but with one difference: the boarders all talked and danced for their own fun, their own pleasure, while she did those things for the others. She always stood there, ready to form a couple with anybody if that person lacked someone to form a couple with, to dance with or do something else with. Most of all, she joined in when they were dancing a broom dance. She took part in such a dance as intensely as the broom did. Just as the broom never grabbed anyone to dance with, but was always grabbed, and just as anyone had no choice but to grab it when he or she had no partner, so too they grabbed Miss Bertha if they didn't want to remain without a partner . . . Yes, that was why she stood there, she never tried to grab anyone, but she was grabbed and pulled into the circle with everyone else; and the moment the fiddle and the piano abruptly stopped, and the broomstick crashed to the floor, she stood there as if not taking part in the game. She stood there, waiting for somebody to grab her instead of grabbing the broom.

Among the rest and with the rest, the prominent border also joined in the dance, and he danced, a man in his fifties, and he kept trying to grab the youngest and prettiest girl. Miss Bertha often noticed that one girl preferred falling into another girl's arms rather than falling into his hands. For Miss Bertha, it was better for him to grab her rather than some other girl, who would suffer if he grabbed her. Dancing and whirling with him, Miss Bertha sensed that even though he chased other girls and not her, his conduct nevertheless indicated that he was far from unhappy with her

. . . She figured that other girls avoided him because he would thrust his foot and his knee into their dancing legs, and it was pleasant for Miss Bertha to help other girls avoid this unpleasant experience . . .

Once, while dancing with him, she asked him whether or not he was married. She wanted to find out because other girls wanted to know. He failed to answer her question; instead, he pulled her entire body against his own and made her an indecent suggestion . . . Miss Bertha was so surprised that she couldn't tell whether this was she or whether she was someone else, and whether he had made that indecent suggestion not to her but to another girl . . . She was so confused that she forgot to feel insulted and she kept dancing, wedged against him and chained by his hands. When the dance was done, she hurried out of the casino and ran away, not knowing where . . . She ran into the deep grass and she heard someone running after her. She didn't know who it was but she assumed it was that same man.

She ran into one of the canvas booths that stood there, white, aslant, and sharply angular like roofs torn from houses, roofs full of dark, gaping holes, virtually concealing the darkness of booths, the gloominess of booths. A short time later, he came lurching in after her and went straight toward her.

"What do you want from me?" she asked, her heart pounding. Her tone of voice was that of a woman who knows the answer but pretends not to know what he wants, because she herself isn't so far from wanting the same thing. However, she, Miss Bertha, was quite far from that, even though she understood (after all, he had made his intentions clear). Still, it failed to sink in . . . Something in her felt hazy, almost dark, incomprehensible, that he didn't mean her, or that he meant something else, not what she already knew he meant. He didn't answer, he simply pounced on her brutally, like a man who's certain that he's in the right place and that he doesn't have to argue with her.

Miss Bertha was utterly lost, and in losing she found herself, and that was by pure chance: at the very moment that he, heavy and virile, pressed her to him, she felt a stab in the chest. She now remembered that she had a needle in her blouse, and, not losing a single moment, she pulled the needle from her blouse and stabbed him. The stabbed man let out a roar like a wild beast and retreated.

. . .   .

SHE WENT TO bed late that night, fully dressed, but she didn't fall asleep. Long after the incident she lay in the dark silence and she could hear the wild noise and wild dancing of the reckless and sated merry-makers . . . At times in her drowsing, she thought that an unfamiliar man who was very familiar in his unfamiliarity was the most reckless and that the wild noise was coming from him, and this wrenched her from her drowsing, and she awoke with a fever in her blood . . . She was terrified of him even though she knew that the danger was past . . . It was only now, after the incident, that she was terrified of him, a lot more than before. She was terrified of him but didn't feel the strong anger that she ought to feel. There were even moments when she regretted that the nee-dle had stabbed him. She knew she could have avoided it anyway.

THE NEXT EVENING, a car arrived at the Sunshine Boardinghouse. It was the same car that drove back and forth, that brought guests and took them away. Now, driving up and breathing like a car, it halted and waited for someone.

If was after supper, the diners had just left the tables after their third fill-ing meal of the day. The diners, who had just finished dining and most of whom were sated even before they finished dining, scattered in pairs and in groups along the hard, dusty road, which, in its dusty hardness and dusty grayness, stretched out in one direction and in another, both directions running over hill and dale, past farms and boardinghouses. The high moun-tain, the highest of all the mountains in the area, cast a huge shadow as on every evening and, early on, long before sunset, that mountain poured its evening shadow over the Sunshine Boardinghouse, and up there, on its necklike height and in its dense, wooded slanting, there were bright patches in the wooded darkness, and it was as if those bright patches had arrived from some fantastic world and were visiting the mountain height and the mountain aristocracy. And now, as always, it was as if the mountain were a high microcosm unto itself, that had grown out of the mother earth and separated from it and now had its own woods, its trees, and it didn't know and would never know about any boardinghouses and boarders.

Miss Bertha came out, clutching a small knapsack in her right hand, and she was followed by someone else, a brother, and by the sister-in-law of the second brother, who did not follow her. Bertha looked sleepy and angry. She ignored everyone, although many boarders told her and one

another how sorry they were about her sudden and unexpected departure. And when she sat down in the car, they tossed flowers in all kinds
of colors at her and twigs and plants—all the things that were yielded by
the summer and the rich mountain nature.

Miss Bertha sat there like an outsider, as if the attention weren't aimed
at her. She was ashamed to raise her eyes, and it was only when the car
started moving that she glanced at one side, then the other, and smiled
a crooked smile at the people seeing her off and she couldn't figure out
who they were, all those people so warmly seeing her off. They were
strangers, and yet not so long ago all these strangers had been so close to
her. She had played such an active part in the personal, intimate lives of
many of them and she knew so many intimate things about some of them,
in which she had shown so much interest not so long ago . . .

She was taking it all along, all of it, like an unnecessary, a sickening
burden, and what did anyone know about her? Nobody knew anything
about her and nobody was interested in knowing anything about her, as
if she had no personal life of her own and were merely an empty vessel
into which only other people's interests were poured . . .

She was leaving, and nobody knew that she was looking for someone,
someone who had so brutally offended her . . . He wasn't there; and it
was obvious that he couldn't be there . . . But she wanted him to be there
. . . It was a deep, inner longing. She couldn't want it on the surface
because . . . Really because—because it was only after that incident that
she . . . fell in love with that man. . . .

They tossed flowers at her, poured flowers over her, and twigs, and various wild, blossoming plants and they shouted after her in English:
"Goodbye, Miss Bertha! Miss Bertha, goodbye!"

And she drove away, Miss Bertha did.

YOYSEF SMOLAZH *(1907–1942)*

*Born in Chmelnik, Poland, Smolazh moved to Lodz, then Warsaw, where
he was living at the outbreak of World War II. He was murdered at the
Treblinka death camp.*

The Open Grave (*1937*)

CROWDS OF PEOPLE had been gathering since dawn at the morgue next to the city hospital. Drowsy, shivering, in damp gray clothes, they warmed themselves by huddling in one another's breath. Their faces were remote and gloomy, their lips pressed together in harsh sorrow, their eyes blinked naively and awkwardly. A damp autumn fog shrouded these people, isolating them from the rest of the city.

Now and then, however, the faded yellow light of a municipal streetcar flickered in the distance. A grating shriek shook them up, reminding them that living creatures were bustling on the other side of the fog. But they, virtually cast out on a wild steppe, stood there, silent, melancholy, motionless.

Somewhat later, new people tore through the foggy cloud. The air grew freer, the light vaster, and the fog evaporated like steam.

A red-hot strip cut the horizon more sharply, pouring like blood into the blue, cadaverous day.

The sleepy people, who, in their damp gray clothes, had come to pick up their dead relatives, breathed more easily with the arrival of the day, shaking courage into their cold, drowsy legs, peering at the growing crowd—God help us!

A Jewish woman wrapped in a blanket flung her arms apart and yelled in a dry, hoarse voice: "Why are we standing like wooden poles? Today's a Friday in winter. We won't be able to bury the dead! What an awful business!" She sobbed more vehemently. "My son set out a week ago . . . to save our home and his poor mother . . . Then he tried to hang himself. And then peasants cut him down, untied the noose—his face was blue, he was scarcely breathing, his head was twisting every which way! He kept gasping: 'Leave me alone! I don't wanna live! I don't wanna live!' My poor son! Your wish came true!"

The woman began shaking, writhing, she collapsed, bending and buckling. The throng was petrified.

Two men pulled her to her feet and kept her standing. Her head thrashed about as if she'd been slaughtered. Her face was flooded with tears, her entire body was sobbing, her heart was pounding recklessly, and in a staccato voice she bellowed: "You dogs! Why don't you say something? Five suicides—six young men starved to death, and my son—" She burst into wild laughter. "And my son was the twelfth—is that a tiny number?" Her eyes flashed insanely. "Like in the epidemic—epidemic—epidemic!"

Two strong orderlies in blue scrubs took her into the hospital waiting room. A young doctor, clad in a white smock with a stiff, shiny collar, earnestly listened to her heart and then mumbled: "An attack of nerves."

The people in the crowd grew agitated; some of them were listening closely to a tall, red-haired young man with lean, drawn cheeks. Spraying saliva through his bared yellow teeth, he proclaimed that the dead were better off, they had already gotten across. "But we," he asked hopelessly, "what are we gonna do? This winter we'll be escorting a lot more people to the cemetery."

An old, bowed Gentile with a gray, tobacco-stained mustache opened the brown, rusty door to the morgue. At first the people shoved their way in, but a short while later they jumped back in disgust.

The long, narrow room, resembling a dark corridor, had thick walls, a high, black, vaulted ceiling, and tiny barred windows. The day seeping through the panes was heavy, overcast. The floor gave off a darkness like black, wind-tousled hair. The corners shuddered in mysterious terror. The blankness emitted the coolness of the damp smell of corpses. And corpses, covered with black rags, were laid out from one end of the room to the door. Tags stuck out between the crooked yellow toes, bearing the names of the dead. The bowed Gentile pulled out the tags and read the names aloud as if deafened by the noise:

"Moshek Shtein, thirty-two years old! Stefan Volotshuk, twenty-eight years old! Antonyova Kraftshik, nineteen years old!"

The crowd trembled. Nineteen . . . But the bowed Gentile's voice grew calmer, as if he were handing out mail parcels.

The hospital plaza resounded with the clattering of horses' hooves. And then came several black wagons drawn by horses with sad, lowered heads. A soft lament rose from the crowd. The corpses were carried out, and some of the people moved on.

A long, gray throng moved through the frosty autumn day, trudging across the slightly frozen earth. Their faces were drawn and gloomy, their lips narrow and sullen, their eyes moist and dark and submerged in an ocean of sorrow. Straight, stiff male backs in ragged jackets stuck out of the throng. Prematurely aged women with thin, feeble legs kept colliding with one another.

No bells were ringing, no Catholic priests in long cassocks were singing prayers of comfort, no Jewish women were naming the good angels that were to welcome the dead. Just a silent throng with grim, bony faces shuffled wearily through the noisy, clamorous streets.

The hospital plaza was completely deserted by now. The heavily charged air weighed down on me. The sun was soaking dimly in the dark clouds, floating tediously from one to the other.

In the morgue two corpses were left—homeless strangers perhaps. I uncovered one face. A pupil wedged inside out in a torn corner of an eye glared angrily at me. The head lay flung to the side. Filthy stickiness darkened the twisted yellow features. I gazed at the face for several minutes. Suddenly I shuddered. Then I stared hard. Yes, someone I knew. I pulled out the tag and I read: Sorre Rozen. My eyes darkened with memories that were struggling in my mind. Yes, Sorre Rozen, the girl with the flaming cheeks, the quiet girl with the modest smile in the corners of her mouth. Our paths had constantly crossed in the workers' homes; she had always worn a black apron on her slight figure, and she usually had a verse by Bovshover, the anarchist poet, on her dry lips:

"How can I, brothers, sing for joy?"

I looked around—there was no one here . . . I wanted to shriek: "Sorre, I never knew that you were this lonely. I never knew why your eyes were so sad."

It was almost dusk; a black wagon drove by, accompanied by a grinding streetcar and a peasant dozing on a wagonload of coal. I sat with a Jewish graveyard worker on the coachbox. Surprised looks drilled into my back. I wanted to shriek: "What indifference! A human being has died! A human being!"

The graveyard workers grumbled at me: "Hey, listen, why are you so late?"

I tried to point out that this was a homeless girl, a stranger.

"Fine!" they snapped. "Forget it!"

Three short, fat women with dark faces and warty chins, trudged out from the ritual cleansing house.

"Where's the shroud? Where's a candle? What a world!" they sighed heavily.

I stood there dumbfounded. What was this? Sorre Rozen . . . A girl had worked in a factory, then lost her job, gone hungry, and now—a tag on her toes: Sorre Rozen, twenty-five years old. And that was that!

I carried her on my shoulder. An old Jew slogged ahead of me. The wind whistled in his beard. His mouth shook out a grumbling Psalm Ninety-one, which is traditionally recited at Jewish funerals: "He that dwelleth in the secret place of the most High shall abide under the shadow of the Almighty . . ."

We halted at the end of the field, next to a brick barrier. A cavernous shout came from a grave: "Beryl, is this the last one already?"

"Yeah, thank God! The last one!"

I stood at the open grave. The corpse had been cleansed and it was shining. The shroud lent it a delicate charm. A human being had been purified . . . The sun blazed up, igniting the horizon. The mound of dug-up soil was aflame.

Suddenly a huge mob of people emerged before my eyes. They hurried like a wall toward the open grave. I recognized them—these were the people in the damp gray clothes. Forming a circle, they gaped down into the open grave. Then I heard a loud wailing: "People! Why are you silent? Can't you see that the graveyard is shut down, nailed up? We've been wandering through it since daybreak like cursed souls and we can't find a way out!"

The wailing grew louder: "We're trapped in the graveyard! We're doomed! The open grave is devouring us!"

I looked around. The woman in the blanket was writhing convulsively, pouring her words like sparks on the cold, mute mob.

The graveyard trees rustled eerily. The wailing grew softer, more profound. The western sky gazed like a blind man. Dark and cold, like lead. The night slid nimbly from the trees and settled like a huge black cat on the freshly dug grave.

MENAKHEM KIPNIS (1878–1942)

In Ashkenazi folklore, Khelm is the Jewish Gotham—a town of fools. The Khelmites are generally called "fools" or "sages," whereby the Yiddish noun khokhem *(sage) has degenerated so terribly that it now also means fool. What else can you expect of a culture that uses* ristotl *(from Aristotle) to mean fool? Khelm itself is actually located in Poland, although its Jews were wiped out under the German occupation.*

No one knows why Khelmites have their foolish renown. Some of the Khelm stories parallel stories about Schildburg (1598), a German town of fools: several collections of these German narratives were translated into Yiddish during the eighteenth century. The first German Schildburg collection goes back to the anonymous German folk book The Lale Book *(1597); its pro-feudal antics take place in a land called Utopia, a name coined by Thomas More in his satire* Utopia *(first published, in Latin, in 1516). The Jewish Khelm is actually a dystopia, which, though not intending to do so, excoriates shtetl life as viciously as the most ferocious maskil might have done.*

The piece selected for this anthology is longer and far more complex than the usual Khelm anecdotes, which were collected and adapted by numerous Yiddish authors. Kipnis himself, active in many areas of Yiddish culture, including folklore, was murdered in the Warsaw Ghetto.

What Became of the Fools of Khelm?

FROM *THE FOOLS OF KHELM* (1930)

NOT SO FAR from Khelm there lived a smart Jewish villager named Beryl. His business was going badly, so it occurred to him: since Khelm was practically at the end of his nose, why shouldn't his sharp mind think of a way for the Khelmites to help him?

After reflecting, he bought an old, scrawny horse, drove to town, and halted not far from the synagogue. He then unhitched the horse and had it stand with its face toward the wagon. Next he inserted a gold imperial halfway under its tail and then he sat down on the side to see what would happen.

A Jew returning from synagogue noticed that gold was shining from the horse's backside. Wondering what this was all about, he walked over.

"Why are you so surprised, my friend?" asked Beryl. "If you feed this horse oats, its backside emits gold imperials—that's the kind of horse it is."

Seeing this treasure, the man offered to buy the horse.

Another man, who saw them haggling, came over. Upon hearing about the miraculous horse, he insisted on buying it. They were joined by a fourth man, a fifth, a sixth—until all of Khelm had learned that if you fed the horse oats, its backside emitted a gold imperial. A huge crowd gathered around the villager and his horse, arguing and quarreling. Each Khelmite wanted to grab the horse for himself, and no matter how much he offered, someone else offered more—until they came to blows. Finally they summoned the rabbi.

When the rabbi reached the square and saw what was going on and what the fight was all about, it didn't take him long to issue a verdict. He determined that the horse should belong not to an individual but to the entire Jewish community, so that everyone could benefit.

Now the rabbi started dickering with the villager: "How much do you want for the horse, Beryl?"

Beryl hesitated. He said he didn't really want to sell it.

"You have to, Beryl," the rabbi pressured him. "Our congregation is poor, and God Himself has sent you here."

"If that's the case, I want five hundred ducats for the horse."

Upon hearing the price, the rabbi handed Beryl five hundred ducats and took the horse.

The townsfolk gathered for an assembly and tried to resolve where they should keep the horse. One person said they should put the horse in the rabbi's home. Someone else suggested that they put it in the women's section of the synagogue. In short, they thought and thought and then decided that they should dig a deep hole in the synagogue courtyard and lower the horse into the hole. In front, they would set up a device for pouring in oats; and in back, a large hollow for the imperials . . .

And that's what they did. They dug a deep hole in the synagogue courtyard, lowered the horse, and waited three days for a heap of imperials to collect.

On the third day they had another assembly. They debated who should go down into the hole and pick up the imperials. They decided that they couldn't trust anyone but the rabbi. So they took him and lowered him into the hole.

The rabbi scratched and scratched but came up with nothing.

The townsfolk refused to rely on the rabbi, and instead they lowered the head of the community. But after quite a while, he too came up with nothing.

Was that the story? Khelm was in turmoil. Was Beryl a swindler? Had he cheated the whole of Khelm? Well, off to his home! The rabbi and two trustees marched to the villager's home, intending to read him the riot act.

The villager knew perfectly well what was going on. The rabbi and the trustees would arrive any minute. So Beryl devised a new trick.

Beryl had two rabbits in his home. He gave one to his wife, telling her that when the rabbi and the two trustees arrived and asked for him, she should take the rabbit, open the window, and say, "Hurry, rabbit, run to the woods and bring Beryl back!" Beryl would then come in through the back door, holding the second rabbit. That way, the rabbi and the trustees would think that this was the same rabbit his wife had sent out through the window. They would witness a fresh miracle and forget all about the horse with the imperials.

And that's what happened.

When the rabbi and the trustees came in and angrily snapped, "Where is Beryl?", his wife grabbed the rabbit, peered into its eyes, and said, "Hurry, rabbit. Hurry to the woods and bring Beryl home!" And she released it through the window.

The rabbi and the trustees witnessed the miracle: the wife had talked to the rabbit, sent it to bring Beryl home, and the rabbit had bounded to the woods. And they were even more astonished when Beryl walked in through the back door, with the rabbit over his shoulder, and cried out: "Here I am!"

The rabbi and the trustees were dumbstruck, they could scarcely believe their eyes.

Instead of bringing up the horse and the imperials, they had another idea: they wanted Beryl to sell them the rabbit. The rabbi began: "Beryl! We came here to buy your rabbit. Our congregation is poor and we can't really afford a beadle to run errands. So we've come here to buy your rabbit and make it our town beadle."

Beryl again hesitated; he couldn't sell the rabbit, he needed it for errands. But the rabbi and the trustees wouldn't back off, and so he squeezed a thousand ducats out of them and gave them the rabbit. The rabbi and the trustees took the rabbit and proudly returned to Khelm.

The townsfolk were delighted. "Wonderful. Now we don't need a beadle! And when the rabbi convenes an assembly, it won't take hours. The rabbit will notify everyone quickly, and it'll be cheaper too."

The community fired all the beadles and made the rabbit the town beadle.

An assembly was scheduled for the next day, and so the rabbi took the rabbit and said: "Hurry, rabbit, summon the Jews to an assembly: Shoel the head beadle, Dovid the assistant beadle, Meyer-Simkhe the kosher-meat-tax collector, Ali the butcher, Meyer the juggler, Yosle the mailman, Peysye the cantor, Shakhne the candlemaker, Yoyl the wild boar, Hershl the skullcap, Shmonye the tailor, and Zisye the ragamuffin. And step on it, do you hear?" And the rabbi released the rabbit through the window.

An hour dragged by—and no rabbit. Two hours, three hours, it was already evening and no rabbit. It was already time for evening prayers, it was already time for the assembly—and there was no rabbit and no assembly.

If that was the case, then Beryl the villager was a tremendous swindler. Not only had he cheated them with the horse that had made imperials, he had also pulled the wool over their eyes with the rabbit as a town beadle.

And the rabbi and the trustees again furiously headed toward the villager's home to settle his hash, which he deserved for playing such a nasty trick.

BERYL AGAIN KNEW perfectly well what was going on in Khelm, and he expected the rabbi and the trustees to come and carry out their verdict and take back the money. So he hit on another trick. He told his wife that as soon as they saw the rabbi and the trustees in the distance, she should lie on the ground and pretend to be dead. Beryl would mourn her and then remove an egg from the cabinet and tap the egg on her forehead. And she would then come back to life and stand up.

And that was what happened.

When the rabbi and the trustees came in furiously, planning to rip Beryl to shreds, they suddenly saw a corpse lying on the ground and covered with a sheet. Beryl was bending over the corpse, tearfully shouting: "What a radiant soul—my dear Khanna! Who are you leaving me with in this foolish world!"

The rabbi and the trustees quieted down, they halted, terror-stricken, gazed at the dismal scene, and joined in Beryl's weeping.

All at once, Beryl stood up and yelled: "No, you mustn't die, you haven't lived out your seventy years!" He went over to the cabinet, removed an egg, stepped over to the "dead" woman, and tapped the egg on her forehead. His wife then stood up and, sound and strong, she went straight to the kitchen.

When the rabbi saw this, he forgot all about the horse with the imperials and the rabbit as town beadle. He said: "Beryl, do you know why we've come here? We want you to sell us that egg, which can raise the dead. Our congregation is poor, and the town can't afford any doctors and healers. Please sell us the egg!"

Beryl wouldn't hear of it: No, he couldn't, he had inherited the egg from his great-great-grandfather, who had inherited it from his great-great-grandfather, and so on and so forth. The egg went all the way back to the spies that Moses sent out to reconnoiter Canaan. "No, I can't sell it!"

"But you have to!" the rabbi and the trustees pleaded. "If not for us, then for our poor congregation."

"Well," the villager finally voiced his desire. "It'll cost you a thousand ducats."

The rabbi and the trustees didn't falter for an instant. They paid Beryl the thousand ducats and took his egg back to Khelm.

The town was delighted! People were no longer scared of the Angel of Death! To hell with the healers and barber-surgeons! The town had an egg that could bring back the dead!

Soon they convened a large assembly to figure out where to keep the egg and they decided that it was nowhere so safe as with the rabbi himself. He should keep the egg in the silver box in which he stored the ethrog for the Feast of Tabernacles.

And that was what they did.

Suddenly, who should fall ill but no less a person than Feygele, the rabbi's wife? People were delighted, ecstatic. They didn't call a healer, a doctor—or anyone. The hell with them all! People simply waited for her to die. Then they could use the egg to bring her back to life.

And that was what happened.

She died at a propitious moment, and as soon as she was stretched out on the ground, the rabbi himself took the egg and tapped it on his wife's forehead. She didn't stir. So he tapped harder. But she absolutely refused to stir. So he tapped her even harder, until the egg shattered altogether.

Upon witnessing this, the town was up in arms. What a swindler, what a trickster! And by the rabbi's wife's grave, they decided: "A life for a life!" And this time not the rabbi but the whole of Khelm should go to Beryl.

When the entire town beleaguered Beryl's home, he couldn't escape. And so they promptly convened an assembly to determine what to do to him. They cited not just the four traditional kinds of Jewish execution—stoning, burning, slicing, strangling—but also breaking, hanging, shooting, roasting, pulling, ripping, biting. They pondered so many different death penalties for Beryl, but in the end they decided not to shed any blood. Instead, they would tie him up in a sack and toss it into the river, so he'd die on his own.

And that was what they did. They put the culprit in a sack and dragged it over to the river. However, the river was frozen, and there was no hole where they could toss in the sack.

What did they do? They needed an ax.

But this was Khelm, and the whole of Khelm went off to get an ax, leaving Beryl all alone in the sack, under the bridge.

As he lay there, Beryl heard a Polish nobleman driving along, and he hit on a trick. He started yelling: "I don't want to be an emperor! I don't want to!"

The nobleman heard someone yelling under the bridge, so he stopped his carriage, got out, climbed under the bridge, untied the sack, and asked Beryl what was going on and why he was yelling: "I don't want to be an emperor!"

Beryl told him that the whole of Khelm had ganged up on him and wanted to make him emperor, and because he didn't want to, they had tied him up in the sack. And now they came to him every two hours and asked him if he wanted to be an emperor.

"Well, if I were you, I'd want to be emperor," said the nobleman avidly.

"You know what? Why don't you get into the sack? I'll tie it up, and when they come and ask you if you want to be emperor, you should say: 'I want to,' and then you'll become emperor."

"Fine!" the nobleman agreed. He pulled Beryl out and then climbed into the sack.

Beryl tied the sack up firmly and took off in the carriage.

When the Khelmites returned with the ax, they quickly hacked a hole in the ice and tossed in the sack with the nobleman inside.

Within a month, Khelm had calmed down. One day, a fine coach drawn by thoroughbreds rolled into the marketplace and stopped outside the rabbi's home. Someone climbed down from the coach and entered the rabbi's home.

The townsfolk had a good look: it was Beryl!

"Where are you coming from, Beryl? From the Other Side?"

People came scurrying over, men, women, and children. The whole town laid siege to the rabbi's home. They all wanted to see Beryl the villager, who'd been tossed into the river just one month earlier. They wanted to hear what he had to say about the Other World.

Beryl stood in front of the whole town and told them what had happened to him. The instant he'd been thrown into the river, he'd found treasures — gold and silver, precious stones, brilliants and diamonds. And since he'd come flying in with his head up, his hands had grabbed as much of the priceless treasures as he could and he had stuffed them into his pockets. Then he'd climbed out the other end, safe and sound.

After hearing his story, the Khelmites had a huge assembly and they decided that, in order to take care of the congregation, the whole of Khelm was to cross to the Other Side and gather gold, silver, and precious stones.

And so early the next morning, everyone, from the rabbi to the bathhouse owner, jumped into the river under the ice in order to reach the Other Side and fill up on gold, silver, and precious stones for the congregation of Khelm.

And that was how they perished and vanished — those old and beloved fools of Khelm, about whom the world tells so many beautiful tales and wonderful folk legends.

MOYSHE KULBAK (*1896–?1949*)

Kulbak, born in Lithuania, started out as a Hebrew teacher. After publishing his first Yiddish poem in 1918, he spent three years in Berlin, which during the twenties contained a small but hyperactive Yiddish community.

Kulbak resettled, first in Vilna, then in the Soviet Union (1926), which at that time seemed to be promoting secular Jewish culture, particularly Yiddish. His corpus includes Expressionist plays, and fiction—especially mystical novels, but also comical poetry. Turning away from the mysticism frowned on by the new state, Kulbak wrote Zelmenyaners *(1931), his humorous saga about Soviet Yiddish farm life. However, in 1937, Russia's antisemitic purges caught up with him: he was arrested for "ideological deviation" and sent to Siberia, where he reportedly died in 1949. The Soviet government rehabilitated him in 1956.*

Zelmenyaners (1931)

BOOK I, THE OLDSTERS (EXCERPTS)

1. Zelmenyaners

THIS IS GRAMPA Zelmele's courtyard.

An ancient brick wall with crumbling mortar and two rows of houses filled with Zelmeles. There are also stables, cellars, and attics. The whole thing looks like a narrow lane. In summer, at the first glint of dawn, short Zelmele would come out wearing nothing but his underpants. He would shift a brick here, carry a spadeful of dung there with all his strength.

Where does Grampa Zelmele come from?

The family always explains that he came from "deep in the Ukraine." In any case, it was here that he married Gramma Bashe, who was obviously a girl back then, and it was here that she began to have kids.

Gramma Bashe, we are told, had kids without premeditation, a whole series of kids, in a kind of frenzy. And the fruits of her womb were tall and dark, with broad shoulders—true Zelmenyaners. Later on, the kids came under Zelmele's jurisdiction—but he didn't pamper them. He would wait a bit and then have them learn a craft.

He made one of them, Folye, a tanner at ten years of age, because of some business about a horse.

Nobody noticed that these kids were starting to have kids of their own. Daughters-in-law with varying degrees of fertility joined the clan, as did all sorts of sons-in-law, all with new energy, until the neighbors started making an effort. All the houses were chockful of dark, lively little Zelmeles. Blondes were few and far between and only among the girls: in general, a meager blond sprinkle that made little impact. A few red-heads have come in during the last few years. But so far, nobody has offered an explanation.

THE ZELMENYANERS ARE dark and bony, with broad, low foreheads. A Zelmenyaner has a fleshy nose. A Zelmenyaner has dimpled cheeks. Normally he's calm, a man of few words, who looks at everything from the side. However, mainly in the younger generation, there are some Zelmenyaners, both male and female, who can talk a blue streak; and some are even nervy. But they too are basically shy Zelmeles who have come under outside influences and pretend to be something they're not. Zelmenyaners are patient and not nasty. They hold their tongues whether mournful or cheerful, although there is a Zelmenyaner style that glows like red-hot iron.

In the course of generations, the Zelmenyaners have developed an aroma of their own—a mellow smell, like that of freshly stacked hay and something else.

Jews may sometimes be riding in a packed railroad car, yawning into the cold morning. All at once a Jew rubs his eyes and asks:

"Excuse me, aren't you from N.?"

"Yeah."

"Aren't you a grandson of Zelmele's?"

"Yeah, a grandson of Zelmele's."

The Jew tucks his hands into his sleeves and keeps traveling. In his sleep, he caught a whiff of Zelmele's aroma, although certainly no one in town ever gave it a second thought; it's never struck anybody that the Zelmenyaners have a particular smell.

The clan has another peculiarity that is characteristic of the men:

A Zelmele likes to sigh—about nothing special. He holds his breath while his lips emit a kind of cheery, tender neighing such as you can over-hear only in a stable where horses are standing and munching oats.

All this proves that Grampa Zelmele was raised on a farm. It also shows that a Zelmenyaner is thoroughly down to earth, like a piece of bread.

None of the women are barren. And none of them die before their time (except Aunt Hesye).

And if a man is bald, then he's no chip off the old block, even if he smells of hay, a small pile of hay.

WHEN THE SPROUTS of the fourth generation started blossoming, Grampa Zelmele began preparing for his journey. He wrote his will inside the cover of a religious tome, aimlessly wandered a bit, and then actually died.

He was a down-to-earth man. He wrote his will in Yiddish with the appropriate Hebrew phrases, and since we're not quite sure of the whereabouts of the book, it may be useful to reconstruct the will from memory, italicizing the Hebrew phrases:

Monday, Portion 16 of the Torah in the year [erased]. . . .

While I am still among the living, I propose to divide my legacy among my children as it will be *after my one hundred years*. This is what I propose: my children should keep living *in my courtyard*. My little cemetery plot is to be sold *for about four hundred rubles*. And my pew in the synagogue should likewise be sold for *about one hundred fifty rubles*.

Also, there are *about a thousand* rubles hidden behind the sixth right-hand brick in the stove, and this money should be divided as follows: *To my son* Itshe—one hundred fifty rubles, since he has already taken an *advance of one hundred fifty rubles* against his share of the inheritance. *To my son* Zishe—two hundred rubles, and *to my son* Yude—likewise *two hundred rubles*; and *to my son* Folye—likewise *two hundred rubles*; and *to my daughter* Khaye-Mashe—one hundred rubles; and *to my daughter* Matle—likewise *one hundred rubles*; and *to my daughter* Rashe—likewise *one hundred rubles*.

Hurvits should be repaid *one hundred sixty rubles*, which I borrowed from him to give *my son* Itshe an *advance* on his share of the inheritance, while I was still alive. And *twenty-five rubles* should be donated to charity. The balance of the money should cover the funeral expenses for conveying me to Life Everlasting.

The household items belong *to my wife* Sorre-Bashti. *After her one hundred years*, they should be divided among all three of my daughters. However, two pillows should be given to Itshe's unmarried daughter

Khayke; and that is how my daughters should divide their inheritance; however, they should give my clothes to my sons. The lambskin overcoat should go to whoever needs it or whoever wins it by lots; but there should be no fighting over it, everything should be done in an agreeable fashion, and the shares should be handed out according to my instructions and not by any outsider. I hope that everyone enjoys and appreciates his inheritance. I wish that with all my heart. But they should not forget me *after my one hundred years*—at least say kaddish if at all possible.

　　Signed: Zalmen-Elye, son of Leyb Khvost

Gramma Bashe outlived Grampa by many years, and one can say that she is still alive today. True, she can't see properly or hear properly or walk properly—but at least she's alive. Nowadays she's more like an old chicken than a human being and she doesn't even know that the world has changed.

　　Gramma Bashe is involved only with herself, and if she does any thinking, her thoughts must be bizarre, made of a wholly different cloth than normal thoughts.

　　On some evenings, when she is wandering in the darkness, she suddenly addresses a red necktie: "Motele, why aren't you going to synagogue?"

　　Dark Motele, who is gradually beginning to smell of hay, goes over to her, peels the kerchief off her ear, and yells into it: "Gramma, I'm a Pioneer." (That's the Communist Children's Organization.)

　　She nods her head. "Yes, yes, he's already been to synagogue. In which one did you pray?"

　　That's how she'll leave the world, in a peaceful, old-fashioned frame of mind. The homestead is solid where Zelmele established it, and Gramma sees that every year there are new dark and silent people—Zelmeles.

　　In the summer, when Gramma Bashe steps out and settles on the threshold, she beams as she watches the Zelmeles pouring and pouring out of every door like black poppy seeds.

　　The huge sun shines down on the new Zelmenyaner offspring.

　　And that is Gramma Bashe.

. . .　　. . .　　. . .

THE SECOND GENERATION of Zelmenyaners spread out in three mighty streams and several tributaries. The pillars of the clan have always been and have remained: Uncle Itshe, Uncle Zishe, and Uncle Yude.

Uncle Folye goes his own way. Uncle Folye goes his own separate, hardworking way in life. The Zelmenyaner homestead should not concern him because he says that when he was young, he was insulted. He's a glutton with a weakness for potato cake. And no one knows his thoughts because he never expresses them.

The others in the clan are slim pickings, barely revealing their source, although they were formed according to Grampa Zelmele's specifications, and now they carry his odor through the world.

Uncle Zishe occupies a special niche in the clan, enjoying great prestige. A chubby watchmaker with a rectangular forehead and a rectangular beard, Uncle Zishe is a weakling or else pretends to be a weakling.

In earlier times, people would bring him documents to read. Uncle Zishe would remove the loupe from his eye, ask the visitor to be seated, and patiently go through the document word by word. But even if Uncle Zishe couldn't make out the document, he had one virtue: he would recite the text from memory.

He had a fine understanding.

However, his chief virtue in reading was that he could give you on-the-spot advice about your "lawsuit."

People say that a great power lay hidden inside him.

His wife, Aunt Gitte, bore him two daughters with a lot more difficulty than is appropriate for Zelmenyaners. One daughter is Tonke—a pure Zelmenyaner. The second daughter has a touch of sweet melancholy, which Aunt Gitte, with all due respect, has smuggled into the family. But one has to forgive Aunt Gitte, for they all maintain that it's not her fault—she's descended from rabbis.

Uncle Itshe is the king of paupers. He was so impatient that he got part of his share of the inheritance while Grampa Zelmele was still alive. Uncle Itshe is a tailor, a patcher. His tall sewing machine, skinny and sluggish, clatters along day and night.

The machine deafens the courtyard.

Uncle Itshe produces true Zelmenyaners of the purest water. The others feel that in this respect he has outshone even Grampa Zelmele.

Among all the peculiarities marking the entire clan, Uncle Itshe has developed a habit of his own: he sneezes with a shriek.

Once, a sneeze of his made a woman faint.

In the perilous times of the Civil War, the family members were quite worried about his sneezes. Uncle Zishe even found it necessary to visit him and discuss this issue.

"Itshe," said Uncle Zishe, "do you realize that your sneezes threaten our very lives?"

Now what could Uncle Itshe have replied? After all, he did sneeze with a violent shriek.

The family kept hatching plans, but when push came to shove, Aunt Malkele herself hit on a solution:

If he felt a sneeze coming on, Uncle Itshe would grab his nose and collapse on his bed, Aunt Malkele would throw a pillow on him and lie down on him full force. Or, if she had no time, she put a child on top of him. There, under the bedding, the sneezer would sneeze his heart out, shake off the feathers, and get back to work.

In peacetime, however, he posed no danger.

Quite the contrary!

Daybreak in summer, half the courtyard was still in shade, a well-kempt Uncle Itshe was already sitting at the open window, gunning away at his machine. All at once he sneezed. He emitted the dark, yammering shriek of a dying man. The courtyard began to awaken, they rubbed their eyes, a few people got out of bed: "What's wrong?"

"Nothing," someone replied. "Uncle Itshe is sneezing."

"Nothing, nothing!"

Meanwhile windows large and small were opening everywhere, and all sorts of Zelmenyaner heads with shaggy black hair poured out into the dawn, and shouts rang from all sides:

"Good health to you, Uncle!"

"Long life to you, Uncle!"

"Good health to you and long life to you, Uncle!"

NOW UNCLE YUDE was a very different sort, a different person and a strange person. He was a carpenter, a scrawny man with a small, shiny beard and with spectacles on the tip of his nose, and he always peered over those spectacles. That was why he always seemed angry. But maybe he wore his spectacles for beauty and for dignity. He would do his planing in the spectacles, eat in the spectacles, though apparently never sleep in them.

Uncle Yude was a philosopher and a widower.

His wife, Aunt Hesye, died during the German invasion [in World War I], together with a kosher slaughterer named Yehezkl, and it was not a pretty death. Uncle Yude went to synagogue, sat behind the stove for the seven days of mourning, and refused to get up at all. He resolved to abandon all worldly concerns and devote himself purely to serious pondering: a highly respectable occupation, one must admit. But the town kept nagging away at him, until he finally returned to his workshop.

What had happened to Aunt Hesye?

Our town had lain under artillery fire. All the housewives on our street locked up their homes and took refuge in Grampa Zelmele's basement. Suddenly Aunt Hesye developed a yen for chicken soup. How come? In that stifling cellar, she'd been gaping and gaping at Yehezkl the slaughterer until she felt a hankering for chicken. So she caught a hen, the slaughterer pulled out his ritual knife, and they stepped outside in order to slaughter the fowl. A savage fire crashed in the courtyard, shattering every window.

Later on, a neighbor knocked on the basement door, signaling that they could come out. Aunt Hesye lay on the ground, pale and calm, as if nothing had happened. Near her, with the beard pointing up, lay the slaughter's head, while he, the slaughterer himself, lay on the fallen fence, clutching his knife.

Next to him stood the hen, philosophizing.

Uncle Yude lapsed into gloom and silence, while the other Zelmenyaners maintain a cheerful silence. Aside from this minor deviation, he has remained loyal to Grampa Zelmele's traditions.

He also, incidentally, expresses a love of nature, which is so dynamic throughout the clan. Uncle Yude used to raise geese in his enclosed porch! There was talk about one of his hens. Whenever it rained, Uncle Yude put a tub outdoors to catch the water; and in springtime he felt he needed to get up before dawn and go sorrel-picking. His love of logs and boards probably also derives from that same urge for nature. Uncle Yude would plane a board with love and fervor—in a word: he adored carpentry. Plus he had a terrible weakness for fiddling, singing, and musical stuff in general.

Uncle Yude's children each had a different value. Only two are of interest to us: Khayele and Tsalke.

BEFORE I CONCLUDE, it would be worthwhile to focus more sharply on the younger Zelmenyaners—say, Uncle Itshe's older son, Berre Khvost.

Now there's a young man for you, a hero, a silent tanner! During the Civil War, he was decorated with an Order of the Red Banner for his cool, Zelmenyanerish heroism in the battles of Kazan.

He went to Warsaw with Gai Gaia, that renowned military and political activist. Berre nearly got killed when he fell into Polish hands, but he miraculously managed to change clothes and return home on foot.

When he stepped inside, they whooped it up. The entire clan came running. So did Uncle Zishe. Berre sat down and, slowly removing his boots, he told Aunt Malkele: "Mama, get me food!"

With wild intensity, he gobbled down the banquet while gazing at the ceiling. Uncle Yude spat and left. Little by little the others went home. Berre finished eating, pulled on his boots, and headed back to the war.

2. A World — Huh?

THE COURTYARD WAS silent.

War and revolutions had finally swept through peacefully. Except that Aunt Hesye suffered a misfortune for no good reason—all on account of a silly bit of soup.

The Zelmenyaners came home from the various front lines: they sported stiff tunics and unraveling winter caps. At first they prowled through the courtyard like wolves, devouring everything they got their hands on. But little by little their families lured them into the houses, spoke with them softly, and somehow helped them regain their earlier appearance. In winter the tunics were nailed to the cold doors as insulation, and the unraveling caps have remained somewhere behind the stoves to the present day. At times during severe frosts, Uncle Itshe may reach into the sand behind the stove, fish out such a cap, put it on, pull it down to his beard, and haul a load of wood for Aunt Malkele.

That's what the war has left.

...   .

THE MOST TIGHT-LIPPED Zelmenyaner is Uncle Folye. He never utters a word because he was insulted here during his childhood. Be that as it may, nobody seems inclined to make him talk!

Second to him in silence is Berre, also a fine fellow, and now a militiaman in the second district. But no one ever catches sight of him, he comes home merely to nap on his father's hard plank bed, so he poses no problem.

If any of the young Zelmenyaners start babbling any current foolishness, the family applies its own remedy. A louder word can stop the culprit, and if it doesn't, then a slap can do the trick.

"High time we knocked the confusion out of your head!" says Uncle Zishe.

"You should try and be a mentsh!" says Uncle Itshe.

"Will that prattling ever stop?" says Uncle Yude.

Uncle Yude must be thinking of his daughter Khayele. We know he'd like her to marry a decent Jew. Lately, he's put aside his plane and he's been roaming the study houses, looking for a true-blue Jew. Uncle Yude would like a kosher slaughterer.

People talk, for example, about the following incident:

The other day, he arranged for his daughter to meet a likely candidate on some out-of-the-way street. That night, there happened to be a blizzard. Nevertheless, Khayele went out, reached the designated corner, and started waiting. No living creature was visible in the storm, not even the candidate. But apparently, Khayele was so fired up to get hitched that she hugged a wall, resolving to wait for her destined bridegroom as long as it took. It's hard to say what she was thinking.

In bed late that night, Uncle Yude remembered her. He dashed out and brought her home more dead than alive.

As for the bridegroom, the Zelmenyaners say: "Isn't it obvious that he didn't want to get married in a frost?"

There's a Zelmenyaner who'd marry Khayele even in a frost. He's an elderly bachelor of about thirty-eight if not more—a man of stony silence. We've already mentioned that he comes to his father every night to sleep on the hard plank bed. People feel that he and Khayele suit one another. But their cold love still has to take shape, for now and then Khayele still goes to appointments with prospective bridegrooms.

Uncle Jude is sure to oppose the match with Berre for the following reasons:

1. A Zelmenyaner dislikes a Zelmenyaner.
2. The suitor isn't Jewish enough.
3. The suitor makes fun of the clan.

That's correct. At this very moment, to spite the world, he played yet another trick on his mother, Aunt Malkele—a trick that shook the old Zelmenyaners to the core.

What happened?

Some time ago, Aunt Malkele made up her mind to visit Berre in the militia.

"Berre, how come you never smile?" That's what she asked. "People might think goodness knows what!"

According to her, he did manage a smile. Maybe yes, maybe no. But he sat there for a long time, peering at his bundled-up mother and snorting.

Then he asked: "Ma, have you got enough to live on?"

Uncle Itshe is a cheerful Jew, so he doesn't need anything to live on.

Berre sighed, neighed elegantly through his lips (check Chapter 1), and said: "Mama, do you realize you're not literate?"

To tell the truth, she hadn't realized it. Berre enlightened her, made it clear to her, and advised her to take a course and liquidate her ignorance.

Then he got up and telephoned the Pedagogical Institute.

IT WAS THE Jewish month of Shebat, the dead of winter. Aunt Malkele was freezing as she trudged home, thinking to herself: "The less you see of Berre, the better."

In the courtyard all hell broke loose.

THE NEXT DAY, a teacher did show up, a boy with a forelock billowing from under his visor.

Aunt Malkele's heart began pounding. She quickly washed, took off her apron, and, terribly embarrassed, she sat down at the edge of the table. Aunt Malkele was terrified, she didn't know what lay in store for her, and she desperately peered into the teacher's eyes. The teacher likewise didn't quite know what to do, and his face reddened under his visor.

Communist Youth (those prattlers) keeps its writing material under lock and key. And it turned out that Aunt Malkele's inkwell contained flies instead of ink. She huffed and puffed into the inkwell, but the teacher explained that it wouldn't help. They pulled out the pen from behind the mirror and wiped off the cobwebs; the teacher pressed the tip of the pen on his fingernail, and it turned out that this was an ancient pen, from before the Revolution.

As a result, Aunt Malkele got into the habit of testing any pen on her fingernail to see if it worked—she feels that this too is a sign of an educated person.

Uncle Itshe was likewise totally upset; still, he offered her his notebook. Reaching into the box on the sewing machine, he took out a scrunched-up notebook, to which a pencil was attached by a tiny string. He smoothed out the notebook on his knee and, with trembling elbows, he handed the notebook to the teacher.

The clan gathered together, the crowd was suffocating, they marveled, they shrugged.

Uncle Itshe couldn't stand it any longer: "A world, huh?"

Uncle Yude glared at him over his spectacles and replied: "Wouldn't we be better off six feet under?" He was alluding to Aunt Hesye, who was exempt from having to attend school.

Only Uncle Zishe stood calmly on the side, plucked a hair from his beard, and smiled. "Nice kids!"

EVENTUALLY THEY GOT used to the idea. The teacher would arrive every evening, and Aunt Malkele, admittedly, did accomplish a lot, for she had the aptitude; though we must also grant that she was a bit lazy about learning.

"My mind's not in it," she used to assert.

In general, Aunt Malkele behaved like a little schoolgirl—which was hard to understand in a woman of such great understanding.

Once, when the teacher failed to find her at home, he deemed it necessary to complain to Uncle Itshe: "Your wife reveals enough aptitude, but she doesn't show enough interest in the work."

"Really?" Uncle Itshe was flabbergasted.

Later on, he reprimanded her: "C'mon!" he snapped. "It may cost us money!"

At first Aunt Malkele was flustered, she even blushed, but then she hit on an excuse: "I don't have a book . . ."

That was something Uncle Itshe simply couldn't fathom: What do you mean? Aren't there enough books in the house? Have you finished all of them?"

Aunt Malkele realized her answer was lame. So she thought up another excuse: "I can't see . . . A lens fell out of my spectacles . . ."

But don't think that Uncle Itshe was always so strict with Aunt Malkele. It doesn't hurt to recall that we're talking about old-fashioned love, forty-two years. Uncle Itshe, alas, sympathized with Aunt Malkele.

Indeed, the following incident occurred:

The teacher was due to arrive at any moment. Aunt Malkele was preparing to escape to town. Suddenly dark-haired Motele dashed in, shouting: "Auntie, the teacher's coming!"

Supposedly Aunt Malkele was so befuddled that she crept into bed, wearing her shoes and her overcoat and clutching her basket. Uncle Itshe tucked her in. Then he folded his hands, tilted his head to one side (Oh! Those Zelmenyaners!), and told the teacher in profound sadness: "My missus is a bit under the weather . . . Look, Comrade Teacher, just register the lesson as given and you can do a make-up lesson some other time."

Nevertheless, Aunt Malkele has accomplished a lot.

THE DEPTH OF winter. The windows covered with snow. Communist Youth is in its clubs, and Aunt Malkele stays up through the night, splattered with ink, working with the pen. On the table a tiny kerosene lamp as used by all tailors. The wind whistles in the chimney. Uncle Itshe sits on one side of the table, ripping and sewing. Aunt Malkele sits on the other side, absorbed in her stationery. The pen scratches. Then, with a radiant face, she passes a note to her husband. Uncle Itshe holds the note by the lamp: he can read only at a distance. Aunt Malkele has written the following:

> I am hellthy, yu are soing, go too the stov, takke out the pott, we will drink tee, from mee, yor highly esteemed wiffe makle khvost.

Uncle Itshe smiles. He is content. Later on, over tea, he has an instructive conversation with her. He doesn't bother with trivia, he promptly gets down to brass tacks.

"That's not how people write," he says. "If you're talking, it doesn't matter, but when you write, you have to be elegant."

Aunt Malkele feels uneasy.

"For instance, here," he says, "you write: 'I am hellthy.' You're not expressing your thought elegantly. You shouldn't write like that."

"Then how should I write?" she asks.

"You should write" (and Uncle Itshe shuts his eyes) "you should write: 'I find myself in the very best of perfect hellth!'"

Aunt Malkele sees that he's right.

"Copy the model texts in a letter manual," says Uncle Itshe. "Newfangled methods are so bland. And you also have to read books! Books make you intelligent. There was a writer named Shomer, who people could learn from" (Uncle Itshe didn't realize that most literate people didn't go in for Shomer's pulp romances). "Today's writers are useless—full of suns and moons."

And outside, in the darkness, the winter lay like a cold silver bowl.

BERTHA LELCHUK *(1901–after 1940)*

*B*orn *in Byelorussia, Lelchuk received both a Jewish and a secular education. After a checkered career in Europe and in Palestine (where she practiced dentistry), she moved to America in 1923. She first published a story in 1925 and continued writing tales, sketches, and articles for Yiddish periodicals worldwide. Lelchuk, who had also done some acting in Europe and America, supposedly ended up in Hollywood in 1940, playing bit roles under various names.*

The Aunt from Norfolk

FROM *SHADOWS ON THE SUN* (1938)

SHE SPOKE SLOWLY, doling out each word as if it had cost her dearly: "How many years has it been since I last saw you all?"

Husband and wife stood facing her, unable to utter a word. They smiled, flustered: Who would have expected the aunt from Norfolk to drop in on them without warning?

"Why are you standing?" They asked her to sit down.

The aunt sat down. She viewed the family calmly, the way you view items in a store. Her eternal "refined" smile lingered on her lips: "You were just a little girl, and now you've already got a daughter of your own."

Six-year-old Stella jerked up as if someone had awoken her from sleep. She was busy viewing the rich aunt's clothing. A diamond brooch sparkled on her bosom. It hit Stella that she herself was wearing an old, raggedy dress. She hurried into the next room, dragged out an old valise from under the bed, and swiftly rummaged through it with her little hands. She eventually unearthed her only festive frock and she quickly changed into it. Now she had no reason to envy the rich aunt from Norfolk: she would certainly buy Stella a lovely frock and also shoes, and a doll that could open and close its eyes.

"Stella, come here! Why are you so bashful? Our aunt wants to see you."

Stella winced, spat on her hands, and smoothed her hair. She went over to the mirrored door and gazed at her reflection.

Then she joined the others and stood next to the aunt. The aunt was giving off perfume. What soft hands she had, not like Stella's mother, whose hands were callused from heavy work.

Stella had often heard her mother talk about the aunt with her maids and her nine rooms. Stella peered at the aunt and wondered: "What does she do in those nine rooms?" The floors there were shiny and slippery, and Stella could have slid across them.

"Your name's Stella?" the aunt asked, and Stella's heart pounded. She couldn't utter a word. Now the aunt would tell them what she had brought the child. She couldn't hear her aunt, it was as if she weren't in the room. Stella tried to see if the aunt had a package, but there was no package. Stella scrutinized the entire room, but she didn't see any package. What? The aunt had brought her nothing?

The mother touched Stella's shoulder: "Stella, why won't you answer? Cat got your tongue?"

Stella smiled, still thinking about the gift. She heard her mother saying to her father: "Go and buy some fruit and other goodies. Tell the grocer that the aunt from Norfolk is visiting, and we're gonna pay off our entire tab. He'll give you credit for now."

The father went down. The mother talked to the aunt while straight-ening the tablecloth. She set out the chairs.

"Did you get our letter? We never received an answer. And these are such bad times."

"Yes, I was very concerned about you, but I had no time to write. I'm always so busy, you know. My husband's absorbed in business, and I . . ." The aunt yawned. The trip had tired her. "These subways in New York are horrible!"

Now the father returned with a dozen packages. His face barely showed through them. Stella imagined what was in those packages.

Her mother took them. Green and purple grapes. Large nuts. Candy. The mother placed everything on the table. Water was already boiling in the kitchen. Tea for the aunt.

The father pushed the table over to the aunt: she should be more com-fortable. The aunt smiled: she felt slightly nauseous, she hadn't had a drop of water for an hour now. The mother was still setting things up. Three glasses of water were already on the table. The mother had forgotten all about Stella. The aunt handed Stella a large nut. Stella took the nut, and a crack resounded within a minute: Stella had broken the nut in the door-way. The pieces had fallen on the floor. Stella picked them up and slipped them into her mouth.

The aunt drank tea and talked about her educated daughter.

The mother and the father didn't touch their tea.

"Haven't you been to New York in all this time?" the mother asked the aunt.

"I have, I have. More than once. But whenever I come here, I'm so busy, you know, I don't have time to visit you . . ."

The mother screwed up her courage: "You know, these are very bad times. My husband hasn't worked in almost a year. So we wrote you a few letters . . ."

The aunt slipped grape after grape into her mouth in a "refined" way and she sighed: "Yes, yes, times are bad."

Yes, the mother wanted to tell the aunt about their debts, about their hope that the aunt would help them out and they would pay her back over time, once the father found a job. These words were on the tip of the mother's tongue, but it was difficult to say them to the aunt.

"Yes, we'll pay you back!" The phrase tore out of the mother's mouth and she smiled, flustered.

The aunt peered around the room. "A fine room. How many have you got? Two? Very fine, very fine."

The mother wanted to tell the aunt that they were three months behind in their rent and that the landlord was threatening to toss them out into the street.

But the aunt kept cracking nuts and talking about her life in Norfolk. "It's a small town, nothing like New York." She sighed. "You must think I don't want to live in New York. But circumstances won't allow it. I've wasted my life in Norfolk, my youth."

She moaned. And little Stella's heart ached for the "good" aunt.

"When I arrived in Norfolk thirty years ago, I was young and beautiful. I've wasted the best years of my life."

Now the aunt slipped a piece of candy into her mouth and called to the little girl: "Stella, darling. Come here. Have some candy, don't be shy. Such a quiet child."

The mother smiled, flustered. She wanted to tell the aunt about so many things that she had to endure for little Stella. The girl had been sick, and they couldn't afford a doctor. She had nearly died, and they had written several letters to the aunt, but no answer had come. And perhaps now . . . The mother had all these thoughts, but she couldn't verbalize them. Her heart felt heavy.

"You're looking good," she said to the aunt.

"Good," the aunt echoed mechanically. "You know, despite the Depression that we're all suffering, life can still be very fine."

The father wanted to respond and tell her the whole truth: tell her that everything on the table had been bought on credit, that if the aunt didn't help, they'd have nothing for breakfast tomorrow, and that a harsh winter was coming. . . .

But the aunt kept talking: "You people in New York are so cheerful. Norfolk is so dismal. You know my husband's absorbed in business, my daughter's in college. The black girl cleans our house. All I can do is drive around in my car. You know, I drive myself. During the day, when everyone's busy, I play cards with my friends. I catch a movie several times a week. That's how I fill out my time. I also do charity work, I go to temple. But generally it's dismal. I long for New York."

She dug her teeth into a fresh, juicy apple, munched, swallowed, and resumed talking: "My daughter visits New York a lot. She comes here a lot on holidays, when her college is shut down. She stays in a hotel of course. It costs money, you know, and a girl alone . . . Don't you think that now that we're friends—wouldn't it be better if she stayed with you?"

She smiled so softly. She was so nice now. The father gave the mother a confused look. Flustered, he nodded: "Sure, sure, why not? We'd be delighted."

The aunt stood up. "I have to go. I need to take care of a few things, you know. Well, goodbye, my darlings, it's been great. You're fine people . . . Goodbye."

She went over to Stella and kissed her head. "Goodbye, sweetie."

The parents stood in the middle of the room, unable to speak, as if someone had cut out their tongues. . . .

The room resonated with the "refined" voice of the aunt from Norfolk: "Goodbye . . ."

SARAH HAMER-JACKLYN *(1905–1975)*

*B*orn *into a Hasidic home in Poland, Sarah Hamer-Jacklyn moved to Canada in 1914 with her parents. At sixteen, she began acting and touring in the Yiddish theater. She also started writing stories and, in 1934, publishing them. Aside from appearing in countless Yiddish journals, she eventually put out several collections of her tales, many of which focused specifically on female characters. She herself "appears" in her fiction, which often reads like P.O.V. docudrama. She died in New York in 1975.*

She's Found an Audience

FROM *TRUNKS AND BRANCHES* (1954)

WE WERE A trio of roommates: Zina, Dora, and I. And each of us aspired to becoming "something." Zina wanted to be a singer. We added "Tetra" to her name, making it Tetrazzini—after the great opera diva. Dora, who dreamed of becoming a famous actress, also studied modern dance, and since she greatly admired Isadora Duncan, we attached Iza to her name, crowning her Isadora. As for me, I would sit up half the night with my pen and ink, fantasizing about becoming a writer—and my two friends did not overlook me: they turned my name Sarah into Sand, after the renowned French writer George Sand. . . .

The house we roomed in was always tumultuous, like a county fair. Tetrazzini sang, rehearsed, and tested her voice. Isadora wandered about, holding a book and declaiming, or else memorizing a part; often she launched into a dance, bending, twisting, cutting different figures. The telephone jangled nonstop, the doorbell jingled frequently, flowers might arrive, sometimes a telegram, often packages of clothes, shoes, and novelties, which Isadora liked to buy and later return. All this was accompanied by mayhem, quarreling, and then cheerful laughter.

Most of the fighting was triggered by the phone. Each of us was always expecting a super-important call from a friend, an admirer, and each of us could yack away for half an hour, while the other two roommates were on tenterhooks, yelling: "Well? C'mon! Finish up already! How long are you gonna keep up this drivel?"

The three of us had very different characters. Isadora was like a real sister, loyal, devoted, but very high-strung and absentminded. She could never remember where she'd left something, and she often wrote down a wrong phone message. And whenever someone was introduced to her, she'd chat amiably as if they were old friends, and then it would suddenly hit her that this was a stranger. So she'd hold out her hand, say "Hello!", and ask him who he was.

Tetrazzini was very romantic. Her brown hair and fiery black eyes fitted her hot temperament. She was always hopelessly entangled in love affairs: she'd get involved quickly and then lose interest even more quickly. With sometimes hidden but more often open irony, we'd listen to her amorous adventures, which she enjoyed describing with enthusiasm and grandiloquence. Sometimes, when she'd been disappointed, she'd weep bitter tears. But experience had taught us that before long she'd be suffering over some new romance while the earlier love would be gone and forgotten.

I was the one who always made peace between the singer and the actress. The two of them couldn't live peacefully with each other. Still, we were bonded by deep love and sincere friendship.

Tetrazzini was already on a career track: she performed solo at a number of concerts, she sang on the radio and at major events arranged by organizations, and she got paid for her singing. But her big dream was the opera, and she spent all her earnings on her operatic studies.

Isadora had also had a taste of applause for her acting, but her triumphs were limited to amateur productions, while she dreamed about Broadway, about the theaters of the world, about leading roles. Most of all, she wanted to play Shakespeare.

Life roared by for us. Each of us lived with her own daydreams and artistic ambitions.

I would sit at my desk, in a corner, thoroughly engrossed in writing a short story. All at once I heard Isadora's clear voice, which rang through the house like a bell, carrying me off to a strange and faraway world. With her tall stature she majestically strode back and forth. She had been studying *Hamlet*, and, looking like a boy with her close-cropped blond hair, her tall, slender figure, and dreamy blue eyes, she was virtually typecast as the noble prince of Denmark. I put down my pen and listened to her reciting, "To be or not to be . . ."

When she was done with her soliloquy, I would applaud. She would bow with great dignity and ask mischievously, "Well, George Sand? Are you making fun of me?"

"No, Isadora. You've got the knack, and with your talent you'll go far. But I beg you: let me write. I need total silence. Half an hour more and I'll be done."

"But I can dance, can't I?"

"Yes, but quietly."

I returned to my desk. All at once I heard Tetrazzini's high voice from the next room: "Do, re, mi, fa, sol, la, ti, do . . . " After warming up for several minutes, she sang whole arias from operas. Meanwhile Isadora was dancing full force, stamping her feet and leaping about. I would ask them to stop and let me write. But they were so absorbed in their studies that my pleas fell on deaf ears. Grabbing my manuscript and my pen and ink, I would hurry to the kitchen and shut the door. By then, however, Isadora had stopped dancing and had started performing a scene from a play. Tetrazzini was singing a high C. The cotton I kept stuffing into my ears didn't work. The thoughts that had been flashing through my mind disappeared. I kept begging my housemates to observe silence for a while. And when that didn't help, I got so angry that I grabbed a flowerpot and hurled it. The flowerpot shattered. The soil poured out on the couch. The crash woke them up, and they were ready to beat me black and blue. Our racket could be heard in the street. But after the stormy battle, silence returned and peace was concluded.

Eventually Isadora was cast in a Broadway play. She was blissful. Her knocking on the doors of agents and producers, she victoriously declared, had paid off. True, she only had a few lines, but she was certain that the doors leading to her success as an actress had finally opened, and that directors, who are always on the lookout for new talent, would now get to see her.

But the play ran for just three performances. Isadora, with more faith and determination than ever, knocked away at all theatrical doors. The instant she got wind of any new play, she would dash to the auditions.

One day Isadora came home all afire. She opened her purse and, with trembling hands, she pulled out some notes and shouted: "A part! At last the part that I've been waiting for and dreaming about! My career is taking off!"

"What kind of part?" we inquired.

"Shylock's daughter, Jessica! I read for the part, and they really liked me! Rehearsals are starting in a couple of days." She was talking feverishly. "It's being done by a famous British director, Sir Arthur Roy! Until he arrives, my friend, the young director Gavan, is preparing the cast for him."

Isadora studied the role day and night. We didn't disturb her. Quite the contrary. We tiptoed around and often went out so as not to bother her. Tetrazzini and I already looked upon her as the great future actress. We endured all her whims and defended her outbursts. We understood the source of her tension: she was about to work under a director who, she'd heard, was extremely severe and capricious. However, she was certain that her star was in the ascendant, and that her big role would be her big break. She was certain that her dream would come true, and that her artistic life was now beginning.

Finally it was the day of the first rehearsal. Isadora had already memorized her entire part. We wished her luck. Proud and self-assured, she headed for the theater.

Several hours later, she came back. One glance at her, and we knew she wouldn't be playing the role. She could barely drag her feet. Her tall figure was bent as if someone had beaten her and she didn't have the strength to straighten up again. Exhausted, she collapsed on a chair. Her eyes were filled with distress. Her lips were tightly shut. She stared at a single point. She didn't appear to see anything or hear what we said.

Tetrazzini served her some coffee. I brought her some cake. She didn't touch it. Tetrazzini couldn't stand it any more—she exclaimed: "For God's sake, Isadora, what happened?"

Isadora shook herself, woke up as if from a deep sleep, and murmured: "Someone else got my part! The director brought someone from London. She's done Jessica before . . ."

All at once Isadora jumped up, dashed into the bedroom, and locked the door. A stifled weeping emerged.

For a while, Isadora remained shut off. She didn't eat, she didn't go out, and she refused to talk to us. She stayed in bed, living on black coffee and cigarettes. Eventually she staggered to her feet as after a serious illness, put on makeup, and went back to Broadway. She started knocking more obstinately on the doors of agents and casting directors. She was constantly promised "something." She lived in a feverish expectation that finally, finally, she would receive her long-cherished dream role and make a name for herself in the theater.

At that very moment Tetrazzini's star began to rise. She sang at a concert attended by critics, who gave her very fine reviews. She came home, clutching a newspaper, joyfully showing us her picture and reading us the reviews, which predicted a great career for her. She practically danced in sheer delight.

I too had a surprise. I pulled out a newspaper and showed an announcement: the paper would very soon be publishing a short story by a new writer—and my name was printed in large letters.

Zina produced a bottle of champagne, which she had brought from somewhere. She filled three glasses, and we drank to our further triumphs.

Isadora smiled, congratulated us, and said: "For now, we'll drink to your success—mine is still to come . . . Well, hand me a glass."

We kept pouring refills—time to make merry . . . But then our revelry deteriorated into a fight. We concluded that in order to preserve our deep friendship, we should stop rooming together. That would give us time to work on our art undisturbed.

Within several weeks, each of us had her own place, a quiet nook. But this didn't harm our friendship. Quite the opposite, we really missed one another. Aside from phone calls, we got together a lot. Something had always happened to us, there was always something to talk about.

Zina traveled a lot to nearby towns. Her name was heard more and more. I was engrossed in preparing a book for publication and fixing up my new home. Isadora was still trying to get to Broadway, knocking on doors that were impenetrable for a young, unknown actress.

She listened to us attentively, but was more interested in our artistic lives. She was unconcerned about our private doings. She seemed content with the bits and pieces of success that came our way. She would often murmur: "I have to become 'something' too—I will!"

Late one night, when I was fast asleep, the telephone woke me up. In the darkness, with half-closed eyes, I found the receiver and I snarled: "What's wrong? Who's this?"

"It's Tetrazzini."

She was hysterical, confused, screaming, weeping. I couldn't understand her. "Aha!" I thought. "She's going through some kind of drama in her love life . . ."

I yelled at her: "That's why you ring me up in the middle of the night? Because of some shattered romance? Couldn't it wait till morning?"

"What's the matter with you? Are you deaf? Didn't you hear me? It's Isadora—our Dora!"

"What do you mean?"

A second later I was wide awake. And suddenly I grasped my friend's bizarre words, her terrible words: "Isadora is sick . . . She's had a sudden breakdown. She's in an asylum." Tetrazzini had just found out!

I stopped hearing. Spasmodic sobs tore out of my throat. A fearful weeping spread across the dark room. The voice at the other end of the line stopped speaking. Zina wanted to let me cry my eyes out. All at once, the dead receiver regained its voice:

"That's enough, Sarah! Isadora's got good prospects. She's in a private sanitarium on Long Island, her brothers and sisters are picking up the tab . . . Get over to my place at the crack of dawn, and we'll both go and visit her and check how bad it is." She hung up, the line went dead.

I lay back down, but I couldn't doze off. Horrible images flashed before my eyes. I switched on the lamp: it was one a.m. Terror-stricken, I twisted and turned. The hours dragged by like boring days. The clock said three. I felt as if I were the one losing her mind. I abruptly sprang out of bed, dressed, and charged over to Tetrazzini's home.

She wasn't surprised by my nocturnal visit. She couldn't sleep either. We sat up all night, speculating, trying to figure it out. What had happened to our smart, fine, sane Isadora? Why this sudden rupture in her lucid mind? We drew comfort by assuming she'd suffered a mild nervous breakdown. It would pass, and she'd regain her health.

Early in the morning we phoned a mutual friend, a well-known doctor. He too was shaken by the dismal news. He instantly left his office, and the three of us went to the asylum to which Isadora had been committed.

But we were highly disappointed because they wouldn't let us see her. She had just gone through shock therapy. They only admitted our doctor friend. That calmed us down a bit: he'd be able to inform us about her condition.

On the way home, the doctor explained that Isadora was very ill. She hadn't recognized him. But that was often the case after shock treatment. Still, he said, her prognosis looked very good. Only time would tell how long it would take her to become normal again.

After four months in a private sanitarium, she came home, and she appeared to be the same Isadora as before. She resumed her efforts in the theater, and, as luck would have it, she got a walk-on in a major Broadway production. Her role consisted of four words. But she was glad that agents would see her on stage, and her dream of becoming "something" seemed about to materialize.

The play ran for only one week, and Isadora again remained unknown and unemployed. Zina traveled a great deal, and we saw very little of her. And I myself was often away.

Eventually Isadora fell ill again. Her brothers and sisters again sent her to a private sanitarium, where she stayed a while. And again she came home with what looked like a sound mind. But not for long. She had periods of melancholy and often wild fits of insanity. She had a serious relapse. This time, her family put her in a public asylum.

In the course of time, I found her in various moods, both at home and in the hospital. But to my great astonishment, she always spoke normally and calmly. Except that she kept repeating too often: "I have to become something."

Six years passed, and Isadora remained in the public asylum. I'd usually been out of town during the last two years. But I'd kept writing to both her and Tetrazzini. Isadora ignored my letters, but Tetrazzini did respond. She wrote me detailed letters about how well off she was. Her mind was teeming with plans for the future. She seldom mentioned

Isadora. And if she did bring her up, she sounded resigned, the way you talk about someone who's doomed.

Late one summer, when I came back to New York, I promptly went to visit my sick friend, Isadora, in the asylum, which was located far from the city. A lot of the train passengers were going to see their nearest and dearest. The train halted and released the travelers. The guard pointed to a high, white building which, from a distance, looked like a castle. The area was surrounded by hills, large pines, and chestnut trees. Colored flowers were scattered over a grassy carpet. Indian summer cast a spell with its reddish and yellow-brown leaves. From a clear sky the sun cast golden rays, cheering my heavy heart.

A nurse in white, slipping through the trees, reminded me that this was a hospital.

I approached the building, and all at once I saw that the high windows had iron bars. From there, strange noises emerged. I shuddered, fully conscious of where I was.

My heart pounded as I entered the building. A nurse showed me the way. I was in a huge, bare hall with bare walls. Patients of different ages, races, and appearances—from black to white—were sitting on chairs. Each patient seemed to be in a world of his own. Some were walking quickly, others sat on the floor, barefoot. One woman was hurrying about with an open umbrella, shaking her dress, as if it were raining.

An open door led to a wide, barred balcony. I looked around for Isadora, but she was nowhere to be seen. I went out on the balcony—she was standing in a corner. Her tall, thin figure had become taller and thinner. Her eyes agape, she was staring into space. I drew nearer, called out her name. She didn't move or seem to hear. Her bulging eyes were glassy. She appeared to have been swept away to a distant, mystical world.

I nudged her arm: "Dora! Isadora!"

Terrified, she looked around and saw me.

"Oh . . . It's you . . . How'd you get here?"

"I've come to see you and find out how you're doing."

Instead of replying, she asked me a strange question: "How would you feel in a madhouse? Well, have a seat." She courteously pointed to a chair. "Tell me what's happening out in freedom. And how are the sane people? How's the leading lady? Is she already singing at the opera or in a wine cellar?" Nasty questions came hailing down. And she never waited for an answer. "And how's our great and famous George Sand? . . . Have you written your great and famous opus? . . . Or are you struck in the middle?" She kept hurling words like heavy rocks. And her sarcastic smirk never left her lips. "Well, I've managed to become 'something' too. You'll soon see . . ."

Suddenly she walked to the center of the huge hall and clapped her hands to signal the others. She was completely surrounded by the patients, who began shouting: "Hurry up! Isadora is performing!"

Isadora waited for a few minutes until all of them were circling her. She pointed to a place for me. After a long pause, she smoothed her hair upward, bowed majestically, and began in a clear and quiet diction, and gradually her rich voice sounded more solid, more certain:

"To be or not to be . . ."

She recited the entire soliloquy and received a stormy ovation. There were different cries:

"Isadora, dance!"

"The serpent dance!"

"No, the canine dance!"

"The swan dance!"

She motioned toward a female patient, who handed her a white sheet. Isadora wrapped it around half her body and gracefully draped the other half of the sheet over her left shoulder. She kicked off her slippers, drew up her head, and clapped her hands as a sign that she was starting. And soon her thin, bare feet glided over the shiny floor. She floated across the hall like a butterfly, scarcely grazing the floor. She soared high, high, under the heavens. Now her long neck pointed downward, her figure bent toward the ground, and then she awoke once again and soared far, far into space. Isadora was dancing the swan dance!

I crept into a corner and wept softly. Suddenly she noticed me and came dashing over: "You're crying? Why? Aha, you're jealous. You resent my bit of joy, the two of you always resented me! . . . Only you and Tetrazzini, the singer and the writer . . . You and her . . . You and her . . . I never existed. I wanted to become 'something' too! and I *have* become 'something'! If you've got talent and persistence, you'll become 'something'! I've acquired a dear and loyal audience . . . What's the difference where I perform? . . . What did Shakespeare say? The world's a stage, and people are players . . . My stage is here . . . You saw how much my audience loves me . . . They yearn for my artistry. They wouldn't trade me for any other actress. Wipe your tears and stop envying me . . . You have to resent me? Huh?

Who sent for you anyhow? Go away!" she yelled imperiously. "I never want to see you again! You and the singer won't take my audience away!"

All the while she glared at me victoriously. Then she stalked off and launched into another wild dance.

ROKHL KORN (*1898–1982*)

*K*orn, who grew up among Christian and Jewish farmers in Poland, first *wrote in Polish. But then, taught by her husband, she switched to Yiddish after the pogroms following World War I. Her husband was killed by the German invaders during World War II; she and her daughter fled to the Soviet Union. After spending several postwar years in Lodz, she immigrated to Canada in 1949. Aside from two volumes of short stories, Korn also published nine collections of poetry and an autobiography.*

The End of the Road (*1957*)

BY MORNING, THE whole town had learned about the new German decree. But in Hersh-Layzer Sokol's household, they virtually pretended not to know about it. As on any other day, Beyle, his wife, put on the pot of grits and half-rotten potatoes, the ghetto's ration, and punctually set the table for the entire family. Seven plates and seven spoons laid out in two rows as if to fend off all the evil lurking beyond the door.

Every so often Beyle hurried to the door or the window, where she wiped the steamy pane with her apron and peered down into the street. But on that autumn day in 1942 not a single Jew could be seen in the small Galician shtetl. Now and then, a Jewish policeman with a pack of documents under his arm passed by and vanished in the alley leading to the *Judenrat*, the Jewish Council.

"Papa still isn't here," she said, more to herself than to the others. Her elderly mother-in-law, who sat next to the stove plucking feathers into a patched sieve, turned her half-deaf ear toward her: "What did you say, Beyle?"

"Nothing!"

All at once, a loud commotion resounded from the corner where the two youngest children were playing. Duvid had yanked Sorke's doll from her hands and was waving a stick: "When I order you to give up your baby, you have to give him up! Otherwise I'll grab you too, and you'll be beaten as well!"

Beyle dashed over to the children. "What are you making a racket for? What's gotten into you?"

"Mama, he's hitting me!" Sorke burst into tears, feeling her mother's protection.

"Go away, Mama, go way right now!" the eight-year-old boy insisted, pulling over his little sister. "We're playing resettlement, and there's no mother in resettlement. You have to obey the policeman. Since she didn't want to give her baby up, she has to go with her baby. See? I've got my rifle." He brandished his stick.

"Damn it! Damn it to hell! Throw your stick away—now! And get over here! Some game! Is this what you call a game?"

"That's what happened to our neighbor, Malke. You know it yourself. Joseph's son, the policeman, took Malke along with her baby. Don't you remember?"

"I don't want you playing games like that, do you hear? You're a big boy, but you don't get it! Go over to Lippe!"

Whenever the mother couldn't cope with Duvid, she'd send him to her eldest child, Lippe, the only person Duvid would obey.

Lippe was sitting at the table in the next room, propping his head on his left arm and writing. He didn't turn around, didn't respond with a single word, when his mother stood behind him, waiting for him to help her calm his wild little brother. Duvid was also waiting for something: he suddenly quieted down and strenuously gaped at his older brother. The pen in Lippe's hand raced swiftly, swiftly across the white paper as if heading toward some inevitable goal, for which Lippe was a mere accessory, carrying out someone else's will.

Beyle's ears, alert to the slightest sound, caught the peculiar rustle of swishing silk. Turning her head, she saw the wardrobe and, between its wide-open doors, her daughter Mirl taking out frock after frock and trying them on in front of the mirror.

"What damn holiday are you celebrating?"

"Mama, I just wanna try on all my dresses again."

Beyle looked askance at her as if eying a stranger who'd just walked in. During the past two years of constant terror and torture, she had viewed her children as a flock that she had to tend and to shield against all the lurking dangers. Only now did she see that her fourteen-year-old daughter had grown up. Her thin, juvenile shoulders were curved as if preparing for the burden of new and unknown yearnings. Her brown, doe-like eyes were filled with her first soft, womanly submission to fate.

And as if owing this blossoming daughter an inexplicable and unpayable debt, Beyle, like a bankrupt debtor, collapsed on a chair and burst into an uncontrollable wailing. All her pent-up alarm, her fear of the unavoidable future had abruptly found some out-of-the-way channel, releasing a flood of tears. Beyle rocked her head in both hands, with a staccato moaning and sniveling, as if her chest were being ripped to shreds.

The two youngest children tiptoed into the kitchen and rummaged among the pots and pans like kittens. Sorne dragged Mirl away from the wardrobe: "C'mon! Stick a fork into the potatoes, check if they're done!"

Duvid hurried to the front door. "I wanna see what's keeping Papa."

"Don't you dare!" Beyle awoke from her daze. "Do you want something terrible to happen to us? —God forbid!"

Now, a heavy trudging could be heard from the stairs, as if the legs had to wrangle with each single step. Lippe thrust his pages into his breast pocket and ran to open the front door, which had been steadily locked and bolted ever since the Germans had marched in.

For a while, father and son gazed at one another. The son's eyes asked, demanded to learn what the father knew and what would be kept secret from the others.

The father's head was stooped as if he himself bore the guilt for what was happening, the guilt for having married and brought children into the world, for now being unable to protect them. Beyle took one look at her husband and realized she didn't need to question him. The creases in his face had suddenly grown deeper and were covered with gray as if they had gathered all the dust from the street; his nose was drawn out and pointed like that of a corpse, and his usually tidy, darkish beard was so disheveled that it exposed its normally hidden grayness.

"Are you gonna wash your hands, Hersh-Layzer?"

"Yes, let's eat," he softly replied.

They ate in silence, and nobody paid any heed to how full his or her spoon was; each bite they swallowed was only half-chewed. Even the children, accustomed to fear and terror, sensed that something dreadful was in the offing and they shouldn't even ask what.

Whenever a spoon unexpectedly clanked against the edge of a plate, they were startled, trembling, and they glared at the source of the noise. Only the grandmother, as if thoroughly absorbed in the food, slowly lifted one spoonful after another to her toothless gums.

Hersh-Layzer was the first to rise. Wiping his mustache with the back of his hand, he began striding up and down with a heavy, measured tread. When the mother started clearing the table, he waved his hand at her: "Don't, Beyle."

Dropping both hands as if they'd become useless, she suddenly confronted her husband, blocked his path. "Have you had any news? Is what people are saying all true?"

"True, all true, Beyle." His voice was hoarse and muffled, as if something dense and brambly were growing in his throat. "They've already put up posters on walls and pillars. Within two hours from now, each family has to hand over one member—do you understand? The family has to choose the victim themselves. They have to make the choice, otherwise the Germans'll take everyone, the entire household, no exceptions. And so they're giving us free choice. Do you hear, Beyle? *Free choice!*"

They were all stunned. But they weren't surprised. You could expect anything from the Germans. The family members exchanged glances. Who? Who would go? Go to a place from which no one ever came back?

All at once, a wave of estrangement swept over them. Each person saw the next as a victim. Each person saw the next as an enemy.

And who would be chosen and who would do the choosing? With what yardstick would they measure, with what scales would they do the weighing in order to decide who should die now and who was worthy of living—for now?

"If that's the case . . . ," said Lippe very calmly, not looking at the bowed heads. He broke off. As if the burden of those spoken words were too great a load for their quaking legs, they all sat down. Each person tried to sit as low as possible as if observing the seven days of mourning for himself.

Beyle threw her arms around the two youngest as if covering them, as if blocking all access to them.

The grownups started mentally reckoning each person's age, the years he had lived, the years he was granted. They reckoned the creases in a face and the veins on a hand.

The father couldn't go, that was clear. He was the provider, the bread-winner for the whole family. The mother certainly couldn't go. What would become of the smallest children without her? Lippe? What had he already gotten out of life in his twenty-four years, the last two dark-ened under Hitler's reign? Let him think for a while. Perhaps he should have trudged out, and that would be that. His mother would lament, tear out her hair. His father would roar with grief when he'd recite Kaddish, the prayer for the dead, for his son. Duvid would look for Lippe every day, unable to grasp that his brother was gone. But in the first moment, they would sigh with relief because Lippe would have redeemed them, freed them from the necessity of executing their own flesh and blood.

He began mentally saying goodbye to everyone. Tomorrow, he would no longer be here. Everything would remain in its place, but he would no longer be here. No longer see the sun, the sky, the old clock on the bureau. Touching his breast pocket, he took out his watch and the bit of money he kept there. Making sure that nobody saw him, he tucked the money under the clock. He also slipped in the pages he had written. Yes, that was the letter to Elke. He would have to entrust it to a Pole. Because Elke mustn't receive a letter from the ghetto. She was living out there with forged Aryan papers. Just recently she had let him know that she was getting Aryan papers for him too, with the necessary seals and signatures. The two of them would move to a large city, where it was easier to hide.

Was there no one who could go instead of him? What about grandma? The old grandma? Lippe's eyes, seeking his grandma, encountered his parents' gaze above her head. They had stripped the leaves from her years the way falling autumn leaves expose the naked and vulnerable tree trunk. But no one dared to say what they were thinking, no one dared to say, "Go!" No one dared to take control of the few ragged years she had left.

Their eyes dug into her so sharply that the old woman started droop-ing, her entire body pushed into her chair, as if she were vanishing from the surface, growing into the bit of floor beneath her, taking root there so that no one could pull it out from under her feet. At that instant, each person's senses grew more acute, more alive. Each person's thoughts were open for everyone else in these moments of intense spiritual strain. The grandma's mind was the only one that stayed shut, just like her two half-extinguished eyes. She was locked up inside herself, warding off death. Suddenly she felt so alone, so lonely in the midst of her own fam-ily, next to her son, whom she had born and raised. Her own flesh and blood. And his eyes were searching for her too, focusing on her. And that would enable her to defend herself against all of them, with her last ounce of strength. There was no one who would take her part, no one who would at least put up a wall around her, protect her with a warm gaze. That would have made it easier for her to draw the final balance. Dying is less arduous if you know you'll be missed.

They figured it was less difficult for an old person to die. Maybe that was true when death came on its own, to your own bed. But going like this, bringing death your bundle of wornout bones. Shush! She wasn't done with everything. She had to look back at her life once more, from start to finish. The time when she had been a child with her mother. She too had once been a child, after all, like her son, like her grandchildren. Her mother had held her in her lap, like Beyle with Sorke. "Mama, mama!" her blue lips murmured, calling her back from the hereafter. "Mama," she pleaded as she had done in her childhood when they had wanted to hit her. She had pretty much forgotten what her mother looked like, her features had blurred with the passing years. Two large, heavy tears rolled down from under her closed lashes, fell into the mesh of wrinkles, and spread down the full length of her face.

And she recalled herself as later—as ready for marriage. She had seen Duvid, her betrothed, only once, at the engagement ceremony, but all her girlish dreams were filled with his presence. When they had prepared her wedding garments, she stubbornly insisted on having the costliest fabrics, the iridescent blue silk with its rosy glow and the pink flowers woven into it. She wanted her intended to find her attractive.

All these years, her wedding gown had been hanging in the closet until recently. She hadn't let anyone touch it. Then, a few months ago, she had let them make it over for Mirl. Because her granddaughter was her spit and image: when she looked at Mirl, she saw herself as she had been long ago.

The clock struck sharply. Once, then twice. Everyone came to. Soon, very soon. Until now, everyone had been waiting for something to happen. Some miracle. But now, less than an hour was left.

Mirl stood up, to her full height. She grabbed her coat from its hanger and stood in the middle of the room.

"I'm going."

They all turned their heads toward her.

She stood in the iridescent blue-and-rosy dress, which had been made over from her grandma's wedding gown. Mirl had forgotten to take it off when her mother had yelled at her; or perhaps she had deliberately left it on. Whether it was the gown or her tight, stubborn lips that made her look older, more adult, everyone felt that Mirl had grown a lot taller during those past few hours.

"Go where? What are you talking about?" Her father went over to her with bulging, bloodshot eyes.

"You know where! Goodbye everyone!"

She was already at the door.

With a broad, wild jump, her father caught up with her and grabbed her sleeve.

"Get back here right now! Right now! Or there'll be hell to pay! Do you hear?"

As Mirl tried to free herself from her father's grip, they heard a loud swish, which sounded like a whip. The old, lengthened silk sleeve had ripped.

They all gaped at this scene, but no one stirred, no one held back the father or assisted Mirl.

Hersh-Layzer clutched his daughter with one hand while removing his belt with the other.

No one could grasp what happened next. Was the father going to hit Mirl, his radiant child, after never so much as lifting a finger against her? He had always brought home a present for her — not for the two youngest, but for her, Mirl. The insanity, which each person felt growing inside himself and which they kept pushing back with all their strength, must have suddenly ripened in the father like an abscess that drew and drew until it burst.

He finally gripped the belt and whirled it over Mirl's head like a noose. He lowered it to her shoulders, then cinched it around her waist, the way a farmer ties up a sheaf of wheat. The father tested his belt several times to make sure it was tight enough. Then, grabbing the loose end, he dragged Mirl like a hog-tied calf to the oak table. He bent over and looped the end of the belt three times around the heavy table leg. Next, he tied a knot on the other end of the belt and, using his teeth, he pulled the belt through its tiny hole. Now he wiped his hand across his wet forehead as if trying to rub away the beads of sweat. He remained in his chair, both hands in his lap, his breathing heavy and choppy.

Mirl stayed on her knees, just as her father had put her, with her head against the edge of the table. She was rigid and completely drained by her exertion. For the very first time in her young life, she had striven for something—and so what if it was death! She had walked the way a bride walks toward her groom. She had been preparing for it all morning. And her grandma's wedding gown was now shamed. And she had been humiliated by her father, her devoted father, who understood her better than anyone else, even better than her mother. He had refused to let God accept her sacrifice. Isaac had been permitted to go, but not she? And Abraham had led Isaac himself, led him by his hand, and he had known, known all the while, what God was demanding of him. And here, everyone—yes, she could see it—everyone wanted the grandmother to go. But did the grandmother have the strength to drag herself far, far away on her bad legs? And how worthy was the sacrifice of an old person who was bound to die soon anyhow?

For the first time in her life, Mirl hated her father. She furiously tried to get free, to stand up. But the belt, which she had already forgotten about, cut deeper into her flesh. She fell back and lay on the floor, burying her face in her hands.

The streak of light coming through the window kept shifting, shifting across the floor, until it reached her legs. The light made the rosy blossoms shimmer in the blue, iridescent silk, awakening them to a new life. The room was hushed again. They could clearly hear the buzzing of a final fly looking for a safe corner from which no one could drive it away—the corner for its final hibernation.

The family members sat there with bowed heads. Let come what may. Let the decision come from outside, from beyond them. And if they all had to go instead of just one, so be it. If the good Lord wanted it, permitted it, then they would have to resign themselves.

With its quiet ticking, the clock on the bureau measured the silence, and the hands moved around the face toward the appointed moment as if to cut into that moment with black tongs.

Suddenly the father turned his head and all eyes followed his look. Grandma's chair was empty. They had all been so deeply absorbed in their own thoughts that no one had noticed her getting to her feet. Where was she? When had she stolen out so softly that no one had heard her? It could only have been just minutes ago.

They all peered around, focusing on each nook and cranny. Suddenly a shadow appeared on the glass door leading to the front room. The shadow grew nearer and nearer until it covered the entire pane. All eyes focused on it. Yes, it was Grandma, in her old, black holiday cloak. She was holding a small package under her arm, like a prayer book when she'd gone to synagogue. One hand clutched her cane, her other hand slowly unchained and opened the front door. The door then instantly swung to on its hinges.

No one stood up. No one called her back. They all remained seated. And their heads bowed deeper, deeper, as if their place were down there, by their feet, in the dust on the floor.

AVROM KARPINOVITSH *(b. 1918)*

Born and raised in interwar Vilna, Karpinovitsh settled in Israel after two years in a British detention camp in Cyprus. In 1952, he became manager of Israel's Philharmonic Orchestra. A prolific storyteller, he has won many literary prizes. His subject matter is drawn mainly from interwar Vilna, including its seamy side. He now lives in Tel Aviv.

Zubak *(1967)*

THE VILNA THEATER mounted *The Jewish Hamlet* every single season, and Zubak always played the father's ghost. He had to stand there for an entire act, draped in a white sheet and lit up from behind by a small lamp, until the curtain fell. Shtraitman, the director of the play, demanded a long, handsome corpse, and the role fit the tall and scraggy Zubak like a glove. At first Zubak had raised a rumpus, threatening to leave the troupe unless they gave him a few lines before he returned to the grave. But everyone knew he was just bluffing. Zubak loved acting much too much. He asked the director to revise the play and have him die earlier, so that he, Zubak, could get home before the front door of his building was locked. That way he wouldn't have to tip the janitor to unlock the door.

But Shtraitman had yelled at the top of his lungs: "You beanpole! Have respect for Shakespeare!" And Zubak, with his tail between his legs, hurried off to whiten his face.

Recently, Zubak hadn't been doing so well. He hadn't been cast in any part. His salary had been cut. For several seasons now he'd had to hold his tongue ever since the scene in which he'd flubbed his line: he'd exclaimed, "General, the lady's face is tailed" instead of "veiled." Shtraitman had thereupon become Zubak's mortal enemy, and frankly, he had good reason: the scene was supposed to be tragic, but the audience had rolled in the aisles. One spectator had even yelled: "Zubak, what does she need a tail for!"

And now there was this whole business about the janitor's tips, which had added up mightily in the course of a month. Zubak quite simply needed the money to make ends meet. The back door of Svirsky's bakery opened into Zubak's courtyard. The curtain was usually rung down just as the baker was starting to set the dough. Zubak would dash through the store, trying not to disturb the work—and he was already on the other side. But some time ago, when he was about to hop over the hearth broom next to the fired-up oven, Svirksy had blocked Zubak's path and explained that Wincenty the janitor had been grumbling that the baker was poaching on his preserve. The janitor was continually asking how Zubak managed to come home at night without passing through the front door. Now they didn't give a tinker's damn about the janitor, but it made no sense for the baker to let the actor through and not get something for it. Zubak, a very honorable man, raised an eyebrow, waiting to hear how he could reward the baker. Svirsky whispered something to his two workers—those devils Shneyke and Tevele. The baker then announced that by way of a fee, Zubak would have to either dance or sing for them. Whichever he preferred. In the twinkling of an eye, the two assistants were at Zubak's side, urging him: "Zubak, sing the hit from *Shloyme Gorgl*." And not waiting for him to say yes or no, they burst into song themselves:

> Oh, I don't much care for this—
> This whole business makes me hiss.

Tevele did a jig—and he crashed into a trough of dough.

Zubak was dismal. He felt as if he'd fallen into a real hell. And indeed he had. Sparks were flying from the open oven. Svirsky, clutching a hearthbrush, was up to his ears in soot. The two assistants were singing and dancing around him like devils (please don't utter that word at night!). Zubak shuddered from head to toe. He felt faint. The trough of dough didn't look like a trough, God help us, it looked like a barrel of pitch. And Shneyke and Tevele seemed about to throw Zubak into the pitch and roast him.

The two assistants ended their songfest and stood there, content, waiting to hear what Zubak had to offer. At first Zubak wanted to curse the living daylights out of them and he even spit into the full trough. But then he turned and headed toward the door. His exit would have looked solemn, indeed theatrical, if he hadn't tripped over a shovel.

Svirsky was the first to realize that they had gone too far. He scampered after the actor and shouted through the open door: "Zubak, c'mon! We didn't mean it! We were just kidding around—that's all!"

But Zubak didn't respond, he charged toward the front door. Svirsky turned to the oven and angrily yelled at his assistants: "Set the dough, God damn you! You wanted to perform—and all you did was humiliate him for nothing!"

Zubak rang the janitor's bell as if it were a fire alarm. The whole courtyard awoke. The woman next door cursed Zubak loudly: he should fall down the stairs and break every bone in his body! Zubak was so furious that he couldn't hit on the right retort. He bounded into his room, undressed in the dark, lay down, pulled the covers over his head, and inscribed the following words in his memory with blood red ink: "I'll make those bakers perform all right—the rats!"

All night long Zubak dreamed that Svirsky was playing the ghost of Hamlet's father, while he, Zubak, kept raving and ranting. All his lines, which for a long time now no one had entrusted him with delivering properly, tore out of him. Bits and pieces of one play mingled with a whole act of another, a soliloquy from a tragedy got wedged into a scene from a comedy. And the baker—that rat!—was standing with floury clodhoppers sticking out from under his winding sheet, his eyes blinking with fear.

When Zubak got up the next morning, he was hoarse. He practically wept with chagrin. A new play was being cast today, he was ready to fight like a lion for a role—and now he was hoarse. He remembered last night's scene in the bakery, and the insult burned inside him like a jigger of brandy on an empty stomach. Zubak sat up on the side of the bed and took spiritual stock. It's an actor's lot for some green kid to be buddy-buddy with him. The kid ought to say: "Good evening, Mr. Zubak, please pass through—careful! Don't get any flour on you." Instead, they played nasty jokes on him.

He actually felt like crying, but no tears came to his eyes. At the theater, people would say he was so obstinate and foul-tempered that you could slice up whole sacks of onions right in front of his eyes and it wouldn't faze him in the least. Even in the most tragic scenes, each of his tears was worth gold. Older actors denied it, they remembered that he could laugh and cry and grumble and what not. In good moments they would remember him playing Bar-Kokhba, bare-chested, waving his sword at the Romans, while the female spectators pinched one another and whispered, "Just look, he's blazing away, just look at those shoulders!"

In the shtetl of Rudzishek the drama club had wanted him as their steady director. They offered him a bride, a divorcée with a haberdashery. Friends nudged him: "Grab the dowry, you jerk! You can go on tour in style!" But how could Zubak have thought of getting hitched? He'd been young, fit, and he'd had top billing on the posters!

All morning long, Zubak, in his underpants, sat on the edge of the bed, pouring tubs of pity on himself, until it dawned on him that he had to hurry to the theater to keep Shtraitman from casting someone else in the role. He threw his clothes on and went out, intending to have tea at Velfke's tavern.

The courtyard was all astir. Shneyke and Tevele were scrubbing the troughs, and their jaws were flapping nonstop. They paid more attention to every young female tenant. Svirsky stood nearby, unable to control his two demons. Upon spotting Zubak, the baker wished him a broad "Good morning" and tried to add some friendly words and a floury pat on the back in order to wipe away last light's fiasco. But Zubak refused to kiss and make up. They had touched his honor as an actor. Zubak cut across the courtyard without even deigning to glance in the baker's direction. He did, however, glare at the two assistants, virtually tossing them a bone as if they were barking dogs. Zubak walked through the front doorway, comforting himself: "It doesn't matter, Zubak's still alive. He'll bring the house down with a scene that people will remember him by."

AT THE THEATER they were up in arms. Shtraitman, the director, was shouting that the new play would set Vilna on its ear. The actors shouted back that the play was a piece of crap, not worth washing the floor with. No jokes, no dancing, there wasn't even room to slip in a comical old crone. Shtraitman practically had a stroke; he gave a long speech about art and the classic repertoire. The actors exchanged glances. Bombe the Dandy made faces, and the entire troupe laughed their heads off. But Shtraitman was imbued with his faith. He said that if they trimmed the cheese and squeezed out the water, the play would be a hit. It would even outdo *My Wife's Husband.* And all in all, they should stop doing garbage and aim at a better theater.

Zubak likewise wanted to put in his two cents, but they wouldn't let him. Besides, his voice was so hoarse that he couldn't be heard anyway. He thought he'd explode! He wanted to play the Devil, who lures a saint into all kinds of sins. He was to urge him on for two whole acts plus a pro-logue. It was a meaty role. For goodness knows how many seasons all Zubak had done on stage was carry a pole of a wedding canopy. And recently he had the plum part of Hamlet's dead father! The poor man wanted to play the Devil more than anything in the world! Vilna was starting to forget him, and he wanted to make at least one more appear-ance, cross the boards one more time in a black cloak, his eyes cunning under arched eyebrows, and recite so eloquently that the theater would explode!

The actors shrugged and said to one another: "Let's give it a try."

When the director cast the parts, he chose Maximov, a rising star in the troupe, to play the Devil. And Zubak left with empty hands. Shtraitman, who wasn't quite sure what to do with Zubak, promised he'd come up with something during rehearsals: Zubak shouldn't worry. He'd manage to squeeze out a salary this week.

VELFKE'S TAVERN WAS in high spirits. The celebration was headed by the poet Itsik Manger, who'd come wandering to Vilna from Czernowitz or Jassy or wherever. Clutching a jigger of slivovitz, he recited his rhymes, and the throng devoured every last word. Curvaceous girls, practitioners of all sorts of tricks, breathed through half-open mouths like hens during the dog days, yearning for the slightest glance from those dark eyes. But how? Manger strode from verse to verse with his tousled forelock. When he finished his recital, the tavern grew even more tumultuous. There was no end of people shouting, "*L'khaim!*" Actors yelled their heads off, writers hollered for all they were worth. Respectable Jews, who'd help out in an emergency and liked the barefoot riffraff as if they were their own kids, licked their fingers—both from the carrot pudding and from the entire hurly-burly.

Zubak sat in the front room, peering through the door, watching the party, and his blood boiled. How greedy Vilna was for new gods! Maximov, still wet behind the ears in regard to the stage, was table-hopping, cozying up to everybody. Nor did the other actors keep their distance. They all guzzled liquor donated by patrons and they poured out witticisms like so many beans. But no one asked Zubak to join the fun. He sat with the coachmen on the covered porch. Velfke, hauling platters and bottles through the room, didn't even raise his tongue to say: "Zubak, you old beanpole! C'mon in and wet your whistle!" As if Zubak hadn't been on the stage for some forty years now! As if he were a scurvy coach-man! The town was filled with young snotnoses. New fashions were being introduced—people were reading plays, looking for literature . . . Zubak was a nobody for them . . .

Clutching their whips, the coachmen beleaguered the door to the back room the better to hear the melody that, Gershteyn, a teacher, drew out in such honeyed tones. If Zubak had managed to catch even a glimpse of the next room, he was now fully cut off. He got to his feet and stomped off, nursing his grudge.

The frost was lingering in the Jewish district, waiting for customers. It took his breath away. Burrowing deeper into his coat, he wondered: Should he head back to the tavern and wait for an opportunity or should he maintain his self-respect and go home? He decided his self-respect came first. Ultimately, he wasn't the last man in Vilna.

Fast as he trudged through the snow, he was frozen by the time he reached his front door. His fingers were burning and he barely managed to fish out the janitor's tip from his trouser pocket. The janitor took for-ever, probably because of the frost. Hopping from one foot to the other, Zubak had time to go through his hit list: from Svirsky the baker to Shtraitman the director.

THE THEATER WAS mobbed. Women tried to place several kids on one seat. Vilna did not care for extravagance. The spectators had also brought food along to avoid squandering money at the buffet. The atmosphere was friendly. People were delighted to find one another as if they hadn't crossed paths in years. Children, clutching pieces of buckwheat cake, scurried about like squirrels, poking their heads under the curtain, playing hide-and-seek. Moms dispensed slaps, sunflower seeds, and chunks of challah, dads fought over occupied seats. But things settled down by the time the lights were dimmed. With each child wedged in between a parent's knees, the audience was all ears and all eyes. Mendke, the stagehand, hammered in a final nail, and the performance was ready to begin.

Zubak, sitting in the dressing room, was as dark as loam. He was still upset that he hadn't been cast. Actors stared at him, wondering what was wrong. He had come to the theater some three hours before curtain time. At least according to Mendke. And now he wasn't even made up.

Shtraitman stormed into the dressing room all set to shoot: "You beanpole! Are you trying to wreck the production?" But when he saw Zubak, Shtraitman's heart tightened. Zubak was gaping into the mirror as if the face weren't his. And what sort of face? Painfully wrenched and twisted as if a molar had been yanked out. Shtraitman realized that Zubak was feeling wretched because he had to play the father's ghost. So the director sat down and started comforting him.

"Zubak, be a mentsh, don't go temperamental on me! What's a bad role? Nothing! Castor oil! You take it, you gulp it down! And that's that!

"You're an actor, aren't you? You're standing on the boards, aren't you? That's the crux! Art, my brother, art demands sacrifices!" Shtraitman pointed his forefinger at the ceiling: "Huge sacrifices!"

Zubak didn't look very comforted. So Shtraitman poured it on even thicker: "Don't be upset, Zubak, I'll try to find you something in the new play. You'll be such a hit that all your colleagues'll blow a gasket! You'll see what Shtraitman can do for a pal! And now put on your makeup. It's curtain time!"

THE REHEARSALS FOR the new play were going badly. Maximov was pulling some fast ones. He was trying to get the cast to rebel against Shtraitman. Maximov argued that the play was crap and that Shtraitman didn't know his ass from his elbow. The actor incited the others: "A director is not a tailor! You gotta know what you're doing!"

The actors stood on the stage, clutching their scripts, munching whole sentences like starving geese and choking on every intellectual word.

Throughout their careers they had always ad-libbed, and now they had
to recite as if from the prayer book (please excuse my mentioning them
in the same breath!). Shtraitman was ecstatic, he knew his people, whatever, but they were professionals. Once they'd memorized their lines,
their actor's instinct would find a path.

And indeed, that's what happened. At the fourth rehearsal, Bombe
went to the director and said, "Ya know, Shtraitman, this *is* a play. Who
slapped it together?"

Shtraitman drew himself up as if for a salute. "Goethe indited it, and
I adapted it . . ."

"Goethe? Hmm! Not bad."

The rehearsals went as smoothly as greased lightning. Only Maximov
gave him a hard time.

The actors knew why. Maximov's suitcase contained a play in which
he'd do the lead and which he'd also direct. So he did everything he could
to malign Shtraitman and get him kicked out of the theater. Friends
added fuel to the fire. War was unavoidable.

At one rehearsal Shtraitman told Maximov that he, the Devil, should
not sneak up behind the sinner—after all, he wasn't going to pick the
man's pocket. Instead, the Devil should saunter elegantly, in patent
leather shoes. Maximov, as was his wont, disagreed. The whole world
knew that a Devil has hooves and that hooves clatter. That was why
Maximov had to clatter like that. Shtraitman hit the roof! He snapped
something about shady characters and finally asked Maximov just who
was the director here. To which Maximov replied: "You're the director,
but you know a lot more about door-to-door peddling!"

Shtraitman couldn't believe his ears. "What? What did you say?"

So Maximov added an explanation: "I said that you like to sleep late,
that's the reason you work in the theater. Why else are you here?"

Shtraitman wanted to tear Maximov from limb to limb. Mendke the
stagehand and several bolder actors pulled the antagonists apart. Mendke
clutched Shtraitman's arms. Shtraitman yelled: "Mendke, hold me tight!
I'm gonna rip his heart out! That asshole!"

Maximov said goodbye to the cast: "So long, kids, I'm gonna start my
own company. I'll show you what theater is! Anybody who wishes me bad
luck should keep working with this hack!" And not waiting for someone
to hurl a prop at him, Maximov exited.

Shtraitman was very bitter. He was stranded without a Devil. What should he do? Apparently, somebody in Heaven must have liked Zubak. As he sat in the empty auditorium, glaring at the rehearsal, Shtraitman spotted him, and a golden light went on in the director's brain: Why not cast Zubak in the part? Why not? He may have been out of style, but he was still a thespian. And an old thespian at that. Why drive him away? He'd have to be taught not to roll his gaping eyes and not to wave his arms like a windmill. Then he wouldn't be half bad. And Maximov would choke on his own bile because he, the great analyst, would be replaced by Zubak, and the show would go on.

The actors stood on the stage, at a loss about what to do. Some had already folded up their scripts and were ready to head home: why stand around gawking?

Then they heard Shtraitman shout: "Zubak! Get on stage!"

Zubak's heart flipped over. It had been pounding violently throughout the confrontation: Maybe Shtraitman would remember him? Zubak had waited for the call the way an aging warhorse waits for the blare of trumpets. And the call came. He was paralyzed from head to foot. He could barely drag himself to the stage.

Shtraitman was frantic: "Well, get a move on! You did want to play the Devil, didn't you? It's yours! But remember: if you flub even one word . . ."

And Zubak, with a touch of a tear in one eye, could barely whisper: "I'm coming, Mr. Shtraitman, I'm coming . . ."

ZUBAK HAD A new lease on life. Once he'd gotten that part, the whole world was his. He even straightened his body, which had been stooped for years. People figured he was bent from all his troubles, but actors knew the truth. Something terrible had happened to him. He had fallen in love with Pérele the chorist. Instead of getting hitched, he'd fooled around with her in the wings. He'd cop a feel, a kiss, a squeeze between exits and entrances.

Pérele realized that when push came to shove, Zubak turned a deaf ear. So one day she asked him: "Mr. Zubak, how long do you plan to keep feasting on me without a marriage contract? Who are you playing hide-and-seek with?"

Zubak, as was his habit, wanted to hug Pérele and say, "Sweetie pie!" But she kneed him in a noble place. Luckily, there was a doctor in the house. Zubak barely revived. Pérele gave up the stage and she married Ruvke the fireman. She still loved Zubak, while Ruvke was a coarse drunkard. He died, and so Pérele became a widow. Zubak grew surly and started walking with a stoop. He remained a bachelor, and he switched from romantic leads to character roles.

Eventually he realized he'd made a big mistake letting Pérele slip through his fingers. Both of them were known far and wide. Pérele had blazed on stage. People prophesied that she'd be a star. One day, the soubrette had fallen ill and been replaced by Pérele. What a performance! Artel the butcher cut himself because of her. And no wonder! When Pérele entered, sporting breeches and red bootlets, with a cinched waist that made her breasts stick out into the proscenium—what man could sit there without ants in his pants? Moreover she had marvelous features and a head of hair like a crown. But how could Zubak have dreamed of attaching himself? He was a guest performer and he also caroused every night away in Shuman's *café-chantant*.

Nevertheless, Zubak and Pérele stayed friends. Pérele had become an invalid, and Zubak, even in the worst theatrical season, managed to bring her something. He now intended to drop by and tell her about his new role. But then he felt it wasn't right to visit her with empty hands. Besides, he had rehearsals every day.

Shtraitman scheduled the premiere for Saturday night, and they had to work their tails off. Zubak decided to visit Pérele Saturday morning, when there'd be no rehearsal. He'd spend half the day with her, cheer her up a little. If the theater paid advances, he'd bring her a couple of zlotys. Zubak also planned to take Dr. Pergament to examine her after the premiere. Her lungs were whistling, and her legs were unsteady.

Meanwhile Zubak was fully absorbed in his role. He sat in bed for whole days at a time, learning the text. Shtraitman had announced the awful news that the cast had to memorize their lines thoroughly, because there wasn't going to be any prompter in the prompter's box.

SATURDAY MORNING, ZUBAK got up bright-eyed and bushy-tailed. His script was under his bed. Zubak knew it by heart. All the long, alien sentences were lined up in his brain like soldiers, just waiting to charge through his mouth and attack! He washed, dressed, and stepped into the courtyard for a breath of fresh air. A thought flashed through his mind:

Why not go to the bakery and buy a baked good on credit? That way, he'd be able to bring Pérele something for tea. Besides, why nurse a grudge against the baker? They were neighbors, after all. He'd kill two birds with one stone: Make up with the baker and bring something to Pérele. Whether it was the fresh snow or the new role, the world on that Saturday morning seemed purer and cheerier to Zubak, and his quarrel with the baker not so important.

No sooner said than done. Zubak crossed the threshold of the back door with a "good shabbes" on the tip of his tongue. But Svirsky wasn't there. The Sabbath pots had been moved from the oven to the floor. Zubak was intoxicated by the aromas of puddings and roast potatoes as if he'd stepped into an orangerie filled with rare blossoms. He nearly passed out. He stood there for an instant, overwhelmed by that culinary miracle. For quite a number of years now, nobody had thought of asking him to a Sabbath dinner. Once upon a time, people had fought over him. But ever since his name had vanished from the posters, not even Velfke the tavernkeeper noticed him. In his imagination, Zubak could picture the covered pots. A shiny burnished derma floated among fragrant piles of beans. Puddings like paving stones pressed down upon breast meat. Potatoes lurked on the edges of cauldrons, just waiting to be torn away. And Zubak saw a sweet bite in even the lowliest, most battered little pot. And even if there was no beef, wasn't there a calf's foot somewhere? Weren't there a few decent bones? It was all good enough for him.

Inhaling the spicy bouquets, Zubak stepped gingerly among the pots as if they were priceless vases. All at once he burst out laughing, louder than in many years. He felt his joy in the pit of his stomach. He chortled, he held his sides, he waved his arms as if driving away a prankster, a buffoon telling an unbelievable joke. And he did have someone to drive away. His own prankster, raised on theatrical tours, in small-town rooming houses, in dark stage wings, told him a good joke. His prankster, no less and no more, pestered him to take one of these Sabbath stews to Pérele.

His prankster nagged and nagged him, until Zubak started feeling that it wouldn't be such a crooked thing. Pérele was sick. It would be a mitsva, a good deed, to revive her. As for the premiere: a bit of stew would cheer Zubak's heart. You act better on a full stomach. He knew his lines, he knew the staging. And once he'd downed a plate of Sabbath stew, who would outact him? And most important of all. Pérele would rally a little.

His excuse would be: the celebration of the premiere. For once, Pérele wouldn't have to make do with a herring and fill up on chicory.

Now that the sin had a face, Zubak got cold feet. If he yielded to temptation, might he be depriving a poor family? God only knew which pot was whose! Common sense inferred that a huge cauldron belonged to Leyzer or to Gitke Toybe with their gaggles of children, and nothing came from any wealthy home. So Zubak had to focus on the smaller pots and let God decide. And that's what Zubak did. He leaned over, closed his eyes, and stretched out both hands.

The winner was a tall cauldron. On the brownish rim of the newspaper that lay under the lid, a name and address stood out: *Berger, Shvartsova Street.* When Zubak saw those words, a new soul entered his body. A celestial angel must have guided his hands. Zubak's conscience was clear. Berger, the rich kvas manufacturer. For him and his family, the stew was merely a tidbit, an hors d'oeuvre. The prosperous Jews began their Sabbath dinner with a piece of fish, eggs and onions, chopped liver, then soup, a quarter of a chicken with plum preserves, and what not. So they'd celebrate the Sabbath without a stew—big deal! After the premiere, Zubak would go to Berger, and the whole town would have a good laugh.

Zubak slipped the pot under his coat, holding it through his torn pocket. And then he softly hurried to Pérele.

That Sabbath, all hell broke loose in the bakery. Every last stew was cold. On Friday, Svirsky had awkwardly lifted a sack of mail and twisted his ribs. He therefore asked his two assistants to hand out the Sabbath pots. But the two revelers had been invited to a party. So they'd come to work very early, lugged the pots from the oven at breakneck speed, and left the bakery to its own devices.

The customers had dragged Svirsky from his bed to make him feast his eyes on the mess. As if that wasn't enough, Berger's maid grabbed hold of the baker: her Sabbath stew was missing! Svirsky tried to ask her whether she'd merely dreamed up a stew, maybe she hadn't brought it this time. The maid burst into tears and showed a receipt. Svirsky froze. He had indeed put her stew in the oven on Friday. It was a three-layer cauldron with a newspaper, *Evening Courier,* under the lid. He even remembered yelling at that lazy bum, Tevele, who'd leaned over the grate to read the latest installment of *Bloody Sonya.*

Svirsky wasn't so scared of the maid. Even though she wailed that she couldn't go home without the cauldron. Berger's oldest daughter had a guest from abroad, practically her fiancé, and the family wanted to overwhelm him with the stew. However, the baker was worried about something else. Recently there'd been a quarrel in his underworld club, The Golden Banner, and he'd sort of joined one faction. Orke had wanted to give Zelik the philanthropist a dressing-down. But since Svirsky did business with Zelik, Orke had hit on a revenge: he'd sent the baker a cauldron containing a small-scale grenade instead of pudding. Shortly after Svirsky had placed the pots in the oven and closed the oven door, Orke's cauldron had burst, shattering all the pots to bits.

The town was in an uproar. Vilna had always despised violence. The rabbi summoned both parties. Orke was as innocent as a lamb: he didn't know from nothing. The government got involved. It cost hundreds of zlotys to settle the issue.

This had all happened six months ago (may we be spared!), and now the situation looked awful again. A Sabbath cauldron had disappeared. Svirsky saw new troubles ahead. He sent the maid home with all kinds of excuses, swearing that he himself would go to Berger promptly and clear up the whole matter. But instead he went to the club secretary, Kivke the Beet, and asked what they had against him now. Kivke said they had nothing against him, things were quiet. No one had thought of anything. Orke and Zelik had agreed to conclude any argument without bloodshed, without weapons.

But Svirsky's mind was not at ease. He ran back to the bakery and searched every nook and cranny. You couldn't trust those thieves. Svirsky shuddered at the slightest rustle. He was terrified that he and the bakery would explode at any moment. Wiping the soot from his hands, he tried to guess: If it wasn't those bandits, then who could've done such a thing? Unless it was burglars. They were greedy for even a worn-out hearth broom. And tomorrow, God willing, they'd try and fence the empty cauldron. Then he'd know for sure.

Svirsky headed home, determined to confront those fiends, his assistants, after the Sabbath and not mince his words. He'd teach them to leave the bakery in a lurch!

"WELL, DID IT taste good?"

"Yes, I'd nearly forgotten its taste . . ."

"Have a little more derma."

"Zubak, c'mon, I'm stuffed to the gills."

Zubak and Pérele had wolfed down their Sabbath feast, assuring themselves that nothing remained on the other person's plate. Zubak had done his best to get her to eat, as if he wanted to make up for all the Sabbath dinners she had missed. Warmed up, shifted away from the table because of his overcrammed belly, he was beaming with pride and joy, gazing at the color that Pérele had gotten after the second portion of pudding. He'd told her that he'd received the meal from a neighboring woman in exchange for writing something for her: a letter, passages from a play. It was all aimed at her husband, who'd run out on her and sailed to America. Pérele had laughed and eaten, and praised the neighbor's pudding.

Zubak had joined in the laughter. "You know what, Pérele? I copied the second-act monologue, and so he mailed her a ten-spot and promised to send her a ticket for a passage to America."

Pérele shook her head. "Oh, Zubak, you're as much of a sweet-talker as ever, and you're going to die a sweet-talker. Did you behave any differently with me?"

Zubak held out his arms. "Well, whose fault is it that you ran away from the theater? If you'd stuck it out and gone on tour with us, we'd 've definitely tied the knot."

Between potatoes, Zubak described several funny incidents in the theater. They both laughed their heads off, failing to notice that nothing was left of the Sabbath food.

ZUBAK CARRIED HIS belly to the theater like a klezmer toting his kettledrum. He could barely bend over. It was only when sitting in the dressing room that he managed to recall everything he'd gorged on. He was no longer used to rich fare. He felt a pressure in the pit of his stomach, and his hiccups banged away at his throat. Zubak moaned: "What can you do? I'm doomed."

The other actors in the dressing room saw that something was wrong with him. Between moans, he assured them that he was all right. A bit of pudding had bothered him. It would soon pass.

He had a hard time pulling on his bootlets, and he was drenched with sweat when climbing into his velvet breeches and tying the devilish cape to his neck. The hiccups knocked Zubak's head back as if he'd been handed a live ember. He was unable to make up his eyes. The mascara dripped on his nose, leaving black spots.

By the time he was finished, Borodov, who'd been transformed from prompter to stage manager, had shouted twice into the dressing room: "Zubak, you're on!"

Zubak pulled himself together for all he was worth and stepped out on the boards. Mendke the stagehand pulled up the curtain.

When it was time for Zubak's cue, he tossed a corner of his cloak over his shoulder and started gearing up for the soliloquy he had so ardently yearned for. But when he opened his mouth, he hiccupped so violently that his eyes practically popped out of his head. His belly reared, and he collapsed amid the cramps. You could have freighted him off to the grave-yard! The audience panicked. Women squealed, spectators began dash-ing across the auditorium. Mendke rang down the curtain.

ZUBAK LEFT THE theater. Shtraitman threatened to shoot him. He foamed at the mouth: How could an actor, a civilized man, do such a thing? And where? In Vilna. Stuff his guts on the Sabbath right before a premiere! And what a premiere!

Pérele nestled close to Zubak on a cot in her tiny room. She was grow-ing sicker. But she was surviving for Zubak. Once, she asked him: "Zubak, why in God's name did you need that whole business with the Sabbath meal?"

Zubak looked at her, his face wreathed in smiles. "It was for you, Pérele, for you. I wanted you to have some joy . . . ."

Pérele grabbed his hand and wept into it. "Well, darling, you can see that we don't appear fated to have much joy. We brought joy to others, but we ourselves . . . ."

Zubak exclaimed: "Never mind, Pérele, don't let it get you down. If we don't have the stage, we still have each other. We've got nothing else . . . ."

Zubak succeeded in comforting her, but he didn't tell her the truth about the stage.

Sometimes he attends a performance. He sits way back, in the last row. But he always leaves in the middle. First of all, he's managed to shed a tear like an ordinary Jew, but he doesn't want those bastards to see it. Secondly, he can't stand the fact that everyone's acting but him. What wouldn't he give to be up there on the stage with the others!

Zubak, more stooped than ever, trudges out of the dark auditorium and goes back to Pérele's room. There he transfers his clippings into a new album. These old reviews of his performances are the only comfort he's got left.

FRUME HALPERN *(n.d. —1966)*

Halpern, who arrived in America in 1905, published stories in Di Frayhayt *(a Communist Yiddish newspaper) and in anthologies. Eventually she brought out a book of short stories in 1963. She died three years later in New York.*

Dog Blood

FROM GEBENTSHTE HENT (BLESSED HANDS) (1963)

THE GUEST, WHO went over to the Shtroms, was beside himself. For politeness' sake, he avoided using curse words with his friends, with whom he had wandered through the Holocaust years until he managed to reach these shores. He thought to himself: "How is it possible? They were torn out together, they suffered horribly, they lived like hunted animals. So how can a person come up with something like that? Something must have gone wrong in their brain!" He would never have expected it! Instead of kissing the hand that had welcomed him so humanely, instead of blessing the land that had given him a roof over his head, he complained that he'd been forced against his will!

The Shtroms, husband and wife, were way into middle age. They bore the traces of agonies that shrieked without words. Shtrom was a short, heavyset man with a burned-off eyebrow and a scarred face. He spoke from time to time. But his wife was always silent. Talking was a strain for her. She would listen to her husband and nod in agreement. She barely enjoyed the milk and honey dripping from the trees in this country. Her face was skeletal, her eyes were big and shiny, and it was astonishing how she clung to life.

Shimkhe Shtrom responded to the guest's complaints: "How can I enjoy all these good things here if the soil is alien and empty? Back home everything was mine, after all! You're smiling! You're thinking: 'A fine home! Those blood-soaked fields!' I know what you're thinking! But I want you to know that the blood-soaked fields, the trees, and even the wild grass on the grave mounds were all mine and dear to me. When have Jews ever fled the graves of their own flesh and blood? And despite fire and slaughter, aren't the graves still graves? We should have remained where our bones lie."

He nodded toward his wife. "She—certainly! Do you really believe that we were rescued by being dragged here? It's all the same whether she sits on a chair or I trudge around. We're still there! Over there our eyes were glued to the earth. Every grain of sand, every stone reminded us of something. And here? There's nothing to look at. The wealth numbs your eyes, you want to run away, run to the graves!" He then added: "And you should know, my friend, that there's going to be a Jewish life wherever Jews have remained. It's already begun! If we'd stayed there, we'd find some solace for the blood we lost, we'd have revenge and consolation. But here they resent it if we find enjoyment even far away. They paint everything in dark colors, as if their lives depended on their poisoning whatever they can."

Shtrom spoke in a strained voice even though it wasn't too loud, and his wife stared at him with her frozen face, as if she were waiting for something.

The guest, an emaciated manikin with high cheekbones, was a lot younger than the Shtroms. He never removed his right hand from his pocket, while his left hand kept tugging at his throat as if to indicate that even though he was absorbed in his thoughts, he could hear what was being said.

Shtrom drew closer to him, saying: "Would you like to know what I think of your philanthropists with their millions? I think they've gorged themselves on their piled-up riches and they're scared stiff that some day they're going to be called to account for remaining silent when the ground rose under the jackboots of drunken Nazis. And the dead are stirring."

Shtrom's face was the color of tinder. He felt his breast pocket, took out an old leather wallet, glanced at his wife, and put it back into his pocket. He smoothed his threadbare jacket and said more softly: "Don't be angry. Maybe I shouldn't have mentioned all this. I know that we both have deep wounds. Both of us are victims, but you're younger. She and I won't adapt here. Not me with the dog blood running in my guts and not her with her skeletal face."

The guest winced. Shtrom had a strange smile as he continued: "And didn't we eat rats? Dog meat was a festive banquet. We fed on whatever we could lay our hands on. And you think that these people here can or want to heal our souls? I don't believe it! I can still remember how I called out to them—that's all I want!"

The guest, scowling now, twisted on his chair. He wanted to say something, but couldn't find the appropriate words. All he did was rummage in his pocket and pull out a pack of crushed cigarettes and a box of matches. But when he tried to light a match, his fingers wouldn't obey. Shtrom helped him. The guest greedily devoured the smoke, gazed at the floor, and said: "You see these hands? What wouldn't I have done without them? And if I'd remained there, would the graves have helped me much? You're angry at the do-gooders here because they didn't hear our shrieks. But I ask you, Where was God? Why aren't you angry at Him?"

He spoke very swiftly as if scared of being interrupted. "Nonsense, please don't be offended, nonsense, drivel!"

Shtrom shifted away from his guest to have a better view of him. Fuming, he said: "Did God come to me and give me the choice to go to Israel or America? I'm not saying that everything those people do is worthless. God grant that they do good with their fortunes, but one shouldn't hide the truth. The truth is that they didn't dare run, they shouldn't have dragged us!

"Believe me, if people only knew with what deep love and dedication the Jews who've remained are rebuilding the country—the country that's now free for every citizen! Not just they but also the graves of the murdered Jews are shielded and protected. I'm ashamed to face my murdered mother, who's weeping from her grave . . ."

Shtrom stood next to his wife, who sat there, gazing to the side. For a while Shtrom looked at her, then he turned back to the guest. "Oh, how we screamed and moaned, but their brains were stuffed. Don't think they're giving away the shirts on their backs! They'll have something left over for themselves." His voice was already tearing from him. He felt his wife's mute eyes begging him to rest. He sat down on the sofa and again produced the old, worn wallet from his breast pocket.

His wife's hands reached out, and for the first time she stammered something: "Don't!"

When he slipped the wallet back into his pocket, she lowered her feeble hands.

Suddenly, as if forgetting his wife and the guest, Shtrom stood up, hurried over to the small table at the window, yanked forth the wallet with both hands, and started laying out photographs. In an orderly, unhurried manner, he placed them one by one in straight lines, counting out four generations. He put young next to young, old next to old, calling them by name and title: rabbis, doctors, lawyers. There were radiantly smiling faces of bridal couples in wedding clothes, students clutching diplomas, playful children with joyous faces and defiant eyes. Clouds of smoke, clouds of all colors hovered in front of Shtrom . . . Black, red . . . His eyes prickled, his ears buzzed . . .

Shtrom's one hand held the table and his other hand summoned the guest. The guest was in no hurry, he knew what he'd see there. His face quivered as if he were about to view a corpse; and before he could reach the table, Shtrom dropped to the floor . . .

Now they were all sitting again. The four generations were back in the wallet inside the breast pocket. The room was filled with a chilly, gloomy hush. The guest was preparing to leave. After a long silence, the guest regained his power of speech. His first few words, almost inaudible as if frightened, barely pierced the shadows:

"Lawyers, engineers, rabbis . . . And since I come from a simple, ordinary background, since my boys were born to be craftsmen, were born with big hands and feet, like their granddads, like their father—" He gazed mechanically at his dangling hands. "Do you believe my pain is less acute than yours?"

Shtrom snapped up as if he'd been bitten. His head and his hands were shuddering with agitation. "My God! How can a person, a Jew talk like that? Do I give a damn about family background, about titles? It's the worthlessness that manures everything, and it's tearing me apart! Dung and dog blood mix together in my guts, and I can't endure it! And you believe that we have to stand in front of them with bowed heads because of their charity, because of their activities? No—not me! Should I do it for the dog blood that's inside me? Or for her? For the face and for the eyes that keep searching? No and no again! I'm not going to bless them for this bit of foul life! You claim that if it hadn't been for them, the few survivors wouldn't have survived. And I say, Blessed are those who wouldn't be led astray. The ones over there have managed to get back on their feet. As for those of us who are here: What are we? What are we doing here?"

The grayness of the walls spread across the three faces. A moaning wind angrily shook the loose window frames, and the three people in the room felt ice-cold.

Shtrom struggled to his feet and trudged over to the window. A scraggy, quivering little tree stuck out between two small cottages. The tree shook and circled hastily as if trying to escape. Shtrom trembled to the rhythm of the small, parched branches, which reminded him of human hands that he had once seen sticking out of hills of soil.

The guest said, "Goodnight." But the Shtroms didn't hear him.

Y. Y. TRUNK (1887–1961)

Y. Y. Trunk, who was born near Warsaw, spent his adolescence in Lodz, studying both religious and secular subjects. It was Y. L. Peretz who influenced him to turn from Hebrew to Yiddish. Trunk's early fiction describes his radical leanings; he also wrote essays, criticism, and poetry. After spending a year in Palestine and World War I in Switzerland, he lived in Lodz, then Warsaw. When the Germans invaded Poland, Trunk fled eastward, eventually settling in New York in 1941. Aside from a wealth of fiction, some of it based on Jewish history and folklore, he produced a vast amount of criticism, including an incisive analysis of Oscar Wilde's The Picture of Dorian Gray. *Trunk's most important work was his seven-volume* Poland, *a docudrama of Jewish life in Poland.*

A Roman Philosopher Writes a Letter (1958)

LUCIUS ANNERS SENECA, who owned vast landed properties, was a government minister and a member of Nero's court as well as a usurer and municipal philosopher.

Once, when returning home from the imperial palaces on the Palatine, he had to spend a few moments at the Forum. Sualius had publicly accused him of forging wills and usury. Many of Seneca's debtors, under the pretext that their IOUs were forged, were trying to extricate themselves from their responsibilities.

The accusations brought by Sualius and other enemies against the divine Seneca were taken up by him with a truly stoic peace of mind. He recalled how the Athenians had accused Socrates. How calmly Socrates had died. But Seneca the philosopher lost his equilibrium in regard to the ugly swindle that his debtors were trying to perpetrate. He was threatened with a huge monetary loss. (We must add: The divine Seneca viewed his weakness for gold as a sickness and incomprehensible punishment inflicted by the gods.) With genuine anger, he perceived the people you see at the Forum and at the Circus as seething with evil plans to harm one another. No, there was no peace among all the wearers of togas.

The debtor with whom Seneca the Stoic was involved in a money quarrel at the Forum today was a lame freedman, Pandaros, a Greek. With the extreme slyness characteristic of slaves and cripples, Pandaros refused to pay the interest. He even tried to prove that the IOUs in the philosopher's possession did not bear the Greek's signature. He bowed to Seneca with canine servility (despite his own significant fortune). Flattered him. Spoke softly. But absolutely refused to pay his debt. Seneca sneered at him, but not without philosophical commiseration. A man's soul, whose place is in the highest spheres of Platonic Ideas, can be lowered to a miserable level in the body of a Pandaros. The ways of the gods are wondrous. In facing this debtor, Seneca maintained his spiritual tranquility. His library contained a document that proved the ex-slave's obligations with absolute certainty. That was why the philosopher Seneca could watch every last movement of this petty soul with utter objectivity.

Upon leaving the Forum, he went straight home.

He walked slowly. Step by step. He was wearing an old, threadbare toga to make it seem that he was not rich, a state minister, who knew that wealth and honor are ephemeral. Eternal are philosophical thought and a tranquil spirit. The minister and philosopher Seneca was now in the blissful mood of the world-poorest Stoic. He thought about destiny. Through an antagonism toward philosophy, a hatred defying any simple explanation, destiny sometimes burdens a philosopher's life with gold and landed estates. Destiny constrains the philosopher in gold chains just as it constrains the lowliest slave. It looms like a wall that blocks the philosopher's path toward great tranquility. When our Zeno learned that his entire fortune was lost at sea, he said: "Destiny wants me to philosophize unhampered."

"The gods own no property!" Seneca whispered to himself. "They have no estates and no gardens. They don't charge usurious interest at the Forum."

All at once, Seneca bumped into a throng of slaves accompanying a fat Patrician clad in purple. The well-known and stingy Quintus Mucius. Raising his eyes and staring a while at the throng surrounding Mucius, Seneca then started gazing at the motley commotion in the Roman streets. At the same time, he remembered how happy Diogenes had been in his barrel.

After many days of aggravation with his debtors, this new day was starting to become a true day for an unpropertied Stoic.

He thought of his friend and pupil Novatus.

Novatus, a young and very rich Roman, resided in his country estate on the northern border of Italy. While in Rome, Novatus had been in contact with the Stoic school and made friends with Seneca. Now Novatus was completely isolated. His house, made of white Grecian marble, stood on the shores of a calm blue lake, where he lived in great wealth. He was surrounded by slaves, who served him as if he were a young god. His wealth had become loathsome to him. He read books. Mused about the ephemeralness of the world. Fed up with himself, he tortured his slaves. The most trivial thing made his blood boil. The young Stoic did not have a tranquil conscience.

He sent extensive letters to his master Seneca in Rome. He wanted the great philosopher to advise him how to overcome his vile temper.

Seneca felt it was his conscientious duty to help his friends. Especially when it came to philosophical advice.

He therefore indited a three-volume treatise discussing all the causes of ugly and damaging irascibility. He also set down various kinds of moral advice for quelling anger. This opus, in the guise of a letter to young Novatus, was meant as both a response and an immortal monument for future generations. In this letter, Seneca also strove to gain a solid foundation for his own soul. He saw this opus as the mirror of an ethical credo. In it he described various episodes in the lives of great men in order to hold their deeds up constantly. The deeds of great men show what we can achieve with true peace of mind.

The victory that the philosopher Seneca had won today over his own human foibles (in regard to his debtor, the ex-slave Pandaros) strengthened his conviction that it was purely thanks to philosophy that he had remained tranquil and indifferent to the lame and malevolent Greek. Philosophy is a comforting mother to its children. It puts their minds at ease. At that very moment, Nero's minister felt like a silent, innocent child in the shadow of his philosophical thoughts. He remained sanguine in his contempt for the world. "Spiritual grandeur is not to be found among bad people," Seneca murmured to himself. "The sage Diogenes tranquilly endured it when someone spit in his face. He would say: 'I am not angry.'"

Seneca mulled over a few other important points for finishing his letter to Novatus. Soon he found himself in front of his own house.

Seneca the Stoic's fortune came to three hundred million sesterces, and his mansion in Rome was splendid and sumptuous. However, his study, his library, were very modestly arranged. In his library, Seneca did not care to see himself as the man of the world, the celebrity, the teacher, Nero's friend and minister; Seneca wanted to see himself as a philosopher. And he wished to live there as a philosopher. "The philosopher should spend no more than half a sesterce a day," Seneca would state. Though he was unable to stick to that, given his fortune and his social status. At least in the library, where he would be alone with his thoughts, he wanted to indulge in the illusion that he was no richer than Socrates.

Seneca's library was indeed modest. Without the slightest hint of luxury. Nearly poor. All you could smell was dust and parchment. The book scrolls were heaped up on plain stone chairs and tables. The philosopher did not buy books just for looking at, like people who collect paintings and Corinthian vases. What he sought in the books was the call of eternity, the tranquility and equilibrium of his mind. Furthermore the library was very far from all the other rooms, beyond the slightest worldly noise. In the middle of the imperial city of Rome, among his wealth and slaves, the state minister Seneca lived in his library like Diogenes in his barrel. How wise are they who walk in the ways of wisdom!

The only items of furniture that the philosopher used in this room were a simple table and a marble chair devoid of decorations and bas-reliefs.

The only luxury was to be found amid the diverse scrolls and written parchments on Seneca's desk—namely, the oil lamp. It was made of bronze and bore the image of a cunningly stylized lemon tree. Small oil pans hung like ripe fruits among the bronze branches and hammered leaves. In the high grass under the trunk, the artist had depicted a flirtation between a small Cupid and three nude nymphs. Seneca kept this sole de luxe object in his library not to look at it and enjoy it. In that erotic game, Seneca the Stoic, in the solitude of his thoughts, wanted to have not merely the weaknesses of men but also the weaknesses of the gods.

He now softly and slowly entered his library. Shut the door firmly behind him. Drew the curtain across the door in order to close himself off completely from the world. His mind was filled with lofty thoughts. Filled with spirit. Filled with inner calm. Seneca intended to weave these thoughts into the conclusion of his letter to Novatus. The letter against anger. From the pockets of his toga he produced a small volume of writings by the immortal Epicurus. Seneca always had Epicurus writings with him. He liked to dip into them while setting down his moral and philosophical tractates or even when sitting with Nero and talking about various court or state matters.

And in his work as Nero's minister, Seneca did not forget the soul. The immortal part of the human being!

However, he remembered Pandaros the Greek and he made a decision: before settling down to write, he ought to review the document that confirmed the ex-slave's obligations. To make sure he took it along to the Forum tomorrow, the philosopher planned to wrap this document in his favorite book by Epicurus. Seneca wanted to shut himself off completely from all his monetary concerns. When writing to his pupil Novatus, Seneca preferred to maintain a spiritual equilibrium. Virtue alone is lofty and sublime. The soul cannot achieve grandeur if one is not tranquil and passionless.

Seneca gracefully settled on his chair and began rummaging through the scrolls and parchments scattered on the desk. He then promptly jumped up. His pallid, ascetic face had suddenly turned purple.

The document was nowhere to be found.

Profoundly agitated, Seneca dug through the heaps of parchments with both his hands. More and more nervous, he flung them to and fro. He bit his lips. His face kept switching color—now white, now red.

He loudly clapped his hands.

The door flew open very softly. A slave came tiptoeing swiftly. Bowed deep. Waited for an order.

Seneca yelled: "Who removed a written parchment from my desk?" His chalky lips and the jaws of his longish face were trembling.

The slave's body shrank. He knew it was no trivial matter if the great Seneca was in such a state.

"I have no idea . . . ," the slave barely managed to stammer.

The philosopher screamed even louder. Both his hands were charging through the piles of scrolls and parchments on his desk.

"You bastard, you!" the philosopher shouted. "That lame Pandaros bribed you to give him that parchment! What a financial loss! You're all in it together, you dirty gang of slaves!"

The slave stammered, "I don't know any Pandaros, divine lord!"

The philosopher's hands stormed more ferociously through his desk. His pale, parched lips were covered with foam. "Hand over the parchment, you bastard!" he gasped.

The slave trembled like a leaf. He barely managed to stay on his feet. "I'm innocent, divine lord!"

"And you talk back to me too?" the philosopher hollered in a strange voice. Grabbing the bronze lamp with both hands, he threw it at the slave with all his strength.

There was a loud crash. The artwork fell on the library's mosaic floor. The slave wobbled and collapsed next to the lamp like a sheaf of wheat. His skull was shattered. Blood mixed with marrow was oozing out. The slave lay on the floor like a slaughtered calf.

A small oil pad had broken off the lamp. The Cupid was leaning slightly to one side.

Seneca kept tossing the scrolls and parchments about for a brief while. All at once, a smile lit up his face.

The document he was hunting lay where the bronze lamp had stood.

He heaved a great sigh of relief. Sat down on the marble chair as if after hard labor. With both hands, which were still trembling, he clutched the document. Read it.

Once more he smiled with relief. Kept reading the parchment.

Suddenly he stopped reading and looked at the murdered slave. The slave was lying calmly, his feet barely quivering.

The philosopher clapped his hands several times.

Two slaves hurried in. They bowed deeply. Waited.

"Take him away!" the philosopher ordered. He didn't even glance at them. He kept poring over the document with a satisfied smile.

The slaves picked up the murdered man and quietly carried him out of the library.

The philosopher slowly rolled up the document and slipped it into the small volume of writings by the divine Epicurus. Then he sat straight up. Fully absorbed, he started to conclude his letter to Novatus.

Among the various episodes in the lives of great men—episodes that Seneca was describing—among the various sublime thoughts he set down, the philosopher focused on the following idea (he regarded it as immortal):

"Nothing proves a man's spirit more," he wrote, "than his ability to remain calm in all the vicissitudes of his life. There are no storms and no whirlwinds among the stars. Nothing but complete tranquility exists in those astral areas."

DOVID-LEYB MEKLER*

Made famous by S. Ansky's supernatural drama, a dybbuk is a spirit that takes possession of a living person. This Yiddish creation, recurrent since the Middle Ages, entered Yiddish fiction in 1602 ("The Possession," from The Mayse Book) *and has haunted Jewish literature ever since. The word "dybbuk" itself was coined in Yiddish in 1680. (For a more detailed treatment, see Joachim Neugroschel,* The Dybbuk and the Yiddish Imagination *[Syracuse, NY: Syracuse University Press, 2000].)*

The Dybbuk *(1931)*

RABBI DÚVIDL OF Tolne was famous both for his great wisdom and for his great miracles.

Many of his miracles were simply based on wisdom, but his followers were as delighted with those expressions of wisdom as they were with the tales of his real miracles.

Rabbi Dúvidl was also renowned as a healer, and people with all sorts of illnesses would visit his court, hoping that he would cure them.

*From *Dem Rebns Hoyf/Tolne* (New York: Jewish Book Publishing Co. 1931), vol. 1, pp. 135–41.

The remedies he offered were not only blessings but also herbs, compounds, and salves as well as amulets, talismans, and the like.

The rabbi had a medical book that had been handed down through several generations: it contained treatments and remedies for various illnesses.

As a result his court was constantly besieged by patients with all sorts of mental or physical complaints and deformities—men, women, and children.

And Hasids tell one another all kinds of stories about his miraculous cures. Why, he even resurrected the dead. . . .

Needless to say, the most interesting stories are about dybbuks.

And there are many such stories. But they can be divided into two categories. In one group, the treatments are based on wisdom, intelligent ideas, and exact understanding of the human soul; while in the other group, the treatments derive from the rebbe's great power as a Cabalist and miracleworker.

One story is about a man who had convinced himself that his legs were made of glass. He refused to sit down, scared as he was that if he bent his legs, they would shatter. Glass doesn't bend, and a man with glass legs is a miserable creature.

So he always stood on his straight legs or else walked about as if on stilts, and when he lay down, he would twist and turn, making sure not to bend his knees so that the glass wouldn't shatter.

People kept telling him that he had normal legs just like anyone else, that he could sit and walk and even dance. But no matter how much they talked away at him, it did no good. He stuck to his guns—his legs were made of glass.

So people said that a "dybbuk" had entered him and they took him to Talne, so that Rabbi Dúvidl could expel the "dybbuk."

And expel him he did. The man stopped imagining that his legs were glass, and they became flesh and blood and bones again.

How did the rebbe pull it off? This is the story that the Hasids tell:

WHEN THE MAN was brought before the rebbe, the rebbe, without further ado, told him to have a seat.

"I can't, rebbe," he said. "My knees won't bend, my legs are made of glass."

"But I order you to sit down!" the rebbe shouted. "I order you to sit down immediately!"

The man was terrified. When the rebbe orders you to do something, you must obey no matter what may happen—even if your glass legs shatter.

The man sat down, and as he did so, they heard a loud racket like the breaking of glass. The "glass" legs burst, shattered, but they were mobile again—like the legs of a normal person.

"Now you can stand up and walk and sit and move like everyone else," the rebbe told him. "The glass has been shattered."

And the man left, fully convinced that his glass legs had returned to what they should have been.

What had happened? Not much. The rebbe had told his assistant to wait in the next room and break some glass the instant the man sat down. The man would then think that the glass fettering his legs had burst.

The idea was based purely on wisdom, and the rebbe's followers always cited it as an example of his great wisdom.

* * *

A VERY DIFFERENT dybbuk tale concerning Rabbi Dúvidl is told as follows:

In a remote shtetl, a feud erupted over a cantor. Such feuds were not unusual in the little Jewish towns. They would often end peacefully but very often flare up into a bitter war that lasted for years, making entire families miserable.

The whole shtetl was Hasidic; there was virtually no anti-Hasids there. But the Hasids were divided up, they were followers of different rebbes, and these various sects were battling with one another. They fought every day of the year and they fought over nothing.

Naturally the war reached its climax when a new cantor had to be hired for the synagogue.

The shtetl had an old cantor who had his friends and foes. Still, when a man has held a position for a long time, you don't hassle him.

But with age his voice became weak and raspy.

And so his old opponents reared their heads. "Enough," they argued. "We need a new cantor."

And the dissatisfaction with the old cantor grew by the day until they brought in new cantors and tried them out.

The feud worsened. It erupted into an all-out war.

But the faction that wanted a new cantor was larger and stronger, and the other faction realized that there would be no peace in the shtetl until they hired a new and younger cantor, who could lead the prayers.

After managing to conciliate the old cantor, they took on a new one.

The shtetl was now finally at peace. The new cantor did a good job of leading the prayers, and the congregation was satisfied.

The only dissatisfied person was the old cantor, whose broken heart could not be mended. There was no question of his finding another position. That was something a man of his age and with his voice could hardly expect.

So he had to remain in the shtetl and find some other line of work. But a wound remained in his heart, a deep, bleeding wound. His heart bled when he saw another man reigning in his stead and when he was rejected by all the world. No one so much as glanced at him or felt his great sorrow.

The old cantor started weakening by the day. He grew senile, he was bent and twisted, a shadow of his former self. His life was ebbing slowly, he was dying a bit more every day—until one day they discovered his corpse.

Only now did some people realize that the old cantor had been the victim of persecution and that his life had been shortened because the synagogue had replaced him with a new cantor.

His fiercest opponents now felt bad.

Unhappiest of all was the new cantor, who had pangs of guilt about the old cantor's premature death.

The old cantor died shortly before Rosh Hashanah (the New Year), a time when every Jew has a need to repent.

The new cantor was miserable. You could tell that he was suffering, that his heart was broken, that he felt guilty about something.

And then Rosh Hashanah arrived. The new cantor was standing with his choirboys, ready to sing the added morning prayer for the Sabbath and for holidays.

It was the first day of Rosh Hashanah. The beadle had already knocked on the Torah table, signaling the cantor to start.

The cantor, in his smock and with his prayer shawl around his head, stood by his pulpit, surrounded by his choir, which was ready to accompany him.

The synagogue was filled with a deathly hush, aside from a few moans and a soft weeping from the women's section.

The cantor began.

He cried out the opening words, and the congregants shuddered.

It wasn't his voice, it was the voice of the old cantor, who had died.

It was exactly the same voice.

The cantor himself was frightened. He too felt that it wasn't his voice. Still, he tried to sing on. Perhaps it was only his imagination. But no, it *was* the old cantor's voice. There could be no doubt.

The congregation panicked.

A dybbuk had entered the cantor . . . The old cantor's dybbuk . . .

The old cantor had returned to take his position at his pulpit, where he had stood for so many years and which he had come to love and cherish . . .

In mortal terror, the new cantor threw down his prayer shawl and his smock and dashed home.

But even in his home, the old cantor's voice sang through him.

The old cantor's dybbuk refused to leave him.

And the dybbuk haunted him and occupied him more and more obstinately.

"I want to be cantor here again," the dybbuk asserted, and he sounded exactly like the old cantor. "I couldn't do it while I was alive, so I'll do it now that I'm dead, through the new cantor."

The townsfolk tried everything. They prayed at the old cantor's grave, they measured the graveyard, they applied all sorts of remedies. But nothing helped. The dybbuk refused to leave the new cantor.

Finally they decided to take the cantor to the Rebbe of Talne. Rabbi Dúvidl had performed so many exorcisms that he would certainly be able to drive out this dybbuk too.

The rebbe ordered them to bring the new cantor to his home.

"Sing me something," said the rebbe to the cantor.

The cantor began, but all that came out was the weak and raspy voice of the old, dead cantor.

"I want to hear some singing!" snapped the rebbe. "That isn't singing. Try it again!"

The cantor began anew, but out came the same weak and raspy voice.

"Can't you sing?" the rebbe snapped angrily. "You want to pray at the pulpit with a voice like that? Go back to your rest. You're merely disturbing the Jews who are trying to worship God as they should."

For a while there was silence. But then they heard a soft weeping.

"I love my pulpit so much."

"'It is not the dead who will praise God,'" said the rebbe in response to what the dybbuk had said.

And the dybbuk didn't say another word.

"You cannot sing and you cannot stand at the pulpit anymore," the rebbe concluded.

A short time later, the rebbe, calm and collected, again ordered the new cantor to sing:

"Now sing yourself in your own voice. The old cantor has returned to his rest. He has nothing more to do at your pulpit."

The cantor began to sing, and this time he sang in his own voice. The dybbuk had left him forever.

ISAAC BASHEVIS SINGER *(1904–1991)*

One of the best-known Yiddish authors and the only one to receive a Nobel Prize (1978), I. B. Singer was born into a Hasidic home near Warsaw. He was educated at Warsaw's Rabbinical Seminary. In 1935 he settled in New York City, where he worked as a reviewer and journalist for the Jewish Daily Forward. Many of his stories, novels, children's books, and memoirs have been translated into a number of languages.

The Mirror *(1957)*

FROM GIMPEL THE FOOL
TRANSLATED BY NORBERT GUTERMAN

1

THERE IS A kind of net that is as old as Methuselah, as soft as a cobweb and as full of holes, yet it has retained its strength to this day. When a demon wearies of chasing after yesterdays or of going round in circles on a windmill, he can install himself inside a mirror. There he waits like a spider in its web, and the fly is certain to be caught. God has bestowed vanity on the female, particularly on the rich, the pretty, the barren, the young, who have much time and little company.

I discovered such a woman in the village of Krashnik. Her father dealt in timber; her husband floated the logs to Danzig; grass was growing on her mother's grave. The daughter lived in an old house, among oaken cupboards, leather-lined coffers, and books bound in silk. She had two servants, an old one that was deaf and a young one who carried on with a fiddler. The other Krashnik housewives wore men's boots, ground buckwheat on millstones, plucked feathers, cooked broths, bore children, and attended funerals. Needless to say, Zirel, beautiful and well-educated—she had been brought up in Cracow—had nothing to talk about with her small-town neighbors. And so she preferred to read her German song book and embroider Moses and Ziporah, David and Bathsheba, Ahasuereus and Queen Esther on canvas. The pretty dresses her husband brought her hung in the closet. Her pearls and diamonds lay in her jewel box. No one ever saw her silk slips, her lace petticoats, nor her red hair which was hidden under her wig, not even her husband. For when could they be seen? Certainly not during the day, and at night it is dark.

But Zirel had an attic which she called her boudoir, and where hung a mirror as blue as water on the point of freezing. The mirror had a crack in the middle, and it was set in a golden frame which was decorated with snakes, knobs, roses, and adders. In front of the mirror lay a bearskin and close beside it was a chair with armrests of ivory and a cushioned seat. What could be more pleasant than to sit naked in this chair, and rest one's feet on the bearskin, and contemplate oneself? Zirel had much to gaze at. Her skin was white as satin, her breasts as full as wineskins, her hair fell across her shoulders, and her legs were as slender as a hind's. She would sit for hours on end delighting in her beauty. The door fastened and bolted, she would imagine that it opened to admit either a prince or a hunter or a knight or a poet. For everything hidden must be revealed, each secret longs to be disclosed, each love yearns to be betrayed, everything sacred must be desecrated. Heaven and earth conspire that all good beginnings should come to a bad end.

Well, once I learned of the existence of this luscious little tidbit, I determined that she would be mine. All that was required was a little patience. One summer day, as she sat staring at the nipple on her left breast, she caught sight of me in the mirror—there I was, black as tar, long as a shovel, with donkey's ears, a ram's horns, a frog's mouth, and a goat's beard. My eyes were all pupil. She was so surprised that she forgot to be frightened. Instead of crying, "Hear, O Israel," she burst out laughing.

"My, how ugly you are," she said.

"My, how beautiful you are," I replied.

She was pleased with my compliment. "Who are you?" she asked.

"Fear not," I said. "I am an imp, not a demon. My fingers have no nails, my mouth has no teeth, my arms stretch like licorice, my horns are as pliable as wax. My power lies in my tongue; I am a fool by trade, and I have come to cheer you up because you are alone."

"Where were you before?"

"In the bedroom behind the stove where the cricket chirps and the mouse rustles, between a dried wreath and a faded willow branch."

"What did you do there?"

"I looked at you."

"Since when?"

"Since your wedding night."

"What did you eat?"

"The fragrance of your body, the glow of your hair, the light of your eyes, the sadness of your face."

"Oh, you flatterer!" she cried. "Who are you? What are you doing here? Where do you come from? What is your errand?"

I made up a story. My father, I said, was a goldsmith and my mother a succubus; they copulated on a bundle of rotting rope in a cellar and I was their bastard. For some time I lived in a settlement of devils on Mount Seir where I inhabited a mole's hole. But when it was learned that my father was human I was driven out. From then on I had been homeless. She-devils avoided me because I reminded them of the sons of Adam; the daughters of Eve saw in me Satan. Dogs barked at me, children wept when they saw me. Why were they afraid? I harmed no one. My only desire was to gaze at beautiful women—to gaze and converse with them.

"Why converse? The beautiful aren't always wise."

"In Paradise the wise are the footstools of the beautiful."

"My teacher taught me otherwise."

"What did your teacher know? The writers of books have the brains of a flea; they merely parrot each other. Ask me when you want to know something. Wisdom extends no further than the first heaven. From there on everything is lust. Don't you know that angels are headless? The

Seraphim play in the sand like children; the Cherubim can't count; the Aralim chew their cud before the throne of Glory. God himself is jovial. He spends his time pulling Leviathan by the tail and being licked by the Wild Ox; or else he tickles the Shekhinah, causing her to lay myriads of eggs each day, and each egg is a star."

"Now I know you're making fun of me."

"If that's not the truth may a funny bone grow on my nose. It's a long time since I squandered my quota of lies. I have no alternative but to tell the truth."

"Can you beget children?"

"No, my dear. Like the mule I am the last of a line. But this does not blunt my desire. I lie only with married women, for good actions are my sins; my prayers are blasphemies; spite is my bread; arrogance, my wine; pride, the marrow of my bones. There is only one other thing I can do besides chatter."

This made her laugh. Then she said: "My mother didn't bring me up to be a devil's whore. Away with you, or I'll have you exorcised."

"Why bother," I said. "I'll go. I don't force myself on anyone. *Auf wiedersehen.*"

I faded away like mist.

2

FOR SEVEN DAYS Zirel absented herself from her boudoir. I dozed inside the mirror. The net had been spread; the victim was ready. I knew she was curious. Yawning, I considered my next step. Should I seduce a rabbi's daughter? deprive a bridegroom of his manhood? plug up the synagogue chimney? turn the Sabbath wine into vinegar? give an elflock to a virgin? enter a ram's horn on Rosh Hashanah? make a cantor hoarse? An imp never lacks for things to do, particularly during the Days of Awe when even the fish in the water tremble. And then as I sat dreaming of moon juice and turkey seeds, she entered. She looked for me, but could not see me. She stood in front of the mirror but I didn't show myself.

"I must have been imagining," she murmured. "It must have been a daydream."

She took off her nightgown and stood there naked. I knew that her husband was in town and that he had been with her the night before although she had not gone to the ritual bath—but as the Talmud puts it, "a woman would rather have one measure of debauchery than ten of modesty." Zirel, daughter of Roize Glike, missed me, and her eyes were sad. She is mine, mine, I thought. The Angel of Death stood ready with his rod; a zealous little devil busied himself preparing the cauldron for her in hell; a sinner, promoted to stoker, collected the kindling wood. Everything was prepared—the snow drift and the live coals, the hook for her tongue and the pliers for her breasts, the mouse that would eat her liver and the worm that would gnaw her bladder. But my little charmer suspected nothing. She stroked her left breast, and then her right. She looked at her belly, examined her thighs, scrutinized her toes. Would she read her book? trim her nails? comb her hair? Her husband had brought her perfumes from Lenczyc, and she smelled of rosewater and carnations. He had presented her with a coral necklace which hung around her neck. But what is Eve without a serpent? And what is God without Lucifer? Zirel was full of desire. Like a harlot she summoned me with her eyes. With quivering lips she uttered a spell:

> Swift is the wind,
> Deep the ditch,
> Sleek black cat,
> Come within reach.
> Strong is the lion,
> Dumb the fish,
> Reach from the silence,
> And take your dish.

As she uttered the last word, I appeared. Her face lit up.

"So you're here."

"I was away," I said, "but I have returned."

"Where have you been?"

"To never-never land. I was at Rahab the Harlot's palace in the garden of the golden birds near the castle of Asmodeus."

"As far as that?"

"If you don't believe me, my jewel, come with me. Sit on my back, and hold on to my horns, and I'll spread my wings, and we'll fly together beyond the mountain peaks."

"But I don't have a thing on."

"No one dresses there."

"My husband won't have any idea where I am."

"He'll learn soon enough."

"How long a trip is it?"

"It takes less than a second."

"When will I return?"

"Those who go there don't want to return."

"What will I do there?"

"You'll sit on Asmodeus' lap and plait tresses in his beard. You'll eat almonds and drink porter; evenings you'll dance for him. Bells will be attached to your ankles, and devils will whirl with you."

"And after that?"

"If my master is pleased with you, you will be his. If not, one of his minions will take care of you."

"And in the morning?"

"There are no mornings there."

"Will you stay with me?"

"Because of you I might be given a small bone to lick."

"Poor little devil, I feel sorry for you, but I can't go. I have a husband and a father. I have gold and silver and dresses and furs. My heels are the highest in Krashnik."

"Well, then, good-by."

"Don't hurry off like that. What do I have to do?"

"Now you are being reasonable. Make some dough with the whitest of flour. Add honey, menstrual blood, and an egg with a bloodspot, a measure of pork fat, a thimbleful of suet, a goblet of libatory wine. Light a fire on the Sabbath and bake the mixture on the coals. Now call your husband to your bed and make him eat the cake you have baked. Awaken him with lies and put him to sleep with profanity. Then when he begins to snore, cut off one half of his beard and one earlock, steal his gold, burn his promissory notes, and tear up the marriage contract. After that throw your jewels under the pig butcher's window—this will be my engagement gift. Before leaving your house, throw the prayer book into the rubbish and spit on the *mezuzah*, at the precise spot where the word *Shadai* is written. Then come straight to me. I'll bear you on my wings from Krashnik to the desert. We'll fly over fields filled with toadstools, over woods inhabited by werewolves, over the ruins of Sodom where serpents are scholars, hyenas are singers, crows are preachers, and thieves are entrusted with the money for charity. There ugliness is beauty, and crooked is straight; tortures are amusement, and mockery, the height of exaltation. But hurry, for our eternity is brief."

"I'm afraid, little devil, I'm afraid."

"Everyone who goes with us is."

She wished to ask questions, to catch me in contradictions, but I made off. She pressed her lips against the mirror and met the end of my tail.

3

HER FATHER WEPT; her husband tore his hair; her servants searched for her in the woodshed and in the cellar; her mother-in-law poked with a shovel in the chimney; carters and butchers hunted for her in the woods. At night, torches were lit and the voices of the searchers echoed and reechoed: "Zirel, where are you? Zirel! Zirel!" It was suspected that she had run off to a convent, but the priest swore on the crucifix that this was not so. A wonder worker was sent for, and then a sorceress, an old Gentile woman who made wax effigies, and finally a man who located the dead or missing by means of a black mirror; a farmer lent them his blood-hounds. But when I get my prey, it is reprieved by no one. I spread my wings and we were off. Zirel spoke to me, but I did not answer. When we came to Sodom, I hovered a moment over Lot's wife. Three oxen were busy licking her nose. Lot lay in a cave with his daughters, drunk as always.

In the vale of shadow which is known as the world everything is subject to change. But for us time stands still! Adam remains naked, Eve lustful, still in the act of being seduced by the serpent. Cain kills Abel, the flea lies with the elephant, the flood falls from heaven, the Jews knead clay in Egypt, Job scratches at his sore-covered body. He will keep scratching until the end of time, but he will find no comfort.

She wished to speak to me, but with a flutter of wings I disappeared. I had done my errand. I lay like a bat blinking sightless eyes on a steep cliff. The earth was brown, the heavens yellow. Devils stood in a circle wiggling their tails. Two turtles were locked in an embrace and a male stone mounted a female stone. Shabriri and Bariri appeared. Shabriri had assumed the shape of a squire. He wore a pointed cap, a curved sword; he had the legs of a goose and a goat's beard. On his snout were glasses, and he spoke in a German dialect. Bariri was ape, parrot, rat, bat, all at once. Shabriri bowed low and began to chant like a jester at a wedding:

Argin, margin,
Here's a bargain.
A pretty squirrel,
Name of Zirel.
Open the door,
To love impure.

He was about to take her in his arms when Bariri screamed, "Don't let him touch you. He has scabs on his head, sores on his legs, and what a woman needs he doesn't have. He acts the great lover, but a capon is more amorous. His father was like that also, and so was his grandfather. Let me be your lover. I am the grandson of the Chief Liar. In addition I am a man of wealth and good family. My grandmother was lady-in-waiting to Machlath, daughter of Naama. My mother had the honor to wash Asmodeus' feet. My father, may he stay in hell forever, carried Satan's snuffbox."

Shabriri and Bariri had grasped Zirel by the hair, and each time they pulled they tore out a tuft. Now Zirel saw how things were and she cried out, "Pity, pity!"

"What's this we have here?" asked Ketev Mariri.

"A Krashnik coquette."

"Don't they have better than that?"

"No, it's the best they've got."

"Who dragged her in?"

"A little imp."

"Let's begin."

"Help, help," Zirel moaned.

"Hang her," Wrath, the Son of Anger, screamed. "It won't help to cry out here. Time and change have been left behind. Do what you are told; you're neither young nor old."

Zirel broke into lamentations. The sound roused Lilith from her sleep. She thrust aside Asmodeus' beard and put her head out of the cave, each of her hairs, a curling snake.

"What's wrong with the bitch?" she asked. "Why all the screaming?"

"They're working on her."

"Is that all? Add some salt."

"And skim the fat."

This fun has been going on for a thousand years, but the black gang does not weary of it. Each devil does his bit; each imp makes his pun. They pull and tear and bite and pinch. For all that, the masculine devils aren't so bad; it's the females who really enjoy themselves, commanding: Skim boiling broth with bare hands! Plait braids without using the fingers! Wash the laundry without water! Catch fish in hot sand! Stay at home and walk the streets! Take a bath without getting wet! Make butter from stones! Break the cask without spilling the wine! And all the while the virtuous women in Paradise gossip; and the pious men sit on golden chairs, stuffing themselves with the meat of Leviathan, as they boast of their good deeds.

Is there a God? Is He all merciful? Will Zirel ever find salvation? Or is creation a snake primeval crawling with evil? How can I tell? I'm still only a minor devil. Imps seldom get promoted. Meanwhile generations come and go. Zirel follows Zirel, in a myriad of reflections—a myriad of mirrors.

YEHUDA ELBERG *(b. 1912)*

Born into a rabbinical family in Poland, Elberg himself was ordained as a rabbi. Active in the Polish underground during World War II, he is a prolific author of stories, novels, and plays in both Yiddish and Hebrew. He now resides in Montreal.

The Empire of Kalman the Cripple *(1997)*

Chapters 1–2

1

WHEN THE COMMUNITY elder Reb Jonah Swerdl passed away, he left only one heir, his young grandson, Kalman, who dutifully recited the

Kaddish at the open grave. But when the townspeople came to the deceased's house to conduct evening services, as is the custom, they found the doors locked. Kalman did not show up at the synagogue to say the mourner's prayer. An outrageous thing like this had never once happened since Jonah had built the prayer house, making Dombrovka a respected Jewish community. But who can argue with Kalman the Cripple?

Only recently was Lowicz Road, the main thoroughfare of Dombrovka, renamed Lowicz Street in recognition of its role as the commercial center of the town. Here a professionally constructed building could be found alongside an old wooden structure a peasant had built for himself, with the helping hands of neighbors. No one knew whether the little wood house, smack in the center of the street, was the oldest, but it certainly looked ancient. Stooped and sunken into the ground, it would have toppled long ago if not for the wooden posts, and the supporting beams holding up the ceiling. Rarely did a sunbeam reach so low that it crawled through the tiny windows. Several crooked steps led from the street down to a little store; from the store, a door opened onto a series of dark rooms. Jonah had purchased this old house when he was still poor, and now his heir, Kalman, considered it the choice business location of Dombrovka.

People did not recall ever having heard sounds of merriment coming from this gloomy old house, but now suddenly, in this period of mourning, strains of music burst through the open window — music was being played on the first gramophone in town. Kalman the Cripple had assembled it from parts of broken-down machines he had acquired from God knows where. When asked about it, Kalman would laugh and say that his grandfather had a part in the music, for after all it was the spring from Jonah's timepiece that made the gramophone work.

"You didn't take apart your grandfather's cherished clock?!" they asked him in disbelief.

"I resurrected it in something that gives much nicer melodies than the chimes of that old clock."

Childhood diseases had cut down old Jonah's entire household. His son, Boruch, had attended six funerals before he turned thirteen: five for his younger brothers and sisters, and the sixth for his mother, who followed these five children of hers into the next world.

Boruch left home very young, and settled in another town, where he married and had a son, Kalman. After a childhood disease crippled the boy, Boruch vanished without a trace. Some years later, Jonah rode off to the funeral of his daughter-in-law and returned with his orphaned grandson.

When Jonah died it was rumored that he had left a lot of money, but that he had hidden it away so well that Kalman would probably never find it. It seemed, however, that Kalman did find something after all. New shelves appeared in the store, filled with new kinds of merchandise. In Dombrovka, people were accustomed to buying food in a grocery store, linens and materials for making clothing in a dry goods store, and leather and shoe fittings in a leather shop. But Kalman was offering so many new things that old Jonah's grocery was transformed into a sort of general store. One could still buy a kilo of flour, a few chunks of yeast, a liter of oil. But one could also find a pot or a baking pan, or dish towels with a red stripe for meat and a blue stripe for dairy dishes. One could order a whole trousseau from Kalman, even a wig for the bride and a *shtrayml* for the groom, a fancy fur hat for the Sabbath. One could certainly order a gold wedding band, for there was no goldsmith in Dombrovka. When a peasant needed a new scythe, plough, pitchfork, or thresher, he could buy these from Kalman on credit and not pay until after the harvest. Kalman sold tools for every trade and, if necessary, he could even repair them.

* * *

THE CUSTOM OF crowning people with nicknames had its rhyme and reason: Moyshe Longlegs was tall and skinny; Matus Pulpit always wanted to lead the services from the pulpit in the synagogue; Sarah Stargazer was constantly murmuring some prayer, her eyes raised piously toward heaven. Generally, a cripple would not be humiliated this way, but they dubbed Kalman "the Cripple" only because he himself invited it. "Ask Kalman the Cripple," he would say, or "You can depend on Kalman the Cripple!"

Kalman expanded his shop into the long room behind the store. Soon a barn was erected in the courtyard behind the house, full of shelves with even more merchandise. Although the old, sunken house could not be lifted out of the ground, it no longer looked so drab. The tiny windows near the ground could not be made into showcases, but a big sign across the front proclaimed: BUY EVERYTHING YOU NEED FROM THE CRIPPLE.

One day Kalman gave some candy to a group of schoolboys, in

exchange for which they walked the streets of the town shouting, "Buy from Kalman the Cripple!" "Kalman sells cheaper!" The people of Dombrovka weren't used to such wild innovations, but Kalman enjoyed making people open their eyes and turn their heads.

2

KALMAN SEEMED TO remember an illness in his childhood but wasn't sure whether it was then that he had become paralyzed. The good years, when he was like other children, had completely flown out of his head. He only remembered himself as a cripple.

Did he love his parents? He had no recollection of when his father disappeared or when his mother died. Maybe that was why he vented all his bitterness on his grandfather. He remembered the trip to Dombrovka with Old Jonah very clearly. He had resisted his grandfather's efforts to remove him from his house. They had promised him many wonderful things, but he struggled with his grandfather and clung to the doorknob. When Jonah pulled at his hand, he had sunk his teeth into the old man's fingers. That was the beginning of the feud between them. During the trip he had fought incessantly with his grandfather, and he tried to jump out the train window. He couldn't run anywhere, of course. At that time he couldn't even move around very well on his behind. All he knew was that he had been happy "there" and "back then." Here, in Dombrovka, in his grandfather's house, he always felt miserable. To annoy Jonah, he would yell, "Pissin' shittin'—bah!" and stick out his tongue like a goat. He learned his spitefulness early.

Kalman's years in *heder* were filled with dreaded days for him. The other kids played terrible pranks on him. At night he would stuff his pillow into his mouth so Jonah wouldn't hear him crying. He kept biting holes in his pillowcase until he discovered he could use his head to get even. At first he only avenged himself on those who had wronged him, but he soon decided that if others could play dirty tricks on him for no reason at all, he could do the same. And when Kalman the Cripple did a thing, he tried, successfully, to do it better than anyone else. Up to that time Kalman had only pretended to laugh, but after each of his successful pranks he laughed freely, genuinely, and with all his heart. After all, he had a right to laugh too . . .

In *heder* the teacher would go over the same portion of the Bible from

Sunday to Friday, and on Saturday the children would be examined by one of the town's learned people. One day—it must have been a Monday, because they were going over the section for the second time—the teacher noticed that Kalman wasn't looking at the book. The teacher motioned to the class to stay quiet, and told Kalman to read the next part. Kalman had no idea which sentence they were at. All the boys burst out laughing.

The teacher twisted Kalman's ear. "A boy must always follow the reading in the Bible; a boy must study even if he is not going to be examined by anyone at all!"

Kalman's ear turned red and his face grew white from anger. "If the rebbe wants to examine me," he challenged, "let him examine me right now!" Without waiting for the teacher's response, he turned back to the beginning of the chapter, read the Hebrew words flawlessly, and translated them into Yiddish.

The teacher couldn't believe his ears. "Is your grandfather tutoring you? We only started this section yesterday."

"Once is enough for me," Kalman replied brazenly.

The children roared with laughter, certain that this was impossible.

"If I want to," Kalman continued, "I can learn the section all by myself. It's all in the Yiddish translation, printed right here."

This infuriated the teacher. Usually the children understood the Bible text only when it contained a story, such as Joseph and his brothers. The rest they learned by rote, word for word. When they grew older they would understand the meaning.

"Really?" said the teacher mockingly. "Maybe you also know the portion for next week—and the *haftorah*, the reading from the Prophets, too?"

Kalman unflinchingly turned the pages, found the excerpt from the Prophets, and began reading the Yiddish translation. "And a woman of the disciples of the prophets, the wife of Obadiah, cried out to Elisha . . ."

The teacher stared, openmouthed, and the children gaped. Kalman surveyed the room triumphantly.

It was a great victory, but no good came out of it. The next day the teacher informed Jonah that Kalman had outgrown his *heder*. Jonah then enrolled Kalman in a Talmud class, where all the boys, who were a few years older, considered it an affront to their dignity to have a five-year-old brat in their class.

Kalman kept pace with the other boys on the subjects of the Bible and Rashi commentary, but Mishna was entirely unfamiliar to him. Aware that everyone hoped he would fail, he studied even when the teacher was not watching him, and he wouldn't join in the games the boys played under the table and behind the rebbe's back. When he didn't understand something in the text he asked questions, and then he asked questions about the answers, until even the teacher lost patience. Eventually he learned enough that he no longer had to ask questions to follow the rebbe.

The other boys now realized that this upstart knew as much as they did, and they made his life even more miserable. Before class or during recess, the boys horsed around and wrestled with each other, mostly in fun but sometimes in earnest. There was no way they could fight with Kalman, who could do nothing but sit. It often happened, however, that one of the boys would "accidentally" bump into him and knock him over. He would have endured all this gladly if any one of them had talked with him or had a good word to say about him.

* * *

WHEN THE TEACHER noticed what was going on, he lectured the boys: "You are a gang of heartless scoundrels! How can you not feel sorry for an orphan—and a crippled orphan at that!" But even before the teacher had finished reproaching them, one boy thumbed his nose at Kalman and another stuck out his tongue. But the teacher's words hurt him even more than their taunting gestures.

Kalman had just about gotten used to the Hebrew Mishna text when they began to study the Aramaic Gemarah. Many of the words were similar to those in the Mishna, but others were as foreign to him as Chinese. He didn't always catch the rebbe's translation or remember it when he did hear it. It was difficult for the other boys too, only they could afford not to care what it meant. But he *had* to know.

He tried asking Jonah, but sometimes the Aramaic words were unfamiliar to his grandfather, too. Once, when the rebbe said the word *kaka*, the boys laughed so loud that Kalman didn't hear the translation. He asked an older student in the synagogue, but he didn't know what it meant either. Kalman screwed up his courage and asked the Rabbi. The *shammes*, standing nearby, also laughed at the word *kaka*. But the Rabbi sat down with Kalman and answered him with great patience:

"It depends on where the word occurs and in what form. K-A-K or

K-A-K-I can mean a white goose. K-A-K-A means neck. However, KA-AKA means tattoo—a kind of writing etched into the skin—something Jews are not permitted to do. What is your name, little boy?"

"Kalman."

"Kalman who?"

Didn't the Rabbi have eyes? How many cripples were there in Dombrovka? Or was he pretending that Kalman was just like all the other boys? Finally Kalman answered, "I'm Kalman—old man Jonah's Kalman."

"Oh, Reb Jonah's grandson! If you continue to study this way, you'll be a rabbi yourself some day and help other Jews understand the Torah." The Rabbi rose, and Kalman moved aside to make way for him. But the Rabbi continued: "Come with me, Kalman, I want to show you something."

He led the boy to the bookcase, took out a volume, and showed it to him. "You see this? It is the *Sefer He-Arukh*. It's a kind of dictionary of all the words in the Gemarah, in alphabetical order." He opened the book and helped Kalman find the root K-K. "But if you have a question, don't be shy. And, if you wish, come in sometimes and I'll examine you in your studies."

Not long afterward, Kalman took up the Rabbi's invitation. The Rebbetsin even gave him an apple and a cookie. He was so proud that he boasted about his visit in the *heder* the next day, but the boys only laughed: "And maybe it was *you* who examined the Rabbi, Kalman?"

Later, when the boys were playing soccer, one boy threw the ball at him, possibly intending to hurt him. Kalman reached up and caught it, but couldn't kick it back. The boy came over to get the ball, and Kalman hoped to hear him say it was a good catch. But apparently his classmate could not forgive his boasting. "If you weren't a cripple, Kalman, which would you rather be: a rabbi or a soccer player?"

Kalman realized that it was utter folly for him to show off his cleverness. At that moment he swore to keep his mouth shut and pretend to be a dunce like everyone else, but it was hard to restrain himself.

Then came the incident with the burrs. By now, he was almost a member of the Rabbi's household. The Rabbi was the only person in the world he loved, and he was sure that if the Rabbi had been his grandfather, life wouldn't have been so bitter.

He was now studying with Mendel the Talmud teacher. The boys in the class who harassed him also tormented a boy named Shloimele, calling him "Red Chicken" or "Red Pig" because of his red hair and freckles. Kalman sat beside Shloimele and tried to make friends with him. On the other side of Shloimele sat Beryl Bass. Beryl butted Shloimele and said, "Go wash your shitty face!" Shloimele started to cry, but stopped in surprise when Kalman said, "Beryl Bass, with a head like an ass, has touched your face, you had better go wash it!" The other boys smothered their laughter as the teacher entered the room, but the nickname stuck: "Beryl Bass, with a head like an ass!"

The truth was, Shloimele wasn't very smart. When the other boys teased him, he waited for Kalman to tell him how best to respond. On the day of Tisha b'Av, everyone went to the synagogue, where the men sat on the floor reciting lamentations for the destruction of the Holy Temple. Outside, the boys were fooling around. Kalman, skillfully ducking the seed-burrs the boys were pelting him with, didn't think he had anything to worry about from Shloimele; after all, Shloimele was his friend. But Shloimele, apparently trying to ingratiate himself to the other boys, stuck a handful of burrs under Kalman's shirt. The more Kalman scratched, the more the itching spread around his body. "Scratch, Kalman, scratch!" the boys taunted him. "Your lice will eat you up alive!"

He went home, washed, put on a fresh shirt, and the itching let up a bit. Shloimele's betrayal, however, left an itching in his head that was impervious to scratching. His usual fantasy of an older brother who would avenge him brought him no relief—he would have to fend for himself.

There was an abundance of plum trees in the vicinity of Dombrovka. In the town itself there was a sugar refinery. Since plums and sugar were both plentiful and cheap, every housewife had a supply of plum jam in her pantry. Dvosha, the woman who came in every day to cook and clean for Jonah, had put up plum jam for him and his grandson. Kalman knew that Shloimele had an insatiable sweet tooth; whenever he brought bread and plum jam to class, he shared it with his friend.

After the incident with the burrs, Kalman thought of mixing some poison into the jam before giving it to Shloimele. Let him croak, the red-headed pig! Obtaining the poison would be no problem—Jonah sold rat poison in the store. But Kalman knew that he couldn't carry out that plan, no matter how outraged he was, though it gave him malicious pleasure to think of it.

The next morning, Kalman was watching Jonah mixing up a powder with water—a laxative he took every morning—when the answer popped into his head. A little of that powder in the plum jam and that traitor Shloimele would be shitting in his pants in front of everyone!

As he expected, Shloimele gobbled down the Kaiser roll he offered him so fast that he didn't notice any difference in taste. Soon after, Shloimele stood up to ask the teacher's permission to leave the room, and Kalman knew that the laxative was having its effect. He quickly moved off the bench and, before Shloimele could get the words out of his mouth, Kalman was already out the door with a desperate, "I've got to go right away!" There was only one outhouse in the courtyard, and, on general principle, the teacher never let two boys go out at the same time, because they might use it as an excuse to stay outside and play. Shloimele continued to plead for permission to leave the room, but the Rebbe's rule was ironclad: "As soon as Kalman comes back . . ."

By the time Kalman finally returned, the cramps in Shloimele's stomach had overwhelmed him, and he soiled his pants before he reached the door. "Shitface has a shitty ass!" the boys mocked, as Kalman observed the scene with an innocent look.

He had designed his prank well and had executed it to perfection, but the result was just the opposite of what he had planned. Because he was Shloimele's best friend, the teacher instructed him to take the sick boy home. All the way along Wilki Street, the mess dripped down Shloimele's pants; his face was ash-gray, his red earlocks turned dirty brown with perspiration, and the tears running down his face looked red as drops of blood. Kalman, taking pity on him, went into Jancze's feed store and got a bundle of straw to wipe the excrement from Shloimele's shoes.

Shloimele did not return to the *heder* the next day, or the day after that. Several days later, Ita, Shloimele's redheaded sister, appeared at the *heder* to ask the children to recite psalms and pray for Shloimele, for he was very sick. The following day, all the children went to the synagogue to recite psalms with the congregation in front of burning candles. The boys stood around the prayer leader, and the Rabbi noticed that Kalman was weeping uncontrollably. After the service, the Rabbi tried to console Kalman: "The One above will certainly listen to the prayers of the children, who are pure and without sin. He will undoubtedly send a cure for Shloimele's illness."

But the One above, it seemed, paid no attention to the prayers. A few days later, Kalman, along with the other boys from the *heder*, attended his friend's funeral. After Shloimele's father said the Kaddish, the teacher appealed to his pupils: "Boys, many things can happen among friends. If any of you ever quarreled with Shloimele, if any of you ever said a bad word to him or about him, come closer now and beg forgiveness at his open grave."

None of the children moved. Each clod of earth fell on the coffin like a thunderclap. All the mourners held their breath.

"Go near the grave and beg his forgiveness," Kalman prodded himself. "You didn't say any bad words to him, you just killed him!"

He had edged toward the grave when Ita started wailing: "Look, none of his friends ever quarreled with him. No one ever wanted to harm him. Shloimele was goodness itself, an angel from God, why do we deserve such cruel punishment?" The whole family began to sob: "An angel from God! Never quarreled with anyone!"

"Beg forgiveness before it's too late," Kalman kept telling himself. But everything within him froze. He could neither move a muscle nor utter a sound. And he barely got home on arms that seemed to have lost all their strength.

That night he couldn't fall asleep. When his eyes finally closed, frightful nightmares gripped him: he was on his way to *heder,* he was in Jancze's feed store, he had to go and get some straw. In the store there were great heaps of sacks of oats, bundles of hay, he had to get some straw . . . The big brown seed-oil cakes smelled like—like freshly dug earth. Where was the straw? Suddenly, the shutters of the store slammed shut behind him, the heavy doors banged shut. He went further into the darkness; he had to find the straw. He bumped into a stack of seed-oil cake and knocked them over; the cakes hit the floor, sounding like clods of earth falling on a coffin. Stacks of seed-oil cakes marched toward him. A freckled hand reached out of the bundles of straw. Kalman retreated, but the hand grew longer and longer, and seized him by the neck. He wanted to scream for help! But the bony fingers tightened around his throat and choked off his voice. From all the bundles of straw, from all the sacks of oats, from all the stacks of seed-oil cakes, long, bony fingers stretched out toward him. The straw and the oats turned as brown as the seed-oil cakes, then they turned into seed-oil cakes and fell upon him with a dull thud, like clods of earth falling onto a coffin. HELP!

He woke up in a cold sweat, afraid to open his eyes, and afraid to keep them shut in case he fall asleep again. For the first time since he had arrived in Dombrovka, he crawled into his grandfather's bed. He was grateful for Jonah's snoring—anything except the sound of seed-oil cakes thudding down onto floorboards . . .

When he finally fell asleep, the dream recurred. And it recurred night after night, in various guises. Every detail of the dream became so familiar to him that he could no longer distinguish between it and reality. Night and day intermingled in a cruel nightmare.

Jonah realized that something was wrong with Kalman. Dvosha noticed that he left the food on his plate. Was he sick? They called Leiybush Feldsher, the town barber-surgeon, who applied his usual remedy, cupping. They summoned the doctor, who prescribed cod-liver oil. When Jonah forced him to swallow it, he vomited it right up. They ordered him to stay in bed, but now he didn't want to miss a single day in *heder*, nor did he skip any opportunities to go to the synagogue for the daily services. He didn't want to be left alone, he was afraid to fall asleep. . . He ate little, and seldom said anything. The dark grief in his eyes reminded Jonah of his wife, Liebele, when she got depressed. Kalman followed his grandfather to the synagogue for the Shabbes services, but hardly moved his lips at the prayers. Jonah asked the Rabbi's advice.

"He's not eating, you say?" the Rabbi responded. "Maybe he doesn't like Dvosha's cooking. Kalman loves to eat with us." He approached the boy. "Kalman, it's true you're a big boy now, but you can still come to see me once in a while so I can examine you in your studies. Or you could just drop in for a visit—we are distantly related, did you know that?"

Kalman nodded his head.

"It so happens that the Rebbetsin has prepared a very delicious tsimmes. Why don't you come and eat with us? Your grandfather won't mind."

Kalman didn't answer.

"And there's a kugel too, a noodle kugel. I remember you used to like that very much."

The Rabbi started to walk away, but Kalman didn't move.

"Well, Kalman?"

"I'm not hungry," Kalman finally replied in a low voice.

"When have you had to be hungry to eat my wife's kugel? Come, Kalman, don't be stubborn." The Rabbi waited, and Kalman had no choice but to follow him, but he barely touched his food. During the *zemirot* he moved his lips, but soundlessly. After the meal, when everyone else had left the table, the Rabbi asked him to come into his study.

"Proverbs advise us that if we are worried about something we should talk about it to someone. Can you tell me what's troubling you, Kalman?"

How could he tell the Rabbi what he had done?

"I know what happened to your friend," the Rabbi began, consolingly. Kalman almost jumped out of his skin. How could the Rabbi know?

"It's a great accomplishment to become attached to a friend and to love him as David and Jonathan loved each other. But the Almighty knows better than we do what is right. Maybe Shloimele was destined to have a life full of troubles, and the Father of Mercy took him up to Himself in order to save him from that—"

"Why didn't he save *me* from that?" Kalman's accusation was almost a scream.

The Rabbi put an arm around him. "I know, Kalman, how bitter it is to lose a loved one." The warm hand on his shoulder released something inside Kalman. His whole body shook. The Rabbi drew him closer. The boy' useless legs dragged behind him, and he hung limply in the old man's arms. His face buried in the Rabbi's silk Sabbath coat, he choked out his story, exactly as it had happened.

"Kalman, Kalman, you're such a clever boy—how did you ever convince yourself of such foolishness? Shloimele died of pneumonia, God protect us. A laxative has nothing to do with the lungs. He must have already been walking around with the disease for several days when he fell ill at the *heder* . . ."

A huge rock rolled away from Kalman's heart, but he could not stop crying.

"Maybe you should have begged his forgiveness," the Rabbi added, "but it's not too late for that. Those who are in the next world can still hear us. Do it now, Kalman. I'll say the words and you repeat them after me, all right?"

Kalman nodded.

"*Mes tohur Shlomo ben Yaakov* . . ."

Kalman broke into sobs again.

"If it's too hard for you to say the words aloud, say them in your heart. In the next world they can hear the voice of the heart too. I'll start again. *Mes tohur habachur Shlomo ben Yaakov*—I, your friend Kalman son of Boruch, beg your forgiveness for all the wrongs I did to you both deliberately and unintentionally. And for all the good things I did for you I beg you to bestow loving kindness upon me and to intercede for me in the next world."

That night Kalman finally slept without dreaming. He slept through the night and the next day. When he opened his eyes, Dvosha was standing at his bedside.

"The Rabbi's son Berish is here. The Rabbi wants to see you."

Although Kalman felt weak, he hurried to the Rabbi's.

"Kalman, I've got to go to the cemetery. I always ask someone to accompany me. Will you come with me?"

"I haven't said my prayers yet. I just woke up."

"Have you said the Shema?"

"I was asleep. When Dvosha woke me I got dressed and came right over."

"Say the Shema. The Rebbetsin will give you a glass of milk. You'll finish your prayers when we get back."

At the cemetery, the Rabbi suggested to Kalman that he stop for a moment at Shloimele's grave. Kalman was able to beg for forgiveness, saying the words out loud without crying.

On the way back, they happened to pass Jancze's feed store. The Rabbi held Kalman's hand as they went inside, and then asked questions about every sack and bundle—what it was and how it was made. He said that he smelled a foul odor in the straw and asked that everything be moved and inspected. Jancze shrugged: "The hay smells of clover, and even the seed-oil cakes are fresh." But the Rabbi insisted, and so Jancze moved everything around.

Kalman's eyes went from the Rabbi to Jancze and back again, trying to fathom what was going on. He thought the Rabbi meant to intone some sort of incantation, some formula to drive away evil spirits, but the Rabbi wasn't moving his lips. Only later did Kalman understand that the Rabbi wanted him to see that Jancze's store contained only ordinary bundles of straw, without any bony fingers. There was nothing there for Kalman to fear.

CHAVA ROSENFARB *(no birth date)*

*B*orn in Lodz, Poland, Chava Rosenfarb survived the Lodz Ghetto and several concentration camps. The main theme of her fiction is the Jewish past. The recipient of numerous literary prizes, she now resides in Canada.

Bociany *(2000)*

Chapter 1

THROUGH THE WINDOW of the garret, the first gray of dawn crowded in. It was late summer, and the sky outside was very deep and slightly hazy, as if filled with transparent cotton. In the east its color turned to a pale orange. A cock began to crow, then another. A few birds responded. The crickets had been singing all night, and now, with the oncoming day, their tunes became louder, sawing through the stillness with a gnawing, irritating monotony.

Hindele Polin, the scribe's wife, was fully dressed. She adjusted the wig on her head, wrapped herself in her plaid shawl, and picked up an empty jug from the shelf where the kitchen utensils were stored. She faced the room. Although its corners were still steeped in darkness, the familiar contours of everything in it were outlined quite discernibly by the gray light coming in through the window. What a cheerless, dingy dwelling it was! The crooked floor was cracked, and it swayed under the slightest step. The slanted roof descended almost to Hindele's head. It was only in the middle, where the table stood, that it was possible to raise a hand and not touch the beams. In the summer it was suffocatingly hot, in the winter freezing cold, and the roof leaked. Yet Hindele liked this home of hers very much, despite its dreariness and the misfortunes it seemed to attract.

She turned her puffy eyes to the bed where the two sick ones lay, her husband, Hamele the Scribe, and her eldest son, Itchele. Itchele was an *ile*, a genius, whose name was renowned not only in Bociany, but even in the town of Chwosty. He had been stricken with consumption just when it had been decided that after his bar mitzvah he would leave for the yeshiva in Sielce. His father had contracted the same disease two years earlier.

Both father and son breathed with difficulty, emitting heavy, labored sighs. Each sigh cut into Hindele's heart like the blade of a sharp knife, causing a fresh wave of tears to come to her eyes. The tears seemed to pour directly from the wounds of pain within her. The whites of her enormous black eyes were red, her eyelids were puffed like bluish boils, her checks were swollen. She no longer had any strength to cry, and yet whenever she was alone, the tears refused to stop, as if her entire body were made of weeping, and the tears issued from a bottomless well. She could no longer feel her tears, nor did she wipe them away. They would go their way undammed, and she would go hers. In spite of them, she did all that she had to do. There was no time to devote herself, even for a moment, solely to the luxury of crying.

She turned her overflowing eyes to the rumpled bed at the opposite side of the room. There she made out the empty space that still held the imprint of her body. Close to the wall, at the foot of the bed, slept her two youngest, the girls. From there, her gaze wandered toward the straw mattress on the floor under the window, where the other two sons slept entangled in a feather quilt, their limbs braided together.

Yacov, the younger of the two, stirred as she looked at him, as if he had felt his mother's glance in his sleep. Quickly she turned away, afraid that her eyes might awaken him. But as soon as she moved toward the door, she heard his voice, "I'm coming too, Mameshie!"

Afraid that he might start crying, she went back to the table and cut him a slice of bread from the quarter loaf she had placed there. "Hurry then," she whispered. "Wash and say the benediction." She wiped her face quickly with the edge of her plaid shawl. As soon as the boy had disengaged himself from the feather quilt and slipped out, she went over to cover his brother. Then she leaned out through the open window and inhaled deeply as she continued to dry her face with the palms of her hands.

The storks on the roofs were quiet. Only the crickets and a few birds, early risers, disturbed the stillness with their tuneful chattering. Hindele's gaze wandered over the roofs of the shtetl and halted for a while on the church tower, which pierced the deep, hazy gray with its pale, shimmering cross. Then, as she leaned a little further out the window, her eyes fell on the garden of the neighboring cloister.

Two nuns, dressed in black, with spotless white wimples and bibs, were walking among the flower beds, holding little prayer books in their hands. They were already up and about, eager to enjoy a last summer's day in peace. It did not occur to Hindele to envy them. They were too alien to be envied. Yet the sight of them was soothing; they made her think of her own faith. She sighed and whispered, raising her eyes to the sky, "Father in Heaven, show me your kindness with this new day."

A tiny, hopeful smile appeared at the corners of her mouth, which harbored a salty aftertaste of tears. She knew that this day would differ little from any other, and she was far from considering herself fortunate, yet the arrival of a new day was uplifting, even if accompanied by tears. She did not hope for a miracle. The hope she nourished every morning fed on the power of her faith, the capacity to accept the judgment of the Almighty, to surrender to His will and not falter in her trust in Him. "God will help," she muttered. Yet the grief in her heart quickened as she inhaled the intoxicating fragrances that reached her from the nuns' garden, the perfume of roses, jasmine, and acacias. The crickets chirped stubbornly, pricking the mind like a million pins. Hindele turned back toward the room, where the scents of the flowers mingled with the stale inside air and shadows hovered like the outstretched wings of a monstrous bird of prey.

The slice of bread she had cut for Yacov had vanished. He was standing at the door, manipulating the bolt, which hung loosely on its screws. Hindele placed a pitcher of fresh water on the stool near the sickbed. Her eyes met the hot, glassy stare of her husband. "You feel better, don't you?" she asked in a tone that sounded more like a statement than a question.

"Blessed be the Almighty," he replied in a weak voice, his thin nose struggling for air, the wings of his nostrils fluttering. "Move the stool with the books closer, too," he muttered.

She frowned, then moved the stool laden with heavy tomes closer to the bed. Her voice was soft. "It's still dark in here. Why don't you sleep some more?" She turned towards Yacov. "Have you said the prayer?"

He nodded. She picked up the empty jug, which she had deposited on the table, and they left the room, carefully finding their way down the flight of stairs in the dark. The wooden stairs were winding and shaky.

Some boards were partially broken off, while others were missing completely. The banister shook and groaned with the stairs as she and the boy descended. In the dark, they felt with the soles of their shoes for the strong spots that would support their weight, so that they might descend without mishap. On the landing they came eye-to-eye with Manka the Washerwoman's cow, which occupied the ruined room on the ground floor.

In the yard, Hindele noticed that Manka, who did the laundry for the lessee and a few other wealthy families, was already at work in front of her house. Her arms and legs bare, she was standing over a steaming washtub, her thick torso swaying energetically back and forth over the scrubbing board. At the sight of Hindele, she stopped for a moment to wipe the sweat off her face with her bare arm, and asked, "How are they?"

"God will help," Hindele replied hurriedly, dragging Yacov with her by the hand. When she had passed Manka, she turned her head, adding as an afterthought, "You can kindle the stove in an hour and put the pot on to warm up."

"Shall be done," Manka replied without looking up, again engrossed in her work.

As she walked on, Hindele thought about Manka, whose luck was similar to hers. Manka was a widow, and nearly three years earlier, her house, which had stood across the street, burned to the ground. If not for the heroic exertions of her cousin, the fire chief Vaslav Spokojny, the whole street, and perhaps all of Bociany as well, would have gone up in flames. Now Manka lived in a hut that bordered on Hindele's backyard.

Hindele and Manka had always been civil to one another, but until the time of her misfortunes, Hindele had never allowed herself to establish a close personal contact with the gentile woman. Now that every day at dawn she had to hurry to Reb Faivele the Miller's farm on the Blue Mountain in order to get a jug of fresh goat milk for her sick men—this being one of Reb Faivele's charitable gestures—Hindele had accepted Manka's offer to keep an eye on her window. At the slightest sound from upstairs, Manka would go up, kindle the stove, and put the breakfast pot on the fire to warm.

"How strange," Hindele shook her head in amazement as she plodded with Yacov through the wheel-rutted alley. "If not for our misfortunes, we would never have come in contact with one another like human beings."

As the road grew wider, Hindele marched with more energy, holding on to the boy's hand. She did not mind taking him along. True, he needed those few hours of sleep in the morning, yet she was certain that this walk with her compensated for it somehow. Although he said nothing—her boys were not overly given to talking—she could feel that he enjoyed walking beside her as much as she enjoyed having him do so. To her it was a consolation to hold his tiny hand, rest her eyes on his dreamy, delicate face, and see there a contented smile. That little smile was very precious to her, especially since he had recently become such a crybaby. Well, not quite a crybaby. He did not cry at all like a child, but rather like herself, silently, letting the tears roll down his cheeks.

If she asked him why he was crying, he would reply, "I'm not crying, Mameshie. My eyes are sweating."

"Why are your eyes sweating?"

"Because I'm scared."

"What are you scared of, Yacov?"

"I don't know, Mameshie."

She would not insist that he tell her. Her little girls would often cry as well, but as children do, noisily, with a persistent urgency that often tested her patience. But when Yacov cried, her heart would fill with such dread and premonition that she could hardly bear it.

A few men with prayer bags under their arms went by on their way to the synagogue. As Hindele and Yacov passed the beautiful wooden structure, they could see through the open door a number of praying men wrapped in prayer shawls. Other men were standing on the threshold, arguing about something. The street was dotted with peasants. The field boys and serving men of the landowner hurried in the opposite direction, toward the Narrow Poplar Road, which led to the manor. A sleepy shepherd boy was herding some cows to the nearby pasture.

As Hindele and Yacov came out onto the Wide Poplar Road and the sky brightened, they noticed Reb Senderl the Cabalist approaching them from the distance. Yesterday, when she was sitting in front of her shop on the roofed market, which was known as the Potcheyov, Hindele had seen Reb Senderl lock up his store and set out in the direction of this road. Now he was on his way back, with a sack of herbs slung over his shoulder. She knew that he had spent the night near the marshes, bathing in the lake. Perhaps he had even seen the face of the moon on the past moonless night. He had once told her about the moon representing the face of the Divine Emanation, the *Shkhina*, her eyes blinded from crying over the exile she shared with the children of Israel. For even when the moon shone, it was not with its own light, but with the dull light of a blind person's eyes. As Reb Senderl passed them, Hindele greeted him from the side of the road with heartfelt reverence.

"What's new?" he called from the distance.

"Blessed be His holy Name. God will help," she replied, moving on, but allowing her eyes to rest on him a while longer. The sight of this small, elderly man with his magnificent gray beard was soothing. She could feel a healing kindness radiate from his figure. She had no doubt that on his way from his nocturnal escapade he had visited Yoel the Blacksmith, who lived alone in a hut near his smithy on the Wide Poplar Road, far beyond the Blue Mountain. For many years no one in Bociany would have anything to do with Yoel, who was a drunkard and was suspected of ugly deeds. Only wagon drivers and Hasidim on their way to the Rabbi of Chwosty would stop at his place to shoe their horses. Reb Senderl was the only one who befriended the man.

Reb Senderl had once explained this to Hindele. "The Rabbi Reb Mayer," Reb Senderl had said, "carried on a friendship with Elisha Ben Abuya, the sinful infidel. When he was asked why he carried on with such a despicable person, Rabbi Mayer answered, 'I liken Elisha Ben Abuya to a pomegranate. So I throw away its outer husk and take delight in the fruit.'"

This Hindele had learned from Reb Senderl, and she followed his example in her relationships with her women friends, such as Nechele the Pockmarked, the sexton's wife, and even with Manka the Washerwoman. But she followed it particularly with Nechele the Pockmarked, because Nechele was closer to her heart, almost like a relative, and therefore her shortcomings were all the more irritating.

Nechele was so strictly observant of the religious laws that she could not bear to hear Hindele say a single good word about Manka the Washerwoman, because Manka was a devout Christian. Had Nechele known that Hindele did not scold her children for playing with Manka's children, she would have broken off all contact with her. Nechele sat in judgment on everyone's words and deeds, proclaiming her opinion on what people did or said, without taking into account any mitigating circumstances. Nonetheless, Hindele loved Nechele the Pockmarked, despite her rigidity. Nechele's soul was full of yearning. She loved Hasidic and cantorial song, and she was lonesome, without even a child to console her. Moreover, Nechele was goodhearted. More than once had she cooked a soup from her own supplies for Hindele's sick, and she shared with Hindele the bargains that she bought on market days, as Hindele had neither the time nor the patience to go looking for bargains herself.

In the huts people were waking. Barefoot peasant women in white fustian nightshirts were feeding the animals. The cocks started to crow more energetically, while the birds prattled feverishly. The sun came out. Its rays shot through the poplar boughs onto the road, greeting Hindele and Yacov with sudden dazzling light. The world was transformed into a luminous, cheerful place. A passing cart seemed to be rolling straight into the sun's beams. Hindele called after the driver. She knew him, as she knew most of the peasants of the region, from dealings with them in her shop on the Potcheyov. Soon mother and son had clambered into the cart and seated themselves on top of a sweet-smelling stack of hay.

Yacov was engrossed in watching his mother, observing her face as it was washed by the sun's rays. His legs, which had begun to hurt during the long walk, were now nestled deep in the hay under Hindele's skirt. He shut his sleepy eyes but opened them again, so as not to miss his mother's hidden smile or the sight of her delicate stooped body outlined by the sun's quivering rays. His mother was small and thin. Although she worked hard and he could not remember a day when he had seen her lying in bed sick, except when his youngest sister was born, he still trembled for her safety, as if she were so weak the slightest breeze might blow her away. It seemed to him that she was a rare creature, almost holy, made of precious, fragile matter, which had to be handled with care and protected. Yet in her fragility she was his rock of support. He helped her as much as he could, but it was to her that he ran for attention and comfort whenever he needed it. Now the plaid shawl on her shoulders, which before had seemed to him like a mourning hood or the cowl of a ghost, looked like the folded wings of a stork at rest.

"You see the sunflowers?" She sniffled and pointed with her chin in the direction of a plot of land covered with high-stemmed sunflowers.

Yacov turned his head, following her gaze with his eyes. The plot of land looked like an island of suns in a sea of green and gave off a cheerful light of its own. He smiled. "They look funny."

She knew that by "funny" he meant fun, delightful to look at. She nodded and enveloped him in her shawl. She observed him from the corner of her eye. "Between him and me there is a kind of fiddle music playing," she said to herself. "I wonder whether he is aware of it, too." She wiped her nose with the corner of her shawl and adjusted her wig, which had the habit of sitting askew on her head. It was her only wig and, in truth, she should be saving it for the Sabbath and the holidays and wear just a kerchief or a bonnet, as many of the other married women did. But she stood all day in the Potcheyov, exposed to the public and, after all, she was Reb Hamele the Scribe's wife and herself a descendant of the Rabbi from Wurke. Besides, she felt somehow safer in the wig.

They arrived at the foot of the Blue Mountain. Hindele and the boy disembarked and thanked the peasant. She and Yacov began to climb up the hill. After a while, she let go of his hand and left him behind as she darted ahead to leave the jug on the step of the miller's verandah. By the time Yacov reached the top of the hill, his mother was already waiting for him in front of the fence that surrounded the miller's yard.

They sat down beside a cluster of heather in the tussocky grass over which Hindele had spread the edge of her plaid. She fondled the heather with her hand as she and Yacov looked at its tiny flowering heads. Then they watched the revolving sails of the mill and listened to their pleasant squeaking. The air glistened with crystalline brightness, its fragrance sharp and intoxicating. Yacov cradled his head in Hindele's lap, shut his eyes to protect them from the sun's glare, and before long drifted into slumber. She looked down at his delicate, pale face. A curly brown side-lock trembled on his cheek as he breathed deeply, calmly. She put her hand over his head as if to cover it with an additional skullcap and turned her eyes to the distance.

* * *

FAR IN THE valley Hindele saw Bociany wreathed by the two poplar roads, the Narrow and the Wide. It had been by the nearer one, the Wide Poplar Road, that she had arrived in the shtetl to marry Reb Hamele. She had always liked the shtetl's name. Storks built their nests on its rooftops. The Polish word for storks is *bociany*, so the name of the shtetl was Bociany.

As she gazed down upon it, she saw Bociany nestled between the Blue Mountain and the White Mountain, itself looking like a stork's nest. The pointed, dark yellow straw roofs and brick-colored shingle roofs peeked out like the bills of young fowl. It was a remote, forgotten shtetl, where time seemed to arrive very slowly. News, when it reached Bociany through the Wide Poplar Road that led from Chwosty, the closest town, was so old that it had already grown a beard.

The valley in which Bociany lay was an offshoot of the larger Vistula Valley. With the exception of a swampy ring surrounding the shtetl, the region was blessed with good, rich soil. Hindele's eyes wandered over the fields of rye and wheat, oats and potatoes, interspersed by green pastures and orchards, which stretched mile upon mile into the distance. Here and there, like islands dotting the gold and green, were the stark shadows of forest land or the glimmering mirror of a lake or a pond.

The Blue Mountain was blue, and the White Mountain white, because during the summer, the former wore a hood of bluebells and the latter a hood of white daisies. On a day as bright and sunny as this one, the blue-bells and daisies, together with the red poppies and yellow buttercups in the pastures and on the hills, along with the lilies-of-the-valley, the for-get-me-nots in the marshes, the water lilies in the lake, and the sunflow-ers near the huts, joined with the golden fields and green pastures, with the bright birch wood and the shadowy pine wood, to create a lively and colorful carpet. The carpet was not only reflected in the sky, but it infused the very air with its shimmer. So crystal clear was the air in that region that one was never sure whether the clouds on the horizon were really clouds, or the outlines of the distant Tatra Mountains. These mountains belonged to the Austrian Empire, whereas the shtetl, located on this side of the mountains, belonged to Russia and Tsar Nicholas II.

Aside from the fact that the noise of the world reached it even later than other Polish shtetlekh, Bociany differed very little from Hindele's home shtetl or the shtetlekh she knew. That is to say, Bociany was some-thing between a little town and a village, and its official representative was not a burgomaster but a county officer. As in the other shtetlekh, Bociany's life centered around the cobblestone marketplace, where the peasants from the countryside gathered to sell their wares on Tuesday market days. The marketplace was surrounded only by a few brick or stone buildings. From where she now sat, Hindele could see the build-ings protruding from the density of wooden huts like a half-circle of uneven teeth, the tallest and pointiest being the Church of All Saints.

And yet Hindele considered Bociany an exceptional shtetl. This fact had struck her as soon as she had approached it for the first time and its rooftops had come into sight. It was amazing. Each one of the roofs, whether it covered a proud brick house or a moldy sunken shack, whether it belonged to a Jewish or to a gentile family, displayed an old wheel attached to its front like a box of phylacteries. On these wheels pairs of storks would build their nests every year, lay their eggs, and sit on them until they hatched, then bring up their young and stay on for the rest of the summer.

The storks of Bociany were majestic white birds, three, sometimes four feet in height, with black flight feathers, dark red bills, and spindly reddish legs. They were inclined to stand motionless on one foot and meditate and would have devoted entire days to this activity—were it not for the prosaic problems of sustenance, which, in comparison to the problems of the hosts on whose roofs they lived, were not inordinately severe.

The storks derived their livelihood from the swamps surrounding the shtetl, which swarmed with frogs, tadpoles, snails, and earthworms. The human habit of storing away supplies against a "black hour" was alien to them. They could fill themselves and their offspring so far and no more, yet the thought of their treasures in the swamps gave them no peace of mind. Several times a day they felt compelled to check on their "gold mines," if only to fish for a snack for their little ones, or merely to survey the marshes by cruising above them. Because of this, the air above the shtetl always resounded with their bustling cries and the clatter of their bills, sounds that expressed with urgency the grave state of stork affairs.

It is therefore no wonder that a wandering band of beggars, which regularly descended on Bociany for the Tuesday market day, had coined the term "a Bociany fair" for any racket loud enough to reach the sky. Every Tuesday, the clamor from the humans below, and the cacophony from the birds above, threatened to deafen the unprepared ears of a stranger, before he even realized that he was actually caught between two towns, a Bociany on earth and a Bociany in the heavens, both towns preoccupied in dead seriousness with practical problems, one with having too much, the other with having too little.

For the earthly Bociany fared not so "heavenly." The land around the shtetl was indeed generous and fertile, but it belonged to a landowner and to his heirs, who lived in a manor house at the foot of the White Mountain. Most of the peasants owned little more than a small piece of swampy land. They labored as field hands on the landlord's property. And as the Gentiles fared, so fared the Jews. The shtetl of Bociany was distinguished by its poverty.

It could not be helped. The pauper could neither escape his home nor his fate. What he could do was wait with iron fortitude, the Christian for the Kingdom of Heaven and the Jew for the coming of the Messiah, and in the meantime be consoled with whatever solace he could find. And the storks were a solace for the shtetl.

When the Polish autumn began to dip leaves in a pallet of sunset colors, when the sheaves of grain appeared on the scythed fields like figures embracing in a melancholy dance, and the time for blowing the ram's horn for the High Holy Days was passed, a peculiar restlessness entered the hearts of the people of Bociany and mixed with the usual autumnal sadness. That was the time when the storks, as if by a prearranged signal, rose from the rooftops, fluttered their wings as if waving good-bye, and soared toward the sky. For a while, they circled the region, as if to fix the familiar panorama in their memory. Then, as if on command, they formed themselves into long lines and, with majestic dignity, flew off toward distant lands.

"Who knows if they'll return," Manka the Washerwoman and the other peasant women would sigh, crossing themselves in awe.

A bird was not like a human being, who died where he was born. A bird was born free, soared high, and could see what was behind and what was ahead. So perhaps the storks could foresee that the abundant swamps would become arid, and they would seek out new homes for future summers. The peasant women blinked their moist eyes toward the sky, until the last quivering string of storks wound itself into the horizon and vanished.

Every year before spring arrived, even before the snow had melted, both the gentile boys and the heder boys ran through the muddy roads to await the arrival of the storks. The gentile boys headed toward the White Mountain and the Jewish boys toward the Blue Mountain, where the windmill stood, and where Hindele now sat. From here, they could see all of Bociany, see the lake where the demons bathed and Kailele the Bride had drowned herself, and see the fields and the woods across the lake. They could also discern, at a great distance, what they believed to be the Mountains of Darkness, which stood on the border of this world and the next. There, at the mysterious Sabbath River, the Sambation, lived the dragons that guarded the land of the eternally happy little red Jews, who knew nothing of exile. It was to the marshes of that happy land, the boys were convinced, that the storks flew every winter, and it was from there that they returned.

These same little boys brought the news to Bociany. "The storks are coming!"

The adults received this information with pretended indifference, as if to say, "May more important tidings be brought to us." But secretly, they sighed with relief. The return of the storks was a good omen. And out of gratitude to the storks for their devotion, the shtetl refused to mark the seasons by the calendar. Instead, the day on which the storks returned was considered the first day of summer, and the day they left, the first day of winter.

As far as the Jewish boys were concerned, most were convinced that one fine day the Messiah Ben David himself would arrive in the shtetl along with the storks. He would ride his donkey through the Wide Poplar Road, and the storks would soar above his head. Together they would pass first the gentile cemetery and afterwards the Jewish. The storks' clucking would help the Messiah waken the dead, so that this particular day would be not only the first day of summer, but also the Day of Resurrection and Deliverance.

All generations of Jewish boys had been preoccupied with the same problem: What would the Messiah do when he rode past the gentile cemetery? Would the gentile dead also profit from the resurrection, or would the Messiah leave them rotting in the ground? And what would he do with the living goyim? Would he redeem them, too—not, of course, for their good deeds to the Jews, but perhaps because of their kindness to the storks? And since they could never make out the answers, the boys themselves would decide the issue, depending whether or not they were involved in a war with the gentile boys at the time.

The favorite pastime for the people of Bociany was to observe with a feeling of kinship how the storks built their nests on the roofs, and to philosophize on the similarity between human family life and that of the birds. This subject was of particular interest to the women, both Jew and gentile, some of whom kept prepared a bundle of good straw and sticks in order to save the storks the trouble of going too far in their search for building materials. And when the "she" became pregnant and was about to lay her eggs, these housewives would send their children to the nearest swamp for frogs, tadpoles, snails, or rain worms, which they offered to the female in a gesture of solidarity. They did not believe that a male bird had any more understanding of a female in such a condition than did the human male. The women would carry on this special attention both when the "she" was laying the eggs and during the entire month when the pair were sitting on the eggs. That the male sat on the eggs along with the female was regarded as further proof of male laziness. It was no great trick to join in the act of life-giving, if the wife bore all the pains of labor.

The women would watch the young storks set out for their first flight with their parents. They would smile wistfully, and then remind themselves that they had more important business to see to. The storks once again became a part of day-to-day life and were paid no more attention, unless danger threatened the shtetl, in the form of a fire or a storm.

The Jewish and gentile fire brigades, each of which had its own horses and wagons, its own water barrels and equipment, usually worked together. They had even worked out a special technique for saving the storks in dangerous situations. At such moments they were supposed to resort to a long pole with hooks. That was what they were supposed to do; in practice they hardly ever did so. There were more important things to remember during a fire than the pole with the hooks, or the storks. The houses of Bociany, except for those few brick or stone structures surrounding the marketplace, were made entirely of wood, the roofs were straw, and it took no more than a spark and a little breeze for the fire to spread. The only advantage in this situation was that since the pogrom after the death of Tsar Alexander II, when half the shtetl had gone up in flames, the Gentiles did not dare set fire to any Jewish house during an attack on the Jews. In this violent way they had learned that fire does not discriminate.

As far as the storks were concerned, they managed better without the fire brigades than their hosts did with the fire brigades. They usually escaped with their families intact, before the firemen even discovered where the fire was.

On the whole, thanks to the storks, harbingers of good fortune for humans—provided one behaved humanely to them in turn—the shtetl of Bociany, except in matters of livelihood, was a fortunate place for both Jew and Gentile. Since the storks, like nature in general, took no notice of the racial differences among their hosts, they saw to it that the wombs of both the kosher Jewish matrons and those of their gentile neighbors were never empty. Moreover, for the most part, Jew and Gentile lived quite peacefully together. Mutual needs called forth mutual support, in spite of mutual distrust. Although the two communities were worlds apart in their way of life, there was a certain civil contact between them; there were even friendships formed, although of a casual character. Friendships like the one between Hindele and Manka the Washerwoman were rather the exception than the rule.

Jewish peddlers who wandered through the villages, Jewish butcher boys and wagon drivers would drink with the peasants at the Jewish inn. Gentiles bought merchandise on credit in the Jewish stores on the Potcheyov. Often Jewish shopkeepers received bags of potatoes, cabbage, onions, or fruits as gifts from "their" peasants. If the bailiffs from the district office arrived to mark down a peasant's belongings as security against unpaid taxes, his Jewish acquaintances would organize a collection, just as if it were a Jewish cause, and help to save the threatened household. By the same token, through the intercession of a peasant, a Jewish father could influence the county officer to register his newborn son in the army recruitment books as having been born much later than he was, thus giving the Messiah a chance to arrive and cancel the recuitment altogether. And during a drought, or a plague among the cattle, if the Hasidim were on their way to visit the Rabbi of Chwosty and were in their wagons passing the peasant huts along the Wide Poplar Road, the peasants would call after them, "Don't forget, in God's name, to ask the *tsadik* for rain. Ask for a miracle for us, too!"

And yet, although the gentiles and Jews got along well, they became strangers, even enemies, as soon as Sunday or any other Christian holiday arrived. On Christian holy days, the Jews disappeared like mice into their holes, while the goyim took over Bociany. As a rule, Jewish fears ran wild automatically—for through the ages, the Jews had developed to perfection the art of worrying ahead of time, and their worries had seldom proved unfounded. True, in Bociany there was a great probability that they were worrying for nothing; still, they allowed their hearts to toll with alarm as soon as they heard the church bells toll for prayer.

Small wonder. On Christian holy days, the Gentiles of the shtetl, as well as those from the surrounding villages, and the nuns from the cloister, which was located on the border of the gentile district where Hindele lived, filled all the streets as they moved toward the market place, carrying holy pictures. Choir songs and incense made the familiar atmosphere seem alien, especially as the day wore on and the gaily dressed crowd began to pour out of the church door, overflowing into the town square, the marketplace, and the sidewalks around the Potcheyov. Soon bottles of the vodka known as *monopolka* appeared from behind the Sunday camisoles. The peasants would begin with a dance and end with a fight. A Jew would have had to be out of his mind not to lock the doors and windows and secure them with iron or wooden bars; he would have to be crazy not to tighten the wires that fastened the shutters, especially if he lived in one of the unfortunate houses that bordered directly on the areas where the Gentiles congregated.

With the exception of a few attacks on the Jews, however, everything had been quiet since Hindele had first arrived in Bociany. One of these attacks had been inspired by the unexplained death of a gentile boy; another had occurred after a too passionate sermon by the priest, a third after a baptism. There had also been one after a wedding and another after a funeral, when the intoxicated crowd had required more than the usual distraction.

After all, the heart of the shtetl was not inhabited by the Gentiles. True, the church stood at the shtetl's very center, in the marketplace, flanked by the parsonage on its right and by the country officer's stone house on its left. Adjoining the county officer's house stood the house where the gendarmes lived, which also contained the jail. But aside from these gentile structures, the marketplace was surrounded by Jewish houses, a few fashionably built with brick, the rest of wood, decrepit, mildewed, and rotting. All these houses were inhabited by the elite of the Jewish congregation. The brick houses were occupied by the families of such important people as the lessee, the wood merchant, or the landlord's Jewish bookkeeper, who was known as "the writer"; the other houses were occupied by the members of the Jewish clergy, the barber-surgeon, and Fishele the Butcher. As for the Potcheyov, it contained only Jewish shops.

From the marketplace, the crooked, muddy streets and alleys extended like the sun's rays in all directions. The nearer to the center they were, the more likely they were to be occupied by Jews. The further toward the countryside, the more likely they were to be inhabited by Gentiles. The distribution of the Jewish population was such that the more money one had, or the greater one's say in public affairs, the closer one lived to the heart of the shtetl. The view from the windows of these houses may have been unfortunate, but within them, life was good, or almost so.

* * *

AS SHE LOOKED now down on Bociany, Hindele asked herself how long it had actually been since that day when she had arrived there to marry Reb Hamele. She could hardly count the number of years that had passed, although the day of her arrival and her wedding day stood out in her memory very vividly. How long was it since she had seen her family? She missed her sisters, but more than anyone else, she missed her deceased mother. "Even very old people," Hindele thought, "still feel the need for their mothers, especially during hard times."

It was strange how she was prone to misfortune. The wise saying, "A change of place, a change of luck," could not be applied to her. Her distinguished lineage of descent in a straight line from King David's house had done nothing to alter her bad luck, even after she had moved to Bociany. Her more recent parentage, which derived from the house of the Rabbi of Wurke, also had no bearing on it, nor did her husband's descent from the very cream of the rabbinical world.

She tried to recall the features of her father's face, but she could see them only vaguely. She barely knew him, barely remembered him. He had been a fanatically devout Hasid who had lived with the Rabbi and for the Rabbi. His real home had been the Rabbi's court. Her mother however . . . Hindele could recall her mother's face down to the smallest detail; she saw her stooped figure, the way she had walked, talked, and gestured. Proud as her mother had been of her social position and of her pious husband, and joyful as she had always tried to be, in keeping with Hasidic tradition, she hardly ever had time to catch her breath. Not only did she have a house full of children and a husband to support, but she also had to receive and lodge visiting Hasidim from other towns whom her husband brought home as guests. She had to make ends meet as well as she could by taking on all kinds of business, especially peddling, and leaving the care of the household to Hindele, her eldest daughter. Only when her mother grew weaker and Hindele grew older was the procedure reversed. The mother stayed home, while the daughter went out to earn the daily bread for the family.

Hindele could not recall a single day when she had sat idle, even on the Sabbath, except when she was obliged to go to the synagogue with her family. To go for a walk with no purpose but pleasure in mind was an unheard-of thing. She was the firstborn, a second mother to her siblings, privileged by nature to carry most of the family's burden on her shoulders. More than once, while still a very young girl, she had to remind her preoccupied mother to suckle her youngest brother, Zishele. Zishele later returned the favor in kind, when he taught Hindele all that he himself had learned in heder. Later still, when Zishele had begun studying the *Mishne*, they would go over the text together, in secret, because Zishele thought it was not proper for him to be seen studying with his sister, not even when she was occupied with mending socks while they studied. Yet those hours were so precious to them both that they were reluctant to give them up even when Zishele became a bat mitzvah boy. Then fate intervened, and Zishele died of an unknown disease.

Because of these studies with her brother, Hindele developed a love of reading. Before her husband's and son's illnesses, she was always doing business with the book peddler who visited Bociany a couple of times a year, his cart laden with phylacteries, mezuzahs, amulets, talismans for women in labor, and stacks and stacks of books, sacred and profane, hard and soft-covered, at the sight of which Hindele's head always began to swim. For a few kopeks a month, she would borrow whatever she saw: morality books, books of verse and wise sayings, books of Hasidic lore, or interesting stories in Yiddish. But her favorites were stories from the Jewish past, tales woven around the heroes whom she had read about in the women's Bible. Such books fortified and sustained her in her daily life.

She had married very late, at eighteen. This was not because there had been a lack of matchmakers with interesting proposals, but because her mother had fallen ill, and Hindele had to wait for the next sister to grow experienced enough to take over the household duties. Only then did Hindele get the kind of groom she deserved. Oh, the time between her engagement and her wedding! It was then that Hindele had heard for the first time that she was "not an ugly" girl. When she came to Bociany to marry, she had long chestnut hair, which she wore braided in a huge bun at the nape of her neck. True, she was slight of build and seemed fragile, but in reality she was well developed, sturdy and healthy at the same time that she was slender, supple, and light-footed. At that time, she had moments when she worried about being pleasing to the eye and rejoiced when she discovered that she was.

Now this fussing over herself seemed like plain vanity. It was so alien to her present nature that she thought of herself in those times as if she had been living a dream. Now her life belonged exclusively to her husband and her children. It had become entirely dissolved in their lives, while she continued to try to make her "selfishness" vanish even more completely. Even her love of reading was not entirely linked to seeking self-gratification. In the back of her mind there was always the hope that in this manner she could more closely approach her husband's inner world and understand him better, so that she might serve him better. Or she memorized the stories that she read, in order to be able one day to recount them to her children. It seemed to her that only her body bore the traces of hardship and suffering, while her soul, enriched, continued to grow like a fertile tree, thanks to her life with her dear ones.

Hindele had followed in her mother's footsteps by supporting her family. She had opened a shop of odds and ends on the Potcheyov. She saw to it that the pipe leading from the stove in her garret to the neighboring shed should always be warm, so that her husband could do all his work in peace and comfort at the table inside. She made sure that he did not lack oil for his lamp, bread for his herring, an onion or a few potatoes, and that there should even be a leg of chicken on his plate for the Sabbath meal. Her husband was not just anybody, and what he was doing was no small thing. He had to invest all of his being in his work. He had once quoted the saying of Rabbi Reb Mayer to her. "I am a scribe," Rabbi Reb Mayer had said, "so I must pay attention to my work, for it is sacred. It is God's work. And if one leaves out a single letter, or adds one letter too many, one can, Heaven forbid, destroy the whole world."

Hindele's husband, Hamele the Scribe, was a Talmudic scholar whose name was well known throughout the province of Sielce. Not only did he occupy himself with the sacred task of writing Torah Scrolls for the surrounding communities, but he was also the author of a number of books devoted to close examination of the Scriptures, as well as question-and-answer books and a small volume of his own sharp thoughts about Jewish faith. His whole life had been one struggle to deserve this good fortune of being a scholar among Jews. But Hindele was aware that the greatest difficulty in that struggle lay in his daily life with his own family. He always felt that he owed his family a debt, owed his wife on account of her hard work, owed his little daughters because he rarely noticed them and when he did, he mixed up their names, and owed his sons because he devoted too little time to them. So he tried to pay them back, to reward them through the diligence of his work, through the effort he invested in his writings, and through his modesty and self-composure.

* * *

AS SHE SAT on the grass, waiting for Reb Faivele the Miller's goats to be milked, Hindele felt the night creep back into her heart along with thoughts about her husband. She tried to concentrate on Yacov, who was sleeping with his head cradled in her lap. She marveled at the boy's finely drawn eyebrows and his thin, almost transparent eyelids fringed with glistening brown lashes. She loved his eyes. They seemed like two dishes of honey, full of brown sweetness. She loved his mouth as well, so delicately red and shiny. She loved his chin, his ears, the shape of his entire face, and the form of his thin body, which made her think of a small, swaying tree. And he had a good mind as well. Of course, neither he nor Shalom, his elder brother, could compare with her eldest, Itchele, who was a genius; none of her sons resembled their father as much as Itchele did. Yet she was proud of her other sons just as much as she was of Itchele. She was proud of her two little girls as well, although no one saw any exceptional qualities in them. But Itchele—he was the most important of them all, not because of his gifts, but because he was so very ill.

The tears welled up and burst from Hindele's eyes, causing her body to convulse with spasms, as if it were nothing but a vessel filled to the brim with bitter, salty water. At that moment she heard Fredka, the miller's housekeeper, calling her. With the tears still lying fresh on her face, she lifted Yacov's head from her lap and made him sit up. She jumped to her feet and dashed into the yard, trying to control her sobs so as not to wake the miller's family, which slept on obliviously in the silent whitewashed house.

Fredka was waiting on the verandah. "Have they gotten worse?" she asked.

"God will help," Hindele stammered, choking on the words and the tears. She took the jug from Fredka's hand and bowed deeply, as if Fredka were the mistress of the house. "May God bless you," she added and turned around. She let her gaze drop into the jug, and her tears dripped into the white foam. The sight of the warm, bubbly milk calmed her. She stopped for a while outside the fence to regain her composure, then walked swiftly over to Yacov and took him by the hand, and they walked down the path in the direction of the Wide Poplar Road.